English
for
Competitive Examinations

Practice Tests for Language Proficiency

English for Competitive Examinations

Practice Tests for Language Proficiency

Dr. Mrs. SWARN CHAWLA
Reader in English,
Vivekananda College,
University of Delhi

Academic Advisor & Co-ordinator
Institute of UN Studies, Indian Federation of UN Associations

Deputy Chairperson
National Federation of UNESCO Associations in India

VIKAS PUBLISHING HOUSE PVT LTD

VIKAS PUBLISHING HOUSE PVT LTD
576, Masjid Road, Jangpura, **New Delhi**-110 014
Phones: 24376605, 24375313 • Fax: 24370879
E-mail: ***helpline@vikaspublishing.com***
Website: ***www.vikaspublishing.com***

- First Floor, N.S. Bhawan, 4th Cross, 4th Main, Gandhi Nagar, **Bangalore**-560 009 • Phone: 22204639
- Damodhar Centre, New No. 62, Old No. 59, Nelson Manickam Road, Aminjikarai, **Chennai**-600 029 • Phone: 23744547, 23746090
- 35, Palm Avenue, **Kolkata**-700 019 • Phone: 22833494
- F-20, Nand Dham Industrial Estate, Marol, Andheri (East), **Mumbai**-400 059 • Phone: 28502333, 28502324

Distributors:

UBS PUBLISHERS' DISTRIBUTORS PVT LTD
5, Ansari Road, **New Delhi**-110 002
Ph. 23273601, 23266646 • Fax: 23276593, 23274261
- 10, First Main Road, Gandhi Nagar, **Bangalore**-560 009 • Ph. 2253903
- 143, M P Nagar, Zone-1, **Bhopal**-462 011 • Ph. 5203183, 5203193
- 60, Nelson Manickam Road, Aminjikarai, **Chennai**-600 029 • Ph. 23746222
- 40/7940, Convent Road, **Ernakulam**-682 035 • Ph. 2353901, 2363905
- NVK Towers, 2nd Floor, Adjacent to old Hyderabad Stock Exchange, 3-6-272 Himayat Nagar, **Hyderabad**-500 029 • Ph. 36999108
- 8/1-B, Chowringhee Lane, **Kolkata**-700 016 • Ph. 22521821, 22522910
- 1st Floor, Halwasiya Court Annexe, 11-MG Marg, Hazratganj, **Lucknow**-226 001 Ph. 2294134
- 2nd Floor, Apeejay Chambers, 5 Wallace Street, Fort, **Mumbai**-400 001 • Ph. 56376922
- GF, Western Side, Annapoorna Complex, Naya Tola, **Patna**-800 004 • Ph. 2672856, 2673973
- 680 Budhwar Peth, 2nd Floor, Appa Balwant Chowk, **Pune**-411 002 • Ph. 56028920

ISBN: 81-259-1661-X

Printed at Gajendra Printing Press, Delhi-110032

Dedicated to
Saraswati,
the goddess of learning
and
to my late mother Smt. Kaushalya Devi Mehra
who was like an incarnation of Saraswati

FOREWORD

Dr. Swarn Chawla, bestowed with a profundity of thought, and an excellent sense of criticism based on continuous research, has been teaching successfully as a teacher of English as a second/third language at various universities for the last about three decades, Since 1982, after the award of doctoral degree to her, she has been teaching and constructing tests of English in Delhi University with Reader in English as her present designation.

Having evolved innovative techniques of testing of English at her doctoral and post-doctoral levels, and having further polished the MCQ technique of testing by having academic involvement with a number of prestigious research centres, she resolved to produce a book of proficiency test of English for students at higher education level.

The present book titled *English for Competitive Examinations* (Practice Tests for Language Proficiency) is going to be a landmark in the history of English testing in India as it comprises validated tests of English for students preparing for various competitive examinations at national and international levels, and for professionals who wish to excel in the global market of the day by having excellent command over English language skills.

I wish this book a brilliant success in colleges, universities and professional institutes not only in India but all over the world where English is taught as L2/L3. The book is the brainchild of my former student who has always exhibited a keen desire for progress by possessing an unquenchable thirst for knowledge.

I most heartily congratulate Dr. Swarn Chawla for her sincere hard work for the student community, for the teaching community, and for the research community at large. I am very sure she will continue working further and writing more such books with same enthusiasm.

Prof. D D Sharma, Ph D (Edin)
An ELT Expert, Former Head of the Deptt. of English and Modern European Languages, and Pro-VC Lucknow University.

ACKNOWLEDGEMENTS

'There is always a woman behind a man's success' is a popular saying but let me admit vociferously that ***there is a man behind my success***, and that man is none else but my dynamic husband Mr. J.P. Chawla (A Professional Chartered Accountant) – my only motivational force behind the successful production of this practice book.

I take this opportunity for expressing my gratitude to my teacher and guide Prof. Dr. D.D. Sharma for giving me constructive suggestions and advices during the time I was writing this book. I further owe my thanks to Prof. R.W. Desai, Prof. S. Panja. Dr, P. Batra, my colleagues, friends and students for their contribution and encouragement at all stages.

I thank two of my students Ms. Poornima Banerji and Ms. Shubhangi and a young computer typist Deepak Khanna for helping me in preparing rough drafts for the practice tests. Further, I thank my sons Rajat and Rachit for their cooperation and unbiased constructive criticism from time to time in their capacity of being examinees for English Language Tests.

Finally, I thank all members of my family for their wishes and blessings.

Swarn Chawla

PREFACE

This book is an outcome of my many years of experience in ELT and my specialisation on Testing. With more than thirty years of experience of teaching English as a second language, I have been able to appreciate the problems students face in gaining proficiency in the language and handling the various examinations that test it. My journey with learners of English and with other ELT and testing experts strengthened my resolve to prepare a book that would help students prepare for the various tests of English they need to face. I undertook a detailed study of the various syllabi of competitive and regular examinations at the national and international levels including the TOEFL, SAT, IELTS, CA, CS, ICWA, CAT, MAT, XAT, UPSC Civil Services, Bank Services, NDA, CDS and the various undergraduate courses in universities and colleges.

This book covers the broad spectrum of tests that are used to gauge proficiency in English language. All the tests in the book have been administered on students before being selected for the book. The aim of the book is to provide a 'training course' for examinees to successfully clear English language examinations. The book deals with reading skills, vocabulary, grammar and writing skills.

The tests include multiple choice questions (MCQs), cloze, modified cloze procedures, C-type and question-answer type. Tests employ internationally recognized and acceptable criteria for testing, for instance, 'distractors' or wrong options following the MCQs have been framed as per authentic theoretical foundations. Every new type of test is preceded by a brief and relevant introduction to help the reader understand what is being tested and how this type of test needs to be tackled. A separate chapter has been compiled containing tests of précis writing, paragraph writing, essay type question-answers and complete answers of productive type. The book thus would also prove useful to ELT experts and researchers as a good compilation of validated tests for English.

As a whole, the book seeks to help students gain proficiency in English and acquire the necessary skills to tackle the examinations. Students are requested to follow a regular schedule by practising these tests regularly. They need to remember: "Genius begins great works, labour alone completes them."

January 2006

Dr (Mrs) Swarn Chawla

CONTENTS

6. Practice Tests 189-263

"Reading maketh a full man"
– Bacon, *Of Studies*

CHAPTER 1

READING SKILLS

INTRODUCTION

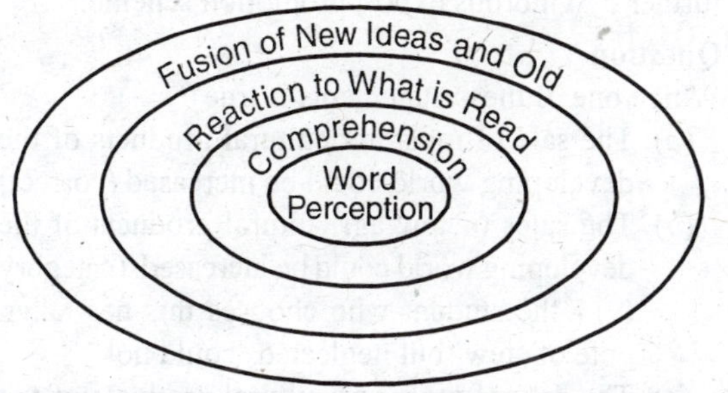

As you can see in the figure above, word perception is at the centre of all reading skills; without it, comprehension and analysis is just not possible. It will help you to know that there are three kinds of comprehension: first, literal comprehension, which is to grasp exactly what is written. The second is determining the implicit or inferred meanings. The third level relates to understanding the implications and significance of the author's ideas beyond what is actually stated. Or to put it simply, reading comprehension is the ability to read the lines, to read between the lines and to read beyond the lines.

Reaction, the third concentric band, is actually nothing but 'critical reading', i.e., reaching conclusions, making judgements or emotional responses to the content of the text. The final band, assimilation or fusion of ideas comes from combining information provided in the current text with the reader's existing knowledge or ideas. Important factors to keep in mind, which have not been shown in the figure above, are the rate of reading and the immense scope for improvement in all these aspects of critical reading, i.e., word perception, comprehension, reaction and fusion.

During practice for comprehension exercises, keep in mind that the questions that can be asked would cover the following:

- Questions that need factual answers – information directly available in the text;
- Questions that require answers to be inferred in the text;
- Questions that require the selection, arrangement, interpretation etc. of information available in the text.

Introductory notes on the various techniques employed in the chapter

1. MULTIPLE-CHOICE

To begin with, in this chapter, you will find Prose passages, poems, communicative passages and Dialogues followed by multiple choice question items. You will see that there will be mainly four options after each question-item, out of which one is a correct answer and three are distractors. For your help, you can go through the following **categorization of distractors** (with examples) on the basis of functional analysis before solving the question items for the multiple-choice comprehension passages:

(i) Spatial proximity

This is a choice which is to be found very close spatially to the stem or stem equivalent in the passage and, therefore, spatially close to the correct answer but which, in fact, is incorrect or irrelevant.

Text

Corresponding advances in agricultural science and techniques are necessarily shown in taking effect. Reserves of marginal land which have been relied upon to feed recent increases in population are virtually exhausted....

Question

Improvements in agriculture

(*a*) are slow (Category (*x*), explained ahead)
(*b*) do not produce results quickly (correct)

(*c*) do not necessarily produce result (category (*ii*))
(*d*) have virtually exhausted any spare land (category (*i*) close in space but in this case, nonsense).

(ii) Word-form confusion

A distractor which consists of or includes an item which is in form close to or identical with the correct form but which is not relevant or is used wrongly.

Text

The summit meeting started off on an unpromising note.

Question

The start of the meeting
(*a*) was uncompromising (category (*ii*) looks like unpromising)
(*b*) was noteworthy for promise (category (*ii*) - takes up 'promise' and note)
(*c*) was not hopeful (correct)
(*d*) was hopeful (category (*ix*))

(iii) Structural confusion

A distractor which hinges on a potential misunderstanding of the structure of a sentence or part of a sentence.

Question

'He spoke German as well as he spoke French' means:
(*a*) He spoke German better than he spoke French (category (*iii*))
(*b*) He spoke a mixture of German and French (category (*iii*))
(*c*) He spoke both German and French (category (*iii*) – this is the confusion the question is aimed at)
(*d*) He spoke German and French equally well (correct).

(iv) Irrelevance

A statement which may be perfectly correct but is not the relevant answer to the question.
(*a*) Correct from the evidence of another area of the text but not the correct answer to **this** question
(*b*) correct according to general knowledge or information outside the text itself.
(*c*) incorrect **and** irrelevant.

(v) Modification

Choices which are unacceptable because they neglect or misinterpret the various forms of modification, including :

A. The force of negatives, double negatives, implied negativisation.

Text

Yet there are few agricultural products of the developing world whose sales could not be expanded further by vigorous export promotion scheme.

Question

Which one of these statements is true ?
(*a*) The sale of most agricultural products of the developing world could be increased (correct)
(*b*) The sales of few agricultural products of the developing world could be increased, (category (*v*) - the student who chooses this has taken note of 'few' but neglected 'could not').
(*c*) The sale of most agricultural products of the developing world could not be increased, (category (*v*) - B's error reversed).
(*d*) The sales of only a few agricultural products of the developing world could be increased, (category (*v*) - similar to B).

B. The force of adverbial and adjectival modifiers of time, frequency, quantity, degree, etc.

Texts

—— in a number of countries these new varieties are now multiplying yields by as much as three and four items.

Question

The new varieties are multiplying yields
(*a*) whenever they have been tried.
(*b*) in most of the countries where they have been tried.
(*c*) in a few countries where they have been tried. Category (*v*)
(*d*) in some countries (correct - 'some' is equivalent to 'a number'.

Question

The yields have increased
(*a*) by up to three and four times (correct 'by up to' is equivalent to 'as much as')
(*b*) by three or four times (category (*v*))

(*c*) several times over (category (*v*))
(*d*) in a small number of countries (category (*iv*))

(vi) Auxiliaries

Distractors which misinterpret the force of auxiliary verbs such as **will, would, shall, should, may, might, can, could.**

Text

It is also participating in the development of other high protein foods, including oilseeds, meat, fish, protein concentrates and other less conventional products, which might, in future, make up an important part of mankind's food.

Question

It is

(*a*) certain (category (*vi*))
(*b*) possible (correct)
(*c*) unlikely (category (*vi*))
(*d*) probable (category (*vi*))

That the new high protein foods will make up an important part of man's food in the future.

(vii) Connectives

Choices which misinterpret the force of connectives and link words.

Text

—— advances in preventive medicine and improved public health programmes have dramatically reduced death rates and prolonged life. Consequently, populations are rising as never before in developing countries where birth rates have remained high.

Question

Population is rising

(*a*) in spite of medical progress (category (*vii*)) misinterpretation of 'consequently')
(*b*) because of medical progress (correct)
(*c*) although it has never done so before in developing countries (category (*vii*) - misinterpretation of 'consequently' and (*v*) - misinterpretation of 'as never before')
(*d*) and consequently there have been advances in medicine and public health (category (*ix*) - the wrong way round).

(viii) Lexis

Multiple choice is frequently used to test the student's knowledge of word meaning and a meaning of a word in a particular context. Concentration on 'known' words in varieties of contexts would seem to be the most valid use of this type of question in the field of lexis.

Question

The possibilities include :

(*a*) spatial proximity
(*b*) word form confusion
(*c*) semantic confusion — close but not sufficiently close in meaning
(*d*) neglect of context — a meaning which is 'correct' but is not the relevant meaning of the item in its context in the passage.

(ix) Contrast or opposition confusion

The confusion of contrasted or opposed items or points.

Text

Mr. X put the release of the 90000 prisoners and Y's withdrawal from the areas its forces have occupied at the top of the agenda.

Question

Mr. X wanted first :

(*a*) the fundamental questions to be settled (this was precisely what Mr X wanted)
(*b*) An agreement with Y (this was wanted by Mr X and Mr Y)
(*c*) the return of prisoners and occupied areas (correct)
(*d*) an agreement not to start hostilities again (this was wanted by Mr X).

This is the classic 'getting the wrong end of the stick' situation.

(x) Partial Vs. Complete correctness

Choices which are partially right, which constitute a small part of a larger factor, or give an answer which might suffice if a more precise or complete answer were not also present.

Text

——— the rate of population increase must slow down; there must be a substantial increase in productivity — and there must be equitable distribution. All three parts of the answer are included in FAO policy, increased productivity is the ultimate reason for everything that FAO does.

Question

The basic purpose of FAO's actions is

(*a*) to slow down the increase in the world population (category *x* - part of the answer)

(*b*) to increase productivity (correct)

(*c*) to share production in a fairer way (category (*x*) part of the answer, less precise)

(*d*) to feed the hungry (category (*x*) : part of the answer, less precise).

Text

Labour intensive off - form projects — when undertaken within the contexts of national plans, offer partial solutions.

Question

(*a*) will solve the problem of under employment (category (*x*) overstated and incomplete)

(*b*) will solve the problem of under employment to some extent (category (*x*) - closer than '*A*' but needs modification)

(*c*) are part of national planning (category *I*)

(*d*) will help to solve the problem of under-development if they are part of national planning (correct).

This is the classic 'getting the wrong end of the stick' situation.

2. CLOZE PROCEDURE (CP) (Subjective Type)

Cloze procedure (CP) is a testing technique accepted as a global measure of language proficiency. Technically, a Cloze procedure text consists of a passage from which every 7th/6th/9th word has been deleted. No deletions are made in the first two or three lines, to allow the theme of the passage to become established. Your task is to fill the blanks appropriately.

A Model CP Test Follows

I assume that the desirability of a school book-stall need no urging. Many schools sell food and toys. If we do not sell books, it is surely strange. Many schools serve areas where book shops do not exist and the only books brought before children for buying are the dubious selections of supermarkets. Moreover even in communities where a good book ______**(1)** is available, the guidance which can be given ____**(2)** the book–stall is valuable, as we soon ______**(3)**.

Essentially the school book-stall is an extension ______**(4)** the encouragement and guidance in private reading which ______**(5)** part of the work of the English teacher. ______**(6)** first essential then, in setting up shop is ______**(7)** teacher particularly interested in children reading and in ______**(8)** up as wide as possible a knowledge of ______**(9)** to suit the school's range of pupils.

ANSWERS

1. shop	**2.** at	**3.** found
4. of	**5.** is	**6.** The
7. a	**8.** building	**9.** books

With the passage of time, a variety of cloze passages have evolved, for example, deletions are made on the basis of the purpose of the test envisaged by a test constructor. You will confront the variety in the following exercises which will prepare you for all types of cloze passages, occurring in various examinations.

Among the methodological questions concerning the Cloze tests, which have been investigated systematically with non-native speakers, the most important question has been that of the **scoring method** to be employed for evaluating their reading comprehension/ability.

The scoring method most frequently used with native speakers is to count only exact word replacements as correct. But with non-native speakers, it seems unlikely that the exact word method is superior to a method which allows contextually acceptable response. The research data supports the conclusion that with non-native speakers the method of allowing any contextually acceptable response is significantly superior to the exact word scoring technique.

3. MODIFIED CLOZE PROCEDURE (MCP) (Objective Type)

The Modified Cloze Procedure tests comprehension pure and simple, without the obtrusion of other language–ability. In the MCP exercises, we supply a set of words for each gap – in other words, we marry the CP to the multiple-choice test. The advantage in modifying a CP test in this manner would introduce an element of control and flexibility. You will have a controlled set of choices whereas in CP test, the choice was open to you.

In the modified CLOZE procedure test, you will be given a passage where every nth (5th, 7th, 9th) word is deleted and supplied multiple choices for filling these blanks. You will have to choose from these the word which is felt to fit the context best.

A Model MCP Test for Students

Read the following passage. **ONE** word in each bracket is correct. Mark the number of the word with a cross on the right hand side of the page like this: –

Alica looked round. 'There isn't any'

1 2 3 4 ×

she (said/talked/believed/asked). 1 – 2 – 3 – 4

It is among the white youth of the world that the greatest change is taking place. It is they who are experiencing the great psychic pain of waking up to find their inherited heroes turned by events into villains. Communication and understanding between the older and younger

1 2 3 4

(*a*) (People/progeny/generations/persons)

1 – 2 – 3 – 4

(*b*) of whites has entered a crisis. The elders,

1 2 3 4

(as/if/who/whose)

1 – 2 – 3 – 4

are in the tradition of privileged classes or races,

1 2 3 4

(*c*) (really/frankly/genuinely/clearly)

1 – 2 – 3 – 4

do not understand the youth. They trapped by old

1 2 3 4

(*d*) (ways/modes/methods/sources)

1 – 2 – 3 – 4

of thinking and blind to the future, have

1 2 3 4

(*e*) (always/only/ever/also)

1 – 2 – 3 – 4

just begun to be vexed–because the youth

1 2 3 4

(*f*) (has/have/had/will have) 1 – 2 – 3 – 4

only just begun to rebel.

4. C-TEST (SUBJECTIVE TYPE)

The C-Test is another variety of Cloze. Instead of deleting whole words as in the Cloze type, it is the second half of every 2nd/5th/7th/9th word which is deleted. It is easier for you to practise such tests, as you do not have to read as much text as you are required to do for the Cloze Procedure tests. Besides, C-Test functions well as a rough measure of your overall ability in a foreign language. You are advised to practise a few C-Tests before attempting other types of Cloze tests. An example follows.

A Model C-Test

There are usually five men in the crew of a fire engine. One o- them dri—— the eng—. The lea— sits bes— the dri—. The oth— firemen s—inside t—cab o— the f—engine. T—leader h— usually be—in t—Fire Service for ma—— years. H—will kn—how t—fight diff—— sorts o— fires. S—, when t—firemen arr— at a fire, it is always the leader who decides how to fight a fire. He tells each fireman what to do.

Now follow the various types of Practice tests.

READING COMPREHENSION AND READING ABILITY

TEST PASSAGES

Objective and Subjective Type

PROSE

Note: You are advised to keep in mind the guidelines given in the introductory part of this chapter before practising the test passages for comprehension purposes by allowing yourself an average of 30 seconds for attempting each of the question items following each passage.

TEST – 1
(OBJECTIVE TYPE MULTIPLE-CHOICE TEST)

Directions: Read through the passage once only as quickly as you can without suffering loss of comprehension and answer the questions that follow.

An orator, whose purpose is to persuade men, must speak the things they wish to hear; an orator, whose purpose is to move men, must also avoid disturbing the emotional effect by any obtrusion of intellectual antagonism, but an author, whose purpose is to instruct men, who appeals to the intellect, must be careless of their opinions and think only of truth. It will often be a question when a man is or is not wise in advancing unpalatable opinions, or in preaching heresies, but it can never be a question that a man should be silent if unprepared to speak the truth as he conceives it. Deference to popular opinion is one great source of bad writing and is all the more disastrous because the deference is paid to some purely hypothetical requirement. When a man fails to see the truth of certain generally accepted views, there is no law compelling him to provoke animosity by announcing his dissent. He may be excused if he shrinks from the lurid glory of martyrdom; he may be justified in not placing himself in a position of singularity. He may even be commended for not helping to perplex mankind with doubts which he feels to be founded on limited and possibly erroneous investigation. But if allegiance to truth lays no stern command upon him to speak out his immature dissent, it does lay a stern command not to speak out hypocritical assent. There are many justifications of silence, there can be none of insincerity.

1. A man who dissents with generally accepted views:
   (*a*) must be sincere.
   (*b*) should announce his dissent.
   (*c*) should assent to the accepted view to achieve harmony.
   (*d*) marks himself as an individualist.

2. To persuade people, it is wise to:
   (*a*) instruct.
   (*b*) tell them what they want to hear.
   (*c*) show them their errors.
   (*d*) avoid disturbing their peace of mind.

3. A good speaker:
   (*a*) is prejudiced.
   (*b*) has due respect for the reaction of his audience.
   (*c*) does not appeal to emotions.
   (*d*) tells his audience his own attitude toward the topic.

4. Among the justifications for silence, the author does not include:
   (*a*) fear. (*b*) modesty.
   (*c*) uncertainty. (*d*) dishonesty.

5. The underlined word 'allegiance' is
   (*a*) a noun. (*b*) an adjective.
   (*c*) an adverb.

6. The underlined word 'animosity' means
   (*a*) jealousy. (*b*) opposition.
   (*c*) envy. (*d*) hilarity.

TEST – 2
(OBJECTIVE TYPE MULTIPLE-CHOICE TEST)

Directions: Read through the passage only once as quickly as you can without suffering loss of comprehension and answer the questions that follow.

Immigration is frequently an uneven transaction. When a scientist from India or a professor from Guatemala or a physician from the Philippines moves to the U.S., America's gain is the native land's loss. Since few American professionals head out to settle elsewhere in the world, the redistribution of talent serves only to widen the gap between the land of plenty and the lands of poverty. Worse still, the cycle tends to perpetuate itself: as more people leave their native country for the U.S., more are likely to leave, to join relatives or cash in on the connections or simply follow examples.

Though nothing new, the brain drain has recently seemed more than ever to be taking from the poor and giving to the rich: whereas 30 years ago most well-qualified new comers to the U.S. arrived from Europe, now they stream in from the poorer countries of the Third World. "It is indeed paradoxical," says Dr. D.N. Misra, advisor to the India's Council of Scientific and Industrial Research, "the underdeveloped countries, which have the greatest need for scientists, engineers, managers and other professionals, are in fact losing many of their best educated young men to the developed countries." Even among unskilled workers, the U.S., tends to attract the most enterprising – those who are adventurous enough to quit their homes and strike out for new opportunities in America.

The first to leave are outstanding people who win admission to U.S. universities and who, not surprisingly, accept challenging jobs and high salaries in America upon their graduation. Each year, for instance, some 6,000 Taiwan Chinese arrive to study in the U.S.; no more than 20% ever return home. Many of the top achievers at the prestigious Indian Institute of Technology at Kharagpur are snapped up by the U.S. National Aeronautics and Space Administration. "These students are dedicated individuals of discipline, diligence and dignity," says Robert Ringler, an associate dean of the University of California, Los Angeles, who is an advisor to Asian students. "They are a treasure to any country, and it is a shame that their homes sometimes don't have the resources to nurture and hold on to them."

No less costly to Third World nations is the steady migration of well-trained professionals in search of a life, any life, in America. The wage differential between the U.S. and Mexico, for example, is 15 to 1. For many others, even poverty in the U.S. is preferable to an uneasy prosperity at home: thus lawyers and doctors from Central America may be found washing cars or working as bellhops in Miami. Other highly skilled people are driven to emigrate not by economic choice but by political circumstances. During their genocidal 45-month reign in Kampuchea, the Khmer Rouge killed roughly 2 million people, many of them white-collar workers. As a result, around 70% of the Kampucheans in the U.S. are professionals.

Whatever the cause, the cost of countries that lose minds and hearts to the U.S. can be high. The presence of 8,000 Israeli engineers in the U.S. has, according to Yosef Kicik, emigration to Israeli government, "created a severe bottleneck in the development of sophisticated industry in Israel." Around half of the 1,000 students who graduate each year from the 27 medical schools in the Philippines go abroad, leaving one doctor tending to as many as 20,000 people in some of the Archipelago's rural areas.

Inevitably, many countries have mounted efforts to counter the outflowing tide. An Israeli professional in the U.S. who considers going home, for example, receives a banquet of blandishments. The local consulate sends his or her resume to at least three prospective employers in Israel and helps the applicant finance a trip back home for job interviews. If the candidate accepts the position, the Israeli government makes available a host of benefits, including a handsome mortgage on a new house, loans to cover moving costs and a waiver of customs duties on everything except a car.

Other nations, by contrast, actually encourage emigration. Mexico's population is growing so fast that the country would have to create at least 7,50,000 jobs a year just to keep its unemployment rate mounting further. Small wonder, then, that Mexico makes scant effort to assist the U.S. in reversing the tide. Ex-president Ferdinand Macros had cited the annual exodus of 35,000 Filipinos to the U.S. as a help in offsetting two of his country's most obstinate problems: unemployment (now running at 45%) and a lopsided balance of payments. In South Korea, the departure of workers has eased some of the strains triggered by a population boom; in overcrowded Hong Kong (pop. 5.5 million), departing workers have reduced competition for professional jobs.

Few countries, however, can afford to take satisfaction from the departure of their best and brightest. In the process, they lose not only the resources of those who leave but also the confidence and commitment of those who remain. That loss is poignantly dramatized in an image common to most Third World capitals: the long line that snakes each weekday around the U.S. embassy. In Mexico, most applicants must wait eight years for an U.S. immigrant visa. In India, 1,40,000 people are on the waiting list for 20,000 annual U.S. immigrant visas. Most difficult of all, perhaps, is Hong Kong, where nearly 31,000 people have applied for the 600 places available each year. That could mean a wait of more than 50 years. And the line is growing longer.

Questions

1. Migration of trained professionals to the U.S. would not widen the gap between the rich and the poor nations
(*a*) if there were migration of trained American professionals to less privileged countries
(*b*) if the cycle did not tend to perpetuate itself
(*c*) (*a*) & (*b*)
(*d*) none of the above

2. The main reason why most of the brilliant students from the Third World stay back in the U.S. is because
(*a*) of the challenging jobs in the U.S.
(*b*) of the high salaries
(*c*) of the spirit of adventure
(*d*) their own countries lack resources to nurture and hold them

3. The lawyers and doctors found doing odd jobs have left their own countries in search of
(*a*) better wage (*b*) a better life
(*c*) security (*d*) adventure

4. Most Kampuchean professionals migrated to the U.S.
(*a*) in search of better life
(*b*) because of fear of persecution
(*c*) because of lack of opportunities in Kampuchea
(*d*) none of the above

5. When an Israeli settled in the US wishes to take up a job in his home country, the Israeli government does all except
(*a*) send his resume to prospective employers
(*b*) finance his trip to Israel for job interviews
(*c*) offer him a handsome mortgage on a new house
(*d*) waive custom duties on all his belongings

6. Of all the Third World Countries, the one that appears to be least perturbed by the adverse consequence of brain drain is
(*a*) Israel (*b*) India
(*c*) Kampuchea (*d*) Mexico

7. Philippines considers the exodus of a large number of its citizens to the U.S. as providing a solution to its problem of
(*a*) unemployment
(*b*) surplus population
(*c*) adverse balance of payment
(*d*) (*a*) & (*c*)

8. In Hong Kong, exodus of professionals has
(*a*) helped the colony to straighten up its balance of payments
(*b*) created a bottleneck in its industrial development
(*c*) reduced competition for professional jobs
(*d*) eased some of the problems triggered by a population boom

9. The most important psychological harm that brain drain can cause is
(*a*) severe bottlenecks in development
(*b*) severe bottlenecks, especially, in the development of sophisticated industry
(*c*) loss of confidence among those who remain
(*d*) lack of diligent, disciplined team of trained professional

10. The underlined word 'poignantly' in the last paragraph is
(*a*) a noun (*b*) an adverb
(*c*) an adjective

TEST – 3

(OBJECTIVE TYPE MULTIPLE-CHOICE TEST)

Directions: Read through the passage once only as quickly as you can without suffering loss of comprehension and answer the questions that follow:

1. You are walking down a long dark tunnel which gets narrower and hotter and louder. The clamour of many voices and machines makes it impossible for you to think; the air seems too oppressive to breathe. You feel yourself enclosed in too little space from which there is no escape; you can go only in the direction of the crowd, which becomes more and more claustrophobic. It is a nightmare, except that you are awake.

2. For this unpleasant experience, thousands of New Yorkers are paying a dollar a head and are expected to continue doing so in increasing numbers, for the next two years. The event is a unique exhibition at the American Museum of Natural History, the first of its kind in the world. It is called Can Man Survive? and it is a serious attempt to pose that question.
3. In the early stages the exhibition is a delight. One enters a broad, carpeted hallway from which all exterior sounds are excluded. It is cool and softly lighted; there is an impression of much space, and the sound of birds singing. The world of nature is projected on film, and a commentator gently drives home the message that for millions of years life has been maintained by a self-regulating natural balance between the amount of food and oxygen available, and the number of animals which survived.
4. The point is made that nature's methods are sometimes harsh; one beast devours another. From then on the corridor narrows and darkens as films and photographs trace man's advance into the industrial age. At first the positive side of this is shown, but then the tunnel gets even narrower, the background noise of machines, factory furnaces and automobiles becomes noisier. There are film flashes projected from every wall, crowding in on the visitor, with the impression of conveyor belts, tractors and teeming masses of people.
5. Amid the noise there is a shot of a new-born baby, and the visitor is immediately attracted to it as the one thing endearing and innocent. But a voice from somewhere in the tunnel comments: 'This baby's chances of survival are excellent. So are every baby's. There are twice as many mouths to feed as there were 40 years ago, and already there is not enough food to go round......'
6. By the end of the exhibition the tunnel has become so narrow and oppressive that the visitor almost stumbles over a beat-up bus and a pile of garbage cans which half-blocks the exit. There, written in red on the wall, is the message 'Can Man Survive? It is up to you.'
7. After such bombardment of the senses it is a sweet relief to walk out of the museum into the Manhattan traffic.
8. The scientist who planned the exhibition is Dr. Harry L. Shapiro, chairman of the museum's Department of Anthropology. He feels that the picture as presented is not in the least overdrawn. 'I think the prospects for survival are very grim', he said in an interview. 'Our only hope is to make people aware of it in time, because in the last analysis nothing can be done to regulate the consequences of our technology unless people are conditioned to accept regulation. A government cannot tell a family that it must have no more than two babies and one car. Instead we have to make people understand that survival depends upon their co-operation.
9. Of all the threats to survival – air and water pollution, food shortage, pesticides and noise – Dr. Shapiro believes that by far the greatest is the population explosion. 'This problem is overwhelming, and we do not have much time to solve it', he said. 'Already we have a situation far more insidious and far more dangerous than the atomic bomb. At least for the moment that is under control. But the population explosion is getting bigger day by day, and the prospects of getting an international consortium on this are not good.'
10. Dr. Shapiro said that if he had an entirely free hand there was one further point he would have had the exhibition make. 'There used to be so many hazards to man's survival that it was necessary for him to produce numbers of children. Now we – the developed nations – have created a terrible problem for the under-developed people. We have gone into their countries and killed off the bugs that were decimating them. We have changed the entire pattern of living for them, while they have not changed theirs one scrap. But for all sorts of reasons we have still not succeeded in showing them how to adjust to the new pattern by limiting their reproduction rate. So in a generation or two we may have a major disaster – a famine or a revolution which could irrevocably affect the entire world.'

Write down the time taken to read this passage and then attempt the Comprehension Test.

Comprehension Test

Select the most suitable answer in each case. Do not refer back to the passage.

1. The 'Can Man Survive?' exhibition took place in
(*a*) London. (*b*) Paris.
(*c*) Washington. (*d*) New York.

2. There are now twice as many mouths to feed in the world as there were
(*a*) 4 years ago. (*b*) 40 years ago.
(*c*) 140 years ago. (*d*) 400 years ago.

3. The message at the exit from the exhibition read
(*a*) 'There are too many children in the world.'
(*b*) 'Please mind the garbage cans.'
(*c*) 'Can man survive? It is up to you'
(*d*) 'Can man survive? Not without birth control.'

4. Dr. Shapiro believes that by far the greatest threat to human survival is
(*a*) the population explosion.
(*b*) air and water pollution.
(*c*) food shortage.
(*d*) pesticides.

5. Dr. Shapiro said that, as a result of our failure to show undeveloped people how to limit their reproduction rate, in a generation or two there may be
(*a*) more people in the world than land for them to live on.
(*b*) a plague or an epidemic to restore the balance of nature.
(*c*) a considerable increase in the birth rate.
(*d*) a famine or a revolution which could irrevocably affect the entire world.

6. '......you can only go in the direction of the crowd, which becomes more and more claustrophobic.' Claustrophobic is
(*a*) a dread of confined spaces.
(*b*) a state of intoxication.
(*c*) a fear of heights.
(*d*) a fear of the dark.

7. The world of nature, as portrayed in the early stages of the exhibition is
(*a*) idyllic. (*b*) cool.
(*c*) noisy. (*d*) lifeless.

8. At the end of the exhibition the 'beat-up bus and a pile of garbage cans' symbolize
(*a*) the world of nature as it is today.
(*b*) the failure of man to develop beyond the primitive stage.
(*c*) the condition of western industrial civilization.
(*d*) the problems facing the underdeveloped countries.

9. Dr. Shapiro proposes that, to secure people's co-operation in limiting the size of their families, governments should
(*a*) tell them they must have no more than two babies.
(*b*) use persuasion.
(*c*) form persuasion, to look into the problem.
(*d*) use force.

10. The most important single point made by the exhibition was that
(*a*) the answers to man's problems are single ones.
(*b*) There was no hope for man's problems.
(*c*) It was up to governments to get together if man was to survive.
(*d*) It was up to the individual to act if man was to survive.

11. The underlined word 'harsh' in paragraph 3 contextually means
(*a*) brilliant. (*b*) cruel.
(*c*) challenging. (*d*) unpalatable.

12. The verb for the underlined word 'reproduction' in paragraph to is:
(*a*) reproductivity. (*b*) reproductible.
(*c*) reproduce. (*d*) produce again.

TEST – 4

(OBJECTIVE TYPE MULTIPLE-CHOICE TEST)

Directions: Read through the passage once only as quickly as you can without suffering loss of comprehension and answer the questions that follow.

Both plants and animals of many sorts show remarkable changes in form, structure, growth, habits and even mode of reproduction in becoming adapted to different climate, environment, types of food supply, or mode of living. This divergence in response of evolution is commonly expressed by altering the form and functions of some part or parts of the organism, the original identity of which is clearly discernible. For example, the creeping foot of the snail is seen in related marine peteropods to be modified into a flapping organ useful for swimming, and is changed into prehensile arms that bear suctorial disks in the squids and cephalopods. The limbs of various mammals are modified according to several different modes of life for swift running (cursorial) as in the horse and antelope, for swinging in trees (arboreal) as in monkeys, for flying (volant) as in the bats, for swimming (aquatic) as in the seals, whales and dolphins, and for other adaptations. The structure or organs that show main change in connection with this adaptive divergence are commonly identified readily as homologous, in spite of great alterations. Thus the finger and wrist bones of a bat and whale, for instance, have virtually nothing in common except that they are definitely equivalent elements of the mammalian limb.

1. The best title for this passage is
(*a*) Our changing Times.
(*b*) Unusual Structures.
(*c*) Adaptive Divergence.
(*d*) Evolution.

2. "Homologous" means
(*a*) corresponding. (*b*) simple.
(*c*) altered. (*d*) divergent.

3. Plants and animals change in form
(*a*) in swimming
(*b*) as they evolve
(*c*) to adjust to environment
(*d*) because of their structure.

4. Horses, monkeys, moles, bats and whales are
(*a*) mammalian (*b*) aquatic
(*c*) fossorial (*d*) Volant.

5. Cephalopods have
(*a*) discernible organs.
(*b*) homologous organs.
(*c*) creeping feet. (*d*) suctorial disks.

6. Marine peterpods
(*a*) swim. (*b*) crawl.
(*c*) grab. (*d*) suck.

7. The noun for the underlined word 'modified' is:
(*a*) modification (*b*) modality
(*c*) modify (*d*) modificance

TEST – 5
(OBJECTIVE TYPE MULTIPLE-CHOICE TEST)

Directions: Read through the passage once only as quickly as you can without suffering loss of comprehension and answer the questions that follow:

1. Advances in the field of science in the nineteenth century produced three important scientific theories – the conservation of energy, the conservation of matter and evolution. The first two pointed towards materialism; the third produced a revolution in thought similar to that which occurred in the seventeenth century.
2. The increase in knowledge was so great that science began to split up into the sub-branches we know today. Specialisation in rather narrow fields became more and more necessary.
3. An important characteristic of intellectual life in the nineteenth century was a growing respect for science. Comte (1798–1857), a French philosopher, evolved a system called 'positivism' in which science finally took the place of theology and metaphysics.
4. Attempts were made to make use of the scientific method in almost all branches of thought; to treat history, for example, as a science rather than an art.
5. For the first time, men of science came into open conflict with the views of philosophers. The leading philosopher of the beginning of the nineteenth century, Hegel (1770–1831), knew nothing of science. His view was that everything in the universe, including matter, was essentially moral or spiritual. His philosophy was reasonable when applied to history and morals, but seemed absurd to men of science, when applied to the natural sciences.
6. The great scientific principles of the

indestructibility of matter and of the conservation of energy led to the view that the essential reality of the universe was matter and that the behaviour of matter obeyed scientific laws. Organic matter, the chemists showed, obeyed laws just as inorganic matter did, and life itself, according to the theory of evolution, had developed mechanistically.

7. John Tyndall, the physicist, stated that just as atoms and molecules combined to produce the beautiful and complicated forms of crystals, so they also form the more complicated living matter, plants and animals. Thoughts are the result of chemical activity in the brain. If the brain is damaged, the mind cannot function normally. So the mind is a product of matter. Tyndall also stated publicly that what had prevented the advance of science until comparatively recent times had been the opposition of the Church.

8. The conflict between science and religion went on all through the later part of the nineteenth century. While people like W.G. Ward believed that knowledge is gained by intuition and revelation, and believe in the supernatural, others like Thomas Huxley held that knowledge could be gained only by experience and the scientific method and did not accept the supernatural. Huxley invented the word 'agnostic' to describe his own attitude to religion.

9. The attitude of the Roman Catholic Church during the conflict was unmoved. As a result of the dogma of the infallibility of the Pope, made public in 1870, there could be no argument about his utterances on matters of faith and morals. Catholics who were guilty of 'modernism' were excommunicated. Among Protestants there was a group of fundamentalists who believed in the absolute truth of the Bible story of the creation and refused to accept evolution.

Questions:

1. An important characteristic of intellectual life in the 19th century was:
   (*a*) a love of literature.
   (*b*) a growing respect for science.
   (*c*) a respect for metaphysics.
   (*d*) a belief in God.
2. The philosophical system called 'positivism' was evolved by:
   (*a*) Hegel. (*b*) Tyndall.
   (*c*) The Pope. (*d*) Comte.
3. Hegel's view was that everything in the universe was:
   (*a*) based on science.
   (*b*) essentially moral or spiritual.
   (*c*) essentially religious.
   (*d*) the result of accident.
4. John Tyndall believed that thoughts were the result of:
   (*a*) electrical activity in the brain.
   (*b*) the movement of atoms.
   (*c*) chemical activity in the brain.
   (*d*) blood circulation in the brain.
5. The dogma of the infallibility of the Pope was made public in:
   (*a*) 1798. (*b*) 1831.
   (*c*) 1857. (*d*) 1870.
6. The theory of the conservation of energy held that:
   (*a*) the total quantity of energy in the universe was invariable.
   (*b*) energy could be stored up for future use.
   (*c*) the universe came into being as a result of natural causes.
   (*d*) the dogma of the infallibility of the Pope was incorrect.
7. It would be reasonable to suppose that 'positivists' were:
   (*a*) Christians. (*b*) Deists.
   (*c*) Catholics. (*d*) Atheists.
8. The important scientific theories of the 19th century:
   (*a*) confirmed the existence of God.
   (*b*) challenged the existence of God.
   (*c*) converted everyone to Catholicism.
   (*d*) turned everyone against religion.
9. An agnostic is one who:
   (*a*) believes in God.
   (*b*) sometimes believes in God.
   (*c*) doubts the existence of God.
   (*d*) denies the existence of God.
10. In the 19th century:
    (*a*) no Catholics were scientists.
    (*b*) few Catholics were scientists.

(*c*) many Catholics were scientists.
(*d*) all Catholics were scientists.

11. The opposite for the underlined word 'gained' in paragraph 8 can be:
(*a*) failed. (*b*) attained.
(*c*) lost. (*d*) retained.

TEST – 6

(OBJECTIVE TYPE MULTIPLE-CHOICE TEST)

Directions: Read through the passage once only as quickly as you can without suffering loss of comprehension and answer the questions that follow:

1. The Germans, because they led the world in theoretical chemistry, were the leaders in the fine chemical industry, producing dyes, perfumes, drugs and explosives. The First World War obliged other countries to set up their own chemical industries, with the result that production in Britain and the USA later became greater than that of Germany.
2. Germany led too in the optical industry, again because of her superior science and because she set up research laboratories for industry. She produced the finest cameras, microscopes, spectrometers and other scientific instruments.
3. Towards the end of the century industrialised Europe could no longer produce enough food to feed its greatly increased population. Food was imported from North America, where machines like the combine harvester were invented to help to meet the demand for greater production. Refrigeration and canning enabled meat, fish and fruit to be transported to Europe over the oceans of the world. The first cargo of frozen meat reached England in 1880.
4. The nineteenth century was a period of great public optimism based on enormous scientific and technological advances and rising standards of living. People believed in automatic and inevitable progress.
5. The origin of the idea of progress goes back about 300 years, to the time of Francis Bacon and the beginnings of modern science. It was an unknown idea in classical times. In the Middle Ages men looked backward to a Golden Age. In the eighteenth century, however, the idea of the progress of knowledge, the result of the development of reason and science, became very general.
6. The theory of evolution seemed to support the idea of inevitable progress. Everything is evolving, said Spencer, and the direction of evolution must be good. Spencer was convinced that mankind was becoming better and better and would finally reach perfection.
7. In spite of the horrors of the two world wars, which showed that modern man is still capable of the greatest cruelty, many people still believe in the idea of progress. But it is a belief in purely material progress, the product of technological advance.
8. Most scientific advances of the nineteenth century were made in France, Britain and Germany. The science of these three countries had some distinctive characteristics. French science was often perfect in form and thought; English science was individualistic and often highly original; German science was thorough and very well organised.
9. For the first quarter of the century, Paris was the scientific centre of the world. In 1794 the Ecole Polytechnic and the Ecole Normale Superieure were founded and these trained many of finest French scientists throughout the century. In 1795, the Academy of Sciences, closed during the Revolution, was re-opened. Although later in the century France produced an outstanding figure, Pasteur, she never again was as great a leader in science as she had been in the past.
10. From about 1830 until 1865 the most important scientific developments came from Britain, in the work of Lyell, Faraday, Joule, Darwin and Maxwell. Of these five men Joule, Darwin and Lyell were amateurs with private incomes and Faraday worked at the Royal Institution.

Questions:

1. The leaders in the fine chemical industry in the nineteenth century were:
(*a*) the British. (*b*) the French.
(*c*) the Germans. (*d*) the Americans.

2. The leaders in the optical industry were:
(*a*) the British. (*b*) the French.
(*c*) the Germans. (*d*) the Americans.

3. In the nineteenth century, people believed progress was:
(*a*) unlikely. (*b*) possible.
(*c*) likely. (*d*) inevitable.

4. Spencer was convinced that mankind:
(*a*) was becoming better and better.
(*b*) was getting worse and worse.
(*c*) was perfect.
(*d*) was doomed.

5. From 1830 to 1865, the most important scientific developments came from:
(*a*) Britain. (*b*) France.
(*c*) Germany. (*d*) USA.

6. The First World War obliged several countries to set up their own chemical industries because of:
(*a*) the need for paint.
(*b*) the need for explosives.
(*c*) the need for perfumes.
(*d*) the need for food.

7. The belief in the perfectibility of man suffered a setback as a result of:
(*a*) the theory of evolution.
(*b*) the World Wars.
(*c*) the progress of science.
(*d*) the ideas of Spencer.

8. Inventiveness in science was a distinctive characteristic in:
(*a*) USA. (*b*) Germany.
(*c*) France. (*d*) Britain.

9. In becoming the scientific centre of the world in the first quarter of the nineteenth century, Paris was helped by:
(*a*) its educational facilities.
(*b*) the Revolution.
(*c*) the competition from Germany.
(*d*) Britain.

10. Most of the important nineteenth century British scientists were:
(*a*) French. (*b*) poor.
(*c*) engineers. (*d*) amateurs.

11. The word 'distinctive' in question 8 means:
(*a*) different (*b*) basic
(*c*) mysterious (*d*) typical

TEST – 7

(OBJECTIVE TYPE MULTIPLE-CHOICE TEST)

***Directions*:** Read through the passage once only as quickly as you can without suffering loss of comprehension and answer the questions that follow.

Adopting the Korean pattern of waging war without declaring it, of nominating only a few to do the killing while the rest stayed home to make a killing, we corrupted a whole generation. Young men were openly counselled in ways to beat the system; innumerable college men took education courses so they could become elementary-school teachers when they had no vocation for such work but only a desire to evade the draft. The poor went to war and the rich stayed home. Ghetto youths were sent to Vietnam while members of professional athletic teams were provided with escape hatches. Young men joined the National Guard to avoid service overseas, and girls were coached on how to marry quickly and become pregnant even more quickly so as to help their men beat an evil system.

Questions:

1. From the passage, we can infer all of the following except
(*a*) The war on Korea was not officially declared.
(*b*) The soldiers for the war were nominated by the Government.
(*c*) A number of people avoided being drafted by using loopholes in the law.
(*d*) The system of drafting gave some people with the wherewithal, the opportunity of avoiding the draft.

2. According to the passage, all the following categories of people were exempted from being drafted except
(*a*) members of the National Guard.
(*b*) college students.
(*c*) members of professional athletic teams.
(*d*) elementary school teachers.

3. The author seems to see the tragedy of the Korean war in

(*a*) the widespread corruption in Government.

(*b*) creating an evil system of drafting.

(*c*) a generation being taught how to cheat.

(*d*) the injustice of a war waged but not declared.

4. According to the passage, all the following were consequences of the Korean war except

(*a*) people took up occupations in which they had no interest or aptitude.

(*b*) injustice was perpetrated on the less fortunate in society.

(*c*) the young were taught to beat a system.

(*d*) a new generation learnt that killing is bad for the system.

5. The underlined word 'it' is a

(*a*) noun (*b*) pronoun

(*c*) adjective (*d*) preposition

TEST – 8

(OBJECTIVE TYPE MULTIPLE-CHOICE TEST)

***Directions*:** Read through the passage once only as quickly as you can without suffering loss of comprehension and answer the questions that follow:

1. One of the unfortunate features of the human condition is that the natural exploratory behaviour of human infants has to be curtailed, especially in conditions of civilization, where the hazards of traffic, electricity, gas, stairs and many other complex dangers have been added to those which are found in primitive, rural circumstances. We are forced to overprotect our children psychologically, because we live in an artificial environment; and, because small children are ill-equipped to look after themselves when surrounded by the dangerous trappings of civilization; we tend to guard them too carefully in situations where this is not necessary.

2. In a recent experience, Eleanor Gibson constructed a 'visual cliff', that is, a floor which appears to end in a sheer drop, but which is actually safe since the floor continues as a sheet of tough glass. Babies crawl to the apparent edge but will not venture on to the glass even if encouraged to do so, since they are already aware of the danger of the drop. This is not to say that it is safe to leave a baby on the edge of a real cliff, since the child may turn round and fall off backwards.

3. The pioneer doctors who started the Pacham Health Centre discovered that quite tiny children could be safely left in the sloping shallow end of a swimming bath. Provided no adult interfered with them, they would teach themselves to swim, exploring the water gradually and never venturing beyond the point at which they began to feel unsafe. Similarly, children would teach themselves to ride bicycles and use gymnasium equipment and did so more confidently and quickly than if adults tried either to urge them on or warn them to be careful. The American analyst Clara Thompson writes:

4. "Aggression is not necessarily destructive at all. It springs from an innate tendency to grow and master life which seems to be characteristic of all living matter. Only when this life force is obstructed in its development do ingredients of anger, rage or hate become connected with it."

5. It is a pity that our culture makes such obstruction inevitable; and one reason why aggressiveness is a problem to modern man is that the natural exploratory urge to grasp and master the environment has perforce to be limited in a way which is bound to cause frustration. There are far too many things which children must not do or must not touch; so that within all of us who have been brought up in Western civilization, especially in urban civilization, there must be reserves of repressed, and therefore dangerous, aggression which originate from the restrictions of early childhood.

Questions:

1. A suitable title for the passage would be

(*a*) Aggression and the Western Man.

(*b*) Repression the cause of Aggression.

(*c*) Let the Child Alone.

(*d*) Dangers of Urban Civilization.

2. According to the author, aggression

(*a*) is natural to all of us.

(*b*) gets invariably frustrated.

(*c*) is a predominant characteristic in urban children particularly.
(*d*) cannot be fully repressed.

3. According to the doctors of Pacham Health Centre, the best way the adults could contribute towards the child's learning such activities as swimming and bicycle riding is:
(*a*) by being indifferent to the children.
(*b*) by encouraging them to be aggressive.
(*c*) by warning them of obvious dangers.
(*d*) by not interfering.

4. Which of the following statements is true:
(*a*) In rural surroundings it was not necessary to protect children.
(*b*) In rural communities life was free from hazards.
(*c*) Civilization with its complexities adds to the list of dangers already existing.
(*d*) In cities it becomes necessary to overprotect children.

5. Ms. Eleanor Gibson's experiment indicates that:
(*a*) children are born free and fearless, but adults tend to dampen their spirits.
(*b*) parental overprotection leads to frustration and excessive aggression in children.
(*c*) children are conscious of common dangers.
(*d*) it may not be wise to leave a baby on the edge of a real cliff.

6. Which of the following, if true, would seriously undermine the validity of Ms. Gibson's findings that:
(*a*) babies are not aggressive by nature.
(*b*) some babies did fall off the visual cliff.
(*c*) some babies did crawl beyond the apparent edge of the cliff.
(*d*) some babies did not venture to climb even up to the edge of the cliff.

7. According to the author, dangerous aggression is the result of:
(*a*) rage and anger.
(*b*) repression and frustration.
(*c*) hate and disbelief.
(*d*) parental dominance.

8. It can be inferred that the passage is excerpted from:
(*a*) a book advising mothers on the upbringing of children.
(*b*) a guide to town planners advocating more sensible planning of urban environs.
(*c*) a technical study of child behaviour meant for psychologists.
(*d*) none of the above.

9. The author is clearly against adults:
(*a*) guarding the children carefully.
(*b*) making their children less aggressive.
(*c*) overprotecting the children.
(*d*) not encouraging their children to be brave and daring.

10. The adjective for the underlined word 'carefully' in paragraph 1 is
(*a*) care (*b*) care taking
(*c*) careful (*d*) careless

11. In context, the opposite for the underlined word 'Pity' in paragraph 5 can be
(*a*) pride (*b*) greatness
(*c*) tragedy (*d*) stupidity

TEST – 9

(SUBJECTIVE TYPE CLOZE TEST)

Directions: Fill in the blanks with appropriate words in context. You can read the whole passage before beginning the task.

This bitterness, which is the bitterness of fear, made some shopkeepers bawl out rudely to many beggars who came hourly to beg at their doors. It made men ruthless in paying small fares _______ [1] the rickshaw-pullers, of which there were ten times _______ [2] many as could be used, because the refugees _______ [3] trying to earn something thus. Even the usual _______ [4] of rickshaws who followed this as their profession _______ [5] the refugees because, being starved, they would pull _______ [6] anything given to them, and no fares were low _______ [7] anyone, and everyone suffered. With the city full _______ [8] refugees, then, begging at every door, swarming into _______ [9] unskilled trade and service, lying dead on the ______[10] at every frozen dawn, why should one look ______[11] this fresh horde coming in now at twilight ______[12] a winter's day?

TEST – 10

(SUBJECTIVE TYPE CLOZE TEST)

Directions: Fill in the blanks with appropriate words in context. You can read the whole passage before beginning the task.

The Land, the human settlements, the forests, the flora and fauna, the water bodies and the envelope of air all constitute a spatial entity. Some of these components are more ________[1] and fragile than others and are ________[2] susceptible to degradation due to pollution. ________[3] planning is vital to protect these ________[4] areas. However, this concept or tool ________[5] seldom been used in India. Proper ________[6] of newly planned industries and industrial ________[7] is a strong pollution preventive instrument ________[8] ensures environmental sustainability of the industrial ________[9]. It is the site that ultimately ________[10], which water bodies might be affected ________[11] effluents streaming out of an industry, ________[12] air shed might be affected by air ________[13] or which ecosystem might be harmed. ________[14] above urgency can also be emphasized ________[15] the Bhopal Gas Tragedy'. Had there ________[16] a sufficient compatibility between the industry ________[17] the surrounding land uses, the impact ________[18] the accident would have been less ________[19].

TEST – 11

(OBJECTIVE TYPE MCP TEST)

Directions: Read the following passage carefully. A few words in the beginning have been written without any bracketed words. This will facilitate you to understand the context. Each bracket contains 4 (four) choices; 1 (one) choice is correct and 3 (three) are incorrect. Choose the correct choice so that the whole passage becomes a coherent piece of writing.

"Do what I say, not what I do". Most parents know that command just doesn't work. Our children learn from watching what we do. They (learn, watch, work, think)[1] what we think is important by (a, this, the, that)[2] way we spend our time and (the, those, many, numerous)[3] activities we're involved in. Young children (were, had been, have been, are)[4] great imitators, and, in a very (real, false, rare, common)[5] sense, parents are their children's first (but, or, and, though)[6] most important teachers. What parents value, (growing, elderly, young, infant)[7] children learn to value – especially in (literacy, education, studies, reading)[8].

Learning to enjoy and value reading (and, or, without, with)[9] writing starts at home. Parents can (think, encourage, makė, help)[10] their children see reading and writing (as, very, too, much)[11] important as well as fun by (taking, creating, having, making)[12] these activities part of family life. (The, when, now, where)[13] families participate in activities together related (for, with, to, about)[14] reading and writing, it demonstrates the (weightage, importance, impotence, value)[15] placed on those subjects. When you (allot, dedicate, give, permit)[16] your children time and encouragement to (read, study, prepare, develop)[17] and write you help them practice (or, except, but, and)[18] develop these skills.

Summer is the (absolute, perfect, great, true)[19] time for parents to make reading (and, without, or, with)[20] writing a part of regular family, (life, entertainment, problem, trees)[21]. Many studies show that young children (gain, prepare, lose, misuse)[22] some of their reading skills over (a, this, the, one)[23] summer for lack of practice. Activities (in, at, from, from, into)[24] home can help children sharpen their (crafts, skills, intelligence, brain)[25] and be ready for school after (the, a, one, some)[26] break.

This booklet contains over twenty (ideas, items, requests, commands)[27] you can use to help make (those, that, this, the)[28] summer a "family reading" summer. You (can't, won't, shouldn't, don't)[29] need a formal education or a (crore, lot, sum, collection)[30] of money to help your children (love, develop, stop, continue)[31] reading; just a little time, some (ideas, thoughts, theories, philosophy)[32] and desire.

TEST – 12

(OBJECTIVE TYPE MCP TEST)

Directions: Read the following passage carefully. A few words in the beginning have been written without any bracketed words. This will facilitate you to understand the context. Each bracket contains 4 (four) choices; 1 (one) choice is correct and 3 (three) are incorrect. You are instructed to choose the correct choice so that the whole passage becomes a coherent piece of writing.

What will man be like in the future – in 5,000 or even 50,000 years from now? We can only (construct, fabricate, imagine, make)[1] a guess, of course, but we (may, can, should, must)[2] be sure that he will be (separate, similar, different, apart)[3] from what he is today. For (human, man, he, person)[4] is slowly changing all the (way, same, period, time)[5]. Let us take an obvious example. Man (even, still, just, as)[6] five hundred years ago, was shorter (around, than, as, to)[7] he is today. Now, on an (average, account, increase, inch)[8] men are about three inches (tall, taller, short, shorter).[9] Five hundred years is quite a short (term, period, era, quantity)[10] of time, so we may assume (instead, however, that, how)[11] man will continue to grow taller. (Since, Now, Then, Again)[12] in the modern world we use (the, all, our, many)[13] brains a great deal, but we (practice, make, apply, attempt)[14] use of only about 20% of (a, our, the, others')[15] brain's capacity. As time goes on, (however, whenever, moreover, nevertheless)[16], we shall have to use our (hands, bodies, brains, wits)[17] more and more – eventually we shall (need, demand, deserve, desire)[18] larger brains. This may bring about (the, one, a, this)[19] physical change too: the head, in (end, last, fact, particular)[20] the forehead, will grow larger.

Nowadays, (all, we, people, they)[21] use our eyes all the time. (With, In, To, For)[22] fact, we use them so much (which, when, that, whenever)[23] very often they become weaker and (they, we, all, you)[24] have to wear glasses. However, it (was, will be, isn't, is)[25] likely that over a (long, longer, longest, lengthy)[26] period of time, man's eyes will grow stronger (otherwise, instead, rather, now)[27] than weaker.

On the other hand, (we, they, people, I)[28] tend to make less use of (their, my, our, ours)[29] arms and legs. These, as a (finality, conclusion, result, cause)[30] may grow weaker. At the same (juncture, time, interval, rate)[31] however, our fingers will grow more (sensitive, competent, eligible, insensitive)[32] because they are used a great (sort, part, type, deal)[33] in modern life, as in computer (programming, management, operation, printing).[34]

But what about hair? This will (probably, unlikely, hopefully, definitely)[35] disappear from the body altogether in (period, interval, passage, course)[36] of time because it does not (serve, work, do, become)[37] a useful purpose any longer. In (a, the, coming, our)[38] future then, both men and women (may be, were, are, aren't)[39] likely to be bald.

Perhaps all (that, this, what, which)[40] gives the impression that the future (creature, human, person, man)[41] will not be a very attractive (individual, animal, creature, man)[42] to look at. This may be (fact, lie, real, true)[43]. But, in spite of all these (transformations, facts, changes, developments)[44] the future man will still have (the, a, his, this)[45] lot in common with us. He (may, can, would, will)[46] still be a human being, with (ideas, notions, views, thoughts)[47] and emotions similar to our own.

TEST – 13

(SUBJECTIVE TYPE C-TEST)

Directions: Fill in the blanks. Each blank begins with one or more than one letter. Taking a clue from that, you are directed to fill in the blanks in the following passage:

Four weeks ago I was late for work. I left my house five minutes later than usual and I saw **m**__________[1] bus approaching the bus stop. I began to **r**__________[2], but I was too slow. I waited ten **mi**__________[3] for another bus and I was still gasping **f**__________[4] air when it arrived. The next day I **g**__________[5] up smoking. For the first few days I **w**__________[6] very irritable, but now I feel much better. **N**__________[7] I can ask: Why do people smoke?

Every **y**__________[8] teams of doctors publish reports saying that smoking **i**__________[9] dangerous for your health. Every year the Government

p________[10] for advertisements telling people that smoking is bad **f**________[11] for them. But there are millions of people who **st**________[12] smoke twenty or thirty cigarettes a day.

In **s**________[13] countries advertisements for cigarettes are not allowed on **tel**________[14]. If you read a newspaper or a magazine **y**________[15] will see cigarette advertisements but at the bottom **o**________[16] each advertisement you will see the government health **wa**________[17] – Cigarette Smoking is Injurious to Health. You can **re**________[18] this warning on cigarette packets also. And yet **pe**________[19] die every year from the effects of smoking. **O**________[20] wonders why people smoke.

Experts in various fields **s**________[21] that it is difficult to understand why people **be**________[22] to smoke and why they make it a **ha**________[23]. Most people start smoking because other people around **th**________[24] do it. Children feel it makes them seem **ad**________[25] to smoke, and other children also encourage them **t**________[26] smoke. Some children see their parents smoking, so **th**________[27] start smoking too. The effect that smoking has **o**________[28] a person helps to make it a habit. **Cig**________[29] contain nicotine which has an effect on the **he**________[30] and the nervous system. Smoking one or two **Cig**________[31] causes an increase in the heart rate and **a**________[32] slight rise in blood pressure. The effect of **sm**________[33] on the nervous system is that it reduces **te**________[34] and helps to relax. People want these effects **o**________[35] feel they need them and start depending on **th**________[36] and so they go on smoking.

TEST – 14

(SUBJECTIVE TYPE C-TEST)

Directions: Fill in the blanks. Each blank begins with one or more than one letter. Taking a clue from that, you are directed to fill in the blanks in the following passage:

Fashion is a term commonly used to describe a style of clothing worn by a large number of **pe**________[1] in a country. However, popular styles **o**________[2] furniture, homes and many other products **a**________[3] also fashions. The kinds of art, **m**________[4], literature and sports that many people **pr**________[5] can also be fashions. Thus, a **fa**________[6] is – or reflects – a form of **beh**________[7] accepted by most people in a **so**________[8].

A fashion remains popular for a **f**________[9] months or years and then another **fa**________[10] takes its place. A product or **ac**________[11] is in fashion or is fashionable **du**________[12] the period of time that many **pe**________[13] in society accept it. After a **t**________[14], however, the same product or activity **be**________[15] old – fashioned when the majority of **pe**________[16] no longer accept it.

A clothing **st**________[17] may start as a fashion but **i**________[18] use becomes a custom if it **i**________[19] handed down from generation to generation. **To**________[20], wearing long trousers is a custom **f**________[21] men in most countries. But changes **i**________[22] the colour and shape of trousers **h**________[23] taken place through the years. A **fa**________[24] that quickly comes and goes is **ca**________[25] a fad. The majority of people **d**________[26] not accept fads. Some people may **be**________[27] involved in faddish behaviour because fads **g**________[28] a lot of publicity.

Today people **fo**________[29] fashions for many reasons. For example, **th**________[30] want others to think that they **be**________[31] to a special class of society. **N**________[32] fashions may be adopted immediately by **w**________[33] known people, including athletes, film stars **a**________[34] political figures. Then, other people follow **th**________[35] fashions so that they can also **l**________[36] important. Some people think that fashionable **cl**________[37] and surroundings raise their status in **l**________[38].

People also follow fashions to make **th**________[39] more attractive. Standards of beauty change **th**________[40] the years, and people decorate themselves **ac**______[41] to the changing standards. Ideas of **be**______[42] also change from culture to culture. **F**______[43] example, people in many countries use **co**______[44] to look attractive. In some countries **pe**______[45] decorate themselves with tattoos.

Men and **wo**______[46] have always enjoyed changing their appearance. **Fol**______[47] new fashions in clothes, hairstyles **a**______[48] makeup allow people to change their **ap**______[49] in a way which is generally **ac**______[50].

TEST – 15
(SUBJECTIVE TYPE C-TEST)

Directions: Fill in the blanks. Each blank begins with one or more than one letter. Taking a clue from that, you are directed to fill in the blanks in the following passage:

Perhaps the most important contribution of forests to modern civilization is that they provide the raw material for making **pa**______[1]. The Chinese who invented paper several thousand **ye**______[2] back used the inner bark of certain **t**______[3] for making paper. Today, paper is made **mo**______[4] from wood, bamboo and certain types of **gr**______[5]. The paper on which this book has **b**______[6] printed must have been made out of **w**______[7] or bamboo and certain types of grasses. **V**______[8] little work can be done these days **wi**______[9] the use of paper, and we can **e**______[10] say that modern civilization depends on paper.

T______[11] are a large number of other raw **mat**______[12] which come from the forests. Pine trees **yi**______[13] resin from which resin and turpentine are **man**______[14]. Resin is used in the sizing of **pa**______[15] and textiles and for making paints, varnishes, **po**______[16] and adhesives. Turpentine is used for making **p**______[17] and varnishes. It is also used for **ma**______[18] medicines, and is now being used for **t**______[19] manufacture of artificial camphor, which is used **f**______[20] medicines, and during religious ceremonious. Natural camphor **i**______[21] also produced by forests and it comes **f**______[22] the wood and leaves of the camphor **w**______[23] tree which is mostly found in China **a**______[24] Taiwan. But now in our country all **ca**______[25] is obtained from turpentine. Some forest trees **yi**______[26] gums which are not only used for **st**______[27] paper but are also used in the **pre**______[28] of sweets and ice-creams.

Medicinal herbs and **pl**______[29] are another important gift of the forests **t**______[30] mankind. They are used in the Ayurvedic **a**______[31] Unani as well as the modern systems **o**______[32] medicine. The Ayurvedic and Unani systems of **med**______[33] have been practiced in our country for **cen**______[34] and they both rely on medicinal plants **a**______[35] herbs. In every village shop in India, **o**______[36] can buy dried roots, barks, leaves, flowers **o**______[37] fruits of different medicinal plants which are **u**______[38] for common diseases.

In the life of **o**______[39] rural people products from the forests play **a**______[40] important role. They provide people with material **t**______[41] make huts and to thatch roofs, wood **f**______[42] making bullock carts, agricultural tools and household **fur**______[43] and fibres for making ropes, nets, mats, **ba**______[44] and many other items of daily use.

TEST – 16
(OBJECTIVE TYPE MCP-TEST)

Directions: Read the following passage carefully. A few words in the beginning have been written without any bracketed words. This will facilitate you to understand the context. Each bracket contains 4 (four) choices; 1 (one) choice is correct and 3 (three) are incorrect. You are instructed to choose the correct choice so that the whole passage becomes a coherent piece of writing.

The parents in Family Reading progress were concerned about helping their children manage money. They developed these activities to help turn money management into reading (progress, improvement, innovation, upliftment)[1].

"I take my sons to the bank (for, alongwith, with, around)[2] me and teach them how to deposit (or, and, instead, besides)[3] withdraw money from our account and to (scribble, draft, write, read)[4] cheques the proper way. Sometimes they fill (out, in, down, around)[5] the deposit slips or write down the (slip, cheque, paper, draft)[6] themselves. This way I can also show (children, them, others, sons)[7] how to balance their money and be (responsible, answerable, questionable, responsive)[8] for it."

"We have our children help (them, others, parents, us)[9] sort the mail each day, using a (packet, drawer, folder, box)[10] as file for each type of bill. (Others, They, We, Parents)[11] show the children how to mark the (paper, item, thing, bill)[12] 'paid' after we pay for it, then how (to, about, in, inside)[13] file it in the proper space. We (only, just, always, also)[14] show them that it is easier to (file, fill, tag, list)[15] the most recent bill in front so (that, this, it everything)[16] is easy to find if we need (to, in, about, for)[17] check our bill again. This activity teaches, (many, other, some, our)[18] children how to alphabetize and how to (detect, estimate, find, think)[19] what our bills will be. For example, (children, they, bills, things)[20] are different in the winter months as (opposed, opposite, contrast, contradictory)[21] to the summer. It is a very (beautiful, practical, theoretical, idealistic)[22] activity".

"My kids, always want new clothes—(always, never, seldom, sometimes)[23] expensive ones—because 'that's what everybody else (was, is, has been, had been)[24] wearing". Before school starts each year, we (decide, resolve, determine, use)[25] how much money we can afford to (expend, waste, spend, use)[26] on new clothes. Then my children make (the, an, one, this)[27] inventory of what they currently have. They (narrow, write, scribble, describe)[28] down what they have of each piece, (the, a, some, any)[29] colour, the size etc. Then they write (up, in, about, down)[30] what they want to buy and how (many, much, cheap, costly)[31] each item costs. Then we look at (the, their, these, any)[32] two lists together and make a final (list, activity, size, estimate)[33] of what they actually need and will (want, spend, use, have)[34] their money to buy. This also stops (a, the, however, therefore)[35] lot of fights at the shops. If (everything, anything, one, something)[36] is not on their list or in (one, the, their, a)[37] budget, they know not to ask for (it, something, one, some)[38].

TEST – 17

(SUBJECTIVE TYPE CLOZE TEST)

***Directions*:** Fill in the blanks with appropriate words in context. You can read the whole passage before beginning the task.

Some families created home literacy exercises designed to help children learn about family history, religion and values. For example:

"We live far away__________[1] our families and we want our__________[2] to know them and how important__________[3] are to us. Even though we __________[4] see them often, we can write __________[5] letters. Sometimes, my children write their__________[6] letters, sometimes they write for me. __________[7] tell them what I want to __________[8] then they write it down for __________[9]. Their 'Naniji' – grandmother likes the letters__________[10] children write because she can see__________[11] hand-writing. I have then address the__________[12] too. Sometimes we go to the __________[13] office together to mail the letters. __________[14] try to write a letter each__________[15] to a different relative. I save__________[16] of the letters the relatives send__________[17] us because I think my children__________[18] like to read them again when__________[19] are older. It will help them __________[20] their grandparents and what life was __________[21] in our country."

"Our family goes__________[22] church together. We bring home the__________[23] each week and use it to__________[24] reading. Sometimes we read prayers from__________[25] prayer book or stories from the__________[26]. Frequently my children write down the__________[27] they learn at church."

"I use__________[28] to help my children learn about__________[29]. For example, I told my daughter '__________[30] is only skin deep.' Then we __________[31] about what that meant. We made __________[32] whole list of sayings and wrote __________[33] the lesson that each one taught. __________[34] think these are important values for __________[35] daughter to learn."

TEST – 18

(SUBJECTIVE TYPE CLOZE TEST)

Directions: Fill in the blanks with appropriate words in context. You can read the whole passage before beginning the task.

A puppet is an artificial figure whose movements are controlled by a person. Puppets can be moved by hand ______[1] by strings, wires or rods. A figure ______[2] represent a person, an animal, a plant ______[3] an object. Puppets usually appear as characters ______[4] plays called PUPPET SHOWS. A person who ______[5] a puppet is called a PUPPETEER.

Many ______[6] make puppets from such cheap materials as ______[7] and wood or from such items as ______[8] packing and rags. They write puppet shows ______[9] operate the puppets, varying their voice for ______[10] character. A table or bookcase can be ______[11] as a stage for a puppet show. ______[12] puppeteer can also work behind a blanket ______[13] a sheet tied across the lower part ______[14] a doorway. We cannot see the puppeteer. ______[15] see only the puppets performing in the ______[16] part of the doorway.

Hand puppets are______[17] most common puppets. One variety, the glove ______[18] fist puppet, consists of a hollow head ______[19] to a glove or a piece of______[20] used as the puppet's body. The body ______[21] over the hand of the puppeteer who ______[22] a thumb into one of the puppet's ______[23], one or two fingers go into the ______[24] arm and the remaining fingers in the ______[25]. These puppets can pick up and throw______[26] and can gesture strongly with their head ______[27] arms. Most glove puppets have no legs ______[28] feet.

Another type of puppets are those ______[29] are controlled by strings or by wires. ______[30] are known as marionettes. A marionette has ______[31] complete body with head, trunk, arms, hands, ______[32] and feet. Strips of cloth or other ______[33] material connect the various parts of the ______[34]. Most marionettes have strings that run ______[35] the head, the shoulders, the hands and ______[36] knees to a small wooden frame. One ______[37] more puppeteers, who are hidden above the ______[38], operate the marionettes by moving the strings ______[39] they are tied to the frame.

TEST – 19

(SUBJECTIVE TYPE CLOZE TEST)

Directions: Fill in the blanks with appropriate words in context. You can read the whole passage before beginning the task.

A rich old lady was steadily losing her eyesight, so she called in a famous doctor who examined her and offered to cure her completely. He ______[1] a very big fee, and ______[2] rich lady gladly agreed to ______[3] him the money if he ______[4] restore her sight. The doctor ______[5] her eyes and carried out ______[6] treatment, which took several days. ______[7] he was very greedy. He ______[8] many beautiful pieces of furniture ______[9] which the house of his ______[10] was furnished, and each day ______[11] carried away one of the ______[12] pieces till there was hardly ______[13] left.

In the course of ______[14], the lady was completely cured. ______[15] bandage was taken off, and ______[16] could see everything clearly. Then ______[17] discovered that almost all her ______[18] was gone. When the doctor ______[19] for his payment, she said, '______[20] here, doctor I am by______[21] means cured, for I cannot ______[22] my furniture in my house. ______[23] not going to pay you ______[24]. The doctor was thus paid ______[25] his own coin.

TEST – 20
(SUBJECTIVE TYPE CLOZE TEST)

Directions: Fill in the blanks with appropriate words in context. You can read the whole passage before beginning the task.

This lack of food was confirmed when one looked closely into the faces of the people. In the first glance in the twilight they ______[1] well enough, but when one looked more closely ______[2] saw they were the faces of people starving ______[3] moving now in despair to a last hope. ______[4] saw nothing of the strange sights of a ______[5] city because they were too near death to ______[6] anything. No new sight could move their curiosity, ______[7] were men and women, who had stayed by ______[8] land until starvation drove them forth. Thus they ______[9], silent, alien, as those who know themselves ______[10] are alien to the living.

POETRY
TEST – 1
(OBJECTIVE TYPE MULTIPLE-CHOICE TEST)

There Isn't Time

There isn't time, there isn't time
To do the things I want to do

With all the mountain tops to climb
And all the woods to wander through

And all the seas to sail upon,
And everywhere there is to go,

And all the people, every one,
Who live upon the earth to know,

There's only time, there's only time,
To know a few, and do a few,

And then sit down and make a rhyme
About the rest I want to do.

Questions:

1. The poet says that there is no time because
   (*a*) he is a very busy man.
   (*b*) life is short.
   (*c*) he is very old.
   (*d*) All of the above.
2. In the lines "And all the people, every one, / who live upon the earth to know," the poet means that
   (*a*) everyone should know everyone on earth.
   (*b*) we should know all living things, people and animals on earth.
   (*c*) we would like to know everyone on earth.
   (*d*) All of the above.
3. In this poem, the poet is
   (*a*) sad. (*b*) dissatisfied.
   (*c*) happy. (*d*) insecure.
4. For those things which the poet does not have any time, he wishes to
   (*a*) sit down and compose a poem.
   (*b*) find the time.
   (*c*) be satisfied with a few things in life.
   (*d*) imagine them.
5. In the poem, the poet wants to know
   (*a*) all the mountains, forests and seas
   (*b*) everyone existing on this earth
   (*c*) all that is available on earth
   (*d*) All of the above

TEST – 2
(OBJECTIVE TYPE MULTIPLE-CHOICE TEST)

Nobody To Help Me

Mrs. O'Neill

There's nobody to help me
If I want a cup of tea,
No one to talk to
Except my old TV.

There's nobody to lift me
When I can't get out of bed
No one to cry on
Or to stroke my poor old head.

There's nobody to rely on
When I want my shopping done,
No one to be my friend,
For friends I have none.

Questions:

1. The poetess says that there is nobody to help her if
   (*a*) she wants to go out.
   (*b*) she wants a cup of tea.
   (*c*) she wants to sit.
   (*d*) she wants to have her shopping done.
2. The poetess is in this condition because
   (*a*) she has been turned out of her home.
   (*b*) she has grown old.
   (*c*) she is poor.
   (*d*) She is issueless.
3. In this poem, the poetess is
   (*a*) cheerful (*b*) thoughtful
   (*c*) sad (*d*) reminiscent
4. In this poem, the poetess talks to
   (*a*) herself (*b*) her friend
   (*c*) her TV (*d*) her pet
5. In the poem, the poetess talks about
   (*a*) her old TV
   (*b*) her illness
   (*c*) her loneliness
   (*d*) her chores to be done

TEST – 1

(OBJECTIVE TYPE MULTIPLE-CHOICE TEST)

The Lake Isle of Innisfree

I will arise and go now, and go to Innisfree,
And a small cabin build there, of clay and wattles made:
Nine bean rows will I have there, a hive for the honey-bee,
And live alone in the bee-loud glade.

And I shall have some peace there, for peace comes dropping slow,
Dropping from the veils of the morning to where the cricket sings;
There midnight's all a glimmer, and noon a purple glow,
And evening full of the linnet's wings.

I will arise and go now, for always night and day
I hear lake water lapping with low sounds by the shore;
While I stand on the roadway, or on the pavements grey,
I hear it in the deep heart's core.

Questions:

1. The poet intends to go to Innisfree because he wants to
   (*a*) start a business there by setting up a honey industry.
   (*b*) build a small cabin of clay and wattles to live in.
   (*c*) swim and enjoy in the lake water.
   (*d*) enjoy the quiet and natural environment.
2. Pick out a word from the poem which means the same as – 'shine faintly'.
   (*a*) Glade
   (*b*) Glimmer
   (*c*) Glow
   (*d*) None of the above.
3. In the poem, the word 'Wattles' refers to:
   (*a*) twigs (*b*) bricks
   (*c*) wood (*d*) leaves
4. 'Veils of the morning' implies:
   (*a*) cloudy weather of the morning.
   (*b*) early hours of the morning.
   (*c*) layers of mist in the morning
   (*d*) gusts of wind in the morning.
5. The poet lives in
   (*a*) Innisfree.
   (*b*) near a lake.
   (*c*) in a lake isle.
   (*d*) in a city.
6. Write whether the following statements are 'True' or 'False':
   (*a*) The poet wishes to build a cabin of bricks.
   (*b*) The poet wishes to live alone far from the madding crowd of the cities.
   (*c*) In the lap of nature peace comes gradually.
   (*d*) The poet likes the buzzing of the bees.

TEST – 4

(OBJECTIVE TYPE MULTIPLE-CHOICE TEST)

On Killing a Tree

It takes much time to kill a tree,
Not a simple jab of the knife
Will do it. It has grown
Slowly consuming the earth,
Rising out of it, feeding
Upon its crust, absorbing
Years of sunlight, air, water,
And out of its leprous hide
Sprouting leaves.

So hack and chop
But this alone won't do it.
Not so much pain will do it.
The bleeding bark will heal
And from close to the ground
Will rise curled green twigs,
Miniature boughs
Which if unchecked will expand again
To former size.

No,
The root has to be pulled out-
Out of the anchoring earth;
It has to be roped, tied,
And pulled out-snapped out
Or pulled out entirely,
Out from the earth-cave,

And the strength of the tree exposed,
The source, white and wet,
The most sensitive, hidden
For years inside the earth.
Then the matter
Of scorching and choking
In sun and air,
Browning, hardening,
Twisting, withering,
And then it is done.

Questions:

1. A 'simple jab of knife' cannot kill a tree because
   (*a*) it has 'leprous hide' and fresh green leaves.
   (*b*) it has no blood flowing in it.
   (*c*) it has been fed by the crust of the earth.
   (*d*) it has been grown and nurtured by soil, sun, air and water.
2. The strength of the tree lies in
   (*a*) the root (*b*) the branches
   (*c*) the leaves (*d*) None of the above
3. What is it that finally kills the tree?
   (*a*) Lack of food
   (*b*) Lack of water
   (*c*) Getting uprooted
   (*d*) Getting exposed to the sun.
4. Find out a word from the poem which means the same as <u>'burning'</u>
   (*a*) Choking (*b*) Withering
   (*c*) Anchoring (*d*) Scorching
5. Find out a word from the poem which is the *opposite* of the word <u>'hidden'</u>.
   (*a*) Pulled (*b*) Consuming
   (*c*) Exposed (*d*) Leprous

TEST – 5

(OBJECTIVE TYPE MULTIPLE-CHOICE TEST)

Sympathy

I know what the caged bird feels, alas!
When the sun is bright on the upland slopes;
When the wind stirs soft through the springing grass,
And the river flows like a stream of glass;

When the first bird sings and the first bud opes,
And the faint perfume from its chalice steals-
I know what the caged bird feels!
I know why the caged bird beats his wing
Till its blood is red on the cruel bars;
For he must fly back to his perch and cling
when he fain would be on the bough a-swing;
And a pain still throbs in the old, old scars
And they pulse again with a keener sting-
I know why he beats his wing!

I know why the caged bird sings, ah me,
When his wing is bruised and his bosom sore-
When he beats his bars and would be free;
It is not a carol of joy or glee;

But a prayer that he sends from his heart's deep core,
But a plea, that upward to Heaven, he flings-
I know why the caged bird sings!

Questions:

1. State whether the following statements are <u>True</u> or <u>False</u>.
   (*a*) The caged bird beats his wings against the cage bars in an attempt to gain his freedom.
   (*b*) The caged bird sings out of joy.
   (*c*) The caged bird prays to God to set him free.
   (*d*) The bird prefers his cage to the bough of a tree.
   (*e*) The caged bird feels very uneasy when the sun is bright.
   (*f*) The caged bird feels miserable for not being out with the rest of the flock.
   (*g*) The old scars on the bird's body pain afresh every time he attempts to escape.
   (*h*) At midday the river water turns into Liquid glass.
2. The hour of the day depicted in the first stanza is that of
   (*a*) midday (*b*) morning
   (*c*) afternoon (*d*) evening
3. The phenomena described in the first stanza is
   (*a*) supernatural (*b*) natural
   (*c*) barbaric (*d*) rural
4. The poet's attitude towards the caged bird is
   (*a*) sympathetic and loving
   (*b*) apathetic and offensive
   (*c*) inimical and attacking
   (*d*) rational and evidential
5. The poet is sad because
   (*a*) the bird cannot fly out freely.
   (*b*) the caged bird feels very uneasy when the sun is bright.
   (*c*) the almighty God does not listen to the caged bird's prayer.
   (*d*) someone has put the bird in a cage.
6. Find out words from the poem which are the opposite of
   (*a*) Kind (*b*) Free
   (*c*) Dark (*d*) Sorrow
7. Find out words from the poem which mean nearly the same as the following
   (*a*) Joy (*b*) Throb
   (*c*) Sting (*d*) Sore

TEST – 6
(MISCELLANEOUS TYPE TEST)

Two Armies

Deep in the winter plain, two armies
Dig their machinery, to destroy each other.
Men freeze and hunger. No one is given leave
On either side, except the dead, and wounded.
These have their leave; while new battalions wait
On time at last to bring them violent peace.

All have become so nervous and so cold
That each man hates the cause and distant words
Which brought him here, more terribly than bullets.
Once a boy hummed a popular marching song,
Once a novice hand flapped the salute;
The voice was choked, the lifted hand fell,
Shot through the wrist by those of his own side.

From their numb harvest all would flee, except
For discipline drilled once in an iron school
Which holds them at the point of a revolver.
Yet when they sleep, the images of home
Ride wishing horses of escape
Which herd the plain in a mass unspoken poem.

Finally, they cease to hate: for although hate
Bursts from the air and whips the earth like hail
Or pours it up in fountains to marvel at,
And although hundreds fell, who can connect
The inexhaustible anger of the guns
With the dumb patience of these tormented animals?

Clean silence drops at night when a little walk
Divides the sleeping armies, each
Huddled in linen woven by remote hands.
When the machines are stilled, a common suffering

Whitens the air with breath and makes both one
As though these enemies slept in each other's
arms.

Only the lucid friend to aerial raiders,
The brilliant pilot moon, stares down
Upon the plain she makes a shining bone
Cut by the shadow of many thousand bones,
Where amber clouds scatter on no-man's-land
She regards death and time throw up
The furious words and minerals which kill life.

1. Who in the army are granted leave during the war?
   (*a*) The soldiers fighting the war
   (*b*) The dead soldiers
   (*c*) The wounded soldiers
   (*d*) Both (*b*) & (*c*)

2. "The wishing horses" tend to take the riders to
   (*a*) the battlefield (*b*) their home
   (*c*) the open fields (*d*) None of the above.

3. Who is the 'She' in the last stanza?
   (*a*) The battlefield (*b*) The moon
   (*c*) The clouds (*d*) None of the above.

4. Pick out six words from the poem which denote warfare.

5. The actual subject of the poem is:
   (*a*) to depict the two armies destroying each other.
   (*b*) to applaud the new battalions trying to bring peace.
   (*c*) to bring out the ironical situation of the war.
   (*d*) to portray the soldiers dreaming of their home.

6. Soldiers remain in the deadly battle field because:
   (*a*) they can dream of home while asleep.
   (*b*) they were drilled in an iron school at the point of a revolver.
   (*c*) they are out to destroy the enemy army.
   (*d*) they wish to die at the battle field.

7. Each man hates distant words more terribly than bullets because:
   (*a*) These were the words of orders given to them in the battle field.
   (*b*) They were words of abuse shouted at them by officers.
   (*c*) These seemingly inspiring words mislead them into joining army life.

8. The <u>'numb harvest'</u> refers to:
   (*a*) Farmers numbed by warfare reaping a harvest.
   (*b*) Silently reaped harvests in the fields around the battle field.
   (*c*) Harvest of skilled soldiers reaped by death.
   (*d*) Harvest destroyed due to lack of rains.

TEST – 7

(OBJECTIVE TYPE MULTIPLE-CHOICE TEST)

The Greenland Fishery

In seventeen hundred and ninety-four
On March the twentieth day
Our gallant ship her anchor weighed
And for Greenland bore away, brave boys
And for Greenland bore away.

The bosun at the mast-head stood
With a spy-glass in his hand;
He cried "A whale, a fine great whale,
And she blows at every span, brave boys
And she blows at every span."

Our boat was launched with all hands in;
The whale was full in view.
Each seaman bold was then resolved
To steer where the whale-fish blew, brave boys,
To steer where the whale-fish blew.

We struck that whale and the line went out,
But she gave a flourish with her tail;
The boat capsized and we lost four men,
And we never caught that whale, brave boys,
We never caught that whale.

"To lose a whale," our captain said,
"It grieves my heart full sore,
But the losing of those four gallant men,
It hurts me ten times more, brave boys,
It hurts me ten times more."

Greenland is a dreadful place,
A land that's never green;
There's ice and snow, and the whale-fish blow,
And the sunlight's seldom seen, brave boys
And the sunlight's seldom seen,

1. On 20th March 1794, the ship began:-
   (*a*) to sail for Greenland.
   (*b*) to fight the pirates.
   (*c*) to go to the North pole.
   (*d*) to enjoy the scenic beauty of the sea.
2. The sailors launched the boat in order to:-
   (*a*) go for swimming in the sea.
   (*b*) catch the whales
   (*c*) go for fishing
   (*d*) discover hidden treasures.
3. The Greenland is never green because-
   (*a*) it is dreadful.
   (*b*) it is full of whales.
   (*c*) there is no sunshine there.
   (*d*) it is all white due to snow.
4. Find another word in the poem which means the same as **brave:-**
   (*a*) Resolved (*b*) Bosun
   (*c*) Gallant (*d*) Great.

TEST – 8
(MISCELLANEOUS TYPE TEST)

What Has Happened To Lulu?

What happened to Lulu, mother?
What has happened to Lu?
There's nothing in her bed but an old rag-doll.
And by its side a shoe.

Why is her window wide, mother,
The curtain flapping free,
And only a circle on the dusty shelf
Where her money-box used to be?

Why do you turn your head, mother,
And why do the tear-drops fall?
And why do you crumple that note on the fire
And say it is nothing at all?

I woke to voices late last night,
I heard an engine roar.
Why do you tell me the things I heard
Were a dream and nothing more?

I heard somebody cry, mother,
In anger or in pain,
But now I ask you why, mother,
You say it was a gust of rain?

Why do you wander about as though
You don't know what to do?
What has happened to Lulu, mother,
What has happened to Lu?

A. Say whether the following statements are True (T) or False (F):

1. The speaker in this poem is Lulu's brother or sister.
2. The mother is crying because she is sick and has pain.
3. From the poem we come to know that Lulu was in pain and had gone to hospital.
4. The window was open because Lulu had jumped out of it.
5. The mother found out from Lulu's note that Lulu had gone.

B. What do the following refer to:

1. It's (stanza 1, line 4)
   (*a*) The rag-doll (*b*) The Bed
   (*c*) Lulu
2. It (stanza 3, line 4)
   (*a*) The fire (*b*) The tear-drops
   (*c*) The note
3. The things (stanza 4, line 3)
   (*a*) The voices (*b*) An engine roar
   (*c*) Both of the above
4. It (stanza 5, line 4)
   (*a*) A gust of rain (*b*) The cry
   (*c*) Somebody.

C. Complete the following:

(*a*) Lulu took __________ with her.
(*b*) Lulu left __________ and __________ behind.
(*c*) __________ was angry because __________.
(*d*) In place of the money box, there was __________ on the shelf.

D. Answer the following questions by choosing the best alternative from below:

1. How did Lulu leave?
   (*a*) Through the main door
   (*b*) Through the back door
   (*c*) Through the window
2. Why did Lulu leave her home?
   (*a*) Because she was unhappy.
   (*b*) Because her mother had scolded her in the might.
   (*c*) Because she wanted money.

TEST – 9

(OBJECTIVE TYPE MULTIPLE-CHOICE TEST)

When Autumn Came

This is the way that autumn came to the trees:
it stripped them down to the skin, left their
ebony bodies naked.
It shook out the yellow leaves which were their
hearts,
scattered them over the ground.
Whoever wanted, trampled them out of shape;
not a single moan of protest was heard.

Birds that herald dreams
became strangers to their voice
when their song was throttled.
They dropped into the dust
even before the hunter strung his bow.

Oh, God of May, have mercy.
Bless these withered bodies
with the passion of your resurrection,
make their dead veins flow with blood.

Give some tree the gift of green again.
Let one bird sing.

Questions:

1. State whether the following statements are **True** or **False**.
   (*a*) During autumn, trees blossom.
   (*b*) Autumn shakes out the yellow leaves from the trees.
   (*c*) Birds are enthralled in the autumn season.
   (*d*) 'Ebony bodies' refers to the black wooden bodies of trees.
2. Find out a word from the poem which means the same as <u>'renewal of life and hope'</u>
   (*a*) scattered (*b*) resurrection
   (*c*) withered (*d*) strung
3. The autumn strips-
   (*a*) the skin of the trees.
   (*b*) the leaves.
   (*c*) the trees.
   (*d*) the birds.
4. '<u>The gift of green</u>' suggests:
   (*a*) The leaves (*b*) The life
   (*c*) The spring (*d*) The rain
5. The colours yellow and green in the context of the poem symbolize:
   (*a*) dry and fresh leaves
   (*b*) death and life
   (*c*) dead veins and fresh blood
   (*d*) autumn and spring
6. The autumn referred to in the poem relates to:
   (*a*) the major features of the autumn season
   (*b*) the changes taking place in the spring season
   (*c*) the cycle of seasons
   (*d*) the images related to the autumn and spring seasons

TEST – 10

(OBJECTIVE TYPE MULTIPLE-CHOICE TEST)

Night of the Scorpion

I remember the night my mother
was stung by a scorpion. Ten hours
of steady rain had driven him
to crawl beneath a sack of rice.
Parting with his poison-flash
of diabolic tail in the dark room,
he risked the rain again.
The peasants came like swarms of flies
and buzzed the Name of God a hundred times
to paralyse the Evil One.
With candles and with lanterns
throwing giant scorpion shadows
on the mud-baked walls
they searched for him: he was not found.

They clicked their tongues.
With every movement that the scorpion made
his poison moved in Mother's blood, they said.
May he sit still, they said.
May the sins of your previous birth
be burned away tonight, they said.
May your suffering decrease
the misfortunes of your next birth, they said.
May the sum of evil
balanced in this unreal world
against the sum of good
become diminished by your pain.
May the poison purify your flesh
of desire, and your spirit of ambition,
they said, and they sat around
on the floor with my mother in the centre,
the peace of understanding on each face.

More candles, more lanterns, more neighbours
more insects and the endless rain.

My mother twisted through and through
groaning on a mat.
My father, sceptic, rationalist,
trying every curse and blessing,
powder, mixture, herb and hybrid.
He even poured a little paraffin
upon the bitten toe and put a match to it.
I watched the flame feeding on my mother.
I watched the holy man perform his rites
to tame the poison with an incantation.
After twenty hours
it lost its sting.

My mother only said
Thank God the scorpion picked on me
and spared my children.

Questions:

1. State whether the following statements are **True** or **False**.
   (*a*) Suffering reduces the sins of the previous birth.
   (*b*) Father believes in myths.
   (*c*) The scorpion clicked his tongue.
   (*d*) The scorpion lost its sting after twenty hours.
2. The 'Evil One' in the poem refers to
   (*a*) the devil (*b*) the scorpion
   (*c*) the mother (*d*) the poison
3. Mother is thankful because
   (*a*) she herself is safe.
   (*b*) she is purified.
   (*c*) her children were spared.
   (*d*) her sins are reduced.
4. The theme of the poem is
   (*a*) the mutual love of mother and father.
   (*b*) the endless suffering of a mother.
   (*c*) the nearly fatal effects of a scorpion- bite.
   (*d*) selfless love of a mother.
5. Find out a word from the poem which means the same as 'sinister'
   (*a*) diabolic (*b*) sceptic
   (*c*) rationalist (*d*) sting
6. "With every movement that the scorpion made his blood moved in Mother's blood, they said"
   The above line shows that the people were
   (*a*) worry (*b*) afraid
   (*c*) superstitious (*d*) caring

TEST – 11
(OBJECTIVE TYPE MULTIPLE-CHOICE TEST)

Last Lesson of the Afternoon

When will the bell ring, and end this weariness?
How long have they tugged the leash, and strained apart,
My pack of unruly hounds! I cannot start
Them again on a quarry of Knowledge they hate to hunt,
I can haul them and urge them no more.

No longer now can I endure the brunt
Of the books that lie out on the desks; a full threescore
Of several insults of blotted pages, and scrawl
Of slovenly work that they have offered me.
I am sick, and what on earth is the good of it all?
What good to them or me, I cannot see!

So, shall I take
My last dear fuel of life to heap on my soul

And kindle my will to a flame that shall
consume
Their dross of indifference; and take the toll
Of their insults in punishment?-I will not!-

I will not waste my soul and my strength for
this.
What do I care for all that they do amiss!
What is the point of this teaching of mine, and
of this
Learning of theirs? It all goes down the same
abyss.

What does it matter to me, if they can write
A description of a dog, or if they can't?
What is the point? To us both, it is all my aunt!

And yet I'm supposed to care, with all my might.
I do not, and will not; they won't and they
don't; and that's all!
I shall keep my strength for myself; they can
keep theirs as well.
Why should we beat our heads against the wall
Of each other? I shall sit and wait for the bell.

Questions:

1. The poet is sick of
   (*a*) The books (*b*) The students.
   (*c*) The teachers (*d*) The work
2. The unruly hounds in stanza I refers to
   (*a*) the despicable students in a class- room.
   (*b*) the irrelevant books.
   (*c*) the ringing of the bells.
   (*d*) the impatient teachers.
3. The phrase 'all my aunt' in stanza V means
   (*a*) confusion (*b*) fun
   (*c*) indifference (*d*) pun
4. Find out a word from the poem which means the same as: - 'untidy'.
   (*a*) slovenly (*b*) dross
   (*c*) blotted (*d*) unruly
5. The poet is waiting for
   (*a*) his aunt (*b*) the next class
   (*c*) the bell to go (*d*) None of the above
6. The whole poem is
   (*a*) an emotional outburst of a teacher's anger on the prevailing system of education and its goals.
   (*b*) an expression of indifference on the part of teachers and students both.
   (*c*) a dialogue between a teacher and a student on the prevailing system of teaching and learning
   (*d*) an outburst of sympathy for the students on the part of the teacher.

TEST – 12

(OBJECTIVE TYPE MULTIPLE-CHOICE TEST)

Ars Poetica

A poem should be palpable and mute
As a globed fruit,
Dumb
As old medallions to the thumb,
Silent as the sleeve-worn stone
Of casement ledges where the moss has grown-
A poem should be wordless
As the flight of birds,
A poem should be motionless in time
As the moon climbs,
Leaving, as the moon releases
Twig by twig the night-entangled trees,
Leaving, as the moon behind the winter leaves,
Memory by memory the mind-
A poem should be motionless in time
As the moon climbs.
A poem should be equal to:
Not true.
For all the history of grief
An empty doorway and a maple leaf,
For love
The leaning grasses and two lights above the
sea-
A poem should not mean
But be.

Questions:

1. The poem should make an __________ on the reader's mind.
   (*a*) expression (*b*) impression
   (*c*) exposition (*d*) None of the above.
2. A poem need not always be
   (*a*) Meaningful (*b*) Good
   (*c*) Lyrical (*d*) Rhythmic

3. Choose a word from the poem which means the same as 'soundless'
   (*a*) Wordless (*b*) Maple
   (*c*) Mute (*d*) Palpable
4. State whether the following are **True** or **False**.
   (*a*) A poem should be full of words.
   (*b*) A poem should be timeless.
   (*c*) The poet compares the poem to a globed fruit.
   (*d*) A poem should be silent as the flight of birds.

TEST – 13

(OBJECTIVE TYPE MULTIPLE-CHOICE TEST)

The Human Seasons

Four seasons fill the measure of the year;
There are four seasons in the mind of man:
He has his lusty Spring, when fancy clear
Takes in all beauty with an easy span:
He has his Summer, when luxuriously
Spring's honey'd cud of youthful though he loves
To ruminate, and by such dreaming high
Is nearest unto heaven: quiet coves
His souls has in its Autumn, when his wings
He furleth close; contented so to look
On mists in idleness-to let fair things.
Pass by unheeded as a threshold brook.
He has his Winter too of pale misfeature,
Or else he would forego his mortal nature.

Questions:

1. Life of a man has been compared to
   (*a*) months (*b*) seasons
   (*c*) climates (*d*) All of the above
2. In spring, man is
   (*a*) dreamer (*b*) idle
   (*c*) lusty (*d*) None of the above.
3. Find out a word from the poem which is the opposite of 'imperishable'.
   (*a*) Mortal (*b*) Furleth
   (*c*) Ruminate (*d*) Coves
4. Find out a word from the poem which means the same as 'stream'.
   (*a*) Span (*b*) Spring
   (*c*) Coves (*d*) Brook
5. In the poem, 'Lusty spring' means
   (*a*) vigorous period of growth and full of animal energy.
   (*b*) a period full of sexual energies.
   (*c*) a period of exuberance.
   (*d*) a rumination of the stored up impressions of youth and beauty.

TEST – 14

(OBJECTIVE TYPE MULTIPLE-CHOICE TEST)

Bright Star

BRIGHT star! would I were steadfast as thou art-
Not in lone splendour hung aloft the night,
And watching, with eternal lids apart,
Like Nature's patient, sleepless Eremite,
The moving waters at their priestlike task
Of pure ablution round earth's human shores,
Or gazing on the new soft-fallen mask
Of snow upon the mountains and the moors-
No-yet still steadfast, still unchangeable,
Pillow'd upon my fair love's ripening breast,
To feel for ever its soft fall and swell,
Awake for ever in a sweet unrest,
Still, still to hear her tender-taken breath,
And so live ever-or else swoon to death.

Questions:

1. 'Bright Star' refers to
   (*a*) The sun (*b*) The moon
   (*c*) The Pole star (*d*) The Constellations
2. In the first two lines the poet says that just like the Bright star
   (*a*) he wants to be steadfast.
   (*b*) he wants to be splendid.
   (*c*) he does not want to be lonely.
   (*d*) he wants to be steadfast but not lonely.
3. The phrase 'priest-like task' means
   (*a*) like a priest moving around earth in shores full of human beings.
   (*b*) like a priest who purifies the worshippers with holy water.
   (*c*) like a priest who watches everything.
   (*d*) None of the above.

4. The word 'moor' means
   (*a*) valleys.
   (*b*) plains.
   (*c*) tract of open waste lands.
   (*d*) water bodies.

DIALOGUES
(OBJECTIVE TYPE SPEEDED TESTS)

TEST – 1

At The Bank

Bank Manager : So, you wish to open an account with us?

Mohit : Yes, that's right.

Manager : What kind of account do you wish to open, Current or Savings?

Mohit : What's the difference?

Manager : If you open a Current account, you pay bank charges and you do not get interest on your money.

Mohit : Oh, but I want interest on my money and I also want a cheque book.

Manager : Then a Savings account will be better for you. Actually, Current accounts are more useful for business people.

Mohit : Why only for the business people?

Manager : Because a businessman needs to withdraw and deposit money all the time, i.e., with the Current account he can take out money as many times as he likes, but if you have a Savings account you can take out money only once or twice a week.

Mohit : I see! Well, I am a student, so I would like to open a Savings account. My father has given me a cheque for a hundred rupees. Can I open an account with that?

Manager : I'm sorry, but you will have to open an account with some cash because if you want a cheque book, you will have to open the account with a hundred rupees in cash. We will then deposit your cheque in it. Is your cheque a crossed one or an uncrossed one?

Mohit : What do you mean by a crossed and an uncrossed cheque?

Manager : A crossed cheque is one which has two lines drawn across it. So if you are sending a cheque through post and the letter is lost or stolen, the person who has got the crossed cheque cannot bring it in here and ask for money. A crossed cheque has to be put into an account only. It's a question of safety.

Mohit : You mean that an uncrossed cheque is not safe?

Manager : That's what I mean. Any person can withdraw money on an uncrossed cheque, if he can identify himself.

Mohit : I'd better check my father's cheque. Ah! Here it is. Yes, it is crossed. So, I will have to deposit it in my account after I have opened the account. Right?

A/C Payee

Date: 10.1.2001

Pay Mohit Sharma

Rupees One hundred only

A/C. No.: 27 Rs. 100/-

Indian Overseas Bank
86/A21, Rajori Garden, New Delhi – 110027
RJG

P.Sharma

"047934" 1100200121

Manager : Yes, that's right. Here is a form. Please fill it in and deposit hundred rupees with the cashier.

Questions:

A. Say whether the following statements are true (T) or false (F).

1. Mohit opened his account by depositing a cheque.
2. You cannot encash a cheque that has lines across it.
3. Mr. Sharma found an uncrossed cheque and went to the bank and was able to encash it.
4. We should never post any cheques.

B. Answer the following questions

1. An uncrossed cheque is
   (*a*) safe (*b*) risky
   (*c*) accountable (*d*) None of the above.
2. Businessmen open current account because
   (*a*) they get a lot of interest.
   (*b*) they can withdraw cash a number of times.
   (*c*) Both (*a*) and (*b*)
   (*d*) None of the above.
3. In savings account you can
   (*a*) deposit money. (*b*) withdraw money.
   (*c*) get interest (*d*) All of the above.
4. One can withdraw money against an uncrossed cheque by
   (*a*) identifying himself.
   (*b*) crossing the cheque
   (*c*) depositing it in his account
   (*d*) requesting the manager.
5. The opposite for the underlined word 'deposit' is
   (*a*) withdraw (*b*) draw
   (*c*) submit (*d*) lose
6. The noun for the underlined word 'Actually' would be:
   (*a*) Actual (*b*) Actuality
   (*c*) Actualize (*d*) Act

TEST – 2

Jacko Wins Again

Jacko, the famous New York detective, is interviewing a murder suspect, Maria. Her lover, Bruno Foscoli, was found shot dead in his room last night.

Jacko : Come on! If you admit now, we can help you in court. Why did you kill him?

Maria : I didn't kill him. He was my lover. I loved him.

Jacko : Oh, come on now. We've found your coat in his room.

Maria : I didn't leave it there... I mean... it's not mine. It must be his.

Jacko : Have you ever seen a man button his coat from right to left?

Maria : It could be Gina's.

Jacko : Gina? Who's Gina?

Maria : ... a girl he knew about two years ago.

Jacko : Oh, yes? And how long have you known him?

Maria : Oh, I've known him for about a year and a half.

Jacko : Right! Now I know you are jealous. You killed him because Gina had come back.

Maria : You can't prove that.

Jacko : Oh, yes I can. This cigarette end was picked up in his room. It's got lipstick on it.

Maria : I could have smoked that myself.

Jacko : Oh no, you couldn't. We've checked your cosmetic supplier. You've never used a shade like that in your life. You never smoked that cigarette with lipstick on it. That was Gina. Now, where's the knife?

Maria : Knife? He was shot.

Jacko : How did you know that? You haven't seen the body, and nobody's spoken to you except me.

Maria : I...I... thought you said he was shot.

Jacko : No. I didn't. But you are right, of course. So, Maria, where's the gun?

Maria : I've got a gun at home, of course, for self-protection, but I've never used it.

Jacko : That's what you say. We found it at your house this morning. Nice and clean, isn't it?

Maria : Yes... I cleaned it...

Jacko : Early this morning?

Maria : No, I cleaned it last night. I clean it regularly every Friday night. Just as Bruno told me to... (She bursts into tears). I didn't kill him. I've already told you. I haven't seen Gina for two years.

Jacko : Oh, so you did meet her, didn't you?

Maria : Yes, I met her two years ago.

Jacko : Do you swear that you haven't seen Gina Broccoli for two years, and that she never visited your room last night to tell you she had been blackmailing Bruno?

Mario : It's all lies. There was nobody in my room last night except myself.

Jacko : Plaisir d' Armour

Maria : (looking blank) What?

Jacko : Plaisir d' Armour

Maria : What are you talking about?

Jacko : Have you ever heard or read these words before?

Maria : I don't know what you're talking about.

Jacko : Plaisir d' Armour is the name of the scent which we smelt in your room when we visited it this morning. You have never heard of it. Gina Broccoli has worn it since she was sixteen. We've already arrested her for blackmail, but now I'm arresting you for the murder, (he calls to his assistant) Crocker! Now, Miss Casetti, if you admit that you have done it we may be able to help you .....

Questions:

A. Say whether the following statements are true (T) or false (F):

1. Bruno's friendship with Gina was not as old as his friendship with Maria.
2. Maria killed Bruno because she thought that Bruno was in love with Gina too.
3. The cigarette found in Bruno's room belonged to Maria.
4. Jacko examined Maria's gun in his house.
5. Maria was right in saying that she had not met Gina for two years.
6. Plaisir d' Amour is the dress that Gina had worn since she was sixteen years old.
7. Lipstick is a kind of cosmetic.

B. Tick (✓) the correct answer:-

1. How did Jacko find out that Maria had gone to Bruno's room before he was murdered?
   (*a*) Because Maria had been smoking in Bruno's room and had left the cigarette stub there.
   (*b*) Because Maria had left her coat in Bruno's room.
   (*c*) Because Jacko had smelt her perfume in Bruno's room.
   (*d*) Because Gina had told him.
2. Why was Gina arrested?
   (*a*) For attempted murder
   (*b*) For conspiring with Maria against Bruno.
   (*c*) For murdering Bruno
   (*d*) For blackmailing Bruno.
3. Maria killed Bruno
   (*a*) out of hatred (*b*) out of love
   (*c*) out of jealousy (*d*) out of revenge
4. Jacko is
   (*a*) a world famous police inspector.
   (*b*) a renowned New York sleuth.
   (*c*) a probing reporter.
   (*d*) a well-known interviewer.
5. From the passage, find a word which means the same as 'taking an oath'.
   (*a*) suspect (*b*) self-protection
   (*c*) swear. (*d*) blackmailing
6. The opposite for the underlined word 'arrested' would be
   (*a*) discharged (*b*) released
   (*c*) escaped (*d*) convicted

TEST – 3

Examinations

Dilip : How I wish these examinations were over. I am sick of studying. What is the use of examinations, anyway?

Kishore : Well, I too think they are a great nuisance but I don't see how we could get on without them.

Dilip : But why?

Kishore : Well, you see, there must be, from time to time, some sort of test of what you really know, and how far you have progressed in your studies. In what other way could a University tell whether you were fit to write "B.A." after your name?

Dilip : I don't know; but I do not believe examinations are a real test. You can get through an examination by last minute work and cramming; but cramming is not education, and the crammer generally forgets all he ever knew as soon as the examination is over. Then there is a good deal of luck about it. Your papers may be examined by a strict examiner, and mine by a lenient one; I may pass, and you may fail - and yet you may really be the better student.

Kishore : This is true; but to show that the examination system has defects, does not prove it useless or unnecessary. In general, I think examinations are a fair test.

Dilip : I am afraid, I am not convinced.

Kishore : Very well, can you suggest any other way of testing a man's fitness?

Dilip : No. I can't but I can say that not only are examinations unnecessary, they are positively harmful, very often the hard study necessary for an examination affects a student's health. Some students get quite ill with over-study.

Kishore : If you waste most of your time at college and then try to cram a year's course of study in a few weeks, it is quite likely you will break down. But examinations don't hurt students who work methodically and regularly throughout their course.

Dilip : Well, I think we would study much better if we do not always have some examination awaiting us.

Kishore : A few might; but many students would not work at all. It is only the fact that they will be examined which makes some students study at all. An examination is very useful for it makes idle students work.

Dilip : Well, have it your way. All our talk will not put off our examination, which is next month.

Questions:

1. When is their examination due?
   (*a*) They are already over.
   (*b*) Next month.
   (*c*) In a few weeks.
   (*d*) After two months.
2. According to Dilip examinations are
   (*a*) Necessary. (*b*) Positive.
   (*c*) Unnecessary. (*d*) A waste of time.
3. Why are examinations necessary?
   (*a*) To secure a better position in class.
   (*b*) To prove our knowledge to others.
   (*c*) To test our progress from time to time.
   (*d*) To be eligible for further studies.
4. Examinations are not a real test of one's abilities because
   (*a*) everyone can pass a test by cramming.
   (*b*) luck may overshadow hard work in an examination.
   (*c*) last minute studying may help a student to secure marks but may not add to his/her knowledge.
   (*d*) stress during examinations may lead to health hazards and students may not perform well due to that.
5. The two boys are
   (*a*) studying in a school.
   (*b*) pursuing a B.A. course.
   (*c*) pursuing a B.Sc. course.
   (*d*) pursuing an M.A. course.
6. Select a word from the options given below which means the opposite of 'methodically'.
   (*a*) systematically (*b*) skilfully
   (*c*) haphazardly (*d*) scientifically
7. Find out a word from the passage which means the same as 'to memorize'
   (*a*) Cram. (*b*) Study.
   (*c*) Learn. (*d*) None of the above.
8. Find out a word from the passage which is the opposite of 'strict'.
   (*a*) nuisance (*b*) idle
   (*c*) lenient (*d*) None of the above.

TEST – 4

A Dialogue Between a Countryman and a Townsman

Smith : Good morning, Mr. Jones. It's a long time since I saw you in town. Are you staying long?

Jones : Good morning Mr. Smith. Nice to meet you. No I won't be staying long; I'm leaving tomorrow.

Smith : Running away so soon? Why don't you stay for a few days and enjoy?

Jones : You see, I like the quiet and the fresh air of the country.

Smith : Well, I grant that you have the advantage of purer air in the country; but as for the noise, you soon get used to it.

Jones : Why don't you come over and try the country for a few days?

Smith : Ah! My friend, do not forget what Dr. Johnson said: "When you have seen one green field, you have seen all green fields; come with me down Fleet Street and study man."

Jones : Every village has its own charm and for your kind information country life is very exciting.

Smith : But what in the world do you do with yourself in the village? It must be a very dull and slow life, with no theatres, no concerts, no cinemas, no public lectures and no exciting political meetings. You must lead a stupid vegetable life, like a cabbage!

Jones : What you call "stupid vegetable life" is actually very productive and has been a source of inspiration for many poets.

Smith : Well, every man to his taste. But to me, yours would be a dull life.

Jones : Ours is not a dull life but a long, healthy and active life.

Smith : Yes, you may live longer in the country, but you don't get so much out of life as we do in town. A short life, but a merry one I'd say.

Questions:

1. Why doesn't Mr. Jones stay long in the town?
(*a*) Because he hates Mr. Smith.
(*b*) Because he likes the peaceful environment of the country.
(*c*) Because the town is very dirty.
(*d*) All of the above.

2. Living in a city is disadvantageous because of
(*a*) the high pollution level.
(*b*) annoying neighbours.
(*c*) less space.
(*d*) unproductive lifestyle.

3. From the above conversation we can conclude that
(*a*) life in a city is short yet exciting.
(*b*) life in a country is long but dreary.
(*c*) both city life and country life have their own advantages and disadvantages.
(*d*) one should be able to adjust himself/herself both according to the city and country.

4. Opposite of the word 'lethargic' is
(*a*) Crazy (*b*) Active
(*c*) Slow (*d*) Swift.

5. State whether the following statements are 'True' or 'False'.
(*a*) Smith enjoys hustle and bustle of a town.
(*b*) Jones feels that life in a town is unhealthy.
(*c*) Smith believes that one lives longer in a village.
(*d*) Jones wishes to shift from his village to a town.

TEST – 5

A Dialogue Between a Master and a Pupil

Master : Well Ram Narain, I heard you are taking part in a speech competition.

Pupil : Yes sir; what you have heard is correct indeed. I would be obliged if you help me in the matter sir.

Master : With pleasure, Ram Narain. Have you prepared your speech?

Pupil : I have not only prepared it, but also memorized it.

Master : Oh! But that is a great mistake. Always prepare carefully what you want to say, but never try to learn it off by heart.

Pupil : Why not sir?

Master : Because when you are speaking, you should watch your audience to see whether they are following what you say. You can see through their expressions whether they've caught what you said; and if they haven't, you can win their attention by adding, or emphasizing, or changing something. But if your speech is learnt by heart, you can't do that.

Pupil : But just as I have prepared it now, I can very well alter it at the last moment.

Master : It is not so in the end. Memorizing is a great strain. Also, if you forget one sentence, you may break down altogether.

Pupil : So what should I do now?

Master : At first you may take a short note of the outline, or the main points of your speech, last you should forget; but when you get used to speaking in public, it is best to do without notes altogether.

Pupil : I see...

Master : You must prepare carefully, and think about what you want to say; and learn the main points, or the outline, of your speech. Then, when you get up to speak, you will find that the words are striking you spontaneously.

Pupil : I am a little nervy about the whole business.

Master : That's natural, especially at the initial stage. But as you get used to speaking in public, you'll overcome that fear. Even seasoned speakers may often feel a bit nervous before starting their speech; but when they get on to their feet, they grow fluent.

Pupil : Sir, what if I stammer?

Master : Well, you must practise speaking slowly and distinctly. And don't shout- it strains your voice and prevents people from comprehending your speech; nor should you speak too low. Speak naturally, so that the audience can follow you easily.

Pupil : Thank you very much sir. I'll positively follow your guidelines as I'm sure to gain much from it.

Questions:

1. The dialogue between the master and the pupil is on the method for
   (*a*) preparing a speech for a competition.
   (*b*) preparing for a competition.
   (*c*) preparing a lecture for a class-room.
   (*d*) All of the above.

2. The master advises the pupil against memorising because
   (*a*) it is a great strain.
   (*b*) it can't be altered later on.
   (*c*) it may interrupt him, leading to a breakdown in the speech.
   (*d*) All of the above.

3. Even experienced speakers often get
   (*a*) stuck while speaking
   (*b*) nervous before speaking.
   (*c*) excited while speaking.
   (*d*) indistinct while speaking.

4. 'Obliged' means
   (*a*) to be indebted (*b*) to be thankful.
   (*c*) to be servile. (*d*) None of the above.

5. 'Stammer' means
   (*a*) To speak with embarrassment.
   (*b*) To speak haltingly.
   (*c*) To speak nothing due to nervousness.
   (*d*) None of the above.

6. Find a word or phrase from the above dialogue, which means the same as 'cram'.
   (*a*) prepare. (*b*) learn by heart.
   (*c*) memorise. (*d*) swot.

7. State whether each of the following is True or False:
   (*a*) Preparing is the same as memorising.
   (*b*) By following his master's guidelines, the pupil will not lose anything.
   (*c*) Notes are absolutely essential while speaking.
   (*d*) One should always shout while speaking so as to make himself heard.

TEST – 6

A Dialogue Between Two Boys

George : I am in luck, Will. My uncle has just sent me a letter from Japan, where he is on business which deals with some Japanese stamps. He knows that I collect them and he often sends me foreign stamps from the places he visits. I am so glad because I had no Japanese stamps before.

Will : Can you show me your collection?

George : Yes, here it is. I have got quite a nice collection now.

Will : Wow! This is a real gem of a collection.

George : Oh! There's a lot which I haven't got as yet. And some rare ones are very expensive, and cost many a pounds.

Will : Why do you collect stamps?

George : Oh well, it's one of my hobbies. It teaches you some Geography; and sometimes it even brings money.

Will : How does it bring money?

George : Why, a really good collection sometimes sells for hundreds of pounds. Why don't you go in for stamp-collection too?

Will : No, I am more interested in collecting coins.

George : But what do you do with them once you get them?

Will : Well, I display them on important occasions.

George : And what is its benefit?

Will : When I have collected enough, I intend to organise a big exhibition and become a member of the International Coin Collector's Club.

Questions:

1. George and Will are discussing:
   (*a*) George's uncle.
   (*b*) Japanese stamps.
   (*c*) stamps and coins.
   (*d*) their hobbies.
2. George collects stamps because
   (*a*) it teaches him some geography.
   (*b*) it brings money.
   (*c*) it keeps him occupied.
   (*d*) All of the above.
3. The phrase 'real gem of a collection' means
   (*a*) George also collects gems.
   (*b*) the collection is very expensive.
   (*c*) it is an exclusive collection.
   (*d*) it is an authentic collection.
4. State whether each of the following statements is true (T) or false (F).
   (*a*) George is feeling lucky because he has received a letter from his uncle.
   (*b*) Some of the stamps are very expensive and rare.
   (*c*) Will prefers collecting coins.
   (*d*) Will never displays his collection because he intends to exhibit them on a large scale later on.
5. The opposite for the underlined word 'collecting' would be
   (*a*) distributing (*b*) classifying
   (*c*) dividing (*d*) gathering

TEST – 7

A conversation between two boys, one of whom is habitually despondent and thinks luck is against him, whereas the other is of a more practical bent of mind.

Vicky: Come, Sunny, you are taking your failure too much to heart. I know it is a great disappointment, and I sympathize with you; but you must not allow it to make you so unhappy.

Sunny: It is all very well for a lucky chap like you, Vicky. You have passed the first time, and this is my second failure. You would not feel so cheery if you were in my place.

Vicky: I know; but you must pull yourself together, and make up your mind. You will pass the next time. Remember the old saying, " If at first you don't succeed, try, try, try, again!"

Sunny: I think the other version of the saying has more sense in it-"if at first you don't succeed, quit, quit, quit at once!"

Vicky: Oh nonsense! You'll never do anything if you don't persevere. Now why do you think you failed?

Sunny: This entire year fate has been against me. First, I was ill with typhoid, which lost me a whole term. Then just before my examination my grandfather expired, and that upset me so much that I could not prepare properly.

Vicky: Well you certainly did have bad luck. I am sorry. But I am sure that you will succeed next time. So you must make up your mind to win through.

Sunny: It's no use. I think I was born unlucky. I seem to fail in everything I touch. I tried several times to get a scholarship, but some other boy always got it instead. I shall give it up.

Vicky: Indeed you must not. Remember that it's the darkest hour before the dawn. Often when things are at their worst, they begin to improve. I don't believe in all the talk about bad and good luck. A brave man makes his own luck. You have a whole year before you; you have brains, and if you will only pull yourself together and put your heart into your work, you will win through.

Sunny: I wish I had your hopeful disposition. Still, I will take your advice and have another try.

Vicky: That's the style! And I am sure you will succeed and break your so-called "bad luck" once and for all.

Questions:

1. What does the phrase "Once and for all" mean?
   (*a*) Forever (*b*) Never
   (*c*) Always (*d*) Once
2. In the passage, Sunny says, "I shall give it up". This shows that he is
   (*a*) cynical (*b*) hardworking
   (*c*) sanguine (*d*) All of the above
3. If Sunny heeds the advice of Vicky, it would be
   (*a*) his first attempt to pass the class.
   (*b*) his second attempt to pass the class.
   (*c*) his third attempt to pass the class.
   (*d*) his fourth attempt to pass the class.

4. According to Vicky, to succeed one should
   (*a*) have a positive attitude.
   (*b*) have a strong will power.
   (*c*) work hard.
   (*d*) All of the above.
5. Pick out a word from the above passage which means the opposite of 'cheerful'.
   (*a*) persevere (*b*) upset
   (*c*) despondent (*d*) unlucky
6. State whether the following are 'True' or 'False'.
   (*a*) Sunny is practical.
   (*b*) Vicky does not believe in luck.
   (*c*) Sunny's grandfather was ill with typhoid.
   (*d*) Vicky is happy that Sunny has failed.
7. Another word for the underlined word 'quit' can be
   (*a*) leave (*b*) go
   (*c*) stop (*d*) correct

TEST – 8

An imaginary conversation between a bookish student and an athletic student on the comparative merits of mental and physical culture:

Dilip Singh : Hello, Swarup! swotting away as usual. Come out, man; shut up your old books, and come and have a game of tennis.

Swarup : I'm sorry I can't do that Dilip. The examination is drawing near, and I want every hour I can get for study.

Dilip Singh : Oh! Hang all examinations! I don't worry about mine. What's the use of them, anyway?

Swarup : Well, you can't get a degree if you don't pass the examinations; and I have set my heart on being a B.A.

Dilip Singh : And pray what good will a B.A. degree do you? You may get a clerkship in a government office; but that's all. And there are hundreds of fellows who have got their degrees, but are nowhere nearer to getting a job of any sort.

Swarup : That may be so; but I'm not studying so much as to pass the examination and obtain a degree, as to store my mind with knowledge and develop my intellectual faculties.

Dilip Singh : My word! How fine you "highbrows" can talk! "Develop my intellectual faculties", indeed! I tell you, all a man wants to get on in the world is some brains, plain common sense, and plenty of push. And you can't learn these things from books. And while you're "developing your intellectual faculties," you are spoiling your health. You'll soon be a thin, white, narrow-chested, half-blind weakling if you stick to your beloved books like this. Look at my broad chest and feel my biceps! Anyway I am developing my physical powers with my games and athletics.

Swarup : Well, if I have to choose, I would rather have a learned and cultivated mind than a strong and well developed body; for the mind is far more superior than the body.

Dilip Singh : Oh, I see! You mean to say that a man who plays football and hockey and is as strong as a horse, cannot, have any brains?

Swarup : I didn't say that; but you may remember what Kipling said about " Muddied oafs and flannelled fools."

Dilip Singh : Well, I must say you are very complimentary! Kipling must have been an ass if he said that. Anyway I would rather be "a muddied oaf" than a white-faced, spectacled bookworm, as blind as an owl.

Their teacher (coming in) **:** Hello! What are you two fellows quarrelling about?

(They explained)

Teacher : I see. Well, you are both right and both wrong. Swarup a little more physical exercise will do you good and will not interfere with your mental culture; and Dilip Singh, a little more study will not in any way spoil your physical strength. So, go and have a game of tennis, Swarup; and afterwards you, Dilip, settle down to a few hours' study.

Questions

1. Swarup is studying hard in order to
   (*a*) pass the B.A. examination.
   (*b*) become a clerk in a government office.
   (*c*) store his mind with knowledge and develop his intellectual faculties.
   (*d*) All of the above.

2. According to Dilip Singh, to get on in the world, a man needs
   (*a*) some brains.
   (*b*) some common sense.
   (*c*) some reference and contacts.
   (*d*) All of the above.
3. According to Swarup
   (*a*) the mind is more important than the body.
   (*b*) the body is more important than the mind.
   (*c*) one who is physically developed cannot have good mental faculties.
   (*d*) B.A. degree is more important than physical development.
4. By talking about Kipling's "muddied oafs and flannelled fools", Swarup is being
   (*a*) complimentary (*b*) sarcastic
   (*c*) ironic (*d*) flattering
5. According to the teacher
   (*a*) both physical and mental prowess are necessary for an individual.
   (*b*) both Dilip Singh and Swarup are wrong.
   (*c*) both Dilip Singh and Swarup are correct.
   (*d*) all of the above.
6. 'Swotting' is a slang for
   (*a*) reading. (*b*) writing
   (*c*) studying hard (*d*) none of the above.
7. In the phrase 'cultivated mind', 'cultivated' can also be substituted by
   (*a*) creative (*b*) productive
   (*c*) cultured (*d*) all of the above
8. Complete the following phrase
   'As blind as______________
   (*a*) an eagle (*b*) a rat
   (*c*) a bat (*d*) an owl

TEST – 9

Inflation

Bill : Have you noticed how the price of everything seems to go up almost every week now?

Charles : Yes, that's what inflation does to a country. Soon we'll be paying twenty rupees for a cup of tea.

Bill : Twenty rupees for a cup of tea? Don't be silly!

Charles : Well, if I'd told you a few years ago that soon we'd be paying more than Rs. 29 for a litre of petrol, you'd have said the same thing, wouldn't you?

Bill : Yes, I suppose I would. But where's it all going to end? It can't go on much longer.

Charles : Excuse me, but it can! In some South American countries the annual rate of inflation has been more than 250% for years.

Bill : But how do they manage, then?

Charles : Well, everything goes on rising at the same rate-wages, salaries, pensions, and so on – nobody notices it. Of course, they can't travel abroad much, or import things, because their money is falling the whole time, so expenses abroad become impossible for them to incur.

Bill : But why doesn't the government stop inflation?

Charles : It tries to now and then, but that causes a lot of unemployment, so there's trouble and they have to stop.

Bill : What I'd like to know is, how does it cause unemployment?

Charles : Inflation means printing or borrowing more and more money each month to keep industry going and to pay the workers. When you stop printing or borrowing, industry gets short of money for investment and for paying its workers, so there is a recession, which means less goods produced and more people out of work.

Bill : But wait a minute! That's happening now-with inflation going on!

Charles : Exactly! That's the strange thing that the experts can't explain to us. We manage to have the worst of both worlds at the same time.

Questions:

A. Choose the best answers:

1. Bill and Charles are talking about
   (*a*) the price of a cup of tea.
   (*b*) rise in prices.
   (*c*) increase in production.
   (*d*) unemployment in the country.
2. In the sentence, 'That is what inflation does to a country', 'inflation' means
   (*a*) more money in circulation.

(*b*) increase in unemployment.
(*c*) increase in wages.
(*d*) increase in production.

3. 'Twenty rupees for a cup of tea!' These words of Bill show that
(*a*) he is angry. (*b*) he is worried.
(*c*) he is surprised. (*d*) he is shocked.

4. The South American countries have tried to solve the problem of inflation by
(*a*) paying more to the people.
(*b*) by not permitting people to go abroad.
(*c*) by not allowing people to buy foreign goods.
(*d*) by making it impossible for them to spend money abroad.

5. When a Government does not increase the circulation of money, it leads to:
(*a*) unemployment.
(*b*) less production of goods.
(*c*) a recession in the industry.
(*d*) All of the above.

6. The phrase, 'their money is falling' means:
(*a*) prices are coming down.
(*b*) money is in short supply.
(*c*) money is losing its value.
(*d*) to lose money.

7. The verb for the underlined word 'unemployment' would be
(*a*) unemployed (*b*) employ
(*c*) employee (*d*) unemployable

TEST – 10

Woman : "Good Morning, Mr. Whiteacre. I understand you are applying for this job as a welder.

Man : "Yes. And I'm an experienced welder. You might say I know just about all there is to know about welding."

Woman : "That's interesting. Now this job is in a manufacturing company. They need a welder as a regular part of their staff, and they have only one welder. You will take the place of their old welder who is leaving."

Man : "That's OK with me. What does the company manufacture?

Woman : "They make different kinds of electrical controls. Can you do any soldering?

Man : "Of course. I can do anything."

Woman : "You're very sure of yourself. They might want you to do some soldering and it's also possible that they may want to train you to assemble circuit boards. You wouldn't do that regularly, however. You would be just filling in whenever the circuit board assemblers have too much work."

Man : "That's good. I could do it, but I wouldn't want to do too much of that. It's women's work, you know."

Woman : "Oh Well, if they hire you, when could you start?"

Man : "Two weeks from yesterday. I gave notice at my old job yesterday."

Woman : "Good. One more thing. At this manufacturing company your boss will be a woman."

Man : "What? How can a woman be a boss?"

Woman : "Easy. This woman knows the business inside out. What's the matter, are you a male chauvinist?"

Man : "No, but I'm not going to work for a woman boss."

Woman : "Then you are a male chauvinist. You'd better look somewhere else for a job. You wouldn't be happy at this one."

Man : "But, where can I look?"

Woman : "That's your problem. Good bye, Mr. Whiteacre."

Questions:

1. What job is Mr. Whiteacre applying for?
(*a*) Boss. (*b*) Welder.
(*c*) Circuit board assembler.
(*d*) Solderer

2. Why does the manufacturing company need to hire someone?
(*a*) To replace their old welder.
(*b*) To get an additional welder.
(*c*) To get a trainee.
(*d*) To solder some things from time to time.

3. What would Mr. Whiteacre have to do with circuit boards?
(*a*) Fill them.
(*b*) Substitute them.
(*c*) Assemble them when necessary.
(*d*) Train them.

4. When did Mr. Whiteacre tell his old company that he would be quitting?
   (*a*) At the last minute.
   (*b*) Not yet.
   (*c*) Two weeks ago.
   (*d*) Yesterday.
5. What is Mr. Whiteacre's prejudice?
   (*a*) He dislikes circuit boards.
   (*b*) He likes being a welder.
   (*c*) He does not respect women.
   (*d*) He has already given notice.
6. The underlined word 'manufacturing' is
   (*a*) noun (*b*) verb
   (*c*) adjective (*d*) adverb

COMMUNICATIVE PASSAGES
(OBJECTIVE TYPE MULTIPLE-CHOICE TESTS)

TEST – 1

ELECTRONIC WIREMEN

— Permanent, full-tme positions
— 2 – 3 years experience
— Day Shift

Wiring and soldering of chassis and P.C. Boards. Excellent Company benefits. Salary commensurate with experience.
Phone 548-3889

TEKNICIRCLE LABORATORIES
899, Robin Road
Long Hill, Pa.

Equal Opportunity Employer

Questions:

1. Approximately what hours would the applicant expect to work?
   (*a*) midnight to 7 A.M.
   (*b*) commensurate with experience.
   (*c*) 8 A.M. to 5 P.M.
   (*d*) 3.30 P.M. to midnight.
2. What would the applicant's job be?
   (*a*) full-time position.
   (*b*) shifting.
   (*c*) company benefits.
   (*d*) wiring and soldering.
3. State whether the following are True or False:
   (*a*) Deepak has an experience of 2.5 years. He can get the job.
   (*b*) The positions are temporary.
   (*c*) There are two phone numbers.
   (*d*) Preference would be given to more experienced candidates.

TEST – 2

ADMISSION NOTICE

PG. DIPLOMA in IT and Systems	B.Sc. in Information Technology
(1 year Full Time Programme)	(3 years Full Time Programme)
Eligibility:	*Eligibility :*
Graduate in any stream	10 +2

AMITY
RESOURCE CENTRE FOR INFORMATION TECHNOLOGY

An Institution of Ritnand Balved Education Foundation
Application forms available at the addresses given below or can be downloaded from the website

Amity Campus,
Sector-44, Noida-201 303.
Ph.: 91-4578242/3/4 *RBEF: E-27

Questions:

1. You can do the following course/courses from the Amity Resource Centre for Information Technology:
   (*a*) One year full time PG Diploma in IT & Systems.
   (*b*) Three years part time B.Sc. in Information Technology.
   (*c*) One year full time PG Diploma, and three years full time B.Sc.

(*d*) Three years full time B.Sc. in Information Technology, and one year full time PG Diploma in IT & Systems.

2. The application forms for the courses can be
   (*a*) downloaded from the website.
   (*b*) obtained from the Noida office.
   (*c*) obtained from the Defence Colony office.
   (*d*) All of the above.
3. You can apply for the B.Sc. course in Information Technology if you
   (*a*) are a graduate in any stream
   (*b*) have passed class XII.
   (*c*) are studying for a graduate course.
   (*d*) are studying for class XII.
4. You can apply for the Diploma in IT and Systems if you
   (*a*) are studying for class XII.
   (*b*) have a bachelor's degree.
   (*c*) are studying for a graduate course.
   (*d*) have passed class XII.

TEST – 3

A leading
Chartered Accountants Firm
based in South Delhi
Requires

SECRETARY

Candidate should be a Graduate with proficiency in Computers & Stenography. Candidates with experience of 2-3 years will be preferred.

Please send in your resume within 7 days to:

Box No. 335784-CD
The Hindustan Times,
New Delhi - 110 001.

Questions:

1. For the applicant, experience of 2-3 years is
   (*a*) optional (*b*) compulsory
   (*c*) obligatory (*d*) preferable
2. The salary for the post is
   (*a*) fixed (*b*) negotiable
   (*c*) to be fixed after a trial
   (*d*) None of the above.
3. The qualifications for the post is/are
   (*a*) graduation.
   (*b*) graduation with command over computers.
   (*c*) graduation with command over computers and stenography.
   (*d*) graduation with command over computers or stenography.
4. The resume should reach the given address within:
   (*a*) 8 days (*b*) a week
   (*c*) 5 days (*d*) None of the above.

TEST – 4

CIPLA

GENERIC DIVISION

Requires

MARKETING MANAGER

(For All India Operations)
Location: Bangalore
(For North Eastern Operations)
Location: Delhi

Pharmacy/Graduate or preferably a Post Graduate in Marketing with 5-6 years experience in promoting Generic Products, would find this a challenging opportunity.

ZONAL SALES MANAGER

Location: Bangalore, Mumbai,
Kolkata and Delhi

Graduate in Science/Pharmacy, having at least 2-5 years experience in Generic selling will be considered.

For suitable candidates the remuneration package will be attractive and not a constraint.

Interested candidates should send their detailed resume stating current emoluments, superscribing the envelope with the position and apply within 10 days

to:

The Personnel Manager
CIPLA LTD.,
Mumbai Central, Mumbai-400008
E-mail: hrd@cipla.com

Questions:

1. Marketing Manager is required for
   (*a*) All India operations.
   (*b*) North Eastern operations.
   (*c*) For (*a*) and (*b*)
   (*d*) For Mumbai, Kolkata, Delhi.
2. For Zonal Sales Manager, the candidates need to be
   (*a*) graduate/ post-graduate in Marketing with 5-6 years experience.
   (*b*) graduate in Science/ Pharmacy.
   (*c*) graduate in Pharmacy.
   (*d*) graduate in Science/ Pharmacy with 2-5 years experience.
3. The candidates need to send their applications by
   (*a*) post (*b*) e-mail
   (*c*) post or e-mail (*d*) hand
4. Find out another word from the advertisement which means the same as 'salary'.

TEST – 5

FOR SALE

1992 Estrella, auto., 2 dr. convert. A/C, AM/FM, tape deck, built-in CB, good mpg, red/black, power steer & brks., tilt wheel, $ 2600 negot. Call 672-6970 after 8.

Questions:

1. What feature would make this car seem economical?
   (*a*) A/C (*b*) power steer & brks.
   (*c*) good mpg (*d*) built-in CB
2. What is the model of this car?
   (*a*) tilt wheel (*b*) Estrella
   (*c*) convert. (*d*) CB
3. Interested customers should call after:
   (*a*) 8 days (*b*) 8 hours
   (*c*) 8 P.M. (*d*) 8 o'clock
4. State whether the following are true or false.
   (*a*) The car has a manual transmission.
   (*b*) The car has four doors.
   (*c*) The car does not have a radio.
   (*d*) The car has air conditioning.
   (*e*) The price is firm.
   (*f*) The colour of the car is red or black.

TEST – 6

LONDON SCHOOL OF MANAGEMENT

STUDY IN LONDON FOR BBA/MBA DEGREE

London School of Management (LSM) is **accredited by the British Accreditation Council (BAC),** which means it is recognised as a Bona Fide private education institution that meets the requirement of paragraph 57(i) (b) of the Immigration Rules. **LSM offers degree programmes validated and awarded in association with Fairfax University of USA.**

The **Principal** of the London School of Management will be holding a **free seminar** and conducting interviews to select students for the above programmes.

***Venue:* Maple Hall, India Habitat Centre, Gate No. 3, Lodhi Road, New Delhi**
Date: 12 June
Time: 2 p.m. to 6 p.m.

MAKE LSM YOUR NUMBER ONE CHOICE

For further details: Contact:
LONDON SCHOOL OF MANAGEMENT (INDIA) PVT. LTD.
E-14 (1st Floor), Kalkaji,
New Delhi- 110 019
Tel: 622 8204, 642 3907,
Fax: 011-622-2275
E-mail: lsm@cableinet.co.uk
Web Site: www.lsm.ac.uk

Questions:

1. What are the courses offered by LSM?
   (*a*) BBA (*b*) MBA
   (*c*) BBS (*d*) BBA and MBA.
2. The word 'Bona Fide' in the advertisement means:
   (*a*) genuine (*b*) in good faith
   (*c*) popular (*d*) acceptable
3. The institute is accredited by:
   (*a*) BAC (*b*) LSM
   (*c*) Fairfax University (*d*) none of these

4. State whether the following are True or False:
   (*a*) The institute meets the required needs of paragraph 57(i) (*d*) of immigration rules.
   (*b*) LSM offers degree programmes.
   (*c*) Free seminar is being conducted by the principal.
   (*d*) Selection would be done on the basis of merit.

TEST – 7

LET THERE BE LIGHT VISION CENTRE
1451 Broadview Rd.
661-9281
More Than a Quarter of a Century Serving
Holly Heights
Registered Opticians

One-day Prescription Service
Custom-Fitted Glasses to Suit Your
Individual Needs

HARD AND SOFT CONTACT LENSES

HRS. M 10-9
T-F 8:30-5
Sat 10-4
Call for an Immediate Appointment

Questions:

1. Which phrase indicates that the company is an established firm?
   (*a*) More than a quarter of a century serving holly heights.
   (*b*) Registered opticians.
   (*c*) One-day prescription service.
   (*d*) Call for an immediate appointment.
2. The establishment deals only in
   (*a*) spectacles.
   (*b*) spectacles and hard lenses.
   (*c*) soft and hard lenses.
   (*d*) spectacles, hard and soft lenses.
3. Which evenings will this establishment be open?
   (*a*) Tuesday through Friday.
   (*b*) Monday only. (*c*) Saturday only.
   (*d*) Monday and Saturday.
4. Who would most likely go to this establishment?
   (*a*) a person needing surgery for an eye disease.
   (*b*) a person who has a prescription for antibiotics to be bought.
   (*c*) a person who does not have an appointment.
   (*d*) a person who needs a new pair of contact lenses.
5. Which of the following is **NOT** true about this business?
   (*a*) It is closed on Sundays.
   (*b*) It is open later in the evening on Monday than on other days.
   (*c*) It has the same hours from Tuesday through Saturday.
   (*d*) It does not open as early in the morning on Monday and Saturday as it does on the other days.

TEST – 8

SNOWFLAKE CAKE

2 cups plus 2 tbsp. sifted flour
½ cup soft shortening
1½ cups sugar, 1 cup milk
3 ½ tsp. Baking powder, 1 tsp. flavouring
1 tsp. salt, 4 egg whites unbeaten
Heat oven to 350°. Grease and flour two layer pans, 8 or 9 × 1 ½″, or an oblong pan, 13 × 9½ × 2″. Sift together into bowl flour, sugar, baking powder, and salt. Add shortening, milk and flavouring. Beat 2 minutes, medium speed on mixer, or 300 vigorous strokes by hand. Scrape sides and bottom of bowl constantly. Add egg whites. Beat 2 more minutes, scraping bowl frequently. Pour into prepared pans. Bake layers 35 to 40 minutes, oblong 40 to 45 minutes, or until cake tests done. Cool.

Questions:

1. Which of the following ingredients is measured by a tablespoon?
   (*a*) Flour. (*b*) Baking powder.
   (*c*) Salt. (*d*) Flavouring.

2. If you are using an oblong pan to bake this cake, how long would you bake it?
   (*a*) 35 to 40 minutes.
   (*b*) 45 to 50 minutes.
   (*c*) 40 to 45 minutes.
   (*d*) 50 to 55 minutes.
3. Which of the following ingredients is *not* called for in this recipe?
   (*a*) Baking powder. (*b*) Milk.
   (*c*) Salt. (*d*) Egg yolk.
4. What is the total amount of time that this cake must be beaten using an electric mixer?
   (*a*) 2 minutes. (*b*) 35 minutes.
   (*c*) 4 minutes. (*d*) 13 minutes.
5. Which of the following is added after the mixture has been beaten one time?
   (*a*) Egg whites. (*b*) Salt.
   (*c*) Shortening. (*d*) Flour.

TEST – 9

POLYTECHNIC FOR WOMEN
SOUTH EXTENSION, NEW DELHI ESTD. 1979

THE POLYTECHNIC was established by a Registered Society which has been providing educational & technical training for nearly two decades. The society has been running International Polytechnic for Women (IPW) which is one of the premier institutes in the country for providing vocational training **(Approved by AICTE, Govt. of India).**

Admission open for 2001–2002 Session

1. Fashion Designing
2. Textile Designing
3. Garment Manufacturing Technology
4. Interior Design and Display
5. Commercial Art / Graphic Design
6. Beauty Culture & Hair Design
7. Nursery and Primary Teachers Training
8. Modern Office Management /S.P.
9. Marketing, Advertisement & P.R.
10. Tourism & Ticketing
11. Journalism & Mass Media
12. Home Science
13. Information Technology
14. Airhostess Training

(State-of-the-art Computer Labs in all departments)
For prospectus, send Rs. 100/-
(By DD or MO) to or Contact:
A-3, South Extension-I, Ring Road, New Delhi-49.
Phones: 4624049, 4699855, 4623517. Telefax: (011) 4644500

Visit www.womenpolytechnic.com
Bus facility available
No other branch in Delhi

Questions:

1. Polytechnic for women has the following facilities
   (*a*) Hostel and bus.
   (*b*) Computer labs and hostel
   (*c*) Hostel, bus and computer labs
   (*d*) Computer labs and bus
2. The institute is approved by
   (*a*) a private body
   (*b*) a governmental body
   (*c*) a public-sector body
   (*d*) a registered society
3. For obtaining a prospectus, send money through
   (*a*) DD only (*b*) DD or MO only
   (*c*) MO only (*d*) person
4. For imparting vocational training to the women in the country, it is
   (*a*) the only institute for women
   (*b*) a major institute
   (*c*) one of the major institutes
   (*d*) one of the few institutes

TEST – 10

No: E/Tech/V/00-01/16
DT: 13.10.01

ADVERTISEMENT

Applications are invited from Indian Nationals for filling up 3 posts (1 General, 1 S/C and 1 S/T) FOR Crane operator in the scale of pay allowances as admissible under the rules and orders of the D.E.S.U. in force from time to time.

QUALIFICATION & EXPERIENCE:

(I) Middle Class pass or equivalent from a recognized Board/School or equivalent.
(II) 3 years experience on electric overhead cranes, crawler crane /mobile crane of minimum capacity of 50 tons.

DESIRABLE: Experience of attending to minor defects in cranes.

AGE: Between 18 and 25 years. (Relaxation for Govt. Servants and employees of Munici-pal Corporation of Delhi). Also relaxable upto 5 years for candidates belonging to S/C and S/T.

Applications on plain paper stating full particulars along with attested copies of certificates and testimonials together with crossed postal order for Rs. 8/- (Rupees eight only). (Not applicable in case of S/C - S/T candidates, who are exempted from making payment of this fee). It should be drawn in favour of Assistant ACCOUNTANT Delhi Electric Supply Undertaking, Rajghat Power House, New Delhi-02 and should reach the Administrative Officer (PV), Delhi Electric Supply Undertaking, Shakti Bhawan, Nehru Place, New Delhi-19 latest by 28.10.01. S/C-S/T candidates called for interview will be paid single 2nd class railway fare by passenger train by the shortest route to and from the nearest railway station of their place of residence if the distance travelled exceeds 80 kms. If return tickets are available, same should be availed of. This concession will not be admissible to the Central/State Govt. employees.

Persons already in service should apply through proper channel. Incomplete application and/or received after the stipulated date will not be entertained.

PR/915/906

Sd/-(JYOTI PARSAD)
ASSISTANT PERSONNEL OFFICER (HQ.)1

Questions:

1. What is the minimum age required for the post advertised above?
   (*a*) Above 18yrs.
   (*b*) Below 18yrs.
   (*c*) 18yrs.
   (*d*) 25 yrs.
2. What should the applicant send along with the application.
   (*a*) Attested copies of certificates
   (*b*) Testimonials
   (*c*) Crossed postal order for Rs. 8/-
   (*d*) All of the above.
3. "Incomplete application and/or received after the stipulated date will not be <u>entertained</u>". In this sentence 'entertained' refers to:
   (*a*) considered (*b*) disqualified
   (*c*) excepted (*d*) none of the above.
4. State whether the following are True or False.
   (*a*) S/C-S/T candidates do not have to pay the postal order fee
   (*b*) All the candidates will be paid railway fare.
   (*c*) Candidates must have an experience of 3 years.
   (*d*) The candidates should be Middle class pass.
   (*e*) The Pay scale is negotiable
5. Write down opposites of the following words
   (*a*) Admissible (*b*) Incomplete
   (*c*) Shortest (*d*) Received.

ANSWER KEY

Reading Comprehension and Reading Ability

Prose

Test-1

1. a 2. b 3. b 4. d 5. a 6. b

Test-2

1. c 2. d 3. c 4. b 5. d
6. d 7. d 8. c 9. c 10. b

Test-3

1. D 2. B 3. C 4. A 5. D 6. A
7. A 8. C 9. B 10. D 11. B 12. C

Test-4

1. C 2. A 3. B 4. A
5. D 6. A 7. A

Test-5

1. b 2. d 3. b 4. c
5. d 6. a 7. d 8. b
9. c 10. b 11. c

Test-6

1. c 2. c 3. d 4. a
5. a 6. b 7. b 8. d
9. a 10. d 11. d

Test-7

1. b 2. b 3. c 4. d 5. b

Test-8

1. b 2. a 3. d 4. c
5. c 6. c 7. b 8. d
9. c 11. c 11. a

Test-9

1. to 2. as 3. were
4. pullers 5. cursed 6. for
7. for 8. of 9. every
10. streets 11. at 12. of

Test-10

1. sensitive 2. more 3. environmental
4. sensitive 5. has 6. siting
7. estates 8. that 9. development
10. determines 11. by 12. which
13. pollutants 14. the 15. by
16. been 17. and 18. of
19. severe

Test-11

1. learn 2. the 3. the
4. are 5. real 6. and
7. young 8. education 9. and
10. help 11. as 12. making
13. when 14. to 15. importance
16. give 17. read 18. and
19. perfect 20. and 21. life
22. lose 23. the 24. at
25. skills 26. a 27. ideas
28. this 29. don't 30. lot
31. love 32. ideas

Test-12

1. make 2. can 3. different
4. man 5. time 6. even
7. than 8. average 9. taller
10. period 11. that 12. Again
13. our 14. make 15. the
16. however 17. brains 18. need
19. a 20. particular 21. we
22. In 23. that 24. we
25. is 26. longer 27. rather
28. we 29. our 30. result
31. time 32. sensitive 33. deal
34. operation 35. probably 36. course
37. serve 38. the 39. are
40. this 41. man 42. creature
43. true 44. changes 45. a
46. will 47. thoughts

Test-13

1. my 2. run 3. minutes
4. for 5. gave 6. was
7. Now 8. year 9. is
10. pays 11. for 12. still
13. some 14. television 15. you
16. of 17. warning 18. read
19. people 20. One 21. say
22. begin 23. habit 24. them
25. adult 26. to 27. they
28. on 29. Cigarettes 30. heart
31. cigarettes 32. a 33. smoking
34. tension 35. or 36. them

Test-14

1. people 2. of 3. are
4. music 5. prefer 6. fashion
7. behaviour 8. society 9. few
10. fashion 11. activity 12. during
13. people 14. time 15. becomes
16. people 17. style 18. its
19. is 20. Today 21. for
22. in 23. have 24. fashion
25. called 26. do 27. become
28. get 29. follow 30. they

31. belong	32. New	33. well
34. and	35. these	36. look
37. clothes	38. life	39. themselves
40. through	41. according	42. beauty
43. For	44. cosmetics	45. people
46. women	47. Following	48. and
49. appearance	50. accepted	

Test-15

1. paper	2. years	3. trees
4. mostly	5. grasses	6. been
7. wood	8. Very	9. without
10. even	11. There	12. materials
13. yield	14. manufactured	15. paper
16. polishes	17. paints	18. making
19. the	20. for	21. is
22. from	23. wood	24. and
25. camphor	26. yield	27. sticking
28. preparation	29. plants	30. to
31. and	32. of	33. medicine
34. centuries	35. and	36. one
37. or	38. used	39. our
40. an	41. to	42. for
43. furniture	44. baskets	

Test-16

1. improvement	2. with	3. and
4. write	5. in	6. cheque
7. them	8. responsible	9. us
10. box	11. we	12. bill
13. to	14. also	15. file
16. it	17. to	18. our
19. estimate	20. bills	21. Opposed
22. practical	23. sometimes	24. is
25. determine	26. spend	27. an
28. write	29. the	30. down
31. much	32. their	33. list
34. use	35. a	36. something
37. their	38. it	

Test-17

1. from	2. children	3. they
4. can't	5. them	6. own
7. I	8. say	9. me
10. the	11. their	12. envelopes
13. post	14. we	15. week
16. some	17. to	18. might
19. they	20. remember	21. like
22. to	23. bulletin	24. practice
25. the	26. Bible	27. prayers
28. sayings	29. values	30. beauty
31. talked	32. a	33. down
34. I	35. my	

Test-18

1. or	2. may	3. or
4. in	5. operates	6. children
7. cloth	8. milk	9. and
10. each	11. used	12. a
13. or	14. of	15. we
16. upper	17. the	18. or
19. attached	20. cloth	21. fits
22. puts	23. arms	24. other
25. head	26. things	27. and
28. or	29. that	30. they
31. a	32. legs	33. such
34. marionette	35. from	36. the
37. or	38. stage	39. where

Test-19

1. demanded	2. the	3. pay
4. could	5. bandaged	6. the
7. but	8. saw	9. with
10. patient	11. he	12. best
13. anything	14. time	15. The
16. she	17. she	18. furniture
19. came	20. Look	21. no
22. see	23. I'm	24. anything
25. in		

Test-20

1. seemed	2. one	3. and
4. They	5. new	6. see
7. They	8. their	9. passed
10. dying		

Poetry

Test-1

A 1. b 2. c 3. a 4. a 5. b

Test-2

A. 1. b 2. b 3. c 4. c 5. c

Test-3

1. d 2. b 3. a 4. c
5. d 6. (*a*) F (*b*) T (*c*) T (*d*) T

Test-4

1. d 2. a 3. c 4. d 5. c

Test-5

1. (*a*) T (*b*) F (*c*) T (*d*) F
(*e*) T (*f*) T (*g*) T (*h*) F
2. b 3. b 4. a 5. d
6. (*a*) cruel (*b*) caged (*c*) bright (*d*) Joy
7. (*a*) Glee (*b*) Pulse (*c*) Pain (*d*) Bruised

Test-6

1. d **2.** b **3.** b

4. marching song, bullets, guns, aerial raiders, armies, battalions.

5. c **6.** b **7.** c **8.** c

Test-7

1. a **2.** b **3.** c **4.** c

Test-8

A. 1. T **2.** F **3.** F **4.** T **5.** T

B. 1. (*a*) **2.** (*c*) **3.** (*c*) **4.** (*b*)

C.(*a*) her money-box

(*b*) an old rag-doll and a shoe behind.

(*c*) Lulu was angry because her mother had shouted at her badly.

(*d*) a circle.

D. 1. (*c*) **2.** (*b*)

Test-9

1. (*a*) F (*b*) T (*c*) F (*d*) T

2. b **3.** c **4.** a **5.** a **6.** a

Test-10

1. (*a*) F (*b*) F (*c*) F (*d*) T

2. b **3.** c **4.** c **5.** a **6.** c

Test-11

1. b **2.** a **3.** c **4.** a **5.** c **6.** a

Test-12

1. b **2.** a **3.** c

4. (*a*) F (*b*) T (*c*) T (*d*) F

Test-13

1. b **2.** c **3.** a **4.** d **5.** a

Test-14

1. c **2.** d **3.** b **4.** c

Dialogues

Test-1

A. 1. F **2.** T **3.** F **4.** F

B. 1. b **2.** b **3.** d **4.** a **5.** a **6.** b

Test-2

A. 1. F **2.** T **3.** F **4.** F

5. F **6.** F **7.** T

B. 1. b 2. d 3. c 4. b 5. c 6. b

Test-3

1. b **2.** c **3.** c **4.** c

5. b **6.** c **7.** a **8.** c

Test-4

1. b 2. a 3. c 4. b

5. (*a*) T (*b*) T (*c*) T (*d*) F

Test-5

1. a **2.** d **3.** b **4.** a **5.** b **6.** b

7. (*a*) F (*b*) T (*c*) F (*d*) F

Test-6

1. d **2.** d **3.** c

4. (*a*) F (*b*) T (*c*) T (*d*) F 5. a

Test-7

1. a **2.** a 3. c 4. b 5. c

6. (*a*) F (*b*) T (*c*) F (*d*) F 7. a

Test-8

1. c **2.** d **3.** a **4.** b

5. d **6.** c **7.** c **8.** d

Test-9

1. b **2.** a **3.** d **4.** a

5. d **6.** c **7.** b

Test-10

1. b **2.** a **3.** c **4.** d **5.** c 6. c

Communicative Passages

Test-1

1. c **2.** d

3. (*a*) T (*b*) F (*c*) F (*d*) F

Test-2

1. d **2.** d **3.** b **4.** b

Test-3

1. a **2.** d **3.** c **4.** b

Test-4

1. c **2.** d **3.** a **4.** emoluments

Test-5

1. c **2.** b **3.** d

4. (*a*) F (*b*) F (*c*) F (*d*) T

(*e*) F (*f*) F

Test-6

1. d **2.** a **3.** a

4. (*a*) F (*b*) T (*c*) T (*d*) F

Test-7

1. a **2.** d **3.** b **4.** d **5.** c

Test-8

1. a **2.** c **3.** d **4.** c **5.** a

Test-9

1. d **2.** b **3.** b **4.** c

Test-10

1. c 2. d 3. a

4. (*a*) T (*b*) F (*c*) T (*d*) T (e) F

5. (*a*) inadmissible (*b*) complete (*c*) longest (*d*) given

ADDITIONAL TESTS OF READING COMPREHENSION

OBJECTIVE TYPE MCP TESTS

TEST – 1

Cigarettes Are Risky

Four weeks ago I was late for work. I left my house five minutes later than usual and I saw (his, my, here, their)[1] bus approaching the bus stop. I began to (walk, move, fall, run)[2], but I was too slow. I waited ten (months, steps, minutes, o'clock)[3] for another bus and I was still gasping (in, for, with, about)[4] air when it arrived. The next day I (gave, stopped, started, left)[5] up smoking. For the first few days I (am, was, became, turned)[6] very irritable, but now I feel much better. (Then, When, Now, How)[7] I can ask: *Why do people smoke*?

Every (years, year, time, moment),[8] teams of doctors publish reports saying that smoking (is, becomes, grows, turns)[9] dangerous for your health. Every year the Government (cries, gives, pays, buys)[10] for advertisements telling people that smoking is bad (for, regarding, about, with)[11] them. But there are millions of people who (now, will, still, then)[12] smoke twenty or thirty cigarettes a day.

In (the, some, any, no)[13] countries, advertisements for cigarettes are not allowed on (television, paper, newspaper, magazines)[14]. If you read a newspaper or a magazine, (anyone, you, he, one)[15] will see cigarette advertisements but at the bottom (in, of, with, at)[16] each advertisement, you will see the government health (threat, warning, advertisement, publicity)[17] – *Cigarette Smoking is Injurious to Health*. You can (watch, see, read, perceive)[18] this warning on cigarette packets also. And yet (they, persons, people, individuals)[19] die every year from the effects of smoking. (Everyone, One, Each, None)[20] wonders people smoke.

Experts in various fields (say, speak, tell, deny)[21] that it is difficult to understand why people (stop, think, begin, start)[22] to smoke and why they make it a (habit, schedule, hobby, routine)[23]. Most people start smoking because other people around (us, them, you, one)[24] do it. Children feel it makes them seem (huge, big, adult, boyish)[25] to smoke, and other children also encourage them (for, about, regarding, to)[26] smoke. Some children see their parents smoking, so (all, they, adults, we)[27] start smoking too. The effect that smoking has (for, on, upon, over)[28] a person helps to make it a habit. (They, All, Many, Cigarettes)[29] contain nicotine which has an effect on the (valve, heart, vein, artery)[30] and the nervous system. Smoking one or two (types, varieties, things, cigarettes)[31] causes an increase in the heart rate and (the, a, also, always)[32] slight rise in blood pressure. The effect of (cigarettes, smoking, nicotine, drug)[33] on the nervous system is that it reduces (strain, pressure, tension, burden)[34] and helps to relax. People want these effects (but, or, however, whenever)[35] feel they need them and start depending on (drugs, them, smoking, nicotine)[36] and so they go on smoking.

ANSWERS

1. my	**2.** run	**3.** minutes
4. for	**5.** gave	**6.** was
7. Now	**8.** year	**9.** is
10. pays	**11.** for	**12.** still
13. some	**14.** television	**15.** you
16. of	**17.** warning	**18.** read
19. people	**20.** One	**21.** say
22. begin	**23.** habit	**24.** them
25. adult	**26.** to	**27.** they
28. on	**29.** Cigarettes	**30.** heart
31. cigarettes	**32.** a	**33.** smoking
34. tension	**35.** or	**36.** them

TEST – 2

Fashion is a term commonly used to describe a style of clothing worn by a large number of (individuals, persons, men, people)[1] in a country. However, popular styles (of, about, regarding, for)[2] furniture, homes and many other products (have, were, are, had)[3] also fashions. The kinds of art, (melody, music, singing, tone)[4], literature and sports that many people (prefer, like, love, desire)[5] can also be fashions. Thus, a (tradition, style, fashion, fad)[6] is – or reflects – a form of (style, behaviour, conduct, convention)[7] accepted by most people in a (nation, world, group, society)[8].

A fashion remains popular for a (many, few, less, several)[9] months or years and then another (style, fad, convention, fashion)[10] takes its place. A product or (action, activity, thing, style)[11] is in fashion or is fashionable (during, for, in, about)[12] the period of time that many (persons, members, people, men)[13] in society accept it. After a (gap, time, duration, century)[14], however, the same product or activity (is, became, becomes, grows)[15] old – fashioned when the majority of (public, society, community, people)[16] no longer accept it.

A clothing (fashion, style, fabric, design)[17] may start as a fashion but (its, that, a, the)[18] use becomes a custom if it (was, will be, is, were)[19] handed down from generation to generation. (Now, When, Then, Today)[20], wearing long trousers is a custom (among, for, regarding, with)[21] men in most countries. But changes (in, about, for, regarding)[22] the colour and shape of trousers (has, have, had, will have)[23] taken place through the years.

A (style, convention, rope, fashion)[24] that quickly comes and goes is (said, described, called, named)[25] a fad. The majority of people (has, have, does, do)[26] not accept fads. Some people may (become, grow, get, be)[27] involved in faddish behaviour because fads (receive, get, supply, bring)[28] a lot of publicity. Today people (adopt, copy, pursue, follow)[29] fashions for many reasons. For example, (we, people, men, they)[30] want others to think that they (belong, go, attend, classify)[31] to a special class of society. (Fresh, Adaptable, New, Lively)[32] fashions may be adopted immediately by (all, well, nicely, lets)[33] known people, including athletes, film stars (but, and, except, including)[34] political figures. Then, other people follow (all, those, these, some)[35] fashions so that they can also (sound, grow, be, look)[36] important. Some people think that fashionable (rokes, garments, clothes, apparel)[37] and surroundings raise their status in (life, age, youth, time)[38].

People also follow fashions to make (them, others, ourselves, themselves)[39] more attractive. Standards of beauty change (in, after, during, through)[40] the years, and people decorate themselves (according, as per, in spite, however)[41] to the changing standards. Ideas of (ugliness, attraction, charm, beauty)[42] also change from culture to culture. (For, With, Without, Regarding)[43] example, people in many countries use (powder, perfumes, cosmetics, herbs)[44] to look attractive. In some countries (people, persons, individuals, men)[45] decorate themselves with tattoos.

Men and (ladies, women, girls, spinsters)[46] have always enjoyed changing their appearance. (Pursuing, Following, Chasing, Neglecting)[47] new fashions in clothes, hairstyles (including, along with, and, excluding)[48] makeup allow people to change their (bodies, appearance, glimpse, faces)[49] in a way which is generally (rejected, accepted, admired, acknowledged)[50].

ANSWERS

1. people	**2.** of	**3.** are
4. music	**5.** prefer	**6.** fashion
7. behaviour	**8.** society	**9.** few
10. fashion	**11.** activity	**12.** during
13. people	**14.** time	**15.** becomes
16. people	**17.** style	**18.** its
19. is	**20.** Today	**21.** for
22. in	**23.** have	**24.** fashion
25. called	**26.** do	**27.** become
28. get	**29.** follow	**30.** they
31. belong	**32.** New	**33.** well
34. and	**35.** these	**36.** look
37. clothes	**38.** life	**39.** themselves
40. through	**41.** according	**42.** beauty
43. For	**44.** cosmetics	**45.** people
46. women	**47.** Following	**48.** and
49. appearance	**50.** accepted	

TEST – 3

Perhaps the most important contribution of forests to modern civilization is that they provide the raw material for making (furniture, paper, houses, sheets)[1]. The Chinese who invented paper several thousand (months, centuries, years, decades)[2] back used the inner bark of certain (goods, wood, trees, adhesives)[3] for making paper. Today, paper is made (mostly, only, almost, not)[4] from wood, bamboo and certain types of (fibres, straws, grasses, trees)[5]. The paper on which this book has (to be, been, got to be, had)[6] printed must have been made out of (tree, garbage, pulp, wood)[7] or bamboo and certain types of grasses. (Very, The, So, Great)[8] little work can be done these days (with, without, about, for)[9] the use of paper, and we can (just, as well, still, even)[10] say that modern civilization depends on paper.

(Their, There, Where, Those)[11] are a large number of other raw (prints, food, fruit, materials)[12] which come from the forests. Pine trees (contribute, donate, yield, generate)[13] resin from which resin and turpentine are (made, fabricated, grown, manufactured)[14]. Resin is used in the sizing of (cloth, material, sheet, paper)[15] and textiles and for making paints, varnishes, (paints, polishes, papers, medicines)[16] and adhesives. Turpentine is used for making (polishes, paints, herbs, furniture)[17] and varnishes. It is also used for (inventing, developing, synthesizing, making)[18] medicines, and is now being used for (a, the, any, quick)[19] manufacture of artificial camphor, which is used (in, regarding, for, from)[20] medicines, and during religious ceremonious.

Natural camphor (is, may be, can be, will be)[21] also produced by forests and it comes (for, from, about, regarding)[22] the wood and leaves of the camphor (wood, herbal, bush, fresh)[23] tree which is mostly found in China (in, and, except, or)[24] Taiwan. But now in our country all (wood, camphor, paper, furniture)[25] is obtained from turpentine. Some forest trees (develop, grow, give, yield)[26] gums which are not only used for (fixing, sticking, clinging, separating)[27] paper but are also used in the (manufacture, preparation, cooking, baking)[28] of sweets and ice-creams.

Medicinal herbs and (plants, branches, leaves, shoots)[29] are another important gift of the forests (for, to, from, towards)[30] mankind. They are used in the Ayurvedic (or, and, including, excluding)[31] Unani as well as the modern systems (in, about, with, of)[32] medicine. The Ayurvedic and Unani systems of (medicine, science, technology, practice)[33] have been practiced in our country for (months, decades, years, centuries)[34] and they both rely on medicinal plants (or, and, except, including)[35] herbs. In every village shop in India, (we, I, one, all)[36] can buy dried roots, barks, leaves, flowers (or, except, but, with)[37] fruits of different medicinal plants which are (made, practiced, used, kept)[38] for common diseases.

In the life of (their, our, my, all)[39] rural people products from the forests play (an, the, one, only)[40] important role. They provide people with material (and, to, or, but)[41] make huts and to thatch roofs, wood (in, for, and, or)[42] making bullock carts, agricultural tools and household (goods, utensils, things, furniture)[43] and fibers for making ropes, nets, mats, (baskets, ropes, tools, pots)[44] and many other items of daily use.

ANSWERS

1. paper	2. years	3. trees
4. mostly	5. grasses	6. been
7. wood	8. Very	9. without
10. even	11. There	12. materials
13. yield	14. manufactured	
15. paper	16. polishes	17. paints
18. making	19. the	20. for
21. is	22. from	23. wood
24. and	25. camphor	26. yield
27. sticking	28. preparation	29. plants
30. to	31. and	32. of
33. medicine	34. centuries	35. and
36. one	37. or	38. used
39. our	40. an	41. to
42. for	43. furniture	44. baskets

TEST – 4

Like all sports, hunting has its own rules but there is no referee present to make sure that rules are (pursued, followed, accepted, rejected)[1]. The entire responsibility of following the rules depends (in, for, over, on)[2] the sportsman himself. The forest and wild life (people, persons, staff, members)[3] are there to keep a check but it (was, is, may be, isn't)[4] the sportsman who has to keep a control (upon, in, within, on)[5] himself and has to ensure that our wild (forest, animal, greenery, life)[6] is not destroyed completely. The most serious and (great, heavy, dangerous, light)[7] damage to our wild life is caused by (thieves, robbers, poachers, rogues)[8] from villages next to the forest. Damage is (just, only, merely, also)[9] done by gangs from big towns who kill (green, wild, bird, plant)[10] life so that they can sell skins and (legs, horns, feet, eyes)[11]. If we are careful and follow the rules (of, about, regarding, for)[12] the game strictly, we can continue to hunt (with, without, for, about)[13] any loss of our fauna at present.

In order to (create, develop, improve, save)[14] our wild life, a number of national parks (or, and, with, in)[15] game sanctuaries have been established. The difference between (a, the, one, any)[16] national park and a game sanctuary is that (as, through, while, them)[17] a national park is established through an Act (with, of, in, for)[18] parliament or a state legislature, sanctuaries are established (with, for, about, through)[19] an administrative order of the government. National parks (may be, are, were, have been)[20] permanent and their boundaries cannot be changed whereas (parks, zoos, sanctuaries, playgrounds)[21] are established for a fixed period of time (who, whom, same, which)[22] may or may not be increased; and also (the, many, some, all)[23] boundaries can be changed or modified. In India

(they, people, we, states)[24] have forty five national parks. The most famous (is, was, were, are)[25] the Kanha National Park in Madhya Pradesh, (a, the, one, some)[26] Corbet National Park and Dudwa National Park (in, at, written, on)[27] Uttar Pradesh.

In these National Parks the wild (animal, life, forest, plant)[28] gets an opportunity to exist and multiply in (the, a, some, any)[29] natural manner without any interference or danger from (woman, person, man, humanity)[30]. In the game sanctuaries (210 at present), similar (safety, protection, danger, shelter)[31] is given to all forms of wild life. (A, The, One, Only)[32] most famous game sanctuary in India is (the, a, only, also)[33] Gir Lion Sanctuary in Gujrat. Here lives the Asiatic (lion, animal, giant, bird)[34] which once roamed freely all over Northwest (World, India, Continent, Ocean)[35] Pakistan, Iraq and Arabia. This is the only (part, nation, zoo, land)[36] of the earth where the Asiatic lion still (besides, dwells, puts up, exists)[37] in its natural environment owing to the strict (vigilence, discipline, protection, food)[38] given to it for the last eighty years (and, or, also, nearly)[39] more.

All our national parks and sanctuaries are (a, the, only, also)[40] source of great pleasure and recreation to thousands (of, accountable, countable, countless)[41] visitors each other because they given an opportunity (for, to, from, about)[42] people to see the rich fauna of our (earth, forests, life, country)[43] in their natural surroundings

ANSWERS

1. followed	**2.** on	**3.** staff
4. is	**5.** on	**6.** life
7. heavy	**8.** poachers	**9.** also
10. wild	**11.** horns	**12.** of
13. without	**14.** save	**15.** and
16. a	**17.** while	**18.** of
19. through	**20.** are	**21.** sanctuaries
22. which	**23.** the	**24.** we
25. are	**26.** the	**27.** in
28. life	**29.** a	**30.** man
31. protection	**32.** The	**33.** the
34. lion	**35.** India	**36.** part
37. exists	**38.** protection	**39.** or
40. a	**41.** of	**42.** to
43. country		

"When all things began, the word already was"

– *New English Bible Version*

CHAPTER 2 VOCABULARY

In the multiple-choice type, it is advisable to practise the following types

(i) Definition:

This "classic" type of vocabulary item consists of a test word followed by several possible definitions or synonyms. For example **Nap**

(*a*) a brief sleep (*c*) a sharp rock
(*b*) a happy song (*d*) a short meeting

The above version of the definition item type has the advantage of being highly economical in terms of the number of problems that can be answered in a short period of testing time. It would be good to practise such question – items for about 5-7 minutes daily and test yourself on these items the next day before proceeding further. You are advised to employ these words in your daily conversation as well as in your productive written pieces.

(ii) Completion:

A second item type places the problem words in context, e.g., The old woman was too______to push open the heavy door.

(*a*) feeble (*b*) sincere
(*c*) deaf (*d*) harsh

The above item type has the advantage of placing the problem words in a contextual setting, a procedure felt by many as better to text your ability actually to use the test words actively in a real-life situation.

(iii) Paraphrase:

A third method of testing vocabulary, combining elements of two of the previously discussed devices, is to underline/italicise a word in context and provide universal possible meanings.

John was **astounded** to hear her answer

(*a*) greatly amused (*b*) greatly relieved
(*c*) greatly surprise (*d*) greatly angered

The advantage of this item type is, as with type 2, that it puts the test words in a context. The Chapter tests your knowledge and application of the following vocabulary types.

(*i*) Synonyms
(*ii*) Antonyms
(*iii*) Use of appropriate word/phrases in context
(*iv*) Collocation of words and phrases
(*v*) Idioms and Phrases
(*vi*) Specialized Vocabulary for Students of English Literature, and Medicine
(*vii*) One word Substitution
(*viii*) Homophones, Homonyms, and Homographs

TEST – 1

1. SYNONYMS

Directions: Select the word which is closest to the meaning of the following word:

1. Brevity
(*a*) stupidity (*b*) helplessness
(*c*) conciseness (*d*) incongruity
2. Overawe
(*a*) agitate (*b*) validate
(*c*) abstain (*d*) restrain
3. Licentious
(*a*) liberal (*b*) lewd
(*c*) ravishing (*d*) calm
4. Ingenious
(*a*) shrewd (*b*) supplementary
(*c*) frank (*d*) dull
5. Languish
(*a*) continue (*b*) suppress
(*c*) reduce speed (*d*) grow feeble
6. Vista
(*a*) view (*b*) argument
(*c*) illusion (*d*) screen
7. Allege
(*a*) declare without proof
(*b*) form a new group
(*c*) greatly
(*d*) prove guilty

8. Pittance
(*a*) a small amount (*b*) a feeling of sorrow
(*c*) a narrow inlet (*d*) a large amount

9. Plaudit
(*a*) darkness (*b*) criticism
(*c*) fancy (*d*) applause

10. Morose
(*a*) strong and hardy
(*b*) lenient and courteous
(*c*) dismal and fretful
(*d*) shy and bashful

11. Glee
(*a*) hilarity (*b*) gleam
(*c*) adhesive (*d*) discovery

12. Skittish
(*a*) playful (*b*) naughty
(*c*) silent (*d*) frightened

13. Provoked
(*a*) instigated (*b*) encouraged
(*c*) inclined (*d*) dissuaded

14. Ruthless
(*a*) urbane (*b*) bestial
(*c*) frail (*d*) irrational

15. Demur
(*a*) objection (*b*) creation
(*c*) attraction (*d*) rejection

16. Unseemly
(*a*) improper (*b*) assiduous
(*c*) agitated (*d*) filthy

17. Pester
(*a*) bribe for one's selfish end
(*b*) spoil out of excessive love
(*c*) annoy with frequent requests
(*d*) agonize out of anger

18. Fillip
(*a*) imagination (*b*) impunity
(*c*) infusion (*d*) incentive

19. Precise
(*a*) slump (*b*) final
(*c*) short (*d*) exact

20. Throng
(*a*) congestion (*b*) crowd
(*c*) group (*d*) explosion

21. Dictatorial
(*a*) offensive (*b*) wordy
(*c*) eccentric (*d*) domineering

22. Discover
(*a*) invent (*b*) unwrap
(*c*) find out (*d*) search for

23. Pristine
(*a*) primitive (*b*) bland
(*c*) immaculate (*d*) refined

24. Onslaught
(*a*) assault (*b*) skirmish
(*c*) war (*d*) revolt

25. Pretences
(*a*) whims (*b*) odds
(*c*) excuses (*d*) fallacies

26. Brusque
(*a*) abrupt (*b*) extrinsic
(*c*) unexpected (*d*) witty

27. Indict
(*a*) reprove (*b*) cause
(*c*) catalogue (*d*) accuse

28. Affluent
(*a*) parasitic (*b*) fortified
(*c*) affected (*d*) prosperous

29. Fragile
(*a*) intrinsic (*b*) hardy
(*c*) beneficial (*d*) frail

30. Asylum
(*a*) galaxy (*b*) sanctuary
(*c*) establishment (*d*) hospital

31. Indelible
(*a*) that cannot be understood
(*b*) that cannot be read
(*c*) that cannot be eaten
(*d*) that cannot be removed

32. Flair
(*a*) aroma (*b*) excitement
(*c*) qualification (*d*) natural ability

33. Replete
(*a*) deprived (*b*) worked
(*c*) filled (*d*) lacked

34. Genial
(*a*) natural (*b*) kindly
(*c*) fascinating (*d*) hereditary

35. Retaliation
(*a*) keeping score
(*b*) attack in return
(*c*) open disrespect
(*d*) long-lasting hatred

36. Hibernation
(*a*) Irish dancing step
(*b*) inactivity
(*c*) foreign holiday
(*d*) retirement

37. Manger
(*a*) carpenter's tool-rack
(*b*) feeding– trough
(*c*) device for closing stable door
(*d*) haystack

38. Deciduous
(*a*) decisive (*b*) referring
(*c*) temporary (*d*) low-alcohol

39. Corrosive
(*a*) devious (*b*) destructive
(*c*) intense (*d*) unpleasant

40. Extant
(*a*) lengthy (*b*) long-dead
(*c*) stationary (*d*) surviving

41. Gamut
(*a*) stimulus (*b*) complete range
(*c*) homeless child (*d*) obstacle

42. Herculean
(*a*) immensely difficult
(*b*) violent
(*c*) reckless
(*d*) extraordinarily brave

43. Winsome
(*a*) odd (*b*) fickle
(*c*) angelic (*d*) attractive

44. Virtual
(*a*) actual (*b*) partial
(*c*) simulated (*d*) extended

45. Evangelist
(*a*) wanderer
(*b*) enthusiastic preacher
(*c*) faithful follower
(*d*) eccentric

46. Meritocracy
(*a*) system based on achievement
(*b*) system based on red-tapism
(*c*) the democratic process
(*d*) temporary authority

47. Acumen
(*a*) exactness (*b*) potentiality
(*c*) shrewdness (*d*) assurance

48. Premonition
(*a*) understanding (*b*) forewarning
(*c*) determination (*d*) forecast

49. Criterion
(*a*) explanation (*b*) essence
(*c*) standard (*d*) turning-point

50. Extricate
(*a*) frustrate (*b*) isolate
(*c*) get rid of (*d*) set free

2. SYNONYMS IN CONTEXT

TEST – 2

Directions: Read the following passages and from the alternatives given below choose the word closest to the meaning of the *underlined* words/phrases in the passage.

Passage I.

A background questionnaire, seeking information on such matters as age, gender, self-rated English proficiency[1], reasons for learning English, etc., was also administered. Results indicated that Indian college students use a variety of language learning strategies[2] and that they use them with high to moderate[3] frequency. Significant differences were found in the strategy use of males versus females and between students who went to English-medium school ("the high proficiency group") as opposed to[4] the ones who went to vernacular-medium schools ("the low proficiency group"). Implications[5] of the study for college teachers are discussed.

1. Proficiency
(*a*) knowledge. (*b*) efficiency
(*c*) expertise (*d*) intelligence

2. Strategies
(*a*) tactics (*b*) plans
(*c*) processes (*d*) procedures

3. Moderate
(*a*) normal (*b*) medium
(*c*) middle (*d*) low

4. Opposed to
(*a*) contrasting (*b*) contradicting
(*c*) against (*d*) confronting

5. Implications
(*a*) results (*b*) effects
(*c*) proposals (*d*) grounds

Passage II.

What does it boil down to? To control but not to invade[1] or unduly interfere. To watch over but not to peer[2] or scrutinize[3]. To advise but not to harass[4] with counsel[5].

1. Invade
(*a*) misbehave (*b*) supersede
(*c*) encroach upon (*d*) trespass

2. Peer
(*a*) glance (*b*) glare
(*c*) look keenly (*d*) peep

3. Scrutinize
(*a*) examine (*b*) penetrate
(*c*) indicate (*d*) control

4. Harass
(*a*) trouble (*b*) insult
(*c*) terrify (*d*) disturb

5. Counsel
(*a*) instruction (*b*) advice
(*c*) suggestion (*d*) arrangement

Passage III.

The dynamic[1], passionate change of attitude that occurred in America has not been achieved to shake secondary school complacency[2] out of its mediocre[3] rut, to force it to pursue excellence, to tell it forth forthrightly that the old slovenly[4] second-rateness is not good enough, and that nothing short of perfection will do if we are not to perish as an independent entity. It is not enough today to have good teachers; we need to have superlatively good teachers now and at all times.

1. Dynamic
(*a*) dashing (*b*) motivating
(*c*) dull (*d*) boring

2. Complacency
(*a*) sluggishness (*b*) completeness
(*c*) carefulness (*d*) cleverness

3. Mediocre
(*a*) second-rate (*b*) middle-class
(*c*) simple (*d*) passive

4. Slovenly
(*a*) out-dated (*b*) unintelligible
(*c*) unmethodical (*d*) out-caste

Passage IV.

Another ghost that needs to be laid at once stalks[1] surprisingly through intellectual homes. It is that if teaching is intrinsically[2] good, it is not necessary to think of character-building, as an activity by itself. In practice, this is a wholly fallacious[3] view. Children outstandingly good at mathematics, who have had the good fortune to get good teaching and the good sense to respond to it, are often dishonest, given to subterfuge and intrigue[4] and are deeply impregnated with inherited prejudice[5] which is the negation of mental and moral clarity.

1. Stalks
(*a*) attacks (*b*) peeps
(*c*) haunts (*d*) disturbs

2. Intrinsically
(*a*) inwardly (*b*) essentially
(*c*) really (*d*) automatically

3. Fallacious
(*a*) receptive (*b*) truthful
(*c*) deceptive (*d*) fearful

4. Intrigue
(*a*) confusion (*b*) cheating
(*c*) deception (*d*) plotting

5. Prejudice
(*a*) misconception (*b*) preconception
(*c*) precondition (*d*) presumption

Passage V.

And with this backdrop of bricks and mortar, with the compelling drive of superlatively[1] good teaching and a code, such as I have described, of conduct for children, we shall have the best students in the world. Then, and then only, will patriotism become what it should be, not an emotional, irrational and isolated impulse[2], but a daily, silent, corporate quality of service without vanity[3], as silent, corporate and serviceable as the bricks and mortar that symbolize the abiding[4] triumph[5] of man over the dark hosts of ignorance.

1. Superlatively
   (*a*) exclusively (*b*) exceptionally
   (*c*) reasonably (*d*) particularly
2. Impulse
   (*a*) urge (*b*) compulsion
   (*c*) force (*d*) attraction
3. Vanity
   (*a*) display (*b*) pride
   (*c*) prejudice (*d*) conceit
4. Abiding
   (*a*) promising (*b*) enduring
   (*c*) temporary (*d*) permanent
5. Triumph
   (*a*) creation (*b*) victory
   (*c*) discovery (*d*) depiction

TEST – 3

Directions: Read the following sentences and from the alternatives given below choose the word closest to the meaning of the *italicised* word in the sentence.

1. I am quite *content* to stay here.
   (*a*) eager (*b*) compelled
   (*c*) reluctant (*d*) happy
2. He gave me a detailed *account* of the meeting.
   (*a*) summary (*b*) report
   (*c*) history (*d*) analysis
3. There is no *gainsaying* that the country is in difficulties.
   (*a*) exaggeration (*b*) doubt
   (*c*) forecast (*d*) contradiction
4. Our art treasures must be kept for *posterity*.
   (*a*) prosperity
   (*b*) all succeeding generations
   (*c*) all preceding generations
   (*d*) artisans
5. He is so *meticulous* that he can never do anything in a hurry.
   (*a*) patient (*b*) careless
   (*c*) lethargic (*d*) careful
6. This was his *maiden* performance on the stage and he did very well.
   (*a*) opening (*b*) girlish
   (*c*) first (*d*) primary
7. The man *vehemently* denied all the charges of corruption that were levelled against him.
   (*a*) forcefully (*b*) serenely
   (*c*) hysterically (*d*) devoutly
8. *Eventually* vision is affected and the patient is only able to see if light is present.
   (*a*) primarily (*b*) obviously
   (*c*) gradually (*d*) ultimately
9. Reading of poetry is not *congenial* to his taste.
   (*a*) appealing (*b*) helpful
   (*c*) beneficial (*d*) suited
10. He had a *penchant* for fine phrases.
    (*a*) fondness (*b*) distaste
    (*c*) eagerness (*d*) hunger
11. *Sagacity* increases with age.
    (*a*) kindness (*b*) love
    (*c*) wisdom (*d*) senility
12. He entertains a sense of *rancour* against the colleague who superseded him.
    (*a*) hatred (*b*) disrespect
    (*c*) ill-will (*d*) malice
13. '*Frailty* thy name is woman.'
    (*a*) Shyness (*b*) Fragility
    (*c*) Cowardice (*d*) Delicacy
14. It is not for *lay* readers to evaluate a great poet.
    (*a*) ordinary (*b*) common
    (*c*) non-professional (*d*) unskilled
15. The nurse was well appreciated by the patients for her *benign* acts.
    (*a*) kind (*b*) loving
    (*c*) sweet (*d*) entertaining
16. His strange behaviour is a source of *mirth* for his fellow workers.
    (*a*) anger (*b*) talk
    (*c*) embarrassment (*d*) amusement
17. It is strange that John has begun to make decisions. He was always *reluctant* to do so.
    (*a*) hesitant (*b*) helpless
    (*c*) illiberal (*d*) ill-equipped
18. The disaster left millions of people in *destitution.*

(*a*) disgrace (*b*) misery
(*c*) poverty (*d*) desperation.

19. We have a rigid programme ahead but we still persist in dealing with *trivial* matters.
(*a*) unimportant (*b*) unpopular
(*c*) irrelevant (*d*) impractical

20. When the teacher saw John looking idly at the walls, he *admonished* him to study.
(*a*) warned (*b*) guided
(*c*) punished (*d*) implored

21. Soon after the slaves were *emancipated* the industry collapsed.
(*a*) imprisoned (*b*) released
(*c*) punished (*d*) enslaved

22. The government can only afford to provide the poor with a meagre *subsistence.*
(*a*) material (*b*) food
(*c*) assistance (*d*) salary

23. A *posthumous* award was given to the poet.
(*a*) postal (*b*) after-death
(*c*) creditable (*d*) literary

24. I doubt the *veracity* of your statement.
(*a*) application (*b*) thoughtfulness
(*c*) truthfulness (*d*) appreciation

3. ANTONYMS

TEST – 4

Directions: Select the word which is closest to the opposite in meaning of the word in bold letters.

1. Virile
(*a*) effeminate (*b*) synthetic
(*c*) malignant (*d*) robust

2. Demur
(*a*) concur (*b*) disagree
(*c*) dissipate (*d*) consume

3. Apogee
(*a*) sinister (*b*) perigee
(*c*) callow (*d*) chary

4. Bias
(*a*) unfairness (*b*) subjective
(*c*) absoluteness (*d*) objectivity

5. Abortive
(*a*) successful (*b*) defeated
(*c*) unfruitful (*d*) fixed

6. Foolhardy
(*a*) quick (*b*) sensitive
(*c*) futile (*d*) wise

7. Auspices
(*a*) award (*b*) legal remedy
(*c*) non-sponsorship (*d*) divinity

8. Consonant
(*a*) abundant (*b*) uniform
(*c*) ambiguous (*d*) incongruous

9. Inadequate
(*a*) rapid (*b*) sufficient
(*c*) glossy (*d*) insufficient

10. Analysis
(*a*) dialysis (*b*) synthesis
(*c*) nemesis (*d*) emphasis

11. Concede
(*a*) object (*b*) refuse
(*c*) grant (*d*) accede

12. Suppress
(*a*) grow (*b*) encourage
(*c*) praise (*d*) permit

13. Furious
(*a*) unrestrained (*b*) witty
(*c*) flourishing (*d*) restrained

14. Prosaic
(*a*) usual (*b*) acceptable
(*c*) extraordinary (*d*) gregarious

15. Temerity
(*a*) reticence (*b*) composure
(*c*) establishment (*d*) trial

16. Abscond
(*a*) depart (*b*) disappear
(*c*) appear (*d*) hide

17. Sedate
(*a*) excited (*b*) calm
(*c*) sleepy (*d*) alert

18. Tirade
(*a*) submit (*b*) abuse
(*c*) praise (*d*) help

19. Punctilious
(*a*) sloppy (*b*) hidden
(*c*) timely (*d*) unexpected

20. Enervate
(*a*) assemble (*b*) fortify
(*c*) destroy (*d*) assume

21. Faze
(*a*) erase (*b*) avoid
(*c*) perturb (*d*) encourage

22. Feigned
(*a*) resigned (*b*) natural
(*c*) artificial (*d*) unclear

23. Opulent
(*a*) dishonest (*b*) affluent
(*c*) eager (*d*) impoverished

24. Zest
(*a*) silence (*b*) enthusiasm
(*c*) apathy (*d*) joke

25. Pellucid
(*a*) transparent (*b*) insane
(*c*) similar (*d*) opaque

26. Balm
(*a*) irritant (*b*) imperfection
(*c*) ointment (*d*) comfort

27. Analgesia
(*a*) difference (*b*) relief of pain
(*c*) synthesis (*d*) sensitivity to pain

28. Vigilant
(*a*) cautious (*b*) oblivious
(*c*) secretive (*d*) careful

29. Abrogate
(*a*) enact (*b*) cancel
(*c*) validate (*d*) reduce

30. Centrifugal
(*a*) circular (*b*) rotary
(*c*) centripetal (*d*) turbulent

31. Abbreviate
(*a*) enlarge (*b*) reduce
(*c*) abridge (*d*) expand

32. Abeyance
(*a*) expectancy (*b*) suspension
(*c*) dormancy (*d*) action.

33. Alacrity
(*a*) animation (*b*) briskness
(*c*) eagerness (*d*) indifference

34. Amass
(*a*) dissipate (*b*) accumulate
(*c*) aggregate (*d*) hoard

35. Alteration
(*a*) conformity (*b*) dissension
(*c*) brawl (*d*) debate

36. Baffle
(*a*) balk (*b*) foil
(*c*) outwit (*d*) abet

37. Benevolence
(*a*) almsgiving (*b*) beneficence
(*c*) malignity (*d*) goodwill

38. Bleak
(*a*) white (*b*) bright
(*c*) dull (*d*) cold

39. Candid
(*a*) frank (*b*) transparent
(*c*) distorted (*d*) crafty

40. Defile
(*a*) contaminate (*b*) disinfect
(*c*) pollute (*d*) clarify

41. Defer
(*a*) prorogue (*b*) expedite
(*c*) protract (*d*) suspend

42. Endeavour
(*a*) strive (*b*) assay
(*c*) try (*d*) abandon

43. Fallacy
(*a*) refinement (*b*) sophism
(*c*) sureness (*d*) subterfuge

44. Formidable
(*a*) dangerous (*b*) impregnable
(*c*) powerless (*d*) invincible

45. Frugality
(*a*) miserliness (*b*) extravagance
(*c*) parsimony (*d*) providence

46. Incongruous
(*a*) conflicting (*b*) general
(*c*) ill-matched (*d*) compatible

47. Latent
(*a*) dormant (*b*) apparent
(*c*) hidden (*d*) explicit

48. Perverse
(*a*) compliant (*b*) fraction
(*c*) intractable (*d*) obstinate

49. Heterogeneous
(*a*) mingled (*b*) inhomogeneous
(*c*) identical (*d*) conglomerate

50. Reproof
(*a*) approbation (*b*) comment
(*c*) condemnation (*d*) criticism

4. ANTONYMS IN CONTEXT

TEST – 5

Directions: Read the following sentences and from the alternatives given below choose the word *opposite* to the meaning of the *italicised* word in the sentence.

1. The growing *disparity* among the several states has been a subject of discussion for the politicians in India.
   (*a*) brotherhood (*b*) equality
   (*c*) diversity (*d*) fraternity
2. His *extravagant* spending will affect the growth of his business.
   (*a*) excessive (*b*) decreased
   (*c*) miserly (*d*) wild
3. During his stay at the office he dealt with *essential* matters.
   (*a*) insignificant (*b*) important
   (*c*) silly (*d*) useless
4. Jack is too *fickle* minded.
   (*a*) like (*b*) firm
   (*c*) narrow (*d*) broad
5. In certain cases, *docile* girls may be rejected by their prospective life partners.
   (*a*) determined (*b*) submissive
   (*c*) obedient (*d*) obstinate
6. It is difficult even for the psychologists to predict delirious moments in the life of mentally challenged people. Betty was *delirious* struggling to survive typhoid fever.
   (*a*) sane (*b*) mad
   (*c*) hysterical (*d*) sensible.
7. The *pungent* smell of farmland tells me I'm close.
   (*a*) repellant (*b*) sweet
   (*c*) attractive (*d*) uneasy
8. Jim came back to find his house *in shambles.*
   (*a*) neat and clean (*b*) in a mess
   (*c*) in ruins (*d*) all decked up.
9. He has reached across the world, *fomenting* violence against the west.
   (*a*) planning (*b*) subduing
   (*c*) instigating (*d*) negating.
10. The *comic* figure can never be forgotten.
    (*a*) interesting (*b*) laughing
    (*c*) tragic (*d*) unhappy
11. He was *economical* in his expenses.
    (*a*) frugal (*b*) spendthrift
    (*c*) extravagant (*d*) waster
12. John's *erratic* behaviour was a subject of discussion among the teachers.
    (*a*) variable (*b*) punctual
    (*c*) consistent (*d*) unreliable
13. The playwright *vividly* describes the beauty of nature.
    (*a*) unintentionally (*b*) unscrupulously
    (*c*) unimpressively (*d*) unwillingly.
14. For of his activities, the man was *exonerated* by the court,
    (*a*) accused (*b*) rejected
    (*c*) contracted (*d*) admit.
15. Jim is very *inquisitive* about the life of birds.
    (*a*) ignorant (*b*) uninterested
    (*c*) indolent (*d*) careful
16. Jack used *devious* ways to set up his business.
    (*a*) direct (*b*) random
    (*c*) abnormal (*d*) indirect
17. "The teacher passed *derogatory* remarks about Rina's performance in exams.
    (*a*) critical (*b*) complimentary
    (*c*) heinous (*d*) important
18. He led an *ascetic* life but his wife followed her own philosophy of life.
    (*a*) austere (*b*) pompous
    (*c*) hedonistic (*d*) artificial
19. There is something *repulsive* about the way he handles people.
    (*a*) attractive (*b*) reflective
    (*c*) distinctive (*d*) smooth
20. His plans for Seema showed his *churlish* behaviour.
    (*a*) naughty (*b*) coarse
    (*c*) courteous (*d*) modest

5. MULTIPLE-CHOICE COMPLETION TYPE

TEST – 6

Directions: Complete each sentence with one of the words underneath.

Example: If you had the opportunity, which of these would you ____________?

(*a*) ask (*b*) choose
(*c*) envisage (*d*) accept

The answer is (*b*)

1. They were ready for a ____________ with the enemy.
 (*a*) retaliation (*b*) combat
 (*c*) confrontation (*d*) hostility
2. Wearing odd socks would be classed as ____________ behaviour.
 (*a*) awkward (*b*) eccentric
 (*c*) exotic (*d*) ecstatic
3. The building burned down because no ____________ against fire had been taken.
 (*a*) alarms (*b*) precautions
 (*c*) protections (*d*) protectives
4. To make the house more comfortable, we have decided to have central heating ____________.
 (*a*) installed (*b*) established
 (*c*) settled (*d*) involved
5. A good way of ____________ food is by keeping it in a refrigerator.
 (*a*) extending (*b*) prolonging
 (*c*) preserving (*d*) maintaining
6. The fire soon ____________ the wooden hut.
 (*a*) extinguished (*b*) squashed
 (*c*) dissolved (*d*) consumed
7. Our preferences are often so ____________ that we can give no logical reason for them.
 (*a*) irrational (*b*) unreasonable
 (*c*) unthinkable (*d*) baseless
8. A lot of misunderstanding about student politics ____________ at present.
 (*a*) prevails (*b*) reports
 (*c*) exists (*d*) predominates
9. Animals should not be locked in cages. They should be in their normal ____________.
 (*a*) residence (*b*) environment
 (*c*) position (*d*) home
10. There were few young people in the group; most of the others were ____________.
 (*a*) ripe (*b*) mature
 (*c*) elderly (*d*) senior
11. A ____________ of care often leads to accidents.
 (*a*) lack (*b*) shortage
 (*c*) want (*d*) deficiency
12. He promised to attend to his office without ____________
 (*a*) doubt (*b*) fail
 (*c*) miss (*d*) mistake
13. The only sure means by which success may be ____________ is hard work and persistence.
 (*a*) achieved (*b*) obtained
 (*c*) bought (*d*) got
14. For your own sake, I ____________ you to think again before making such a decision.
 (*a*) insist (*b*) urge
 (*c*) demand (*d*) invite
15. I was invited to ____________ in the forthcoming competition.
 (*a*) take over (*b*) take part
 (*c*) take up (*d*) take place
16. Mr. Kalra is in ____________ and can, therefore, maintain a car easily.
 (*a*) job (*b*) profession
 (*c*) service (*d*) business
17. Louka is too ____________ of Raina to obey his instructions.
 (*a*) jealous (*b*) contemptuous
 (*c*) proud (*d*) tolerant
18. No new ____________ could arouse their curiosity.
 (*a*) picture (*b*) sight
 (*c*) look (*d*) people
19. Although the ____________ was light it was too much for the old man.
 (*a*) load (*b*) cart
 (*c*) horse (*d*) elephant
20. He was ____________ to such labour.
 (*a*) abled (*b*) disliked
 (*c*) unaccustomed (*d*) unwanted
21. He ____________ in his clothes and brought out of his ragged girdle a bit of a silver coin.
 (*a*) nervously (*b*) fumbled
 (*c*) awkwardly (*d*) uncomfortably

22. He said to the old man, 'Let me see you ________ noodles'.
(*a*) drink (*b*) chew
(*c*) gulp (*d*) eat

23. He felt ________ in his apron and happily brought out the two coins.
(*a*) eagerly (*b*) pathetically
(*c*) disinterestedly (*d*) angrily

24. Two sparrows ________ a nest in a cosy corner in the roof of Ramayya's house.
(*a*) destroyed (*b*) built
(*c*) constructed (*d*) bought

25. You are always starving the servants, don't be that ________', said the wife to her husband.
(*a*) greedy (*b*) mean
(*c*) self centred (*d*) careless

26. He has no ________, only stubs.
(*a*) fingers (*b*) legs
(*c*) head (*d*) back

27. I had to acknowledge that his ________ was diminished, when his wife started abusing his friend's children in a party.
(*a*) rank (*b*) station
(*c*) prestige (*d*) title

28. The bullocks seemed glad of the water, for already their ________ were dusty and glistened with sweat in the sunlight.
(*a*) hides (*b*) leather
(*c*) sole (*d*) feet

29. The cats are ________.
(*a*) mewing (*b*) grumbling
(*c*) growling (*d*) roaring

30. How well I ________ the good old days!
(*a*) forget (*b*) recall
(*c*) decide (*d*) call

31. What ________ indeed my husband must have had, to put up with me uncomplainingly during the early days of our married life!
(*a*) anger (*b*) patience
(*c*) nervousness (*d*) unwillingness

32. The ________ of Chris, a dominating attribute of his character, may be considered a negative feature of the play *All my Sons*.
(*a*) love (*b*) violence
(*c*) morality (*d*) generosity

33. Through the play 'All my sons', Miller points to our inescapable social ________.
(*a*) irresponsibilities (*b*) responsibilities
(*c*) character (*d*) rights

34. It meant that those killed in the war had sacrificed themselves in ________.
(*a*) vain (*b*) pity
(*c*) compulsion (*d*) danger

35. The neighbours were inclined to believe that Joe Keller was ________.
(*a*) guilty (*b*) good
(*c*) cunning (*d*) smart

36. They were awaiting official ________ of the news they had heard from a friend.
(*a*) sanction (*b*) recommendation
(*c*) confirmation (*d*) ratification

37. It ________ to me that she was incurable.
(*a*) happened (*b*) occurred
(*c*) flashed (*d*) suggested

38. My father was too ________ to push open the heavy door.
(*a*) faint (*b*) feeble
(*c*) timid (*d*) faltering

39. Every Shakespearean hero has an internal ________ in his character.
(*a*) defect (*b*) weakness
(*c*) flaw (*d*) fault

40. Anita ________ me of a girl I used to know.
(*a*) recalls (*b*) remembers
(*c*) reminds (*d*) recollects

41. They are refugees in need of ________.
(*a*) restoration (*b*) rehabilitation
(*c*) recapitulation (*d*) renovation

42. Many women in developing countries experience a cycle of poor health that ________ before they are born and persists through adulthood passing from generation to generation.
(*a*) originates (*b*) derives
(*c*) rotates (*d*) establishes

43. I enjoy ________ the children playing in the garden.
(*a*) examining (*b*) staring
(*c*) watching (*d*) viewing

44. The passengers were afraid but the captain ____________ them that there was no danger.
(*a*) promised (*b*) assured
(*c*) advised (*d*) instructed

45. The shirt is not expensive, I bought it very ____________.
(*a*) cheaply (*b*) low
(*c*) dearly (*d*) cheap

46. This is not a lesson that I like to ____________ about.
(*a*) meditate (*b*) comment
(*c*) beat (*d*) think

47. He wanted to know if I had ____________ a house.
(*a*) bought (*b*) shopped
(*c*) marketed (*d*) brought

48. The silk merchant will give a ____________ dowry to his daughter, won't he?
(*a*) vast (*b*) high
(*c*) big (*d*) rich

49. The sun is shining brightly so please ____________ the light.
(*a*) put off (*b*) put out
(*c*) put on (*d*) put over

50. She did not ____________ me or my friend.
(*a*) see (*b*) observe
(*c*) watch (*d*) look

51. The traveller had not drunk water for three days and his throat was ____________.
(*a*) sore (*b*) unmoist
(*c*) hoarse (*d*) parched

52. Dilip with his two brothers had entered their ____________.
(*a*) house (*b*) abode
(*c*) dwelling place (*d*) habitation

53. He looks ____________ like his father.
(*a*) practically (*b*) genuinely
(*c*) realistically (*d*) exactly

54. She ____________ from the crowd because of her height and flaming red hair.
(*a*) stood out (*b*) stood off
(*c*) stood up (*d*) stood away

55. When I was a child, I ____________ to school every day instead of going by cycle.
(*a*) crawled (*b*) walked
(*c*) placed (*d*) hurried

56. The lovers were meeting each other secretly, but their ____________ affair was soon known to everyone.
(*a*) clandestine (*b*) covert
(*c*) unknown (*d*) candid

57. I listened, but I had no idea what he was ____________ about.
(*a*) saying (*b*) talking
(*c*) telling (*d*) discussing

58. At one point, it looked as if an area of agreement would ____________, specially over the issue of productivity linked wages.
(*a*) develop (*b*) come out
(*c*) emerge (*d*) grow

59. The river overflowed its ____________ and flooded the area.
(*a*) edges (*b*) fronts
(*c*) limits (*d*) banks

60. In hot weather I like lying in the ____________ of a tree.
(*a*) shade (*b*) shelter
(*c*) protection (*d*) shadow

61. She ____________ Rs. 80 out of the bank every Friday.
(*a*) obtains (*b*) draws
(*c*) pulls (*d*) extracts

62. He is too dull ____________ this problem.
(*a*) solving (*b*) to solving
(*c*) to solve (*d*) solves

63. People who ____________ on horses usually lose in the end.
(*a*) gamble (*b*) play
(*c*) risk (*d*) place

64. His father-in-law ____________ him up in business.
(*a*) put (*b*) made
(*c*) set (*d*) built

65. The robbers were arrested and ____________ prison yesterday.
(*a*) brought into (*b*) brought to
(*c*) taken into (*d*) taken to

6. COLLOCATION

TEST – 7

Introduction:

Collocation represents a major area of difficulty even for advanced learners of English as a second/third / foreign language all over the world. The causes of difficulty are very apparent; collocation does not lend itself very readily to rule-making, to generalization, and so it has to be learnt to a large extent on an item-by-item basis. In the absence of the amount of exposure to English which a native speaker of the language has, the foreign learner is bound to find this element of the language extremely difficult.

Memory will play a large part for learning these items. In order to test your knowledge and understanding of such items, they have been placed in some context by using them in simple sentences.

1. The ________ was sent to the prison.
(*a*) culprit (*b*) convict
(*c*) guilty (*d*) accused

2. I had my ears ________ so that I could wear my grandmother's diamond earrings.
(*a*) bored (*b*) pricked
(*c*) pierced (*d*) stitched

3. Three children were ________ to death in the fire.
(*a*) charred (*b*) burned
(*c*) fired (*d*) butchered

4. I need to have my hair ________ an inch.
(*a*) trimmed (*b*) chopped
(*c*) cut (*d*) scissored

5. Beer production needs to be ________
(*a*) enhanced (*b*) increased
(*c*) speeded up (*d*) improved

6. They want to ________ English as a language of instruction.
(*a*) remove (*b*) abolish
(*c*) exterminate (*d*) eliminate

7. The lecture would be delivered by ________ professors.
(*a*) eminent (*b*) prominent
(*c*) famous (*d*) honourable

8. The speech was ________ by Mr. Jones
(*a*) vocalised (*b*) delivered
(*c*) given (*d*) produced.

9. The audience started cheering as soon as the wrestlers stepped into the ________
(*a*) ring. (*b*) enclosure
(*c*) arena (*d*) stage

10. Fox is a ________ animal.
(*a*) shrewd (*b*) cunning
(*c*) greedy (*d*) clever

11. Before the rains came, the grain was stored in the ________
(*a*) godown (*b*) granary
(*c*) storehouse (*d*) shed

12. By his statement, the officer ________ that the mission had been accomplished.
(*a*) implied (*b*) inferred
(*c*) meant (*d*) summarised

13. The rowers ________ the boat off the land.
(*a*) shoved (*b*) pushed
(*c*) pulled (*d*) heaved

14. Harris took a day off his work to ________ the lawn.
(*a*) cut (*b*) trim
(*c*) mow (*d*) shear

15. Aditya fed the ________ to his dog after dinner.
(*a*) crumbs (*b*) morsels
(*c*) debris (*d*) left overs

16. Arunima is as ________ as an ant.
(*a*) organised (*b*) industrious
(*c*) intelligent (*d*) small

17. He brought back a ________ from all the places he visited.
(*a*) relic (*b*) reminder
(*c*) souvenir (*d*) gift

18. She has a ________ skin.
(*a*) spotless (*b*) flawless
(*c*) faultless (*d*) blotless

19. She has a ________ character.
(*a*) blotless (*b*) flawless
(*c*) faultless (*d*) blameless

20. The twins are ________
(*a*) similar (*b*) ditto
(*c*) identical (*d*) likewise

21. Ayesha ____________ her to write.
(*a*) instilled (*b*) instigated
(*c*) promoted (*d*) inspired

22. The child was ___________ about the toy.
(*a*) unyielding (*b*) adamant
(*c*) determined (*d*) obstinate

23. How is the ___________ outside?
(*a*) weather (*b*) climate
(*c*) temperature (*d*) condition

24. The number of the sheep is becoming ________ by the day.
(*a*) little (*b*) fewer
(*c*) lesser (*d*) lower

25. Our school stresses on all-round ___________
(*a*) growth (*b*) education
(*c*) knowledge (*d*) development

7. IDIOMS AND PHRASES

TEST – 8

Directions: Each item below consists of an idiom or a phrase, followed by three options. Choose the option that most nearly expresses the meaning of the given Idiom or Phrase.

1. To bring laurels
(*a*) To bring shame
(*b*) To earn distinction
(*c*) To earn favours

2. In one's good books
(*a*) To enjoy one's favour.
(*b*) To keep one's books properly.
(*c*) To read good books.

3. To throw cold water on
(*a*) To step into cold water.
(*b*) To discourage.
(*c*) To show bravery.

4. To come off with flying colours
(*a*) To wear a colourful dress.
(*b*) To fly in a colourful aeroplane.
(*c*) To make a great success of something.

5. Crocodile tears
(*a*) Insincere grief.
(*b*) Tears of a crocodile.
(*c*) Sad about something.

6. To lead a dog's life
(*a*) To take care of a dog.
(*b*) To lead a faithful life.
(*c*) To lead a miserable life.

7. Play ducks and drakes
(*a*) To waste money wildly.
(*b*) To do hard work.
(*c*) To show cunningness.

8. To throw dust in someone's eyes
(*a*) To fight with someone.
(*b*) To deceive someone.
(*c*) To play in the dust.

9. To end in smoke
(*a*) To produce no result.
(*b*) To destroy in fire.
(*c*) To smoke a cigarette.

10. To take one's eye off
(*a*) To stop paying attention to.
(*b*) To operate upon the eyes.
(*c*) To direct one's attention to.

11. To have an eye for
(*a*) To have a good vision.
(*b*) To be a good judge of.
(*c*) To be a sincere person.

12. To be hand in glove with
(*a*) To be closely associated with.
(*b*) To wear new pair of gloves.
(*c*) To be very sensitive.

13. To tear one's hair out
(*a*) To get a new haircut.
(*b*) To show great sorrow or irritation.
(*c*) To become mad.

14. A snake in the grass
(*a*) A very poisonous snake.
(*b*) A secret enemy or danger.
(*c*) Not a reliable person.

15. To bell the cat
(*a*) To make noise.
(*b*) To be alert of the enemy.
(*c*) To take lead in danger.

16. To live in the lap of luxury
(*a*) To sit in the lap of a rich person.
(*b*) To live lavishly.
(*c*) To be extravagant.

17. To grease one's palm
    (*a*) To cheat someone.
    (*b*) To take advantage of.
    (*c*) To bribe someone.
18. To have a finger in every pie
    (*a*) To show concern in every matter.
    (*b*) To eat like a glutton.
    (*c*) To be very fond of cooking.
19. A dog in the manger
    (*a*) A dog that has no kennel of its own.
    (*b*) A person who prevents others from enjoying something useless to himself.
    (*c*) A person who puts himself in difficulties on account of other people.
20. A bird's eye view
    (*a*) General survey of a subject.
    (*b*) Careless summing up of a case.
    (*c*) Professional interpretation of a problem.

Idioms and Phrases-II

1. To worship the rising sun
    (*a*) To become pious
    (*b*) To work honestly
    (*c*) To work for the welfare of people
    (*d*) To welcome the coming events
2. To draw a line
    (*a*) To impose certain restrictions
    (*b*) To turn out the visitors
    (*c*) To have fair game
    (*d*) To divide evenly
3. To show the door
    (*a*) To welcome the visitors
    (*b*) To turnout the visitors
    (*c*) To behave rudely
    (*d*) To dismiss a person
4. To put down in black and white
    (*a*) To distinguish clearly
    (*b*) To write down on paper
    (*c*) To seal the envelope
    (*d*) To tell the truth
5. To sail under false colours
    (*a*) To falsely implicate
    (*b*) To tell everything but the truth
    (*c*) To provide leverage
    (*d*) To pretend to be what one is not
6. To eat humble pie
    (*a*) To face failure
    (*b*) To be undernourished
    (*c*) To work secretly
    (*d*) To be highly annoyed
7. To gild pill
    (*a*) To cover something disagreeable with some pleasant thing
    (*b*) To work hard
    (*c*) To die fighting
    (*d*) To meet with humiliation
8. With a high hand
    (*a*) In a dictatorial way
    (*b*) With massive support
    (*c*) Out of experience
    (*d*) In an advantageous position
9. To crow over
    (*a*) To criticize bitterly
    (*b*) To become unwanted
    (*c*) To exult in triumph
    (*d*) To compromise
10. To rise from the ranks
    (*a*) To get a rank in the examination
    (*b*) To succeed in life from a low level
    (*c*) To get undue promotions
    (*d*) To fall and again rise
11. To keep the powder dry
    (*a*) To be enthusiastic
    (*b*) To become aggressive
    (*c*) To look for enemy
    (*d*) To be on alert
12. To be at sea
    (*a*) To wait for an opportunity
    (*b*) To be perplexed and confused
    (*c*) To watch the events
    (*d*) To make futile efforts
13. A bird's eye view
    (*a*) A general view
    (*b*) Narrow mindedness
    (*c*) Honest like a bird
    (*d*) One who acts fast like birds
14. An eye for an eye
    (*a*) Transplantation
    (*b*) Revenge
    (*c*) Association
    (*d*) Creation

15. A feather in one's cap
(*a*) An achievement to be proud of
(*b*) As light as a feather
(*c*) An ornament
(*d*) An honour

16. To chew the cud
(*a*) To reunite
(*b*) To cleanse
(*c*) To ruminate
(*d*) To avoid unpleasantness

17. To set one's heart upon
(*a*) To think of something imaginary
(*b*) To desire something that cannot be achieved
(*c*) To become intensely desirous of
(*d*) To assure help in hour of need

18. The small hours
(*a*) Evening time
(*b*) Periodically
(*c*) Early morning hours
(*d*) Now and then

19. To bring to light
(*a*) To shape nicely (*b*) To reveal clearly
(*c*) To revive (*d*) To cause

20. To cut one's coat according to one's cloth
(*a*) To be well dressed
(*b*) To reduce one's expenses
(*c*) To live within means
(*d*) To work under the directions of someone

Idioms and Phrases-III

Directions: Read the following sentences carefully and from the alternatives given below choose the correct alternative for the underlined phrase.

1. The strike would have been successful but for a black leg.
(*a*) one who misleads
(*b*) one who betrays
(*c*) one who shows no sympathy
(*d*) one who is emotional

2. Do not blow your own trumpet.
(*a*) speak what you like
(*b*) speak unnecessarily
(*c*) boast
(*d*) produce music

3. One should be wide awake while taking part in politics.
(*a*) alert
(*b*) with wider knowledge
(*c*) broad in thinking
(*d*) posted with the latest

4. He is a gentleman to the backbone.
(*a*) completely (*b*) firmly
(*c*) definitely (*d*) surely

5. Keeping the old status of English is a cry in wilderness.
(*a*) impossible (*b*) in vain
(*c*) under process (*d*) in demand

6. A true patriot dies in harness.
(*a*) for the country
(*b*) for oneself
(*c*) while working
(*d*)while singing

7. Do not indulge in double dealing in your industrial houses.
(*a*) deceit
(*b*) two standards
(*c*) two works
(*d*) back biting

8. As the manager of the estate, he feathered his own nest.
(*a*) made money
(*b*) built a house
(*c*) worked hard
(*d*) made money by dishonest means

9. You should not leave your friends in the lurch.
(*a*) finally
(*b*) temporarily
(*c*) when help needed
(*d*) when they are alone

10. For his own interests to serve he has made a mess of the whole affair.
(*a*) confused
(*b*) destroyed
(*c*) corrected
(*d*) improved.

11. Do not mince matters ; tell the truth.
(*a*) tell in pieces
(*b*) keep secret
(*c*) restrain the truth
(*d*) cut short

12. Nip the evil in the bud.
   (*a*) see the evil
   (*b*) kill the evil in the initial stages
   (*c*) bypass the evil
   (*d*) nurse the evil
13. I can see through your trick.
   (*a*) understand emotionally
   (*b*) grasp mentally
   (*c*) penetrate visually
   (*d*) discover physically
14. The child takes after the mother.
   (*a*) follows (*b*) meets
   (*c*) resembles (*d*) loves
15. He turned down my proposal.
   (*a*) criticized (*b*) accepted
   (*c*) amended (*d*) rejected

8. WORDS OFTEN CONFUSED

TEST – 9

Directions: In each item below, a choice of words that are often confused is offered in parentheses. Write in the blank the letter indicating the best choice for the context.

1. ___ The chairman's statement (A. implied; B. inferred) that the matter would be reconsidered at the next meeting.
2. ___ Walter's talents were a (A. complement; B. compliment) to Jim's. Walter could give order, and Jim could follow them.
3. ___ I learned from my (A. counsel; B. council) that he will be out of town soon.
4. ___ The chairman of the board is only a (A. figurehead; B. leader) the executive secretary does all the work.
5. ___ She assured me (A. orally; B. verbally) of her good intentions, but she never confirmed her message in writing.
6. ___ Not wishing to (A. detract; B. distract) my neighbours, I didn't begin typing until they were awake.
7. ___ We had many excellent convocation speakers, but the governor was the most (A. eminent; B. imminent).
8. ___ The general restlessness in the audience suggested that people were (A. disinterested; B. uninterested) and wanted to leave.
9. ___ Such behavior cannot be too strongly (A. censored; B. censured).
10. ___ Moving from one place to another is always a shock, and it takes some time to become (A. adapted; B. adopted) to city life.
11. ___ Mr. Jeffers often (A. indulged in; B. took part in) fund-raising drives.
12. ___ Even though the movie was a serious one: He could not (A. refrain; B. restrain) from laughing.
13. ___ He had taught at the university for nearly 40 years and had many amusing (A. anecdotes; B. antidotes) about visiting professors.
14. ___ Mr. Harrold had the (A. allusion; B. delusion; C. illusion) that he was George washington.
15. ___ This was not the first trial in which the prisoners had (A. flaunted; B. flouted) all courtroom decorum.
16. ___ He looked at me (A. incredibly; B. incredulously) and said that he didn't believe a word I had said.
17. ___ One of the rights guaranteed us by the Constitution is the right to (A. descent; B. dissent).
18. ___ The (A. persecution; B. prosecution) of the Christians during the Roman empire ceased with the reign of Constantine.
19. ___ After finishing her internship, Dr. Walsh made her (A. residence; B. residents) in a small town in Minnesota.
20. ___ The Furmans' (A. marital; B. martial) problems appeared regularly on the court calendar.
21. ___ Every time an impromptu essay was announced, George would lean over and whisper."(A. Borrow; B. Lend) me some paper."

22. ___ Saint Augustine was troubled throughout his life by problems of (A. conscience; B. conscious).

23. ___ If the secretary left any work unfinished. She depended on an (A. aid; B. aide) to complete it for her.

24. ___ The buffet was a generous one, and we saw before us baked ham, fried chicken, potato salad, cole slaw, (A. and etc; B. etc.).

25. ___ While in college Terry was always solitary and never was one of the (A. click; B. clique) of fellows who played pool every evening.

26. ___ The vote was unexpectedly heavy in our favour, and I was happy to be (A. appraised; B. apprised) of the outcome.

27. ___ It was an annual joke for Mr. Walworth to say on his birthday that the (A. amount; B. number) of his gray hairs had increased by only ten.

28. ___ Reba seemed to be able to swim as soon as she could walk, and she (A. learned; B. taught) all her younger brothers to swim. .

29. ___ The colour scheme of the apartment was (A. predominately; B. predominantly) red.

30. ___ Miss Lasker does not suffer fools gladly, and she finds it hard not to look (A. contemptible; B. Contemptuous) in their presence.

31. ___ One of the finest sights in Stockholm is an exhibition of her (A. sculptor; B. sculpture) at her home far above the sea.

32. ___ One of the (A. famous; B. notorious) residents of the village for many years was the great frank Lloyd wright.

33. _________ Ellery gave us an (A. ingenious; B. ingenuous) smile and said that he han't the least idea who had used the sailboat last.

34. ___ The (A. moral; B. morale) of this story is that if you're going to tell a lie, tell a big one.

35. ___ Avery had a perfectly clear (A. conscience; B. conscious) and told where he had been all afternoon.

36. ___ All these old movies seem to have a scene in which the heroine say, "(A. Leave; B. Let) me go or I'll never speak to you again."

37. ___ The weather had turned very hot for May, and it seemed only (A. human; B. humane) to clip the dog's hair.

38. ___ Directions for the procession were confused, but all the participants found their (A. respective; B. respectful) Places.

39. __________ Although Dr. Getty's practice is (A. formally; B. formely) limited to children. She will on occasion treat adults.

40. ___ We had reserved a big room and were disappointed when (A. fewer; B. less) members than we had expected showed up.

41. ___ Their new apartment was furnished comfortably but not (A. luxuriously; B. luxuriantly).

42. ___ This final and most crucial debate on television between the two candidates was (A. figuratively; B. literally) a battle to the death.

43. ___ Although Father rarely scolded us, his high standards were (A. explicit; B. implicit) in everything he did.

44. ___ Mead asserted that mind was superior to body, (A. whereas; B. whereby) McDonald said that body was superior.

45. ___ Many of the (A. manufactures, B. manufacturers) have withheld delivery until shipping conditions become more favorable.

46. _________ It was his customary (A. manner; B. mannerism) to greet his wife as soon as he entered the door.

47. ___ Not finding his keys in his pocket, Ralph (A. rationalized; B. reasoned) that he had left them on his bureau.

48. ___ Everyone (A. accepted; B. excepted) from attendance in class should read ahead in the text.

49. ___ In spite of spending so much time in the sun, Mrs. Bailey remained (A. fair- complected; B. fair-complectioned).

50. ___ If you visit Washington, D.C., seeing the National Gallery is a (A. must; B. necessity).

ANSWER KEY

Vocabulary

Test-1: Synonyms

1. c	2. d	3. b	4. a	5. d
6. a	7. a	8. a	9. d	10. c
11. a	12. a	13. a	14. b	15. a
16. a	17. c	18. d	19. d	20. b
21. d	22. c	23. c	24. a	25. c
26. a	27. d	28. d	29. d	30. b
31. d	32. d	33. c	34. b	35. b
36. b	37. b	38. c	39. b	40. d
41. b	42. a	43. d	44. a	45. b
46. a	47. c	48. b	49. c	50. d

Test-2

I.	1. **c**	2. **a**	3. **b**	4. **c**	5. **a**
II.	1. **c**	2. **c**	3. **a**	4. **a**	5. **b**
III.	1. **b**	2. **a**	3. **a**	4. **c**	
IV.	1. **c**	2. **b**	3. **c**	4. **c**	5. **b**
V.	1. **b**	2. **a**	3. **d**	4. **b**	5. **b**

Test-3

1. d	2. b	3. b	4. b	5. d
6. c	7. a	8. d	9. d	10. a
11. c	12. e	13. b	14. c	15. a
16. d	17. a	18. c	19. a	20. a
21. b	22. a	23. b	24. c	

Test-4: Antonyms

1. a	2. a	3. b	4. d	5. a
6. d	7. c	8. d	9. b	10. b
11. b	12. b	13. d	14. c	15. a
16. c	17. a	18. c	19. a	20. b
21. d	22. b	23. d	24. c	25. d
26. a	27. d	28. b	29. c	30. c
31. a	32. d	33. d	34. a	35. a
36. d	37. c	38. b	39. d	40. b
41. b	42. d	43. c	44. c	45. b
46. d	47. b	48. a	49. c	50. a

Test-5: Antonyms in Context

1. b	2. c	3. a	4. b	5. d
6. a	7. b	8. a	9. b	10. c
11. c	12. c	13. c	14. a	15. b
16. a	17. b	18. c	19. a	20. c

Test-6: Multiple-choice Completion Type

1. c	2. a	3. b	4. a	5. c
6. d	7. a	8. a	9. b	10. c
11. c	12. b	13. a	14. b	15. b
16. d	17. a	18. b	19. a	20. c
21. b	22. d	23. a	24. b	25. b
26. a	27. c	28. a	29. a	30. b
31. b	32. b	33. b	34. a	35. a
36. c	37. b	38. b	39. c	40. c
41. b	42. a	43. c	44. b	45. d
46. d	47. a	48. c	49. b	50. a
51. d	52. a	53. c	54. a	55. b
56. a	57. b	58. c	59. d	60. a
61. b	62. c	63. a	64. c	65. d

Test-7: Collocation

1. a	2. c	3. b	4. a	5. b
6. b	7. a	8. b	9. c	10. b
11. b	12. a	13. a	14. c	15. d
16. b	17. c	18. b	19. c	20. c
21. d	22. b	23. a	24. b	25. d

Test-8: Idioms and Phrases-I

1. b	2. a	3. b	4. c	5. a
6. c	7. a	8. b	9. a	10. a
11. b	12. a	13. b	14. b	15. c
16. b	17. c	18. a	19. b	20. a

Idioms and Phrases-II

1. d	2. a	3. d	4. b	5. d
6. a	7. a	8. a	9. c	10. b
11. d	12. b	13. a	14. b	15. a
16. c	17. c	18. c	19. b	20. c

Idioms and Phrases-III

1. c	2. c	3. d	4. a	5. b
6. c	7. a	8. d	9. c	10. a
11. c	12. b	13. b	14. c	15. d

Test-9

1. B. inferred **2.A.** complement **3. A.** counsel
4. A. figurehead **5. B.** verbally **6. B.** distract
7. A. eminent **8. B.** uninterested **9.B.** censured
10. A. adapted **11. B.** took **12.A.** refrain
13. A. anecdotes **14. B.** delusion **15.B.** flouted
16. B. incredulously **17. B.** dissent **18. A.** prosecution
19.A. residence **20.A.** marital **21.B.** Lend
22.A. conscience **23.B.** aide **24.B.** etc. **25. B.** clique
26.B. apprised **27. B.** number **28. B.** taught
29.B. predominantly **30.B.** contemptuous
31.B. sculpture **32.A.** famous **33.B.** ingenuous
34.A. moral **35.A.** conscience **36.B.** Let **37. B.** humane
38.A. respective **39.A.** formally **40.A.** fewer
41.A. luxuriously **42.A.** figuratively **43. B.** implicit
44.A. whereas **45.B.** manufacturers **46. B.** mannerism
47.B. **48.B.** excepted **49.B.** fair-complectioned
50. A. must

ADDITIONAL TESTS OF MULTIPLE CHOICE VOCABULARY

Multiple Choice Type

Directions: Fill in the blanks choosing the suitable option from the choices given after the end of this passage:

Gifts of Forests

Perhaps the most important [1] ____________ of forests to modern [2] ____________ is that they [3] ____________ the raw material for [4] ____________ paper. The Chinese who [5] ____________ paper several thousand years back used the inner bark of certain trees for making paper. Today, paper is made [6] ____________ from wood, bamboo and [7] ____________ types of grasses. The paper on which this book has been [8] ____________ must have been made out of wood or bamboo and certain types of grasses. Very [9] ____________ work can be done these days without the use of paper, and we can even say that modern civilization [10] ____________ on paper.

1. (*a*) contribution (*b*) blessing (*c*) creation (*d*) accomplishment
2. (*a*) culture (*b*) environment (*c*) humanity (*d*) civilization
3. (*a*) sell (*b*) provide (*c*) present (*d*) manufacture
4. (*a*) making (*b*) designing (*c*) constructing (*d*) publishing
5. (*a*) created (*b*) developed (*c*) invented (*d*) made
6. (*a*) almost (*b*) mostly (*c*) sometimes (*d*) never
7. (*a*) other (*b*) any (*c*) great (*d*) certain
8. (*a*) printed (*b*) written (*c*) made (*d*) designed
9. (*a*) brief (*b*) few (*c*) little (*d*) small
10. (*a*) lives (*b*) depends (*c*) commits (*d*) dwells

ANSWER KEY

1. a **2.** d **3.** b **4.** a **5.** b
6. b **7.** d **8.** a **9.** c **10.** b

VOCABULARY IN CONTEXT (MULTIPLE CHOICE)

Fill in the Blanks Type

Directions: The following passage contains seven (7) blanks. For each blank 4 choices are given at the end of the passage. You are directed to choose a suitable word and mark (✔) against the same. The whole passage should result into a coherent piece of writing.

The Rule of the Road

A stout old lady was walking with her basket down the middle of a street in Petrograd to the great ____________ [1] of the traffic and with no small ____________ [2] to herself. It was pointed out to her that the pavement was the place for ____________ [3], but she replied: "I'm going to walk where I like. We've got ____________ [4] now." It did not occur to the dear old lady that if liberty ____________ [5] the pedestrian to walk down the middle of the road, then the end of such liberty would be universal ____________ [6]. Everybody would be getting in everybody else's way and nobody would get anywhere. ____________ [7] liberty would have become social anarchy.

1. (*a*) amazement (*b*) confusion (*c*) help (*d*) pleasure
2. (*a*) peril (*b*) punishment (*c*) fun (*d*) credit
3. (*a*) travellers (*b*) passengers (*c*) passersby (*d*) pedestrians
4. (*a*) license (*b*) liberty (*c*) law (*d*) brain
5. (*a*) brought (*b*) facilitated (*c*) disciplined (*d*) entitled
6. (*a*) triumph (*b*) peace (*c*) chaos (*d*) law
7. (*a*) Legal (*b*) Limited (*c*) Everyone's (*d*) Individual

ANSWER KEY

1. b **2.** a **3.** d **4.** b
5. d **6.** c **7.** d

FOR ENGLISH LITERATURE

OBJECTIVE TYPE

TEST – 1

Q. Write True or False:

1. **Emaciated** prisoners sometimes look to be *cadaverous.*
2. **Discreet** people are **imprudent.**
3. **Eccentric** people sometimes do **bizarre** things.
4. **Effusive** people are **impassive.**
5. A **dyspeptic** fellow is **affable** and has buoyant spirits.

Q. Write the letter that indicates the best synonym for the italicized word or phrase:

6. a mean **Cowardly** deed: (*a*) clandestine, (*b*) arrogant, (*c*) dastardly, (*d*) avaricious.
7. an **ever–talking** fellow: (*a*) garrulous, (*b*) astute, (*c*) delusive, (*d*) facetious.
8. a **self–satisfied** chef: (*a*) complacent, (*b*) callow, (*c*) exotic, (*d*) flippant.
9. a **skillful machinist:** (*a*) impeccable, (*b*) fluent, (*c*) deft, (*d*) flamboyant.
10. **tradition – smashing** policies: (*a*) iconoclastic, (*b*) esoteric, (*c*) fatuous, (*d*) blatant.

Q. Match each word with its definition:

11. enigmatic	(*a*) pure; spotless
12. impious	(*b*) rural
13. destitute	(*c*) authoritarian
14. buxom	(*d*) comical
15. boorish	(*e*) ill-mannered
16. bucolic	(*f*) mentally unsound
17. dogmatic	(*g*) very poor
18. bovine	(*h*) canine
19. immaculate	(*i*) perplexing
20. droll	(*j*) cow-like
21. insane	(*k*) plump and healthy
22. dog like	(*l*) ungodly

ANSWERS

1. True		**2.** False		**3.** True
4. False		**5.** False		**6.** c
7. a	**8.** a	**9.** c	**10.** a	**11.** i
12. l	**13.** g	**14.** k	**15.** e	**16.** b
17. c	**18.** j	**19.** a	**20.** d	**21.** f
22. h				

TEST – 2

Q. Supply the missing word in each sentence. The first letter of each answer is given.

1. The rebirth of learning in Europe was called the R________
2. A literary type, such as epic or novel, is a G________
3. The language of England during 1100–1500 was M________ E________
4. A short final speech to the play audience is an E________
5. The pursuit of art for art's sake is A________
6. The eighteenth century revival of classicism is N________
7. Teaching or moralizing in poetry is D________
8. A list of sources of information is a B________
9. A traditional, recurring theme or story or event is an A________
10. The largest book printed is the F________

Q. Write true or False:

11. **Explication** is the critical analysis of literary passages.
12. **Biographies** are usually classed as fiction.
13. **Beowulf,** an eighth-century epic, was written in **old English.**
14. An **epigram** is a night letter which goes at special rates.
15. The **epigraph** is placed at the end of a novel or poem.
16. Emotionalism, imaginativeness, and love of nature are common aspects of **romanticism.**
17. **Platonic** thinking tends to be idealistic and mystical.
18. **Regionalism** in literature reflects the life of a region.

19. **Calvinism** maintained that if you did good deeds you would go to heaven.
20. According to transcendentalism, man has divinity within himself and therefore intuitive wisdom.

Q. Write the letter that indicates the best completion:

21. Modern English has been used since about (*a*) 900, (*b*) 1100, (*c*) 1500, (*d*) 1890.
22. The quarto is smaller than the (*a*) average book today, (*b*) duodecisno, (*c*) Octavo, (*d*) folio.
23. The Aristotelian approach is (*a*) metaphysical, (*b*) speculative, (*c*) practical, (*d*) idealistic.
24. Humanism emphasized (*a*) mythology, (*b*) human activities, (*c*) religious speculation (*d*) medieval learning.
25. Greek Classicism is notable for (*a*) restraint, (*b*) emotionalism, (*c*) novelty, (*d*) distortion.

Q. Write the letter that indicates the best definition:

26. Age of Reason	(*a*) creative, imaginative, literature
27. belles-lettres	(*b*) the entire authenticated works of an author.
28. canon	(*c*) an introduction to a literary work
29. memoirs	(*d*) the enlightenment.
30. prologue	(*e*) a record of personal observations.

ANSWERS

1. Renaissance	**2.** genre	**3.** Middle
4. epilogue	**5.** aestheticism	**6.** neoclassicism
7. didacticism	**8.** bibliography	**9.** archetype
10. Folio	**11.** True	**12.** False
13. True	**14.** False	**15.** False
16. True	**17.** True	**18.** True
19. False	**20.** True	**21.** c
22. d	**23.** c	**24.** b
25. a	**26.** d	**27.** a
28. b	**29.** e	**30.** c

FOR MEDICOS

OBJECTIVE TYPE (MULTIPLE CHOICE)

TEST – 1

Directions: The following passage contains five (5) blanks. For each blank 4 choices are given in the end of the passage. You are directed to choose a suitable word and mark (✔) against the same. The whole passage should result into a coherent piece of writing.

Blood Supply of Stomach

Arterial supply is from branches of coeliac axis artery. The left and right ________[1] arteries run along the ________[2] curvature of stomach. The left and right [3] arteries run along the greater curvature of stomach. The short ________[4] arteries supply the ________[5] of stomach.

1. (*a*) colic (*b*) ileal (*c*) oesophageal (*d*) gastric

2. (*a*) greater (*b*) lesser (*c*) mesenteric (*d*) none of the above

3. (*a*) pancreatico-duodenal (*b*) right gastric (*c*) gastroepiploic (*d*) supraduodenal

4. (*a*) jejunal (*b*) pyloric (*c*) cardiac (*d*) gastric

5. (*a*) cardiac end (*b*) pyloric end (*c*) body (*d*) fundus

ANSWERS

1. d **2.** b **3.** c **4.** d **5.** d

TEST – 2

Directions: The following passage contains seven (7) blanks. For each blank 4 choices are given in the end of the passage. You are directed to choose a suitable word and mark (✔) against the same. The whole passage should result into a coherent piece of writing.

Structure of the Small Intestine

The mucous membrane is thrown into permanent ________[1] folds. Its characteristic feature is the presence of ____________[2] These are meant to ____________[3] the surface area for absorption. The muscularis mucosae is thin layer made of outer ____________[4] and inner ____________[5] layer of muscle fibres. Submucosa contains ____________[6] plexus of nerves while muscularis externa contains ____________[7] plexus of nerves.

1. (*a*) longitudinal (*b*) transverse (*c*) oblique (*d*) circular
2. (*a*) folds (*b*) valves (*c*) villi (*d*) plexus
3. (*a*) increase (*b*) decrease (*c*) maintain (*d*) stabilise
4. (*a*) circular (*b*) oblique (*c*) longitudinal (*d*) mixed
5. (*a*) oblique (*b*) circular (*c*) mixed (*d*) longitudinal
6. (*a*) Meissner's (*b*) Auerbach's (*c*) Lymphatic plexus (*d*) Spinal nerve plexus
7. (*a*) Spinal nerve plexus (*b*) Meissner's (*c*) Auerbach's (*d*) Lymphatic

ANSWER KEY

1. d **2.** c **3.** a **4.** c **5.** b
6. a **7.** c

TEST – 3

Directions: Complete each sentence with one of the words underneath. Tick (✔) against the appropriate alternative.

1. Stomach is situated in the upper and left part of the ____________ cavity.
2. Saliva keeps the mouth ____________ and lubricated.
3. Stomach is suspended by two folds of peritoneum (greater and lesser)____________.
4. Salivary amylase digests the cooked starch into ____________.
5. Saliva helps in getting ____________ of food.

1. (*a*) thoracic (*b*) pelvic (*c*) abdominal (*d*) cranial
2. (*a*) dry (*b*) wet (*c*) moist (*d*) hard
3. (*a*) galactose (*b*) maltose (*c*) maltase (*d*) fructose
4. (*a*) smell (*b*) touch (*c*) taste (*d*) consistency

ANSWER KEY

1. c **2.** c **3.** b **4.** c

TEST – 4

Directions: The following passage contains five (5) blanks. For each blank 4 choices are given in the end of the passage. You are directed to choose a suitable word and mark (✔) against the same. The whole passage should result into a coherent piece of writing.

Haemoglobin is made up of heme and globin. Synthesis requires ____________[1] in diet, B12 and ____________[2]. Main function of haemoglobin is transport of ____________[3]. It combines with oxygen to form oxyhaemoglobin in red cells and transports ____________[4] from lungs to ____________[5]. Haemoglobin acts as a buffer and maintains blood pH.

1. (*a*) fat (*b*) carbohydrate (*c*) protein (*d*) sodium
2. (*a*) calcium (*b*) manganese (*c*) iron (*d*) sodium
3. (*a*) liquids (*b*) gases (*c*) solids (*d*) chyme
4. (*a*) carbon dioxide (*b*) nitrogen (*c*) oxygen (*d*) nitric oxide
5. (*a*) blood (*b*) heart (*c*) tissues (*d*) brain

ANSWER KEY

1. c **2.** c **3.** b **4.** c **5.** c

TEST – 5

Directions: The following passage contains three (3) blanks. For each blank 4 choices are given in the end of the passage. You are directed to choose a suitable word and mark (✔) against the same. The whole passage should result into a coherent piece of writing.

White Matter of Cerebrum

The white matter lies subjacent to the grey matter. It is made of nerve fibres. These fibres are of three types. __________[1] fibres connect different areas of the same side of cerebral cortex. Thus different lobes and poles are connected to each other. __________[2] fibres connect identical areas of two sides of brain. __________[3] fibres connect various areas in the cerebral cortex with neurons of medulla oblongata, spinal cord.

1. (*a*) Medial lemnisens
   (*b*) Association
   (*c*) Interthalamic adhesion
   (*d*) Superior longitudinal fasciculus
2. (*a*) Projection
   (*b*) Commissural
   (*c*) External arcuate fibres
   (*d*) Cingulum
3. (*a*) Inferior longitudinal
   (*b*) Projection
   (*c*) Internal arcuate fibres
   (*d*) Medial longitudinal bundle

ANSWER KEY

1. b **2.** b **3.** b

TEST – 6

Directions: Complete each sentence with one of the words underneath. Tick (✔) against the appropriate alternative.

1. EPSP is due to ______ of the post synaptic cell membrane.
2. The three-part response, accomodation, convergence of visual axis and pupillary constriction is known as ________.
3. In dogs and cats the spasticity produced by Decerebration is most marked in ________ muscles.
4. The syndrome of adult Hypothyroidism is known as ________.
5. Coronary blood flow to the sub endocardial portion of left ventricle occurs only during ________.

1. (*a*) Hyperopolarisation
   (*b*) Summation
   (*c*) Depolarisation
   (*d*) Facilitation
2. (*a*) Accomodation reflex
   (*b*) Pupillary reaction
   (*c*) Adaptation
   (*d*) Near response
3. (*a*) Extensor (*b*) Upper limb
   (*c*) Flexor (*d*) Lower limb
4. (*a*) Cushing's syndrome
   (*b*) Addison's disease
   (*c*) Myxoedema
   (*d*) Cretinism
5. (*a*) Diastole
   (*b*) Isovolumetric ventricular contraction
   (*c*) Systole
   (*d*) Ventricular ejection

ANSWER KEY

1. c 2. d 3. a 4. c 5. a

TEST – 7

Directions: The following passage contains five (5) blanks. For each blank 4 choices are given in the end of the passage. You are directed to choose a suitable word and mark (✓) against the same. The whole passage should result into a coherent piece of writing.

Biosynthesis and Secretion of Insulin

Insulin is synthesized in the Endoplasmic Reticulum of the [1]__________ cells. It is then transported to the [2]________ apparatus where it is packaged in membrane bound granules. These granules move to the cell wall by a process that appears to involve [3]__________, and their membranes fuse with the membrane of the cell, expelling the [4]________ to the exterior by [5]________.

1. (*a*) Delta (*b*) Alpha
   (*c*) Gamma (*d*) Beta
2. (*a*) Mitochondrial (*b*) Golgi
   (*c*) Vesicular (*d*) Microfilaments

3. (*a*) Migration (*b*) Chemotaxis
(*c*) Microtubules (*d*) Diapedesis
4. (*a*) Granules (*b*) Insulin
(*c*) Glucagen (*d*) Lipids
5. (*a*) Exocytosis (*b*) Endocytosis
(*c*) Diffusion (*d*) Active transport

ANSWER KEY

1. d **2.** b **3.** c **4.** b **5.** a

TEST – 8

Directions: The following passage contains five (5) blanks. For each blank 4 choices are given in the end of the passage. You are directed to choose a suitable word and mark (✔) against the same. The whole passage should result into a coherent piece of writing.

This class of lipoproteins are found in [1] ________ formed only by [2] ________ system draining the intestine. Their concentration fluctuates with the load of [3] ____________ absorbed. The bulk of plasma lipoprotein [4] ________ is hepatic in origin and transports to from [5] ________ to extrahepatic tissues.

1. (*a*) chyle (*b*) microvilli
(*c*) duodenum (*d*) bile duet
2. (*a*) circulatory (*b*) biliary
(*c*) lymphatic (*d*) enterohepatic
3. (*a*) cholesterol (*b*) triacylglycerol
(*c*) fatty acids (*d*) phosphoglycerides
4. (*a*) IDL (*b*) LDL
(*c*) VLDL (*d*) HDL
5. (*a*) liver (*b*) brain
(*c*) heart (*d*) intestine

ANSWER KEY

1. a **2.** c **3.** b **4.** c **5.** a

TEST – 9

Directions: Complete each sentence with one of the words underneath. Tick (✔) against the appropriate alternatives.

1. Increased ________ concentration in brain enhances glutamine formation from glutamate.
2. A high plasma sodium concentration does not necessarily mean that the total body sodium content is increased, but infers that the ________ sodium is excessive relative to water.
3. Metabolic role of selenium is established as the prosthetic group of selenium enzyme ________ which functions to reduce hydro-peroxidase.
4. The location of genes on chromosomes can be mapped by hybridizing with ________ probes.
5. ________ forms a membrane cytoskeleton that makes erythrocytes resist to shear.

1. (*a*) aminoacids (*b*) ammonia
(*c*) glutathione (*d*) glutamic acid
2. (*a*) intracellular (*b*) extracellular
(*c*) tissue (*d*) interstitial
3. (*a*) catalase
(*b*) glutathione synthase
(*c*) glutathione peroxidase
(*d*) superoxide dismutase
4. (*a*) Z-DNA (*b*) C-DNA
(*c*) B-DNA (*d*) RNA
5. (*a*) glycoprotein (*b*) collagen
(*c*) spectrin (*d*) syringomyelin

ANSWER KEY

1. b **2.** b **3.** b **4.** b **5.** c

MISCELLANEOUS

1. HOMONYMS/HOMOPHONES /HOMOGRAPHS

Go through the list given below and use them in written/spoken form. For example, look at the meanings of **credible** and **creditable, of discreet** and **discrete, of appraise** and **apprise,** of **presumptive** and **presumptuous,** or **factious** and **factitious,** of **disburse** and **disperse,** of **illusive** and **elusive,** of **clique** and **claque,** of **affect** and **effect,** of **monetary** and **monitory** and their usage in exams, such a list will prove immensely helpful.

Homonyms—are words with same sound or spelling but different in meaning.

Homophones—are words with different spelling but same sound

Homographs—are words spelt alike but with different meanings.

Note: Though a separate list will be provided for homographs, yet while going through the list of homonyms and homophones also, you will find different meanings given of the same word. So they can note down some homophones in the List of Homonyms and Homophones as well.

1. A LIST OF HOMONYMS/HOMOPHONES

1. *Adapt*—to change, to adjust
   Adept—skilled
2. *Advice*—counsel (n)
   Advise—to give advice/instruction (v)
3. *Accept*—to agree or admit
   Except—to omit; to exempt
4. *Affect*– to cause change in something (v)
   Effect– result (n)
5. *Afflicted*—stricken
   Inflicted—caused or imposed something negative
6. *Allude*—to refer to indirectly
   Elude—to evade
7. *Allusion*—a reference to
   Illusion—unreal image
8. *Apprise*—to let know
   Appraise—to estimate the value of
9. *Assay*—to make an experiment
   Essay—to make an intellectual or physical effort
10. *Beside*—near
    Besides—in addition
11. *Birth*—bringing forth
    Berth—a sleeping place in a train or aboard a ship
12. *Canvas*—a strong, coarse cloth
    Canvass—to discuss; to solicit
13. *Capital*—money; punishable by death; large form of letter
    Capitol– the U.S. house of legislature
14. *Caret*—a mark used in proofreading
    Carat—unit of gem weight
    Carrot—a variety of vegetable
15. *Censor*—one who screens objectionable material
    Censure—condemnation
    Censer—an incense–burning vessel
16. *Cite*—to quote
    sight—vision
    site—location
17. *Collision*—violent encounter of moving bodies
    Collusion—fraudulent secret understanding between ostensible opponents
18. *Complacent*—self-satisfied
    Complaisant— obliging
19. *Command*—to order
    Commend—to praise
20. *Confidant*—a person to whom one confides one's private affairs
    Confident—feeling or showing assurance
21. *Compile*—to collect
    Comply—to consent
22. *Complement*—to make complete
    Compliment—to praise
23. *Conscientious*—diligent
    Conscious—aware; awake
24. *Depositary*—person with whom a thing is deposited
    Depository—storehouse
25. *Deprecate*—to plead against
    Depreciate—to belittle; to reduce its value
26. *Desert*—a barren place
    Dessert—course of fruit, sweetmeats etc. ending dinner
27. *Discreet*—showing prudence; modest
    Discrete—separate or distinct
28. *Diverse*—varied, different
    Divers—several
29. *Draught*—current of air; one continuous act of drinking; artist's sketch for picture
    Draft—sketch of work to be done; order for drawing money
    Drought—continuous dry weather; thirst
30. *Egoist*—self-seeking,
    Egotist—self-centred & boastful
31. *Elegant*—graceful;
    Eloquent—fluent (in speech or writing); persuasive
32. *Elicit*—to draw out
    Illicit—unlawful
33. *Eligible*—suitable
    Illegible—unreadable
34. *Emigrant*—one who leaves one's country to settle in another

Immigrant—one who comes to a new country to settle

35. *Eminent*—famous
Imminent—impending
Immanent—inherent

36. *Epic*—a long poem dealing with heroic deeds
Epoch—a period of time marked by noteworthy people or events

37. *Endemic*—regularly found among people
Epidemic—spreading rapidly like a disease

38. *Enquiry*—a request for information—a set of questions
Inquiry—investigation

39. *Euphemism*—substitute of mild for blunt expression
Euphuism—high flown style of writing

40. *Exalt*—to elevate
Exult—to rejoice greatly

41. *Facility*—ease; an aptitude
Faculty—an ability to do something specified; a department at a college or university

42. *Factitious*—artificial
Facetious—given to or marked by pleasantry

43. *Fain*—well-pleased
Feign—pretend

45. *Faint*—dizzy; weak; a brief loss of consciousness
Feint—a misleading movement

46. *Farther*—more far (distance)
Further—in addition to; promote

47. *Fay*—a fairy
Fey—whimsical

48. *Flaunting*—to show off
Flouting—to scorn

49. *Forbear*—to refrain (v)
Forebear—an ancestor (n)

50. *Foreboding*—something unpleasant in advance
Forbidding—impeding or discouraging

51. *Forego*—precede
Forgo—to relinquish

52. *Foreword*—introduction to a book
Forward—toward the front

53. *Fount*—a fountain or source
Font—the baptismal water basin in a church; printing a set of type of one size

54. *Gage*—pledge; security; challenge
Gauge—standard measure; measure exactly

55. *Gamble*—risky undertaking
Gambol—frisk; caper

56. *Gaol*—prison
Goal—destination; object of effort

57. *God*—God with a capital *G* refers only to the one God of the monolithic religions
god—All other deities are referred to by small *g*

58. *Gourmand*—a person who eats heartily or plentifully or greedily
Gourmet—a person who is an expert in fine food

59. *Gorilla*—an ape
Guerilla—a soldier of the underground

60. *Graceful*—elegant
Gracious—kind, sympathetic and courteous; leisurely and refined

61. *Historic*—noted in history
Historical—belonging to past

62. *Honorary*—unpaid
Honourable—deserving or bringing honour

63. *Horde*—a crowd
Hoard—to store up a supply

64. *Human*—belonging to the race of man
Humane—compassionate

65. *Hypocritical*—playing a part, grossly insincere feigning beliefs or feelings or virtues
Hypercritical—excessively critical

66. *Idle*—without work
Idol—an image of a deity

67. *Imaginary*—existing only in imagination
Imaginative—full of imagination

68. *Immoral*—without a sense of morality
Immortal—able to live for ever

69. *Impassable*—that cannot be traversed
Impassible—not liable to pain or injury
Impossible—most difficult; not possible

70. *Imperial*—supreme; royal; of an empire; of an emperor
Imperious—urgent; domineering

71. *In*—within
Inn—a pub or hostel

72. *Incite*—to urge to action
Insight—quality of perceptiveness

73. *Incredible*—unbelievable
Incredulous—doubting
74. *Indict*—accuse, especially by legal process
Indite—put into words
75. *Industial*– of industries
Industrious—diligent
76. *Inequity*—inequality
Iniquity—a sin or immoral act
77. *Ingenious*—clever
Ingenuous—frank
78. *Inflammable/Flammable*—highly combustible; extremely volatile
Inflammatory—causing swelling; arousing strong emotions
79. *Informant*—a person who discloses information
Informer—someone who discloses information in exchange for money
80. *Inhuman*—to lack all essentially desirable qualities of humankind
Inhumane—cruel
81. *Instantly*—Immediately
Instantaneously—at the same instant or simultaneously
82. *Inveigh*—to protest vehemently
Inveigle—to entice
83. *Irrelevant*—having no bearing on matter
Irreverent—lacking respect
84. *Judicial*—of or by a court of law
Judicious—sensible, skilful
85. *Junction*—meeting point
Juncture—at this moment (e.g., at this juncture)
86. *Knave*—rogue
Nave—body of church apart from chancel and aisle
87. *Languid*—drooping' lacking in energy
Languorous—gracefully slow moving
88. *Last*—after all others
Latest—most recent
89. *Laudable*— deserving praise
Laudatory—giving praise
90. *Lea*—piece of meadow or pasture land
Lee—shelter given by a neighbouring object
91. *Lifelong*—during the whole length of life
Livelong—complete; whole
92. *Lightning*—electric flashes in the sky
Lightening—making lighter
93. *Litany*—prayer; a repetitive sequence of questions and answers
Liturgy—ritual form of worship in any religion; ritualistically repeated and unchanging language
94. *Loath*—reluctant
Loathe—to hate
95. *Loose*—not tight
Lose—to be deprived of
96. *Luxuriant*—profuse; florid
Luxurious—self-indulgent; having an aura of wealth
97. *Main*—Chief; the high sea
Mane—long hair on horse's or tiger's neck
98. *Malicious*—wishing to cause harm
Malignant—actively evil in nature; extremely dangerous
99. *Mantle*—a covering
Mantel—a shelf over a fireplace
Mental—relating to mind
100. *Mean*—ignoble; intermediate
Mien—person's bearing or look
101. *Mendacious*—untrue
Mendicant—a beggar
102. *Momentary*—short-lived
Momentous—of great importance
103. *Naught*—nothing
Nought—the figure zero
104. *Negligent*—heedless
Negligible—that need not be taken account of
105. *Notable*—worthy of note
Notorious—known to deserve an ill name
106. *Oar*—bladed pole worked with both hands by one of the rowers of a boat
Ore—Native mineral yielding metal
107. *Official*—properly authorized
Officious—meddling
108. *Ordinance*— decree
Ordnance— department for military stores
109. *Peal*—long ringing of bells
Peel—rind of fruit; thin soft bark of young shoots
110. *Perpetuate*—to cause to continue
Perpetrate—to do (something evil)

111. *Persecute*—subject to ill-treatment
Prosecute—institute legal proceedings
112. *Personal*—private
Personnel—employees
113. *Perspective*—Appearance as determined by distance and position
Prospective—likely
114. *Perspicacious*—having sight; discerning
Perspicuous—lucid
115. *Physic*—the medical art or profession
Physique—bodily structure or development
116. *Popular*—of the people; generally liked
Populous—thickly populated
117. *Precede*—to come before
Proceed—to continue
118. *Prescribe*—lay down authoritatively; to advise (as medicine)
Proscribe—exile; ostracize
119. *Principle*—a fundamental law
Principal—the head of an institution; primary; the amount of a debt
120. *Profuse*—excessive
Profess—to claim
121. *Raise*—make stand up; set upright
Raze—wipe out
122. *Relay*—to convey; a race between teams
Relate—to connect; to tell
123. *Repel*—to reject
Repeal—to cancel
124. *Respectful*—showing regard for
Respective—particular
125. *Rightly*—with good reason
Rightfully—having a lawful claim
Righteously—acting in a virtuous way
126. *Sanatory*—curative
Sanitary—of the conditions that affect health
127. *Seam*—line of junction between two edges especially those of the pieces of cloth, etc. turned back & sewn together
Seem—have the appearance of being
128. *Sensual*—of the body; licentious
Sensuous—aesthetic
129. *Sensible*—having or showing good sense
Sensitive—touchy or quick to take offence
130. *Sequel*—upshot; who follows after; after–effects
Sequence—successive;
131. *Significance*—importance; meaning
Signification—sense or exact meaning of a term
132. *Spacious*—having ample space
Specious—apparently good, but not genuine
133. *Spiritual*—concerned with soul or spirit
Spirituous—containing distilled spirit
134. *Staple*—a pin holding papers together; basic commodity
Stable—firm; a shed for horses
135. *Stationary*—immobile
Stationery—writing materials
136. *Straight*—without curves or angles
Strait—narrow; strict
137. *Team*—a side of players
Teem—be prolific with
138. *Temperance*—avoidance of excessive indulgence
Temperament—natural disposition; idiosyncrasy
139. *Temerity*—boldness
Timidity—shyness
140. *Temporal*—earthly; secular
Temporary—lasting for a short time
141. *Tortuous*—twisting; complex
Torturous—extremely painful
142. *Vacation*—fixed period of cessation from work
Vocation—occupation
143. *Vain*—conceited
Vein—tube that carries blood from any part of the body to the heart
Vane—weathercock
144. *Vale*—valley
Veil—curtain
145. *Verbal*—oral
Verbose—prolix
146. *Venal*—mercenary; guilty of taking money
Venial—excusable
147. *Vertex*—the highest point of a hill or structure; upright triangle standing on its base
Vortex—a flow round an axis or a whirl—of air, water, or flame

148. *Virtual*—such in practice though not in name
Virtuous—morally good

149. *Wander*—to roam; to digress
Wonder—to be filled with great surprise

150. *Wave*—undulate; a long body of water curling into an arched form and breaking on the shore
Waive—forego

151. *Way*—road
Weigh—to measure the weight of
Whey—a part of milk that is separated from the curds in cheese making

152. *Weather*—atmospheric conditions
Whether—if

153. *Whit*—particle; jot
Wit— combination of intelligence and humour

154. *Willing*—cheerfully ready or given
Wilful—committed intentionally

155. *Wreck*—destruction or disablement
Wreak—give play to

156. *Yoke*—the connecting crossbar; a bond
Yolk—the yellow part of an egg

157. *Zealot*—a fanatic
Zealous—enthusiastic

2. A LIST OF HOMOGRAPHS

1. *Abstract*– existing in thought or as an idea.
Abstract– a short summary of a book etc.

2. *Address*– details of where a particular place is.
Address– to make a speech to a person or an audience.

3. *Advance*– a forward movement
Advance– to pay money before it is due.

4. *Aim*– to point or direct a weapon etc. towards an object.
Aim– to try to achieve something.

5. *Angle*– the amount of distance between the directions of two lines.
Angle– to catch fish with a line and a hook.

6. *Back*– situated behind.
Back– to give help or support to somebody or something.

7. *Bail*– money paid as guarantee for an accused to be released until his/her trial.
Bail– either of the two small pieces of wood resting on a set of three stumps in cricket.

8. *Bank*– an organization providing financial service.
Bank– the ground on the sides of a river.

9. *Bat*– a piece of wood with a handle used for hitting the ball in cricket.
Bat– a small animal like a mouse with wings.

10. *Bear*– a large wild animal with thick fur.
Bear– to carry something

11. *Boot*– a covering for the foot, ankle and often for the leg below the knee.
Boot– the space in a car for putting luggage etc.

12. *Can*– a metal or plastic container for liquids.
Can– is used to say that somebody has the ability to do something.

13. *Canon*– a general rule, standard etc. by which something is judged.
Canon– a priest with special duties in a cathedral.

14. *Cant*– insincere talk especially about religion or moral issues.
Cant–to turn over or make something turn over.

15. *Check*– to examine something in order to make sure that it is correct.
Check– a pattern of crossed lines forming squares.

16. *Cross*– a mark made by drawing one line across another.
Cross– annoyed and rather angry.

17. *Dark*– with no or very little light.
Dark– not fair in colour or complexion.

18. *Dart*– a small pointed missile, often with feathers attached to it.
Dart– a sudden fast movement.

19. *Date*– a specific numbered day of the month.
Date– a sweet brown fruit that grows on a palm tree.

20. *Dawn*– the time of day when light first appears.
Dawn– to become clear to one's mind.

21. *Desert*– to go away from a place without intending to return.
Desert– a large area of land with very little water and covered with sand.

22. *Edge*– the outside limit or boundary of an object, an area etc.

Edge– to move or move something slowly and carefully in a particular direction.

23. *Egg*– a small oval object with a thin hard shell which contains young birds, reptiles etc. in the initial stages of development.
    Egg– to urge or strongly encourage somebody to do something.
24. *Exhaust*– to make a person or animal very tired.
    Exhaust– waste gases, steam etc. released by an engine or machine.
25. *Faint*– not intense in colour, sound or smell.
    Faint– to lose consciousness.
26. *Fair*– treating each person, side etc. equally and according to rules.
    Fair– an exhibition of commercial and industrial goods.
27. *File*– a line of persons or things one behind the other.
    File– any type of holder, cover etc. for keeping loose papers together and in order.
28. *Grave*– serious and important.
    Grave– a hole dug in the ground for a dead body.
29. *Gum*– the firm pink flesh at the base of the teeth.
    Gum– glue used for sticking things together.
30. *Hack*– to cut with rough heavy blows.
    Hack– to gain access to a computer's memory without permission.
31. *Hard*– stiff, firm or solid and not easily bent or broken.
    Hard– difficult to do, understand or answer.
32. *Index*– a list of names or topics referred to in a book etc. and arranged in alphabetical order.
    Index– a figure showing the relative level of prices or wages compared with that of a previous date.
33. *Joint*– a place, line or surface at which two or more things are joined.
    Joint– shared, held or done by two or more people together.
34. *Kid*– a child or a young person.
    Kid– to deceive somebody in a playful way.
35. *Lap*– a single circuit of a track or a race-course.
    Lap– the flat area between the stomach and knees when a person is sitting.
36. *Leave*– to go away from a person or a place.
    Leave– time when one has permission to be absent from work etc.
37. *Light*– easy to lift; not heavy.
    Light– the natural force that makes things visible.
38. *Major*– important or more important.
    Major– an army officer of middle rank.
39. *Match*– to be like or correspond to somebody or something else.
    Match– a small stick used for lighting a fire.
40. *Note*– a short written record to help one remember something.
    Note– a single sound of a certain pitch and length, made by the voice or a musical instrument.
41. *Orange*– a round juicy edible fruit with a thick skin.
    Orange– the reddish-yellow colour of an orange.
42. *Order*– the state of being carefully and neatly arranged.
    Order– a command or an instruction given by somebody in authority.
43. *Palm*– the inner surface of the hand between the wrist and the fingers.
    Palm– a tree that grows in warm or tropical climates.
44. *Patient*– having or showing patience.
    Patient– a person receiving medical treatment.
45. *Rash*– a patch of tiny red spots on the skin.
    Rash– done without careful consideration of the possible results.
46. *Refuse*– rubbish; waste.
    Refuse– to say or show that one is unwilling to give, accept or do something.
47. *Scale*– the relative size, extent etc. of something
    Scale– an instrument for weighing people or things.
48. *Score*– a number of points, goals etc. made by a player or team in a game etc.
    Score– a set or group of twenty.
49. *Tone*– a sound with reference to its quality, pitch, strength etc.

Tone– to make something less intense, extreme etc.

50. *Tear*– to pull something apart or into pieces with force.

Tear– a drop of salty water coming from the eyes when one cries etc.

3. FOREIGN WORDS & TERMS COMMONLY USED IN ENGLISH

1. abattoir – Slaughter house.
2. ablation – surgical removal of body tissue.
3. abnegate – give up or deny oneself.
4. babushka – an old woman.
5. carafe – a glass container for water or wine.
6. spaghetti – pasta made in solid strings, between macaroni and vermicelli in thickness.
7. fiasco – an ignominious result.
8. graffiti – inscriptions or drawings scribbled, on public walls
9. etch – reproduce by engraving a design on a metal plate with acid.
10. replica – an exact copy.
11. siesta – an afternoon sleep or rest esp. in hot countries.
12. spree – a lively extravagant outing.
13. camouflage – disguise.
14. gourmet – a connoisseur of good food.
15. palaver – profuse or idle talk.
16. cliché – a hackneyed phrase or opinion.
17. blarney – flattery
18. etiquette – the conventional rules of social behaviour.
19. rendezvous – an agreed or regular meeting place.
20. verve – enthusiasm.
21. coup d'état – a violent or illegal seizure of power.
22. coup de main – a sudden vigorous attack.
23. bêtise – a foolish or ill-timed remark or action.
24. bête noire – a person or thing one particularly dislikes.
25. macho – showily manly.
26. coleslaw – a dressed salad of sliced raw cabbage, carrot, onion etc.
27. nouveau riche – a person who has recently acquired wealth.
28. hors concours – unrivalled
29. hors d'oeuvre – an appetizer served at the beginning of a meal.
30. hortus siccus – an arranged collection of dried plants.
31. cul-de-sac – a street or passage closed at one end.
32. culpa – negligence
33. tête-à-tête-private conversation or interview.
34. patella – the Kneecap
35. patio – a paved usually roofless area adjoining and belonging to a house.
36. groove – a monotonous routine.
37. poppy cock – nonsense
38. bolero – a Spanish dance in simple triple time.
39. bourgeois – conventionally middle– class.
40. boulevard – a broad tree-lined avenue.
41. boutonniere – a splay of flowers worn in a buttonhole.
42. bouillon – thin soup ; broth.
43. veld – grassland.
44. blitz – an intensive or sudden attack.
45. delicatessen – a shop selling cooked meats, cheeses and unusual or foreign prepared foods.
46. kitsch – tasteless or sentimental art.
47. rucksack – a bag slung by straps from both shoulders and resting on the back.
48. sotto voce – in an undertone or aside.
49. snorkel – a breathing tube for an underwater swimmer
50. spanner – an instrument for turning or gripping a nut on a screw.
51. chutzpah – shameless audacity.
52. schlep – go or work tediously or effortfully.
53. dolce vita – a life of pleasure and luxury.
54. doppelganger – an apparition or double of a living person.
55. samaritan – a charitable or helpful person.
56. pogrom – an organised massacre.
57. kleptomania – a recurrent urge to steal.
58. bijou – a jewel ; a trinket.
59. horde – a large group, a gang.
60. joie de vivre – a feeling of healthy and exuberant enjoyment of life.
61. masquerade – a false show or pretence.

62. ab initio – from the beginning.
63. ad infinitum – without limit.
64. bona Fide – in good faith, honestly, without fraud, collusion or participation in wrong doing.
65. cadit quaestio – the matter admits of no further argument.
66. cestui que trust – a person for whom another is trustee: a beneficiary.
67. futuro – owed at present, payable in future.
68. de facto – in fact.
69. de jure – by right.
70. de novo – anew.
71. ex contractu – arising out of contract.
72. ex debito justitiae – a remedy which the applicant gets as of right.
73. ex facie – on the face of it.
74. ex lege – according to law.
75. ex parte – proceeding by one party in the absence of, and without notice to, the other party.
76. ex post facto – by a subsequent act, retrospectively.
77. fuctus officio – having discharged his duty.
78. in invitum – against a reluctant person.
79. in specie – in its own form and essence, and not in its equivalent.
80. inter alia – among others.
81. inter se – between or among themselves
82. intra vires – within the power of.
83. ipso facto – by the mere fact.
84. locus standi – a place of standing, the right to be heard in Court or other proceeding.
85. mala fide – bad faith.
86. mandamus – a writ issued by a higher Court to a lower Court.
87. pari passu – with equal pace, without preference.
88. per pro as an agent, on behalf of another.
89. prima facie – on the first view, at first sight.
90. pro forma – as a matter of form.
91. pro rata – in proportion.
92. proviso – a clause in a deed or instrument beginning "provided that…..".
93. qua – in the capacity of, as.
94. raison d'etre – reason for existence.
95. sinequa non – without which not: an indispensable condition.
96. suo moto – on his own motion.
97. supra – above
98. ultravires – beyond the power, an act in excess of the authority conferred by law and therefore invalid.
99. vice versa – the other way round.
100. vis-à-vis – face to face.

4. LITERARY TERMS

1. Imagery – Use of language to represent descriptively– things, actions or even abstract ideas.
2. Epilogue – A short final speech to the play audience.
3. Farce – Low Comedy.
4. Allegory – A story in verse or prose with a double meaning.
5. Anapest – A metrical foot which comprises of two unstressed syllables and one stressed.
6. Epigram – A short poem or saying expressing an idea in a clever and amusing way.
7. Calvinism – Religious teaching of the French Protestant John Calvin and his followers.
8. Belles lettres – Creative, imagination literary writings.
9. Canon – The entire authenticated works of an author.
10. Pseudonym – An assumed name.
11. Thesaurus – Dictionary containing words of a certain type.
12. Parody – Comic imitation.
13. Satire – Composition which attacks foolish or wicked behaviour by making fun of it often by using sarcasm and parody.
14. Novelette – A short novel often of inferior quality.
15. Lampoon – A piece of writing that attacks and ridicules a person, a book, an institution etc.
16. Myth – Traditional strong, widely believed in
17. Saga – A tale of medieval heroes.
18. Blank Verse – Verse written usually in ten syllables, without rhyme.

19. Euphemism – Use of pleasant, mild or indirect words or phrases in place of more accurate or direct ones.
20. Analogy – Similarity of two or more things of different categories.
21. Ballad – A poem meant to be sung, usually with a refrain.
22. Colloquialism – Word or expression found in speech, and reproduced in informal writing.
23. Comedy – Light, humorous element in drama or fiction, or life.
24. Dialect – A variety of language used by people of a specific geographical and social area, which is different in some words, grammar, or pronunciation from other forms of the same language.
25. Dramatic monologue – A poem in which a single speaker speaks, usually to a silent auditor, in a specific dramatic situation.
26. Exposition – Prose writing used to explain a point or subject.
27. Fable – A short and usually simple tale to teach a moral.
28. Irony – An indirect means of conveying meaning sometimes by saying the exact opposite of what is meant.
29. Tragedy – A play or story with an unhappy conclusion.
30. Realism – Depiction of life as it is.
31. Symbolism – Use of objects to stand for something abstract.
32. Antonyms – Words opposite in meaning to each other.
33. Synonyms – Words which are similar in meaning.
34. Mood – A feeling or emotional state that characterizes a piece of writing.
35. Metaphor – A figure of speech in which a comparison is made between two unlike things, by stating that one thing is the other.
36. Metonymy – Naming of a thing to represent something closely associated with it.
37. Narration – Account of an action over a period of time.
38. Paradox – A statement which sounds contradictory.
39. Personification – A figure of speech in which objects, abstract ideas, or nonhuman creatures are seen as persons having human traits and characteristics.
40. Simile – Explicit comparison of two unlike things.
41. Tone – Writer's attitude towards the subject or the readers.
42. Epistolary novel – Telling a story through an exchange of letters.
43. Parable – Simple Biblical tale that illustrates moral truth.
44. Anthology – A collections of essays, stories or poems.
45. Pornography – Obscene writing without redeeming social value.
46. Coincidence – A remarkable chance occurrence of events at the same time.
47. Tetralogy – Four inter-related works of an author.
48. Tetrameter – A metrical line of four feet.
49. Inversion – Twisting poetic words into unnatural order.
50. Trochee – A metrical foot consisting of a stressed syllable followed by an unstressed syllable.
51. Hyperbole – A gross exaggeration.
52. Quatrain – A four line stanza.
53. Hexameter – A verse with six Metric feet.
54. Pentameter – A verse with five metric feet.
55. Scansion – Analysis of rhythm and meter.
56. Renaissance – Rebirth of learning in Europe.
57. Genre – A literary type such as epic or moves.
58. Aestheticism – The pursuit of act for art's sake.
59. Neoclassicism – The eighteenth century revival of classicism.
60. Didacticism – Teaching or Moralising in poetry.
61. Bibliography – A list of sources of information.
62. Archetype – A traditional, recurring theme or story elegant.
63. Folio – The largest book printed.
64. Prologue – An introduction to a literary work.
65. Memoirs – A record of personal observations.
66. Terza Rima – Three line stanza, the first line

rhyming with the third, the middle rhyming with the first and third of the next stanza and soon.

67. Pastiche – Literary or other work of art composed of matter, style, etc. borrowed from others.
68. Cliché – An expression that has become stale by repeated use.
69. Alexandrine – A line of six iambic feet.
70. Alliteration – The use of the same initial letter in successive words
71. Anapaest – A foot of two unaccented syllables followed by an accented one.
72. Avant-garde – ultramodernists and innovators in literature.
73. Baroque – Over-ornate style
74. Burlesque, a piece of comic writing imitating a person or style designed to produce ludicrous effect.
75. Caesura – a slight break or pause in the line with or without punctuation.
76. Dactyl – A metrical foot consisting of one accented and two unaccented syllables.
77. Doggrel – unmetrical verse.
78. Eclogue – Short pastoral poem.
79. Elegy – a poem of mourning.
80. Epic – A long narrative poem celebrating the achievements of a national hero or heroes in a dignified style.
81. Foot – Unit of metre consisting of syllables accented and unaccented.
82. Verse – without regular metre.
83. Iambic – A metric foot of two syllables, the first unaccented, the second accented.
84. Idyll – Short verse or prose piece depicting pastoral or romantic scene.
85. Magnum – an author's greatest book.
86. Masque – Amateur dramatic entertainment comprising songs, music, dancing, elaborate costumes and scenic splendour.
87. Mime – a dumb show in which action is shown by gestures.
88. Opera – Theatrical entertainment with music predominating.
89. Ottava rima – Stanza of eight iambic lines rhyming a b a b a b c c.
90. Pantomime – an elaborate Christmas entertainment based on fairy tales with lively music, singing, dancing and broad clowning.
91. Pastoral – It presents shepherds or simple rustic life in an idealised manner.
92. Penny Dreadful – Cheap novel of sensational character.
93. Periphrasis – round about manner of expressing oneself.
94. Potboiler – Work written to make a living, popular fiction of little literary value
95. Protagonist – Chief or leading character in a play or a novel.
96. Rhythm – arrangement of words so as to have musical effect.
97. Sarcasm – Irony of a bitter kind intended to give pain to its victim.
98. Sonnet – Lyric poem of fourteen lines.
99. Spondee – Metric foot of two accented syllables.
100. Trochee – Metric foot of two syllables, the first accented, the second unaccented.

5. MEDICAL VOCABULARY

1. **Adhesive:** Sticky; tenacious; producing adhesion.
2. **Al'kyl:** Any univalent alcohol radical.
3. **Alopecia:** Loss of the hair.
4. **Amniorrhea:** A flow of liquor amnii.
5. **Amphibia:** A class of vertebrate animals capable of living both on land and in water.
6. **Amputation:** The removal of a part of the body.
7. **Anatomy:** The science of organic structure.
8. **Anemia:** Deficiency of blood or of red corpuscles.
9. **Anesthesia:** A state of insensibility.
10. **Angina:** A sense of suffocation.
11. **Angiography:** A description of the vessels.
12. **Antiparasit'ic:** 1. Destroying parasites. 2. An insecticide.
13. **Antiseptic:** Preventing, or destroying, the germs of putrefaction, or suppuration.
14. **Apoplexy:** Paralysis from rupture of a cerebral vessel.

15. **Appendicitis:** Scolecoiditis, Inflammation of appendix vermiform.
16. **Aromatic:** Spicy; fragrant. A spicy, stimulant drug.
17. **Asphyxia:** The condition caused by nonoxygenation of the blood.
18. **Assimilation:** Capable of being assimilated.
19. **Asthma:** Paroxysmal dyspnea with oppression.
20. **Ath'lete's Heart:** Aortic incompetence from strain.
21. **Athete's foot:** Ringworm of the foot. Trichophytosis.
22. **Atonic, Atony:** Want of tone; power. Debility.
23. **Autism:** Morbid or phantasmic day dreaming.
24. **Autoplasty:** The repairing of a wound by grafting fresh parts taken from the patient's body.
25. **Aux'in:** A growth promoting hormone.
26. **Cat'aplexy:** Muscular rigidity induced by sudden emotion, fright or shock.
27. **Cataract:** Opacity; of the crystalline lens.
28. **Catarrh:** Inflammation of a mucous membrane.
29. **Cavernous:** Having hollow places.
30. **Cerebrosu'ria:** The occurrence of cerebrose in the urine.
31. **Cervical:** Pertaining to the neck or to a cervix.
32. **Cesarean** Op'eration: Extraction of the fetus by abdominal incision.
33. **Denti'tion:** The cutting of the teeth, and the period of the same.
34. **Diagnosis:** The recognition of a disease from its symtoms.
35. **Dyspepsia:** Impaired digestion.
36. **Ec'zema:** Psydracia, Salt rheum, Tetter.
37. **Egesta:** The discharges of the bowels.
38. **Elevator:** 1. A muscle lifting a part. 2. A surgical instrument for raising a depressed bone or the periosteum.
39. **Gastropathy:** Any disease of the stomach.
40. **Genetic:** Pertaining to generation.
41. **Germ:** 1. A microbe or bacterium.
42. **Glaucoma:** A disease of the eye, characterized by increased intraocular tension which results in hardness and blindness.
43. **Globule:** A small spheric body.
44. **Gynecology:** The science of the diseases of women.
45. **Imbecile:** Feeble in mind.
46. **Immunity:** Freedom from risk of infection.
47. **Incest:** Sexual intercourse between near relatives.
48. **Incision:** The act of cutting into.
49. **Incoherent:** Not connected or coherent.
50. **Incontinence:** 1. Involuntary evacuation. 2. Venereal indulgence.

"The Greater Part of this World's troubles are due to questions of Grammar."

– Montaigne, *Essais*

CHAPTER 3 GRAMMAR

Objectives of Learning Grammar

At higher levels, the main purposes of the study of grammar are seen as follows:

(*a*) To establish the system and provide a terminology for the description of (*i*) the spoken language (*ii*) the written language;

(*b*) To supplement and if necessary modify the description by close and extended examination of language in action (*i*) in speech situations (*ii*) in written contexts;

(*c*) To pass judgement on usage as 'correct' or 'wrong.'

Grammar is generally seen as dull and boring. This chapter will help you use English effectively in a number of situations. Our methodology will be:

(*i*) presenting sentences in situations and/or identifying sentences in textual contexts,

(*ii*) helping students make significant generalisations,

(*iii*) working out a formula to function as a mnemonic device,

(*iv*) producing sentences in situations based on rules already learnt —— what emerges out of this organisation is a cyclic order:

Sentences in situations	→	Rules
↑		↓
Rules	←	Sentences in situations

For example, the following sets of sentences can be examined:

1. (*a*) The juice is very chilled
(*b*) We cannot drink it.

2. (*a*) The almirah is very heavy
(*b*) We cannot lift it.

3. (*a*) The issue is very delicate
(*b*) We cannot solve it.

In each set, (*a*) and (*b*) sentences can be combined into one sentence, using **too** in place of **very** in (*a*) and making (*b*) a constituent of (*a*) by introducing certain changes in it. The sentences thus formed will be:

The juice is too chilled (for us) to drink.
The Almirah is too heavy (for us) to lift.
The issue is too delicate (for us) to solve.
Notice the central point of this pattern, which is:
too + adjective + to verb.

That is, **too** comes before an adjective. The adjective is followed by the verb of the second sentence in its infinitival form. Between the adjective and the infinitive, we can have, *for example*: The issue is too delicate for Alan to solve. Grammar tests aim at evaluating your knowledge, application and communication skills. Objective type questions are useful for checking your skill in grammar. Please remember that a good grasp of grammar will also help your composition skills.

TYPES OF PRACTICE TESTS OF GRAMMAR

1. MULTIPLE CHOICE

(a) Completion

The most common type of multiple choice structure item presents a context in which one or more words are missing, followed by several alternative completions. The following examples illustrate three versions of this basic type.

(*i*) Dr. Peter Dry (lives) (is living) (has lived) in England since 1970.

(*ii*) Dr. Peter Dry_______ in England since 1970.
(*a*) lives
(*b*) is living
(*c*) has lived

(*iii*) "Is Dr. Peter Dry still in India?"
"No, _________ in England since 1970.

(*a*) he lives (*b*) he'd lived
(*c*) he's living (*d*) he's lived

All the three versions have been employed in the exercises that you will confront in this section. A model exercise illustrating version I in detail follows:

Directions: In this part, each question consists of a sentence with four parts underlined. Select that part (A or B or C or D) which is **not acceptable** for standard written English.

Example 1

Although John **has attended** college
A B
until recently, he left **without** getting his degree.
C D

A B C D
☐ ☑ ☐ ☐

Answer

Choice B is incorrect because the past tense ("attended") – not the present perfect tense ("has attended") – must be used to express a completed action in the past.

Example 2

Pakistan's football captain **could pass**, block,
A B
and tackle **better** than **anyone** on the team.
C D

A B C D
☐ ☐ ☐ ☑

Answer

Choice D is incorrect because "anyone else" not "anyone" —— should be used in this case since the captain is incorrectly included with the other players on the team.

Model Exercise

1. **When** the movie **was over**, John and
A B
me went for a **quick** walk.
C D

A B C D
☐ ☐ ☐ ☐

2. Mrs. Kumar was **surprise** that her son and his
A
friend had **gone** to the concert **which was held**
B C D
at the school, so he gave his sister his tickets.

A B C D
☐ ☐ ☐ ☐

3. Mohan **himself** could not **gone** to the concert,
A B
which was held at the school, so he gave his
C D
sister his tickets.

A B C D
☐ ☐ ☐ ☐

4. **Although** Abrahms did not look **like** his
A B
brother, **there** personalities **were** very similar.
C D

A B C D
☐ ☐ ☐ ☐

5. Mrs. Kumar was **having** trouble controlling
A
the children **because there was** so many of
B C D
them.

A B C D
☐ ☐ ☐ ☐

6. **Between** one thing and another Julie **does not**
A B
finish her work in time to **go to the show** last
C D
night.

A B C D
☐ ☐ ☐ ☐

7. **Having seen** the **children's** work, Miss Peters
A B
approves their **requesting** to go to home.
C D

A B C D
☐ ☐ ☐ ☐

8. If Mohan **had wanted** to pass his exams,
A
he would have study much harder **for them.**
B C D

A B C D
☐ ☐ ☐ ☐

9. **Tom calling** Marie made **her** angry **so** she
A B C

hung up on him.
D

A B C D

10. **Except for you and I,** everyone **is enjoying**
A B C

this new play, **it seems.**
D

A B C D

11. Dolly and Paul **want to go** to Simla **this**
A B

summer which sounds like a good idea **to me.**
C D

A B C D

12. **Having attended** college **since** four years,
A B

Nina is **quite** proficient **at taking** notes.
C D

A B C D

13. My Counsellor **suggested** that I make my
A

professor **to change** my grade since I was sick
B

the day of the exam.
C D

A B C D

14. **As** his sister, David **needed** a ride from
A B

some generous person **in order** to get home.
C D

A B C D

15. Martha **on violin**, accompanied by Saul on
A

piano, **were** a great hit **at the annual recital**
B C

last week.
D

A B C D

16. **Each** girl and boy **must sign their** full name
A B C

before entering the examination hall.
D

A B C D

17. Kutty and Engineer went to **his apartment**
A

for drinks, and then drove **across town** to pick
B C D

up their friends.

A B C D

18. **From the top** of the hotel, he was able
A

to clearly and easily see the **whole city**
B C.

stretched out below him.
D

A B C D

19. **As soon as** I saw the smoke, **I called** the fire
A B

department, but **they haven't** arrived **already.**
C D

A B C D

20. I **have studied** very hard for my finals this term
A

because unless I pass **all of them,** its the end
B C D

of my scholarship.

A B C D

21. **To** the finalists, **Bob and I,** the last high jump
A B

was the most exciting **as well as** the
C

most difficult.
D

A B C D
☐ ☐ ☐ ☐

22. The day **before yesterday,** she **had had** dessert
A B

at the ice-cream parlour, but today she **will buy**
C

pastries **at** the bakery.
D

A B C D
☐ ☐ ☐ ☐

23. **To get a scholarship,** the bursar's office **called**
A B

Jaime in **<u>to discuss</u>** **his** application.
C D

A B C D
☐ ☐ ☐ ☐

24. Asha is **<u>only</u>** **<u>an</u>** amateur, but she sings **<u>sweeter</u>**
A B C

<u>than</u> most professionals.
D

A B C D
☐ ☐ ☐ ☐

25. **By this time** next week, Raju **<u>not only</u>**
A B

<u>will have memorised</u> the words, but he
C

<u>will also learn</u> the melody of the new song.
D

A B C D
☐ ☐ ☐ ☐

ANSWER KEY

1. C	**2.** A	**3.** B	**4.** C	**5.** D
6. B	**7.** D	**8.** B	**9.** A	**10.** B
11. C	**12.** B	**13.** B	**14.** A	**15.** B
16. C	**17.** A	**18.** B	**19.** D	**20.** D
21. B	**22.** B	**23.** A	**24.** C	**25.** D

Explanation for the Model Exercise

1. (C) "Me" should be "I" because "John and I" make up the subject of the sentence.
2. (A) "Surprise" should be "surprised". Surprise is a verb or a noun, surprised is an adjective. An adjective is needed here as predicate adjective following the verb "to be", here in the form "was".
3. (B) "Gone" should be "go". "Gone" is the past participle and is therefore not correct with the helping verb "could". It is correct with the helping verb "have".
4. (C) "There" should be the possessive adjective "Their".
5. (D) "Was" should be "were". "There" is not the subject of the clause; it merely stands in (as an expletive) for the subject. The subject of the clause is "so many", referring to "children", which is plural.
6. (B) "Does not" should be "did not", the past tense, since not finishing her work took place "last night".
7. (D) "Their requesting" should be "their request". This is a matter of idiom and logic rather than of grammar. Miss Peters is not allowing them to request that they go home – she is allowing them to go home.
8. (B) "Would have study" should be "would have studied". "Studied" is the past participle and must be used with the helping verb "have".
9. (A) "Tom calling" should be "Tom's calling". "Calling" is a gerund which is a noun form, and therefore Tom must be in the possessive case.
10. (B) "You and I" should be "You and me" because it is the compound object of the compound preposition "except for".
11. (C) "Which" has no definite antecedent. Therefore, it is incorrect. This is a common error in English. One has to be very careful and should not make this type of error.
12. (B) "Since" should be "for".
13. (B) "To change" should be "Change". The infinitive prefix "to" is not used in this case in which the infinitive is an objective complement.
14. (A) "As" should be "like". David and his sister are being compared.
15. (B) "Were" should be "was" because "Martha" is the subject of the sentence. "Saul" is the object of the proposition "by", not part of the subject.
16. (C) "Their" should be "his" or "his and her". The antecedent is "each" which is singular.
17. (A) "His" is incorrect because its antecedent is unclear. The antecedent could be either "Kutty" or "Engineer". Use the person's name in the possessive case. If the apartment belongs to both, "Their" should be used.

18. (B) The infinitive "to see" is split for no reason. Say "to see the whole city clearly and easily ———".
19. (D) "Already" should be "yet".
20. (D) "Its" should be It's". "Its" is the possessive of it; "It's" is the contraction for "It is".
21. (B) "Bob and I" should be "Bob and me" because "Bob and me" is in apposition to "the finalists" and "the finalists" is the object of the preposition "to". Therefore, "Bob and me" must be in the objective case.
22. (B) "Had had" should be "had". There is no reason to use the past perfect tense. "The day before yesterday" is before "today" but "today" is the present, not the past, so the simple past may be used to indicate "the day before yesterday".
23. (A) "to get the scholarship" is a dangling infinitive phrase. It seems to modify "the bursar's office" when it should modify Jaime".
24. (C) "sweeter" should be "more sweetly", an adverb, not an adjective, since it modifies "sings", a verb.
25. (D) "will also learn" should be "will also have learned", the future perfect; not the simple future because the future perfect indicates an action which will be completed in the future but before a particular time or event. "By this next week" indicates a particular time in the future before which the actions of memorising and learning will be completed.

Version 2 may be felt less confusing by some students, but they have to be tackled with equal care. For an illustration a Practice Test is given below:

Directions: In Part A, each question consists of an incomplete sentence. In your test booklet there will be four words or phrases. Choose that one word or phrase which best completes the sentence according to standard written English. Mark your choice on your answer sheet.

Example 1

If you would rather, we can take ________

(A) of the bus (B) the bus
(C) in the bus (D) for the bus

A ☐ B ☐ C ☐ D ☐

Answer

Choice B is correct because it provides a direct object for the verb "Take". The other choices are incorrect grammatically.

Example 2

John has not seen Mary ________

(A) during a week
(B) next week
(C) last week
(D) for a week

A ☐ B ☐ C ☐ D ☐

Answer

Choice D is correct because it completes the sentence with the only expression that makes sense with the form used in this sentence.

Practice Test

1. Would you like to go ________ a ride?

(A) with (B) on
(C) for (D) in

A ☐ B ☐ C ☐ D ☐

2. They were here, but they have gone back to ________ apartment.

(A) they're (B) theirs
(C) his (D) their

A ☐ B ☐ C ☐ D ☐

3. ________ of us are staying home.

(A) Some (B) A little
(C) Couples (D) Less

A ☐ B ☐ C ☐ D ☐

4. There isn't ________ food in the house.

(A) none (B) no
(C) some (D) any

A ☐ B ☐ C ☐ D ☐

5. I could have done better if I ________ more time

(A) have had (B) had
(C) had had (D) will have had

A ☐ B ☐ C ☐ D ☐

6. I will talk to the children ________.

(A) one and then the other
(B) first one then the next

(C) one by one
(D) in singles

A ☐ B ☐ C ☐ D ☐

7. While he________the poster a door somewhere behind him opened.
(A) is staring at
(B) did stare to
(C) looked carefully upon
(D) was staring at

A ☐ B ☐ C ☐ D ☐

8. After __________ on his couch more than a dozen times, he gave up his attempt to sleep.
(A) he overturned
(B) turning over
(C) his having turned
(D) turning up

A ☐ B ☐ C ☐ D ☐

9. He __________ move the piano in.
(A) helped in to
(B) does help for us
(C) helped ourselves
(D) helped us to

A ☐ B ☐ C ☐ D ☐

10. The assassination attempt __________ millions, because the speech was on television.
(A) was seen by
(B) was saw by
(C) seen by
(D) was seen for

A ☐ B ☐ C ☐ D ☐

11. Real wealth is __________ avoid doing what one would rather not.
(A) being able as to
(B) to be able to
(C) to
(D) to find yourself able to

A ☐ B ☐ C ☐ D ☐

12. If he __________ the storekeeper's scissors, he would have forgotten to buy a pair.
(A) would of seen
(B) had not seen
(C) had not of seen
(D) has seen

A ☐ B ☐ C ☐ D ☐

13. Isabel can't stand it __________ noise during a concert.
(A) when people to
(B) if the music is disturbed by people's
(C) if people have
(D) when people make

A ☐ B ☐ C ☐ D ☐

14. Despite his broken leg, Alan can walk __________ get around.
(A) good enough to
(B) good to
(C) well enough to
(D) fine enough to

A ☐ B ☐ C ☐ D ☐

15. When we get our tickets, __________ be marked "first class".
(A) it is to
(B) it will
(C) they were to
(D) they will

A ☐ B ☐ C ☐ D ☐

ANSWER KEY for the Practice Test

1. C	**2.** D	**3.** A	**4.** D	**5.** C
6. C	**7.** D	**8.** B	**9.** D	**10.** A
11. B	**12.** B	**13.** D	**14.** C	**15.** D

Explanation for the Practice Test

1. (C) You go "with" someone for a ride, but you go "for" the ride.
2. (D) "They're" is a contraction for "they are". It is not a possessive. "Their" is used when no noun accompanies the possessive pronoun. In this sentence we are given the noun "apartment", "This" is incorrect because it does not agree in number with the plural pronoun "They" at the beginning of the sentence.

3. (A) "Some" is an indefinite number or amount. It can be used to refer to individual items grouped together. "A little" and "less" are used only for lump sums, so they cannot be used when referring to "us", who are individuals, "Couples of us" is not correct usage, although "a couple of us" would be correct.
4. (D) "None" and "no" would be double negatives in this sentence since "isn't" means "is not" Therefore, choices A and B are incorrect. "There isn't any food" means "There is no food". We might say "There is some food", but we would not say "there isn't some food". Choice c is incorrect.
5. (C) "Had had" is the past perfect (or plu–perfect) tense. Since the speech occurred in the past, preparing for it must have occurred before that past. To indicate action completed in the past before another action in the past, the past perfect is used. Choice A is in the present perfect tense, choice B is in the past tense, and choice D is in the future perfect tense.
6. (C) The only correct choice is the idiom "One by One".
7. (D) The progressive past tense "was staring" is the correct verb for this sentence.
8. (B) The gerund phrase "After turning over" is the only correct introduction for this sentence.
9. (D) The past tense plus the infinitive "He helped us to move" completes the sentence properly.
10. (A) The past tense in the passive voice "was seen by" is the only correct choice.
11. (B) The infinitive "to be able" followed by another infinitive "to avoid" is the only correct choice for this sentence.
12. (B) The contrary to fact form of the past tense verb "had not seen" is the correct form for the "if" clause of this sentence.
13. (D) The dependent clause of the sentence should correctly start with "When people make".
14. (C) The adverbial phrase "well enough" is correct.
15. (D)The simple future with the plural subject "they will be" must be used here to make the sentence correct.

(b) Sentence alternatives

It is another item type which does away with the item stem altogether and simply presents several sentences from which the examinee chooses the acceptable version.

A. Mary is living in New York since 1960.
B. Mary lives in New York since 1960.
C. Mary has lived in New York since 1960.

(c) Sentence Interpretation

A third type of a structure item presents a stimulus and then asks for an interpretation. This becomes a kind of reading comprehension task in which the crucial clues are structural.

"An old friend of John's family brought <u>him</u> news of his uncle last night". **Him** refers to

(*a*) An old friend
(*b*) John
(*c*) The uncle

More advanced students may find such items extremely easy unless the test writer resorts to very complicated contexts. This is a close imitation of some of the items that have occurred in sentence – interpretation tests:

"The friend of the doctor that John met when he visited his daughter and her husband came to the library today".

The person who visited the library was

(*a*) the friend
(*b*) the doctor
(*c*) John
(*d*) the daughter
(*e*) the daughter's husband.

Sometimes, the test writer may deliberately omit punctuation which would provide an obvious clue to meaning.

"Have your friends come with you" the speaker is

(*a*) making an observation
(*b*) asking a question
(*c*) extending an invitation.

This makes comprehension more difficult as punctuation is an important signalling device in written English.

2. SUPPLY TYPE

(i) Completion

A fill-in exercise type is often used for testing. Such items require a certain amount of composition skills. The exercises, for example, can be set as follows:

Directions: Complete the sentences by writing a form of the verb given in parenthesis.

Mary ______ (live) in New Work since, 1960.

Directions: Complete the sentence by using the prepositions: before, during, since.

Mary has been living in New York ________ 1960.

Another kind of test would be to give a passage and then ask for sentence structures based on the facts in the given passage. For example, "Joe Soap was in a hurry to get to a meeting. He knew that the road was slippery but he was still driving too fast. When he came to a sharp right hand bend, he realised he would have difficulty in getting round it and touched his brakes. The car skidded out of control and spun round back to front off the road. Fortunately there was nothing else on the road".

Fill in the gaps in the sentences below:

They all refer to Joe Soap's misadventure.

Joe Soap ______ driving so fast if he had not been in such a hurry. He thought the corner was ______ sharp ______ take at the speed he was doing. But his great mistake was ______. He could hardly have avoided a nasty accident if ______.

For testing the sense of verb and tense usage, a passage, which will provides context may also be used. A model exercise follows.

Given below is a passage with numbered blanks. Write against each number (1, 2, 3, etc.) the most appropriate form of the verbs that will complete the sentences in the passage.

Do not reproduce the passage:

Fear and its companion pain ____1____(be) two of the most useful things that men and animals possess, if they are properly used. If fire does not hurt when if ______2______(burn), children ______3______(play) with it until their hands were burnt away. Similarly, if pain______4______(exist) but fear______5______(do) not, a child would burn itself again and again, because fear would not warn it to keep away from the fire that______6______ (burn) it before. A really fearless soldier, and some______7______(do) exist, is not a good soldier, because he is soon killed; and a dead soldier is of no use to his army. In our first sentence we ______8______ (suggest) that fear ought to be properly used. If, for example, you never ______9______(go) out of your house because of the danger of______10______(knock down) and killed in the street by a car, you are letting fear ______11______ (rule) you too much. Even in your house you are not absolutely safe: an aeroplane may crash on you in your house, or ants may eat away some of the beams in your roof so that the latter ______12______ (fall) on you, or you may get cancer. The important thing is not ______13______ (let) fear rule you, but instead to use fear as your servant and guide. Fear ______14______ (warn) you of dangers; then you have to decide what action to take. For example, you see a car coming towards you; fear warns you, you ______15______ (jump) out of the way, and all is well.

The above model represents the latest integrative or holistic approach towards language testing.

There is another type in which a student is asked to finish an incomplete sentence in such a way that it means exactly the same as the sentence printed before it. (Test No 16 is an example of the same type)

A model exercise follows:

Finish each of the following sentences in such a way that it means exactly the same as the sentence printed before it:–

Example:

They say Mr. Jones is a very good administrator.

Answer

Mr. Jones is said to be a very good administrator.

Is it absolutely necessary to answer those letters today?

1. Do those letters ______________?
   It is impossible for me to catch an earlier train.
2. There is______________
   How high do you think the tallest building in New York is?

3. What———————?
The Managing Director said very little about the proposed merger.
4. The proposed merger———————
I shan't accept that appointment if the salary is too low.
5. I shall only———————.
Increasing the tax on household goods is bound to cause trouble.
6. It's asking———————
The doctor told Mary to tell her mother he would call in half an hour.
7. "Tell———————
Did anyone reply to your advertisement in the local paper last week?
8. Have there———————?
Music has never been one of John's interests.
9. John has———————.

(ii) Conversion

Another popular type of short–answer structure test requires the students to convert or transform series of sentences in a specified manner – by changing them from present to past tense, from active to passive voice, from singular to plural, from simple to complex sentence, and so forth.

A good type of item is one that requires the student to change one structure for another with as little change of meaning as possible. For example

(*i*) I want another cup of tea, Replace **want** by **like.**

Ans. I would like to have another cup of tea.

(*ii*) A knowledge of grammatical terminology is less useful in everyday life than the ability to – use grammatical signals.

Begin: A knowledge of grammatical terminology is not as useful in everyday life as the ability to use grammatical signals.

(*iii*) He told me the details of his scheme. Replace **told** by **explained.**

Ans. The details of his scheme were explained to me.

Another useful rubric is **Rewrite as one sentence.** This can be made more precise by adding e.g. **using** 'which' **or** 'that' **or** 'where' for example:

(*i*) A man (we saw him working in his garden) told us the road (we were going to take it) was flooded. Use 'who' and 'that'

Ans. (*i*) The man who was working in his garden told us that the road we were going to take was flooded.

(*ii*) In Kansas thousands of people are homeless. The floods are especially serious. Use 'where'

Ans. In Kansas, where the floods are especially serious, thousands of people are homeless.

You may be asked for explanations of differences in meaning between grammatical pairs: For example:

If I see him I'll tell him.

Explanation can be: If I happen to see him, I'll positively tell him.

If I'd seen him, I'd have told him.

Explanation can be: Had I seen him, I'd have definitely told him. OR

At a more difficult level:

If they leave at seven, they'll be here by eight. Only if they leave at seven, they'll be here by eight.

An examiner may even ask for the rewriting to remove ambiguities, e.g. There was a girl in the car that needed a wash.

Ans. The girl in the car needed a wash. OR

The girl, who was travelling in the car, needed a wash.

NOUN

A Noun is a word used as the name of a person, place or thing. It can be divided into four kinds- Proper noun, Common noun, Collective noun and Abstract noun.

A Common noun is a name given in common to every person or thing of the same class or kind.

A Proper noun is the name of a particular person or place.

A Collective noun is the name of a number (or collection) of persons or things taken together and spoken of as one whole.

An Abstract noun is usually the name of a quality, action, or state considered apart from the object to which it belongs, e.g. Rohan is an honest boy. His honesty has won the heart of the jury.

'Rohan' is a Proper noun.
'boy' and 'heart' are Common nouns.
'honesty' is an Abstract noun.
'jury' is a Collective noun.

TEST – 1

Directions: Point out the nouns in the following sentences, underlining the appropriate choice by pointing out whether they are Common, Proper, Collective, Material or Abstract. If there is more than one noun in one sentence name them as N1, N2, etc. and put the same number for example N1, N2, N3 along with the mark (✓) against the appropriate choice.

1. Our class consists of twenty pupils.
   Proper Collective
   Abstract Common Material
2. The crowd was very big.
   Proper Collective
   Abstract Common Material
3. He gave me a bunch of grapes.
   Proper Collective
   Abstract Common Material
4. The streets of some of our cities are noted for their crookedness.
   Proper Collective
   Abstract Common Material
5. The class is studying grammar.
   Proper Collective
   Abstract Common Material
6. Never tell a lie.
   Proper Collective
   Abstract Common Material
7. I recognised your voice at once.
   Proper Collective
   Abstract Common Material
8. I believe in his innocence.
   Proper Collective
   Abstract Common Material
9. Wisdom is better than strength.
   Proper Collective
   Abstract Common Material
10. He sets a high value on his time.
    Proper Collective
    Abstract Common Material
11. What is your verdict, gentlemen of the Jury?
    Proper Collective
    Abstract Common Material
12. Our team is better than theirs.
    Proper Collective
    Abstract Common Material
13. Without health there is no happiness.
    Proper Collective
    Abstract Common Material
14. The soldiers were rewarded for their bravery.
    Proper Collective
    Abstract Common Material
15. Nelson is famous for his victory at Trafalgar.
    Proper Collective
    Abstract Common Material
16. A committee of five was appointed.
    Proper Collective
    Abstract Common Material
17. Cleanliness is next to godliness.
    Proper Collective
    Abstract Common Material
18. We saw a fleet of ships in the harbour.
    Proper Collective
    Abstract Common Material
19. Solomon was famous for his wisdom.
    Proper Collective
    Abstract Common Material
20. We all love honesty.
    Proper Collective
    Abstract Common Material
21. An elephant has great strength.
    Proper Collective
    Abstract Common Material
22. The Nile overflows every year.
    Proper Collective
    Abstract Common Material
23. This room is thirty feet in length.
    Proper Collective
    Abstract Common Material

24. Beauty lies in the eyes of a beholder.
Proper Collective
Abstract Common Material

25. Economics with its widespread range of practical application is of great interest to government leaders throughout the world.
Proper Collective
Abstract Common Material

TEST – 2

Directions: Fill in the blanks with appropriate Nouns from the alternatives given below.

The deceptive lure of money: the influence of money on human behaviour pervades the entire story. Magwitch devotes part of his [1] ______ to making Pip a [2] ______, and Pip himself is at first unable to cope with such unexpected [3] ______, getting into [4] ______ and leading his friend Herbert along the same [5] ______. Miss Havisham's [6] ______ (Matthew Pocket and his family excepted) have greedy [7] ______ of enriching themselves at her [8] ______. Pumblechook and Trabb, as Pip discovers, treat [9] ______ according to their wealth, and Compeyson's whole crime [10] ______ was bound up with the lure of [11] ______.

1. (*a*) wealth (*b*) heritage‘ (*c*) amount (*d*) collection
2. (*a*) human being (*b*) man (*c*) gentleman (*d*) convict
3. (*a*) debt (*b*) aristocracy (*c*) credit (*d*) affluence
4. (*a*) debt (*b*) charity (*c*) credit (*d*) loan
5. (*a*) route (*b*) path (*c*) way (*d*) manner
6. (*a*) relatives (*b*) relations (*c*) close-ones (*d*) families
7. (*a*) intentions (*b*) longings (*c*) hopes (*d*) dreams
8. (*a*) repayment (*b*) place (*c*) loss (*d*) expense
9. (*a*) persons (*b*) human beings (*c*) people (*d*) mobs
10. (*a*) period (*b*) life (*c*) duration (*d*) career
11. (*a*) money (*b*) amount (*c*) currency (*d*) material

PRONOUN

A **Pronoun** is a word used instead of a noun. There are eight kinds of Pronoun:

(*i*) Personal Pronouns
(*ii*) Reflexive
(*iii*) Emphatic Pronouns
(*iv*) Demonstrative
(*v*) Indefinite
(*vi*) Distributive Pronouns
(*vii*) Relative Pronouns
(*viii*) Interrogative Pronouns

Note: Since most exercises are based on Reflexive, Interrogative, and Relative Pronouns only, I'll introduce these only as follows:

Reflexive: When *self* is added to *my, your, him, her, it,* and *selves* to *our, your, them,* we get what are called Compound Personal Pronouns.

They are called Reflexive Pronouns when the action done by the subject turns back (reflects) upon the subject; as,

They hurt themselves.

I hurt myself.

Relative Pronoun: Relative Pronouns (called Conjunctive Pronouns also) refer or relate (*i.e.*, carry us back) to some noun going before, which is called its Antecedent; as,

I saw Mr. Albert who had just come back from Poland. (*Mr, Albert* is the Antecedent of the Relative Pronoun *who* in this sentence).

Note: *who, whose, whom, which, that, what,* etc. can be used as Relative pronouns

Interrogative Pronoun: When the Relative Pronouns –*who, whom, whose, which, what,* are used for asking direct or indirect questions, they are known as Interrogative Pronouns; as,

What is the issue?

Say *which* you would prefer out of these.

TEST – 3

(A) Fill in the blanks with correct pronouns:

1. The boys went to school but ________ were late and the teacher ________ punished ________ by keeping ________ after school hours.
2. The girls went to school but ________ were late and the teacher was angry with ________.
3. The girls flew over the house. Did the children see ________? No, ________ did not see ________.
4. The teacher said to Sheila, "Please tell the girls to come into the room immediately since ________ want to teach ________."
5. The pupils said to the teacher, "Sir, ________ want ________ to teach ________ the use of prepositions."
6. The teacher said to Raman, "Why are ________ late again? Didn't ________ tell ________ to come to school in time?" Raman said, "________ am sorry ________ am late, sir. Please excuse ________ this time."
7. The king said to the queen, "Please take these jewels and put ________ carefully in a box. Then come back to ________ and ________ will tell ________ why ________ must keep ________ carefully."

(B) Fill in the blanks with correct emphasising or Reflexive Pronouns:

1. Sometimes we deceive ________.
2. She killed ________.
3. The king ________ was there.
4. The wall ________ fell.
5. They ________ were present there.
6. The prisoner hanged ________.
7. I ________ went to see her.
8. We enjoyed ________.
9. They blamed ________.
10. We ________ heard her saying so.

(C) Fill in the blanks with suitable Demonstrative Pronouns:

1. ________ is my book; ________ is yours.
2. ________ are sweet grapes; ________ are sour.
3. The climate of the Punjab is better than ________ of Bombay.
4. Both books are good, but ________ is better than ________.
5. The streets of Bombay are wider than ________ of Calcutta.
6. ________ are my pens, ________ are yours.

(D) Fill in the blanks with suitable Interrogative Pronouns:

1. To ________ did you give the message?
2. Of ________ are you speaking ?
3. ________ were you speaking to?
4. ________ was she dancing with?
5. ________ did you give my book to?
6. By ________ was this picture painted?
7. ________ is better, health or wealth?
8. ________ am I speaking to, please?
9. ________ do you consider in the right?
10. ________ of these dolls will you take?
11. ________ do you believe did this?
12. ________ of these girls stood first?
13. ________ is the dog that won the race?
14. ________ is the news?
15. ________ do you prefer, milk or tea?
16. ________ are you waiting for?
17. ________ of you has not done his lesson?
18. ________ of these girls is your sister?
19. ________ is the horse you want to sell?
20. ________ do you consider, is right?

(E) Fill in the blanks with suitable Relative Pronouns:

1. He ________ is content is rich.
2. Take anything ________ you like.

3. God helps those __________ help themselves.
4. Here is the ring __________ Sita lost.
5. This is the boy __________ hit me.
6. This is the man __________ horse won the race.
7. It is only camels __________ can cross the deserts.
8. The man __________ is honest is trusted.
9. These are the boys __________ all praise.
10. They __________ are humble need fear no fall.
11. These are the pictures __________ I bought.
12. The man __________ son stood first in the examination is here.
13. He __________ speaks against me is my enemy.
14. The man to __________ I gave your watch had red hair.
15. Avoid pitfalls into __________ you see others fall.

TENSES

Introduction: Before attempting the test exercises on the use of tenses (Test-4, 5, 6) you should revise the following important notes relating to the area.

There are three tenses—Present, Past, and Future

They are further categorised into four forms: Simple, Continuous, Perfect, and Perfect Continuous (not common in Future tense).

Major uses of the Present Tense

Simple Present Tense

It is used

a. to convey a habitual action; e.g.,
I go for a walk every morning.
He travels by air whenever he goes out.

b. to express universal truths; e.g.,
God is omnipresent.
The sun sets in the west

c. In exclamatory sentences beginning with *here* and *there* to convey what is actually taking place in the present, e.g.,
There he goes
Here enters the hero.

d. In vivid descriptions or narratives, it is used as a replacement for the Simple Past; e.g.,
Napolean now loses the battle of waterloo and goes to St. Helena on exile.
Soon the king rushes back to his capital.

e. to express a future event that is part of a fixed programme; e.g.,
Shatabdi Express leaves Jalandhar at 6.15 a.m.
When does your school reopen?

Other Uses

a. to introduce quotations; as,
Shelley says "The One remains, the Many change and pass."

b. instead of the Simple Future Tense, in clauses of time and condition; as,
I shall sit till you finish your class.
If it rains, we will not play the match.

c. in broadcast commentaries on sport events (instead of Present Continuous) to describe activities in progress.

d. to use verbs of perception, e.g., *hear, smell, see, notice, recognise.*
to use verbs of emotion, e.g., *want, desire, wish, love, feel, like, prefer, refuse, hope, hate*
to use verbs of appearing, e.g., *look, seem*
to use verbs of thinking, e.g., *agree, think, suppose, believe, imagine etc.*
to use the verb *have* (*=possess*), e.g., I *have* a computer.

Present Continuous Tense

It is used

a. for an action that is going on; as,
The girls *are dancing.*

b. For a temporary action; as,
I *am reading* "Great Expectations".

c. An action already planned for the future; as,
He *is going* to the US next month.

Present Perfect Tense

The Present Perfect is used

a. to indicate completed activities in the immediate past (with just); as,
She has just arrived.

b. to express past actions whose time is not given and not definite; as,
My neighbours have been to Germany.

c. to describe past events when we think more of their effect in the present than of the action itself; as
They have finished the match (and they are relaxing now).

d. to denote an action beginning at some time in the past and continuing up to the present moment (often with *since*- and *for*- phrases; as.
We have lived in this colony for five years.

Present Perfect Continuous Tense

It is used:

a. for an action which began at some time in the past and is still continuing; as,
They have been working here since 10 a.m.

b. for some action already finished; as
'Why are your looking so frightened?'—'I **have been reading** a horror book.'

Major uses of Past Tense

Simple Past Tense

It is used:

a. to indicate an action completed in the past; as
He received this award last year.

b. is used sometimes without an adverb of time The time may be either implied or indicated by the context.; as
Mr. Mehta learnt French from the JNU.

c. is also used for past habits; as
He devoted number of hours to meditation.

Past Continuous Tense

It is used:

a. to denote an action going on at some time in the past (the time of the action may or may not be indicated); as
It was getting more and more difficult.

b. with *always, continually* etc. for persistent habits in the past; as
It was continually raining.

Past Perfect Tense

It is used:

a. to describe an action completed before a certain moment in the past; as
She met me in Nagpur in 2001. She had seen me last ten years ago.

b. If two actions took place in the past, it may be necessary to indicate which action happened earlier than the other. The Past Perfect is mainly used in such situations. The Simple Past is used in one clause and the Past Perfect is used in the other; as
It had rained before we reached the airport.

Past Perfect Continuous

The Past Perfect Continuous is used for an action that began before a certain point in the past and continued up to that time; as

When I joined that office, Mr. Albert had already been working there for six years.

Major Uses Of the Future Tense

Simple Future Tense

It is used:

a. to talk about things which we cannot control. It expresses the future as fact. For example,
My son will be fifteen next month.

b. to talk about what we think or believe will happen in the future, e.g.,
I'm sure India will win the match.

c. when we decide to do something at the time of speaking, e.g.,
It is raining. I will take an umbrella.

Future Continuous Tense

It is used:

a. to talk about actions which will be in progress at some time in the future; as
I believe he will be sleeping when we reach his home.

b. to talk about actions in the future which are already planned or which are expected to happen in the normal course of things; as
I will be staying here till Tuesday.

c. We use *be* + base form to talk about official plans and arrangements; as
The President is to visit America next month.
Be is used in a formal style, often in news reports. *Be* is usually left out in headlines, e.g.
"President to visit America."

Future Perfect Tense

It is used:

to talk about actions that will be completed by a certain future time; as

She will have left before he reaches there.

Future Perfect Continuous Tense

It is used:

For actions which will be in progress over a period of time that will end in the future; as

I'll have been teaching for thirty years next December.

TEST – 4

Directions: Choose appropriate Verbs from the alternatives below and fill in the blanks.

Dickens [1] _____ sensitive to every facet of external reality. Very often the effect [2] _______ by the illusion of photography: Miss Havisham's room, which [3] ______ untouched for years as a constant reminder of the betrayal she [4] _________ upon her wedding day, [5] _______ most easily as a set in a film studio. The oddity of Wemmick's house — a wooden cottage with a Gothic door and windows, a flagstaff, a drawbridge which [6] _______ a moat four feet wide, and a gun, protected by a tarpaulin umbrella, which [7] ________ at nine o'clock every night — [8] ________ by the straightforward way in which it [9] ________. Jaggers's office [10] __________ another instance, with its solid furniture, legal papers, and the two plaster-casts of executed criminals.

1. (*a*) was (*b*) has been (*c*) had been (*d*) were
2. (*a*) is gathered (*b*) is collected (*c*) is achieved (*d*) is obtained
3. (*a*) has been deserted (*b*) has been left (*c*) has been dropped (*d*) has been kept
4. (*a*) underwent (*b*) brought (*c*) suffered (*d*) got
5. (*a*) can be conceived (*b*) can be betrayed (*c*) can be prepared (*d*) can be swept
6. (*a*) measures (*b*) reaches (*c*) crosses (*d*) covers
7. (*a*) is fired (*b*) is shot (*c*) is worked (*d*) is practised
8. (*a*) is similarly aggravated (*b*) is similarly increased (*c*) is similarly enhanced (*d*) is similarly raised
9. (*a*) is described (*b*) is painted (*c*) is found (*d*) is criticized
10. (*a*) supplies (*b*) provides (*c*) harbours (*d*) imparts

TEST – 5

Directions: Read the following sentences and complete the incomplete sentences by selecting the most appropriate verb from the alternatives given below:

John Donne (1572–1631), born a Roman Catholic but later converted to Protestantism, was both a poet and priest. Before becoming a priest he ________ [1] a number of love lyrics in various moods such as 'The Sun Rising' and 'The Canonisation'. These poems __________ [2] such vigour and passion that they __________ [3] landmarks in English love poetry. Donne ________ [4] forward to a courtly career, but __________ [5] by circumstances to become a priest. During the last ten years of his life he ___________ [6] sermons and religious works. Donne's poetry ___________ [7] argumentative and persuasive. Realism, introspection and irony ________ [8] its dominant features. As a 'Metaphysical' poet, he successfully _________ [9] emotion and intellectual ingenuity. His poetry _________ [10] by 'wit': apparently unconnected ideas ________ [11] together in a way that the reader __________ [12] out of his complacency and _________ [13] to think. This _________ [14] by a dramatic directness of language which ___________ [15] rhythms of living speech.

1. (*a*) writes (*b*) wrote (*c*) has written (*d*) was writing
2. (*a*) will have (*b*) has (*c*) had (*d*) have

3. (*a*) will become (*b*) had become
(*c*) have become (*d*) are becoming
4. (*a*) looked (*b*) was looking
(*c*) had looked (*d*) has looked
5. (*a*) is compelled (*b*) compelled
(*c*) was compelled (*d*) had compelled
6. (*a*) had written (*b*) wrote
(*c*) writes (*d*) will write
7. (*a*) had been (*b*) has been
(*c*) was (*d*) is
8. (*a*) is (*b*) had been
(*c*) are (*d*) have been
9. (*a*) blends (*b*) grinds
(*c*) unites (*d*) ties
10. (*a*) has been characterised
(*b*) is characterised
(*c*) was characterised
(*d*) had been characterised
11. (*a*) have put (*b*) are put
(*c*) are putting (*d*) will be put
12. (*a*) will be jolted (*b*) is jolted
(*c*) has jolted (*d*) had been jolted
13. (*a*) forces (*b*) will be forced
(*c*) had been forced (*d*) is forced
14. (*a*) has accompanied
(*b*) had been accompanied
(*c*) was accompanied
(*d*) is accompanied
15. (*a*) was (*b*) is
(*c*) has (*d*) will be

TEST – 6

Directions: The following sentences are divided into two parts each. Keeping in view the correct usage of verb and tenses, point out the part of sentence which makes it incorrect.

1. **a** I was swimming in the pool for two hours / **b** and felt very fresh after that.
2. **a** When he came to me / **b** he had been unwell.
3. **a** He believes / **b** that he had committed a mistake.
4. **a** I will come / **b** when he will call me.
5. **a** I am usually going to Kashmir/ **b** when it's summer break for me.
6. **a** He has often boasted of his knowledge/ **b** whenever he was in the company of his classmates.
7. **a** He speaks / **b** as if he is an authority.
8. **a** I wish / **b** I am a first divisioner.
9. **a** I wish / **b** I have wealth of the richest.
10. **a** He does not get / **b** single minute for enjoying life / **c** he always does his work.
11. **a** I have been wanting this book / **b** since the time I join this library.
12. **a** I am hating him for several years/ **b** but he does not know about it.
13. **a** We will leave the airport at 8 a.m. / **b** and reach home at 9 a.m.
14. **a** If I have got money / **b** I would have bought a car.
15. **a** I am to obey the orders of my officers / **b** because I am just a clerk.
16. **a** I talked to him / **b** when he has met me.
17. **a** I forgot / **b** that I am to go to cinema
18. **a** Copernicus discovered / **b** that the earth revolved round the sun.
19. **a** He had appreciated him / **b** more than it is required.

20. a **b**
I will visit that place / so that I learn about it.

21. a **b**
He stood on the bank / when his friend was falling in the river.

22. a **b**
India had defeated Pakistan / when it had been at war with her in 1971.

23. a **b**
The man died / when the doctor arrived.

24. a **b**
He went to the museum / and has come across a friend of his.

25. a **b**
I have taken dinner with him / before I left for Agra.

26. a **b**
I had got admission in M.B.B.S this year / and my parents are extremely happy.

27. a **b**
He had met me many times/ since I have reached here.

28. a **b**
I saw this picture many a times/ and still want to see it again.

29. a **b**
I am in Bombay for two years/ but do not feel settled till date.

30. a **b**
Look / he falls.

TEST – 7

Directions: Read the following passages and fill in the blanks by choosing the appropriate verb from the options given below.

I.

He's a regular at business quizzes—almost every rookie on the quizzing circuit [1] ____________ that the creator of Asian Paint's mascot [2] ____________ cartoonist RK Laxmi. But that question's due for retirement: along with Gattu, which Asian Paints [3] ____________ from its logo and corporate image, in a comprehensive brand overhaul. It's the biggest Asian Paints [4] ____________, at a time when the company [5] ____________ a good last quarter, given the fact the most sectors [6] ____________ under a stubborn slowdown.

1. (*a*) know (*b*) knows (*c*) knew (*d*) had known
2. (*a*) is (*b*) are (*c*) has been (*d*) have been
3. (*a*) are phasing out (*b*) is phasing out (*c*) was phasing out (*d*) has been phasing out
4. (*a*) has ever been undertaken (*b*) was ever undertaken (*c*) has ever undertaken (*d*) is ever undertaken
5. (*a*) did have (*b*) has had (*c*) had had (*d*) did have
6. (*a*) was (*b*) has been reeling (*c*) is reeling (*d*) are reeling

II.

The complicated calculations of advertising elasticity [1] ____________ with hundreds of brands. In 1984, three American analysts, Gert Assmus, John U Farlet and Donald R Lehmann, [2] ____________ a summary of advertising elasticities of 128 separate campaigns. Elasticity [3] ____________ according to category, brand and the campaign.

1. (*a*) is made (*b*) have been made (*c*) has been made (*d*) is being made
2. (*a*) will publish (*b*) publish (*c*) have published (*d*) published
3. (*a*) had varied (*b*) varied (*c*) varies (*d*) will vary

III.

Northumbria is a modern University with an outstanding record for high quality teaching. In assessments of teaching quality conducted by the UK government's Quality Assurance Agency, the University's courses [1] ____________ 'excellent' with a number scoring a maximum of 24 points.

The courses [2] ____________ practical and professional focus and [3] ____________ to the needs of employers in the global work place. Their close links with industry and the high rate of graduate employment [4] ____________ all Northumbria graduates with a major career advantage.

Northumbria [5] ____________ a long tradition of welcoming international students and [6] ________ special efforts to ensure that everyone [7] ________ at home. Their ideal location in Newcastle, excellent facilities and the great social life also [8] ________ for an enjoyable experience. In addition, the cost of living in Newcastle is among the lowest in Britain. A number of Indian scholarships [9] ________ each year for academic merit. Over 200 undergraduate and postgraduate courses in many disciplines [10] ____________ for full time study at the University's campus at Newcastle.

1. (*a*) have been rating
   (*b*) have been rated
   (*c*) have rated
   (*d*) are rating
2. (*a*) have (*b*) had
   (*c*) will have (*d*) have had
3. (*a*) has been geared
   (*b*) were geared
   (*c*) are geared
   (*d*) is geared
4. (*a*) have been providing
   (*b*) provide
   (*c*) provides
   (*d*) have provided
5. (*a*) will have (*b*) had
   (*c*) have (*d*) has
6. (*a*) will make (*b*) have made
   (*c*) makes (*d*) make
7. (*a*) will feel (*b*) feels
   (*c*) feel (*d*) have felt
8. (*a*) will make (*b*) have made
   (*c*) makes (*d*) make
9. (*a*) is awarded (*b*) are awarded
   (*c*) were awarded (*d*) will be awarded
10. (*a*) are offered (*b*) are being offered
    (*c*) were offered (*d*) will be offered

IV.

Since 1891, students from around the world [1] ____________ to the UW-Stout campus by an outstanding curriculum, a faculty with a record of concerned service to students, and facilities that [2] ________ among the finest anywhere. Founded as an experiment in education, UW-Stout [3] ________ national attention from the beginning. Traditionally, UW-Stout's programs [4] ________ students for productive careers in business, industry, technology, education, human development, and art and design. A combination of course work in the humanities, social and natural sciences, as well as work in career fields, [5] ____________ a key part of an educational plan that [6] ____________ graduates who [7] ____________ creatively. The University [8] ________ the prestigious 2001 Malcolm Baldrige National Quality Award presented by the U.S. President George W. Bush. This the first time a University [9] ________ given this award.

1. (*a*) is being drawn (*b*) have been drawn
   (*c*) has been drawn (*d*) were being drawn.
2. (*a*) are (*b*) will be
   (*c*) is (*d*) were
3. (*a*) will attract (*b*) has attracted
   (*c*) attracted (*d*) attracts
4. (*a*) will prepare (*b*) have prepared
   (*c*) prepared (*d*) prepare
5. (*a*) was (*b*) shall be
   (*c*) are (*d*) is
6. (*a*) is producing (*b*) will produce
   (*c*) produces (*d*) produced
7. (*a*) shall be living thinking and working
   (*b*) have been living, thinking and working
   (*c*) are living, thinking and working
   (*d*) live, think and work
8. (*a*) has won (*b*) had won
   (*c*) will win (*d*) is winning
9. (*a*) was given (*b*) has been given
   (*c*) is given (*d*) shall be given

AGREEMENT OF THE VERB WITH THE SUBJECT

Introduction: Before attempting the test exercise (Test-8), the students are advised to read the following notes.

1. A Verb must agree with its Subject in Number and Person. Often, by what is called the "Error of Proximity," the verb is made to agree in number with a noun near it instead of with its

proper subject. This should be avoided as shown in the following example :-
The quality of the mangoes was not good.
His knowledge of Indian vernaculars is far beyond the common.

2. Two or more singular nouns or pronouns joined by *and* require a plural verb; as,
Gold and silver are precious metals.
Are your father and mother at home?
But if the nouns suggest one idea to the mind, or refer to the same person or thing, the verb is singular; as,
Bread and butter is his only food.
Honour and glory is his reward.

3. Words joined to a singular subject by *with, as well as,* etc., are parenthetical. The verb should therefore be put in the singular; as,
The ship, with its crew, was lost.
Sanskrit, as well as Arabic, was taught there.

4. Two or more singular subjects connected by *or* or *nor* require a singular verb; as,
Either the cat or the dog has been here.
Neither praise nor blame seems to affect him.
But when one of the subjects joined by or nor is plural, the verb must be plural, and the plural subject should be placed nearest the verb; as,
Neither the King nor his ministers desire war.

5. When the subjects joined by *or* or *nor* are of different persons, the verb agrees with the nearer; as,
Either he or I am mistaken.
Neither my friend nor I am to blame.
But it is better to avoid these constructions, and to write :-
He is mistaken, or else I am.
My friend is not to blame, nor am I.

6. *Either, neither, each, everyone, many a* must be followed by a singular verb; as,
He asked me whether either of the applicants was suitable.
Neither of the two men was very strong.
Each of these substances is found in India
Every one of the prisons is full.
Many a man has done so.

7. Two nouns qualified by *each* or *every, even though* connected by *and,* require a singular verb; as,
Every boy and every girl was given a packet of sweets.

8. Some nouns which are plural in form, but singular in meaning, take a singular verb; as,
The news is true.
Politics was with him the business of his life.
The wages of sin is death.
Mathematics is a branch of study in every school.

9. *Pains* and *means* take either the singular or the plural verb, but construction must be consistent; as,
Great pains have been taken.
Much pains has been taken.
All possible means have been tried.
The means employed by you is sufficient.
In the sense of income, the word *means* always takes a plural verb; as,
My means were much reduced owing to that heavy loss.

10. Some nouns which are singular in form, but plural in meaning take a plural verb; as,
According to the present market rate twelve dozen cost one hundred rupees.

11. None, though properly singular, commonly takes a plural verb; as,
Cows are amongst the gentlest of breathing creatures; none show more passionate tenderness to their young.

12. A Collective noun takes a singular verb when the individuals of which it is composed are thought of; as,
The Committee has issued its report.
The Committee are divided on one minor point.
But we must be consistent. Thus, we should say :
The Committee has appended a note to its (not their) report.

13. When the plural noun is a proper name for some single object or some collective unit, it must be followed by a singular verb; as,
The Arabian Nights is still a great favourite.
The United States has a big navy.

14. When a plural noun denotes some specific quantity or amount considered as a whole, the verb is generally singular; as,
One hundred paise is equal to one rupee.
Three parts of the business is left for me to do.

TEST – 8

Directions: **A.** Use the appropriate verb in the following sentence choosing the correct verbs from the brackets:-

1. The poet and scholar ________ dead. (is, are, have been)
2. His power and influence ________ very great. (is, are, have been)
3. The peace and order of society ________ promoted by our leaders. (was not, were not, have not been)
4. Bread and butter ________ what they usually have for breakfast. (is, are, have been)
5. Slow and steady ________ the race. (win, wins, are winning)
6. The Ministry ________ much divided in their opinion regarding the foreign policy. (is, are, has been)
7. The crowd ________ forward. (moves, move, are moving)
8. The Committee ________ issued its report. (has, have)
9. The Arabian Nights ________ an interesting book. (is, was, were)
10. Six miles ________ a long distance. (is, are, have)
11. Ten-rupees ________ not a large sum for me. (is, are, were)
12. The news________ very interesting. (is, were, are)
13. All possible means________ tried. (has been, have been, is being)
14. A number of interesting rumours ________ heard. (is, are, was)
15. Plenty of men ________ cowards. (is, are, was)
16. None but the brave ________ the praise. (deserve, deserves, has deserved)
17. Plenty of milk________ supplied to him. (is, are, have been)
18. Ram and not his brother ________ present. (was, were, have been)
19. The commander with all his soldiers ________ killed. (was, were, have been)
20. The teacher together with her students ________ walking in the garden. (was, were, have been)
21. Satish, like Suresh ________ a good musician. (is, are, have been)
22. Silver as well as gold ________ fallen in price. (are, has, have)
23. The house with all its furniture and fittings ________ sold. (was, were, have been)
24. Not only the officer but also the soldiers ________ laughing. (was, were, has been)
25. Either you or your friends ________ stolen my book. (are, has, have)
26. Either you or I ________ in the wrong. (is, am, has been)
27. Neither of the men ________ very strong. (was, were, have been)
28. Everyone of them ________ a blanket. (has, have)
29. Each one of these qualities ________ to be found in his character. (is, are, have)
30. Our only guide ________ the stars. (was, were, has been)
31. None of the students of this class ________ guilty. (is, are, have been)
32. None but fools________ it. (believe, believes, is believing)
33. It ________ raining since six o' clock. (is, has been, have been)
34. The news ________ by him. (was brought, were brought, have been brought)
35. Who ________ the job? (has not finished, is finished)

ACTIVE AND PASSIVE VOICE

Introduction: Before attempting Test exercise 9, you are advised to read the following notes.

Voice is that form of a Verb which shows whether the Subject does something or has something done to it.

A Verb is in Active Voice when its form shows that the person or thing that is the Subject does something; or, in other words, is the does of the action.

A Verb is in Passive Voice when its form shows that something is done to the person or thing that is the Subject. e.g. The cat killed the mouse. (Active Voice) The mouse was killed by the cat. (Passive Voice)

Who did this? (Active Voice)

By whom was this done? (Passive Voice)

TEST – 9

Directions: Read the following sentences in Active Voice. Select the most appropriate of the alternatives given below each sentence. Complete the incomplete sentences in Passive Voice by marking (✔) against the most appropriate alternatives.

1. *Active* : This surface feels rough.
Passive : This surface ......
(*a*) is felt rough.
(*b*) is rough when it is felt.
(*c*) when felt it is rough.
(*d*) is rough and can be felt.

2. *Active* : Your essay can read well.
Passive : Your essay ......
(*a*) is well when read.
(*b*) looks well when it is read.
(*c*) can be read well.
(*d*) reads well when read.

3. *Active* : The cannons are firing.
Passive : The cannons ......
(*a*) are being fired.
(*b*) were being fired.
(*c*) have been fired.
(*d*) fired them.

4. *Active* : I shall have met him yesterday.
Passive : He should ......
(*a*) have met by me yesterday.
(*b*) have been meeting by me yesterday.
(*c*) is being met by me yesterday.
(*d*) have been met by me yesterday.

5. *Active* : I had seen him before he came to me.
Passive : He ...... before he came to me.
(*a*) had seen by me.
(*b*) was seen by me.
(*c*) had been seen by me.
(*d*) would be seen by me.

6. *Active* : The foolish remarks surprised me.
Passive : ...... his foolish remarks.
(*a*) I was surprised at
(*b*) I am surprised at
(*c*) He was surprised at
(*d*) I have been surprised at

7. *Active* : One should always keep one's word.
Passive : One's word
(*a*) should always be kept.
(*b*) are to be kept.
(*c*) will be kept.
(*d*) would be kept.

8. *Active* : It is the time to buy books.
Passive : It is the time ......
(*a*) all the books to be bought.
(*b*) for books to be bought.
(*c*) for books have been bought.
(*d*) for books being bought.

9. *Active* : They like their subordinates to flatter them.
Passive : They like ......
(*a*) to be flattered by their subordinates.
(*b*) flattering by their subordinates.
(*c*) if they have been flattered by their subordinates.
(*d*) when they are flattered by their subordinates.

10. *Active* : Those who live in glass houses should not throw stones at others.
Passive : ...... who live in glass houses.
(*a*) Stones should be thrown on others
(*b*) Others should not throw stones on those
(*c*) Others are not to throw stones on those
(*d*) Stones should not be thrown on others by those

11. *Active* : Bring a glass of water for me.
Passive : ...... for me.
(*a*) A glass of water may be brought
(*b*) Let a glass of water to be brought
(*c*) You are to bring a glass of water
(*d*) A glass of water has been brought

12. *Active* : May I see this photograph?
Passive : May ......
(*a*) this photograph be seen by me?
(*b*) you see this photograph for me?
(*c*) this photograph seen?
(*d*) this photograph see me?

13. *Active* : Is this the time to stop work?
Passive : Is this the time ......
(*a*) to be stopped work.
(*b*) for the work to be stopped.
(*c*) for work being stopped.
(*d*) stopping the work.

14. *Active* : Why do you laugh at him?
Passive : Why is he ......
(*a*) laughed at by you?
(*b*) being laughed at?
(*c*) laughing at you?
(*d*) laughing?

15. *Active* : God helps those who help themselves.
Passive : Those ......
(*a*) are helped by God who help themselves.
(*b*) who are being helped by themselves God helps.
(*c*) help themselves, can be helped by God.
(*d*) are helped by God who help themselves.

ARTICLES

Introduction: Please read the notes before attempting Tests-10, 11,12, 13.

The Adjectives *a* or *an* and *the* are usually called Articles. They are really Demonstrative Adjectives.

A or *an* is called the Indefinite Article, because it usually leaves indefinite the person or thing spoken of. e.g. A doctor; that is, any doctor.

The is called the Definite Article; because it normally points out some particular person or thing. e.g. He saw the doctor; meaning some particular doctor.

While the indefinite article is before singular countable nouns, the definite article is used before singular countable nouns, plural countable and uncountable nouns.

The choice between *a* and *an* is determined by sound. Before a word beginning with a vowel sound *an* is used; as

An ass, an enemy, an hour, an umbrella, an heir.

The article *a* is used before a word beginning with a consonant sound; as

A boy, a woman, a ewe, a European, a unicorn, a horse, a union.

TEST – 10

Directions: In the following sentences tick on the required article (a, an, or the) where it is necessary. If no article is necessary donot tick any.

1. (A, An, The) Statue of liberty was a gift of friendship from France to (a, an, the) United States.
2. Rita is studying (a, an, or the) English and (a, an, or the) Maths this semester.
3. Please give me (a, an, or the) cup of (a, an, or the) coffee with (a, an, or the) cream and (a, an, or the) sugar.
4. When you go to (a, an, or the) store, please buy (a, an, or the) bottle of (a, an, or the) chocolate milk and (a, an, or the) dozen oranges.
5. There are only (a, an, or the) few seats left for (a, an, or the) tonight's musical programme at (a, an, or the) University.
6. (A, An, or The) Lake Erie is one of (a, an, or the) five great lakes in (a, an, or the) North America.
7. On our trip to (a, an, or the) Spain, we crossed (a, an, or the) Atlantic Ocean.
8. (A, An, or The) Mount Rushmore is the site of (a, an, or the) magnificent tribute to (a, an, or the) four great American presidents.
9. Louis played (a, an, or the) volleyball and (a, an, or the) basketball at (a, an, or the) boys' club this year.
10. Rita plays (a, an, or the) violin and her sister plays (a, an, or the) guitar.
11. While we were in (a, an, or the) Alaska, we saw (a, an, or the) Eskimo village.
12. (A, An, or The) political science class is taking (a, an, or the) trip to (a, an, or the) Soviet Union in (a, an, or the) spring.
13. (A, An, or The) Queen Elizabeth II is (a, an, or the) monarch of (a, an, or the) Great Britain.

14. (A, An, or The) Declaration of Independence was drawn up in 1776.
15. Scientists hope to send (a, an, or the) expedition to (a, an, or the) Mars during (a, an, or the) 1980s.

TEST – 11

Directions: Choose the appropriate article out of the three choices given in the brackets and marks a tick (✔) against the same:-

My grandmother, like everybody's grandmother was (the, an, a)[1] old woman. She had been old and wrinkled for (a, the, an)[2] twenty years that I had known her. People said that she had once been young and pretty and had even had (the, a, an)[3] husband, but that was hard to believe. My grandfather's portrait hung above (a, the, an)[4] mantelpiece in (an, the, a)[5] drawing room. He wore (the, an, a)[6] turban and loose-fitting clothes. His long, white beard covered (a, the, an)[7] best part of his chest and he looked at least (the, an, a)[8] hundred years old. He did not look (a, the, a)[9] sort of person who would have (the, an, a)[10] wife or children. He looked as if he could only have lots and lots of grandchildren. As for my grandmother being young and pretty, (a, the, an)[11] thought was almost revolting. She often told us of (a, an, the)[12] games she used to play as (an, the, a)[13] child. That seemed quite absurd and undignified on her part and we treated it like (a, the, an)[14] fables of (a, the, an)[15] prophets she used to tell us.

TEST – 12

Directions: Put articles wherever necessary in the following sentences:

1. Forecasting weather is difficult technique.
2. Such enormous crowd has rarely been seen at the airport.
3. He wanted the beggar to buy a meal with the money.
4. Terai is producing lot of wheat now.
5. He is Englishman, and therefore European.
6. Cow is useful domestic animal.
7. Milk in the cup is sour.
8. Education is not end but means to an end.
9. English proved strong power binding the country together.
10. Shall we go for walk round park?

TEST – 13

Directions: Tick on the article "a" or "an" where necessary in the following:

1. My shirt is made of (a, an) nylon, but I prefer (a, an) cotton one.
2. One of the girls was in (a, an) evening dress.
3. He bought (a, an) iron for thirty rupees.
4. She takes (a, an) glass of (a, an) fruit juice before breakfast.
5. Carpentry is not (a, an) occupation for a (a, an) girl.
6. It is (a, an) honour to be praised by such (a, an) distinguished scholar.
7. He is always complaining that he has (a, an) few neckties.
8. Not many people like poetry but quite (a, an) few like novels.
9. When he is at (a, an) home, he reads two newspapers (a, an) day.
10. (a, an) Fire destroys vast properties every year.

PREPOSITIONS

Introduction: Before attempting Test 14, you are advised to read the following notes.

A Preposition is a word placed before a noun or a pronoun to show in what relation the person or thing denoted by it stands in regard to something else. The word Preposition means 'that which is placed before'.

Prepositions may be arranged in the following classes:

1. *Simple Prepositions* A, by, for, from, in, of, off, on, out, through, till, to, up, with etc.

2. *Compound Prepositions* About, along, below, beneath, amidst, behind, beyond, between, inside, outside, within, without etc.

3. *Phrase Prepositions* (Groups of words used with the force of a single preposition) According to, in addition to, in place of, on behalf of, in comparison to, by means of, for the sake of, with an eye to, in lieu of etc.

TEST – 14

Directions: Choose the appropriate preposition to fill in the blanks. Mark tick (✔) against the appropriate choice:

1. The strain is telling ________ his health.
   (*a*) upon (*b*) of
   (*c*) in (*d*) on
2. I saw ________ the trick.
   (*a*) into (*b*) from
   (*c*) through (*d*) to
3. He is ________ head and ears in debt.
   (*a*) in (*b*) of
   (*c*) upon (*d*) over
4. We are ________ war with them.
   (*a*) at (*b*) in
   (*c*) through (*d*) of
5. He carried ________ his performance.
   (*a*) on (*b*) through
   (*c*) out (*d*) with
6. The thunder was accompanied ________ a heavy rain.
   (*a*) with (*b*) by
   (*c*) up (*d*) through
7. I do not believe ________ what he says.
   (*a*) in (*b*) of
   (*c*) at (*d*) with
8. He was congratulated ________ his success.
   (*a*) on (*b*) by
   (*c*) for (*d*) with
9. The invigilator connived ________ the unfair means.
   (*a*) with (*b*) at
   (*c*) in (*d*) for
10. I tried to dissuade him ________ joining the army.
    (*a*) at (*b*) from
    (*c*) with (*d*) in
11. He is ineligible ________ this post.
    (*a*) to (*b*) of
    (*c*) for (*d*) at
12. A steady mind triumphs ________ difficulties.
    (*a*) in (*b*) over
    (*c*) at (*d*) with
13. Ruin stared him ________ his face.
    (*a*) in (*b*) at
    (*c*) of (*d*) on
14. I was disgusted ________ their treatment.
    (*a*) at (*b*) in
    (*c*) on (*d*) with
15. Be ________ good cheer.
    (*a*) at (*b*) in
    (*c*) of (*d*) on
16. Hope ________ the best and prepare ________ the worst.
    (*a*) at, at (*b*) for, for
    (*c*) in, in (*d*) of, of
17. You are sure to run ________ difficulties.
    (*a*) in (*b*) into
    (*c*) at (*d*) of
18. Let me acquaint him ________ the facts.
    (*a*) in (*b*) of
    (*c*) with (*d*) for
19. I do not agree ________ you on this point.
    (*a*) to (*b*) with
    (*c*) in (*d*) at
20. She accused the servant ________ stealing.
    (*a*) of (*b*) with
    (*c*) in (*d*) at
21. I am quite ________ home in this subject.
    (*a*) in (*b*) to
    (*c*) of (*d*) at
22. I am posted ________ your case.
    (*a*) with (*b*) at
    (*c*) for (*d*) in
23. He resembles ________ his mother.
    (*a*) with (*b*) in
    (*c*) ø (*d*) at
24. The group comprises ________ four persons.
    (*a*) of (*b*) ø
    (*c*) with (*d*) at
25. I am not getting ________ well with him.
    (*a*) with (*b*) at
    (*c*) in (*d*) on

26. This tea is too hot ________ take.
(*a*) to (*b*) at
(*c*) ø (*d*) in

27. He is always boasting ________ his talents.
(*a*) of (*b*) at
(*c*) in (*d*) to

28. The principal called ________ the names of winners.
(*a*) on (*b*) at
(*c*) out (*d*) for

29. He has taken ________ going for long walks.
(*a*) in (*b*) for
(*c*) to (*d*) at

30. We looked forward ________ seeing you.
(*a*) to (*b*) in
(*c*) at (*d*) for

31. We are accountable ________ God for our actions.
(*a*) at (*b*) for
(*c*) to (*d*) in

32. We must lay ________ something for a rainy day.
(*a*) by (*b*) for
(*c*) in (*d*) at

33. Do not believe ________ love at first sight.
(*a*) at (*b*) in
(*c*) for (*d*) to

34. He lives ________ honest labour.
(*a*) with (*b*) at
(*c*) for (*d*) by

35. This dish is not ________ my taste.
(*a*) for (*b*) to
(*c*) in (*d*) with

36. He persisted ________ accusing me.
(*a*) in (*b*) for
(*c*) on (*d*) at

37. Mohan was married ________ Sheela.
(*a*) to (*b*) in
(*c*) with (*d*) at

38. Which hand do you write ________.
(*a*) at (*b*) with
(*c*) of (*d*) in

39. He reached ________ the station in time.
(*a*) to (*b*) at
(*c*) ø (*d*) on

40. A pedestrian was run ________ by the car.
(*a*) down (*b*) by
(*c*) over (*d*) in

41. Under this heavy load the bridge will give ________.
(*a*) way (*b*) in
(*c*) out (*d*) away

42. With great difficulty I brought him ________.
(*a*) about (*b*) in
(*c*) round (*d*) up

43. Without thinking he turned ________ the proposal.
(*a*) out (*b*) up
(*c*) down (*d*) in

44. He will abide ________ the rules.
(*a*) by (*b*) up
(*c*) in (*d*) at

45. She came to the club neatly turned ________.
(*a*) down (*b*) in
(*c*) up (*d*) at

46. You must keep ________ the reputation of the family.
(*a*) down (*b*) in
(*c*) at (*d*) up

47. You must go ________ this book.
(*a*) in for (*b*) in
(*c*) for (*d*) at

48. The thief broke ________ the house.
(*a*) in (*b*) into
(*c*) up (*d*) open

49. He turned ________ to be a cheat.
(*a*) out (*b*) up
(*c*) in (*d*) round

50. The police deals ________ the criminals.
(*a*) out (*b*) in
(*c*) with (*d*) up

CONJUNCTIONS

Introduction: Before attempting Test 15, you are advised to read the following notes.

A Conjunction is a word which joins together sentences and sometimes words. Example, God made the country and man made the town.

Two and two makes four. Conjunctions which are used in pairs are called Correlative Conjunctions or merely Correlatives.

E.g. *Either-or*. Either take it or leave it. *Not only - but also*. Not only is he silly but also obstinate.

We also use many compound expressions as Conjunctions; they are called Compound Conjunctions. e.g. *As if*. He looks as if he is weary. *In order that*. The notice was published in order that all might know the fact.

TEST – 15

Directions: Read the following sentences and select the most appropriate of the alternatives given below. Complete the incomplete sentence by filling in the most appropriate conjunctions.

William Wordsworth is the leader of the Romantic Movement in English poetry, __________ [1] started with the publication of the **Lyrical Ballads** (1798) by Wordsworth __________ [2] Samuel Taylor Coleridge. He __________ [3] with Coleridge __________ [4] Robert Southey belongs to the first generation of Romantic poets. Wordsworth was greatly influenced by the ideals of the French Revolution, __________ [5] was later disillusioned.

1. (*a*) when (*b*) which
   (*c*) that (*d*) what
2. (*a*) as well as (*b*) but
   (*c*) and (*d*) both
3. (*a*) against (*b*) along
   (*c*) accompanied (*d*) both
4. (*a*) both (*b*) and
   (*c*) as also (*d*) as well as
5. (*a*) but (*b*) however
   (*c*) nevertheless (*d*) who

TRANSFORMATION

TEST – 16

Directions: Fill in the blanks by choosing the appropriate option.

1. Bombay is the biggest city in India. ...... Bombay is.
   (*a*) All cities are as big as
   (*b*) A fewer cities are as big as
   (*c*) India has no less cities as big as
   (*d*) No other city in India is as big as
2. Gandhiji was the greatest leader of India. No other leader of India ......
   (*a*) was as great as Gandhiji.
   (*b*) was more greater than Gandhiji.
   (*c*) was the greatest than Gandhiji.
   (*d*) was great than Gandhiji.
3. I will come to meet you if you allow me. I will come to meet you ......
   (*a*) unless you allow me.
   (*b*) till you allow me.
   (*c*) in case you allow me.
   (*d*) lest you should allow me.
4. If you had gone there, you would have settled. ...... would have settled.
   (*a*) Had you gone there, you
   (*b*) Supposing you had gone there, you
   (*c*) Until you had gone there, you
   (*d*) Unless you have gone there, you
5. Provided he gives this book I cannot help him. ...... I cannot help him.
   (*a*) If he gives this book,
   (*b*) Until he gives this book,
   (*c*) Till he gives this book,
   (*d*) Unless he gives this book.
6. Should I start just now I will reach there in time. ...... I will reach there in time.
   (*a*) Unless I start just now,
   (*b*) If I start now,
   (*c*) Until I start just now,
   (*d*) Supposing I start just now.
7. Speak one more word and you die. ...... you die.
   (*a*) Had you spoken one word more
   (*b*) If you had spoken one word more
   (*c*) Had you been speaking one word
   (*d*) If you speak one word more
8. One more goal and the rival will be defeated. ...... the rival will be defeated.
   (*a*) Had you scored one goal more,
   (*b*) If you score one more goal,
   (*c*) Supposing have you scored one goal more,
   (*d*) Would you score one goal more.

9. If your father were to know of your action he will be angry with you.

...... he would have been be angry with you.

(*a*) Had your father known of your action,

(*b*) Would have your father known your action,

(*c*) Had not your father known your action,

(*d*) Did your father know of your action.

10. If I were to pay he will get nothing.

...... he will get nothing.

(*a*) Had I been to pay,

(*b*) Would I to pay,

(*c*) Suppose if he had to pay,

(*d*) If I am supposed to pay,

11. Though he is poor he is very honest.

...... he is honest.

(*a*) If he is poor,

(*b*) Despite his poverty,

(*c*) Had he been poor,

(*d*) If he is poor.

12. Poor as he is, he is honest.

...... he is honest.

(*a*) If he is poor,

(*b*) Though he is poor,

(*c*) Had he been poor,

(*d*) Would he be poor,

13. You are taller than I am.

I am not ......

(*a*) as tall as you are.

(*b*) such tall as you are.

(*c*) less tall than you are.

(*d*) the tallest than you are.

14. As soon he saw me he came to me.

No sooner ......

(*a*) had he seen me than he came to me.

(*b*) he saw me he came to me.

(*c*) did he see me than he came to me.

(*d*) did he see me and then he came to me.

15. You must remember these facts.

You must not ......

(*a*) forget these facts.

(*b*) remember these facts.

(*c*) ignore these facts.

(*d*) neglect these facts.

DIRECT-INDIRECT SPEECH

Introduction: Before attempting the Tests 17 and 18, you are advised to read the following notes.

We may report the words of a speaker in two ways:

(*i*) We may quote his actual words. This is called Direct Speech.

(*ii*) We may report what he said without quoting his exact words. This is called Indirect (or Reported) Speech, e.g.,

Direct: Mohan said to me, " The teacher finished the lesson yesterday".

Indirect: Mohan told me that the teacher had finished the lesson on the previous day.

Some Important Rules for Changing Direct Speech into Indirect

1. When the reporting or principal verb is in the Past Tense, all present tenses of the Direct are changed into the corresponding Past Tense. Thus:

(*a*) A *simple present* becomes a *simple past*.

Direct: He said to me, " I *am* the leader of the group"

Indirect: He told me that he *was* the leader of the group.

(*b*) A *present continuous* becomes a *past continuous.*

Direct: He said, "I *am not running* fast"

Indirect: He said that he *was not running* fast.

(*c*) A *present perfect* becomes a *past perfect.*

Direct: She said, " I have written an essay on the topic."

Indirect: She said that she had written an essay on the topic.

Note : The *shall* of the future Tense is changed into *should.*

The *will* of the future Tense is changed into *would* or *should.*

As a rule, *the simple past* in the Direct becomes *the past perfect* in the indirect.

Direct: Raju said to me, " I *travelled* by air last night."

Indirect: Raju told me that he *had travelled* by air the previous night.

TEST – 17

Directions: The following sentences are changed from direct to indirect speech. Each sentence is followed by four choices a, b, c, d. Select the most appropriate choice.

1. John said, "I am going."
   (*a*) John said he is going.
   (*b*) John said that he is going.
   (*c*) John said that he was going.
   (*d*) John told he was going.
2. He said, "The earth moves round the sun."
   (*a*) He said that the earth moved round the sun.
   (*b*) He said that the earth moves round the sun.
   (*c*) He said the earth moves round the sun.
   (*d*) He told the earth moved round the sun.
3. Sonia says, "I will be going."
   (*a*) Sonia says that she was going.
   (*b*) Sonia says that she is going.
   (*c*) Sonia says that she will be going.
   (*d*) Sonia said that she would be going.
4. He said, "The man has been coming."
   (*a*) He said the man had been coming.
   (*b*) He said that the man had been coming.
   (*c*) He told the man has been coming.
   (*d*) He said that the man has been coming.
5. He said, "I am too ill to speak now."
   (*a*) He said that he was too ill to speak then.
   (*b*) He told he was too ill to speak now.
   (*c*) He said that he is too ill to speak then.
   (*d*) He said he was too ill to speak then.
6. He said, "I will speak here."
   (*a*) He said that he would speak there.
   (*b*) He said he will speak here.
   (*c*) He told that he will speak there.
   (*d*) He said he would speak there.
7. Ram said, "The man came at five."
   (*a*) Ram said that the man came at five.
   (*b*) Ram told the man had come at five.
   (*c*) Ram said the man has come at five.
   (*d*) Ram said that the man had come at five.
8. He said, "We must all die."
   (*a*) He said that we must all die.
   (*b*) He said that they must all die.
   (*c*) He told they must all die.
   (*d*) He said we must all die.
9. Kishan said, "He may go."
   (*a*) Kishan said he may go.
   (*b*) Kishan said that he might go.
   (*c*) Kishan told that he might go.
   (*d*) Kishan said he might go.
10. He said to us, "The carriage has come and we shall start soon."
    (*a*) He said to us the carriage had come and they would start soon.
    (*b*) He said to us that the carriage had come and they will start soon.
    (*c*) He told us that the carriage had come and they would start soon.
    (*d*) He told us that the carriage has come and they would start soon.
11. Ram said to him, "Your fault will be pardoned if you confess it."
    (*a*) Ram told him that his fault would be pardoned if he confessed it.
    (*b*) Ram said to him his fault would be pardoned if he confessed it.
    (*c*) Ram told him his fault will be pardoned if he confessed it.
    (*d*) Ram told him that his fault will be pardoned if he confessed it.
12. The teacher said to us, "The prize will be presented tomorrow."
    (*a*) The teacher told us that the prize would be presented the next day.
    (*b*) The teacher told us that the prize will be presented tomorrow.
    (*c*) The teacher told us the prize would be presented tomorrow.
    (*d*) The teacher told us the prize would be presented the next day.
13. He said to me, "You will be tried before you arrive."
    (*a*) He told me I will be tried before I arrived.
    (*b*) He told me that I would be tried before I arrived.
    (*c*) He told me I would be tried before I arrive.
    (*d*) He said to me I would be tried before I arrived.

14. My son says, "Someone has taken the book I was reading."
   (*a*) My son says that someone had taken the book he was reading.
   (*b*) My son says that someone has taken the book he is reading.
   (*c*) My son said someone had taken the book he was reading.
   (*d*) My son says that someone has taken the book he was reading.
15. He said to me, "I will come if I can."
   (*a*) He told me that he would come if he could.
   (*b*) He said to me he would come if he could.
   (*c*) He told me that he will come if he can.
   (*d*) He told me he would come if he could.
16. I said to him, "I received a phone call from my friend yesterday."
   (*a*) I told him I received a phone call from my friend yesterday.
   (*b*) I said to him that he had received a phone call from his friend yesterday.
   (*c*) I told him that I had received a phone call from my friend, the previous day.
17. Geeta said to me, "Can you accompany me to the library?"
   (*a*) Geeta asked me whether I could accompany her to the library.
   (*b*) Geeta said to me could I accompany her to the library.
   (*c*) Geeta asked me that if I could accompany her to library.
18. The teacher said to the students, "The earth moves round the sun."
   (*a*) The teacher told the students that the earth moved round the sun.
   (*b*) The teacher said to the students that the earth moves round the sun.
   (*c*) The teacher told the students that the earth moves round the sun.
19. Mr. Verma said to his son, "Work hard if you want to succeed in the examination."
   (*a*) Mr. Verma ordered his son to work hard if he wanted to succeed in the examination.
   (*b*) Mr. Verma advised his son to work hard if he wanted to succeed in the examination.
   (*c*) Mr. Verma told his son that work hard if you want to succeed in the examination.

TEST – 18

Directions: Read the following sentences in direct speech. Complete the incomplete sentence in indirect speech by selecting one of the most appropriate options given below.

1. *Direct*: I said to him, "It was very hot the last night."
   Indirect: I told him ......
   (*a*) that it was very hot the previous night.
   (*b*) that it had been very hot the previous night.
   (*c*) that it has been very hot the last night.
   (*d*) it had been very hot the last night.
2. *Direct*: He told me, "Your train will leave if you do not go at once."
   Indirect: He told me that ......
   (*a*) his train would leave if he did not go at that time.
   (*b*) his train would leave if I did not go at that very time.
   (*c*) my train would leave if I did not go at that very time.
   (*d*) my train will leave if I did not go at that time.
3. *Direct*: He said to me, "I shall excuse you for your mistake."
   Indirect: He told me ......
   (*a*) that he should excuse me for my mistake.
   (*b*) that he will excuse me for my mistake.
   (*c*) he would excuse me for my mistake
   (*d*) that he would excuse me for my mistake.
4. *Direct*: He said to me, "Are you going to the cinema?"
   Indirect: He enquired of me......
   (*a*) if I was going to the cinema.
   (*b*) if I had been going to the cinema.
   (*c*) was I going to the cinema?
   (*d*) if I am going to the cinema.

5. *Direct*: He said to me, "Why did you not change your school?"
Indirect: He asked me.....
(*a*) why did I not change my school?
(*b*) why I had not changed my school.
(*c*) that why I had not changed my school.
(*d*) why I did not change my school.

6. *Direct*: He said to me, "When did you borrow this pen?"
Indirect: He asked me ......
(*a*) when I had borrowed that pen.
(*b*) that when I had borrowed that pen.
(*c*) when did I borrow that pen?
(*d*) when I borrowed that pen.

7. *Direct*: He said to us, "Are you meeting me today?"
Indirect: He asked us ......
(*a*) were we meeting him that day?
(*b*) are we meeting him that day?
(*c*) whether we were meeting him that day.
(*d*) whether we are meeting him that day.

8. *Direct*: He said John, "What are you doing?"
Indirect: He asked John ......
(*a*) what was he doing?
(*b*) what is he doing?
(*c*) what he was doing?
(*d*) what he was doing.

9. *Direct*: He said to his servant, "Run and catch the thief."
Indirect: He ordered his servant ......
(*a*) run and catch the thief.
(*b*) to run and catch the thief.
(*c*) to run and to catch the thief.
(*d*) run and to catch the thief.

10. *Direct*: He said to his friend, "Wait here till Mohan comes."
Indirect: He requested his friend ......
(*a*) to wait here till Mohan comes.
(*b*) wait here till Mohan comes.
(*c*) wait there till Mohan came.
(*d*) to wait there till Mohan came.

11. *Direct*: My father said to me, "Don't quarrel among yourselves."
Indirect: My father ......
(*a*) asked me not to quarrel among ourselves.
(*b*) forbade me to quarrel among ourselves.
(*c*) asked me that not to quarrel among ourselves.
(*d*) asked me to quarrel not among ourselves.

12. *Direct*: His mother said to his father, "Please excuse the child."
Indirect: His mother ......
(*a*) implored his father to excuse the child.
(*b*) asked his father to excuse him.
(*c*) asked his father to have excused him.
(*d*) asked his father to have been excused.

13. *Direct*: I said to my friend, "Let us go to the library."
Indirect: I told my friend ......
(*a*) we would go to the library.
(*b*) we shall go to the library.
(*c*) that we should go to the library.
(*d*) that we would go to the library.

14. *Direct*: Ram said to me, "Let us search his pockets."
Indirect: Ram said that ......
(*a*) he should search his pockets.
(*b*) they should search his pockets.
(*c*) we should search his pockets.
(*d*) his pockets be searched.

15. *Direct*: He said to me, "Trust in God."
Indirect: He advised me ......
(*a*) to trust in God.
(*b*) trusted in God.
(*c*) should trust in God.
(*d*) that I should trust in God.

ERROR CORRECTION

TEST – 19

Introduction: After practising all the above tests, the students are advised to attempt the following test exercise.

Directions: In the following test, each sentence has four underlined words or phrases. The four underlined parts of the sentence are marked (A), (B), (C) and (D). Identify the <u>one</u> underlined word or phrase that must be changed in order for the sentence to be correct.

1. The main office of the factory can be found in Maple Street in New York City.
A B C D

2. Because there are less members present tonight than there were last night, we must wait until
A B C
the next meeting to vote.
D

3. David is particularly fond of cooking, and he often cooks really delicious meals.
A B C D

4. The progress made in space travel for the early 1960s is remarkable.
A B C D

5. Sandra has not rarely missed a play or concert since she was seventeen years old.
A B C D

6. The governor has not decided how to deal with the new problems already.
A B C D

7. There was a very interesting news on the radio this morning about the earthquake in Italy.
A B C D

8. The professor had already given the homework assignment when he had remembered that
A B
Monday was a holiday.
C D

9. Having been beaten by the police for striking an officer, the man will cry out in pain.
A B C D

10. This table is not sturdy enough to support a television, and that one probably isn't neither.
A B C D

11. The bridge was hitting by a large ship during a sudden storm last week.
A B C D

12. The company representative sold to the manager a sewing machine for forty dollars.
A B C D

13. The taxi driver told the man to don't allow his disobedient son to hang out the window.
A B C D

14. These televisions are quite popular in Europe, but those ones are not.
A B C D

15. Harvey seldom pays his bill on time, and his brother does too.
A B C D

16. The officials object to them wearing long dresses for the inaugural dance at the country club.
A B C D

17. Janet is finally used to cook on an electric stove after having a gas one for so long.
A B C D

18. He knows to repair the carburetor without taking the whole car apart.
A B C D

19. Stuart stopped to write his letter because he had to leave for the hospital.
A B C D

20. She must retyping the report before she hands it to the director of financing.
A B C D

21. How much times did Rick and Jennifer have to do the experiment before they obtained the results
A B C
they had been expecting.
D

22. Each of the students in the accounting class has to type their own research paper this semester.
A B C D

23. Mrs. Stevens, along with her cousins from New Mexico, are planning to attend the festivities.
A B C D

24. They are going to have to leave soon, and so do we.
A B C D

25. All the students are looking forward spending their free time relaxing in the sun this summer.
A B C D

26. Dresses, skirts, shoes, and children's clothing are advertised at great reduced prices this weekend.
A B C D

27. Mary and her sister just bought two new winters coats at the clearance sale.
A B C D

28. A lunch of soup and sandwiches do not appeal to all of the students.
A B C D

29. Some of us have to study their lessons more carefully if we expect to pass this examination.
A B C D

30. Mr. Peters used to think of himself as the only president of the company.
A B C D

31. She wishes that we didn't send her the candy yesterday because she is on diet.
A B C D

32. They are planning on attending the convention next month, and so I am.
A B C D

33. Today was such beautiful day that I couldn't bring myself to complete all my chores.
A B C D

34. While they were away at the beach, they allowed their neighbours use their barbeque grill.
A B C D

35. The artist tried stimulate interest in painting by taking his students to the museums.
A B C D

36. Mumps are a very common disease which usually affects children.
A B C D

37. Nancy said that she went to the supermarket before coming home.
A B C D

38. Before she moved here, Arlene had been president of the organisation since four years.
A B C D

39. Each of the nurses report to the operating room when his or her name is called.
A B C D

40. The athlete, together with his coach and several relatives, are travelling to the Olympic Games.
A B C D

41. Professor Duncan teaches both anthropology as well as sociology each fall.
A B C D

42. My brother is in California on vacation, but I wish he was here so that he could help me repair my car.
A B C D

43. I certainly appreciate him telling us about the delay in delivering the materials because we had planned to begin work tomorrow.
A B C D

44. The chemistry instructor explained the experiment in such of a way that it was easily understood.
A B C D

45. Rudolph Nureyev has become one of the greatest dancer that the ballet world has ever known.
A B C D

46. While searching for the wreckage of a unidentified aircraft, the Coast Guard encountered severe squalls at sea.
A B C D

47. Although a number of police officers was guarding the priceless treasures in the museum, the director worried that someone would try to steal them.
A B C D

48. Since it was so difficult for American Indians to negotiate a peace treaty or declare war in their language they used a universal understood form of sign language.
A B C D

49. Louis Braille designed a form of communication enabling people to convey and preserve their thoughts to incorporate a series of dots which were read by the finger tips.
A B C D

50. While verbalisation is the most common form of language in existence, humans make use of many others systems and techniques to express their thoughts and feelings.
A B C D

51. The need for a well-rounded education was an idea espoused by the Greeks in time of Socrates.
A B C D

52. Writers and media personnel sell theirselves best by the impression given in their verbal expression.
A B C D

53. In the spirit of the naturalist writers, that author's work portrays man's struggle for surviving.
A B C D

54. Stephen Crane's story is a clinical portrayal of man as an animal trapped by the fear and hunger.
A B C D

55. Their silly, whiny conversation on a child level was meant to create tension and heighten Nancy's fears and anxiety.
A B C D

56. For a long time, this officials have been known throughout the country as political bosses and law enforcers.
A B C D

57. Nora hardly never misses an opportunity to play in the tennis tournaments.
A B C D

58. Air pollution, together with littering, are causing many problems in our large, industrial cities today.
A B C D

59. Because of the severe snow storm and the road blocks, the air force dropped food and medical supplies close the city.
A B C D

60. Hummingbirds are the only birds capable to fly backward as well as forward, up, and down.
A B C D

61. Neither of the girls have turned in the term papers to the instructor yet.
A B C D

62. After studying all the new materials, the student was able to rise his test score by twenty-five points.
A B C D

63. The book that you see lying on the table belongs to the teacher.
A B C D

64. I suggest that he goes to the doctor as soon as he returns from taking the exam.
A B C D

65. She is looking forward to go to Europe after she finishes her studies at the university.
A B C D

66. They said that the man jumped off of the bridge and plunged into the freezing water.
A B C D

67. Mr. Anderson used to jogging in the crisp morning air during the winter months, but now he has stopped.
A B C D

68. The volume four of our encyclopedia set has been missing for two months.
A B C D

69. I do not know where could he have gone so early in the morning.
A B C D

70. The people tried of defending their village, but they were finally forced to retreat.
A B C D

71. The professor considered postponing the examination until the following week because the students' confusion.
A B C D

72. Having lost the election, the presidential candidate intends supporting the opposition despite the
A B C
objections of his staff.
D

73. The congressman, accompanied by secret service agents and aides, are preparing to enter the
A B C
convention hall within the next few minutes.
D

74. Because the torrential rains that had devastated the area, the governor sent the National Guard to
A B C
assist in the clean-up operation.
D

75. Lack of sanitation in restaurants are a major cause of disease in some areas of the country.
A B C D

76. Most Americans would not be happy without a color television, two cars, and working at an extra job.
A B C D

77. The lion has long been a symbol of strength, power, and it is very cruel.
A B C D

78. All the scouts got theirselves ready for the long camping trip by spending their weekends living in the
A B C D
open.

79. Nobody had known before the presentation that Sue and her sister will receive the awards for
A B C D
outstanding scholarship.

80. In 1927 Charles Lindbergh was the first to fly solo and nonstop from New York to Paris in such short
A B C D
time.

81. Until his last class at the university in 1978, Bob always turns in all of his assignments on time.
A B C D

82. When I last saw Janet, she hurried to her next class on the other side of the campus and did not have
A B C D
time to talk.

83. Before we returned from swimming in the river near the camp, someone had stole our clothes, and we
A B
had to walk back with our towels around us.
C D

84. Patrick was very late getting home last night, and unfortunately for him, the dog barking woke everyone
A B C
up.
D

85. He has been hoped for a raise for the last four months, but his boss is reluctant to give him one.
A B C D

86. After driving for twenty miles, he suddenly realised that he has been driving in the wrong direction.
A B C D

87. The Department of Foreign Languages are not located in the new building opposite the old one.
A B C D

88. The Nobel prize winning candidate, accompanied by his wife and children, are staying in Sweden
A B
until after the presentation.
C D

89. Neither of the scout leaders know how to trap wild animals or how to prepare them for mounting.
A B C D

90. Those of you who signed up for Dr. Daniel's anthropology class should get their books as soon
A B C
as possible.
D

91. I put my new book of zoology here on the desk a few minutes ago, but I cannot seem to find it.
A B C D

92. Martha being chosen as the most outstanding student on her campus made her parents very happy.
A B C D

93. Jane said she would borrow me her new movie camera if I wanted to use it on my trip to Europe.
A B C D

94. When Cliff was sick with the flu, his mother made him to eat chicken soup and rest in bed.
A B C D

95. My cousin composes not only the music, but also sings the songs for the major Broadway musicals.
A B C D

96. The geology professor showed us a sample about volcanic rock which dated back seven hundred years.
A B C D

97. The girl whom my cousin married was used to be a chorus girl for the Rockettes in Radio City Music
A B C D
hall in New York.

98. Ralph has called his lawyer last night to tell him about his problems, but was told that the lawyer
A B C
had gone to a lecture.
D

99. Some bumper stickers are very funny and make us laugh, yet another can make us angry because of
A B C
their ridiculousness.
D

100. The results of the test proved to Fred and me that we needed to study harder and watch less movies on
A B C D
television if we wanted to receive scholarships.

ANSWERS

Grammar
Test-1

Nouns

1. class – collective
   pupils – common
2. crowd – collective
3. bunch – collective
   grapes – common
4. streets – common
   cities – common
   crookedness – abstract
5. class – collective
   grammar – common
6. lie – abstract
7. voice – abstract
8. innocence – abstract
9. Wisdom – abstract
   strength – abstract
10. value – abstract
    time – abstract
11. verdict – abstract
    gentlemen – common
    jury – collective
12. team – collective
13. health – abstract
    happiness – abstract
14. soldiers – common
    bravery – abstract
15. Nelson – proper
    victory – abstract
    Trafalgar – proper
16. committee – collective
17. cleanliness – abstract
    godliness – abstract
18. fleet – collective
    ships – common
    harbour – common
19. Solomon – proper
    wisdom – abstract
20. honesty – abstract
21. elephant – common
    strength – abstract
22. Nile – proper
    year – common
23. feet – common
    room – common
    length – abstract
24. Beauty – abstract
    eyes – common
    beholder – common
25. economics – proper
    interest – abstract
    government – collective
    world – collective
    application – abstract

Test-2

1. a	**2.** c	**3.** d	**4.** a	**5.** b
6. a	**7.** c	**8.** d	**9.** c	**10.** d
11. a				

Test-3

Pronouns

A. **1.** they; herself; them; them **2.** they; them
3. them; they; them **4.** I; them
5. We; you; us **6.** you; I; you; I; I; me
7. them; me; I; you; you; them

B.

1. ourselves	**2.** herself	**3.** himself
4. itself	**5.** themselves	**6.** himself
7. myself	**8.** ourselves	**9.** themselves
10. ourselves		

C.

1. This; that	**2.** These; those	**3.** that
4. this; that	**5.** those	**6.** These; those

D.

1. whom	**2.** whom	**3.** Whom
4. Who	**5.** Whom	**6.** whom
7. What	**8.** Whom	**9.** Whom
10. Which	**11.** Who	**12.** Which
13. Which	**14.** What	**15.** What
16. What	**17.** Which	**18.** Which
19. Which	**20.** What	

E.

1. who	**2.** that	**3.** who
4. which	**5.** who	**6.** whose
7. which	**8.** who	**9.** whom
10. who	**11.** which	**12.** whose
13. who	**14.** whom	**15.** which

Test-4

Verbs

1. a	**2.** d	**3.** b	**4.** c	**5.** a
6. c	**7.** a	**8.** c	**9.** a	**10.** b

Test-5

Verbs

1. b	**2.** d	**3.** c	**4.** a	**5.** c
6. b	**7.** d	**8.** c	**9.** a	**10.** b
11. b	**12.** b	**13.** d	**14.** d	**15.** c

Test-5

Tenses

1. a	2. b	3. a	4. b	5. a
6. b	7. b	8. b	9. b	10. b
11. b	12. a	13. a	14. a	15. a
16. b	17. b	18. b	19. b	20. b
21. a	22. b	23. a	24. b	25. a
26. a	27. a	28. a	29. a	30. b

Test-7

Tenses

I.

1. b	2. a	3. b	4. c	5. b
6. d				

II.

1. b	2. d	3. c

III.

1. b	2. a	3. c	4. b	5. d
6. c	7. b	8. d	9. b	10. a

IV.

1. b	2. a	3. c	4. b	5. d
6. c	7. d	8. a	9. b	

Test-8

Subject–Verb agreement

1. is	2. is	3. was not
4. is	5. wins	6. are
7. moves	8. has	9. is
10. is	11. is	12. is
13. have been	14. are	15. are
16. deserve	17. is	18. was
19. was	20. was	21. is
22. has	23. was	24. were
25. have	26. am	27. was
28. has	29. is	30. were
31. is	32. believe	33. has been
34. was brought	35. has not finished	

Test-9

Active – Passive voice

1. b	2. d	3. a	4. d	5. c
6. a	7. a	8. b	9. a	10. d
11. a	12. a	13. b	14. a	15. d

Test-10

Articles

1. The; the	2. ø ; ø	3. a.; ø ; ø
4. the; a; ø; a	5. a; ø; the	6. ø ; the; ø
7. ø ; the;	8. ø; a, ø	9. ø ; ø ; the
10. the; the	11. ø ; an	12. The; a; the; the
13. ø ; the; ø	14. The	15. an; ø; the

Test-11

Articles

1. an	2. the	3. a	4. the	5. the
6. a	7. the	8. a	9. the	10. a
11. the	12. the	13. a	14. the	15. the

Test-12

Articles

1. Forecasting weather is a difficult technique.
2. Such an enormous crowd has rarely been seen at the airport.
3. He wanted the beggar to buy a meal with the money.
4. Terai is producing a lot of wheat now.
5. He is an Englishman, and therefore a European.
6. The cow is a useful domestic animal.
7. The milk in the cup is sour.
8. Education is not an end but a means to an end.
9. The English proved a strong power binding the country together.
10. Shall we go for a walk round the park?

Test-13

Articles

1. My shirt is made of nylon, but I prefer a cotton one.
2. One of the girls was in an evening dress.
3. He bought an iron for thirty rupees.
4. She takes a glass of fruit juice before breakfast.
5. Carpentry is not an occupation for a girl.
6. It is an honour to be praised by such a distinguished scholar.
7. He is always complaining that he has few neckties.
8. Not many people like poetry but quite a few like novels.
9. When he is at home, he reads two newspapers a day.
10. Fire destroys vast properties every year.

Test-14

Preposition

1. a	2. c	3. d	4. a	5. c
6. b	7. a	8. a	9. b	10. b
11. c	12. b	13. a	14. d	15. c
16. b	17. b	18. c	19. b	20. a
21. d	22. a	23. c	24. b	25. d
26. a	27. a	28. c	29. c	30. a
31. c	32. a	33. b	34. d	35. b
36. a	37. a	38. b	39. c	40. c
41. a	42. c	43. c	44. a	45. c
46. d	47. a	48. b	49. a	50. c

Test-15

Conjunctions

1. b	2. c	3. b	4. b	5. a

Test-16

Transformation

1. d	2. a	3. c	4. a	5. a
6. d	7. d	8. b	9. a	10. a
11. b	12. b	13. a	14. d	15. a
16. b	17. d	18. a	19. c	20. a

Test-17

Direct speech – Indirect speech

1. c	2. b	3. c	4. b	5. a
6. a	7. d	8. a	9. b	10. c
11. a	12. a	13. b	14. d	15. a
16. c	17. a	18. c	19. b	

Test-18

Direct speech – Indirect speech

1. a	2. c	3. d	4. a	5. b
6. a	7. c	8. d	9. b	10. d
11. b	12. b	13. c	14. c	15. a

Test-19

Error correction

1. C	2. A	3. D	4. D	5. A
6. D	7. B	8. B	9. D	10. D
11. A	12. B	13. C	14. C	15. D
16. B	17. A	18. A	19. A	20. A
21. A	22. C	23. C	24. D	25. C
26. D	27. D	28. C	29. B	30. B
31. A	32. D	33. A	34. D	35. A
36. A	37. B	38. D	39. B	40. D
41. B	42. C	43. B	44. B	45. C
46. C	47. A	48. D	49. C	50. C
51. D	52. B	53. D	54. D	55. A
56. A	57. A	58. B	59. D	60. B
61. B	62. D	63. C	64. B	65. B
66. C	67. A	68. A	69. A	70. A
71. D	72. B	73. B	74. A	75. B
76. D	77. D	78. B	79. C	80. D
81. B	82. B	83. B	84. C	85. A
86. C	87. B	88. B	89. B	90. C
91. A	92. A	93. A	94. C	95. A
96. C	97. C	98. A	99. C	100. A

"Reading maketh a full man; conference a ready man; and writing an exact man."

– Bacon, *Of Studies*

CHAPTER 4 WRITING SKILLS

WRITING ABILITY/COHERENCE

Composition can be defined as a sequential combination of sentences existing in various structural relationships, which fulfil communicative functions, that cannot be realised through individual sentences.

Composition has two aspects distinguishing it from a set of unrelated grammatical sentences: the formal and the functional. Since form is only the 'visible' realisation of underlying function, the latter is more basic to the nature of composition. At the formal level composition is characterised by the structural relationships between the constituent sentences, combining to form a text. These relationships determine the Cohesion of a written piece of composition.

At the functional level, composition is characterised by the rhetorical relationships between its parts as they combine to form a **message**. Thus the meaning of a compositional piece is conveyed through the rhetoric maintained by a writer. These rhetorical relationships determine the coherence of a written piece.

Thus, the characteristics that distinguish composition from a mere set of grammatical sentences are:

(a) Cohesion, or value–as–text; and

(b) Coherence, or value–as–message.

The advanced skills of composition are related, therefore, to the properties of cohesion and coherence.

Cohesion is purely a linguistic phenomenon, realised in composition through linguistic–chiefly, syntactic and lexical choices. Coherence, on the other hand, is a complex rhetorical phenomenon, realised in part through logical, meaningful use of points as well as socio-linguistic choices determined by the contexts of culture and situation.

In this chapter, you will encounter the following types of multiple choice tests to measure your writing ability.

1. **Jumbled /Scrambled Type:** In the following exercises (Test-1, & 2), the device of jumbled/ scrambled sentences/ paragraph/ short story/ short compositional piece has been employed to develop and test the above mentioned advanced skills. You are required to rearrange a jumbled series of elements so as to form an acceptable sentence/ paragraph/ short story/ a coherent piece of writing. By practising such exercises, you will find it easier to produce coherent and well organised pieces of writing.
2. **Missing Clauses (Test-3)/ Missing Sentences (Test-4) in Context:** By practising these exercises, you will develop cognitive skills of comprehension, analysis, synthesis, and evaluation. As a whole, such practice tests are very interesting and useful.
3. **Spellings Tests (Test 6 & 7):** The students will learn to use correct spellings after practising the following fifty-six test exercises in context. It's followed by a list of sixty-five difficult words which are generally spelt incorrectly by students.

TESTING COHERENCE/ ORGANISATIONAL SKILL

Introduction: In order to develop your coherence skills, you are advised to practise the following tests:

TEST – 1

Directions: For the following questions, read the sentences and choose the order in which they form a coherent piece of writing.

1. **Sentence 1:** His life was not confining and the delight he took in this observation could not be explained by its suggestion of escape.

Sentence 2: The day was beautiful and it seemed to him that a long swim might enlarge and celebrate its beauty.
Sentence 3: He seemed to see, with a cartographer's eye, that string of swimming pools, that quasi-subterranean stream that curved across the country.
Sentence 4: He was not a practical joker nor was he a fool but he was determinedly original and had a vague and modest idea of himself as a legendary figure.
Sentence 5: He had made a discovery, a contribution to modern geography; he would name the stream Lucinda after his wife.

(*a*) 1, 2, 3, 5, 4 (*b*) 3, 5, 1, 2, 4
(*c*) 2, 4, 5, 3, 1 (*d*) 1, 3, 5, 4, 2

2. **Sentence 1:** This is a bit of delta that they want to endure.
Sentence 2: River deltas are difficult places for map makers.
Sentence 3: And the civil engineers are as interested in performance as in speed and size.
Sentence 4: The river builds them up, the sea wears them down; their outlines are always changing.
Sentence 5: An island six kilometres long and with a total area of 1248 hectares is being created there.
Sentence 6: The changes in China's Pearl River delta, however, are more dramatic than these natural fluctuations.

(*a*) 1, 2, 3, 6, 4, 5 (*b*) 1, 3, 6, 2, 5, 4
(*c*) 2, 4, 6, 5, 3, 1 (*d*) 2, 4, 5, 6, 3, 1

3. **Sentence 1:** Updike graduated from high school in 1950; he was the president and the co-valedictorian of class.
Sentence 2: He was born in Reading, Pennsylvania on March 18, 1932.
Sentence 3: Updike was an only child; he lived with his father, his mother and his mother's parents.
Sentence 4: John Updike was one of the greatest modern writers of our time.
Sentence 5: At age thirteen his family moved to a farm in Shillington, Pennsylvania.
Sentence 6: He attended Harvard University from 1950 to 1954 and majored in English; he wrote stories and drew cartoons for the *Harvard Lampoon.*
Sentence 7: Then he and his wife moved to England, and Updike attended the Ruskin School of Drawing and Fine Arts at Oxford until 1955.
Sentence 8: In 1953 he married Mary E. Pennington.

(*a*) 1, 2, 3, 7, 8, 6, 4, 5
(*b*) 4, 2, 3, 5, 1, 6, 8, 7
(*c*) 4, 2, 5, 3, 6, 1, 7, 8
(*d*) 2, 1, 3, 8, 7, 6, 4, 5

4. **Sentence 1:** This was the first time in the history of the world that such a thing had been done.
Sentence 2: In 1909, they were ready to show the government how fast their machine could fly.
Sentence 3: It raised itself by its own power into the air and sailed forward.
Sentence 4: In the year 1902, Wilbur and Orville Wright made a machine that carried a man.
Sentence 5: It landed without damage.

(*a*) 4, 2, 1, 3, 5 (*b*) 4, 3, 1, 5, 2
(*c*) 1, 4, 3, 5, 2 (*d*) 4, 3, 5, 1, 2

5. **Sentence 1:** The Buddha stood in front of him.
Sentence 2: The robber, Angulimala followed.
Sentence 3: His face was shining with kindness for the robber.
Sentence 4: The Buddha walked on fearlessly.
Sentence 5: He swore and shouted at Gautama Buddha, but the latter only smiled at him kindly and continued to walk through the forest.
Sentence 6: This went on for several hours and Angulimala, tired at last sat down.

(*a*) 6, 1, 3, 2, 5, 4 (*b*) 4, 3, 6, 1, 2, 5
(*c*) 4, 2, 5, 6, 1, 3 (*d*) 1, 5, 2, 4, 6, 3

6. **Sentence 1:** For man is slowly changing all the time.
Sentence 2: We can only make a guess, of course, but we can be sure that he will be different from what he is today.
Sentence 3: Let us take an obvious example.
Sentence 4: Now, on an average, men are about three inches taller.
Sentence 5: What will man be like in the future-in 5000 or even 50,000 years from now?

Sentence 6: Man, even five hundred years ago, was shorter than he is today.
Sentence 7: Five hundred years is quite a short period of time, so we may assume that man will continue to grow taller.

(*a*) 5, 2, 1, 3, 6, 4, 7 (*b*) 6, 5, 2, 1, 3, 7, 4
(*c*) 3, 7, 5, 2, 6, 4, 1 (*d*) 4, 2, 5, 1, 7, 3, 6

7. **Sentence 1:** On the other hand, we tend to make less use of our arms and legs.
Sentence 2: Nowadays, we use our eyes all the time.
Sentence 3: However, it is likely that over a long period of time man's eyes will grow stronger rather than weaker.
Sentence 4: At the same time, however, our fingers will grow more sensitive because they are used a great deal in modern life, as in computer operation.
Sentence 5: These, as a result, may grow weaker.
Sentence 6: In fact, we use them so much that very often they become weaker and we have to wear glasses.

(*a*) 1, 5, 2, 6, 3, 4 (*b*) 2, 6, 3, 1, 5, 4
(*c*) 4, 3, 2, 6, 1, 5 (*d*) 2, 3, 1, 4, 5, 6

8. **Sentence 1:** His head and most of his legs, too, were covered with long hair.
Sentence 2: He was quite small, much smaller than the people of today.
Sentence 3: He had seen no fire except the flames of the rumbling volcanoes which filled the earth with their smoke and lava.
Sentence 4: He wore no clothes.
Sentence 5: His forehead was low and his jaw was like the jaw of a wild animal which uses its teeth both as fork and knife.
Sentence 6: The early ancestor of the human race was a very ugly and unattractive mammal.
Sentence 7: The heat of the sun and the biting wind of the cold winter had coloured his skin dark brown.
Sentence 8: He had very thin but strong fingers which made his hands look like those of a monkey.

(*a*) 3, 1, 8, 6, 2, 7, 5, 4
(*b*) 8, 4, 3, 1, 7, 5, 2, 6
(*c*) 1, 7, 2, 5, 3, 6, 8, 4
(*d*) 6, 2, 7, 1, 8, 5, 4, 3

9. **Sentence 1:** Kodaikanal is famous for its bananas and plums.
Sentence 2: It is situated on the southern side of upper Palani Hills.
Sentence 3: Kodaikanal, a charming hill station near Madurai is surrounded by lovely, tall trees.
Sentence 4: The pride of Kodaikanal is the Kunnji which is a very rare flower.
Sentence 5: Its slopes, big rocks and beautiful waterfalls attract many tourists every year.
Sentence 6: Its temperate climate has made it one of the most popular health resorts in India.
Sentence 7: From mid-April to June, Kodaikanal is paradise for holiday makers.

(*a*) 1, 4, 7, 5, 2, 6, 3
(*b*) 3, 2, 5, 7, 6, 1, 4
(*c*) 4, 3, 2, 1, 7, 6, 5
(*d*) 5, 7, 4, 1, 3, 6, 2

10. **Sentence 1:** It may be that they were not irritated by the digressions and irrelevancies that interrupted the narration.
Sentence 2: It is deplorable that on this account they should be less and less read.
Sentence 3: Readers in the past seem to have been more patient than the readers of today.
Sentence 4: But some of the novels that suffer from these defects are among the greatest that have been written.
Sentence 5: There were few diversions and they had more time to read novels of a length that seems to us now inordinate.

(*a*) 5, 1, 3, 4, 2 (*b*) 3, 2, 1, 4, 5
(*c*) 3, 5, 1, 4, 2 (*d*) 5, 3, 1, 2, 4

11. **Sentence 1:** "No," she replied firmly.
Sentence 2: When I questioned her, she repeated the same story that I had over heard.
Sentence 3: Dissatisfied with her replies, I persisted in my questioning, "Did nobody hear any sound? Did nobody wake up?"
Sentence 4: "Well, I did. And what's more, I heard a strange laugh," I said.
Sentence 5: I noticed that Mr Rochester's room was being tidied and when I glanced inside, I was taken aback to see Grace Poole sitting there calmly with her sewing.

Sentence 6: I was shocked at Grace's brazenness, convinced that she was the one who had tried to set the master's room on fire.

(*a*) 2, 3, 6, 1, 4, 5 (*b*) 5, 2, 6, 3, 1, 4
(*c*) 5, 6, 2, 1, 4, 3 (*d*) 5, 6, 2, 1, 3, 4

12. **Sentence 1:** Fearing disappointment I decided to make inquiries myself at Thornfield, and so I hurried on.
Sentence 2: Only the outer shell of the wall remained.
Sentence 3: I thought that I should first make inquiries about Mr Rochester, and find out whether he was in or not.
Sentence 4: There was the silence of death about the place, and not a soul was to be seen.
Sentence 5: In my mind's eye I pictured the beautiful mansion, but when I arrived there I saw, to my horror, not a stately house but a blackened ruin!
Sentence 6: The grounds surrounding it were laid waste.
Sentence 7: No roof, no battlements, no chimneys.
(*a*) 3, 1, 5, 6, 2, 7, 4
(*b*) 5, 6, 4, 7, 1, 3
(*c*) 1, 5, 6, 7, 2, 4, 3
(*d*) 1, 3, 5, 4, 2, 6, 7

13. **Sentence 1:** When lights fuse, furniture gets rickety, pipes get clogged, or vacuum cleaners fail to operate, wives automatically assume that their husbands will somehow put things right.
Sentence 2: Even husbands who can hardly drive a nail in straight are supposed to be born electricians, carpenters, plumbers and mechanics.
Sentence 3: Wives tend to believe that their husbands are infinitely resourceful and versatile.
Sentence 4: It is a question of pride as much as anything else.
Sentence 5: The worst thing about the do-it yourself game is that sometimes husbands live under the delusion that they can do anything even when they have been repeatedly proved wrong.
(*a*) 3, 2, 1, 5, 4 (*b*) 1, 3, 4, 5, 2
(*c*) 5, 4, 3, 2, 1 (*d*) 3, 2, 5, 1, 4

14. **Sentence 1:** Acting on the contention that facts are sacred, reporters can cause untold suffering to individuals by publishing details about their private lives.
Sentence 2: However, this freedom can be easily abused.
Sentence 3: In democratic countries any efforts to restrict the freedom of the Press are rightly condemned.
Sentence 4: Newspapers exert such tremendous influence that they can not only bring about major changes to the lives of ordinary people but can even overthrow a government.
Sentence 5: Though we may enjoy reading about the lives of others, it is extremely doubtful whether we would equally enjoy reading about ourselves.
Sentence 6: Stories about people often attract far more public attention than political events.
(*a*) 3, 2, 5, 6, 1, 4 (*b*) 3, 2, 6, 5, 1, 4
(*c*) 3, 2, 6, 5, 4, 1 (*d*) 3, 6, 2, 5, 1, 4

15. **Sentence 1:** The statistics collected during a survey confirm it in India.
Sentence 2: The beauty of the world doesn't exist for them.
Sentence 3: It is unfortunate that cases of blindness are on the increase in India.
Sentence 4: The blind feel rejected and dejected.
Sentence 5: Increasing number of hospitals and Eye Care Clinics fail to treat people.
(*a*) 3, 1, 2, 5, 4 (*b*) 3, 5, 1, 4, 2
(*c*) 3, 1, 5, 2, 4 (*d*) 3, 1, 5, 4, 2

16. **Sentence 1:** Already most men spend most of their lives looking after and waiting upon machines.
Sentence 2: And if they do not get their meals when they expect them, they grow sulky and refuse to work or burst with rage and blow up and spread ruin and destruction all round them.
Sentence 3: Machines were made to be man's servants.
Sentence 4: And the machines are very stern masters.
Sentence 5: Yet he has grown so dependent on them that they are in a way to become his masters.
Sentence 6: They must be kept at the right temperature.

(*a*) 3, 5, 4, 1, 6, 2 (*b*) 3, 5, 1, 4, 2, 6
(*c*) 3, 1, 5, 4, 6, 2 (*d*) 3, 5, 1, 6, 4, 2

17. **Sentence 1:** Cosmetics, like shampoos and eye make up, are tested on monkeys and rabbits which may lead to serious health problems and even death of the animals.
Sentence 2: We have no right to protest against slavery and other forms of discrimination when we ourselves are party to it.
Sentence 3: Live and let live must be our motto.
Sentence 4: We have the intellectual capacity to realise that the animal's rights and interests should be well guarded.
Sentence 5: Man has, since time immemorial, been cruel towards animals.
Sentence 6: Animals have been hunted, caged, tamed, domesticated and even killed for their hides and other valuable body parts.
(*a*) 5, 6, 1, 2, 3, 4 (*b*) 3, 5, 6, 1, 2, 4
(*c*) 5, 1, 6, 2, 4, 3 (*d*) 5, 6, 1, 2, 4, 3

18. **Sentence 1:** They were very hard working.
Sentence 2: They were both interested in making things that would 'go'.
Sentence 3: When they began a thing nothing discouraged them.
Sentence 4: Wilbur and Orville Wright were two brothers who lived in Ohio, U.S.A.
Sentence 5: So after school hours, they spent much of their time in their father's workshop.
Sentence 6: Whatever they did whether in work or at play, they were always together.
(*a*) 4, 1, 3, 2, 6, 5 (*b*) 4, 1, 3, 6, 2, 5
(*c*) 4, 1, 3, 6, 5, 2 (*d*) 4, 1, 3, 5, 6, 2

19. **Sentence 1:** Some people think that fashionable clothes and surroundings raise their status in life.
Sentence 2: Today people follow fashions for many reasons.
Sentence 3: Then, other people follow these fashions so that they can also look important.
Sentence 4: For example, they want others to think that they belong to a special class of society.
Sentence 5: New fashions may be adopted immediately by well-known people, including athletes, film stars and political figures.
(*a*) 1, 4, 2, 3, 5 (*b*) 2, 1, 4, 5, 3
(*c*) 2, 4, 5, 3, 1 (*d*) 2, 5, 1, 4, 3

20. **Sentence 1:** Very little work can be done these days without the use of paper, and we can even say that modern civilisation depends on paper.
Sentence 2: The Chinese who invented paper several thousand years back used the inner bark of certain trees for making paper.
Sentence 3: Perhaps the most important contribution of forests to modern civilisation is that they provide the raw material for making paper.
Sentence 4: Today, paper is made mostly from wood, bamboo and certain types of grasses.
Sentence 5: The paper on which this book has been printed may have been made out of wood or bamboo and certain types of grasses.
(*a*) 3, 2, 4, 5, 1 (*b*) 2, 3, 1, 5, 4
(*c*) 1, 2, 3, 5, 4 (*d*) 3, 2, 5, 4, 1

21. **Sentence 1:** The body fits over the hand of the puppeteer who puts a thumb into one of the puppet's arms, one or two fingers go into the other arm and the remaining fingers in the head.
Sentence 2: One variety, the glove or fist puppet, consists of a hollow head attached to a glove or a piece of cloth used as the puppet's body.
Sentence 3: These puppets can pick up and throw things and can gesture strongly with their head and arms.
Sentence 4: Hand puppets are the most common puppets.
Sentence 5: Most glove puppets have no legs or feet.
(*a*) 4, 2, 3, 1, 5 (*b*) 4, 1, 2, 3, 5
(*c*) 4, 2, 1, 5, 3 (*d*) 4, 2, 1, 3, 5

22. **Sentence 1:** "In another ten years or so, circuses in India will totally disappear unless the government does something about it soon," warns Shankaran, the owner of Gemini circus.
Sentence 2: Though the owners of the circuses do not tell exactly how much money they earn for every show we can guess that they collect approximately ten thousand rupees per show.
Sentence 3: Circuses are no longer as popular as

they used to be either in urban or in rural areas.

Sentence 4: Even in Delhi during winter, which is the most important season, the shows are only half full.

Sentence 5: The number of people who come to see the circus is decreasing very fast.

(*a*) 5, 1, 3, 4, 2 (*b*) 3, 5, 4, 2, 1
(*c*) 3, 1, 5, 4, 2 (*d*) 1, 3, 5, 4, 2

23. Sentence 1: The highest circus salary is not more than three thousand rupees but in terms of costs the expenses are very high.

Sentence 2: Let us look at some facts about circuses.

Sentence 3: In Delhi, for example rent for a circus ground comes to about Rs. 10,000/- per show.

Sentence 4: The average monthly wage of these workers is not more than one thousand rupees.

Sentence 5: Both Gemini and Amar circuses employ about four hundred people.

(*a*) 2, 1, 3, 5, 4 (*b*) 2, 1, 4, 3, 5
(*c*) 2, 1, 5, 3, 4 (*d*) 2, 1, 3, 5, 4

24. Sentence 1: Money can buy everything but it cannot buy peace or happiness or a ticket to heaven.

Sentence 2: He thinks that money will give him more freedom to enjoy himself and to have lots of fun.

Sentence 3: He is never satisfied with what he has got but always wants something more even though he knows that in the end, he cannot buy peace or happiness or a ticket to heaven.

Sentence 4: The more he has, the more he wants.

Sentence 5: He thinks he will not be anyone's slave but be his own master.

Sentence 6: But soon he becomes the slave of money.

Sentence 7: Man works hard to earn more and more money and saves a lot of it.

(*a*) 7, 2, 5, 6, 4, 1, 3 (*b*) 7, 5, 2, 6, 4, 1, 3
(*c*) 7, 2, 5, 6, 4, 3, 1 (*d*) 7, 5, 2, 6, 4, 3, 1

25. Sentence 1: I left my house five minutes later than usual and I saw my bus approaching the bus stop.

Sentence 2: Now I can ask : why do people smoke?

Sentence 3: I began to run, I was too slow.

Sentence 4: I waited ten minutes for another bus and I was still gasping for air when it arrived.

Sentence 5: The next day I gave up smoking.

Sentence 6: Four weeks ago I was late for work.

Sentence 7: For the first few days I was very irritable, but now I feel much better.

(*a*) 7, 4, 1, 3, 2, 5, 6(*b*) 2, 6, 1, 3, 4, 5, 7
(*c*) 6, 1, 3, 4, 5, 2, 7(*d*) 6, 1, 3, 4, 5, 7, 2

JUMBLED SENTENCES

TEST – 2

Directions: Below are given some words and phrases which have been jumbled up. Choose the correct alternative which rearranges them to form meaningful sentences.

1. [1]spycom scandal has been/ [2]for nearly ten days/ [3]of the/ [4]undoubtedly the most/ [5]the disruption of Parliament/ [6]unfortunate fallout

(*a*) 4, 6, 3, 1, 5, 2 (*b*) 5, 2, 1, 6, 3, 4
(*c*) 1, 2, 4, 3, 5, 6 (*d*) 4, 6, 1, 2, 5, 3

2. [1]before the national legislature/ [2]a minister/ [3]to explain/ [4]rather than/ [5]in a television studio/ [6]his legislation/ [7]has been forced

(*a*) 4, 7, 1, 6, 2, 3, 5
(*b*) 2, 7, 3, 6, 5, 4, 1
(*c*) 2, 1, 3, 4, 6, 5, 7
(*d*) 7, 1, 2, 4, 3, 6, 5

3. [1]strength of/ [2]itself/ [3]is that/ [4]the/ [5]to quantity/ [6]biotechnology/ [7]limit/ [8]it doesn't

(*a*) 2, 7, 8, 1, 5, 3, 4, 6
(*b*) 1, 3, 7, 5, 8, 6, 4, 2
(*c*) 4, 3, 8, 1, 6, 5, 2, 7
(*d*) 4, 1, 6, 3, 8, 7, 2, 5

4. [1]beneficial/ [2]useless/ [3]organic/ [4]sheer scale/ [5]may be/ [6]for the soil/ [7]fertilisers/ [8]but in terms of/ [9]they are

(*a*) 3, 7, 5, 1, 6, 8, 4, 9, 2
(*b*) 1, 3, 5, 6, 8, 9, 7, 4, 2
(*c*) 3, 6, 8, 4, 1, 5, 7, 9, 2
(*d*) 2, 9, 4, 8, 6, 5, 7, 3, 1

5. [1]plunge/ [2]essential/ [3]organised/ [4]take the/ [5]Civil Services/ [6]planning/ [7]before you really/ [8]is very/ [9]into the
   (*a*) 3, 6, 8, 2, 7, 4, 1, 9, 5
   (*b*) 3, 6, 1, 4, 8, 2, 9, 5, 7
   (*c*) 1, 4, 2, 7, 3, 6, 8, 9, 5
   (*d*) 6, 7, 3, 1, 9, 5, 4, 2, 8

6. [1]the state/ [2]itself/ [3]the conflict/ [4]and/ [5]is as old as/ [6]between/ [7]human/ [8]man/ [9]history
   (*a*) 6, 8, 9, 3, 1, 4, 2, 5, 7
   (*b*) 1, 3, 5, 6, 8, 9, 7, 4, 2
   (*c*) 3, 6, 8, 4, 1, 5, 7, 9, 2
   (*d*) 2, 9, 4, 8, 6, 5, 7, 3, 1

7. [1]and rousing them / [2]the terrorist / [3]struggle of / [4]played an / [5]the political / [6]movement / [7]important / [8]conciousness / [9]role in raising / [10]of the people / [11]to move for the / [12]independence
   (*a*) 2, 6, 4, 7, 9, 5, 8, 10, 11, 3, 12
   (*b*) 2, 6, 4, 7, 9, 3, 8, 11, 10, 12, 5
   (*c*) 1, 3, 6, 8, 7, 9, 10, 4, 5, 12, 11, 2
   (*d*) 6, 4, 10, 1, 11, 2, 12, 5, 3, 7, 8, 9

8. [1]next morning / [2]tennis / [3]I could / [4]when I / [5]sound of / [6]woke the / [7]hear the / [8]someone / [9]rolling the / [10]court
   (*a*) 5, 6, 9, 3, 7, 4, 8, 1, 2, 10
   (*b*) 4, 6, 1, 3, 7, 5, 8, 9, 2, 10
   (*c*) 7, 3, 9, 5, 6, 4, 2, 10, 8, 1
   (*d*) 10, 2, 3, 1, 6, 7, 8, 5, 9, 4

9. [1]the wild grapes / [2]smell of wine / [3]that grow / [4]it was late / [5]made the land and / [6]in August / [7]and / [8]profusely all over / [9]wind / [10]the island.
   (*a*) 4, 6, 7, 1, 3, 8, 10, 5, 9, 2
   (*b*) 1, 3, 6, 4, 10, 8, 2, 9, 5, 7
   (*c*) 3, 10, 5, 9, 4, 6, 2, 7, 1, 8
   (*d*) 8, 6, 5, 2, 10, 1, 7, 3, 9, 4

10. [1]we take / [2]women's / [3]more seriously / [4]the business / [5]of / [6]than we have / [7]we run the / [8]done in / [9]but not families / [10]individuals / [11]unless / [12]education / [13]the past / [14]risk of educating / [15]or a nation.
    (*a*) 1, 2, 12, 3, 9, 10, 15, 11, 7, 14, 4, 5, 8, 13, 6
    (*b*) 2, 12, 3, 10, 9, 11, 5, 7, 14, 5, 4, 8, 6, 1, 13
    (*c*) 11, 1, 2, 12, 3, 6, 8, 13, 7, 14, 10, 15, 9, 5, 4
    (*d*) 11, 1, 4, 5, 2, 12, 3, 6, 8, 13, 7, 14, 10, 9, 15

11. [1]remembered / [2]masochistic / [3]the notion / [4]is purely / [5]that instruction / [6]administered / [7]and dated / [8]to be / [9]must be / [10]in discomfort.
    (*a*) 3, 5, 8, 1, 9, 6, 10, 2, 4, 7
    (*b*) 1, 5, 9, 10, 6, 2, 3, 4, 7, 8
    (*c*) 3, 5, 8, 1, 9, 6, 10, 4, 2, 7
    (*d*) 9, 10, 2, 4, 7, 1, 3, 5, 8, 6

12. [1]to make sure / [2]it is the business / [3]to do so / [4]that those willing / [5]highest standards of / [6]of the community / [7]keep them going / [8]secondary education are allowed / [9]and able to put up / [10]in accordance with the / [11]schools and
    (*a*) 2, 6, 1, 4, 9, 11, 7, 10, 5, 8, 3
    (*b*) 2, 6, 3, 9, 10, 11, 5, 4, 1, 7, 8
    (*c*) 1, 4, 3, 5, 6, 10, 11, 8, 7, 2, 9
    (*d*) 10, 5, 6, 7, 9, 11, 1, 2, 8, 3, 4

13. [1]English should be / [2]there are / [3]universities / [4]secondary schools / [5]probably few / [6]who argue that / [7]curriculum of / [8]in India / [9]banished altogether / [10] and / [11]today / [12]from the
    (*a*) 1, 9, 10, 2, 3, 6, 4, 5, 8, 12, 7, 11
    (*b*) 2, 5, 8, 11, 6, 1, 9, 12, 7, 4, 3, 10
    (*c*) 11, 12, 6, 7, 1, 3, 5, 8, 2, 9, 4, 10
    (*d*) 2, 5, 8, 11, 6, 1, 9, 12, 7, 4, 10, 3

14. [1]a language / [2]when it is / [3]it must be / [4]constantly heard / [5] clear to / [6]with any seriousness / [7]can be acquired / [8]any one who has studied / [9]that a language / [10]proficiently only
    (*a*) 1, 2, 4, 6, 7, 10, 3, 5, 9, 8
    (*b*) 3, 5, 8, 1, 6, 9, 7, 10, 2, 4
    (*c*) 9, 7, 6, 2, 4, 2, 10, 1, 3, 5
    (*d*) 7, 9, 1, 4, 10, 6, 5, 3, 2, 8

15. [1]reasons only / [2], / [3]it is not / [4]dislike it / [5]for economic / [6]resist it / [7]possible to / [8]language of / [9]cultivate English as a / [10]and learn it / [11]interaction in people who

(*a*) 5, 8, 4, 6, 11, 9, 10, 3, 2, 1, 7
(*b*) 3, 7, 9, 8, 11, 4, 2, 6, 10, 5, 1
(*c*) 3, 7, 5, 1, 9, 2, 10, 11, 4, 6, 8
(*d*) 4, 6, 11, 9, 10, 3, 2, 1, 5, 7, 8

16. [1]fall / [2] do / [3] birds / [4]through / [5]in the / [6] migratory / [7]fly / [8]here / [9]?
(*a*) 1, 4, 5, 8, 7, 6, 3, 2, 9
(*b*) 3, 2, 7, 6, 5, 1, 4, 8, 9
(*c*) 2, 6, 3, 7, 4, 8, 5, 1, 9
(*d*) 6, 3, 1, 5, 9, 2, 4, 7, 8

17. [1]to concentrate/ [2]and / [3]India / [4]in recent years / [5]upon / [6]science / [7]has / [8]the teaching of / [9]technology / [10]had
(*a*) 3, 4, 7, 10, 1, 5, 8, 9, 2, 6
(*b*) 2, 3, 4, 7, 10, 1, 5, 8, 6, 9
(*c*) 5, 8, 6, 3, 4, 7, 1, 10, 2, 9
(*d*) 3, 7, 10, 4, 1, 5, 8, 6, 2, 9

18. [1]Criterion / [2]what / [3]of / [4]for / [5]kind / [6]excellence/ [7]that / [8]? / [9]is
(*a*) 2, 5, 3, 6, 4, 1, 9, 7, 8
(*b*) 2, 5, 3, 1, 4, 6, 9, 7, 8
(*c*) 1, 4, 6, 2, 3, 7, 9, 5, 8
(*d*) 2, 5, 3, 1, 4, 6, 7, 9, 8

19. [1]November / [2]stable / [3]although / [4]then / [5]on / [6] from / [7]have a / [8]we / [9]again / [10]population / [11]different from / [12]one / [13], / [14] summer / [15] the
(*a*) 3, 2, 1, 6, 4, 5, 7, 10, 11, 14, 9, 13, 8, 12, 15
(*b*) 3, 1, 10, 13, 11, 2, 12, 9, 8, 7, 14, 5, 4, 15, 6
(*c*) 4, 6, 5, 8, 2, 7, 10, 9, 11, 13, 15, 14, 12, 3, 1
(*d*) 4, 6, 1, 5, 8, 7, 2, 10, 9, 13, 3, 11, 15, 14, 12

20. [1]Edison / [2]office / [3]one / [4]of the / [5]New York newspapers / [6]next day / [7]into the / [8]editor / [9]walked / [10]of / [11]biggest / [12]package / [13]with a / [14]under his arm / [15]of the
(*a*) 1, 9, 7, 2, 4, 8, 10, 3, 5, 3, 11, 12, 14, 15
(*b*) 6, 1, 9, 7, 2, 10, 3, 4, 11, 15, 5, 13, 12, 14
(*c*) 6, 1, 9, 2, 4, 8, 10, 3, 15, 11, 5, 13, 12, 14
(*d*) 3, 4, 5, 6, 9, 7, 8, 10, 11, 12, 13, 14, 15, 1, 2

21. [1]I'll / [2]able / [3]that / [4]be / [5]afraid / [6]never / [7]to do / [8]I am
(*a*) 1, 6, 4, 5, 7, 3, 8, 2
(*b*) 8, 5, 1, 6, 4, 2, 7, 3
(*c*) 8, 2, 7, 3, 1, 6, 4, 5
(*d*) 1, 6, 4, 2, 7, 3, 5, 8

22. [1]I was / [2]relieved / [3]once again / [4]heavy / [5]on my / [6]burden / [7]of the / [8]mind / [9]concentrate / [10]able to / [11]studies / [12] on my.
(*a*) 1, 2, 3, 7, 6, 5, 8, 10, 9, 12, 4, 11
(*b*) 3, 1, 2, 7, 4, 6, 5, 8, 10, 9, 12, 11
(*c*) 2, 7, 4, 6, 5, 11, 3, 1, 10, 9, 12, 8
(*d*) 2, 7, 4, 6, 5, 8, 1, 10, 9, 3, 12, 11

23. [1]too / [2]for / [3]led a / [4]existence / [5]I had / [6]long / [7]cloistered
(*a*) 5, 3, 6, 4, 1, 7, 2
(*b*) 5, 3, 7, 4, 2, 1, 6
(*c*) 5, 7, 2, 6, 4, 3, 1
(*d*) 5, 3, 4, 6, 2, 1, 7

24. [1]low / [2]curious / [3]mirthless / [4]was a / [5]laugh / [6]and / [7] , / [8]it
(*a*) 8, 4, 2, 5, 7, 1, 6, 3
(*b*) 8, 4, 5, 2, 7, 1, 6, 3
(*c*) 8, 4, 1, 2, 5, 7, 6, 3
(*d*) 2, 4, 5, 6, 1, 7, 3, 8

25. [1]I / [2]could / [3]work / [4]are the / [5]for my / [6]receive / [7]best / [8]words / [9]your / [10]present / [11]of praise
(*a*) 1, 2, 3, 5, 7, 8, 11, 4, 10, 9, 6
(*b*) 9, 8, 11, 5, 3, 4, 7, 10, 1, 2, 6
(*c*) 1, 2, 3, 5, 10, 8, 6, 9, 7, 11, 4
(*d*) 9, 10, 3, 5, 7, 4, 8, 1, 2, 11, 6

MISSING CLAUSES AND SENTENCES

In order to test their writing skills, the students are advised to practise the following exercises:

Missing Clauses

TEST – 3

Directions: Choose the best alternative from the choices given below to fill in the *Clauses* missed in the following letter.

I

Dear Mr Atherton

Demand for services: your ref 435/ rd

In March this year I bought from you a used red Ultra van, year of manufacture 1987, licence number D 425 OVR, motor number A45693B, prince £ 6,000.

Since then, every time I have driven the vehicle another fault has come to light. [1]____,

John Brook and Sons, which lists 23 major faults. You will note that they also suspect that the mileometer has been tampered with.

I have discussed this matter with you over the telephone and at your showrooms on several occasions. You will have letters [2]____ on 4th April, 14th April, and 29th May, none of which I have received replies to. You took the vehicle back for repairs between 18th April and 8th May, [3]____.

I have now been in contact with Mrs Chowdhary of the Dewsbury Trading Standards Office. [4]____ that it is your legal duty to correct the faults listed and that her office will support my claim for redress. This would include an element to compensate me for loss of business [5]____.

1. (*a*) I enclose a copy of a report made by my garage,
(*b*) I dispatch a copy of a report made by my garage,
(*c*) I enclose a copy of a report sorted out by my garage,
(*d*) I enclose a list of a report devised by my garage

2. (*a*) that I have written to you
(*b*) that I am writing to you
(*c*) that I wrote to you
(*d*) that I would write to you

3. (*a*) but the damages continue to be apparent
(*b*) as the results remain the same
(*c*) however, the condition does not alter
(*d*) but the faults continue to be apparent

4. (*a*) She reminds me
(*b*) Mrs Chowdhary notifies
(*c*) The office corrects me saying
(*d*) She assures me

5. (*a*) as the car has been out of use
(*b*) while the vehicle has been out of service
(*c*) since I couldn't use my car
(*d*) for the obvious reason that the vehicle couldn't be driven by me

II

Directions: Choose the best alternative from the choices given below to fill in the *Clauses* missed in the following passage.

Before Helen Keller was two years old, [1]____. She lived in a world of confusion until [2]____, the woman who was to change Helen's life. On 3rd March 1987, [3]____ at the Keller home. It was three months [4]____. Miss Sullivan's efforts were rewarded. The deaf and blind [5]____ verbally.

1. (*a*) she started having pain in her eyes and ears
(*b*) she went blind and became deaf
(*c*) she lost her sight and her hearing
(*d*) she became deaf and dumb

2. (*a*) her meeting with Anne Mansfield Sullivan
(*b*) Anne Mansfield Sullivan, had not arrived
(*c*) the coming of Anne Mansfield Sullivan
(*d*) she was escorted by Anne Mansfield Sullivan

3. (*a*) Miss Sullivan met
(*b*) Miss Sullivan stopped
(*c*) Miss Sullivan came
(*d*) Miss Sullivan arrived

4. (*a*) before Helen had turned seven
(*b*) ahead of Helen's seventh birthday
(*c*) before Helen's seventh birthday
(*d*) earlier than Helen's birthday

5. (*a*) Helen Keller started hearing and speaking
(*b*) Helen Keller learnt to speak
(*c*) Helen Keller learnt to communicate
(*d*) Helen Keller learnt to gesticulate

III

Although twins have always been a source of curiosity, [1]____, since they occur once in every 86 births.

About one-third of all twins are identical or single twins. Identical twins have the same genes and hence the same sex, hair, eyes, blood type and bone and tooth structure. Some identical twins are mirror images of each other. For example, [2]____ the other right handed. As young children, some identical twins may develop their own private language. Identical twins have an especially keen intuition and [3]____ even when away from each other. In fact, even when they are separated at birth and raised apart, [4]____. They may pursue the same careers, have the same interests or die within days of each other.

In contrast to identical twins, [5]____ and are not necessarily of the same sex. In some families there is a hereditary tendency to produce fraternal twins, but [6]____ in the population.

1. (*a*) they are not so absurd actually
   (*b*) they are not so uncommon statistically
   (*c*) they are a common occurrence
   (*d*) they are infrequent statistically
2. (*a*) some may be left-handed
   (*b*) one may use the left-hand more frequently, which makes
   (*c*) one will be left-handed
   (*d*) one may be left-handed
3. (*a*) they often seem to think alike
   (*b*) they casually contemplate
   (*c*) they infrequently speak alike
   (*d*) they are often seen together
4. (*a*) they confound others alike
   (*b*) they look to each other alike
   (*c*) identical twins develop startling similarities
   (*d*) identical twins develop dissimilarities
5. (*a*) fraternal twins develop a different assortment of genes
   (*b*) fraternal twins are not dissimilar
   (*c*) fraternal twins inherit a separate assortment of genes
   (*d*) fraternal twins inherit the same assortment of genes
6. (*a*) identical twins occur at specific intervals
   (*b*) identical twins occur at random
   (*c*) identical twins develop at random
   (*d*) identical twins occur in abundance

IV

The rattlesnake, often considered the deadliest of all North American snakes, has often been the subject of research and discussions among naturalists. This snake earns its name from the presence of rings of tough skin on its tail that remain when sloughing or the dropping off of skin, occurs. [1]____, it begins to move its tail, a motion that causes the rings of hardened skin to make a rattling noise.

Most naturalists believe that [2]____ that results from the nervousness of the reptile; [3]____ the rattlesnake is attempting to convey a warning to its possible victim. Studies have revealed that the [4]____ that gives a signal before striking and in fact this reptile is the only species that has rattles. However both the bull snake and the fox snake also [5]____ whenever they become nervous. Whether or not the rattlesnake should be called "the gentleman among snakes" because of the noise it makes before striking is an interesting question.

1. (*a*) When a rattlesnake is made angry
   (*b*) However, a rattlesnake grows furious
   (*c*) As a rattlesnake is indignant
   (*d*) Whenever a rattlesnake is agitated
2. (*a*) perhaps the noise is made by the snake unintentionally
   (*b*) this noise is an involuntary reaction
   (*c*) the noise is an infrequent action
   (*d*) this noise is a deliberate action
3. (*a*) because they do not plane that
   (*b*) the naturalists do not infer that
   (*c*) the naturalists cannot, however, imagine
   (*d*) they do not think that
4. (*a*) the rattlesnake is the only decent snake
   (*b*) the rattlesnake is the only venomous snake
   (*c*) it is mainly the only snake
   (*d*) it's the venomous snake only
5. (*a*) vibrate their tails rapidly
   (*b*) move their tails quickly
   (*c*) make a rattling sound
   (*d*) snake themselves violently

V

Birds of paradise have brighter colours than any other birds in the world. [1]____, that they are cousins of the common crow. However, only the male birds of paradise have bright-coloured feathers; [2]____. The more than 30 different kinds of birds of paradise inhabit mostly the hot, rainy forests of New Guinea, [3]____ in Australia.

As long ago as 500 years, the skins of these birds were used in trading in the East Indies. Before their skins were used, [4]____, leading to the misconception that the birds never had feet. There was a popular story told that these beautiful creatures were not able to stop flying until they died. The scientist Linnaeus even [5]____ which means "without feet."

1. (*a*) this should be useless to imagine
   (*b*) it would be difficult to guess
   (*c*) one needs to guess
   (*d*) who will like to guess
2. (*a*) the females are very dull
   (*b*) the feathers of the female are very dull
   (*c*) the feathers of the female are very bright
   (*d*) the feathers of the female have very dull colour
3. (*a*) although a few birds can be seen
   (*b*) nevertheless a few species are found
   (*c*) although many species are located
   (*d*) although a few species are found
4. (*a*) their feet were always cut off
   (*b*) their feet were always buried
   (*c*) their feet were not seen
   (*d*) their toes were always cut off
5. (*a*) baptized them
   (*b*) gave them a name
   (*c*) used to call them
   (*d*) christened them

VI

Laird Gogins is a fifty-seven-year old inventor [1]____ to harness the power of the wind. [2]____ his invention could eventually provide all the electrical power needed by the United States. A network of his wind machines across the country could transfer electricity produced in a windy spot to a place where the air is still. Just one of Gogins' wind machines will produce eighty megawatts of electricity, [3]____ by all the windmills in the United States today. In addition, [4]____ to build than a windmill. Gogins says that if just one percent of the available wind power in the United States were captured, it could provide one hundred percent of the electrical power now consumed. [5]____ that the wind will probably never become the country's sole power source.

1. (*a*) which has found a device
   (*b*) who has developed a device
   (*c*) when he develops a device
   (*d*) by whom a device is found
2. (*a*) He claims that
   (*b*) Gogins declares that
   (*c*) Gogins plans that
   (*d*) Gogins will claim that
3. (*a*) which is ten time the power may be produced
   (*b*) but which is many more than the power produced
   (*c*) what is higher than the power produced
   (*d*) which is ten times the power produced
4. (*a*) the wind machine is cheaper
   (*b*) the wind machine may be cheaper
   (*c*) the wind machine is more cheaper
   (*d*) the wind machine is the cheapest
5. (*a*) So, the inventor states
   (*b*) However, the inventor admits
   (*c*) In spite of it, the inventor admits
   (*d*) Consequently the inventor decides

VII

According to the recent poll, a large majority of Americans are in favour of retaining the present 55-mile-an-hour speed limit. This speed limit was imposed in 1973 when [1]____. Seventy-five percent of the persons surveyed think [2]____. Fuel is saved. Moreover, there is a decrease in the highway death rate. Easterners and older people, rather than young adults, [3]____ for retention of the law.

Likewise, only 23 percent of the people surveyed [4]____ for trucks. The trucking industry contends that truck engines work more efficiently at higher speeds and that trucks travelling at higher speeds reach markets more quickly, thereby saving consumers' money. [5] ____ that trucks on certain highways are already involved in a disproportionate number of fatal highway accidents.

1. (*a*) while fuel shortages became mandatory
   (*b*) when fuel shortages became crucial
   (*c*) when fuel was not to be found at all
   (*d*) when fuel was in plenty
2. (*a*) that the law is a good one
   (*b*) however, that the law is nasty
   (*c*) how the law could be implemented
   (*d*) what the law conveys
3. (*a*) are more likely to argue
   (*b*) more or less argue
   (*c*) can argue mostly
   (*d*) will perhaps argue rarely
4. (*a*) favour a varied speed limit
   (*b*) favoured more speed limit
   (*c*) favour a higher speed limit
   (*d*) favoured a larger speed limit
5. (*a*) Some of the persons polled argue
   (*b*) Some of the men invited state
   (*c*) Taken into account, others argue
   (*d*) Having polled, they think

VIII

A: "Professor Jones, [1] ____"

B: "Of course, Gus. Come in and [2] ____. I have about a half-hour before my faculty meeting. Let me move this chair closer to my desk.

A: "Thanks. I've come to talk to you about my grade on my last economics project. I want to know [3] ____ an "F".

B: "Well, Gus, your approach was so similar to that of another student in the class that [4] ____ that you'd done the calculations yourself."

A: "I did work closely with my roommate Steve, but let me explain why. A week before the project was due, [5] ____ to do my research. Steve agreed to help me with the project the night before it was due. We stayed up all night in order to finish it on time. The calculations were really my own."

B: "Well, you'd been given a month to work on the project. Wouldn't it have been better to get a head start rather than to wait until the last minute? Each student was supposed to prepare this project individually. I'm afraid that my decision remains the same. However, next week we will be studying the government's role in running the economy. If you're willing to make an oral presentation about the subject, [6] ____."

A: "Thank you, Professor Jones. I'll have my oral report ready for class on Friday."

1. (*a*) may I be seen by you a moment?
   (*b*) may I see you a moment?
   (*c*) could I enter and see you a moment?
   (*d*) might I see you a moment?
2. (*a*) have a seat
   (*b*) have a chair
   (*c*) why don't you sit?
   (*d*) could you sit?
3. (*a*) how I was given
   (*b*) why was I given
   (*c*) why I was given
   (*d*) how should I get
4. (*a*) that I seriously doubted
   (*b*) that about you I seriously thought
   (*c*) that I firmly believe
   (*d*) that I seriously doubt
5. (*a*) I was too dependent to do research
   (*b*) I was too bored to do research
   (*c*) I was too lethargic to do research
   (*d*) I was too sick
6. (*a*) I'll be all praise
   (*b*) I'll give you no points
   (*c*) I'll give you extra credit
   (*d*) I'll give you extra work

IX

The value of a Diamond is estimated according to four qualities – carat, clarity, colour and cut. [1] ____, since a diamond's weight in carats can be determined by an electronic scale. The remaining characteristics have a partly subjective basis.

Clarity refers to the external cracks or to the internal flaws left in the diamond [2] ____. The third quality is colour and in general, the less the colour, the better the diamond. A tinge of gray or yellow can lower a diamond's value. On the other hand, a clear, bright yellow diamond, called a 'fancy yellow', commands a higher price than the top-quality white diamonds.

Finally, the cut of a diamond is judged by the shape of the stone, its light refraction and [3] ____.

1. (*a*) However, only carat, a unit of weight, is an objective measure
   (*b*) But, only carat, a unit of weight, is a subjective measure
   (*c*) And, only carat, a weight unit is an objective way
   (*d*) Only carat, a weight unit is a subjective way
2. (*a*) when it succumbs under great heat and pressure
   (*b*) when it is found due to great heat and pressure
   (*c*) when it is formed under intense heat and pressure
   (*d*) when it operates because of intense heat and pressure
3. (*a*) and well it may be
   (*b*) and how well it is polished
   (*c*) but it is polished so well
   (*d*) and however, it is polished so brightly

X

Woman: "If I leave for Europe in two months, [1] ____, I'd better get my passport picture taken soon. Is there a photographer nearby?"

Man: "There's one just off campus, [2] ____. I think there's a cheaper one near the downtown bank, [3] ____. Why don't you check around?"

1. (*a*) as I've been planning
   (*b*) as I'm planning
   (*c*) as I think
   (*d*) as I'm thinking
2. (*a*) but he takes a lot of time
   (*b*) but he's faulty
   (*c*) but he's expensive
   (*d*) but he's cheap
3. (*a*) but could I be mistaken?
   (*b*) but am I mistaken?
   (*c*) but am I can be mistaken
   (*d*) but I could be mistaken

XI

Because goldfish can be kept easily in small ponds and aquariums, [1] ____, but like any other pets, they must have proper care and the right kind of place to live.

A two-inch fish requires a minimum of two gallons of water containing sufficient oxygen to support life. Some oxygen will make its way into the water of an aquarium from the air [2] ____; plants in an aquarium also help to furnish oxygen. Snails help to keep an aquarium clean. Thus, with plenty of plants and snails, the water in an aquarium does not have to be changed frequently. [3] ____ that goldfish not be overfed. They can be fed such things as dried insects and shrimp in addition to commercially prepared goldfish food, [4] ____. Even then, they should not be given more food [5] ____.

1. (*a*) they make domestic companions
   (*b*) they make a good water game
   (*c*) they make intimate friends
   (*d*) they make good pets
2. (*a*) which purifies the surface
   (*b*) that touches the surface
   (*c*) that flows into the surface
   (*d*) which cleans the surface
3. (*a*) It is mandatory
   (*b*) It is significant
   (*c*) It is important
   (*d*) It is beneficial
4. (*a*) since they may not be fed more than once a day
   (*b*) however they should ever be fed once a day only
   (*c*) and they must not be fed more than once a day
   (*d*) but they should never be fed more than once a day
5. (*a*) than can be consumed
   (*b*) than could be consumed
   (*c*) which can be consumed
   (*d*) than could consume

XII

Man: "Would you like to go to the beach this afternoon? Bill and Mary are coming too."

Woman: "I'm sorry, [1]____. I need to get the blouse that goes with my pants suit. They had to order it, [2]____."

1. (*a*) and I was just starting out for shopping.
   (*b*) I was just leaving out shopping
   (*c*) but I was just going out shopping
   (*d*) I was just moving away shopping
2. (*a*) and it should've arrived yesterday
   (*b*) which just arrived yesterday
   (*c*) but it had arrived yesterday
   (*d*) and it just arrived yesterday

XIII

Man: "How did you like the performance?"

Woman: "Generally speaking, it was very good. The part of the maid was played beautifully, [1]____ the man who played the salesman was too dramatic to be realistic."

1. (*a*) but I proposed (*b*) but I planned
   (*c*) but I thought (*d*) but I described

XIV

Woman: "Your room is a mess! Your clothes are all over the floor and [1]____. And when was the last time you [2]____?"

Man: "You ought to try to be neater. Clean it up now, and [3]____, we'll all go on a picnic."

1. (*a*) your bed is unmade
   (*b*) your bed is undone
   (*c*) your bed is unpacked
   (*d*) your bed is unclean
2. (*a*) settled up your toys
   (*b*) stored up your toys
   (*c*) picked up your toys
   (*d*) raised up your toys
3. (*a*) when you're ended
   (*b*) when you're finished
   (*c*) when you're over
   (*d*) when you're concluded

XV

John: "[1]____ that they can send a man between one and three tomorrow afternoon. But someone has to be at home to let him in."

Clara: "[2]____ I'll have to take off from work in the afternoon. We can't go any longer without a telephone."

1. (*a*) The telephone company asks
   (*b*) A telephone company will say
   (*c*) The telephone company says
   (*d*) Telephone company opines
2. (*a*) Well, I guess (*b*) No, I feel
   (*c*) Yes, I assess (*d*) Well, I don't guess

Missing Sentences

TEST – 4

I

Man: [1] ____

Woman: Yes. I'd like to buy a book for my brother. He just started hiking a lot in the mountains recently.

Man: Then do you want to get him this book on hiking gear?

Woman: No, I think he has it.

Man: [2] ____

Woman: Oh, that's too grim. After all, it's going to be a present. Besides, he knows quite a bit about first aid anyway. What I want is something educational about the things he sees on his hikes. For example, the rocks or the plants or the birds.

Man: I see. Well, this little handbook has picture of all the birds.

Woman: Oh, that's too simple.

Man: But it sells very well.

Woman: What kind of criterion for excellence is that?

Man: Then take Peterson's bird guide. He is a recognised authority and his text has a great deal of explanatory material. The only trouble is, I'll have to order it for you, because we're out of it. [3]____

Woman: No, I don't have enough time to wait for an order to come in. [4]____

Man: Yes, Tory's book on plants is similar in quality to Peterson's bird book. And it's lightweight, so your brother can put it in his backpack. In addition, it tells about the edibility of various plants, in case he gets lost and hungry.

Woman: Do you have it in stock?

Man: Yes, here it is.

Woman: [5]____. Thank you.

1. (*a*) Can I do something for you?
   (*b*) May I help you?
   (*c*) Shall I help you?
   (*d*) Will I do a favour for you?
2. (*a*) What about this book on plants and herbs?
   (*b*) How about this book on self-medication?
   (*c*) How about this book on nursing?
   (*d*) What about this first aid book?
3. (*a*) Would that be all right?
   (*b*) That could be all right
   (*c*) How beneficial that would be?
   (*d*) Is it a lovely offer?
4. (*a*) Has Peterson written a book on plants?
   (*b*) I want it at the earliest.
   (*c*) Do you have another good book on birds?
   (*d*) Do you have a similar book on plants?
5. (*a*) I think that's too expensive.
   (*b*) I think I'll take it.
   (*c*) I think I should order it.
   (*d*) I think it's a good book.

II

Man: Hello. Are you the person who has a house for sale?

Woman: [1]____.

Man: Well the ad says that it has four bedrooms and three baths, just what I need for my family of six. [2]____.

Woman: I prefer not to quote a price over the phone, but let's say it's in the neighbourhood of $150,000. I would also require a down payment of $40,000. [3]____.

Man: Well, I'm not sure I can afford such a large down payment, but I guess it wouldn't hurt to see the house. If you tell me how to get to Churchill Avenue from South Florida Street, my wife and I'll be over.

Woman: [4]____.

1. (*a*) Definitely (*b*) Yes, I am
   (*c*) No, I'm not (*d*) Pardon?
2. (*a*) May I ask how much you'll prefer?
   (*b*) May I ask how many you want for it?
   (*c*) May I ask how much you want for it?
   (*d*) May I ask how much will you pay for it?
3. (*a*) Why don't you come by and take a look?
   (*b*) Why shouldn't you come and test the house?
   (*c*) How about living in the house and see?
   (*d*) Why couldn't you look at the model?
4. (*a*) Positively (*b*) Sure, why not?
   (*c*) Indefinitely (*d*) I'll be obliged

III

Kamaladevi Chattopadhyaya was born on 3 April 1903 into an educated family in Mangalore. Her grandmother was a great reader. [1]____. And the more she read the more she learnt. Kamala's mother was also well-read. Those were the days when women were not much cared for [2]____. They were expected to do only household work. Besides, they had no share in the family property.[3]____.

Kamala's mother knew all this. [4]____. She wanted to do all she could to help Indian women become literate and free. [5]____. The first thing that she did for Kamala was to take her to Annie Besant to get her blessings. Now Annie Besant was a great freedom fighter who participated in our country's freedom struggle and fought for the ideas of this extraordinary lady.

1. (*a*) Also she has been a willing learner.
   (*b*) She was a willing learner.
   (*c*) She was also a willing learner.
   (*d*) She too is a willing learner.

2. (*a*) Parents did not believe in educating their daughters.
   (*b*) Parents preferred to use them as drudges.
   (*c*) Parents believed in teaching their daughters.
   (*d*) Parents neglected them to a large extent.
3. (*a*) According to law, women could not inherit the property of their parents.
   (*b*) According to law, women could inherit the property of their parents.
   (*c*) Law said that, the women should not inherit the property of their parents.
   (*d*) Stringent laws deprived them of all rights.
4. (*a*) So she took to domestic work.
   (*b*) So she agreed to be a drudge.
   (*c*) So she took to social work.
   (*d*) So she supported the socialist pattern of society.
5. (*a*) Women's information was up-to-date in her mind.
   (*b*) Women's education was uppermost in her mind.
   (*c*) Her daughter's cause was primary in her mind.
   (*d*) Her ideas were most welcome to her daughter.

IV

Anandwan tells the story of courage and faith. It began with a small piece of forest and, six patients and an investment of just fourteen rupees. [1]____. But the patients were treated with great love and care. [2]____. Today with aid from different agencies and people in India and abroad, Anandwan has many buildings, farms and a fully-equipped hospital. For his remarkable work, Baba Amte has received numerous awards including the Padma Shri in 1971 and the Damien-Dutton Award for Leprosy Aid in 1983. [3]____.

1. (*a*) Everyone lived in thatched shelters.
   (*b*) Each patient was left to himself.
   (*c*) Shelter was a problem of the community.
   (*d*) Courage is a reward in itself.
2. (*a*) Occasionally the water was supplied to them.
   (*b*) By and by wells were dug and the land cultivated.
   (*c*) Arrangements were made for wells and foodgrains.
   (*d*) However, they dig the wells and cultivate the land.
3. (*a*) But he remains assertive and less involved in the work he started more than forty years ago.
   (*b*) Inspite of it he remains humble and occupied in the work he started more than forty years ago.
   (*c*) He remained humble and engrossed in himself all the time.
   (*d*) Yet he remains humble and totally involved in the work he started more than forty years ago.

V

____. I remember how once I almost broke my mother's nose. She used to bowl to me in the small room in our house where we played our 'daily match' with a tennis ball.

(*a*) I started playing tennis when I was an infant.
(*b*) As a kid, I started crying while playing cricket.
(*c*) I started playing cricket when I was a small boy.
(*d*) I started crawling when I was one year old.

VI

Two years passed before the brothers decided to start again on their travels. This time, they took Marco with them. ____. They travelled to Acro and from there rode overland to Hormuz on the Persian Gulf.

(*a*) He was then only seventeen years old.
(*b*) He was then a popular actor.
(*c*) He only is seventeen years old at the moment.
(*d*) He was refused to accompany them.

VII

The novel, however, in the ultimate analysis is not so much about a woman's futile search for emancipation as about her quest for identity which is again seen in terms of a deep-rooted tradition.

____

But as far as her roles of wife and mother are concerned, she finds herself plagued with an inability to do anything actively.

(*a*) The novel revolves around Savitri.
(*b*) Savitri's role in the novel is very much conventional.
(*c*) Savitri seeks self-realization right from the beginning of the novel.
(*d*) Savitri is potrayed as a role model right in the end of the novel.

VIII

Each year there is a period of greatest growth for a tree. [1] ____. During this period, the cells grow, they divide; one cell divides into two, each of these two cells divide again, etc. [2] ____. The outer cells are blast cells; these will grow again next spring.

1. (*a*) In cold weather, this is the period of summer season.
(*b*) During this period, the trees and plants grow rapidly.
(*c*) During this period, the trees are all snow-covered.
(*d*) In cold climates, this period is the season of spring.

2. (*a*) The new cells so formed are of two kinds.
(*b*) The new cells so formed were found to be of two kinds.
(*c*) How can you divide the new cells?
(*d*) Can the new cells so formed be divided further.

IX

Kanrar then got a job with a Calcutta newspaper, but gave it up when he found it too strenuous. ____.

(*a*) Sometime later, he hired the GSI.
(*b*) A few months later he was hired by the GSI.
(*c*) A little later he was invited for a job by the GSI.
(*d*) Later he was called by the GSI.

X

The novel, however, in the ultimate analysis is not so much about a woman's futile search for emancipation as about her quest for identity which is again seen in terms of a deep-rooted tradition. [1] ____. But as far as her roles of wife and mother are concerned, she finds herself plagued with an inability to do anything activity.

1. (*a*) The novel revolves around Savitri.
(*b*) Savitri's role in the novel is very much conventional.
(*c*) Savitri seeks self-realization right from the beginning of the novel.
(*d*) Savitri is potrayed as a role model right in the end of the novel.

XI

____. He died when I was eighteen and I didn't feel as if I'd lost a grandfather; I felt as if I'd lost my closest friend. He was a wonderful man and had been a famous press photographer.

(*a*) As a child, I was particularly close to my maternal grandfather.
(*b*) As a child, I worked very hard for myself.
(*c*) As a child, I was particularly close to my friend
(*d*) As a child, I was particularly close to my photographer.

XII

Alone and sad in the cave, the blind mother elephant tossed her head unhappily. 'Many days have passed.[1] ____? What could have happened to him?

[2] ____. Oh, my son is not by my side to tell me about the trees and plants and grass and the coming rain. Now, indeed, I am blind, for my son was my pair of eyes.'

1. (*a*) Where is my husband?
(*b*) Where is my son?

(*c*) Could I see my son?
(*d*) Will my son come back?

2. (*a*) I hope he has not enjoyed the nature alone.
(*b*) I hope he has not been caught by man.
(*c*) It's not easy to catch him.
(*d*) I can't see with my eyes.

XIII

The King lived for several years in the forest. He gradually learnt about the beauty of the world around him. He learnt to care for creatures smaller than himself. ____.

(*a*) The creatures turned paler and weaker.
(*b*) He grew weaker, cunning and selfish.
(*c*) He grew strong, wise and selfless.
(*d*) He turned by and by a selfish person.

XIV

Once upon a time there lived a king in Central India. ____. He looked at himself constantly, in mirrors, in pools of water, even in other people's eyes when they spoke to him.

(*a*) He was handsome but very vain.
(*b*) He spoke about his smart looks everywhere.
(*c*) Life for him was just beauty and vanity.
(*d*) How handsome did he look!

XV

[1] ____. When it noticed me, it wagged its tail in a playful manner and started jumping around as if challenging me for a game. I ignored it and started reading a magazine while muttering curses under my breath. [2] ____. My chair overturned and I fell backwards with the confounded beast on top of me, still deriving pleasure out of licking my face. Out of terror, fright and disgust I let out a scream for help and struggled to get up. [3] ____. At this point I realised again that hell had broken loose and it was going to land straight on my head any moment.

1. (*a*) The man looked quiet, harmless and docile sitting there in a corner.
(*b*) The beast was creating chaos.
(*c*) The beast looked quiet, harmless and docile sitting there in a corner.
(*d*) The beast pounced on me instantly.

2. (*a*) Then suddenly, it jumped at me and started licking my face.
(*b*) Now it assaulted me with all its strength.
(*c*) How ferociously did it jump at me to bite my ear!
(*d*) Suddenly, it caught my face within its paws.

3. (*a*) During the assault, I caught its tail.
(*b*) In this cacophony I stepped on its tail.
(*c*) But I couldn't succeed.
(*d*) Now I event into a rage.

XVI

The bird has forelimbs which are modified into wings each bearing three clawless digits. [1] ____. The bones forming the skeleton are spongy, light in weight and contain air cavities. Birds have a horny beak. [2] ____. The most important characteristic is that they are oviparous. The egg has a yolk which is covered with albumen. [3] ____.

1. (*a*) The hindlimbs are adapted for walking, perching or swimming.
(*b*) The hindlimbs are used for their activities.
(*c*) The hindlimbs walk, perch or swim.
(*d*) Walking, perching or swimming are done by their hindlimbs.

2. (*a*) Four walls form their heart.
(*b*) The heart has four rooms.
(*c*) The heart is four-chambered.
(*d*) The heart can be divided into four compartments.

3. (*a*) Dawn is the time for them to get up and night to sleep.
(*b*) The birds are up early with the dawn and rest at night.
(*c*) The birds are up early with dawn and rest in night.
(*d*) The birds are early up at dawn and rest in night.

XVII

[1] ____. This means basically that they lack structure that enables us to divide a human utterance into words. Language is a signalling system. [2] ____. In other words, it is a system of vocal sound. [3] ____.

Thus we can sum up and say that language is a signalling system which operates with symbolic vocal sounds, and which is used by some group of people for the purpose of communication and social co-operation.

1. (*a*) Animals' utterances are not audible.
   (*b*) An animal's language is not decipherable.
   (*c*) Man's cries are not articulate.
   (*d*) Animal cries are not articulate.
2. (*a*) Sound is unique to human beings.
   (*b*) It is that which is spoken.
   (*c*) How can you utter a sound?
   (*d*) It is that which is written.
3. (*a*) These sounds then are symbolic as well as representational.
   (*b*) The vocal system is implicit as well as explicit.
   (*c*) These sounds can be treated as symbolic without being representational.
   (*d*) The whole sound system depends on the vibrations of vocal cords.

XVIII

1 ____. I asked her to make a choice between me and that dog. That was it. 2 ____. "Dog? 3 ____? You heartless fiend, you called him a dog? How dare you address my little baby as a dog? If you show your face to me again, I will personally dismantle each and every bone in your body! Understand."

1. (*a*) I decided to reach the veterinary hospital with him.
   (*b*) I decided to come to the point.
   (*c*) How could I call the baby a dog?
   (*d*) I decided to avoid the issue.
2. (*a*) That was when all hell broke loose.
   (*b*) This was when we were living in a fool's paradise.
   (*c*) Hell was broken loose at the juncture.
   (*d*) Life is hellish for a dog.
3. (*a*) Is life hellish for a dog?
   (*b*) You called him a dog?
   (*c*) Dog is a faithful animal.
   (*d*) Aren't you badly mistaken?

XIX

The sky over the valley was blue, something it never was when the factories were operating. ____ Few had gone far this year, of course, because of the fear of retrenchments. The resort towns on the coast, as a result, were having a lean season.

(*a*) The sky was clearer than it had been for six months.
(*b*) It was only blue when the furnaces had been shut down.
(*c*) They were closed, and most of the factory workers were on holidays.
(*d*) It was the Christmas season, when the factories always closed down.

XX

Harry arrived home a little after 7p.m., much later than his daughters had expected. ____. May and Hilda understood, without needing to ask, that he had made few sales that day. They did their best to stay cheerful, talk positively and try to change the gloom that surrounded him.

(*a*) There was a sad, grey look of defeat in his eyes.
(*b*) He told them that things had gone badly again.
(*c*) They demanded that he tell them where he had been.
(*d*) He brought with him presents for Mary and Hilda.

SPELLINGS

In order to write correct English, the students are advised to practise the following Spelling exercises.

TEST – 5

Directions: In each of the paragraphs below, five of the underlined words have been spelt *incorrectly*. Identify the option, which lists the five *incorrectly* spelt words.

1. Bharat Shah's [1]**arrest** will [2]**compell** the film industry to [3]**perge** itself and [4]**prompt** it to look for an [5]**alternative** source of film finance. Film-makers do not avail of legal funds for their projects

due to the [6]**strengent** terms laid down by banks and [7]**financial** [8]**institutions**. An [9]**exorbitent** rate of interest, a [10]**collateral** of Rs 50 lakh and a track record of three hit films are among the [11]**criteria** that these institutions lay down before [12]**disbersing** money. These conditions need to be relaxed in order to make financing easier for film-makers.

The five **incorrectly** spelt words are:
(*a*) 1, 2, 9, 10, and 12
(*b*) 2, 3, 6, 9, and 12
(*c*) 3, 5, 10, 11, and 12
(*d*) 1, 3, 6, 9, and 11

2. It may rightly be concluded the country's ills stem from the fact that the [1]**bureaucracy** is [2]**inefficeint**, [3]**corrupt** and lacks work [4]**ethics**. Of [5]**course**, [6]**politians** have been aiding and [7]**abeting** this [8]**incompetance** all along. [9]**Socialism** is also [10]**responsble** for this. In fact, democracy as it is [11]**practised** in India, is "of the bureaucrats, by the bureaucrats and for the bureaucrats".

The five **incorrectly** spelt words are:
(*a*) 1, 3, 5, 9, 11
(*b*) 2, 5, 6, 9 and 10
(*c*) 2, 6, 7 , 8 and 10
(*d*) 3, 4, 7, 8, and 10

3. Looking at the [1]**dwindling** population of the NDA, it appears that the [2]**poeple** of India want the [3]**Governmont** to play fast, in the manner of one-day cricket, hitting [4]**boundries** and sixers. The NDA [5]**Government** should [6]**serioussly** consider the wake-up call as the Indian citizens are maturing, besides becoming [7]**incresingly** [8]**impatient**. They want a fast game and instant results.

The five **incorrectly** spelt words are:
(*a*) 1, 2, 4, 5, and 8
(*b*) 2, 3, 5, 6, and 7
(*c*) 2, 3, 4, 6, and 7
(*d*) 1, 2, 3, 7, and 8

4. The most passionate and [1]**unpredictable** creature on earth is [2]**arguably** the artist. And when brush strokes of [3]**color** collide with lyrics and melody the result is sure to be a [4]**spectaculer** blend of sensual energy. This ultimate union of sight and sound is [5]**embodid** in Neel Paban Baruah, [6]**eminant** painter and Lalit Kala Akademi member, and Dipali Barthakur, [7]**legendary** singer of the 1950s affectionately known as the "nightingale of Assam". More [8]**specifically** in the way the couple has tackled [9]**personel** tragedy with a [10]**quiet** dignity.

The five **incorrectly** spelt words are:
(*a*) 3, 4, 5, 6, and 9
(*b*) 2, 3, 7, 8, and 10
(*c*) 1, 4, 6, 7, and 9
(*d*) 1, 4, 5, 8, and 10

5. Society cannot live by the service sector alone. Reduction in [1]**industrail** production will result in a shortage of goods in the country. China today has become a [2]**vibrent** economy due to its industrial [3]**development**. India cannot [4]**aford** to ignore its industrial health. [5]**Regenerating** sick industries and creating new ones by [6]**simplifing** procedures should be undertaken as this will increase employment [7]**oppurtunities** for the manpower that does not find openings in the service sector.

The five **incorrectly** spelt words are:
(*a*) 1, 3, 4, 5, and 7
(*b*) 1, 2, 4, 6, and 7
(*c*) 2, 3, 5, 6, and 7
(*d*) 2, 3, 4, 5, and 7

6. Delhi has had a [1]**cheqeured** [2]**existence** right from the [3]**primevial** past to the ultra-modern present. It has been an [4]**eternal** [5]**metropolise** where 17 cities have arisen since the time of the Indraprastha of the Pandavas when Hastinapur was their [6]**kingdom**. The vast [7]**sweap** of the rise and fall of [8]**civilisations** and dynasties finds a befitting chronicle in *The* [9]***Millinium*** *Book on New Delhi*, complete with [10]**colourful** photographs that vividly capture both the past and the present. Truly the city has been the beloved of all and [11]**mistress** of none.

The five **incorrectly** spelt words are:
(*a*) 1, 2, 4, 6, and 9
(*b*) 3, 5, 7, 10, and 11
(*c*) 3, 5, 8, 9, and 10
(*d*) 1, 3, 5, 7 and 9

7. The fact that [1]**ilegal** construction, use of [2]**inferior** material and [3]**improper** [4]**maintainance** of buildings cause [5]**destruction** and high [6]**casaulties** is not unknown. Builders, [7]**buraucrats** and politicians are all [8]**coniving** in [9]**perpetrating** this fraud. Those who make money at the cost of [10]**innocent** lives should be put behind bars.

The five **incorrectly** spelt words are:
(*a*) 1, 4, 6, 7, and 8
(*b*) 1, 2, 4, 5, and 7
(*c*) 2, 3, 6, 8, and 10
(*d*) 1, 3, 5, 8, and 9.

8. Your [1]**assesment** that the problem in Kashmir has gone beyond the [2]**purview** of a [3]**bilatarel** [4]**dialogue** with Pakistan is correct. No self-respecting nation should tolerate such prolonged [5]**indignity**. We need to toughen our stand and adopt counter-[6]**insurgency** as a solution because we will never negotiate with terrorists or with Pakistan. The terrorists should pay a price for the [7]**merciless** killings of [8]**innocent** [9]**civelians**. The Center should provide [10]**assistence** in the [11]**maintainence** of and order as we have already suffered incalculable losses—not just in lives but [12]**prestige** as well.

The five **incorrectly** spelt words are:
(*a*) 1, 5, 8, 10, and 12
(*b*) 2, 4, 6, 8, and 11
(*c*) 3, 5, 7, 9, and 12
(*d*) 1, 3, 9, 10, and 11

9. Having [1]**appointed** vice-[2]**chancelors** of his choice at several Haryana universities, [3]**Cheif** Minister Om Prakash Chautala is [4]**iminently** [5]**qualified** to reap [6]**acedamic** dividends. Next week, at its [7]**anual** [8]**convocation**, the Kurukshetra University will confer an [9]**honorary** D. Litt. on Chautala. Not bad going for a dropout.

The five **incorrectly** spelt words are:
(*a*) 1, 2, 3, 4, and 9
(*b*) 1, 2, 4, 5, and 8
(*c*) 2, 3, 4, 6, and 7
(*d*) 1, 3, 4, 7, and 8

10. Business @ Speed of Thought may be the order of the day but with it comes the stress of [1]**forever** keeping the body going. [2]**Deits** are the first [3]**casulty** and the clock takes its [4]**toll**. Tea should be drunk because it's healthy. As simple as that. [5]**Antioxidents** or free radical [6]**scavengers** from five or six cup of tea a day will go a long way in keeping your [7]**cholestrol** level down, [8]**lesen** chances of heart or cancer attack. It's good for your eyes, teeth and plenty else.

The five **incorrectly** spelt words are:
(*a*) 1, 2, 4, 6, and 8
(*b*) 2, 3, 5, 7, and 8
(*c*) 1, 3, 4, 6, and 7
(*d*) 2, 3, 5, 6, and 7

11. *Zubeida* is work worthy of [1]**aplause**. Benegal offered Karishma that rare thing—a [2]**textured** lead role. And she [3]**imersed** herself in it, becoming a [4]**temptous** girl who [5]**abondans** her child to marry her already married lover. Karishma's performance is [6]**effortless** enough to make her [7]**heavyweight** costars like Manoj Bajpai and Rekha look [8]**strained**. *Zubeida* is easily her best work. It is also a path-breaking [9]**carear** move.

The five **incorrectly** spelt words are:
(*a*) 1, 3, 4, 5, and 9
(*b*) 1, 2, 5, 6, and 9
(*c*) 2, 4, 5, 6, and 7
(*d*) 2, 3, 6, 8, and 9

12. The [1]**continance** of a banking [2]**secratariat** in the Finance Ministry—like many such sagas of [3]**endurence**—has the [4]**politicans'** blessings. Back in 1985, when V.P. Singh was finance minister, he promised to abolish the banking secretary's post. He wove in and out of the prime [5]**ministership** meanwhile, and banking was [6]**libaralised**, but the secretary still stays because he doubles as the politician's finger in the [7]**pie**.

The five **incorrectly** spelt words are:

(*a*) 1, 2, 4, 5, and 7
(*b*) 2, 3, 5, 6, and 7
(*c*) 1, 3, 4, 6, and 7
(*d*) 1, 2, 3, 4, and 6

13. As long as we keep treating a political problem as one of law and order, we will get [1]**tronched**. There is no doubt that in the [2]**diplometic** game—as in hockey and cricket—Pakistan holds all the [3]**aces** and [4]**nuetralises** our efforts to gain [5]**asendancy**. In the [6]**circumstances**, it is also impossible to ensure that [7]**innocent** people do not become [8]**sacrificial** [9]**pauns** in Kashmir.

The five **incorrectly** spelt words are:

(*a*) 1, 2, 3, 6, and 8
(*b*) 2, 4, 6, 8, and 9
(*c*) 1, 2, 4, 5, and 9
(*d*) 1, 3, 4, 7, and 8

14. Madhavrao Scindia's reaction to his mother will shows his true [1]**character**. His mother's [2]**angish**, reflected in her will, shows that he is a Congress [3]**psycophant**. His battle to get hold over his mother's property despite her having [4]**disinherited** him shows the disregard he has for the law. He should [5]**quit** [6]**politices**, [7]**concentrate** on his court cases and [8]**ceese** trying to become a mass [9]**leider**.

The five **incorrectly** spelt words are:

(*a*) 1, 3, 5, 8, and 9
(*b*) 1, 2, 5, 6, and 9
(*c*) 2, 3, 6, 8, and 9
(*d*) 1, 3, 5, 7, and 9

15. T.K. John's tactless comment, despite holding public office was [1]**apalling**. His [2]**irrational** remark about the Gujarat quake being [3]**devine** punishment makes a [4]**mockery** of the concept of a loving and forgiving God. Instead, he made God out to be [5]**cruel** and [6]**vengeful** [7]**tyrent**. John's brash [8]**utterences** had a streak of [9]**proselytising**. This [10]**serreptitious** exercise only brings disgrace to the Christian community.

The five **incorrectly** spelt words are:

(*a*) 1, 3, 7, 8, and 10
(*b*) 1, 2, 4, 6, and 9
(*c*) 2, 4, 7, 9, and 10
(*d*) 2, 3, 6, 8, and 9

16. The four schemes [1]**advertised** by the [2]**Governmont** this year show the great degree of [3]**populiasm** that is packaged into them. They also mirror past schemes, some of which never took off. Says a [4]**senier** [5]**oficial**: "Prime ministers would do well not to make these [6]**announcements**. It's [7]**usualy** their speech writers who get carried away."

The five **incorrectly** spelt words are:

(*a*) 1, 3, 5, 6, and 7
(*b*) 2, 3, 4, 5, and 7
(*c*) 1, 4, 5, 6, and 7
(*d*) 2, 3, 4, 6, and 7

17. In both countries, [1]**oponents** of these [2]**wapons** of mass [3]**destruction** are [4]**derided** as [5]**peaceniks**, even [6]**traiters**, and about the only thing India and Pakistan have agreed on in the past 50 years is that nuclear bombs are a good thing. In the [7]**subcontinent**, it is not just defence experts but even ordinary people who [8]**beleive** that nuclear [9]**weapons** are a [10]**deterant**, perhaps the only one, against another Indo-Pakistani war.

The five **incorrectly** spelt words are:

(*a*) 1, 4, 6, 8, and 10
(*b*) 2, 4, 5, 7, and 9
(*c*) 1, 2, 6, 8, and 10
(*d*) 1, 3, 4, 6, and 8

18. In India we like to [1]**dismis** this kind of [2]**analysise** of our [3]**stratagic** problems as yet more [4]**evidance** of the [5]**foreign** hand trying to stop us moving along the [6]**glorious** road to [7]**millatry** power. I find it hard to [8]**dismiss** it so easily for the simple reason that we do not even speak the same language as Pakistan any more. There is not a single issue I can think of on which India and Pakistan have been able to agree.

The five **incorrectly** spelt words are:

(*a*) 1, 2, 3, 4, and 7
(*b*) 1, 3, 5, 6, and 7
(*c*) 1, 2, 4, 6, and 8
(*d*) 2, 3, 5, 7, and 8

19. There is a [1]**dangerous** [2]**drifft** in [3]**governence** in the quake-[4]**raveged** state which has much to do with Keshubhai's style of functioning. In the time since the earthquake, he has rarely spoken with senior officers in Kutch. Lack of planning and ad-hocism, so [5]**grave** considering the [6]**magnitute** of the [7]**tragedy**, is becoming more and more [8]**prenounced** in Gandhinagar with each passing day.

The five **incorrectly** spelt words are:
(*a*) 1, 4, 5, 7, and 9
(*b*) 2, 3, 4, 6, and 8
(*c*) 2, 3, 5, 6, and 7
(*d*) 1, 2, 4, 7, and 8

20. The result: the Sangam of the rivers was [1]**complemented** by a [2]**cenfluence** of [3]**spiritual** [4]**seblimity** and professional [5]**governence**. The Kumbh township, spread over 5,000 hectares, was divided into 31 administrative and planning sectors for services and security purposes. Each sector was self-sufficient with regard to civic [6]**aminities**, including drinking water, health, [7]**sanitation**, roads, electricity, housing and [8]**bazars** along with police and firestations.

The five **incorrectly** spelt words are:
(*a*) 1, 3, 4, 6, and 8
(*b*) 2, 4, 5, 7, and 8
(*c*) 2, 4, 5, 6, and 8
(*d*) 1, 2, 5, 6, and 7

21. Censuses had far-reaching impact also on [1]**religon.** Kenneth Jones in his noted book *Arya Dharma*, which came out in 1976, has shown how Hindu [2]**conciousness** and Hindu politics was shaped in the early 1900s by data thrown up by censuses. Lala Lajpat Rai himself [3]**acknowleged** that [4]**orthodox** Hinduism became [5]**senstitive** to the issue of [6]**untouchebility** largely due to fears generated by the census data on the [7]**religious** status of Indians.

The five **incorrectly** spelt words are:
(*a*) 1, 3, 5, 6, and 7
(*b*) 1, 2, 3, 5, and 6
(*c*) 2, 3, 4, 6, and 7
(*d*) 2, 4, 5, 6, and 7

22. Unfolding in the past few months is the largest and most [1]**anigmatic** agriculture crisis faced by independent India. largest, because it [2]**engulfs** every state from Punjab to [3]**Kerela**, and Gujarat to Assam, [4]**afflicting** every crop foodgrains to oilseeds to fruits. [5]**Enigmatic**, because it is a crisis that has built up [6]**amist** an [7]**unprecedanted** 12 [8]**succesive** normal [9]**monsoons** and is marked by falling (or stagnating) output and falling prices.

The five **incorrectly** spelt words are:
(*a*) 1, 3, 5, 7, and 9
(*b*) 1, 3, 6, 7, and 8
(*c*) 2, 3, 5, 6, and 8
(*d*) 2, 4, 6, 7, and 9

23. In essence, the [1]**crises** is nothing more than a noble vision gone [2]**horribly** wrong. In the early 1990s, the problem with Indian agriculture was [3]**diagonosed** as rising farm subsidies and falling investment. The solution: improve returns from agriculture so that farmers' [4]**dependance** on subsidies is reduced. The funds from subsidies could then be [5]**plouhed** back into agriculture. [6]**Consequantly**, the minimum support price of wheat was [7]**doubled** while that of rice was raised.

The five **incorrectly** spelt words are:
(*a*) 1, 2, 4, 5, and 7
(*b*) 2, 3, 4, 6, and 7
(*c*) 1, 3, 4, 5, and 6
(*d*) 2, 4, 5, 6, and 7

24. In Kerala rubber and coconut [1]**cultivation** were [2]**profitable** [3]**busineses**. That, of [4]**coarse**, was when [5]**proccessed**, rubber commanded a price of Rs 60 per kg and a coconut sold for about Rs 10. Falling prices, import of rubber and [6]**palmolin** oil from Malaysia and rising [7]**labor** costs have upset the bottom lines.

The five **incorrectly** spelt words are:
(*a*) 3, 4, 5, 6, and 7
(*b*) 2, 4, 5, 6, and 7
(*c*) 1, 2, 4, 5, and 6
(*d*) 1, 3, 5, 6, and 7

25. In this study, tea consumption was [1]**asociated** with a slightly higher [2]**critical** [3]**fliker** [4]**fushion**

[5]**threshold**, which is a measure of a person's ability to [6]**distinguish** [7]**descrete** [8]**sensory** data. Black tea rapidly [9]**revives** by improving and maintaining mental alertness and its regular consumption throughout the day definitely helps to reduce feelings of [10]**fatige**.

The five **incorrectly** spelt words are:
(*a*) 1, 2, 4, 6, and 9
(*b*) 2, 3, 5, 7, and 8
(*c*) 1, 3, 4, 7, and 10
(*d*) 2, 4, 5, 6, and 10

26. The contrast is striking. As head of [1]**millitary** [2]**inteligence** and the [3]**architect** of the cease-fire with ethnic [4]**insergent** groups, Khin Nynt has held confidence-building [5]**negotiations** with Suu Kui. The talks have made progress and Suu Kui reportedly told an EU delegation of her satisfaction with Khin Nyunt. [6]**Pro-opposition** publicatons I Thailand have painted Khin Nyunt as a [7]**reformor** who enjoys the [8]**confidence** of [9]**westernized** army officers, [10]**intellectuals**, businessmen and, most important, China. In short, someone who could be a bridge between the [11]**military** and the opposition.

The five **incorrectly** spelt words are:
(*a*) 1, 2, 5, 8, and 10
(*b*) 2, 5, 6, 9, and 10
(*c*) 1, 2, 4, 7, and 9
(*d*) 2, 3, 6, 9, and 11

27. After the kidnapping, these urban thugs act as [1]**intermedaries** between the victims' families and their kidnappers, [2]**negotiating** the ransom money and the [3]**modelities** of payment. During the negotiations, the victims are kept at hideouts in small towns and villages in the [4]**revines**. Bhind in Madhya Pradesh and the Etawah in Uttar Pradesh have [5]**amerged** as the [6]**favorite** [7]**havens** for hiding victims picked up from as far as Delhi, Kanpur and Gaziabad.

The five **incorrectly** spelt words are:
(*a*) 1, 3, 4, 5, and 6
(*b*) 1, 2, 4, 6, and 7
(*c*) 2, 3, 4, 5, and 6
(*d*) 2, 4, 5, 6, and 7

28. In this [1]**lucretive** business, urban crooks are the new partners of the dacoits. They help identify [2]**potential** victims and pass on information about their movements to the dacoits. Daily [3]**scedules** of rich businessmen and [4]**effluent** professionals are kept under watch and are [5]**crushial** for the planning and [6]**execution** of the kidnapping. Sometimes, like in the case of the treasure hunters from Guna, these crooks even deliver the victims to their [7]**capturs**.

The five **incorrectly** spelt words are:
(*a*) 1, 2, 4, 6, and 7
(*b*) 1, 3, 4, 5, and 7
(*c*) 2, 4, 5, 6, and 7
(*d*) 1, 2, 5, 7, and 8

29. With [1]**perennialy** recharged creative energy and [2]**dexterity**, Gangopadhyay constructs event after event and [3]**carves** out a stream of [4]**vivid** characters one after another. A [5]**rancounter** [6]**parexcellance**, he is comparable to master storyteller Kambar whose characters [7]**perempotorily** narrate stories to each other as they are drowning in the [8]**swirlling** river.

The five **incorrectly** spelt words are:
(*a*) 1, 2, 4, 5, and 7
(*b*) 2, 5, 6, 7, and 8
(*c*) 1, 5, 6, 7, and 8
(*d*) 2, 3, 6, 7, and 8

30. The [1]**narative** is [2]**studded** with [3]**florishes** and [4]**flamboyence**. Words of many [5]**hues** ring [6]**tinsel**: "The Ganga, [7]**repling** and [8]**shimmerring** like a sheet of silk..." And. "He saw the stars [9]**winking** and glowing, pale and gold against a people sky". When Shashibhushan sees Bhumisuta for the first time, she was holding a bunch of white flowers in her hand. Men have "dark eyes and wavy hair".

The five **incorrectly** spelt words are:
(*a*) 1, 2, 5, 8, and 9
(*b*) 2, 3, 4, 7, and 9
(*c*) 1, 3, 4, 7, and 8
(*d*) 1, 2, 6, 8, and 9

31. Many a passage in the novel, right from the first chapter—[1]**discribing** [2]**throngs** of tribals coming out of the forest to attend the village festival like a "rainbow-hued river" [3]**wraped** in [4]**colorful** loin clothes—is [5]**spectaculer**. So are the wedding scenes and the death of Kadambari. The novel, [6]**iminently** [7]**rendered** in English by Aruna Charavarti, is a [8]**spectacle** of life and time. It bares, though, a certain amount of [9]**historical** material, including the fact that Tagore had piles.

The five **incorrectly** spelt words are:

(*a*) 2, 4, 7, 8, and 9
(*b*) 1, 3, 4, 5, and 6
(*c*) 2, 3, 6, 7, and 8
(*d*) 1, 4, 5, 6, and 7

32. "If you don't get it right, blame it on the night", said Mamesh Dangwal, a bartender of the Hyatt Regency at the [1]**inaugral** Rick's Annual Bartender of the Year [2]**competiton** at Taj Mahal Hotel, Delhi. The slow and steady Dangwal, one of the four [3]**participants**, was [4]**elequently** [5]**exenerating** himself in case his very own [6]**conoction**, 'Blame it on the night' that included the [7]**mandatory** Bacardi and peach [8]**schnaps** failed to get the [9]**honours**.

The five **incorrectly** spelt words are:

(*a*) 1, 4, 5, 6 and 8
(*b*) 2, 4, 6, 8, and 9
(*c*) 1, 3, 5, 7, and 8
(*d*) 1, 2, 3, 5, and 9

33. In the [1]**nineteenth** [2]**centuary**, the desire to produce high-quality goods at a low price led to what is now called mass production. The phrase nowadays is especially [3]**asociated** with the name of Henry Ford, who so [4]**successfully**, applied mass-production methods to the manufacture of motor cars. His business [5]**rivels** were quick to [6]**emitate** him, thus proving the truth of the old proverb, 'Imitation is the [7]**sinecerest** form of flattery.'

The five **incorrectly** spelt words are:

(*a*) 2, 4, 5, 6, and 7
(*b*) 2, 3, 5, 6, and 7
(*c*) 1, 3, 5, 6, and 7
(*d*) 1, 2, 4, 6, and 7

34. There are still some of these [1]**craftmen** in the world, Not every thing is mass produced. [2]**Suppose** we find in a village an [3]**eldarly** man who has done nothing all his life but make fine furniture. [4]**Supose** we see and [5]**praize** his handi-work and order a fine chair from him. After some [6]**weaks** have been passed, he sends us word that the chair is finished and we go to take the delivery of it. We [7]**praise** the chair and pay the price. Then we take an axe and break the chair to [8]**pieces** before the eyes of its maker. It is difficult to know what he would do.

The five **incorrectly** spelt words are:

(*a*) 1, 2, 5, 6, and 8
(*b*) 1, 3, 4, 5, and 7
(*c*) 2, 5, 6, 7, and 8
(*d*) 1, 3, 4, 5, and 6

35. How do we start 'thinking what nobody has thought'? Usually it takes a [1]**whak** on the head, like Sir Isaac Newton [2]**supposely** had when an apple striking his skull [3]**awakened** him to the laws of gravity. [4]**Whacks** can range from something as major as [5]**loosing** a job or something as [6]**trivil** as wanting an [7]**unusual** dish for a dinner party. We're more likely to respond [8]**creativly**—which is to say, think of a new idea—if we've already been [9]**chipping** away at the 'mental locks' that close our minds.

The five **incorrectly** spelt words are:

(*a*) 1, 2, 5, 6, and 8
(*b*) 1, 3, 5, 8, and 9
(*c*) 2, 3, 4, 7, and 8
(*d*) 2, 4, 5, 6, and 9

36. Creative people have to be [1]**generelists**, interested in everything and aware that what they learn in one [2]**feild** might prove useful in another. We're all [3]**generalists** at home-chefs, [4]**decoraters**, teachers, gardeners, and [5]**handimen**—and home is a good place to start being creative. The average homemaker is confronted daily with more creative [6]**oppurtunities** than the middle manager in a company sees in a month.

The five **incorrectly** spelt words are:
(*a*) 1, 2, 4, 5, and 6
(*b*) 2, 3, 4, 5, and 6
(*c*) 1, 3, 4, 5, and 6
(*d*) 2, 3, 4, 5, and 6

37. Thank you, my dear friend, thank you! And allow me on this [1]**aspicious** [2]**occasion**, our [3]**anniversory**, to [4]**embrace** you! I am very happy, very happy [5]**indeed**. Thank you for your [6]**unstinting** service, for everything. Thank you, my friend. If I have anything of value while I have had the [7]**honor** of being Chairman of this bank, then it is first and [8]**formost** thanks to my dear [9]**colleages**. Yes, old man, fifteen years! Fifteen years—as sure as my name's Shipuchin!

The five **incorrectly** spelt words are:
(*a*) 1, 2, 6, 8, and 9
(*b*) 1, 3, 7, 8, and 9
(*c*) 2, 3, 5, 7, and 8
(*d*) 2, 4, 6, 7, and 9

38. Now I [1]**reallise** that you invited me in the [2]**absense**, enforced by your [3]**sedentery** ways, of [4]**stuffed** tiger heads or other [5]**trophies** on your walls, a live artist being the [6]**equivelant** of a dead beast as a social ornament. I will not question your motive because it has given me a chance to do a beautiful and good thing. I should like to [7]**entreate** all these gentlemen to redeem the strange, bittersweet [8]**miracle** of their lives, while there is yet time, by giving up the advertising business at once.

The five **incorrectly** spelt words are:
(*a*) 1, 2, 4, 7, and 8
(*b*) 1, 3, 4, 6, and 7
(*c*) 1, 2, 3, 6, and 7
(*d*) 1, 3, 5, 7, and 8

39. None of you however, is anything but well-fed; yet I am sure that until this moment it has never [1]**occured** to you on what a [2]**dubous** your feeding is [3]**accompolished**. I shall tell you exactly how you eat. You [4]**induce** people to use more things than they naturally desire—the more useless and undesirable the article, the greater the advertising [5]**efort** to [6]**dispos** of it—and in all the profit from that unnatural purchasing, you share.

The five **incorrectly** spelt words are:
(*a*) 1, 2, 3, 4, and 5
(*b*) 1, 3, 4, 5, and 6
(*c*) 2, 3, 4, 5, and 6
(*d*) 1, 2, 3, 5 and 6

40. To what end is all this lying, [1]**vandlism** and misuse? You are trying to sell; never mind what, never mind how, never mind to whom—just sell, sell, sell! Small wonder that in good old American slang 'sell' means 'fraud'! Come now! Do you [2]**hesitate** to promise [3]**requitted** love to [4]**miserable** girls, triumph to failures, [5]**virelity** to [6]**weaklings**, even [7]**prowess** to little children, for the price of a mouth wash or a breakfast food? Does it ever occur to you to be ashamed to live by [8]**preying** on the [9]**myraid** little [10]**tragedies** of [11]**unfulfillment** which make your methods pay so well?

The five **incorrectly** spelt words are:
(*a*) 1, 2, 4, 6, and 9
(*b*) 2, 4, 5, 7, and 8
(*c*) 1, 3, 5, 9, and 11
(*d*) 1, 3, 4, 6, and 11

41. Sofas filled the bays of the windows—sofas covered with [1]**tapastry**. The windows, the three long windows, had the proper [2]**allowance** of [3]**discreat** net and [4]**figured** satin. The [5]**mahagony** sideboard [6]**buljed** [7]**discreetly** with the right brandies, whiskies and [8]**liquers**. And from the middle window he looked down upon the glossy roofs of fashionable cars packed in the narrow streets of Piccadilly.

The five **incorrectly** spelt words are:
(*a*) 1, 3, 5, 6, and 8
(*b*) 2, 3, 4, 7, and 8
(*c*) 1, 2, 5, 6, and 8
(*d*) 1, 2, 3, 6, and 7

42. A more central position could not be imagined. And at eight the morning he would have his breakfast brought in on a tray by a [1]**manservent**: the manservant would unfold his [2]**crimpson** dressing-gown; he would rip his letters open with his long pointed nails and would [3]**extract** thick white cards of invitation upon which the [4]**engreving** stood up roughly, from [5]**ducheses**, countesses, viscountesses and [6]**honorable** ladies. Then he would wash; then he would eat his [7]**toast**; then he would read his paper by the burning fire of the electric coals.

The five **incorrectly** spelt words are:
(*a*) 1, 3, 5, 6, and 8
(*b*) 1, 2, 4, 7, and 8
(*c*) 1, 2, 3, 5, and 7
(*d*) 1, 2, 4, 5, and 6

43. Saturday became a part of my regular work [1]**shedule** as a young salesman. And when a snowstorm hit my [2]**region**, it was an [3]**oppurtunity**, not an [4]**abstacle**. The idea that my [5]**rivels** would be hiding from the elements gave me the [6]**impetous** to push my product. It's [7]**amazing** how [8]**receptive** a buyer could be when the snow was waist-deep and I was the only friendly face he'd seen all day.

The five **incorrectly** spelt words are:
(*a*) 1, 3, 4, 5, and 6
(*b*) 1, 2, 5, 7, and 8
(*c*) 2, 3, 4, 6, and 7
(*d*) 2, 4, 6, 7, and 8

44. There had been a [1]**cristening** that afternoon at St. Peter's, Neville Square, and Albert Edward Foreman still wore his [2]**vergar's** gown. He kept his new one, its folds as full and [3]**stiff** as though it were made not of [4]**alpaca** but of [5]**perenial** bronze, for [6]**funearals** and weddings (St. Peter's, Neville Square, was a church much [7]**favored** by the [8]**fashionable** for these [9]**ceremonies**) and now wrote only his second-best.

The five **incorrectly** spelt words are:
(*a*) 1, 2, 4, 6, and 8
(*b*) 1, 2, 5, 6, and 7
(*c*) 2, 3, 5, 8, and 9
(*d*) 2, 4, 6, 7, and 8

45. He wore it with [1]**complasence**, for it was the [2]**dignifyed** symbol of his office, and without it (when he took it off to go home) he had the [3]**disconcerting** [4]**sensation** of being somewhat [5]**insuficiently** clad. He took pains with it; he pressed it and [6]**ironed** it himself. During the sixteen years he had been [7]**vergar** of this church he had a [8]**succession** of such gowns, but he had never been able to throw them away when they were out and the [9]**complete** series, neatly [10]**wrapped** up in brown paper, lay in the [11]**botom** drawers of the [12]**wardrobe** in his bedroom.

The five **incorrectly** spelt words are:
(*a*) 1, 2, 6, 8, and 10
(*b*) 1, 3, 5, 9, and 12
(*c*) 1, 2, 5, 7, and 11
(*d*) 1, 3, 5, 8, and 12

46. The vicar had been recently [1]**appointed**, a red-faced [2]**energetic** man in the early [3]**fortyies**, and Albert Edward still regretted his [4]**predecesor**, a [5]**clergyman** of the old school who [6]**preached** [7]**leisurely** [8]**sermens** in a silvery voice and dined out a great deal with his more [9]**aristrocratic** [10]**parashinors**.

The five **incorrectly** spelt words are:
(*a*) 1, 2, 4, 6, and 8
(*b*) 2, 4, 7, 9, and 10
(*c*) 2, 3, 5, 7, and 9
(*d*) 3, 4, 8, 9, and 10

47. It was a source of [1]**subdude** pride to him that he could nearly always quiet a [2]**wimpering** infant by the manner in which he held it and he was not [3]**unconscios** of the [4]**amused** [5]**admiration** with which mothers and nurses watched him settle the baby in the [6]**crook** of his [7]**serpliced** arm. The [8]**vergar** knew that it pleased him to be [9]**complimented** on this talent.

The five **incorrectly** spelt words are:
(*a*) 1, 2, 3, 7, and 8
(*b*) 1, 3, 4, 6, and 9
(*c*) 2, 5, 7, 8, and 9
(*d*) 2, 3, 5, 7, and 9

48. He stood in a [1]**respectful** but not [2]**obseqious** attitude. He had been in service before he was [3]**appointed** to his [4]**eccesastical** office, but only in very good houses, and his [5]**deportment** was [6]**irreprochable**. Starting as a page-boy in the household of a [7]**merchant**-prince, he had risen by due [8]**degrees** from the [9]**position** of fourth to first footman, for a year he had been single-handed butler to a [10]**widowed** [11]**peress**, and till the vacancy occurred at St. Peter's, butler with two men under him in the house of a retired [12]**ambasador**.

The five **incorrectly** spelt words are:

(*a*) 1, 3, 5, 10, and 12
(*b*) 2, 4, 6, 11, and 12
(*c*) 2, 3, 7, 9, and 11
(*d*) 1, 4, 5, 8, and 10

49. The [1]**attendents** in blue and red uniforms and gold-[2]**braided** top hats are the Stock Exchange 'waiters' — and there is no doubt much more [3]**responsible** and better [4]**orgenised** than that of their coffee-house [5]**predecessors**. From the 'eleven' stands placed [6]**stratagically** about the floor, waiters control much of the [7]**elaborate** internal communication system. With a battery of switches, each waiter operates one of the large boards with [8]**iluminated** figures. These have no [9]**referance** to shares or prices: they are to call members to receive messages.

The five **incorrectly** spelt words are:

(*a*) 1, 3, 5, 8, and 9
(*b*) 2, 4, 5, 7, and 8
(*c*) 1, 2, 5, 6, and 7
(*d*) 1, 4, 6, 8, and 9

50. It takes [1]**insight** and character at his point to [2]**apprehend** that either [3]**forbiding** a union to strike, or requiring management to [4]**arbitrate** a substantive question, is in fact [5]**denial** of the private [6]**enterprise** system. The concept of [7]**arbitation** is one toward which every honest mind is attracted on first [8]**approching** the problem of industrial disputes, but it will prove grossly misleading unless we [9]**reccognise** that it may be employed for two sharply [10]**contrasted** purposes, one proper and one improper.

The five **incorrectly** spelt words are:

(*a*) 3, 6, 7, 8, and 9
(*b*) 1, 4, 5, 7, and 8
(*c*) 2, 5, 6, 8, and 10
(*d*) 1, 2, 3, 6, and 10

51. He has been taught to respect the law, and the sight of men swinging clubs and [1]**hurling** stones at those [2]**seaking** to go about the ordinary tasks of life will be [3]**aborrent** to him. Bloody heads and broken arms and the use of [4]**filthy** [5]**epithets** toward both men and women have not been part of his life, and he won't like it. Nor will he [6]**complicently** accept [7]**anonymos** threats to his wife on the telephone, or signs painted on the houses of those who think differently from the [8]**cowards** who [9]**prepetrate** the wrong.

The five **incorrectly** spelt words are:

(*a*) 2, 3, 6, 7, and 8
(*b*) 1, 4, 5, 8, and 9
(*c*) 2, 3, 6, 7, and 9
(*d*) 1, 3, 4, 5, and 7

52. The man working at the [1]**bargaining** table, however, finds himself these days [2]**skillfully** and [3]**intentionally** blocked from maintaining [4]**jugement** and poise by the field tactics of trained union [5]**bargainars**. They hope that at three in the morning, after eighteen hours of [6]**negotiation**, locked up in a smoke filled room, the man will [7]**felter**. They hope that then they will [8]**concede** almost anything in order to get a contract [9]**signed** or a [10]**grievence** settled.

The five **incorrectly** spelt words are:

(*a*) 1, 3, 6, 8, and 10
(*b*) 2, 4, 5, 7, and 10
(*c*) 1, 2, 5, 6, and 9
(*d*) 2, 4, 6, 8, and 9

53. The [1]**psychlogical** [2]**pattrens** here are quite clear. When a person says "No" and really means it, he is doing far more than saying a word of two letters. His entire [3]**organsim** —[4]**gandular**, [5]**nervous**, [6]**muscular**—gathers itself together into a condition of [7]**rejection**. There is, usually a minute but sometimes in observable degree, a physical withdrawal, or readiness for withdrawal. The whole [8]**nero**-muscular system, in short, sets itself on guard against [9]**acceptence**.

The five **incorrectly** spelt words are:

(*a*) 1, 3, 6, 8, and 9
(*b*) 2, 4, 6, 7, and 8

(*c*) 1, 2, 3, 4, and 8
(*d*) 2, 5, 7, 8, and 9

54. Last night Mr Vajpayee had [1]**conveyed** his [2]**displeasure** to Mr Musharaff himself when the General was making his farewell call on him. He is learnt to have made a specific [3]**referance** to the guest's [4]**controvarsial** remarks at the meeting with senior [5]**journalists** which were telecast by [6]**steelth**. "Your [7]**uttrances** have [8]**vitiated** the atmosphere, " the Prime Minister is believed to have told the Prez, while adding that these things don't help if you are looking for a [9]**breakthorough**.

The five **incorrectly** spelt words are:
(*a*) 1, 3, 5, 6, and 8
(*b*) 2, 4, 5, 7, and 8
(*c*) 3, 4, 6, 7, and 9
(*d*) 1, 2, 5, 8, and 9

55. The [1] **legetimate** fear: will Bush see the world through advisers who were more [2] **adapt** at Cold War [3] **stratagems** than the new [4] **millenium's** realpolitik? [5] **Secretry** of State [6] **General** Colin Powell, the Gulf War hero, was, however, quick to dispel such [7] **notions,** telling the Senate Foreign Relations [8] **Commitee** that the Bush [9] **presidency** would [10] **propound** "a [11] **distinctly** American [12] **internationalism**".

The five **incorrectly** spelt words are:
(*a*) 1, 3, 4, 9, and 12
(*b*) 1, 2, 4, 5, and 8
(*c*) 2, 6, 8, 9, and 10
(*d*) 1, 5, 7, 9, and 11

56. MONTHS BEHIND [1]**SCEDULE.** Cost overruns. Poor quality.[2] **Infrastructure** projects in India [3] **usally** suffer from one or all of these [4] **predicaments.** But January 24 [5] **witnessed** the [6] **unvieling** of a project that [7] **steared** clear of the usual hurdles. The Noida Toll [8] **Bridge** Company's eight-lane [9] **expressway** bridge connecting Delhi to its [10] **thriving** [11] **satallites** Noida and Greater Noida has other firsts to its [12]**claim**.

The five **incorrectly** spelt words are:
(*a*) 2, 4, 5, 8, 9 (*b*) 1, 3, 5, 7, 12
(*c*) 3, 6, 8, 9, 11 (*d*) 1, 3, 6, 7, 11

TEST – 6

1. (*a*) Occasion (*b*) Ocassion
(*c*) Occassion (*d*) Ocasion
2. (*a*) Bizzare (*b*) Bizzarre
(*c*) Bizarre (*d*) Bizare
3. (*a*) Aprehensive (*b*) Apprehensive
(*c*) Appreehensive (*d*) Aprrehensive
4. (*a*) Association (*b*) Asociation
(*c*) Assocciaation (*d*) Asocciation
5. (*a*) Imemmorial (*b*) Imemorial
(*c*) Immemmorial (*d*) Immemorial
6. (*a*) Effluent (*b*) Eluent
(*c*) Eflluent (*d*) Efluuent
7. (*a*) Tommorow (*b*) Tomorrow
(*c*) Tommorow (*d*) Tommorrow
8. (*a*) Statuete (*b*) Stattuete
(*c*) Statuette (*d*) Stattuette
9. (*a*) Efficacious (*b*) Eficacious
(*c*) Efficaccious (*d*) Eficacious
10. (*a*) Assasination (*b*) Asassination
(*c*) Asasination (*d*) Assassination
11. (*a*) Concieve (*b*) Conceeive
(*c*) Conceive (*d*) Conceiv
12. (*a*) Connossseur (*b*) Connosseur
(*c*) Conoisseur (*d*) Connoisseur
13. (*a*) Deffecential (*b*) Deferential
(*c*) Deferrential (*d*) Defferrential
14. (*a*) Bureaucracy (*b*) Bureucracy
(*c*) Beaurocracy (*d*) Bureocracy
15. (*a*) Fluerescent (*b*) Fluorescent
(*c*) Flurescent (*d*) Florescent
16. (*a*) Commissioner (*b*) Commisioner
(*c*) Comissoner (*d*) Commissionor
17. (*a*) Pesimistic (*b*) Pessimmistic
(*c*) Pessimistic (*d*) Pessimmistic
18. (*a*) Commemoration
(*b*) Commemmoration
(*c*) Comemmoration
(*d*) Comemoration
19. (*a*) Feaeability (*b*) Feasibility
(*c*) Feassibility (*d*) Fesibility
20. (*a*) Geneses (*b*) Genasis
(*c*) Genisis (*d*) Genesis

21. (*a*) Heirloom (*b*) Hairloom
(*c*) Hierloom (*d*) Hereloom

22. (*a*) Indigenous (*b*) Indegenous
(*c*) Indiigenious (*d*) Indiginous

23. (*a*) Quarel (*b*) Quarrel
(*c*) Quarell (*d*) Quarrell

24. (*a*) assimilation (*b*) asimilation
(*c*) asimmilation (*d*) ascimilation

25. (*a*) Eccentric (*b*) Ecentric
(*c*) Ecenntirc (*d*) Ecsentric

26. (*a*) Juvenescense (*b*) Juvenecense
(*c*) Juvenesence (*d*) Juvenescence

27. (*a*) knowledgible (*b*) knowlegable
(*c*) knowledgeable (*d*) knowledgeble

28. (*a*) Luekaemia (*b*) Leukaemia
(*c*) Lukemia (*d*) Lukaemia

29. (*a*) Itenirary (*b*) Itinary
(*c*) Itinerary (*d*) Itineiary

30. (*a*) kitesh (*b*) kitsch
(*c*) kitch (*d*) kitsh

31. (*a*) Labyrinth (*b*) Labirynth
(*c*) Labyryinth (*d*) Labirinth

32. (*a*) Massarcar (*b*) Massacer
(*c*) Massacre (*d*) Mascacre

33. (*a*) Committes (*b*) Commitees
(*c*) Comittees (*d*) Committees

34. (*a*) Therirst (*b*) Thrist
(*c*) Thurst (*d*) Thrust

35. (*a*) Inoccuous (*b*) Innocuous
(*c*) Innocuos (*d*) Inoccuoos

36. (*a*) Enterpreneur (*b*) Entreprenner
(*c*) Entrepreneur (*d*) Entrepreuner

37. (*a*) Casteism (*b*) Castiesm
(*c*) Casteesm (*d*) Castism

38. (*a*) Embarrasment (*b*) Embarrassment
(*c*) Embarassment (*d*) Embrassment

39. (*a*) Envirment (*b*) Envirinment
(*c*) Environment (*d*) Envirement

40. (*a*) Euphimesms (*b*) Euphimisms
(*c*) Eufemisms (*d*) Euphemisms

41. (*a*) Milage (*b*) Mileage
(*c*) Milaege (*d*) Milege

42. (*a*) Reservoir (*b*) Reservior
(*c*) Reservoer (*d*) Reservor

43. (*a*) Convinieat (*b*) Conveinient
(*c*) Convenient (*d*) Convenent

44. (*a*) Accesible (*b*) Acessible
(*c*) Acsessible (*d*) Accessible

45. (*a*) Pharmacuetical (*b*) Pharmaceutiele
(*c*) Pharmaceutical (*d*) Pharmacutical

46. (*a*) Questionnaire (*b*) Questionaire
(*c*) Questionneire (*d*) Questionneire

47. (*a*) Ressurection (*b*) Resurrection
(*c*) Ressurrection (*d*) Resurection

48. (*a*) Retreivable (*b*) Retrevable
(*c*) Retrievable (*d*) Retrieveble

49. (*a*) Scursillous (*b*) Scurillou
(*c*) Scuriilous (*d*) Scurrilous

50. (*a*) Ubiquitous (*b*) Ubiqiutous
(*c*) Ubiqutous (*d*) Ubiqitous

51. (*a*) Psycological (*b*) Psychological
(*c*) Psychologicle (*d*) Pcychological

52. (*a*) Gimmiks (*b*) Gimmicks
(*c*) Gimicks (*d*) Gimics

53. (*a*) Neccessary (*b*) Necessary
(*c*) Nesessary (*d*) Neassary

54. (*a*) Desises (*b*) Deseases
(*c*) Diseases (*d*) Deasises

55. (*a*) Exhibition (*b*) Exibition
(*c*) Exibhition (*d*) Exbihition

56. (*a*) Splender (*b*) Spendour
(*c*) Splendour (*d*) Splendore

57. (*a*) Continous (*b*) Continuous
(*c*) Continuos (*d*) Cuntinuous

58. (*a*) Reitiration (*b*) Releration
(*c*) Rieteration (*d*) Reiteration

59. (*a*) Furoare (*b*) Furor
(*c*) Furore (*d*) Furoar

60. (*a*) Convoluted (*b*) Convolated
(*c*) Counvoluted (*d*) Convoulated

61. (*a*) Nusance (*b*) Nuisance
(*c*) Niusance (*d*) Nuisence

62. (*a*) Predecessor (*b*) Predeccessor
(*c*) Predecesor (*d*) Predeccesor

63. (*a*) Hygeine (*b*) Hygien
(*c*) Hygene (*d*) Hygiene

64. (*a*) Expidiently (*b*) Expediently
(*c*) Expedientely (*d*) Expedeiently

65. (*a*) Veterinarian (*b*) Veterenarian
(*c*) Veternarian (*d*) Veterenian

ANSWER KEY

Writing Ability

Test-1

Coherence

1. a 2. c 3. b 4. d 5. c
6. a 7. b 8. d 9. b 10. c
11. b 12. a 13. a 14. b 15. d
16. a 17. d 18. b 19. b 20. a
21. d 22. b 23. a 24. c 25. d

Test-2

Jumbled Sentences

1. a 2. b 3. d 4. a 5. a
6. c 7. a 8. b 9. a 10. d
11. c 12. a 13. d 14. b 15. b
16. c 17. d 18. b 19. d 20. b
21. b 22. d 23. b 24. a 25. b

Test-3

Missing Clauses

I
1. a 2. c 3. d 4. d 5. b

II
1. c 2. a 3. d 4. c 5. c

III
1. b 2. d 3. a 4. c 5. c 6. b

IV
1. d 2. b 3. d 4. a 5. a

V.
1. b 2. b 3. d 4. a 5. b

VI.
1. b 2. a 3. d 4. a 5. b

VII.
1. b 2. a 3. a 4. c 5. a

VIII.
1. b 2. a 3. c 4. a 5. d 6. c

IX.
1. a 2. c 3. b

X.
1. a 2. c 3. d

XI.
1. d 2. b 3. c 4. d 5. a

XII.
1. c 2. d

XIII.
1. c

XIV.
1. a 2. c 3. b

XV.
1. c 2. a

Test-4

Missing Sentences

I.
1. b 2. d 3. a 4. d 5. b

II.
1. b 2. c 3. a 4. d

III.
1. c 2. a 3. a 4. c 5. b

IV.
1. a 2. b 3. d

V. c VI. a VII. c

VIII. 1. d 2. a

IX. b X. c XI. a

XII. 1. b 2. b

XIII. c XIV. a

XV. 1. c 2. a 3. b

XVI.
1. a 2. c 3. b

XVII.
1. d 2. b 3. a

XVIII.
1. b 2. a 3. b

XIX. c XX. a

Spellings

Test-5

1. b 2. c 3. c 4. a 5. b
6. d 7. a 8. d 9. c 10. b
11. a 12. d 13. c 14. c 15. a
16. b 17. c 18. a 19. b 20. c
21. b 22. b 23. c 24. a 25. c
26. c 27. a 28. b 29. c 30. c
31. b 32. a 33. b 34. d 35. a
36. a 37. b 38. c 39. d 40. c
41. a 42. d 43. a 44. b 45. c
46. d 47. a 48. b 49. d 50. a
51. c 52. b 53. c 54. c 55. b
56. d

Test-6

1. a 2. c 3. b 4. a 5. d
6. a 7. b 8. c 9. a 10. d
11. c 12. d 13. b 14. a 15. b
16. a 17. c 18. a 19. b 20. d
21. a 22. a 23. b 24. a 25. a
26. d 27. c 28. b 29. c 30. b
31. a 32. c 33. c 34. d 35. b
36. c 37. a 38. b 39. c 40. d
41. b 42. a 43. c 44. d 45. c
46. a 47. b 48. c 49. d 50. a
51. b 52. b 53. b 54. c 55. a
56. c 57. b 58. d 59. c 60. a
61. b 62. a 63. d 64. b 65. a

CHAPTER 5 SUBJECTIVE TESTS

INTRODUCTION

The tests of Reading Comprehension and Ability that you will face will probably fall into the following basic categories:

1. Interpretation and opinion
2. Direct reference
3. Indirect reference
4. Direct inference
5. Indirect inference

1. Interpretation and Opinion

Questions which involve interpretation and opinion may be difficult initially, but after practicing the earlier three techniques, viz. the Multiple Choice, the Cloze Procedure, and the Modified Cloze Procedure, you will be able to comprehend the implicit meaning and even give your opinion where and when it is demanded. Such questions demand some degree of subjectivity.

Questions of interpretation are notoriously difficult for students learning English as a foreign/ second/third language. Many students at under-graduate level face great difficulty in seeing beyond the literal meaning of the words, being unable to read between the lines so that even most the innocent looking question may stump them. So, tackle such questions with patience and you are bound to improve.

2. Direct Reference

Questions on direct reference involve the recovery of information from the given passage/text.

You will find that this kind of questions have the simplest level of difficulty:

The reference question has the same wording as the passage, and you can copy the answer without any change of structure or vocabulary. Yet, even here, it is found that many students even at under-graduate level fail to copy the words accurately. This kind of question may be called **Direct reference.**

3. Indirect Reference

Questions on indirect reference also involve the recovery of message or information from the given text.

(*a*) The question may not include the words from the text, so that your search for the relevant information is slightly more difficult and involves full understanding of the passage and question.

(*b*) The question may require that the students' answer be different in structure from the passage.

These two types (*a*) and (*b*) of questions may be called **Indirect reference.**

Here follow some examples showing the use of Direct and Indirect reference.

"A radical change in the eating habits of the Japanese in the postwar years has been a dominant factor in inducing changes in the county's agriculture, to the mutual benefit of both producer and consumer".

(*a*) What has been a dominant factor in inducing changes in the Japanese agriculture ?

Answer: A radical change in the eating habits of the Japanese in the postwar years has been a dominant factor.

The question contains verbal references to the relevant sentence, and the answer may simply be copied, even if you do not fully comprehend the meaning.

(*b*) What has been one of the main reasons for the transformation of Japanese farming?

Answer: A radical change in the eating habits of the Japanese has been one of the main reasons. The answer may be copied provided you can locate the correct information in the text.

(*c*) What effect have dietary changes had in postwar Japan?

Answer: They have caused changes in the country's agriculture.

The answer uses the information, but not the grammatical structure, of the text. In questions like this, it is not just your reading ability, but also your overall command of the language, *i.e.* reading and writing ability, which is being tested.

4. Direct Inference

This type of question usually requires the student to relate two or more items in the text and form simple conclusions. The answers to such questions have to be inferred from the facts given in the passage — they are not stated in the passage itself. For example "——— the introduction of new varieties of rice, which mature in about 100 days instead of the normal 150, will release more land for pasture and fodder crops in areas where formerly only rice was grown".

A possible question would be : –

In about how many days less than the old varieties of rice do the new varieties mature?

Answer:

They mature in about fifty days less. (All the necessary information is in the text, but has to be worked out.)

5. Indirect Inference

Not every passage contains suitable opportunities for asking questions of this type, but a reading passage about under-water exploration by means of a bathysphere gave the following information:

"Weighing two tons, the bathysphere had attached to it 3500 feet of non-twisting steel cable and a solid rubber hose containing telephone and electric light wires." The following question can be asked:

To what depth could the bathysphere explore?

The passage does not specifically state that it could explore down to 3500 feet, but that is a simple and justifiable inference for the reader to make from his understanding of the passage. It calls for no general knowledge beyond what is in the text. It is remarkably simple for a native speaker to grasp, but non-native students of the language often fail to make the necessary inference.

It is suggested that the students for whom English is a second/third language will do well by practising all the five techniques of testing reading ability/ comprehension.

Now a number of examination papers with answer keys follow:

TEST – 1

Directions: Read the passage given below and answer the questions that follow on the basis of what you have read.

Mr. Jones, of the Manor Farm, had locked the hen-house for the night, but was too drunk to remember to shut the pop-holes. With the ring of light from his lantern dancing from side to side, he lurched across the yard, and made his way, up to bed where Mrs. Jones was already snoring.

As soon as the light in the bedroom went out, there was a stirring and a fluttering all through the farm building. Word had gone round during the day that old Major, the prize Middle White boar, had had a strange dream on the previous night and wished to communicate it to the other animals. It had been agreed that they should meet in the big barn as soon as Mr. Jones was safely out of the way. Old Major was so highly regarded on the farm that everyone was quite ready to lose an hour's sleep in order to hear what he had to say.

All the animals were now present except Moses, the tame rave, who slept on a perch behind the back door. When Major saw that they had all made themselves comfortable and were waiting attentively, he cleared his throat and began:

'Comrades, you have heard already about the strange dream that I had last night, but I will come to the dream later. I have something else to say first, I do not think, comrades, that I shall be with you for many months longer and before I die, I feel it my duty to pass on to you such wisdom as I have acquired. I have had a long life, have had much time for thought as I lay all alone in my stall, and I think I may say that I understand the nature of life on this earth as well as any animal now living. It is about this that I wish to speak to you.

Now, comrades, what is the nature of this life of ours? Let us face it: our lives are miserable, laborious, and short. We are born, we are given just so much food as will keep the breath in our bodies, and those of us who are capable of it are forced to work to the last atom of our strength: and the very instant that our usefulness has come to an end we are slaughtered with hideous cruelty.

'But is this simply part of the order of nature? Is it because this land of ours is so poor that it cannot afford a decent life to those who dwell upon it? No, comrades, a thousand times no! This single farm of ours would support a dozen horses, twenty cows, hundreds of sheep—and all of them living in a comfort and a dignity that are now almost beyond our imagining. Why then do we continue in this miserable condition? Because nearly the whole of the produce of our labour is stolen from us by human beings. There, comrades, is the answer to all our problems. It is summed up in a single word—Man. Man is the only real enemy we have. Remove Man from the scene, and the root cause of hunger and overwork is abolished forever.

'Man is the only creature that consumes without producing. He does not give milk, he does not lay eggs, he is too weak to pull the plough, he cannot run fast enough to catch rabbits. Yet he is lord of all the animals. He sets them to work, he gives back to them the bare minimum that will prevent them from starving, and the rest he keeps for himself. Our labour tills the soil, our dung fertilizes it, and yet there is not one of us that owns more than his bare skin. You cows that I see before me, how many thousands of gallons of milk have you given during the last year? And what has happened to that milk which should have been breeding up sturdy calves? Every drop of it has gone down the throats of our enemies. And you hens, how many eggs have you laid this last year, and how many of those eggs ever hatched into chickens? The rest have all your labour in the field, what have you ever had except your bare rations and a stall?

Is it not crystal clear, then, comrades, that all the evils of this life of ours spring from the tyranny of human beings? Only get rid of Man, and the produce of our labour would be our own. Almost overnight we could become rich and free. What then must we do ? Why, work night and day, body and soul, for the overthrow of the human race! That is my message to you, comrades: Rebellion: I do not know when that Rebellion will come, it might be in a week or in a hundred years, but I know as surely as I see this straw beneath my feet, that sooner or later justice will be done. Fix your eyes on that, comrades, throughout the short remainder of your lives. And above all, pass on this message of mine to those who come after you, so that future generations shall carry on the struggle until it is victorious.

And remember, comrades, your resolution must never falter. No argument must lead you astray. Never listen when they tell you that Man and the animals have a common interest, that the prosperity of the one is the prosperity of the others. It is all lies. Man serves the interests of no creature except himself. And among us animals let there be perfect unity, perfect comradeship in the struggle. All men are enemies. All animals are comrades.

Questions:

1. Why was the ring of light from Mr. Jones's lantern dancing from side to side?
2. Where had the animals agreed to meet, and why?
3. What does old Major want to share with the animals?
4. Pick out the three words Major uses to describe the lives of the animals. Why does he use these words?
5. How is Man different from the animals?
6. How according to Major, can animals be rich and free?
7. When will this rebellion take place? Does this show that Major is
   (*i*) a realist? (*ii*) an idealist?
   (*iii*) a dreamer?
8. How does Major describe all men; and how does he describe all animals?
9. Why do you think Major calls the animals Comrades?

ANSWERS

1. Because Mr. Jones was drunk and his movement was not steady.
2. In the big barn to hear what Major had to say.
3. His understanding about the nature of life.
4. Miserable, laborious, short. He wanted to tell the animals how bad their living conditions were.
5. Animals produce all the wealth and Man takes it away from them. He does not produce anything himself.
6. By getting rid of Man, so that they can keep all the things they produced by themselves.
7. Major does not know. He is a dreamer.
8. All men as enemies; and all animals as comrades.
9. To remind them that they are all members of a Union.

TEST – 2

Directions: Read the text of the form given below and answer the questions that follow on the basis of what you have read.

INSTITUTE OF COMPUTER SCIENCE, ELECTRONICS & INSTRUMENTATION
DEVI ANUSUYA VISHWAVIDYALAYA, KHANDWA ROAD, INDORE

ADMISSION NOTICE

For academic session starting from July, 2004.

(A)	Master in Computer Management	(M.C.M.)	30 seats
(B)	Master in Computer Applications	(M.C.A.)	30 seats

M.C.M. 3 Years Evening Programme

Eligibility and Qualification: At least II class graduation in any discipline from a recognised University.

Written Test: February 15, 2004

(Time: 5:00 p.m. to 8:00 p.m.)

M.C.A. 3 Years Full Time Programme

Eligibility and Qualification: At least 55% in graduation with Mathematics at 10+2 level.

Written Test: February 16, 2004.

(Time: 5:00 p.m. to 8:00 p.m.)

Application Form: Prescribed Application form can be obtained by sending Rs.50/- by Banker's Cheque/ IPO in favour of the Director ICSEI, D.A.V.V. payable at Indore and a self-addressed envelope in size 14 × 22 cms with stamp of Rs. 10/. Send separate applications for each programme and subscribe the name of the programme on the left hand top corner.

LAST DATE OF RECEIPT OF APPLICATIONS IS 31ST JANUARY 2004

TEST CENTERS FOR M.C.A. INDORE & DELHI
TEST CENTERS FOR M.C.M. INDORE

ADMISSION NOTICE

NIIP'S CAREER PROGRAMMES IN SYSTEMS MANAGEMENT

The Integrated Higher Education Curriculum: Specially designed programmes for a high-profile career in computers. Starts with computer fundamentals, programming language, structured systems, analysis design.

Programme Options

Programme	***Duration***	***Regular***	***Fast Track***
1. Adv. Diploma in Systems Management	(4 Semesters)	24 Months	12 Months
2. Hons. Diploma in Systems Management	(3 Semesters)	18 Months	9 Months
3. Diploma in Systems Management	(2 Semesters)	12 Months	6 Months

Eligibility: Graduates in any discipline. Special Dual Qualification Scheme for Class XII and Undergraduates enabling simultaneous completion of the programme with graduation.

Questions:

1. COMPREHENSION

A. State whether the following are true (T) or false (F):

1. The NIIP has no last date for application.
2. The NIIP is a University.
3. Only graduates are eligible for admission to courses in Devi Anusuya Vishwavidyalaya.
4. The M.C.A. Course will finish in June 2006.
5. You can join NIIP only after graduating.
6. Your sister Madhu who is in class XII and your graduate friend can both do a course at NIIP now.
7. If you fill in the application form correctly, you will surely get admission in Devi Anusuya Vishwavidyalaya.
8. Devi Anusuya Vishwavidyalaya has a branch both in Indore and Delhi.
9. If you are a player, you will definitely get admission in Devi Anusuya Vishwavidyalaya.
10. In NIIP, you can do three courses at the same time.

B. Answer the following questions:

1. What two things will you have to send to get the application form of Devi Anusuya Vishwavidyalaya?
2. To whom will you send these two things?
3. Your friend Amit sent an application to Devi Anusuya Vishwavidyalaya on the 5th of February 2004 but did not get admission. Can you tell why?
4. Mohit of Lucknow wants to take admission in the M.C.A. and has sent his application. What should he do next?
5. Mr. Fernandes wants to do an honours course in Systems Management and wants to finish his course quickly. Where should he apply and how much time will it take him to complete the course?
6. Reshma got 65% marks in B.A. but could not get admission to the M.C.A. Course of Devi Anusuya Vishwavidyalaya. Can you give one reason for this?
7. What do you have to do to get admission in NIIP?
8. How will you send fifty rupees to Devi Anusuya Vishwavidyalaya to get an application form?

2. VOCABULARY

A. Tick (✔) the correct choice:

1. A recognised university is
   (*a*) One that everyone knows about.
   (*b*) A university that has been approved by an authority.
   (*c*) One that is the most popular University.
2. A prescribed application form is
   (*a*) A form prepared and issued by an institution.
   (*b*) A form giving all the necessary details.
   (*c*) A form signed by a gazetted officer.
3. A self-addressed envelope is
   (*a*) Any envelope which has your name on it.
   (*b*) Any envelope that you send to someone in your own handwriting.
   (*c*) One which you send after writing your own name and address on it so that an answer can be sent back to you.
4. A discipline means
   (*a*) A strict rule.
   (*b*) A branch of knowledge.
   (*c*) A kind of computer course.

B. Fill in the blanks with the following words: qualifications, career, availability, eligibility, guidance, completion.

1. Singing is not her hobby, it is her________.
2. We need someone who knows computer science, shorthand, and typing but you do not have the necessary________.
3. On the ________ of this course, you will get a certificate.
4. We are not sure of going to Kerala for a holiday for it depends on the ________ of train tickets.
5. After the death of his mother, he did not get proper________ so he got into bad company.

ANSWERS

1. COMPREHENSION

A. **1.** T **2.** F **3.** T **4.** F **5.** F
6. T **7.** F **8.** F **9.** F **10.** T

B.

1. A self-addressed envelope in size 14 × 22 cms with stamp of Rs. 10/- and Rs. 50/- Banker's cheque/IPO in favour of the Director ICSEI, D.A.V.V., payable at Indore.
2. To the Director ICSEI, D.A.V.V.
3. Because he sent his application late. The last date of receiving the applications was 31st January, 2004.
4. He will appear in a written test either in Indore or Delhi.
5. He should apply to the NIIP'S career programmes in systems Management and if he opts for the fast track programme, he can complete it in 9 months.
6. Perhaps she did not get admission to the M.C.A. course because she had not studied Mathematics at 10 + 2 level and thus did not fulfil the eligibility criteria.
7. You have to contact NIIP student Advisors.
8. We can send fifty rupees by Banker's cheque/IPO.

2. VOCABULARY

A. **1.** b **2.** a **3.** c **4.** b
B. **1.** career **2.** qualifications
3. completion **4.** availability **5.** guidance

CLOZE PROCEDURE (CP) TESTS

NOTES FOR STUDENTS' HELP on the Section titled Cloze Procedure (CP) Test Passages

Cloze procedure (CP) is a testing technique accepted as a global measure of language proficiency. Technically, a Cloze procedure text consists of a passage from which every **7th/6th/9th** word has been deleted. No deletions are made in the first two or three lines, to allow the theme of the passage to become established. Your task is to fill the blanks appropriately.

An obvious rationale of Cloze procedure is that there is a tendency to close broken language patterns in the same way that most people see an incomplete circle or triangle without any breaks or discontinuation.

A Model CP Test Follows

I assume that the desirability of a school book-stall needs no urging. Many schools sell food and toys. If we do not sell books, it is surely strange. Many schools serve areas where book shops do not exist and the only books brought before children for buying are the dubious selections of supermarkets. Moreover, even in communities where a good book **(1)**______ is available, the guidance which can be given **(2)**_______ the book-stall is valuable, as we soon **(3)**_______.

Essentially the school book-stall is an extension **(4)**_________ the encouragement and guidance in private reading which **(5)**_________ part of the work of the English teacher. **(6)**_________ first essential then, in setting up shop is **(7)**_________ teacher particularly interested in children's reading and in **(8)**_________ up as wide as possible a knowledge of **(9)**_________ to suit the school's range of pupils.

ANSWERS

1. shop **2.** at **3.** found
4. of **5.** is **6.** The
7. a **8.** building **9.** books

TEST – 1

Directions: Fill in the blanks with appropriate words in context. You can read the whole passage before beginning the task.

This bitterness, which is the bitterness of fear, made some shopkeepers bawl out rudely to many beggars who came hourly to beg at their doors. It made men ruthless in paying small fares _______ [1] the rickshaw-pullers, of which there were ten times _______ [2] many as could be used, because the refugees _______ [3] trying to earn something thus. Even the usual _______ [4] of rickshaws who followed this as their profession _______ [5] the refugees because, being starved, they would pull _______ [6] anything given to them, and no fares were too low _______ [7] anyone, and everyone suffered. With the city full _______ [8] refugees, then, begging at every door, swarming into _______ [9] unskilled trade and service, lying dead on the _______ [10] at every frozen dawn, how should one look _______ [11] this fresh horde coming in now at twilight _______ [12] a winter's day?

TEST – 2

Directions: Fill in the blanks with appropriate words in context. You can read the whole passage before beginning the task.

The Land, the human settlements, the forests, the flora and fauna, the water bodies and the envelope of air all constitute a spatial entity. Some of these components are more ________[1] and fragile than others and are ________[2] susceptible to degradation due to pollution. ________[3] planning is vital to protect these ________[4] areas. However, this concept or tool ________[5] seldom been used in India. Proper ________[6] of newly planned industries and industrial________[7] is a strong pollution preventive instrument ____________[8] ensures environmental sustainability of industrial ________[9]. It is the site that ultimately ________[10], which water bodies might be affected ________[11] effluents streaming out of an industry, ________[12] air shed might be affected by air ________[13] or which ecosystem might be harmed. ________[14] above urgency can also be emphasised ________[15] the Bhopal Gas Tragedy'. Had there ________[16] a sufficient compatibility between the industry ________[17] the surrounding land uses, the impact ________[18] the accident would have been less ________[19].

TEST – 3

Directions: Fill in the blanks with appropriate words in context. You can read the whole passage before beginning the task.

Some families created home literacy exercises designed to help children learn about family history, religion and values. For example:

"We live far away ________[1] our families and we want our ________[2] to know them and how important ________[3] are to us. Even though we ____________[4] see them often, we can write ________[5] letters. Sometimes, my children write their ________[6] letters, sometimes they write for me. ____________[7] tell them what I want to ____________[8] then they write it down for ________[9]. Their 'Naniji' – grandmother likes the letters ________[10] children write because she can see ________[11] hand-writing. I have them address the ________[12] too. Sometimes we go to the ________[13] office together to mail the letters. ________[14] try to write a letter each ________[15] to a different relative. I save ________[16] of the letters the relatives write ________[17] us because I think my children ________[18] like to read them again when ________[19] are older. It will help them ________[20] their grandparents and what life was ________[21] in our country."

"Our family goes ________[22] church together. We bring home the ________[23] each week and use it to ________[24] reading. Sometimes we read prayers from ________[25] prayer book or stories from the ________[26]. Frequently, my children write down the ________[27] they learn at church."

"I use ________[28] to help my children learn about ________[29]. For example, I told my daughter '________[30] is only skin deep.' Then we ________[31] about what that meant. We made ________[32] whole list of sayings and wrote ________[33] the lesson that each one taught. ________[34] think these are important values for ________[35] daughter to learn."

TEST – 4

Directions: Fill in the blanks with appropriate words in context. You can read the whole passage before beginning the task.

A puppet is an artificial figure whose movements are controlled by a person. Puppets can be moved by hand ________[1] by strings, wires or rods. A figure ________[2] represent a person, an animal, a plant

______[3] an object. Puppets usually appear as characters ______[4] plays called puppet shows. A person who ______[5] a puppet is called a puppeteer.

Many ______[6] make puppets from such cheap materials as ______[7] and wood or from such items as ______[8] cartons and rags. They write puppet shows ______[9] operate the puppets, varying their voice for ______[10] character. A table or bookcase can be ______[11] as a stage for a puppet show. ______[12] puppeteer can also work behind a blanket ______[13] a sheet tied across the lower part ______[14] a doorway. We cannot see the puppeteer. ______[15] see only the puppets performing in the ______[16] part of the doorway.

Hand puppets are ______[17] most common puppets. One variety, the glove ______[18] fist puppet, consists of a hollow head ______[19] to a glove or a piece of ______[20] used as the puppet's body. The body ______[21] over the hand of the puppeteer who ______[22] a thumb into one of the puppet's ______[23], one or two fingers go into the ______[24] arm and the remaining fingers in the ______[25]. These puppets can pick up and throw ______[26] and can gesture strongly with their head ______[27] arms. Most glove puppets have no legs ______[28] feet.

Another type of puppets are those ______[29] are controlled by strings or by wires. ______[30] are known as marionettes. A marionette has ______[31] complete body with head, trunk, arms, hands, ______[32] and feet. Strips of cloth or other ______[33] material connect the various parts of the ______[34]. Most marionettes have strings that run ______[35] the head, the shoulders, the hands and ______[36] knees to a small wooden frame. One ______[37] more puppeteers, who are hidden above the ______[38], operate the marionettes by moving the string ______[39] they are tied to the frame.

TEST – 5

Directions: Fill in the blanks with appropriate words in context. You can read the whole passage before beginning the task.

A rich old lady was steadily losing her eyesight, so she called in a famous doctor who examined her and offered to cure her completely. He ______[1] a very big fee, and ______[2] rich lady gladly agreed to ______[3] him the money if he ______[4] restore her sight. The doctor ______[5] her eyes and carried out ______[6] treatment, which took several days. ______[7] he was very greedy. He ______[8] many beautiful pieces of furniture ______[9] which the house of his ______[10] was furnished, and each day ______[11] carried away one of the ______[12] pieces till there was hardly ______[13] left.

In the course of ______[14], the lady was completely cured. ______[15] bandage was taken off, and ______[16] could see everything clearly. Then ______[17] discovered that almost all her ______[18] was gone. When the doctor ______[19] for his payment, she said, '______[20] here, doctor I am by ______[21] means cured, for I cannot ______[22] my furniture in my house. ______[23] not going to pay you ______[24]. The doctor was thus paid ______[25] his own coin.

TEST – 6

Directions: Fill in the blanks with appropriate words in context. You can read the whole passage before beginning the task.

This lack of food was confirmed when one looked closely into the faces of the people. In the first glance in the twilight they ______[1] well enough, but when one looked more closely ______[2] saw they were the faces of people starving ______[3] moving now in despair to a last hope. ______[4] saw nothing of the strange sights of a ______[5] city because they were too near death to ______[6] anything. No new sight could move their curiosity, ________[7] were men and women, who had stayed by ________[8] land until starvation drove them forth. Thus they ______[9], silent, alien, as those who know themselves _______[10] are alien to the living.

ANSWERS

Test-1

1. to	**2.** as	**3.** were
4. pullers	**5.** cursed	**6.** for
7. for	**8.** of	**9.** every
10. streets	**11.** at	**12.** of

Test-2

1. sensitive	**2.** more	**3.** environmental
4. sensitive	**5.** has	**6.** siting
7. estates	**8.** that	**9.** development
10. determines	**11.** by	**12.** which
13. pollutants	**14.** the	**15.** by
16. been	**17.** and	**18.** of
19. severe		

Test-3

1. from	**2.** children	**3.** they
4. can't	**5.** them	**6.** own
7. I	**8.** say	**9.** me
10. the	**11.** their	**12.** envelopes
13. post	**14.** We	**15.** week
16. some	**17.** to	**18.** might
19. they	**20.** remember	**21.** like
22. to	**23.** bulletin	**24.** practise
25. the	**26.** Bible	**27.** prayers
28. sayings	**29.** values	**30.** beauty
31. talked	**32.** a	**33.** down
34. I	**35.** my	

Test-4

1. or	**2.** may	**3.** or
4. in	**5.** operates	**6.** children
7. cloth	**8.** milk	**9.** and
10. each	**11.** used	**12.** a
13. or	**14.** of	**15.** we
16. upper	**17.** the	**18.** or
19. attached	**20.** cloth	**21.** fits
22. puts	**23.** arms	**24.** other
25. head	**26.** things	**27.** and
28. or	**29.** that	**30.** They
31. a	**32.** legs	**33.** such
34. marionette	**35.** from	**36.** the
37. or	**38.** stage	**39.** where

Test-5

1. demanded	**2.** the	**3.** pay
4. could	**5.** bandaged	**6.** the
7. But	**8.** saw	**9.** with
10. patient	**11.** he	**12.** best
13. anything	**14.** time	**15.** The
16. she	**17.** she	**18.** furniture
19. came	**20.** Look	**21.** no
22. see	**23.** I'm	**24.** anything
25. in		

Test-6

1. seemed	**2.** one	**3.** and
4. They	**5.** new	**6.** see
7. they	**8.** their	**9.** passed
10. dying		

C-TESTS

TEST – 1

Directions: Fill in the blanks. Each blank begins with one or more than one letter. Taking a clue from that, you are directed to fill in the blanks in the following passage:

Four weeks ago I was late for work. I left my house five minutes later than usual and I saw **m**__________[1] bus approaching the bus stop. I began to **r**__________[2], but I was too slow. I waited ten **mi**__________[3] for another bus and I was still gasping **f**__________[4] air when it arrived. The next day I **g**__________[5] up smoking. For the first few days I **w**__________[6] very irritable, but now I feel much better. **N**__________[7] I can ask: Why do people smoke?

Every **y**__________[8] teams of doctors publish reports saying that smoking **i**__________[9] dangerous for your health. Every year the Government **p**__________[10] for advertisements telling people that smoking is bad **f**__________[11] them. But there are millions of people who **st**__________[12] smoke twenty or thirty cigarettes a day.

In **s**__________[13] countries advertisements for cigarettes are not allowed on **tel**__________[14]. If you read a newspaper or a magazine **y**__________[15] will see cigarette advertisements but at the bottom **o**__________[16] each advertisement you will see the government health **wa**____________[17] – Cigarette Smoking is Injurious to Health. You can **re**__________[18] this warning on cigarette packets also. And yet **pe**__________[19] die every year from the effects of smoking. **O**________[20] wonders why people smoke.

Experts in various fields **s**__________[21] that it is difficult to understand why people **be**_________[22] to smoke and why they make it a **ha**__________[23]. Most people start smoking because other people around **th**__________[24] do it. Children feel it makes them seem **ad**__________________[25] to smoke, and other children also encourage them **t**________________[26] smoke. Some children see their parents smoking, so **th**__________[27] start smoking too. The effect that smoking has **o**__________[28] a person helps to make it a habit. **Cig**__________[29] contain nicotine which has an effect on the **he**__________[30] and the nervous system. Smoking one or two **Cig**__________[31] causes an increase in the heart rate and **a**__________[32] slight rise in blood pressure. The effect of **sm**__________[33] on the nervous system is that it reduces **te**__________[34] and helps to relax. People want these effects **o**__________[35] feel they need them and start depending on **th**__________[36] and so they go on smoking.

TEST – 2

Directions: Fill in the blanks. Each blank begins with one or more than one letter. Taking a clue from that, you are directed to fill in the blanks in the following passage:

Fashion is a term commonly used to describe a style of clothing worn by a large number of **pe**________[1] in a country. However, popular styles **o**________[2] furniture, homes and many other products **a**________[3] also fashions. The kinds of art, **m**________[4], literature and sports that many people **pr**________[5] can also be fashions. Thus, a **fa**________[6] is – or reflects – a form of **beh**________[7] accepted by most people in a **so**________[8].

A fashion remains popular for a **f**________[9] months or years and then another **fa**________[10] takes its place. A product or **ac**________[11] is in fashion or is fashionable **du**________[12] the period of time that many **pe**________[13] in society accept it. After a **t**________[14], however, the same product or activity **be**________[15] old – fashioned when the majority of **pe**________[16] no longer accept it.

A clothing **st**________[17] may start as a fashion but **i**________[18] use becomes a custom if it **i**________[19] handed down from generation to generation. **To**________[20], wearing long trousers is a custom **f**________[21] men in most countries. But changes **i**________[22] the colour and shape of trousers **h**______________[23] taken place through the years. A **fa**______________[24] that quickly comes and goes is **ca**____________[25] a fad. The majority of people **d**___________[26] not accept fads. Some people may **be**________[27] involved in faddish behaviour because fads **g**__________[28] a lot of publicity.

Today people **fo**________[29] fashions for many reasons. For example, **th**________[30] want others to think that they **be**________[31] to a special class of society. **N**__________[32] fashions may be adopted immediately by **w**____________[33] known people, including athletes, film stars **a**________[34] political figures. Then, other people follow **th**________[35] fashions so that they can also **l**________[36] important. Some people think that fashionable **cl**________[37] and surroundings raise their status in **l**__________[38].

People also follow fashions to make **th**________[39] more attractive. Standards of beauty change **th**____________[40] the years, and people decorate themselves **ac**________[41] to the changing standards. Ideas of **be**__________[42] also change from culture to culture. **F**__________[43] example, people in many countries use **co**__________[44] to look attractive. In some countries **pe**__________[45] decorate themselves with tattoos.

Men and **wo**_______[46] have always enjoyed changing their appearance. **Fol**_______[47] new fashions in clothes, hairstyles **a**_________[48] makeup allow people to change their **ap**________[49] in a way which is generally **ac**________[50].

TEST – 3

Directions: Fill in the blanks. Each blank begins with one or more than one letter. Taking clue from that, you are directed to fill in the blanks in the following passage.

Perhaps the most important contribution of forests to modern civilization is that they provide the raw material for making **pa**_________[1]. The Chinese who invented paper several thousand **ye**__________[2] back used the inner bark of certain **t**__________[3] for making paper. Today, paper is made **mo**__________[4] from wood, bamboo and certain types of **gr**__________[5]. The paper on which this book has **b**__________[6] printed must have been made out of **w**__________[7] or bamboo and certain types of grasses. **V**__________[8] little work can be done these days **wi**__________[9] the use of paper, and we can **e**__________[10] say that modern civilization depends on paper.

T__________[11] are a large number of other raw **mat**__________[12] which come from the forests. Pine trees **yi**__________[13] resin from which resin and turpentine are **man**__________[14]. Resin is used in the sizing of **pa**__________[15] and textiles and for making paints, varnishes, **po**__________[16] and adhesives. Turpentine is used for making **p**__________[17] and varnishes. It is also used for **ma**__________[18] medicines, and is now being used for **t**__________[19] manufacture of artificial camphor, which is used **f**__________[20] medicines, and during religious ceremonious. Natural camphor **i**__________[21] also produced by forests and it comes **f**__________[22] the wood and leaves of the camphor **w**__________[23] tree which is mostly found in China **a**__________[24] Taiwan. But now in our country all **ca**__________[25] is obtained from turpentine. Some forest trees **yi**__________[26] gums which are not only used for **st**__________[27] paper but are also used in the **pre**__________[28] of sweets and ice-creams.

Medicinal herbs and **pl**__________[29] are another important gift of the forests **t**__________[30] mankind. They are used in the Ayurvedic **a**__________[31] Unani as well as the modern systems **o**__________[32] medicine. The Ayurvedic and Unani systems of **med**__________[33] have been practiced in our country for **cen**__________[34] and they both rely on medicinal plants **a**__________[35] herbs. In every village shop in India, **o**__________[36] can buy dried roots, barks, leaves, flowers **o**__________[37] fruits of different medicinal plants which are **u**__________[38] for common diseases.

In the life of **o**__________[39] rural people products from the forests play **a**__________[40] important role. They provide people with material **t**__________[41] make huts and to thatch roofs, wood **f**__________[42] making bullock carts, agricultural tools and household **fur**__________[43] and fibres for making ropes, nets, mats, **ba**__________[44] and many other items of daily use.

ANSWERS

Test-1

1. my	**2.** run	**3.** minutes
4. for	**5.** gave	**6.** was
7. Now	**8.** year	**9.** is
10. pays	**11.** for	**12.** still
13. some	**14.** television	**15.** you
16. of	**17.** warning	**18.** read
19. people	**20.** One	**21.** say
22. begin	**23.** habit	**24.** them
25. adult	**26.** to	**27.** they
28. on	**29.** Cigarettes	**30.** heart
31. Cigarettes	**32.** a	**33.** smoking
34. tension	**35.** or	**36.** them

Test-2

1. people	**2.** of	**3.** are
4. music	**5.** prefer	**6.** fashion
7. behaviour	**8.** society	**9.** few
10. fashion	**11.** activity	**12.** during
13. people	**14.** time	**15.** becomes
16. people	**17.** style	**18.** its
19. is	**20.** Today	**21.** for

22. in	**23.** have	**24.** fashion
25. called	**26.** do	**27.** become
28. get	**29.** follow	**30.** they
31. belong	**32.** New	**33.** well
34. and	**35.** these	**36.** look
37. clothes	**38.** life	**39.** themselves
40. through	**41.** according	**42.** beauty
43. For	**44.** cosmetics	**45.** people
46. women	**47.** Following	**48.** and
49. appearance	**50.** accepted	

Test-3

1. paper	**2.** years	**3.** trees
4. mostly	**5.** grasses	**6.** been
7. wood	**8.** Very	**9.** without
10. even	**11.** There	**12.** materials
13. yield	**14.** manufactured	
15. paper	**16.** polishes	**17.** paints
18. making	**19.** the	**20.** for
21. is	**22.** from	**23.** wood
24. and	**25.** camphor	**26.** yield
27. sticking	**28.** preparation	**29.** plants
30. to	**31.** and	**32.** of
33. medicine	**34.** centuries	**35.** and
36. one	**37.** or	**38.** used
39. our	**40.** an	**41.** to
42. for	**43.** furniture	**44.** baskets

TESTS OF WRITING ABILITY

PRÉCIS WRITING

Introduction

Précis Writing is an important branch of English studies, and is an outstanding feature of many examinations, public or official.

The ability to produce a good précis implies that the writer possesses, first of all, the power of judgement. That judgement has to be applied not only to the selection of words with which to clothe ideas; but also to the accurate and rapid evaluation of facts and details. For a précis, matter must be sifted until the chaff of unnecessary detail has been separated out and only the good wheat of fact remains.

Again, the student who desires to excel as a précis writer must possess that, which is always an indispensable asset, namely, a good vocabulary, which he can spell accurately, and of the meaning of which he is absolutely sure. Neither a technical nor a highly ornate vocabulary is necessary; but rather one that will provide the writer with suitable synonyms and sufficient variations of expression to enable him to avoid monotony and repetition in the presentation of his ideas.

The third great asset required is the power to write concisely. Every word in a précis must have a definite value. This conciseness should not, however, be allowed to degenerate into telegraphic curtness, or into such brevity as leads to ambiguity of meaning.

To be further specific, a précis is to be written in indirect speech, and it has to follow a logical order of ideas, facts and details, or information.

Major guidelines for students can be embodied as follows:

1. Read through a given piece at least twice, in order to grasp its general purport.
2. Read it through again, and, while doing so, underline everthing that appears relevant and important.
3. It is often found useful to number in the margin, and in logical order, all points thus underlined, since they must appear in logical order in the précis. This numbering helps the writer to deal quickly and easily with his points, while, at the same time, he considerably lessens the chances of omitting some important fact in his draft précis.
4. The student should now prepare the rough draft of his précis, embodying in it all the numbered points. This need not be a polished narrative. It is simply the skeleton upon which the final structure is to be built.
5. Every précis *must* have a heading/title. First of all, a student is advised to write down the heading, and having done so, he /she should forget about it. It has no part in the précis itself. It is not counted in computing the number of words in the narrative, nor, in the course of the narrative, must it be referred to.
6. No extraneous matter whatever may be introduced into the précis.
7. The opening sentences of the précis must give a clear and definite idea of what is to follow.

8. There is no hard and fast rule as to the length of a précis. Some times the writer is asked to compress the salient features/ facts of a narrative into 150, 200, 300 words, and in an examination he/she is supposed to keep *strictly* within the word limit prescribed. If there is no definite word limit, the precis should not greatly exceed one third of the original.
9. Inability to cut down the narrative to its required limit is a sign of a beginner. As a student practises and progresses, he/she will find it easier to keep within the limits. The student must not at any account indulge in abbreviations, or omit such short words, for example, *as, a, an, in, or, of*. There are, however, certain legitimate ways in which he/she may help to cut down the number of words in her/his precis.
    a. Eliminate all adjectives except those that have a special or technical significance.
    b. Conjunctions may be used to give place to semi-colons, except where the elimination of the conjunctions would affect the grammatical accuracy of the sentence.

Practice Tests

TEST– 1

Q. Write a précis of the following passage in about 175 words, and give it a suitable title.

We have the most dishonest tax system in the world. Such high rates of income tax, wealth tax and compulsory deposit have been levied in the past years that we should have turned into a socialist paradise long ago; yet in practice inequalities continue to grow day by day. In this process we penalise only the honest. The rich effortlessly evade tax while the salaried classes are made to pay taxes through their nose. Thundering speeches are made about cracking down on black money, but, after a decent interval of ineffective enforcement, we introduce schemes like voluntary disclosure or bearer bonds, which make black money perfectly legal.

First of all we levy taxes that would make all honest businessmen bankrupt and then we have the audacity to complain that the businessmen are not investing enough. The truth is that, if by some miracle, everybody starts paying all the taxes due, there would be a very large number of bankruptcies and closures in the private sector, and this would possibly force the government to hand back the taxes collected. In such a situation it is difficult to levy taxes.

The dishonesty now extends to political parties with varying economic policies and programmes. If the Finance Minister makes a modest reduction in the rate of income-tax, the leftists describe this as a sell-out to the rich. But on every occasion, a tax cut is followed by increased taxation on something else. There can, in fact, be no genuine tax reduction for the honest tax-payer because there is no such thing as an honest tax payer.

In reality it makes not the slightest difference whether the tax rates are increased or decreased. They result in much the same. It means that the businessmen have already decided in advance how much tax they are going to pay and changing the tax rates does not materially affect them. In reality, therefore, it is not the Finance Minister but the business community that decides the effective rate of tax and this need not be the same as the official rate of tax.

There is an ancient rule in law-making that one should not enact a law which cannot be implemented, as this merely brings the law into disrepute. In India, we have persistently ignored this rule and if there is a growing disrespect for the law today, our approach must share much of the blame for making laws which cannot be enforced.

The atrociously high rates of tax we have introduced in the name of socialism have made tax evasion respectable and an honest folly.

Those, who mistakenly view tax collection as a moral rather than administrative problem, complain bitterly of corruption and inefficiency in tax administration. But there is little evidence of less corruption and inefficiency in the other sectors. Do we have an efficient police or an efficient bus system, or an efficient electricity supply? We must face the fact that we sadly lack the honesty and efficiency required for a modern industrial state and it is no use expecting the tax administration to perform miracles.

Title: Defective tax system in India

Précis. The Indian tax system is the most dishonest one in the world. Heavy taxation is resorted to in order to bridge economic inequalities but this system has helped in perpetuating those inequalities instead. Indian tax system penalises only the honest tax payers because the rich generally evade it. After its failure to enforce the taxation laws, the government often resorts to various schemes to legalise black money. Tax reductions are only façades because there are no genuine tax payers. Changes in the tax rate do not materially affect the tax-evading businessmen. It is rather the businessmen and not the Finance Minister who actually decide the actual rate of tax. We are blamed for ignoring the golden rule of law-making that the laws that cannot be enforced should not be passed. Corruption and inefficiency are peculiar not only to tax-administration but are rampant in other sectors as well. We must, therefore, admit our lack of honesty and efficiency and must not expect miracles from tax administration.

TEST – 2

Q. Write a précis of the following passage in about 175 words, and give it a suitable title.

How often one hears children wishing they were grown-up, and old people wishing they were young again. Each age has its pleasures and its pains, and the happiest person is the one who enjoys what age gives him without wasting his time in useless regrets.

Childhood is a time when there are few responsibilities to make life difficult. If a child has good parents, he is fed, looked after and loved, whatever he may do. It is improbable that he will ever be given so much in his life again without having to do anything in return. In addition, life always presents new things to a child-things that have lost their interest for older people because they are too well known. His first visit to the seaside is a marvellous adventure. But a child has his pains: he is not free to do whatever he wishes, as he thinks older people can. He is continually told not to do certain things and is punished for the wrong he has done. His life is therefore, not perfectly happy.

When the youngman starts earning his own living, he becomes free from the discipline of school and parents; but at the same time he is forced to accept responsibilities. He can no longer expect others to pay for his food, lodging etc., but has to work to live comfortably. If he spends most of his time playing about in the way he used to as a child, he will have to go hungry. And if he breaks the laws of society, as he used to break the laws of his parents, he may have to go to prison. If, however, he works hard, keeps out of trouble, and has good health, he can have the happiness of seeing himself make steady progress in his job and of building up his own position in society.

Old age has always been thought of as the worst age to be in; but it is not necessary for the old to be unhappy. With old age should come wisdom and the ability to help others with advice wisely given. The old can have the joy of seeing their children making progress in life; they can watch their grandchildren growing up around them; and perhaps best of all, they can, if their life had been a useful one, feel the happiness of having come through the battle of life safely and of having reached a time when they can lie back and rest, leaving others to continue their life.

Title: Different stages of human life.

Précis. Children often wish to be grown ups just as the latter wish to be young again. Each stage of human life has its enjoyments and pains. Happiness lies in enjoying each stage without any regrets. If childhood enjoys all cares and pleasures, it has its own constraints as the child is not free to do anything he wishes. In childhood, life is not perfectly happy because if the child violates his parents' instructions, he is punished. Similarly, the life of a grown up is also hedged with many limitations. He cannot afford to play all the time because if he does, he will starve. Also, he cannot break the laws of society as easily as he could flout his parents instructions when he was a child. Hard work can bring many advantages to a grown up. Though old age is supposed to be the worst period, yet it need not be unhappy. In old age one can have the satisfaction of being wise and can give advice to others.

TEST – 3

Q. Write a précis of the following passage in about 175 words, and give it a suitable title.

Unemployment, in the modern society, which is built on the capitalist system, is a necessary evil. The capitalist grows richer with the concentration of wealth in his hands, at the expense of the poor. The feudal system of old was unjust and cruel. But it had no unemployment problems to face. The socialist systems of Russia and China have no unemployment because the capitalist who has a selfish aim of exploitation, does not exist. Industry is state owned. The state guarantees work, food and clothing to every one. Industry is run for the benefit of the workers themselves. Production is always planned. Since returns of production in the shape of wealth are distributed amongst the workers themselves, their purchasing powers also increase. Hence they can consume more and more of the goods manufactured. The Socialist system does not seek to glut the market to ruin the worker. This unemployment is unheard of in Soviet Russia. We read practically daily in the papers about the figures showing unemployment in a wealthy country like America or a highly industrialised country like England.

The capitalist system has to face many crises. These crises are responsible for unemployment. When a slump or a depression comes, the capitalist owner of the industry, who runs it with a profit motive, closes it down at a moment's notice. Thousands are thrown out of jobs and are left either to starve on the roadside or live on government dole. War is the only remedy for unemployment known to this bankrupt system. And what is war? It is again the exploitation of the poor by the rich - the pursuit of vested interests of a country. The remedy for unemployment under this system, then, is more terrible than the disease.

How can we solve the problem of unemployment? Obviously the answer will be either by discarding machines altogether and reverting to the economy of the good old times or by eliminating the capitalist and running the machines for the benefit of the workers. All industry should be nationalised. The government should have a planned economy. This planning should be done keeping in view the welfare of the common men and not a handful of rich industrialists and landlords. New industries should be started to provide more and more work. India is an under-developed country. There is no dearth of workers here. In all spheres of its economy, it requires men and more men. Its natural resources are immense but untapped so far. If we try to exploit its natural wealth in the proper way, we shall find that we need more people for assistance than we can actually provide.

Unemployment is a great curse. It wrecks society. It turns law abiding and honest men into criminals and dacoits. In fact, it brings to the surface the evil sides of human character. It is a great danger to the government itself. Soon discontent gives place to agitation against the government. Agitation may result in political unrest or a revolution. A wise government will always keep an eye on the unemployed and keep down their number as much as it can.

Title: The problem of unemployment.

Précis. The capitalist system concentrates wealth in the hands of a few capitalists and, thus, gives rise to the problem of unemployment. Even the unjust and cruel feudal system of the old did not create unemployment problems. In a socialist system the industry is state-owned and the capitalist cannot exploit the workers for selfish aims. So all the profits go to the workers. Their purchasing capacity increases, thus maintaining a balance between supply and demand. In the capitalist system, the owner of the industry runs it with a profit motive. When a slump or a depression comes, he closes it down throwing thousands out of their jobs. Under this system the only remedy of unemployment is war, which is again the exploitation of the poor by the rich. The unemployment problem can be solved by nationalising all industry, by having a planned economy, by starting new industries and by exploiting natural resources. Unemployment not only wrecks society, it also causes political instability. So a wise government should always be careful to keep the number of the unemployed to the minimum.

TEST – 4

Q. Write a précis of the following passage in about 175 words, and give it a suitable title.

Most people would agree that, although our age surpasses all previous ages in knowledge, there has been no co-relative increase in 'wisdom' and the means of promoting it. I would firstly want to ask what is wisdom, and then what can be done to increase it?

There are, I think, several factors that contribute to wisdom. Of these I should put first a sense of proportion, i.e., the capacity to take account of all the important factors in a problem and to attach each its due weight. This has become more difficult than it used to be, owing to the extent and complexity of the specialised knowledge required for various kinds of technicians. Suppose, for example, that you are engaged in research in scientific medicine. The work is difficult and is likely to absorb the whole of your intellectual energy. You have no time to consider the effect which your discoveries or inventions may have outside the field of medicine. You succeed, as modern medicine has succeeded, in enormously lowering the infant death-rate, not only in Europe and America, but also in Asia and Africa. This has the entirely unintended result of making the food supply inadequate and lowering the standard of life in the most populous parts of the world.

Comprehensiveness alone, however, is not enough to constitute wisdom. There must be, also, a certain awareness of the goals of human life. This may be illustrated by the study of history. Many eminent historians have done more harm than good because they viewed facts through the distorting medium of their own passions. Hegel had a philosophy of history which did not suffer from any lack of comprehensiveness, since it started from the earliest times and continued into an indefinite future. But the chief lesson of history, which he sought to inculcate, was that from the years A.D. 400 down to his own time, Germany had been the most important nation and the standard-bearer of progress in the world. Perhaps one could stretch the comprehensiveness that constitutes wisdom to include not only intellect but also feeling. It is by no means uncommon to find men whose knowledge is wide but whose feelings are narrow. Such men lack what I call wisdom. To take an even more spectacular example, which is in everybody's mind at the present time, we study the composition of the atom from a disinterested desire for knowledge, and incidentally place in the hands of powerful lunatics the means of destroying the human race. In such ways, the pursuit of knowledge becomes harmful unless it is combined with wisdom. But wisdom, in the sense of comprehensive vision, is not necessarily present in specialists in the pursuit of knowledge.

Title: Knowledge and wisdom

Précis. Even though there has been tremendous increase of knowledge in the modern age, there has been no co-relative increase in wisdom. Wisdom comprises many factors, the first of which is a sense of proportion i.e., the capacity to have a comprehensive view of any problem. This can be illustrated by the example of research in scientific medicine. Such a research may sometimes lead to entirely unintended results, as for example, it brought down the infant mortality-rate and hence made food supply scarce because of increased population. Comprehensiveness must be coupled with the awareness of the goals of human life. The study of history can best illustrate the necessity of such awareness as, Hegel's philosophy of history, though no less comprehensive, tended to turn Germany into the most important nation and the standard-bearer of progress in the world. Comprehensiveness should not only include knowledge but also feeling. This can be illustrated by the study of atom, the knowledge of which can prove to be both beneficial and disastrous to mankind. Hence, the pursuit of knowledge becomes harmful unless it is combined with wisdom.

TESTS OF GRAMMAR

TEST – 1

Pronouns

Directions: Join together each of the following pairs of sentences by means of a Relative Pronouns:

1.	He is a rogue.	No one trusts him.
2.	We got into a bus.	It was full of passengers.
3.	I saw a juggler.	He was showing his tricks.
4.	Here is the book.	You lost it yesterday.
5.	Here is the pen.	You were looking for it.
6.	We met a boy.	He had lost his way.
7.	My brother is dead.	I loved my brother.
8.	These are the boys.	Their parents are here.
9.	Bali stole the pen.	Bali was punished.
10.	That is the man.	We saw him yesterday.
11.	The boy tells lies.	He deserves to be punished.
12.	This is the boy.	His book has been stolen.
13.	Look at these boys.	They are singing.
14.	This is the man.	I trusted him.
15.	I am the person.	You sent for me.
16.	This is the man.	His son stood first.
17.	Here is the book.	I told you about it.
18.	We heard some news.	The news astonished us.
19.	This is the road.	It leads to the station.
20.	He does his best.	He should be praised.

TEST – 2

Usage of Verb and Subject-Verb Agreement

Directions: Correct, improve or justify the following sentences:

1. Too great a variety of studies distract the mind.
2. He as well as his sisters were present in the meeting.
3. The whole fleet of their ships were captured.
4. My requirements are as follow.
5. Each of these students have done their work.
6. The horse and carriage are at the door.
7. Many a men have yielded to this temptation.
8. None but fools has ever believed it.
9. He is one of the cleverest boys that has passed through the school.
10. Milk and soda are a refreshing drink.
11. Either of these six teams might win the cup.
12. The 'Three Musketeers' are very interesting to read.
13. My friend, philosopher and guide have come.
14. The majority are opposed to this proposal.
15. His kindness and benevolence are well-known.
16. I had been to Bombay last year.
17. He told me that he saw his father last month.
18. Either you or I are guilty.
19. I never have, and never will allow my son to take meat.
20. If he would have worked hard, he would have passed the examination.
21. I will be drowned, nobody shall save me.
22. Unless he will be more careful, he will not recover.
23. Two or two makes four.
24. The United states easily take the lead in the production of the steel.
25. A fair means do not always bring success.
26. The end was come as the end of such matters generally comes by gradual decay.
27. The temper as well as the knowledge of a modern historian require a more sober and accurate language.
28. Although the guns were raging all round, neither I nor my horse were touched.
29. No action or instruction can be permanent which are not based on reason and morality.
30. To write, to speak, or to act seem uncommonly easy to a number of over-confident persons.
31. This book is regarded by modern scholars as one of the most shining treatises of morality that is available.
32. There are a dozen large hotels in this town.
33. In these phrases of Shakespeare lie the secret of his genius.
34. The sincerity and honesty of the English Government is heartily recognised and thoroughly admired.
35. I would do this if I was allowed.
36. He works hard that he might finish it quickly.
37. Since the date the strike was declared, twenty clerks have been appointed and thirty resigned.
38. You will receive the money, rest sure.
39. Measles have been prevalent in the city.
40. I will do little more than suggest a few things.

41. My spectacles are broken.
42. I am sure I will be dismissed soon.
43. Every flower and every leaf proclaim the glory of God.
44. Where you spent your last summer vacation?
45. I should be glad if you will come in the evening.
46. So quickly we walked that we reached the school in time.
47. Character and not riches win us respect.
48. The sum and substance of his speech are as follow.
49. None but those having teaching experience needs apply.
50. Sixty rupees are not a large sum for that painting.
51. It were the girls that defied their teacher's order.
52. He got angry before I said a word.
53. Never I had seen such a sight.
54. No sooner I had reached the station, than the train started.
55. If you would see him, you would known him.
56. Not only he will go but also he will stay there.
57. Neither she comes nor she writes.
58. He said that he will send him some money.
59. I shall help you in need.
60. He will likely depart in a few days.
61. We have written the letter last evening.
62. He worked three hours when I met him.
63. Nothing but fraud and dishonesty are discernible in his actions.
64. The young and old men were sitting in the room.
65. The soldiers as well as the commander was running away.

TEST – 3

Active – Passive Voice

Instructions: Change the voice in the following sentences from active to passive.

1. Ram kicks the ball.
2. The minister has postponed the meeting.
3. Gavaskar hit the ball for a six.
4. We keep our jewellery in the bank.
5. Raman's father donated this shield to the college.
6. Who wrote it?
7. What caused this defect?
8. Dew wet the grass.
9. She looked after the children well.
10. The security man checks every visitor at the gate.
11. The government will set up a cement plant.
12. How did you get this confidential information?
13. We shall shoulder the responsibility.
14. Are they criticising you?
15. They are clearing the roads of snow.
16. Who has broken this window pane?
17. We were cheering our team.
18. Somebody had struck him on the head with a blunt weapon.
19. Have you given him permission?
20. The artists were demanding higher wages.
21. Are they observing the rules?
22. Are they avoiding me?
23. Have you given the details?
24. The government has appointed many doctors recently.
25. He had made his plans well in advance.
26. They will have declared the results by the time you reach there.
27. Reveal the secret.
28. Let us forget the past.
29. Some one might have poisoned the food.
30. They should dismiss inefficient workers.
31. Bring the food.
32. They had taken precautions to prevent his escape.
33. Have you found your passport?
34. Have you solved the problem?
35. The police was arresting drunken drivers.
36. He has completed his assignment.
37. Will you finish your work punctually?
38. The postman delivered the letter today.
39. How did you catch the thief?
40. Will they declare Friday, a holiday?
41. It will create problems.
42. Our cricket team won most of the matches.
43. They inspect the factory every week.
44. Most children like sweets.

45. Exhaust gases polluted the air.
46. They sold off the old furniture.
47. Send him to prison.
48. Can we forget the past?
49. They should release the prisoners.
50. Edison invented the first gramophone.

TEST – 4

Active – Passive Voice

I. Given below is a newspaper report. Fill in the passive voice of the verbs in the brackets against each blank.

Work on two pontoon bridges

New DELHI, June 11 (HTC)

The proposal for setting up two more pontoon bridges across the Yamuna[1]____________ were (take) today at a high level meeting at Raj Niwas.

Besides the Lt. Governor P.K. Dave, the meeting was [2]____________ (attend) by the Municipal Commissioner, Vice-Chairman DDA and senior officers of the PWD and Traffic Police.

The quick construction of the pontoon bridges[3]____________ (emphasise) in the light of the fact that the completion of new bridges at ITO, Wazirabad and Nizamuddin would entail considerable time.

Pending the construction of these large bridges, the pontoon bridges are likely to relieve the existing bridges from the load of light traffic.

The Lt. Governor issued instructions that the construction of Seelampur over-bridge, railway underpass at Patparganj Road, sliproads to ITO bridges, improvement of Pushta Road and culverts [4]____________(monitor) closely so that the works [5]____________ (complete) as per the schedule.

II. Complete part b of the following sentences by filling in the blanks.

1. (*a*) Someone cleans this room every day.
   (*b*) ____________ is cleaned by someone every day.
2. (*a*) Dangerous driving causes accidents on the roads.
   (*b*) ____________ are caused by dangerous driving.
3. (*a*) My grandmother built this house.
   (*b*) ____________ was built by my grand mother.
4. (*a*) Ram killed Ravana.
   (*b*) Ravana____________ by Ram.
5. (*a*) My sister sang a song.
   (*b*) A song____________ by my sister.
6. (*a*) The doctor gives injections.
   (*b*) Injections ____________ by the doctor.
7. (*a*) The police shot the terrorist.
   (*b*) The terrorist ____________.
8. (*a*) He closed the shop.
   (*b*) The shop ____________.
9. (*a*) She cooked the potatoes.
   (*b*) ____________
10. (*a*) Sahil heated the water.
    (*b*) ____________.

III. Given below is a recipe for making lemon pickle:

Describe how lemon pickle is made by changing the following sentences into a passive voice:

1. Wash and dry the lemons.
2. Cut them into 4 pieces each.
3. Wash and dry the bottle.
4. Put the pieces in the bottle.
5. Squeeze out the juice.
6. Add salt and juice.
7. Replace lid.
8. Leave it in the sun.

IV. Read what happened to Rocky and Micky.

Rocky and Micky broke the safe of Mr. Mani. They took Rs. 5000/- from there. They ran away. Two policemen followed them. The policemen caught them and put them in jail. The next day the police took them to the court. The magistrate asked them many questions about the money. The police found the money in a bag. They had hidden the money bag in a dustbin.

You are a newspaper reporter and have to write the above report. Write it in the passive voice.

TEST – 5

Articles

Directions: Replace the wrong articles by the right ones in the following sentences:

1. The cloth is selling at ten rupees an metre.
2. He is a M.A. in history.
3. A cleverest of my students is Mohan.
4. He is quite the clever boy.
5. Take the few of the chocolates.
6. None but the mule denies his family.
7. Gandhi was a Buddha of his age.
8. A honourable man would not behave thus.
9. I saw a boy; a boy was very clever.
10. A present is more important to some people than the future.

TEST – 6

Articles

Directions: Insert 'the' where necessary in the following:

1. An aeroplane is fastest means of travelling.
2. Book he has been reading was on loan from College library.
3. Various delegates from United States attended conference at Delhi.
4. Camel is the ship of desert.
5. Hindi language has been derived from Sanskrit.
6. Language spoken in Mysore is Kannada.
7. Everest, which is in Himalayas, was conquered by Tensing.
8. Criminal was imprisoned for life.
9. Prime Minister will address nation tonight.
10. When he joined army he was very young.

TEST – 7

Conjunctions

Directions: Fill in the gaps of the following passage with appropriate conjunctions.

[1] ________ as the amendment about promotions is concerned, it negates the original intent of the policy of reservations, [2] ________ was only to facilitate the entry of SC/ST candidates into government employment. [3] ________, even this facility was to last only for ten years although it has now become a never-ending process. [4] ________ what is unfortunate is the extension of this privilege to the matter of promotions, [5] ________ means [6] ________ merit will once again yield place to a candidate's background.

TEST – 8

Conjunctions

Directions: Fill in the gaps of the following passage with appropriate conjunctions.

1. I listened to Bessie sing ________ she worked, ________ the songs sounded plaintive, ________ I continued to weep ________ Mr. Lloyd came into the room.
2. I pleaded for mercy ________ to no avail. ________ they left I fell down in a fit ________ lost consciousness.
3. Weeks went by, ________ I did not hear the subject of school mentioned again, ________ I had regained my normal health.
4. We travelled over fifty miles, ________ it was evening ________ I reached my destination.
5. Once, ________ John complained to his mother about me, she told him to ignore me ________ she did not wish her children to associate with me.
6. It was also a place ________ young ladies learnt to be genteel and precise, ________ acquired various accomplishments such as painting and French. ________, I would step out of Gateshead Hall ________ into a new life.
7. I was relieved ________ the weather did not permit our afternoon walk ________ usually ended with Bessie, the maid, scolding me ________ reminding me of my inferiority to Eliza, John and Georgina Reed.

TEST – 9

Punctuation

Directions: Punctuate the following passages.

1. in industry people are vastly more important than machines we speak of this as the mechanical age

and are rightly proud of our engineering achievements but the human problems are the ones which give to our industrial fabric the most severe test it is natural that the specialised job of dealing with the employees in industry should hold great attraction for students on campuses all over the united states young men and women of promise seem eager to enter the field of industrial relations in my generation the ambitious youngsters all tried to go into the bond business twenty years later they went into advertising but today in astonishing numbers they are eager to take on this significant and extraordinary difficult responsibility

2. if however he should decide as i have done that the free enterprise system and private management bring the largest measure of happiness to the greatest number of people he must know why he thinks that and thereafter he must scrupulously relate all his actions to the maintenance of that system he must seek its preservation with the same tireless devotion with which the communist seeks its destruction all this will be true whether he selects management or the labour union as the field for his lifes work since only within free enterprise do honest labour unions survive

3. a new phenomenon which will come to him as a severe shock and which is almost completely unknown to the general public is the experience called by insiders bargaining by exhaustion

4. in talking with people dont begin by discussing the things on which you differ begin by emphasising and keep on emphasising the things on which you agree keep emphasising if possible that you are both striving for the same end and your only difference is one of method and not of purpose get the other person saying yes yes at the outset keep him if possible from saying no

5. well i suggested wouldnt it be a good idea to keep your hands off those motors well i guess youre right he admitted we continued to chat for awhile then he called his secretary and lined up approximately $35000 worth of business for the ensuing month

6. the chinese have a proverb pregnant with the age old wisdom of the changeless east he who treads softly goes far

7. is it indeed your wifes supposed to be a well bred woman but she came out with something last monday that made my hair stand on end for two whole days all of a sudden she ups and asks me in front of other people is it true that my husband has bought the bank a lot of dongo pongo shares that have fallen on the stock exchange hes so worried in front of strangers i cant think why you confide in her do you want her to put you in the dock

8. i cant be the only man as walks along this street and wants a fag he said i shouldnt wonder but what a fellow might do very well with a little shop here tobacco and sweets you know

9. but this is not the end of the working day as dealings continue on the telephone often up to a late hour in the offices of brokers and jobbers there is always correspondence to deal with and for brokers and jobbers alike the study of industrial and financial reports is neverending for it is on their expert knowledge that the efficiency and reputation of this great market ultimately depends

10. the writers intentions asking what is the writer trying to achieve may not be such an important query where the material is objectively factual but it is essential to ask it of advertising or propagandist in the widest sense writing failure to do this may result in the acceptance of a statement as fact when it is really an inference or a value judgement both of which are open to opinion and discussion

TEST – 10

Direct Speech – Indirect Speech

Directions: Change the following passages from Direct to Indirect speech.

The merchant said to the young man: "I beg you to pardon the liberty which I take in asking you how it happens that you always make use of your left hand,

and never of the right; some accident surely has happened to it." The young man drew out his right arm from his robe. The merchant saw, to his utter astonishment, that his hand was cut off. He then said to the merchant: "You are no doubt much shocked at seeing me eat with my left hand, but will now see that I cannot do otherwise." The merchant asked him: "May I inquire how you had the misfortune to lose your right hand?"

TEST – 11

Direct Speech – Indirect Speech

Directions: Change the following passage from Direct to Indirect speech.

The lover approached the lady and smilingly said, "You look very sweet today. I have never seen such golden hair and such a charming grace in all my life." The lady smiled and replied, "Your compliments are fine, but I don't deserve them. I am a simple country girl and lack the manners of fashionable people in society." The enthusiastic lover warmed up and said with all his gusto, "You are too humble! Your manners are above reproach; your talk is sweet and honeyed; your knowledge of life is admirable and your kindness to all is the talk of the village. I am not in the habit of flattering anyone. Without any hesitation, I can say that you are a model of virtue and piety. Even gods and goddesses are jealous of your perfection."

TEST – 12

Direct Speech – Indirect Speech

Directions: Change the following into indirect speech.

1. Rama said, "I shall come to tea tomorrow."
2. He said to me, "You have helped my brother,"
3. She said, "You play hockey very well."
4. I said to her, "You are a foolish girl."
5. He said to me, "I have often told you not to idle away your time."
6. He said, "Where do you come from?"
7. "What do you want?" he said to her.
8. He said, "How is your mother?"
9. "Do you like this book?" she said to him.
10. The poor woman cried, "Will no one help me?"
11. Bali said to Ashok, "Go away."
12. I said to the boys, "Please allow me to work."
13. The teacher said to Harry, "Show me your notebook."
14. He said, "Please lend me your book."
15. The captain said to his men, "Stand at ease."
16. She cried, "O that I were dead!"
17. The teacher said, "What a foolish boy you are!"
18. "Alas! I am ruined," said the poor man.
19. He said, "Alas! the child is dead."
20. He said, "How sad it is!"
21. My friend said to me. "Why have you kept me waiting when you knew I was in such a haste to go?"
22. "Is there anybody there?" said the traveller knocking on the moonlit door.
23. "You slow old thing!" said the hare, "Why do you not hurry up?" "I may be slow," said the tortoise, "but I could beat you in a race."
24. "Take my advice," said the fox to his friends, "and cut off your tails."
25. "What have you to sell, dear lady?" he asked. "Only one large diamond, Sir," she replied.
26. He wrote to me, "I am unable to come just now because I am ill."
27. The teacher said to me, "You have not done well in the examination."
28. They said, "Yesterday we went to the cinema."
29. The girls said, "It will be stormy tonight."
30. The teacher said, "I shall not teach your class tomorrow."
31. "Do you know the way to the station?" said I.
32. "Which is your book?" I said to her.
33. "Do you really know magic?" said the queen.
34. She said to him, "Can you do this work?"
35. He said to us. "Why are you sitting idle?"
36. The teacher said to the boys, "Look at the blackboard."
37. "Hurry up." he said to his children.
38. "Sit down, boys," said the teacher.
39. "Shoot!" said the officer to his men.
40. He said to me, "Wait till I return."
41. "What a lovely flower!" he said.
42. He said, "What a pity you did not come!"

43. "May God bless you!" she said.
44. "What a clever fellow you are!" he said.
45. "Hurrah! We have won the match," cried the boys.
46. The mother said, "My son, I earn only one or two rupees a day. How can I afford to buy a kite for you?"
47. The queen said to Rama, "Do not desire to have the moon because it is thousands of miles off and it is not a plaything for children and no child ever got it."
48. Her mother said, "There is a wolf in the woods through which you are going; but if you keep to the road he will not do you any harm."
49. "Our emperor is a just man," said the people, "because he is ever ready to lend an ear to the complaints of the people."
50. "Are you angry, my friends," said the king, "because you have lost your leader? I am your king; I will be your leader."
51. "You are old enough to earn your living now," said the father to the son.
52. "I will not give you a single penny," said the old man to the beggar.
53. "It will rain tonight," said the father to the children.
54. The Headmaster said to the boys, "Tomorrow will be a holiday."
55. The princess said, "It gives me great pleasure to be here this evening."
56. "Can you tell me the secret? he said to her.
57. "Why do you cry?" I said to the little boy.
58. He said, "When will the train start?"
59. "Do you believe in ghosts?" she said to the wizard.
60. "Why are you so late tonight?" said the mother to Sita.
61. She said to him, "Take your seat, please."
62. "Stop writing, please," said the teacher to the boys.
63. He said to us, "Work hard if you want to pass."
64. She said to her son, "Be prudent."
65. Sita said to her friend, "Give a rupee to the beggar."

TEST – 13

Direct Speech – Indirect Speech

Directions: Change the following dialogue into Indirect Speech. You can begin like this:-

Laxmi said to Mohit that she was very happy to see him. She..........

After filling in the withdrawal form, Mohit went to the counter and was surprised to see his old classmate Laxmi Pillai sitting there. It was nearly 2 o'clock and Laxmi suggested that Mohit should wait and have lunch with her. Mohit agreed and during lunch the following conversation took place:

Laxmi said, "I am so happy to see you. I have seen you after two years. You look the same."

Mohit said, "It has been a long time. I see your sister at the Pusa Road bus stop sometimes."

Laxmi said, "She goes to Mamta College there."

Mohit then asked about Laxmi's mother who had been working in Dubai. Laxmi said, "My mother has come back from Dubai. She is now working with the Delhi branch. My father is still there."

Mohit said, "I am also looking for a job in Dubai. If I get it, I will see your father there."

TEST – 14

Direct Speech – Indirect Speech

Directions: Change the following paragraph into Direct Speech. You can begin like this: Mrs. Shankar was busy and said, "You will have to wait for five minutes." Mohit said, "....................."

After a month, Mohit went to the bank again to deposit another cheque from his father. He filled in the pay-in-slip and went to Mrs. Shankar's counter.

Mrs. Shankar was busy and told him that he would have to wait for five minutes. Mohit replied that he could not wait and that he was in a hurry because his friends were waiting outside. They were getting late for the film. Mrs. Shankar said that she was sorry but she was busy with another customer. Mohit got angry and said that he did not like the service in that bank. He would transfer his account to another bank.

ANSWERS

TESTS OF GRAMMAR

Test-1

Pronouns

1. He is a rogue whom no one trusts.
2. We got into a bus which was full of passengers.
3. I saw a juggler who was showing his tricks.
4. Here is the book which you lost yesterday.
5. Here is the pen which you were looking for.
6. We met a boy who had lost his way.
7. I loved my brother who is dead.
8. These are the boys whose parents are here.
9. Bali, who stole the pen, was punished.
10. That is the man whom we saw yesterday.
11. This boy who tells lies, deserves to be punished.
12. This is the boy whose book has been stolen.
13. Look at these boys who are singing.
14. This is the man whom I trusted.
15. I am the person whom you sent for.
16. This is the man whose son stood first.
17. Here is the book that I told you about.
18. We heard some news which astonished us.
19. This is the road which leads to the station.
20. He does his best and so he should be praised.

Test-2

Usage of Verb and Subject-Verb Agreement

1. distracts **2.** correct sentence
3. was **4.** follows
5. has done his /her
6. is **7.** Many a man has
8. have **9.** have passed **10.** is
11. Any of these ... (either is one of two) **12.** is
13. has **14.** is **15.** is
16. correct sentence
17. had seen **18.** am guilty
19. I never have allowed, and never will, allow my son to take meat.
20. had worked
21. I will be drowned, nobody will save me.
22. Unless he is more careful, he will not recover.
23. Two and two ... **24.** takes
25. Fair means does not always bring success.
26. The end has come, as the end of such matters generally comes by gradual decay.
27. requires **28.** was touched
29. No action or instruction which is not based on reason and morality can be permanent.
30. seems **31.** correct sentence
32. ... dozen large hotels ...
33. correct sentence **34.** are
35. were allowed **36.** worked
37. Since the date the strike has been declared, twenty clerks have been appointed and thirty have resigned.
38. assured. **39.** has been
40. correct sentence **41.** are
42. correct sentence **43.** proclaims
44. Where did you spend your last summer vacation?
45. I shall be glad if you would come in the evening.
46. So quickly did we walk that we reached the school in time.
47. wins **48.** is as follows
49. need **50.** is
51. correct sentence: It was the girls who defied their teacher's order **52.** had got angry
53. had I
54. No sooner did I reach the station, than the train had started.
55. If you had seen him, you would know him.
56. He will not only go but also stay there.
57. Neither does she come, nor does she write.
58. would send **59.** correct sentence
60. is likely to **61.** wrote
62. had been working for three hours
63. is **64.** correct sentence
65. correct sentence

Test-3

Active – Passive Voice

(The use of words in the brackets is optional)

1. The ball is kicked by Ram.
2. The meeting has been postponed by the minister.
3. The ball was hit for a six by Gavaskar.
4. Our jewellery is kept in the bank (by us).
5. This shield was donated to the college by Raman's father.
6. By whom was it written?
7. By what was this defect caused?
8. The grass was wet by dew.
9. The children were looked after well by her.
10. Every visitor is checked by the security man at the gate.
11. A cement plant will be set up by the Government.
12. How was this confidential information got by you?
13. The responsibility will be shouldered by us.
14. Are you being criticised by them?
15. The roads are being cleared of snow by them.
16. By whom has this window pane been broken?
17. Our team was being cheered by us.

18. He had been struck on the head with a blunt weapon by somebody.
19. Has the permission been given to him by you?
20. Higher wages were being demanded by the artists.
21. Are the rules being observed by them?
22. Am I being avoided by them?
23. Have the details been given by you?
24. Many doctors have been appointed recently by the Government.
25. His plans had been made well in advance.
26. The results will have been declared (by them) by the time you reach there.
27. The secret should be revealed.
28. The past should be forgotten by us.
29. The food might have been poisoned by someone.
30. Inefficient workers should be dismissed by them.
31. The food should be brought OR Let the food be brought.
32. Precautions had been taken by them to prevent his escape.
33. Has your passport been found?
34. Has the problem been solved by you?
35. Drunken drivers were being arrested by the police.
36. His assignment has been completed (by him).
37. Will your work be finished punctually?
38. The letter was delivered today by the postman.
39. How was the thief caught by you?
40. Will Friday be declared a holiday by them?
41. Problems will be created by it.
42. Most of the matches were won by our cricket team.
43. The factory is inspected by them every week.
44. Sweets are liked by most children.
45. The air was polluted by exhaust gases.
46. The old furniture was sold off by them.
47. He should be sent to prison.
48. Can the past be forgotten by us?
49. The prisoners should be released by them.
50. The first gramophone was invented by Edison.

Test-4

Active – Passive Voice

I. 1. was taken 2. was attended
3. was emphasised 4. be monitored
5. were completed

II.1b. This room **2b.** Accidents on the roads...
3b. This house **4b.** was killed **5b.** was sung
6b. are given **7b.** was shot by the police.
8b. was closed by him.
9b. The potatoes were cooked by her.
10b. The water was heated by Sahil.

III.

1. The lemons are washed and dried.
2. They are cut into 4 pieces each.
3. The bottle is washed and dried.
4. The pieces are put in the bottle.
5. The juice is squeezed out.
6. Salt and juice are added.
7. The lid is replaced.
8. It is left in the sun.

IV. (NOTE: Words within brackets are optional). The safe of Mr. Mani was broken by Rocky and Micky. Rs. 5000/- was taken (by them) from there. They ran away. They were followed by two policemen. They were caught by the policemen and were put in jail. The next day, they were taken to the court by the policemen. Many questions were asked by the magistrate about the money. The money was found by the police in a bag. The money bag had been hidden in a dustbin.

Test-5

Articles

1. The cloth is selling at ten rupees a metre.
2. He is an M.A. in history.
3. The cleverest of my students is Mohan.
4. He is quite a clever boy.
5. Take a few of the chocolates.
6. None but a mule denies his family.
7. Gandhi was the Buddha of his age.
8. An honourable man would not behave thus.
9. I saw a boy; the boy was very clever.
10. The present is more important to some people than the future.

Test-6

Articles

1. An aeroplane is the fastest means of travelling.
2. The book he has been reading was on loan from the college library.
3. Various delegates from the United States attended the conference at Delhi.
4. The Camel is the ship of the desert.
5. Hindi language has been derived from Sanskrit.
6. The language spoken in Mysore is Kannada.
7. The Everest which is in the Himalayas, was conquered by Tensing.
8. The criminal was imprisoned for life.
9. The Prime Minister will address the nation tonight.
10. When he joined the army he was very young.

Test-7

Conjunctions

1. So far 2. which 3. Not only that
4. But 5. which 6. that

Test-8

Conjunctions

1. as; but; and; till. 2. but; when; and.
3. but; although 4. and; when
5. when; as 6. where; and; above all; and
7. that; which; and.

Test-9

Punctuation

1. In industry people are vastly more important than machines. We speak of this as the mechanical age, and are rightly proud of our engineering achievements, but the human problems are the ones which give our industrial fabric the most severe test. It is natural that the specialised job of dealing with the employees in industry should hold great attraction for students. On campuses all over the United States young men and women of promise seem eager to enter the field of industrial relations. In my generation the ambitious youngsters all tried to go into the bond business; twenty years later they went into advertising; but today in astonishing numbers they are eager to take on this significant and extraordinary difficult responsibility.
2. If, however, he should decide, as I have done, that the free enterprise system and private management bring the largest measure of happiness to the greatest number of people, he must know why he thinks that. And, thereafter he must scrupulously relate all his actions to the maintenance of that system. He must seek its preservation with the same tireless devotion with which the Communist seeks its destruction. All this will be true whether he selects management or the labour union as the field for his life's work, since only within free enterprise do honest labour unions survive.
3. A new phenomenon which will come to him as a severe shock, and which is almost completely unknown to the general public, is the experience called by insiders 'bargaining by exhaustion'.
4. In talking with people, don't begin by discussing the things on which you differ. Begin by emphasising—and keep on emphasising—the things on which you agree. Keep emphasising—if possible—that you are both striving for the same end and your only difference is one of method and not of purpose. Get the other person saying, 'Yes, yes', at the outset. Keep him, if possible, from saying 'No.'
5. 'Well,' I suggested, 'wouldn't it be a good idea to keep your hands off those motors?' 'Well, I guess you're right,' he admitted. We continued to chat for awhile. Then he called his secretary and lined up approximately $35,000 worth of business for the ensuing month.
6. The Chinese have a proverb pregnant with the age-old wisdom of the changeless East: 'He who treads softly goes far.'
7. Is it, indeed? Your wife's supposed to be a well-bred woman, but she came out with something last Monday that made my hair stand on end for two whole days. All of a sudden she ups and asks me in front of other people: 'Is it true that my husband has bought the bank a lot of Dongo-Pongo shares that have fallen on the stock exchange? He's so worried.' In front of strangers! I can't think why you confide in her. Do you want them to put you in the dock?
8. 'I can't be the only man as walks along this street and wants a fag', he said, 'I shouldn't wonder but what a fellow might do very well with a little shop here. Tobacco and sweets, you know'.
9. But this is not the end of the working day, as dealings continue on the telephone—often up to a late hour—in the offices of brokers and jobbers. There is always correspondence to deal with, and for brokers and jobbers alike, the study of industrial and financial reports is never-ending. For it is on their expert knowledge that the efficiency and reputation of this great market ultimately depends.
10. The Writer's Intentions
    Asking 'What is the writer trying to achieve?' may not be such an important query where the material is objectively factual, but it is essential to ask it of advertising or propagandist (in the widest sense) writing. Failure to do this may result in the acceptance of a statement as fact when it is really an inference or a value judgement, both of which are open to opinion and discussion.

Test-10

Direct Speech – Indirect Speech

Begging pardon of the young man for taking the liberty, the merchant asked the young man how it happened that he always made use of his left hand, and never of the right; he supposed that some accident surely had happened to it. The young man drew out his right arm from his robe. The merchant saw, to his utter astonishment, that his hand was cut off. He then explained to the merchant that he was no doubt much shocked at seeing him eat with his left hand, but he would see that he could not do otherwise. The merchant asked him whether he might inquire how he had the misfortune to lose his right hand.

Test-11

Direct Speech – Indirect Speech

The lover approached the lady and smilingly paid her the compliment that she looked very sweet that day. He said he had never seen such golden hair and such charming grace in all his life. The lady smiled and replied that his compliments were fine but she didn't deserve them. She said she was a simple country girl and lacked the manners of fashionable people in the society. The enthusiastic lover warmed up and exclaimed with all his gusto that she was too humble. Her manners were above reproach; her talk was sweet and honeyed; her knowledge of life was admirable and her kindness to all was the talk of the village. He further clarified that he was not in the habit of flattering anyone. He could say, without any hesitation that she was a model of virtue and piety and that even gods and goddesses were jealous of her perfection.

Test-12

Direct Speech – Indirect Speech

1. Rama said that he would come to tea next day.
2. He told me that I had helped his brother.
3. She said that I played hockey very well.
4. I told her that she was a foolish girl.
5. He told me that he had often told me not to idle away my time.
6. He asked (me) where I came from.
7. He asked her what she wanted.
8. He asked me how my mother was.
9. She asked him whether he liked that book.
10. The poor woman cried and asked whether any one would help her.
11. Bali ordered Ashok to go away.
12. I requested the boys to allow me to work.
13. The teacher asked Harry to show him his book.
14. He requested me to lend him my book.
15. The captain commanded his men to stand at ease.
16. She cried and said that she wished that she were dead.
17. The teacher exclaimed that I was a very foolish boy.
18. The poor man exclaimed sorrowfully that he was ruined.
19. He exclaimed with sorrow (sadly) that the child was dead.
20. He exclaimed that it was very sad.
21. My friend asked me why I had kept him waiting when I had known he was in such haste to go.
22. Knocking at the moonlit door, the traveller asked whether there was anybody there.
23. The hare exclaimed that the tortoise was a slow old thing, and asked why it did not hurry up. The tortoise retorted (or answered back) that it might be slow but it could beat the hare in a race.
24. The fox told his friends to take his advice and cut off their tails.
25. He asked the lady (courteously) what she had to sell. The lady replied that she had only one large diamond to sell.
26. He wrote to me that he was unable to come just then because he was ill.
27. The teacher told me that I had not done well in the examination.
28. They said that the previous day they had gone to the cinema.
29. The girls said that it would be stormy that night.
30. The teacher said that she would not teach our class the next day.
31. I asked whether he knew the way to the station.
32. I asked her which was her book.
33. The queen asked (him) whether he really knew magic.
34. She asked him whether he could do that work.
35. He asked us why we were sitting idle.
36. The teacher instructed (or told) the boys to look at blackboard.
37. He told his children to hurry up.
38. The teacher instructed (or advised) the boys to sit down.
39. The officer commanded his men to shoot.
40. He told me to wait till he returned.
41. He exclaimed that the flower was very lovely.
42. He exclaimed (to me) that it was a great pity that I did not come.
43. She blessed me.
44. He exclaimed (to me) that I was a very clever fellow.
45. The boys exclaimed with joy (happiness) that they had won the match.
46. The mother told her son that she earned only one or two rupees a day and asked him sadly how she could afford to buy a kite for him.
47. The queen advised Rama not to desire to have the moon because it is thousands of miles off and it i[illegible] not a plaything for children and no child ever g[illegible]

48. Her mother told him that there was a wolf in the woods through which he was going; but if he kept to the road it would not do him any harm.
49. The people said that their emperor was a just man because he was always ready to lend an ear to the complaints of the people.
50. The king asked his friends whether they were angry because they had lost their leader. He then (further) told them that he was their king and he would be their leader.
51. The father told the son that he was now old enough to earn his living.
52. The old man told the beggar that he would not give him a single penny.
53. The father told the children that it would rain that night.
54. The headmaster told the boys (or announced to the boys) that the next day would be a holiday.
55. The princess said that it gave her great pleasure to be there that evening.
56. He asked whether she could tell him the secret.
57. I asked the little boy why he cried.
58. He asked when the train would start.
59. She asked the wizard whether he believed in ghosts.
60. The mother asked Sita why she was so late that night.
61. She requested him to take his seat.
62. The teacher politely advised the boys to stop writing.
63. He advised us to work hard if we wanted to pass.
64. She advised her son to be prudent.
65. Sita advised her friend to give a rupee to the beggar.

Test-13

Direct Speech – Indirect Speech

Laxmi told Mohit that she was very happy to see him. She was seeing him after two years but he looked the same.

Mohit replied that it had been a long time since he saw her, though he saw her sister at the Pusa Road bus stop sometimes.

Laxmi told him that her sister went to Mamta college there.

Mohit then asked about Laxmi's mother who had been working in Dubai. Laxmi told him that her mother had come back from Dubai and she was then working with the Delhi branch but her father was still there.

Mohit concluded the conversation by telling her that he was also looking for a job in Dubai and if he got it, he would see her father there.

Test-14

Direct Speech – Indirect Speech

Mrs. Shankar was busy and said, "You will have to wait for five minutes," Mohit said, "I can not wait and I am in a hurry because my friends are waiting outside. They are getting late for the film," Mrs. Shankar said, "I am sorry, but I am busy with another customer." Mohit got angry and said, "I do not like the service in this bank. I will transfer my account to another bank."

CHAPTER 6 PRACTICE TESTS

INTRODUCTION

After traversing through the practice book, the following five practice tests (with Answer keys) — **Practice Test-1, Practice Test-2, Practice Test-3, Practice Test-4, and Practice Test-5** — have been designed with great care for all categories of students. Hence, you are strongly advised to sit with patience, and practise all of them to come off with flying colours in any of the language exams you are planning to appear for. The author wishes them a very good luck.

PRACTICE TEST — I

PART – A
READING COMPREHENSION AND READING ABILITY

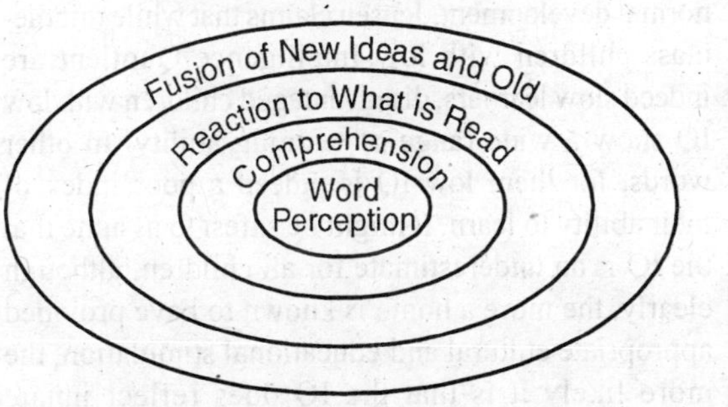

"READING is a unitary act"

– Gray

UNIT – 1

Multiple Choice Type

Directions: Read through the passage only once, as quickly as you can, without suffering loss of comprehension and answer the questions that follow.

The use of intelligence tests has been dominated by the idea that intelligence was an inherited characteristic of the mind that could be reasonably and accurately measured. The tests have been used to find out whether children were 'working up to capacity'. If the intelligence Quotient was well above the attainment level, then clearly the fault lay with factors other than intelligence and, where possible, steps could be taken to remedy the situation. But if both Intelligence Quotient and attainment were low, then nothing could be done since it was assumed that the children were innately dull.

Intelligence was believed to be a fixed entity, some faculty of the mind that we all possess and which determines in some way the extent of our achievements. Since the Intelligence Quotient was relatively unaffected by bad teaching or a dull home environment, it remained constant, at least within the limits of measurement error. Its Value therefore, was as a predictor of children's future learning. If they differed markedly in their ability to learn complex tasks, then it was clearly necessary to educate them differently — and the need for different types of school and even different ability groups within schools was obvious. Intelligence tests could be used for streaming children according to ability at an early age; and at 11 these tests were superior to measures of attainment for selecting children for different types of secondary education.

Today, we are beginning to think differently. In the last few years, research has thrown doubt on the view that innate intelligence can ever be measured and on the very nature of intelligence itself. Perhaps most important, there is considerable evidence now which shows the great influence of environment both on achievement and intelligence. Children with poor home backgrounds not only do less well in their school work and in intelligence tests — a fact which could be explained on genetic grounds — but their performance tends to deteriorate gradually compared with that of their more fortunate classmates. Evidence like this lends support to the view, stressed by Sir Cyril Burt, that we have to distinguish between genetic intelligence and observed intelligence. Any deficiency in the appropriate genes will obviously restrict development, no matter how stimulating the environment. But we cannot observe and measure innate intelligence; whereas we can observe and measure the effects of the interaction of whatever is inherited with whatever stimulation has been received from the environment. Changes may occur in our observations or measurements if the environment is changed. In other words, the Intelligence Quotient is not constant.

Researchers over the past five or ten years, especially in the United States, have been investigating what happens in this interaction. Work in this country has shown that parental interest and encouragement are more important than the material circumstances of the home.

Two major findings have emerged from these studies. Firstly, that the greater part of the development of observed intelligence occurs in the earliest years of life. Professor Bloom in the University of Chicago has estimated that 50 per cent of measurable intelligence at age 17 is already predictable by the age of four. In other words, deprivation in the first four or five years of life can have greater consequences than any in the following twelve or so years. And the longer the early deprivation continues the more difficult it is to remedy.

Secondly, the most important factors in the environment are language and psychological aspects of the parent-child relationship. Much of the difference in measured intelligence between 'privileged' and 'disadvantaged' children may be due to the latter's lack of appropriate verbal stimulation and the poverty of their perceptual experience.

These research findings have led to a revision in our understanding of the nature of intelligence. Instead of it being some largely inherited fixed power of the mind, we now see it as a set of developed skills with which a person copes with any environment. These skills have to be learned and, indeed, one of them – a fundamental one – is learning how to learn. From birth, a baby learns from his environment, and how to react with it. He learns from one experience how to cope with other similar experiences and then with different ones.

It seems equally certain that any built-in mechanism for learning needs to be sustained and encouraged. As Piaget has said, a child must play an active part in regulating his own development; he must be allowed to do his own learning because full intellectual development will not occur if his role is a passive one. The more new things he has seen and heard, the more interested he is in seeing and hearing. The more different things he has coped with himself, the greater his capacity for coping. In this way the intellectual skills of intelligence are built up.

But some children are born into a world where there are few if any, of the basic requirements for normal development. Jensen claims that while middle-class children with low Intelligence Quotient are indeed slow learners, disadvantaged children with low IQ show a wide range of learning ability. In other words, for them low IQ is indeed a poor index of their ability to learn. It might be safest to assume that the IQ is an underestimate for all children, although clearly, the more a home is known to have provided appropriate cultural and educational stimulation, the more likely it is that the IQ does reflect innate potential.

Bloom suggests that most children will master any task or solve any problem provided they are given sufficient time. He admits that a few children, probably less than 5 per cent, may need an impossibly long time to learn some tasks. This fits in well with the changed view of intelligence. High intelligence is not the ability to learn complex tasks so much as the ability to learn rapidly. And a child of relatively low intelligence is not incapable of learning complex tasks but needs a longer time to learn them.

Although educationists have been aware of this idea — the term 'slow learner' is sometimes applied to a child of low IQ — the 'fixed potential' concept of intelligence has tended to dominate our education system. Teachers are being constantly assured through their classroom experience that this concept is apparently sound, and that a system which separates children into groups according to their innate potential, really works. This attitude towards the fixed potential concept intelligence is likely to remain deeply ingrained, since the more successful teachers are at matching pupils' attainments to their apparent abilities, the more successful will any initial streaming or selection process appear to be. This is because the teacher who believes that achievement will strive to see that this happens. Children themselves are obliging creatures and are very inclined to produce the standard of work that their elders regard as appropriate. Thus, streaming and selection procedures are, to some extent, self-fulfilling.

The modern ideas concerning the nature of intelligence put forward here are bound to have some effect on our school system. In one respect a change is already occurring. With the move towards comprehensive education and the development of unstreamed classes, fewer children will perhaps be given the label 'low IQ' which must inevitably condemn a child in his own if not society's eyes. The idea that we can teach them reading or arithmetic may take some getting used to. But perhaps the greatest changes are still to come.

The greatest gains from this view of intelligence must benefit the disadvantaged child, since there can be no doubt that we have in the past underestimated his potential. Not only must we train him in the skills of learning but if necessary we must make our education system more flexible to give him more time for learning if he needs it. Though all children may be to some extent disadvantaged, some are more so than others.

— *Douglas Pidgeon*

COMPREHENSION TEST

Select the most suitable answer

1. The intelligence tests employed regarded intelligence
   (*a*) existing in middle-class children.
   (*b*) developing in good environment only.
   (*c*) an innate feature of mind.
   (*d*) developing in childhood only.
2. Development of observed intelligence occurs mainly in
   (*a*) in middle-class children.
   (*b*) in the early childhood.
   (*c*) in adolescence.
   (*d*) a particular age.
3. At present intelligence is defined as
   (*a*) a set of evolved skills.
   (*b*) a fixed entity.
   (*c*) something beyond measurement.
   (*d*) a prerogative of small children.
4. High intelligence is not the ability to learn complex tasks so much as:
   (*a*) the ability to learn rapidly.
   (*b*) the ability to learn a great deal.
   (*c*) the ability to do well in intelligence tests.
   (*d*) the ability to perform tasks older children find difficult.
5. If required, slow learner should be given
   (*a*) a head-start on other children.
   (*b*) a more congenial environment at home.
   (*c*) higher practice to answer intelligence tests.
   (*d*) more time for learning if he needs it.
6. According to the old view, intelligence would seem to justify:
   (*a*) comprehensive education and unstreamed classes.
   (*b*) the selection of children for different types of schools.
   (*c*) sending the duller children out to work at an early age.
   (*d*) taking 'disadvantaged' children away from their home environment.
7. A 'disadvantaged' child is one:
   (*a*) who belongs to a deprived home environment.
   (*b*) who is unintelligent.
   (*c*) who lacks capability of learning.
   (*d*) who belongs to a poor background.
8. A low IQ (Intelligence Quotient) is a poor index of a disadvantaged child's ability to learn because:
   (*a*) they never found an opportunity to learn.
   (*b*) their intelligence is beyond measurement.
   (*c*) they do not belong to affluent homes.
   (*d*) their parents are probably unintelligent.

9. A 'slow learner' is:
   (*a*) a polite term for someone with a low IQ.
   (*b*) an unintelligent child who makes an attempt but does not quite succeed.
   (*c*) a child who may be as 'intelligent' as others but slow in learning.
   (*d*) a child who just does not perform well in intelligence tests.
10. Teachers are likely to:
   (*a*) welcome the new ideas about the nature of intelligence.
   (*b*) reject completely the new ideas about intelligence.
   (*c*) remain sceptical about the new view of intelligence.
   (*d*) take some time before they generally accept the new view of intelligence.

UNIT – 2

Reading Comprehension (Question-Answer Type)

Lenin was throwing off manifesto after manifesto. There was to be immediate peace with Germany, but civil war to the knife at home. The so-called revolution was nothing but a conspiracy between the Russian capitalists and the French and British to overthrow the Tsar in order to prevent him from making a separate peace with Germany. The proletariat must rally round the Soviet and cast down the Provisional Government, and not only the Provisional Government, but all other revolutionary parties, above all the Mensheviks (themselves Marxists to a man).

This distortion of the situation, as set down in Lenin's *Letters from Afar*, is the key to everything that was going to happen – not only in the summer or autumn of 1917, but for decades to come. 'Our tactics!' he screamed across Europe in a telegram to a group of Bolsheviks in Norway. 'Our tactics: absolute distrust: no support for the new Government: Kerensky especially suspect: arming of proletariat the only guarantee: immediate election Petrograd Duma: no rapprochement with other parties.'

All these demands, had they in fact reached the revolutionaries in Petrograd, would have seemed the ravings of a madman. To those who had been swept up in the intoxication of the past days, who had destroyed the monarchy, made a prisoner of the soldiers in the streets; who were now engaged in consolidating their revolution, in fighting reaction, in trying to feed the country and in getting the factories working, to bring some order out of chaos, and all the time keep Russia from being overrun by the Germans — to all these even such words of Lenin as did reach them were the words of a man completely out of touch.

How could he know what had happened? How could he understand the real nature of the great explosion which made nonsense of all cherished theories? The workers, the soldiers, the peasants, had risen and cast off their chains; and now, guided by professional revolutionaries of every colour working shoulder to shoulder, they were going to fashion a new land. Vladimir Ilyich, who had not set foot in Russia for 10 years, would soon see the new situation for himself and help to lead them to final victory.

They were wrong. It was they, Lenin was to tell them, who were out of touch. It began on the train that brought Lenin into the Finland station in Petrograd. Kamenev, Stalin with him, overwhelmed with emotion, boarded the train outside the station and expected elation and congratulations. Lenin was not elated. 'What on earth do you think you are up to?' he demanded in effect. 'Fraternising with Mensheviks and Socialist Revolutionaries and going on as though you had won a great victory.'

Questions:

1. Who, above all, did Lenin say must be cast down?
2. To whom did Lenin send a telegram?
3. How would Lenin's demands have appeared had they reached the revolutionaries in Petrograd?
4. How long had Lenin been away from Russia?
5. In what kind of mood was Lenin when he arrived in Petrograd?
6. Why did Lenin want 'immediate peace with Germany, but civil war to the knife at home'?
7. Whom does the underlined word 'himself' in paragraph 4 refer to?

8. What do the following underlined words mean:
    (*a*) rapprochement (paragraph 2)
    (*b*) ravings (paragraph 3)
9. What is meant by the underlined phrase in paragraph 3 'the intoxication of the past days'?
10. Why did Lenin consider that it was his supporters who were, in fact, out of touch?

UNIT – 3

Miscellaneous Type

DISTINCTION BETWEEN AN INDIVIDUALIST AND A SOCIALIST

The doctrine of Individualism received a quasi-scientific sanction from the evolutionary theories of Darwin. If existence is, from its very nature, a struggle, the free competition between man and man in which only the fittest survives, is the only basis for society. Assuming, therefore, that human nature must be controlled by the struggle for life, the individualist considered the aim of civilization to be the organisation of that struggle in such a way that the greatest possible amount of life might survive. He thought, that is to say, in terms of quantity of life.

The Socialist, on the other hand, believes it to be possible to transcend the struggle for life, and regards civilization as that by means of which the struggle may be transcended. Life has some purpose other than the mere perpetuation of life. Quality of life is more important than quantity, and it is the business of civilization, by emancipating the individual from the exigencies of the bare struggle for existence, to put within his power the attainment of the highest quality of life.

Questions:

Q.1 Who was the propounder of the evolutionary theory?

Q.2 What does the author hypothesize regarding human nature?

Q.3 How do the individualist and the socialist define the aim of civilization?

Q.4 Do you think that the socialist agrees to the view of the individualist?

Q.5 Answer the following questions by choosing the correct alternative:

(*i*) How did the theory of Darwin react to the individualist theory?
Darwin's theory regarded the individualist theory as:
    (*a*) fully rational.
    (*b*) totally irrational.
    (*c*) irrational, to a large extent.

(*ii*) Whom does the underlined word 'He' in paragraph 1 refer to?
    (*a*) The socialist
    (*b*) The individualist
    (*c*) Darwin

(*iii*) What does the individualist emphasise upon?
    (*a*) Quantity of life.
    (*b*) Quality of life
    (*c*) Struggle of life.

(*iv*) In the socialist pattern of society, what should be the business of civilization?
    (*a*) Preserving his life.
    (*b*) Propagating the species.
    (*c*) Living a meaningful life.

Q.6 Write down the meaning of the following words as used in the passage:
    (*a*) Sanction (*b*) Survive
    (*c*) Transcend (*d*) Perpetuation
    (*e*) Emancipation

UNIT – 4

Cloze Passage Type

Directions: Fill in the blanks with appropriate words in context. You can read the whole passage before beginning the task.

The torch fell from his trembling ________. He turned and scrambled down the ________, running blindly through the trees and ________ for help. He was still running ________ the school buildings when he saw ________ lantern swinging in the middle of ________ path. Mr. Oliver had never before ________ pleased to see the night-________. He stumbled up to the watchman, ________ for breath and speaking incoherently. 'What ________ it, Sahib?' asked the watchman. 'Has ________ been an accident? Why are you running?'

UNIT – 5

Multiple Choice Type

Communicative Passage

Directions: The questions are based on the following advertisement.

ADDING ONE MORE JEWEL TO ITS CROWN

DOEACC 'A' LEVEL COURSE
(Under AICTE & MCIT, Govt. of India scheme)

from

CMC Limited
(A joint venture of Tata Sons Ltd. and Govt. of India)

ONE OF INDIA'S TOP 5 IT TRAINING VENDORS*

CMC, a stalwart in computer education proudly launches the immensely popular DOEACC 'A' level course. Equipped with modern infrastructure facilities and highly talented teaching faculty, CMC offers you the right ambience to realize your dreams.

*DQ July, 2002

Course Venue:

CMC Limited
(Regional Education & Training Centre)
9th floor, Shahpuri Tower, C-58, Community Centre,
Janakpuri, New Delhi-110058
Tel: 5533159, 5525997, 5614969, 5559514
e-mail: e&t@jv.cmc.net.in

Questions:

1. State which of the following statements is TRUE
   (*a*) CMC Limited is one of the world's top five IT Training Vendors.
   (*b*) CMC Limited is a Regional Education and Training Centre
   (*c*) DOEACC 'A' Level course adds another jewel to your crown.
   (*d*) DOEACC 'A' Level course is a reputed private course in IT.
2. Another phrase which means the same as 'jewel to its crown' is:
   (*a*) apple of one's eye
   (*b*) needle in the haystack
   (*c*) feather in one's cap
   (*d*) None of the above
3. The CMC Limited augurs to impart IT training with the help of:
   (*a*) well-equipped machines
   (*b*) modern infrastructure facilities
   (*c*) highly competent teachers and latest infrastructure facilities
   (*d*) its regional education and training centre
4. CMC Limited came into existence with
   (*a*) collaborative efforts of Tata Sons Ltd. and Govt. of India
   (*b*) autonomous efforts of Govt. of India and Tata Sons Ltd.
   (*c*) independent efforts CMC Ltd., Govt. of India and Tata Sons Ltd.
   (*d*) the efforts of AICTE and MCIT
5. CMC Limited promises to impart its computer education through DOEACC 'A' Level course which is :
   (*a*) a reputed course
   (*b*) one of the most reputed courses
   (*c*) the most reputed course
   (*d*) an immensely popular course

UNIT – 6

Multiple Choice Type

Single Sentence Readings

Directions: For each of these questions, choose the answer that is closest in meaning to the original phrase or sentence underlined. Note that several of the choices may be factually correct, but you should choose the one that is the closest restatement of the given phrase or sentence.

1. The principal reason of our failure was quite apparent to those whom we had brought into the venture.
   (*a*) to them whom we had brought
   (*b*) to the ones whom we had brought
   (*c*) to those who we had brought
   (*d*) to those whom we brought
2. Although he was the most friendly of all present and different from others, he had no other friend except me.
   (*a*) different from the others, he hadn't hardly any friends except me.
   (*b*) different from the others, he had no other friend but me.
   (*c*) different from the others, he hadn't hardly any friends except I.
   (*d*) different from the others, he hardly had any friends hardly except I.
3. It was us who had left before he arrived.
   (*a*) we who had left before he arrived.
   (*b*) we who went before he arrived.
   (*c*) us who went before he had arrived.
   (*d*) we who had left before the time he had arrived.
4. Due to the continual rain, a smaller number of spectators witnessed the game than had been expected.
   (*a*) Due to the unending rain, a smaller number
   (*b*) Due to the continual rain, a lesser number
   (*c*) Because of the rain that kept falling now and then, a smaller number
   (*d*) Because of the torrential rain, a smaller number
5. Beside me, there were several persons who were altogether agitated by his manners.
   (*a*) Beside me, there were many persons who were all together aggravated
   (*b*) Besides me, there were many persons who were altogether accelerated
   (*c*) Besides me, there were many persons who were altogether irritated
   (*d*) Beside me, there were many persons who were all together irritated

PART – B
VOCABULARY

UNIT – 1

Vocabulary (Multiple Choice)

Directions: Choose from the options one word or phrase closest to the meaning of the underlined word.

1. Seascape
   (*a*) wave top
   (*b*) ocean debris
   (*c*) picture of the sea
   (*d*) boating accident
2. Aficionado
   (*a*) expert at a game
   (*b*) good friend for a journey
   (*c*) guide for a sport
   (*d*) ardent devotee of a pastime
3. Facsimile
   (*a*) fake comparison
   (*b*) an example
   (*c*) surface comparison
   (*d*) an exact copy
4. Implode
   (*a*) to load
   (*b*) burst inwards
   (*c*) laminate
   (*d*) instigate to action
5. Impresario
   (*a*) magician (*b*) mountebank
   (*c*) organiser (*d*) impersonator
6. Indelible
   (*a*) permanent
   (*b*) doubtless
   (*c*) not worth eating
   (*d*) not worth writing
7. Flair
   (*a*) aroma (*b*) excitement
   (*c*) qualification (*d*) natural ability

8. Replete
   (*a*) deprived (*b*) worked
   (*c*) filled (*d*) lacked
9. Genial
   (*a*) natural (*b*) kindly
   (*c*) fascinating (*d*) hereditary
10. Retaliation
   (*a*) keeping score
   (*b*) repayment of an injury
   (*c*) open disrespect
   (*d*) long-lasting hatred
11. To abdicate
   (*a*) to leave
   (*b*) to renounce formally
   (*c*) to eradicate (*d*) to shift
12. Dike
   (*a*) lake (*b*) wall
   (*c*) river (*d*) ditch
13. Foibles
   (*a*) ailments (*b*) weaknesses
   (*c*) evils (*d*) vulgarities
14. Arbour
   (*a*) a bower (*b*) an orchard
   (*c*) a bush (*d*) a branch
15. Quelled
   (*a*) removed (*b*) stopped
   (*c*) fought (*d*) crushed

UNIT – 2

Multiple Choice

Directions: Each problem in this part of the test consists of a sentence in which one word or phrase has been underlined. From the four choices given, you should choose the one word or phrase which could be substituted for the underlined word or phrase without changing the meaning of the sentence.

1. The question was discarded because it was **ambiguous**.
   (*a*) incorrect. (*b*) biased.
   (*c*) vague. (*d*) dull.
2. Our final assignment for the English class is to give an **impromptu** speech.
   (*a*) eloquent. (*b*) unprepared.
   (*c*) technical. (*d*) unbiased.
3. The television station was **inundated** with enquiries from the elite class of the city.
   (*a*) replete (*b*) reverberated.
   (*c*) overheated. (*d*) flooded.
4. The gunfire was **sporadic**.
   (*a*) intermittent (*b*) frequent
   (*c*) continuous (*d*) distant
5. **Pilfering** by company employers costs many businesses thousands of dollars each year.
   (*a*) tardiness (*b*) stealing
   (*c*) absenteeism (*d*) ignorance

UNIT – 3

Multiple Choice
(One Word Substitution)

Directions: Give one word for the phrase underlined. Under each sentence are given four choices. You are directed to choose the appropriate one.

1. Sexual relations in certain savage tribes are **entirely unrestricted by marriage or any other regulation.**
   (*a*) illegitimate (*b*) promiscuous
   (*c*) free (*d*) unlawful
2. This is an assertion perfectly **capable of being proved.**
   (*a*) approveable
   (*b*) acceptable
   (*c*) demonstrable
   (*d*) believable
3. We used to give each other light, dainty **articles of furniture, dress or food and presents.**
   (*a*) knick-knacks (*b*) gifts
   (*c*) tokens (*d*) items
4. His words left an impression on my mind that can never **be effaced.**
   (*a*) memorable
   (*b*) unforgettable
   (*c*) remarkable
   (*d*) ineffaceable
5. He has this quality **from his parents and forefathers.**
   (*a*) inherited (*b*) hereditary
   (*c*) bequeathed (*d*) naturally

UNIT – 4

Multiple Choice

(One Word Substitution)

Directions: The questions below have a statement followed by four choices. Select the choice which is closest in meaning to the statement.

1. Surrounded on all sides.
   (*a*) Circled. (*b*) Knick-knacked.
   (*c*) Aliened. (*d*) Enveloped.
2. Something no longer in use.
   (*a*) Avaricious. (*b*) Obsolete.
   (*c*) Censured. (*d*) Ineffaceable.
3. Something which cannot be disproved.
   (*a*) Incorrigible. (*b*) Irreversible.
   (*c*) Irrefutable. (*d*) Inevitable.
4. Scientific study of insects.
   (*a*) Ornithology. (*b*) Anthropology.
   (*c*) Entomology. (*d*) Philately.
5. An assumed pen name that enables a writer to conceal his identity.
   (*a*) Pseudonym (*b*) Hypocrisy
   (*c*) Orthodoxy (*d*) Antonym

UNIT – 5

Multiple Choice

1. Mr. Kalra is in __________ and can, therefore, maintain a car easily.
   (*a*) job (*b*) profession
   (*c*) service (*d*) business
2. How well I __________ the good old days.
   (*a*) forget (*b*) recall
   (*c*) discuss (*d*) think
3. No new __________ could move their curiosity.
   (*a*) appearance (*b*) sight
   (*c*) look (*d*) atmosphere
4. Although the __________ was light it was too much for the old man.
   (*a*) load (*b*) capacity
   (*c*) weight (*d*) burden
5. He was __________ to such labour.
   (*a*) unfit (*b*) unable
   (*c*) unaccustomed (*d*) unauthorised

UNIT – 6

Multiple Choice

Synonyms

Directions: Select the word closest to the meaning of the following word:

1. Impediment
   (*a*) stress (*b*) defect
   (*c*) obstruction (*d*) exertion
2. Zealot
   (*a*) figure (*b*) candidate
   (*c*) fanatic (*d*) favourite
3. Confer
   (*a*) bestow (*b*) retrieve
   (*c*) seminar (*d*) hinder
4. Niche
   (*a*) view (*b*) slot
   (*c*) illusion (*d*) hitch
5. Gaudy
   (*a*) rude (*b*) lewd
   (*c*) flashy (*d*) coarse

UNIT – 7

Multiple Choice

Antonyms

Directions: Select the word closest to the opposite in meaning of the following words:

1. Confess
   (*a*) Reject (*b*) Defend
   (*c*) Disown (*d*) Deny
2. Make
   (*a*) Mar (*b*) Undo
   (*c*) Destroy (*d*) Spoil
3. Sacred
   (*a*) Profane (*b*) Unholy
   (*c*) Demonic (*d*) Devilish
4. Stern
   (*a*) Timid (*b*) Mild
   (*c*) Humble (*d*) Meek
5. Hostile
   (*a*) Pleasant (*b*) Attractive
   (*c*) Humble (*d*) Friendly

UNIT – 8

Multiple Choice

Idioms and Phrases

Directions: Each item below consists of an underlined Idiom or a Phrase, followed by four lettered expressions. Choose the expression that most nearly expresses the meaning and can substitute the given Idiom or Phrase.

1. No one likes a person who blows his own trumpet.
   (*a*) gives unsolicited advice.
   (*b*) plays music
   (*c*) creates a lot of noise
   (*d*) boasts about himself.
2. The indolent must go to the wall.
   (*a*) be pushed aside
   (*b*) be smashed against the wall
   (*c*) be punished
   (*d*) be rectified
3. Inspite of the strong opposition, they stood their ground.
   (*a*) did not move
   (*b*) stood on their own feet
   (*c*) maintained their position
   (*d*) retaliated
4. Cowards fight shy of difficulties.
   (*a*) are embarrassed of
   (*b*) avoid
   (*c*) are afraid of
   (*d*) neglect
5. You seem awfully cast down.
   (*a*) repressed (*b*) impoverished
   (*c*) dejected (*d*) useless

UNIT – 9

Multiple Choice

Words Often Confused

Directions: In each item below, a choice of words that are often confused is given in parentheses. Choose the word indicating the best choice for the context.

1. __________ It (A. augers; B. augurs) well for the industry that its present year's profits have beaten last year's level.
2. __________ They had entered into an (A. oral; B. aural) agreement only.
3. __________ His step father's (A. callous; B. callus) treatment led him to leave his home for good.
4. __________ His (A. childish; B. childlike) behaviour with his wife resulted into their separation.
5. __________ The surgeon removed a (A. malicious; B. malignant) tumour from his brain.

UNIT – 10

Multiple Choice

Spellings

Directions: Pick out the option which shows the correct spelling out of the choices given below.

1. (*a*) aserrt (*b*) ascert
   (*c*) asert (*d*) assert
2. (*a*) inherrantly (*b*) inherrently
   (*c*) inherantly (*d*) inherently
3. (*a*) govermental (*b*) govermentle
   (*c*) governmental (*d*) govermentle
4. (*a*) confered (*b*) conferred
   (*c*) conffered (*d*) confferred
5. (*a*) inviobality (*b*) invoibality
   (*c*) inviolability (*d*) invoilability

UNIT – 11

Vocabulary in Context

Modified Cloze Procedure (MCP)

Directions: Read the following passage carefully. Each bracket in the following passage contains 4 (four) choices; 1 (one) choice is correct and 3 (three) are incorrect. You are instructed to choose the correct choice so that the whole passage results into a coherent piece of writing.

The common oral causes of bad breath are [1](decayed, deteriorated, damaged, destructive) teeth, inflammation of the gums, inflammation or [2](swelling, congestion, ulceration, injury) of the mouth and tongue, pyorrhea or [3](unpleasant, putrid, incomprehensible, raw) material in the tonsils, smoking and fever. [4](Intermittent, Periodical, Irregular, continual) and improper brushing and a high [5](sugar, sweet, starch, salt) diet also causes bad breath.

It is [6](necessary, compulsory, urgent, obligatory) to have a regular dental check up to [7](postpone, prevent, halt, decrease) the formation of plaque, a [8](sticky, glued, rough, raw) film produced by bacteria, which [9](irritate, annoy, pressurise, dig) the gums, making them spongy and liable to bleed.

PART – C
GRAMMAR

UNIT – 1

Conversion Type

Direct – Indirect

Directions: Change the following passage from Direct to Indirect speech.

The lover approached the lady and smilingly said, "You look very sweet today. I have never seen such golden hair and such charming grace in all my life." The lady smiled and replied, "Your compliments are fine, but I don't deserve them. I am a simple country girl and lack the manners of fashionable people in society." The enthusiastic lover warmed up and said with all his gusto, "You are too humble! Your manners are above reproach; your talk is sweet and honeyed; your knowledge of life is admirable and your kindness to all is the talk of the village. I am not in the habit of flattering anyone. Without any hesitation, I can say that you are a model of virtue and piety. Even gods and goddesses are jealous of your perfection."

UNIT – 2

Editing

Directions: Edit the following sentences. Eliminate the deadwood and the passive verbs.

1. The dark black train was stopped and halted by the brakeman at the dangerous railroad crossing.
2. The auto-safety report, dealing with safety procedures, was considered for adoption and implementation by the members of the transportation committee.
3. I was being called so often by sales people of all kinds that I demanded and got an unlisted phone number for anonymity purposes.
4. Your refund cheque will be sent by us to you on receipt of the enclosed form.
5. In the course of the campaign, a meeting will be held by some delegates who are engaged in electing a leader.

UNIT – 3

Multiple Choice

Prepositions

Directions: Choose the appropriate alternative to fill in the blanks. Mark tick (✓) against the appropriate choice:

1. We should abide ________ the laws of the country.
   (*a*) with (*b*) for
   (*c*) of (*d*) by
2. Sheila is given ______ telling lies.
   (*a*) to (*b*) into
   (*c*) for (*d*) at
3. The cat jumped ______ the table.
   (*a*) under (*b*) on
   (*c*) upon (*d*) at
4. This road leads ______ Delhi.
   (*a*) at (*b*) into
   (*c*) from (*d*) to
5. He was charged _____ murder.
   (*a*) with (*b*) of
   (*c*) for (*d*) from

UNIT – 4

Multiple Choice

Tenses

Directions: Choose the appropriate tenses from the alternatives given below to fill in the blanks. Tick (✓) against the appropriate choice:

1. The sun ________ when we went out.
   (*a*) was shining
   (*b*) has been shining
   (*c*) had been shining
   (*d*) shone
2. Bad students never ________ hard.
   (*a*) worked (*b*) work
   (*c*) have worked (*d*) had worked

3. He thanked me for what I ________.
   (*a*) did (*b*) was doing
   (*c*) had done (*d*) have done
4. The police ________ the thief last night.
   (*a*) caught (*b*) has caught
   (*c*) have caught (*d*) had caught
5. I ________ here for the last two years.
   (*a*) live
   (*b*) have lived
   (*c*) had been living
   (*d*) have been living

UNIT – 5

Subject Verb Agreement

Directions: Correct, improve or justify the following sentences.

1. Either of these six teams might win the cup.
2. The 'Three Musketeers' are very interesting to read.
3. My friend, philosopher and guide have come.
4. The majority are opposed to this proposal.
5. His kindness and benevolence are well-known.

UNIT – 6

Gender

Directions: Select the feminine genders from the options given below.

1. Administrator
   (*a*) Administratoress
   (*b*) Administratress
   (*c*) Administratrix
   (*d*) Administratorix
2. Duke
   (*a*) Dukess (*b*) Duchess
   (*c*) Duches (*d*) Duchereina
3. Drone
   (*a*) Duck (*b*) Goose
   (*c*) Bee (*d*) Roe
4. Horse
   (*a*) Stallion (*b*) Pony
   (*c*) Colt (*d*) Mare
5. Abbot
   (*a*) Abbotess (*b*) Abbess
   (*c*) Abbotes (*d*) Abbotrix
6. Friar
   (*a*) Friaress (*b*) Friariene
   (*c*) Friarix (*d*) Nun
7. Executor
   (*a*) Executorix (*b*) Executrix
   (*c*) Executoress (*d*) Executress
8. Ram
   (*a*) Doe (*b*) Ewe
   (*c*) Heifer (*d*) Roe
9. Signor
   (*a*) Signora (*b*) Signoress
   (*c*) Signress (*d*) Madam
10. Man-servant
   (*a*) Maid-servant (*b*) Woman-servant
   (*c*) Girl-servant (*d*) She-servant

UNIT – 7

Multiple Choice Global Type

Use of Conjunctions (In Context)

Directions: Read the following sentences and select the most appropriate of the alternatives given below. Complete the incomplete sentence by choosing the most appropriate alternatives.

All animals and plants have their particular habitats ________ [1] they can live successfully ________ [2] multiply. Some voles, for instance, live in holes in a bank. There they make their nests ________ [3] rear their young ones close to their supply of food-insect larvae and wild fruits. Similarly plants can live only in certain habitats-ferns and mosses require damp places, ________ [4] species such as ivy prefer a wall or a tree trunk to climb up ________ [5] they grow.

1. (*a*) in which (*b*) where
   (*c*) wherein (*d*) whereabout
2. (*a*) and (*b*) but
   (*c*) therefore (*d*) hence
3. (*a*) but (*b*) moreover
   (*c*) as also (*d*) and
4. (*a*) not only (*b*) when
   (*c*) while (*d*) as well as
5. (*a*) as (*b*) so
   (*c*) hence (*d*) whenever

UNIT – 8

Multiple Choice

Error Correction

Directions: In questions 1 to10, each sentence has four underlined words or phrases. The four underlined parts of the sentence are marked (A), (B), (C) and (D). Identify the one underlined word or phrase that must be changed in order for the sentence to be correct.

1. He came (A) out of (B) the post office when the (C) airplane appeared going (D) south.

2. Perhaps he did not (A) know that anyone has (B) ever sat in it (C) in the darkness (D).

3. Mr. Tucker was out of (A) sight and then I would (B) put my hat on top of (C) the fence post and leave it there until I see (D) Mr. Tucker coming back.

4. Now we were going (A) fast because we came (B) down the last hill and into (C) the valley where Mottstown was (D).

5. She watches (A) him go on and disappear (B) up the (C) path toward the (D) bench.

PART – D
WRITING ABILITY

"Language is a perpetual orphic song
Which rules with Daidal harmony a throng
Of thoughts and forms,"

—Prometheus Unbound
– P. B. Shelley

UNIT – 1

Précis Writing

Directions: Make a precis of the following passage in about one third of its length.

In democratic countries any effort to restrict the freedom of the press is rightly condemned. However, this freedom can be easily abused. Stories about people often attract far more public attention than political events. Though we may enjoy reading about the lives of others, it is extremely doubtful whether we would equally enjoy reading about ourselves. Acting on the contention that facts are sacred, reporters can cause untold sufferings to individuals by publishing details about their private lives. Newspapers exert such tremendous influence that they cannot only bring about major changes to the lives of ordinary people but can even overthrow a government.

The story of a poor family that acquired fame and fortune overnight, dramatically illustrates the power of the press. The family lives in Aberdeen, a small town of 25,000 inhabitants, in South Dakota. As the parents had five children, life was a perpetual struggle against poverty. They were expecting their sixth child and were faced with even more pressing economic problems. If they had only one more child the fact would have passed unnoticed. They would have continued to struggle against economic odds and would have lived in obscurity. But they suddenly became the parents of quintuplets, four girls and a boy, an event which radically changed their lives. The day after the birth of the five children, an aeroplane arrived in Aberdeen bringing sixty reporters and photographers. The news was of national importance, for the couple had become the parents of the only quintuplets in America.

Their rise to fame was swift. Television, cameras and newspapers carried the news to everyone in the country. Newspapers and magazines offered the family huge sums for the exclusive rights to publish their photographs. Gifts poured in not only from unknown people, but from baby food and soap manufacturers who wished to advertise their products. The old farmhouse the family lived in was to be replaced by a new $ 100,000 home. Reporters kept pressing for interviews, so lawyers had to be employed to act as the spokesman of the family at press conferences. The event brought serious changes to the town itself. Plans were announced to build a huge new highway, as Aberdeen was now likely to attract thousands of tourists. Signposts erected on the outskirts of the town directed tourists not to Aberdeen, but 'Quint-City U.S.A'. The local authorities discussed the possibility of erecting a 'quint museum' to satisfy the curiosity of the public and to protect the family from inquisitive tourists. While the five babies were still quietly sleeping in oxygen tents in a hospital nursery, their parents were paying the price of fame. It would never again be possible for them to lead normal lives. They had become victims of commercialisation, for their names had now acquired a market value. The town itself received so much attention that almost every one of the inhabitants was affected to a greater or lesser degree.

UNIT – 2

Composition

Question: Your college is holding the 14th SAARC 'Letter writing' competition. As the Secretary of Academics, prepare a circular to that effect, giving the details about time, date, venue, topic etc.

UNIT – 3

Paraphrasing

Directions: Reproduce the given passage (poetry or prose) in your own idiom or style without changing the sense.

Breathes there the man, with soul so dead,
Who never to himself hath said,
This is my own my native land?
Whose heart hath ne'er within him burn'd,
As home his footsteps he hath turn'd
From wandering on a foreign strand?

UNIT – 4

Coherence Testing

Multiple Choice

Directions: For the following question, read the sentences and choose the order in which they form a coherent piece of writing.

1. This slim volume of song-offerings catapulted India onto the literary map of the world.
2. Photographers have tried to capture its essence in images, composers in music, and artists in graphic form.
3. Rabindranath Tagore's *Gitanjali* has held a special place of pride in the hearts of all Indians.
4. The literary world has since seen this book in innumerable editions.
5. From the first limited edition in 1912 by the India Society, London, this book has travelled a long way in the last nine decades touching the lives of statesmen, poets and the ordinary man.

(*a*) 5, 4, 1, 2, 3. (*b*) 3, 2, 1, 4, 5.
(*c*) 1, 3, 4, 5, 2. (*d*) 3, 1, 4, 2, 5.

ANSWER KEY-I

Reading Comprehension and Reading Ability

Unit-1

1. c	**2.** b	**3.** b	**4.** a	**5.** d
6. b	**7.** a	**8.** a	**9.** c	**10.** d

Unit-2

1. The Mensheviks.
2. A group of Bolsheviks in Norway.
3. As the ravings of a madman.
4. 10 years.
5. Not elated.
6. He wanted to be able to concentrate on achieving complete success for the aims of Bolshevism.
7. It refers to Lenin.
8. (*a*) compromise
(*b*) frenzied talk
9. The violence and the excitement of the revolution.
10. They had lost sight of the long-term objectives of the revolution in the elation of immediate success.

Unit-3

1. Darwin was the propounder of the evolutionary theory.
2. The author hypothesises that human nature is governed by a neck to neck competition for survival.
3. The individualist defines the aim of civilization as an ordered arrangement of the struggle for survival in a manner by which the greatest number can benefit whereas the socialist defines it as an accomplishment of the most superior quality of life by surpassing that struggle.

4. No.
5. (i) a (ii) b (iii) a (iv) c
6. (i) Approval (ii) Continue to exist
(iii) Surpass (iv) Preservation
(v) Freedom

Unit-4

1. hand	2. path	3. calling
4. towards	5. a	6. the
7. been	8. watchman	9. gasping
10. is	11. there	

Unit-5

1. b 2. c 3. c 4. a 5. d

Unit-6

1. b 2. b 3. a 4. a 5. c

Vocabulary
("Seascape" to MCP Passage)

Unit-1

1. c	2. d	3. d	4. b	5. c
6. a	7. d	8. c	9. b	10. b
11. b	12. d	13. b	14. a	15. d

Unit-2

1. c 2. b 3. d 4. a 5. b

Unit-3

1. c 2. c 3. a 4. d 5. a

Unit-4

1. d 2. b 3. c 4. c 5. a

Unit-5

1. d 2. b 3. b 4. a 5. c

Unit-6

1. c 2. c 3. a 4. b 5. c

Unit-7

1. d 2. c 3. a 4. b 5. d

Unit-8

1. d 2. a 3. c 4. b 5. c

Unit-9

1. B 2. A 3. A 4. A 5. B

Unit-10

1. d 2. d 3. c 4. b 5. c

Unit-11

1. decayed	2. ulceration	3. putrid
4. Irregular	5. sugar	6. necessary
7. prevent	8. sticky	9. irritate

Grammar

Unit-1

The lover approached the lady and smilingly paid her the compliment that she looked very sweet that day. He said he had never seen such golden hair and such charming grace in all his life. The lady smiled and replied that his compliments were fine but she didn't deserve them. She said she was a simple country girl and lacked the manners of fashionable people in the society. The enthusiastic lover warmed up and exclaimed with all his gusto that she was too humble. Her manners were above reproach; her talk was sweet and honeyed; her knowledge of life was admirable and her kindness to all was the talk of the village. He further clarified that he was not in the habit of flattering anyone. Without any hesitation, he could say that she was a model of virtue and piety, and that even gods and goddesses were jealous of her perfection.

Unit-2

1. The brakeman stopped the train at the dangerous railroad crossing.
2. The transportation committee considered the auto-safety report for implementation.
3. The sales people were calling me so often that I acquired an unlisted phone number for anonymity.
4. On receipt of the enclosed form, we shall send you the refund cheque.
5. In the course of the campaign, some delegates will hold a meeting to elect a leader.

Unit-3

1. d 2. a 3. c 4. d 5. a

Unit-4

1. a 2. b 3. c 4. a 5. d

Unit-5

Any of these six teams might win the cup.

1. Either means one of two: Any of these...
2. The 'Three Musketeers' is very interesting to read.
3. My friend, philosopher and guide has come.
4. The majority is opposed to this proposal.
5. His kindness and benevolence is well-known.

Unit-6

1. c	2. b	3. c	4. d	5. b
6. d	7. b	8. b	9. a	10. a

Unit-7

1. b **2.** a **3.** d **4.** c **5.** a

Unit-8

1. C **2.** B **3.** D **4.** B **5.** A

Writing Ability

Unit-1

A check on the freedom of press is aptly criticised, but unrestrained freedom can be misused also. The press reporters give details, which result in attracting the attention of more public. In Aberdeen, a very poor family had got quintuplets. Earlier, their life was one of a continuous struggle against poverty. This event transformed their fate and fortune both. A day after the birth of the five children, reporters and photographers came, as it was news of national importance in America. The news was spread everywhere and to everyone. Newspapers and unknown people offered the couple huge sums and other gifts. Press conferences were organised. This changed the fate of the parents and of the town, as the couple had become the parents of quintuplets. It had even grown overwhelming for them and the city.

Unit-2

NEW ERA COLLEGE

AJMER

14th SAARC

Letter Writing Competition, 2001

15th Aug. 2001

The Department of Post, Govt. of India invites participation from college students for the 14th SAARC Letter Writing Competition.

Subject: "Expectation of the modern day users from the Postal Department."

Composition: A letter not exceeding 1000 words in length.

Eligibility: Bona fide students from recognised colleges and universities.

Date: 1.10.2001

Time: 10.00 a.m.

Venue: New Era College, Ajmer, Rajasthan.

* *Interested students may get their names registered by 25.9.01*

* *Prizes sponsored by the Postal Dept. of India.*

* For further information, please contact:

The Secretary of Academics,
New Era College.

Unit-3

It does not seem probable that a man with so unpatriotic spirit be living in this world, who should never think about his motherland as his own, and who after returning from his travels in foreign countries should never long for the sight and soil of his own native land.

OR

It is hard to imagine a person so soulless that he does not feel love for his native land. A person whose heart has never rejoiced at the thought of returning home to his country after his travels abroad.

Unit-4

Key Ans. d

PRACTICE TEST — II

PART – A
READING COMPREHENSION AND READING ABILITY

UNIT – 1

Multiple Choice Type

Directions: Read through the passage only once as quickly as you can without suffering loss of comprehension and answer the questions that follow.

Newton and his contemporaries believed that God created the universe in essentially the same form as it has today. The nineteenth century view was very different. Laplace put forward the view that the solar system began as a glowing, rotating gas from which the planets condensed and cooled: Hutton and Lyell described the gradual transformation of the surface of the earth during millions of years, how mountains had risen and been worn away, how continents had sunk beneath the sea and risen again; and Darwin offered a picture of the appearance of primitive forms of life which developed during vast periods of geological time into an enormous variety of complex plants and animals and finally into man.

Herbert Spencer (1820-1903), an influential but not a great philosopher, tried to apply the theory of evolution to sociology, psychology and ethics, but without great success. The theory of natural selection was put forward to explain the evolution of living things and cannot be applied to astronomical or geological evolution. The word 'evolution', when used outside the field of biology, can mean little more than 'change', since there is no principle that can be discovered at work in other fields.

Although progress in science in the nineteenth century was very considerable, progress in technology was even greater. The immense development of industry in Europe and the USA produced a rise in the average standard of living greater than that achieved in the two thousand years before. The population of Europe, which had not increased greatly since 1700, rose from 187 millions in 1800 to 400 millions in 1900.

The industrial revolution, begun in Britain in the eighteenth century, continued at increasing speed and spread to other European countries. A method for manufacturing cheap steel was invented by Sir Henery Bessemer in 1856. British coal production rose from 10 million tons in 1800 to 60 million in 1850 and 210 million in 1900.

The steam engine, which helped to make such progress possible, was invented by men who owed little to theoretical science. Although science had little influence on industrial progress in the first half of the nineteenth century, it made possible the creation of entirely new industries in the second half.

Railways and steamships made great changes possible in systems of transport. Railways were built to satisfy the need of industry for a means of transporting raw materials and manufactured goods. The existence of railways in turn helped in the development of industry. By means of railways it was possible for the people of the eastern part of the USA and for the large numbers of people arriving from Europe to spread across the American Continent.

Science made possible the establishment of two entirely new industries, the electrical and the fine chemical industries. The first London telephone exchange was set up in 1879 and the first station for supplying electricity to private users began to operate in New York in 1882. From 1870 a lot of research was carried out on synthetic dyes, mainly in Germany and many new ones were discovered.

— J.G. Bruton

COMPREHENSION TEST

Select the most suitable answer.

1. According to Laplace's view, the solar system began:
   (*a*) as it is today.
   (*b*) as the Garden of Eden.
   (*c*) as a number of dead planets.
   (*d*) as a glowing, rotating gas.
2. Spencer applied the theory of evolution to sociology, psychology, and ethics

(*a*) without considerable success
(*b*) with little success
(*c*) with reasonable success
(*d*) with great success

3. The word 'evolution', outside the field of biology, can only be interpreted as:
(*a*) speed (*b*) change
(*c*) improvement (*d*) progress

4. In the nineteenth century, progress in technology was:
(*a*) more considerable than in Science
(*b*) less considerable than in Science
(*c*) a little more than in Science
(*d*) negligible compared to Science

5. The population of Europe in 1900 was:
(*a*) 200 millions (*b*) 300 millions
(*c*) 400 millions (*d*) 500 millions

6. The purpose of building Railways was:
(*a*) to transport raw materials mainly
(*b*) to meet all the requirements of industry
(*c*) to transport manufactured goods only
(*d*) none of the above

7. The importance of railways in the development of the USA was:
(*a*) considerable (*b*) reasonable
(*c*) small (*d*) negligible

8. Darwin's theory of evolution was:
(*a*) universally applicable
(*b*) only applicable to man
(*c*) only applicable to science
(*d*) of limited application

9. The progress in technology and population increases were:
(*a*) unrelated
(*b*) closely linked
(*c*) mutually dependent
(*d*) unconnected

10. Technological progress can be said to have begun in:
(*a*) USA (*b*) Britain
(*c*) France (*d*) Germany

UNIT – 2

Question-Answer Type

While the Duma Committee wrestled with the formation of an official Government to negotiate with the Tsar, the real business of governing, in so far as there was any, was being conducted by the Soviet in the opposite wing of the palace. Kerensky dashed between the two poles, made himself indispensable, and learnt the secrets of both sides.

Early, on 15th March Milyukov was ready with his Government list. It was a government headed by an enlightened aristocrat, Prince Lvov, which had no imaginable connection with what was happening in the streets. The only concession to the revolutionary mood was the inclusion of Kerensky as Minister of Justice, and Kerensky himself thought twice: he was afraid that the Soviet would disown him for co-operating with what in any country but Russia would have been a conservative cabinet, including as it did such bourgeois politicians as Milyukov, the new Foreign Minister, and Guchkov, Minister for War. At least one member was a millionaire.

Nor was it in any real sense a revolutionary government. It was dedicated to the restoration of order, to forcing Nicholas to abdicate, and to the inauguration of a constitution and the creation of an elected Constituent Assembly. It was determined to pursue the war with Germany and, apart from Kerensky, it wished to retain the monarchy. The battle with the Soviet was now on.

But it was more than the battle with the Soviet; it was a battle with the people. This came out most vividly in Guchkov's resistance to the Soviet's demand that it should control the army. There were many Soviets now, springing up all over the country and in the battle zone. The Petrograd Soviet was supreme; but it had no real control. The troops recognised only the Soviet and the Soviet could not have stopped this even if it had wished to.

The fight to retain the monarchy was kept secret from the Soviet in the first place. When Nicholas was at last run to earth by Guchkov, the new Government's plan was that he should abdicate and surrender the throne to his 13-year old son, Alexis, with his brother the Grand Duke Michael, acting as Regent. Nicholas had tried to get back from Mogilev to Petrograd but his train had been diverted, and now he was held a virtual prisoner at Pskov, about 150 miles away.

He was calm; but he decided that because the Tsarevitch's haemophilia was incurable, the crown should go directly to Michael. It was not to be. When the Soviet heard of the plan there was an uproar. The monarchy must go.

In the end it was the Grand Duke who decided. He would not, he said, accept the crown unless and until it was offered to him by a properly elected Constituent Assembly. That was the end of the road. The Lvov Government was now the official Government of Russia. It was called the Provisional Government because its task was to hold the fort until a Constituent Assembly could be elected. In its pristine form it was doomed to almost immediate failure.

Questions:

1. What was the only concession to the revolutionary mood made in Milyukov's Government list?
2. On which issue did Kerensky disagree with the Milyukov's Government?
3. How old was Nicholas II's son, Alexis?
4. What stopped Nicholas II from getting back to Petrograd?
5. Under what terms would the Grand Duke Michael accept the crown?
6. What is meant by 'the real business of governing'?
7. Why did Milyukov's Government list have 'no imaginable connection with what was happening in the streets'?
8. Why was the fight to retain the monarchy kept secret from the Soviet?
9. Why was Nicholas II prevented from returning to Petrograd?
10. Why did the Lvov Government become the official Government of Russia?

UNIT– 3

Miscellaneous Type

Gandhi went to this meeting out of curiosity; he had no other motive. As he sat and listened to the lip service that a prince paid to a prince, he became uneasy in his chair. At last, he rose in that great assembly of vested interests—a some-what unknown person—and with the President's permission, began to speak on a matter that worried him intensely. He spoke of the police vigilance in honour of the Viceroy and the hordes of policemen that swarmed the city. "It is better to die a thousand times," he said "rather than be followed by a pack of policemen."

A hushed assembly turned around to see who this stranger was in their midst; a murmur came through the whole crowd. On the platform, there was confusion and prince conferred with prince over the identity of this Mr. Gandhi, of whom they had never heard. 'We seek arrest because this so-called freedom is slavery.' They were sure he was of no consequence. 'We are challenging the might of this government because we consider its activity to be wholly evil.' Only Mrs. Annie Besant, who sat on the platform, remembered those Kathiawari features as being those of a young man who had recently appeared at the meeting of the Congress, "a child in politics", she said to those around her. We want to overthrow the government.

Gandhi finished with the Viceroy and his police guard. He then went on to tackle the princes themselves. 'We want to compel its submission to the people's will'. He told them how empty was their pomp and how unimportant they really were in the India that mattered. The President was unaccustomed to such gross impoliteness, for the princes never spoke to each other except with the utmost courtesy. They did not know how to handle this situation. It was unprecedented and had come as a complete surprise to everyone. But this unknown insignificant little man was carrying the crowd. They could now think freely and speak like him without fear. Those on the platform were too dumb-founded to do or to say anything. Eventually the President was seen to get up and leave. He was followed by the other princes, while Gandhi stood there still addressing a meeting which had lost its chairman, its sponsors, its honoured guests. We must refuse to purchase freedom at the cost of our self-respect or our cherished conviction.

Questions:

1. The passage above contains five sentences that do not fit in with the logical development of the passage. Identify these sentences and write them down in the order in which they occur.
2. Answer the following questions :-
   1. What was the reaction to Mr. Gandhi's remarks about the Viceroy and his police guard?
   2. What did Gandhi tell the princes?
   3. How did the crowd react to Gandhi's speech?
   4. What did happen in the end?
3. Find out the right answer to each of the questions below and write it down in your answer book.

   A. Gandhi went to the meeting
   1. to criticise the Viceroy and the princes.
   2. to meet the ordinary people
   3. out of curiosity.

   B. Gandhi told the princes that
   1. he was a child in politics.
   2. they should not be followed by a pack of policemen.
   3. they were quite unimportant in the India that mattered.

   C. The crowd cheered Gandhi because
   1. he spoke their thoughts.
   2. he was a great political leader.
   3. he had shown discourtesy to the princes.
4. Write down meaning of the following words: 1. hordes, 2. swarmed, 3. Conferred, 4. Pomp, 5. unprecedented

UNIT – 4

Cloze Passage (CP)

Directions: Fill in the blanks with appropriate words in context. You can read the whole passage before beginning the task.

Governments have seized on tourism as a way ______[1] creating employment and bringing income – preferably foreign exchange – ______[2] troubled economies. For years tourism's capacity to filter ______[3] through communities has been a major argument in ______[4] favour. The tourist spends money on accommodation, food ______[5] souvenirs, bringing income to the suppliers of these ______[6] and services, whose money will in turn circulate ______[7] the economy.

UNIT – 5

Multiple Choice Type

Communicative Passage

Directions: Read the following Advertisement and answer the following questions by choosing the appropriate option.

DAMP SEAL »2020«

is now available in India

Is your building DAMPSEALED?

All new concrete buildings are susceptible to dampness eating into their life span, gradually.

Damp Seal is silane siloxane aliphatic urethane blend sealer.

Damp Seal 2020 protects buildings from the structure weakening effects of dampness.

Little wonder all leading architects and builders use Damp Seal 2020.

A must do coating for all new constructions.

STERLING

Sterling Decors private limited

Mail us at sterlingmd@vsnl.net; website: www.sterlingdecors.com

Questions:

1. State which of the following statement is TRUE.

   (*a*) New buildings are more prone to dampness.

(*b*) Damp Seal 2020 protects the buildings from bad weather.
(*c*) All builders and architects use Damp Seal 2020.
(*d*) Damp Seal 2020 is important for all new constructions.

2. Damp Seal 2020 is manufactured by:
(*a*) builders and architects.
(*b*) silane siloxane aliphatic urethane blend sealer.
(*c*) Sterling Decors Private Limited.
(*d*) None of the above.

3. Dampness causes:
(*a*) leakage in the buildings.
(*b*) lessening of the life span of buildings.
(*c*) strengthening of the structure of the buildings.
(*d*) None of the above.

4. Pick out a word from the passage which means the same as 'Dank'.
(*a*) Decor
(*b*) Damp
(*c*) Concrete
(*d*) Structure

UNIT – 6

Single Sentence Readings

Directions: For each of these questions, choose the answer that is closest in meaning to the original phrase or sentence underlined. Note that several of the choices may be factually correct, but you should choose the one that is the closest restatement of the given phrase or sentence.

1. The instructor told the student to hold the club lightly, keeping his eye on the ball and drawing the club back quickly, but too much force should not be used on the downward stroke.
(*a*) to hold the club lightly and keeping his eye on the ball, drawing the club back quickly, but too much force should not be used
(*b*) to hold the club lightly, keep his eye on the ball, and drawing the club back quickly, and too much force should not be used
(*c*) to hold the club lightly, keep his eye on the ball, draw the club back quickly, and not use too much force
(*d*) he should hold the club lightly keeping his eye on the ball, drawing the club back quickly, and not using too much force

2. The horse, ridden by the experienced jockey with the broken leg, had to be sold off.
(*a*) The horse ridden by the experienced jockey with the broken leg had
(*b*) With the broken leg, the horse ridden by the experienced jockey had
(*c*) The horse with the broken leg ridden by the experienced jockey, had
(*d*) The horse with the broken leg, ridden by the experienced jockey, had

3. In his last letter our guest let us know that he would be arriving next week.
(*a*) that he was arriving next week.
(*b*) that he will arrive next week.
(*c*) that he will be arriving next week.
(*d*) that he would arrive next week.

4. Whoever objects to my going to the convention ought to state his position promptly.
(*a*) Whomever objects to me
(*b*) Whomever objects to my
(*c*) Who objects to my
(*d*) Whoever has an objection to my

5. There are only five minutes left for us players to recover the initiative we lost because of the delay in the game.
(*a*) There is only five minutes left for us players
(*b*) There is only five minutes left for we players
(*c*) There are only five minutes left for we players
(*d*) There are only five minutes left for all of us (players)

PART – B

VOCABULARY

"The word dwelt with God, and what God was, the word was"

—St. John's Gospel

–New English Bible version

UNIT – 1

Multiple Choice Type

Directions: Choose one word or phrase closest to the meaning of the given word.

1. Farrago
   (*a*) distance (*b*) disorder
   (*c*) medley (*d*) rhyme
2. Inveigle
   (*a*) complicate (*b*) entice
   (*c*) break into (*d*) denounce
3. Marauding
   (*a*) parading (*b*) loitering
   (*c*) brawling (*d*) raiding
4. Database
   (*a*) starting point
   (*b*) system of signals
   (*c*) collection of information
   (*d*) domicile
5. Ensemble
   (*a*) sacred music
   (*b*) old-fashioned dance
   (*c*) musical fanfare
   (*d*) group performers
6. Hibernation
   (*a*) Irish dancing step
   (*b*) inactivity
   (*c*) bacterial infection
   (*d*) retirement
7. Manger
   (*a*) organizer
   (*b*) open feeding-box in a stable
   (*c*) device for closing stable door
   (*d*) haystack
8. Deciduous
   (*a*) resolution (*b*) referring
   (*c*) transitory (*d*) permanent
9. Corrosive
   (*a*) devious (*b*) destructive
   (*c*) intense (*d*) unpleasant
10. Extant
    (*a*) lengthy (*b*) long-dead
    (*c*) stationary (*d*) surviving

UNIT – 2

Multiple Choice

1. To abrogate
   (*a*) to reform (*b*) to repeal
   (*c*) to revise (*d*) to review
2. To abscond
   (*a*) to confront openly
   (*b*) to run off secretly
   (*c*) to be absent
   (*d*) to hide
3. Bland
   (*a*) mild (*b*) soothing
   (*c*) light (*d*) simple
4. Blasphemy
   (*a*) deception
   (*b*) disloyalty
   (*c*) a profane remark about one's nation
   (*d*) a profane remark about God
5. Spruce
   (*a*) meticulous (*b*) neat and smart
   (*c*) methodical (*d*) ridiculous

UNIT – 3

Multiple Choice

Directions: Each problem in this part of the test consists of a sentence in which one word or phrase has been underlined. From the four choices given, choose the word or phrase which could be substituted for the underlined word or phrase without changing the meaning of the sentence.

1. The poem is written in a very <u>**lucid**</u> style.
   (*a*) elaborate (*b*) clear
   (*c*) noble (*d*) intricate

2. A **parsimonious** man is someone who is
   (*a*) cautious (*b*) extravagant
   (*c*) religious in his approach
   (*d*) careful with money
3. If food is **savoury**, it is
   (*a*) healthy (*b*) frozen
   (*c*) insipid (*d*) tasty
4. Few teachers have been spared the problem of **an obstreperous** pupil in the class.
   (*a*) dull (*b*) unruly
   (*c*) lazy (*d*) awkward
5. His visit to foreign countries brought about a **sea change** in his outlook and his attitude to people.
   (*a*) complete change
   (*b*) partial change
   (*c*) favourable change
   (*d*) unfavourable change

UNIT – 4

Multiple Choice

(One Word Substitution)

Directions: Give one word for the phrase underlined. Under each sentence are given four choices. You are directed to choose the appropriate one.

1. Fame is **beyond all power of time to destroy**.
   (*a*) Imperishable (*b*) inevitable
   (*c*) impartial (*d*) intransigent
2. A prolific writer, he **turned out** three novels that year.
   (*a*) conceptualised (*b*) repudiated
   (*c*) produced (*d*) scribbled
3. **A man who spends too much** is not a sensible person.
   (*a*) A spendthrift (*b*) A waster
   (*c*) A spender (*d*) An uneconomical man
4. Small pox is a disease which is **commonly caught from others**.
   (*a*) infections (*b*) contagious
   (*c*) parasitic (*d*) communicative
5. Such negligence is **not only blameable it can be proceeded against in a court of law**.
   (*a*) illegal (*b*) convincible
   (*c*) punishable (*d*) culpable

UNIT – 5

Multiple Choice

(One Word Substitution)

Directions: The questions below have a statement followed by four choices. Select the choice closest in meaning to the given statement.

1. A government by the nobles
   (*a*) Aristocracy (*b*) Democracy
   (*c*) Autocracy (*d*) Bureaucracy
2. That which cannot be believed
   (*a*) Brittle (*b*) Incredible
   (*c*) False (*d*) Illegal
3. An assembly of hearers
   (*a*) Audience (*b*) Assemblage
   (*c*) Crowd (*d*) Congregation
4. A healthy site for invalids
   (*a*) Clinic (*b*) Sanitarium
   (*c*) Hospital (*d*) Dispensary
5. A flotilla means
   (*a*) A fleet of small ships
   (*b*) A flock of birds
   (*c*) A bunch of flowers
   (*d*) A crowd of men

UNIT – 6

Multiple Choice

(In Context)

Directions: Fill in the blanks by choosing the best answer.

1. You must have seen many _______ which deal with smugglers and their evil acts.
   (*a*) theatres (*b*) cinemas
   (*c*) pictures (*d*) films
2. The next paragraph beginning with 'The Social Consequences' could be _______ as 'In the absence of black money, huge dowries would cease to be the practice...'
   (*a*) rewritten (*b*) re-created
   (*c*) re-assembled (*d*) reproduced
3. You are a paid social worker, whose job it is to _______ people away from the bad habit of drinking.
   (*a*) stop (*b*) wean
   (*c*) evade (*d*) discourage

4. As a railway official, you have been sent information by the local _______ about the accident near Mancherial Railway Station.
   (*a*) labour (*b*) people
   (*c*) authorities (*d*) members
5. Armymen on the train jumped in the gushing waters; men, women, and children were _______.
   (*a*) Pumped out (*b*) aided
   (*c*) brought out (*d*) rescued

UNIT – 7

Synonyms

Directions: Select the word closest in meaning to the given word:

1. Vista
   (*a*) view (*b*) argument
   (*c*) illusion (*d*) portable screen
2. Allege
   (*a*) to declare without any evidence
   (*b*) to form a new group
   (*c*) to irritate
   (*d*) to capture
3. Pittance
   (*a*) a small amount (*b*) a feeling of sorrow
   (*c*) a narrow inlet (*d*) a new fashion
4. Plaudits
   (*a*) fits of anger (*b*) praise
   (*c*) suggestions (*d*) creations
5. Morose
   (*a*) hardy (*b*) lenient
   (*c*) fretful/gloomy (*d*) bashful

UNIT – 8

Antonyms

Directions: Select the word which is closest to the opposite in meaning of the underlined word or phrase in the given sentence.

1. <u>Emigration from</u> Europe increased greatly in volume in the 19th century.
   (*a*) Immigration to
   (*b*) Migration from
   (*c*) Transfer from
   (*d*) Shifting from
2. They were writing stories of a more <u>advanced</u> civilization in the continent.
   (*a*) obsolete (*b*) progressive
   (*c*) slow (*d*) backward
3. There is no <u>subjectivity</u> in the author's essay.
   (*a*) attachment (*b*) objectivity
   (*c*) elasticity (*d*) individuality
4. A change in climatic conditions <u>gradually</u> made life more difficult in the region.
   (*a*) speedily (*b*) rapidly
   (*c*) practically (*d*) progressively
5. During his stay at the office he dealt with <u>essential</u> matters.
   (*a*) insignificant (*b*) important
   (*c*) silly (*d*) useless

UNIT – 9

Idioms and Phrases

Directions: Each item below consists of an idiom or a phrase, followed by four expressions. Choose the expression that most nearly expresses the meaning of the given idiom or phrase.

1. To rise from the ranks
   (*a*) To get a rank in the examination
   (*b*) To succeed in life
   (*c*) To get undue promotions
   (*d*) To fall and again rise
2. To keep the powder dry (from gun-powder)
   (*a*) To be enthusiastic
   (*b*) To become aggressive
   (*c*) To look for enemy
   (*d*) To be on the alert
3. An eye for an eye
   (*a*) price (*b*) Revenge
   (*c*) Association (*d*) Importance
4. A feather in one's cap
   (*a*) An achievement to be proud of
   (*b*) As light as a feather
   (*c*) Very slow
   (*d*) Graceful act
5. To cut one's coat according to one's cloth
   (*a*) To be well dressed
   (*b*) To lead a luxurious life
   (*c*) To live within means
   (*d*) To work under the directions of someone

UNIT – 10

Words Often Confused

Directions: In each item below, a choice of words that are often confused is given in parentheses. Write in the blank the letter indicating the best choice for the context.

1. ______ Not wishing to (A. detract; B. distract) my neighbours, I didn't begin typing until they were awake.
2. ______ We had many excellent convocation speakers, but the governor was the most (A. eminent; B. imminent).
3. ______ The general restlessness in the audience suggested that people were (A. disinterested; B. uninterested) and wanted to leave.
4. ______ Such behaviour cannot be too strongly (A. censored; B. censured).
5. ______ Moving from one place to another is always a shock, and it takes some time to become (A. adapted; B. adopted) to city life.

UNIT – 11

Spellings–I

Directions: Answer the questions following the paragraphs. In each of the paragraphs five of the underlined words have been spelt *incorrectly*. Identify the option, which lists the five *incorrectly* spelt words.

1. The receptions I have been **mentioning**[1] **usully**[2] took the form of **buffe**[3], **dinnrs**[4] – they are an **inovation**[5] since my time. Long tables are loaded with Indian food, and **sometimes**[6] one table is **labelled**[7] "**vegitarian**[8]" and the other "**non-vegetarian**[9]."

   The five **incorrectly** spelt words are:
   (*a*) 1, 3, 4, 6, and 8
   (*b*) 2, 3, 4, 5, and 8
   (*c*) 1, 2, 4, 6, and 8
   (*d*) 3, 4, 6, 7, and 8

2. Of modern architecture, the chief example I saw was the great new university at Hyderabad. This is an interesting innovation. It is **built**[1] in the **Amercan**[2] **fashion**[3] on a **campas**[4], a wide open space **severel**[5] miles from the **centar**[6] of the city, in **beautiful**[7] country, among **flowring**[8] **shrubs**[9].

   The five **incorrectly** spelt words are:
   (*a*) 2, 3, 5, 7, and 8
   (*b*) 1, 3, 5, 6, and 7
   (*c*) 2, 4, 5, 6 and 8
   (*d*) 1, 3, 4, 7, and 8

Spellings–II

Directions: Choose the correct spelling from the options given below:

3. (*a*) Subsidiary (*b*) Subsdiary (*c*) Subsediary (*d*) Subisdiary
4. (*a*) Condemed (*b*) Condemned (*c*) Condemnd (*d*) Condemmed
5. (*a*) Inexhastible (*b*) Inixhaustible (*c*) Inexhaustible (*d*) Inexhastable

UNIT – 12

Vocabulary In Context

Modified Cloze Procedure (MCP)

Directions: Read the following passage carefully. A few words in the beginning have been written without any bracketed words. This will facilitate you to understand the context. Each bracket contains 4 (four) choices; 1 (one) choice is correct and 3 (three) are incorrect. Choose the correct choice so that the whole passage results in a coherent piece of writing.

Socrates taught that a man, who is master of himself, is truly free. By knowing one's faults and weaknesses, (one, he, she, it)[1] gains mastery over one's self. The (personal, self, creative, worldly)[2] knowledge enables a man to be (courageous, coward, tricky, wise)[3]. A really courageous person, who is (not, never, seldom, ever)[4] afraid of consequences and felt (conscious, nervous, bound, free)[5] to teach what he thought was (correct, free, sound, sensible)[6]. Socrates made some dangerous enemies by (his, one's, their, its)[7] teachings and asking questions. The rulers (do, can, did, would)[8] not like people asking questions about (his, one's, others', their)[9] actions. Therefore they accused Socrates of teaching (wicked, bad, sad, sensible)[10] things to the youth and condemned (one, him, them, it)[11] to death.

PART – C

GRAMMAR

"For there be woman, fair as she
Whose verbs and nouns do more agree."

– Mrs. Judge Jenkins.

UNIT – 1

Multiple Choice Type

Direct – Indirect

Directions: The following sentences are changed from direct to indirect speech. Each sentence is followed by four choices a, b, c, d. Select the most appropriate choice.

1. Edison said to his technician, "I am serious about the completion of the model I have explained to you."

(*a*) Edison told his technician that he was serious about the completion of the model he had explained to him.

(*b*) Edison told his technician that he was serious about the completion of the model he has explained to him.

(*c*) Edison told his technician that he was serious about the completion of the model he explained to him.

(*d*) Edison told his technician that he is serious about the completion of the model he had explained to him.

2. Jaswant said to his friend, "Have you appeared in the test?"

(*a*) Jaswant asked his friend had he appeared in the test?

(*b*) Jaswant asked his friend whether he had appeared in the test?

(*c*) Jaswant asked his friend had he appeared in the test.

(*d*) Jaswant asked his friend whether had he appeared in the test.

3. Joseph said to me, "When did you visit the Trade Fair?"

(*a*) Joseph asked me when I did visit the Trade Fair.

(*b*) Joseph asked me when I visited the Trade Fair.

(*c*) Joseph asked me when I had visited the Trade Fair.

(*d*) Joseph asked me when I visit the Trade Fair.

4. Sheela said to her servant, "Mop the floor."

(*a*) Sheela said to her servant to mop the floor.

(*b*) Sheela told her servant to mop the floor.

(*c*) Sheela requested her servant to mop the floor.

(*d*) Sheela ordered to her servant to mop the floor.

5. Vinod says to Leena, "Please don't try to befool me."

(*a*) Vinod requests Leena not to try to befool him.

(*b*) Vinod requests Leena that she should not try to befool him.

(*c*) Vinod requests Leena please do not try to befool him.

(*d*) Vinod requests Leena not to please try to befool him.

6. *Direct:* My father said to me, "Don't quarrel among yourselves."

Indirect: My father...

(*a*) asked me to not quarrel among ourselves.

(*b*) forbade me to quarrel among ourselves.

(*c*) asked me that not to quarrel among ourselves.

(*d*) asked me to quarrel not among ourselves.

7. *Direct:* His mother said to his father, "Please excuse the child."

Indirect: His mother...

(*a*) said to his father to excuse the child.

(*b*) asked his father to excuse the child.

(*c*) asked his father that please excuse the child.

(*d*) asked his father that the child could be excused.

8. *Direct:* I said to my friend, "Let us go to the library."

Indirect: I suggested to my friend ......

(*a*) we should go to the library.

(*b*) we shall go to the library.

(*c*) that we should go to the library.

(*d*) that we would go to the library.

9. *Direct:* Ram said to me, " Search his pockets."
Indirect: Ram advised me ......
(*a*) that search his pockets.
(*b*) to search his pockets.
(*c*) to let me search his pockets.
(*d*) to let him search my pockets.

10. *Direct:* He said to me, "Trust in God."
Indirect: He advised me ......
(*a*) to trust in God.
(*b*) that trust in God.
(*c*) that they should trust in God.
(*d*) I should trust in God.

UNIT – 2

Prepositions

Directions: Choose the appropriate alternative to fill in the blanks.

1. Nikhil has been relieved _____ the post.
(*a*) with (*b*) at (*c*) off (*d*) of
2. His services have been dispensed _____.
(*a*) of (*b*) with (*c*) for (*d*) in
3. Anurag spread the sheet _____ the grass.
(*a*) on (*b*) over (*c*) in (*d*) into
4. If you do not heed your elders' advice you will get _____ trouble.
(*a*) in (*b*) into (*c*) through (*d*) at
5. One should not make fun _____ the under-privileged.
(*a*) of (*b*) at (*c*) by (*d*) with

UNIT – 3

Tenses

Directions: Choose the appropriate tenses from the alternatives given below to fill in the blanks. Tick (✔) against the appropriate choice:

1. Yesterday I _____ a new watch as my old one _____.
(*a*) Had bought ; had been stolen
(*b*) bought ; was stolen
(*c*) bought ; has been stolen
(*d*) bought ; had been stolen
2. When the last one _____ I must go too.
(*a*) falls (*b*) fell
(*c*) has fallen (*d*) will fall
3. She usually _____ in black ink.
(*a*) writes (*b*) has written
(*c*) is writing (*d*) has been writing
4. He _____ the English Channel in record time.
(*a*) swims (*b*) swam
(*c*) will swim (*d*) will be swimming
5. After the doctor _____, she went into the work-room.
(*a*) went (*b*) was gone
(*c*) had gone (*d*) had went

UNIT – 4

Active Passive Voice

Directions: Read the following sentences in Active Voice. Select the most appropriate of the alternatives given below each sentence to change the sentence into Passive Voice.

1. We shall not have betrayed our country.
(*a*) Our country would not have been betrayed by us.
(*b*) Our country should not have been betrayed by us.
(*c*) Our country will not have been betrayed by us.
(*d*) Our country shall not have been betrayed by us.
2. Have you completed the assignment successfully by you?
(*a*) Have the assignment been completed successfully?
(*b*) Was the assignment completed successfully by you?
(*c*) Has been the assignment completed successfully by you?
(*d*) Has the assignment been completed successfully by you?
3. I will always stand by you.
(*a*) You will always be stood by me.
(*b*) You will always be stood by by me.
(*c*) You will always have been stood by me.
(*d*) You will always have been stood by by me.
4. Will they have not caught the train?
(*a*) Will the train have been not caught by them?

(*b*) Will the train be not caught by them?
(*c*) Will the train have not been caught?
(*d*) Will the train have not been caught by them?

5. Had she persisted in her demand?
(*a*) Had her demand been persisted in by her?
(*b*) Had her demand been persisted in?
(*c*) Had her demand been persisted by her?
(*d*) Had the demand been persisted in by her?

UNIT – 5

Use of Articles

Directions: Read the following sentences and select the most appropriate of the alternatives given below. Complete the incomplete sentence by choosing the most appropriate alternatives given below.

Alexander Pope (1688–1744), was ____[1] Roman Catholic and ____[2] cripple, and he suffered on account of both. It is, therefore, not surprising that when he became ____[3] poet he wielded ____[4] bitter pen. After some early descriptive poetry he wrote **An Essay on Criticism** (1711) and **The Rape of the Lock** (1712), ____[5] latter poem establishing Pope's greatness as ____[6] satirical poet. ____[7] works of Pope and his contemporaries have many characteristics in common with ____[8] classical Latin literature, ____[9] literature of ____[10] age of Augustus when writers like Virgil, Horace and Ovid were writing. That is why ____[11] period 1660–1780 is often called ____[12] Augustan age. ____[13] Age is also described as ____[14] neo-classical age, or ____[15] age of reason, or the age of prose.

1.	(*a*) a	(*b*) the	(*c*) an	(*d*) ø
2.	(*a*) a	(*b*) an	(*c*) the	(*d*) ø
3.	(*a*) the	(*b*) an	(*c*) ø	(*d*) a
4.	(*a*) ø	(*b*) the	(*c*) a	(*d*) an
5.	(*a*) the	(*b*) an	(*c*) ø	(*d*) a
6.	(*a*) a	(*b*) the	(*c*) ø	(*d*) an
7.	(*a*) A	(*b*) An	(*c*) ø	(*d*) The
8.	(*a*) an	(*b*) the	(*c*) a	(*d*) ø
9.	(*a*) the	(*b*) ø	(*c*) a	(*d*) an
10.	(*a*) an	(*b*) ø	(*c*) a	(*d*) the
11.	(*a*) a	(*b*) an	(*c*) the	(*d*) ø
12.	(*a*) an	(*b*) ø	(*c*) a	(*d*) the
13.	(*a*) ø	(*b*) an	(*c*) the	(*d*) a
14.	(*a*) the	(*b*) ø	(*c*) an	(*d*) a
15.	(*a*) ø	(*b*) the	(*c*) a	(*d*) an

UNIT – 6

Global Test

Directions: Read the following sentences and select the most appropriate of the alternatives given below. Complete the incomplete sentence by choosing the most appropriate alternatives.

John Keats (1795–1821) is perhaps the greatest of the second generation of English romantic poets, who blossomed early and died young. In his lifetime he was neglected and ____[1] as a bad poet. His merits ____[2] a poet were recognised much later. His poetry is characterised by ____[3], Hellenism, continuity of archaic ____[4] and worship of ____[5].

Keats published three volumes of verse. 'On a Grecian Urn' is one ____[6] the several odes written by Keats. In these odes Keats ____[7] his feelings ____[8] shows how they are coloured by ____[9] events of his life. A spirit of sadness ____[10] all his odes. The ____[11] of this poem is said to ____[12] been partly derived from a marble ____[13] belonging to Lord Holland, and still ____[14] in the garden at Holland House; ____[15] it is certain that Keats is ____[16] thinking of Greek Sculpture in ____[17]. Lord Holland's urn represents the scene of ____[18] sacrifice. An altar bearing fruits is carved ____[19] the middle; nearby stands a priest, ____[20] above is a figure playing on a pipe. Other details are two trees and a calf that is brought to be sacrificed.

1.	(*a*) named	(*b*) analysed
	(*c*) appreciated	(*d*) condemned
2.	(*a*) while	(*b*) as
	(*c*) because of	(*d*) of
3.	(*a*) sensuousness	(*b*) sensitivity
	(*c*) senses	(*d*) sensations
4.	(*a*) lexicon	(*b*) languages
	(*c*) words	(*d*) speeches
5.	(*a*) beauty	(*b*) attraction
	(*c*) charm	(*d*) glamour

6. (*a*) with (*b*) of
   (*c*) from (*d*) out of
7. (*a*) cherishes (*b*) serves
   (*c*) nurses (*d*) expresses
8. (*a*) but (*b*) however
   (*c*) rather (*d*) and
9. (*a*) the (*b*) an
   (*c*) a (*d*) none of the above
10. (*a*) prevails (*b*) spreads
    (*c*) pervades (*d*) contains
11. (*a*) aspiration (*b*) inspiration
    (*c*) theme (*d*) motive
12. (*a*) have had (*b*) being
    (*c*) had (*d*) have
13. (*a*) urn (*b*) vessel
    (*c*) pot (*d*) ash
14. (*a*) kept (*b*) preserved
    (*c*) buried (*d*) thrown
15. (*a*) but (*b*) and
    (*c*) therefore (*d*) as also
16. (*a*) too (*b*) well
    (*c*) as (*d*) also
17. (*a*) particular (*b*) general
    (*c*) usual (*d*) casual
18. (*a*) a (*b*) the
    (*c*) an (*d*) none of the above
19. (*a*) within (*b*) about
    (*c*) for (*d*) in
20. (*a*) but (*b*) and
    (*c*) as also (*d*) none of the above

UNIT – 7

Error Correction

Directions: In questions 1 to10 each sentence has four underlined words or phrases. The four underlined parts of the sentence are marked (A), (B), (C) and (D). Identify the one underlined word or phrase that must be changed in order for the sentence to be correct.

1. George is not enough (A) intelligent to pass (B) this (C) economics (D) class without help.
2. There were (A) so much (B) people trying to leave the burning (C) building that (D) the police had a great deal of trouble controlling them.
3. John lived in (A) New York since (B) 1960 to 1975, but he is now living (C) in (D) Detroit.
4. The fire began in (A) the fifth (B) floor of (C) the hotel, but it soon spread (D) to adjacent floors.
5. Mrs. Anderson bought last week a new sports car; (A) however, (B) she has yet to learn (C) how to operate (D) the manual gearshift.
6. The instructor advised the students for (A) the procedures (B) to follow (C) in writing (D) the term paper.
7. Although both of them (A) are trying (B) to get (C) the scholarship, she has the highest (D) grades.
8. The new technique calls (A) for heat (B) the mixture before applying (C) it to the wood (D).
9. The pilot and the crew (A) divided (B) the life preservers between (C) the twenty frantic passengers (D).
10. A five-thousand-dollars (A) reward (B) was offered for (C) the capture of (D) the escaped criminals.

UNIT – 8

Punctuation

Directions: Punctuate the following sentences. Do not turn them into two sentences.

1. If you want another copy of this companys prospectus please phone me at 721-0004 as soon as possible
2. Its going to be a very difficult project it will put great demands on your supervisory skills
3. After more than twenty years of slaving over manuscripts the scholar finally published the manuscript that all his admirers had been waiting for
4. In ten minutes he will be here and the audience will be giving him an ovation
5. The man who wrote my computer program is a consultant to the following three corporations Magma Inc a Brazilian mining company Lamburger a New Zealand fast food company and Westface Manufacturing.

PART – D

WRITING ABILITY

"Knowledge is an arch wherethro' gleams
That untravelled world"

–Lord Tennyson

UNIT – 1

Précis Writing

Directions: Make a precis of the following passage in about one third of its length.

The work of the heart can never be interrupted. The heart's job is to keep oxygen-rich blood flowing through the body. All the body's cells need a constant supply of oxygen, especially those in the brain. The brain cells live only four to five minutes after their oxygen is cut off and death comes to the entire body.

The heart is a specialised muscle that serves as a pump. This pump is divided into four chambers connected by tiny doors called valves. The chambers work to keep the blood flowing round the body in a circle.

At the end of each circuit, veins carry the blood to the right atrium, the first of the four chambers. Its oxygen has been used up and it is on its way back to the lung to pick up a fresh supply and to give up the carbon dioxide it has accumulated. From the right atrium the blood flows through the tricuspid valve into the second chamber, the right ventricle. The right ventricle contracts when it is filled, pushing the blood through the pulmonary artery, which leads to the lungs. In the lungs the blood gives up its carbon dioxide and picks up fresh oxygen. Then it travels to the third chamber, the left atrium. When this chamber is filled, it forces the blood through the mistral valve to the left ventricle. From here it is pushed into a big blood vessel called aorta and sent round the body by way of arteries.

Heart diseases can result from damage to the heart muscle, the valves or the pacemaker. If the muscle is damaged, the heart is unable to pump properly, if the valves are damaged, blood cannot flow normally and easily from one chamber to another, and if the pacemaker is defective, the contractions of the chambers will become uncoordinated.

Until the twentieth century, few doctors dared to touch the heart. In 1953, all this changed. After twenty years of work, Dr. John Gibbon of U.S.A. developed a machine that could take over temporarily from the heart and lungs. Blood could be routed through the machine, bypassing the heart so that surgeons could work inside it and see what they were doing. The era of open-heart surgery had begun.

In the operating theatre, it gives surgeons the chance to replace a defective heart. Many patients have had plastic valves inserted in their heart when their own was faulty. Many people are being kept alive with tiny battery-operated pacemakers. None of these repairs could have been made without the heart-lung machine. But valuable as it is to the surgeons, the heart-lung machine has certain limitations. It can be used only for a few hours at a time because its pumping gradually damages the blood cells.

UNIT – 2

Paraphrasing

Directions: Reproduce the given passage (poetry or prose) in your own idiom or style without changing the sense.

All the performances of human art, at which we

look with praise or wonder, are instances of the resistless force of perseverance; it is by this that the quarry becomes a pyramid, and that distant countries are united by canals. If a man was to compare a single stroke of a pick axe, or of one impression of the spade, with the general design and last result, he would be overwhelmed by the sense of their disproportion; yet those petty operations, incessantly continued, in time surmount the greatest difficulties, and mountains are levelled, and oceans bounded, by the slender force of human beings.

UNIT – 3

Paragraph Development

Directions: Rewrite the following sentences in an order that will demonstrate a coherent paragraph development.

1. The windmill provides a very economical source of energy.
2. This gives it a great advantage over oil, which can seriously pollute the oceans of the world.
3. The day of the windmill may not be over after all.
4. All it needs are fairly constant winds of over ten miles an hour.
5. In addition, the windmill posses another advantage: it does not pollute the environment.

UNIT – 4

Multiple choice

Coherence Testing

Directions: For the following question, read the sentences and choose the order in which they form a coherent piece of writing.

Sentence 1: He had full right by seniority to supervise and instruct me.
Sentence 2: I was the younger, he the elder—I was nine, he was fourteen.
Sentence 3: My big brother was five years older than me but only three grades ahead.
Sentence 4: He wanted to lay a firm foundation for that great edifice, so he took two years to do one year's work; sometimes he even took three.
Sentence 5: He'd begun his studies at the same age I had but he didn't like the idea of moving hastily in an important matter like education.
Sentence 6: If the foundation weren't well-made, how could the edifice endure?
Sentence 7: And I was expected to accept every order of his as law.

(*a*) 1, 2, 3, 6, 4, 5, 7
(*b*) 1, 3, 2, 7, 6, 4, 5
(*c*) 3, 5, 4, 6, 2, 1, 7
(*d*) 3, 4, 5, 6, 2 ,7, 1

But Remember!

'Quiet to quick bosoms is a hell'
–G.G. Byron

ANSWER KEY–II

Reading Comprehension and Reading Ability

Unit-1

1. d	**2.** a	**3.** b	**4.** a	**5.** c
6. b	**7.** a	**8.** d	**9.** b	**10.** b

Unit-2

1. The inclusion of Kerensky.
2. The retention of the monarchy.
3. 13.
4. His train had been diverted.
5. That it should offered by a properly elected Constituent Assembly.
6. The maintenance of law and order.
7. The only 'revolutionary' in it was Kerensky.
8. The Soviet strongly opposed the monarchy.
9. He might have been able to regain power if he had returned.
10. At the time, there was no other body capable of governing because the Soviets were not yet ready to do this. They had no real control.

Unit-3

Ans. 1

1. 'We seek arrest because the so-called freedom is slavery' (para 2)
2. 'We are challenging the might of this government because we consider it's activity to be wholly evil' (para 2)
3. We want to overthrow the government (para 3)

4. 'We want to compel its submission to the people's will' (para 3)
5. We must refuse to purchase freedom at the cost of our self-respect or our cherished conviction (para 3)

Ans. 2

1. The crowd reacted by turning around to see who this stranger was in their midst and the whole gathering grew curious and a bit alarmed. On the platform there was confusion and the princes started conferring about the identity of Mr. Gandhi. Mrs. Annie Besant reacted by remarking that he was a child in politics.
2. Gandhi told the princes how shallow was their glamour and how insignificant they really were in the India that mattered.
3. The crowd reacted to Gandhi's speech by cheering him.
4. In the end, the President got up and left the meeting, leaving Gandhi to address a meeting which had lost its chairman, sponsors, and its honoured guests.

Ans. 3

A 3 B 3 C 1

Ans. 4

1. large groups 2. gathered
3. consulted with each other
4. a splendid display
5. having no precedent; something novel.

Unit-4

1. of 2. into 3. wealth
4. its 5. and 6. goods
7. through

Unit-5

1. a 2. c 3. b 4. b

Unit-6

1. c 2. a 3. d 4. d 5. d

Vocabulary

Unit-1

1. c 2. b 3. d 4. d
5. d 6. b 7. b 8. c
9. b 10. d

Unit-2

1. b 2. b 3. a 4. d 5. b

Unit-3

1. b 2. d 3. d 4. b 5. a

Unit-4

1. a 2. c 3. a 4. b 5. d

Unit-5

1. a 2. b 3. a 4. b 5. a

Unit-6

1. c 2. a 3. a 4. b 5. d

Unit-7

1. a 2. a 3. a 4. b 5. c

Unit-8

1. a 2. d 3. b 4. b 5. a

Unit-9

1. b 2. d 3. b 4. a 5. c

Unit-10

1. B 2. A 3. B 4. B 5. A

Unit-11

Spellings

1. b 2. c 3. a 4. b 5. c

Unit-12

Vocabulary in Context

1. one 2. self 3. courageous
4. not 5. free 6. correct
7. his 8. did 9. their
10. wicked 11. him

Grammar

Unit-1

1. a 2. b 3. c 4. b 5. a
6. b 7. b 8. c 9. b 10. a

Unit-2

1. d 2. b 3. a 4. b 5. a

Unit-3

1. d 2. a 3. a 4. b 5. c

Unit -4

1. c 2. d 3. b 4. d 5. a

Unit-5

1. a 2. a 3. d 4. c 5. a
6. a 7. d 8. d 9. a 10. d
11. c 12. d 13. c 14. a 15. b

Unit-6

1. d 2. b 3. a 4. c
5. a 6. b 7. d 8. d

9. a	10. c	11. b	12. d
13. a	14. b or a	15. a	16. d
17. b	18. a	19. d	20. b

Unit-7

1. A	2. B	3. B	4. A	5. A
6. A	7. D	8. B	9. C	10. B

Unit-8

1. If you want another copy of this company's prospectus, please phone me at 721-0004 as soon as possible.
2. It's going to be a very difficult project; it will put great demands on your supervisory skills.
3. After more than twenty years of slaving over manuscripts, the scholar finally published the manuscript, that all his admirers had been waiting for.
4. In ten minutes, he will be here, and the audience will be giving him an ovation.
5. The man, who wrote my computer program, is a consultant to the following three corporations: Magma Inc., a Brazilian mining company; Lamburger, a New Zealand fast food company; and Westface Manufacturing.

Writing Ability

Unit-1

The heart works constantly without break and supplies blood to all body cells. It is a specialised muscle divided in four compartments connected with valves. Oxygenless blood goes first to the right atrium and then to the right ventricle through the tricuspid valve. When full, the right ventricle contracts and pushes the blood through pulmonary artery into lungs. Lungs purify it and send it through left atrium and left ventricle into aorta. The important diseases of heart concern muscles, valves or pacemakers. With the invention of heart lung machine, it has been possible to treat them all.

Unit-2

It is the irresistible force of human perseverance which is at the back of all the achievements of art which inspire praise or wonder in us. The construction of pyramids and joining together of countries by canals are the results of this very perseverance. A single stroke of a pickaxe or one impression of the spade seem insignificant in themselves as compared to their results. But when such petty operations are continued incessantly, real human force which seems meagre otherwise, is at play, such that even mountains are thus levelled, oceans bounded and the greatest difficulties surmounted.

Unit-3

1. The day of the windmill may not be over after all.
2. The windmill provides a very economical source of energy.
3. All it needs are fairly constant winds of over ten miles an hour.
4. In addition, the windmill possesses another advantage: it does not pollute the oceans.
5. This gives it a great advantage over oil, which can seriously pollute the oceans of the world.

Unit-4

Ans. Key c

PRACTICE TEST — III

PART – A
READING COMPREHENSION AND READING ABILITY

"Our sweetest songs are those that tell of saddest thought".

–P. B. Shelley

UNIT – 1

Multiple Choice Type

Directions: Read through the passage once only as quickly as you can without suffering loss of comprehension and answer the questions that follow.

Logic is a poor *hors d' oeuvre* for the feast of philosophy; it dulls a thousand appetites for everyone it whets. We suspect logic because we have learnt that most reasoning is desire dressed in a little rationality; we pretend to be constructing edifices of impartial thought, when actually we are selecting only such facts and agreements as will give some dignity to some personal and patriotic wish.

At the very outset, we find the main problem of logic clearly caught and clearly answered by those unappreciated freelances of the ancient world — the Sophists. Knowledge, they said (Locke, two thousand years later, was thought to have discovered this), comes from the senses only; therefore the test of truth, the answer to Pilate's question, is Sensation: truth is what you taste, touch, smell, hear, and see. What could be simpler? But Plato was not satisfied: if this is truth, he said there is no truth, for we all taste, smell, hear, touch, and see things differently; the baboon, then, is the measure of truth equally with the sage — and who shall decide between them? Plato was sure that reason was the test of truth; the ideas of reason were to the reports of the senses what statesmen were to the populace — unifying centres of order for a chaotic mass.

Aristotle agreed with him, and made logic for the first time a separate study by seeking to formulate the laws of reason. Nothing should be judged true unless it might be made the conclusion of a perfect syllogism: so man is a rational animal (this credulous proposition is still found in the books of logicians); but Socrates is a man; therefore is a rational animal. Not at all, said Pyrrho; every syllogism is a *petito principii* — a begging of the question. For your major cannot be true unless your conclusion is true in advance — which you have no right to assume; and unless you presume that Socrates is rational you must not start with the proposition that man (who includes Socrates) is a rational animal; perhaps he is merely a rationalising animal. Reason, therefore, is always uncertain. Very well, said Epicurus, let us go back to the Sophists, and trust to our senses. But again, asked the Sceptics, how can this be? To our sense the sun is as small as a pumpkin, and the stars might be "a rash on the sky"; shall we believe our senses here? Nothing is certain, concluded Pyrrho; and when he died his students, though they loved him, did not mourn him, for they could not be sure that he was dead.

Questions:

1. On the basis of the first paragraph we find the author regarding logic as
   (*a*) absolutely unbiased
   (*b*) partially biased
   (*c*) absolutely biased
   (*d*) some times biased and some times unbiased.
2. Knowledge what was felt by the senses was first thought by:
   (*a*) Pilate (*b*) the Sophists
   (*c*) Locke (*d*) Plato
3. Plato's theory could be certainly contradicted if
   (*a*) it were proved with reason that the baboon was a rational animal
   (*b*) the fallacy of syllogisms were brought out
   (*c*) the theory of relative perceptions was introduced
   (*d*) none of the above
4. A paragraph concluding this passage mostly deals with
   (*a*) what finally happened to Pyrrho's body

(*b*) how Epicurus countered the Sophists
(*c*) the tussle between the sense and reason in the next era
(*d*) a further elucidation of Pyrrho's "*petitio principii*"

5. Which of the statements below would Plato NOT regard as "knowledge" or "truth"?
(*a*) Two plus two equals four
(*b*) Sensation is one of the guides of truth
(*c*) The baboon's perceptions will be different from that of the sage
(*d*) None of these

6. Which of the following would be the most appropriate title for the passage?
(*a*) Philosophy of truth
(*b*) Plato — The father of modern philosophy
(*c*) TRUTH — The other version
(*d*) None of these

7. From the passage, it can be inferred that Pilate's question was
(*a*) What could be simpler than truth?
(*b*) What is truth?
(*c*) Why is logic a poor hors d'oeuvre?
(*d*) What is the peptitio principii?

8. The author feels about logic that it
(*a*) acts like an appetiser for the feast of philosophy.
(*b*) can be substituted with intuition.
(*c*) is the most important factor in explaining philosophy.
(*d*) acts like a deappetiser for its followers.

9. The author would tend to agree with the Sophists because the Sophists
(*a*) were countered by Epicurus
(*b*) did not attach much importance to logic
(*c*) had a liking for the under dog
(*d*) none of these

10. The Sceptics countered the Sophists by
(*a*) frowning on their free lancing style
(*b*) resorting to syllogistic examples
(*c*) asserting that sensory perceptions do not often give the right "picture"
(*d*) introducing the theory of relativity

11. The tone of the passage can be best described as
(*a*) narrative (*b*) analytical
(*c*) cynical (*d*) judgmental

12. The underlined word 'whets' in Para 1 means
(*a*) stimulates (*b*) works
(*c*) means (*d*) aims at

13. The underlined word 'edifices' in Para 1 means
(*a*) concepts (*b*) buildings
(*d*) layers (*d*) foundations

UNIT – 2

Question Answer Type

Meanwhile, Lenin, in Zurich, was at first wholly sceptical. Nothing, he was sure, had really changed. There had been strikes and demonstrations and even Soviets before; these would be again, perhaps many times, before the day of revolution dawned. The men and women of his generation would probably not live to see that day, he was saying. He was not quite 47.

It almost seemed as though he wanted it that way. For 14 years all his energies had gone into laying down the law about the true nature of a Bolshevik revolution and intriguing, manoeuvering, bullying, anathematising. Only those who agreed absolutely with him were regarded as fit workers for the cause; those who were not with him were against him, and during all these years his closest supporters were constantly being excommunicated and then, recanting, welcomed back into the fold. The supreme task was to keep Bolshevism pure and uncorrupted even though, as it sometimes appeared, the solitary pure and uncorrupted Bolshevik was Lenin himself.

Even after the news of the Tsar's abdication reached Zurich he could write to one of his most loyal supporters, Madame Kollontai, Stockholm, saying that the so-called revolution in Russia was nothing but a capitalist upheaval. On the whole he thought it best that the Provisional Government should outlaw the Social Democrats; if Marxism were made legal in Russia, then Bolsheviks and Mensheviks might be tempted to draw together, and this would be the deadly sin.

Soon, however, even Lenin began to be affected by the vulgar enthusiasm of his fellow exiles who were sure that indeed something new had happened in Russia, and it was their imperative duty to hurry home and take charge. But how? More arguments, endless discussions — all leading to the famous sealed train provided by the German General Staff to convey Lenin and his friends through the heart of Germany in order to let them loose there and make the Provisional Government's confusion worse.

The Germans were disappointed by the evident determination of the Provisional Government to honour its obligations to their Allies and go on defending Russia. Not only the Provisional Government, the Soviet too. And even those Bolsheviks left in Russia, now coming out of hiding and returning from exile in Siberia, were caught up in the mood. Kamenev and Stalin both thought the revolution was a wonderful thing, that all revolutionaries, no matter how much they had disagreed in the past, must stand together and defend the revolution not only from reaction at home but also from the German Kaiser. They wanted peace, but 'peace with honour.'

Lenin was not interested in honour. He had made this clear enough for the Germans to see. They did not expect him to return to Petrograd and assume command, but they were fairly sure that he could multiply confusion and weaken the Russian will to fight.

Questions:

1. Whom did Lenin regard as 'fit workers for the cause'?
2. What was 'the supreme task', according to Lenin?
3. How did Lenin and his friends travel to Russia?
4. By whom was the transport provided?
5. What was the intention in assisting Lenin and the revolutionaries to return to Russia?
6. Why was Lenin sceptical at first?
7. Why did Lenin think it would be a sin if Bolsheviks and Mensheviks were tempted to draw together?
8. Why did the Germans think the Bolsheviks would cause greater confusion in Russia?
9. What is meant by 'peace with honour'?
10. Why did the Germans not expect Lenin to assume command in Petrograd?

UNIT – 3

Miscellaneous Type

Many years ago there lived a Bishop who, besides being a great religious leader, was also a very kind man. Once a convict escaped from prison and came to the Bishop's house asking for shelter. The Bishop not only gave him shelter, but also fed him and put him at night. But the convict was accustomed to steal. So he got up when all were fast asleep.

"Let me take some expensive articles from this house and run away from the place at once," the convict said to himself. He looked around and found two silver candlesticks on the altar. In no time he hid them under his coat and vanished into the darkness of the night.

The night was dark and cold but luck ran against him. The police who were looking for the convict were only too glad to arrest him. They tied his hands and brought him back to the Bishop. If the Bishop were to say that the man had stolen the articles, the convict would have to be punished. The Bishop felt pity for the man and decided to forgive him. So he told the police that he had given him the candlesticks and saved him from a severe punishment. He fell at the Bishop's feet and asked his pardon. From that day, he decided to lead a good life. By forgiving, the Bishop brought back a man to the path from which he had strayed. It is better to forgive than to punish.

Questions:

A. Answer the following questions:

1. How did the Bishop look after the convict?
2. What did the convict do at night?
3. What did the police do to the convict?
4. How did the Bishop help the convict?
5. What would have happened if the Bishop were to hand the convict over to the police?
6. Do you appreciate the Bishop's action? Why?
7. What would you do in such a situation?

B. Say whether the following statements are true or false and write T or F against them.

1. The Bishop was a kind-hearted man.
2. Two silver candlesticks were gifted to the convict by the Bishop.

3. It was a dark and cold night when the convict ran out of the Bishop's house.
4. The Bishop wanted him to be punished by the Police.
5. Punishment is better than forgiveness.

C. Which words in the passage have the following meanings:

1. a person committing a crime
2. costly
3. disappeared
4. pardon
5. moved away from morality

UNIT – 4

Cloze Passage Type

Directions: Fill in the blanks with appropriate words in context. You can read the whole passage before beginning the task.

This bitterness, which is the bitterness of fear, made some shopkeepers bawl out rudely to many beggars who came hourly to beg at their doors. It made men ruthless in paying small fares _______ [1] the rickshaw-pullers, of which there were ten times _______ [2] many as could be used, because the refugees _______ [3] trying to earn something thus. Even the usual _______ [4] of rickshaws who followed this as their profession _______ [5] the refugees because, being starved, they would pull _______ [6] anything given to them, and no fares were too low _______ [7] all, and all suffered. With the city full _______ [8] refugees, then, begging at every door, swarming into _______ [9] unskilled trade and service, lying dead on the _______ [10] at every frozen dawn, how should one look _______ [11] this fresh horde coming in now at twilight _______ [12] a winter's day?

UNIT – 5

Question-Answer Type

Communicative Passage-I

Directions: Read the following advertisement and answer the questions given below.

No: E/Tech/V/00-01/16
DT: 13.10.01

ADVERTISEMENT

Applications are invited from Indian Nationals for filling up 3 posts (1 General, 1 S/C and 1 S/T) FOR Crane operator in the scale of pay allowances as admissible under the rules and orders of the D.E.S.U. in force from time to time.

QUALIFICATION & EXPERIENCE:

(I) Middle Class pass or equivalent from a recognised Board/School or equivalent.

(II) 3 years experience on electric overhead cranes, crawler crane /mobile crane of minimum capacity of 50 tons.

Desirable: Experience of attending to minor defects in cranes.

Age: Between 18 and 25 years. (Relaxation for Govt. Servants and employees of Municipal Corporation of Delhi). Also relaxable upto 5 years for candidates belonging to S/C and S/T.

Applications on plain paper stating full particulars along with attested copies of certificates and testimonials together with crossed postal order for Rs.8/- (Rupees eight only). (Not applicable in case of S/C-S/T candidates, who are exempted from making payment of this fee). It should be drawn in favour of Assistant ACCOUNTANT Delhi Electric Supply Undertaking, Rajghat Power House, New Delhi-02 and should reach the Administrative Officer (PV), Delhi Electric Supply Undertaking, Shakti Bhawan, Nehru Place, New Delhi-19 latest by 28.10.01. S/C-S/T candidates called for interview will be paid single 2nd class railway fare by passenger train by the shortest route to and from the nearest railway station of their place of residence if the distance travelled exceeds 80 kms. If return tickets are available, same should be availed of. This concession will not be admissible to the Central/ State Govt. employees.

Persons already in service should apply through proper channel. Incomplete application and/or received after the stipulated date will not be entertained.

PR/915/906

Sd/-(JYOTI PARSAD)
ASSISTANT PERSONNEL OFFICER (HQ.)

Questions:

1. What is the minimum age required for the post advertised above?
2. Can a person of twenty years apply for the job?
3. Mention the minimum qualifications required.
4. What should the applicant send along with the application?
5. What is the last date for the receipt of the application?
6. Whom should the application be addressed to?
7. List three reasons for which the application can be rejected.
8. Rohit lives in Mumbai and he wants to apply for the job. If he is called for an interview, will he be paid railway fare?
9. Rohan is a graduate and he has celebrated his 27th birthday. Can he apply for the job? If not, why?
10. Gaurav is 18 years old and is studying in 8th standard. Can you give reasons why he cannot apply for the job?

Multiple Choice Type

Communicative Passage-II

Directions: Questions 1 and 2 are based on the following advertisement. Choose the correct answer.

ELECTRONIC WIREMEN

—Permanent, full-time positions
—2–3 years experience
—Day Shift

Wiring and soldering of chassis and P.C. Boards. Excellent Company benefits. Salary commensurate with experience.

Phone 548-3889

TEKNICIRCLE LABORATORIES

899, Robin Road
Long Hill, Pa.

Equal Opportunity Employer

Questions:

1. Approximately what hours would the applicant expect to work?
   (A) midnight to 7 A.M.
   (B) commensurate with experience
   (C) 8 A.M. to 5 P.M.
   (D) 3.30 P.M. to midnight
2. What would the applicant's job be?
   (A) full-time position
   (B) shifting
   (C) company benefits
   (D) wiring and soldering

UNIT – 6

Multiple Choice

Single Sentence Readings

Directions: Read each of the following sentences carefully. You are instructed to choose an alternative nearest to the meaning of the underlined part in each one of them.

1. The reason that the number of accidents this year is greater than that of last year is because the Americans are uninterested in safety techniques.
   (*a*) are greater than last year is because
   (*b*) is greater than last year is that
   (*c*) is greater than that of last year is that
   (*d*) is greater than the number of accidents last year is because
2. I was asked not only to contribute to the cause by giving money, but also by participating in its activities.
   (*a*) Not only was I asked to contribute to the cause by giving money, but also by participating
   (*b*) Not only was I asked to contribute to the cause by giving money, but also to participate
   (*c*) I was asked not only to contribute to the cause by giving money, but also to participate
   (*d*) I was asked not only by giving money to contribute to the cause, but also to participate

3. Julio did not find the new job preferable to the one he had been selected for, so he decided to continue for a while.
   (*a*) more preferable to the one he had been selected for, so he decided to continue on
   (*b*) preferable to the one he had left so he decided to continue
   (*c*) more preferable to the one he had left so he decided to continue on
   (*d*) preferable to the one he was to leave, so he decided to continue
4. Since we are living in New York for five years, we are reluctant to move to another city.
   (*a*) Being that we are living
   (*b*) Being that we have been living
   (*c*) Since we have been living
   (*d*) Since we were living
5. As a child, my parents took me to Chicago to visit my grandfather.
   (*a*) My parents, as a child, took me to Chicago to visit my grandfather.
   (*b*) My parents took me to Chicago to visit my grandfather as a child.
   (*c*) My parents took me, as a child, to Chicago to visit my grandfather.
   (*d*) When I was a child, my parents took me to Chicago to visit my grandfather.

PART – B
VOCABULARY

"Action is eloquence."

–William Shakespeare

Multiple Choice

UNIT – 1

Directions: Choose the word or phrase closest to the meaning of the given word.

1. Commodious
   (*a*) spacious
   (*b*) sheltering
   (*c*) plentiful
   (*d*) orderly
2. To stymie
   (*a*) to obstruct
   (*b*) to stimulate
   (*c*) to confuse
   (*d*) to disgrace
3. Communiqué
   (*a*) propaganda
   (*b*) speech
   (*c*) announcement
   (*d*) lecture
4. Sough
   (*a*) to plough a piece of land
   (*b*) to howl
   (*c*) to abuse
   (*d*) to make a rushing sound
5. Wassail
   (*a*) to dance
   (*b*) horn cup
   (*c*) to toast
   (*d*) beer hall
6. Gamut
   (*a*) stimulus
   (*b*) complete range
   (*c*) homeless child
   (*d*) obstacle
7. Herculean
   (*a*) immensely difficult
   (*b*) most violent
   (*c*) reckless
   (*d*) creative
8. Winsome
   (*a*) odd
   (*b*) fickle
   (*c*) angelic
   (*d*) attractive
9. Virtual reality—an environment
   (*a*) which is actual
   (*b*) which is partial
   (*c*) generated by computer software
   (*d*) extended by stage artists
10. Evangelist
    (*a*) wanderer
    (*b*) enthusiastic preacher
    (*c*) faithful follower
    (*d*) eccentric

UNIT – 2

Multiple Choice

1. Gaily
   (*a*) humorously (*b*) brightly
   (*c*) seriously (*d*) happily
2. Constant
   (*a*) continuous (*b*) continual
   (*c*) permanent (*d*) persistent
3. Abstruse
   (*a*) illogical (*b*) non-existent
   (*c*) hard to understand
   (*d*) hard to please
4. To abut
   (*a*) to touch or lean upon
   (*b*) to get into
   (*c*) to pledge
   (*d*) to clarify
5. Sucker
   (*a*) an idiot (*b*) a simpleton
   (*c*) a person easily deceived
   (*d*) a person easily impressed

UNIT – 3

Multiple Choice

Directions: Each problem in this part of the test consists of a sentence in which one word or phrase has been underlined. From the four choices given, you should choose the one word or phrase which could be substituted for the underlined word or phrase without changing the meaning of the sentence. Mark your choice on the answer sheet. Put (✔) against the appropriate choice.

1. The climate in the Great Plains is **arid**.
   (*a*) hot and dry (*b*) hot and wet
   (*c*) cold and wet (*d*) cold and dry
2. American **legend** says that Johnny Apple Seed planted apple orchards throughout Ohio.
   (*a*) tale. (*b*) myth.
   (*c*) history. (*d*) epic
3. The time I spent in the library was the most **rewarding** one, as I could add a number of fresh facts to my data.
   (*a*) profitable (*b*) taxing
   (*c*) serviceable (*d*) repetitive
4. Mr. White plays a character of enormous **affability**.
   (*a*) capability (*b*) rudeness
   (*c*) pleasantness (*d*) stoutness
5. Self-denial is one of the **tenets** prescribed for their followers.
   (*a*) reasons (*b*) doctrines
   (*c*) ranters (*d*) figures

UNIT – 4

Multiple Choice

Directions: Give one word for the phrase underlined. Under each sentence are given four choices. You are directed to choose the appropriate one.

1. That word is **no longer in use**.
   (*a*) obsolete (*b*) absent
   (*c*) still-born (*d*) useless
2. His injured leg was **cut off by a doctor**.
   (*a*) dislocated (*b*) disconnected
   (*c*) operated (*d*) amputated
3. Mohan was admired by his comrades because his behaviour was marked by **open and effusive** exhibition of his feelings.
   (*a*) reticent (*b*) flowing
   (*c*) kind (*d*) chivalrous
4. Napoleon always relied most on **skilfully planning the movements of** his troops.
   (*a*) planning (*b*) manoeuvring
   (*c*) designing (*d*) contriving
5. The manager was asked **to postpone** the function as the date did not suit the Chairman of the ICCI.
   (*a*) extend (*b*) dismiss
   (*c*) refer back (*d*) procrastinate

UNIT – 5

Multiple Choice

(One Word Substitution)

Directions: The questions below have a statement/word followed by four choices. Select the choice closest in meaning to the statement. Mark (✔) against the appropriate choice.

1. One who is at the stage of **growth between boyhood and youth**.

(*a*) adolescent. (*b*) equilibrium.
(*c*) adulthood. (*d*) development

2. **Soliloquy** means
(*a*) an act of addressing people
(*b*) an act of speaking to oneself
(*c*) an act of talking to the animals
(*d*) an act of thinking

3. **Contemporary** means
(*a*) Persons living at the same time
(*b*) Act of sacrilege
(*c*) Act of blasphemy
(*d*) Those who existed in the past

4. **Extempore** means
(*a*) Speaking without any preparation
(*b*) Speaking after due preparation
(*c*) Speaking after thinking
(*d*) Speaking at the behest of others

5. **Omniscient** means
(*a*) One who is all powerful
(*b*) One who knows everything
(*c*) One who looks at one side of things
(*d*) One who is present everywhere

UNIT – 6

Multiple Choice

Directions: Complete each sentence with one of the words underneath. Tick (✓) against the appropriate alternative.

1. If you had the opportunity, which of these would you ___________?
(*a*) ask (*b*) avail
(*c*) plan (*d*) accept

2. Our preferences are often so ____________ that we can give no logical reason for them.
(*a*) irrational (*b*) impractical
(*c*) tricky (*d*) thoughtful

3. A lot of misunderstanding about student politics ____________ at present.
(*a*) prevails (*b*) reports
(*c*) mounts (*d*) situates

4. There were few young people in the group; most of them were ____________.
(*a*) ripe (*b*) mature
(*c*) elderly (*d*) senior

5. A _______________ of care often leads to accidents.
(*a*) lack (*b*) shortage
(*c*) want (*d*) deficiency

UNIT – 7

Idioms and Phrases

Directions: Each item below consists of an idiom or a phrase, followed by four lettered expressions. Choose the lettered expression that most nearly expresses the meaning of the given idiom or phrase.

1. To worship the rising sun
(*a*) To become pious
(*b*) To work honestly
(*c*) To work for the welfare of people
(*d*) To welcome the coming events

2. To draw a line
(*a*) To impose certain restrictions
(*b*) To restart
(*c*) To have fair game
(*d*) To divide evenly

3. To show the door
(*a*) To welcome the visitors
(*b*) To receive a party
(*c*) To behave rudely
(*d*) To dismiss a person

4. To put down in black and white
(*a*) To distinguish clearly
(*b*) To write down on a paper
(*c*) To seal the envelope
(*d*) To tell the truth

5. To gild pill
(*a*) To cover something disagreeable with some pleasant thing
(*b*) To work hard
(*c*) To die fighting
(*d*) To meet with humiliation

UNIT – 8

Synonyms

Directions: Select the word closest to the meaning of the given word.

1. Unseemly
(*a*) improper (*b*) cruel
(*c*) agitated (*d*) ugly

2. Pester
   (a) tenacity (b) discourteous
   (c) disturb (d) acme
3. Fillip
   (a) incentive (b) imagination
   (c) impunity (d) infusion
4. Precise
   (a) slump (b) final
   (c) replaced (d) exact
5. To throng
   (a) to prosper (b) to crowd
   (c) to butcher (e) to explode

UNIT – 9

Antonyms

Directions: Select the word which is closest to the opposite in meaning of the word in bold letters.

1. Consonant
   (a) abundant (b) uniformly
   (c) harmonious (d) incongruous
2. Perspective
   (a) two-dimensional
   (b) one-sidedness
   (c) irrelevant
   (d) punitive
3. Furious
   (a) unrestrained (b) witty
   (c) progressive (d) restrained
4. Prosaic
   (a) usual (b) acceptable
   (c) extraordinary (d) gregarious
5. Temerity
   (a) diffidence (b) composure
   (c) establishment (d) trial

UNIT – 10

Words Often Confused

Directions: In each item below, a choice of words that are often confused is given in parentheses. Write in the blank the letter indicating the best choice for the context.

1. ______ The Chairman's statement (A. implied; B. inferred) that the next meeting would be reconsidered at the next meeting.
2. ______ Walter's talents were a (A. complement; B. compliment) to Jim's. Walter could give orders, and Jim could follow them.
3. ______ learned from my (A. Counsel ; B. Council) that he will be out of town soon.
4. __________ The Chairman of the board is only a (A. figurehead; B. leader), the executive secretary does all the work.
5. ______ She assured me (A. orally; B. verbally) of her good intentions, but she never confirmed her message in writing.

UNIT – 11

Spellings (Multiple Choice)

Directions: Answer the questions following the paragraphs. In each of the paragraphs five of the underlined words have been spelt *incorrectly*. Identify the option, which lists the five *incorrectly* spelt words.

1. He stood in a [1]**respectful** but not [2]**obseqious** attitude. He had been in service before he was appointed to his [3]**eclesiastical** office, but only in very good houses, and his [4]**deportment** was [5]**irreprochable**. Starting as a page-boy in the household of a [6]**merchant**-prince, he had risen by due [7]**degrees** from the position of fourth to first footman, for a year he had been single-handed butler to a [8]**widowed** **peeress**, and till the vacancy [9]**occured** at St. Peter's, butler with two men under him in the house of a retired [10]**ambasador**.

   The five **incorrectly** spelt words are:
   (a) 1, 3, 5, 8, and 10
   (b) 2, 3, 5, 9, and 10
   (c) 2, 3, 7, 8, and 9
   (d) 1, 4, 5, 8, and 10
2. He has been taught to respect the law, and the sight of men swinging clubs and [1]**hurling** stones at those seeking to go about the [2]**ordnary** tasks of life will be [3]**aborrent** to him. Bloody heads and broken arms and the use of [4]**filthy** [5]**epithets** towards both men and women have not been part of his life, and he won't like it. Nor will he [6]**complicently** accept [7]**anonimous** threats to his wife on the telephone, or signs painted on the houses of those who think differently from the [8]**cowards** who [9]**prepetrate** the wrong.

The five **incorrectly** spelt words are:

(*a*) 2, 3, 6, 7, and 8
(*b*) 1, 4, 5, 8, and 9
(*c*) 2, 3, 6, 7, and 9
(*d*) 1, 3, 4, 5, and 7

3. The man working at the [1]**bargaining** table, however, finds himself these days [2]**skillfully** and [3]**intentionally** blocked from maintaining judgement and [4]**piose** by the field tactics of trained union [5]**bargainars**. They hope that at three in the morning, after eighteen hours of [6]**negotiation**, locked up in a smoke filled room, the man will [7]**falter**. They hope that then they will [8]**consede** almost anything in order to get a contract [9]**signed** or a [10]**grievence** settled.

The five **incorrectly** spelt words are:

(*a*) 1, 3, 6, 8, and 10
(*b*) 2, 4, 5, 8, and 10
(*c*) 1, 2, 5, 6, and 9
(*d*) 2, 4, 6, 8, and 9

4. The [1]**psychlogical** [2]**patterns** here are [3]**quiet** clear. When a person says "No" and really means it, he is doing far more than saying a word of two letters. His entire [4]**organsim** —[5]**glanduar**, [6]**nervous**, [7]**muscular**—gathers itself together into a condition of [8]**rejection**. There is, usually a minute but sometimes in observable degree, a physical withdrawal, or readiness for withdrawal. The whole [9]**neuro**-muscular system, in short, sets itself on guard against [10]**acceptence**.

The five **incorrectly** spelt words are:

(*a*) 1,3, 6, 8, and 9
(*b*) 2, 4, 6, 7, and 8
(*c*) 1, 3, 4, 5, and 10
(*d*) 2, 5, 7, 8, and 9

5. Last night Mr. Vajpayee had [1]**conveyed** his [2]**displeasure** to Mr. Musharraf himself when the General was making his farewell call upon him. He is learnt to have made a specific [3]**referance** to the guest's [4]**controversal** remarks at the meeting with senior [5]**journalists** which were telecast by [6]**steelth**. "Your [7]**utterences** have [8]**vitiated** the atmosphere," the Prime Minister is believed to have told him, while adding that these things didn't help if one were looking for a [9]**breakthorough**.

The five **incorrectly** spelt words are:

(*a*) 1, 3, 5, 6, and 8
(*b*) 2, 4, 5, 7, and 8
(*c*) 3, 4, 6, 7, and 9
(*d*) 1, 2, 5, 8, and 9

UNIT – 12

M.C.P.

Directions: Read the following passage carefully. A few words in the beginning have been written without any bracketed words. This will facilitate you to understand the context. Each bracket contains 4 (four) choices; 1 (one) choice is correct and 3 (three) are incorrect.Choose the correct choice so that the whole passage results into a coherent piece of writing.

"Do what I say, not what I do". Most parents know that command just doesn't work. Our children learn from watching what we do. They (learn, watch, work, think)[1] what we think is important by (a, this, the, that)[2] way we spend our time and (the, those, many, numerous)[3] activities we're involved in. Young children (were, had been, have been, are)[4] great imitators, and, in a very (real, false, rare, common)[5] sense, parents are their children's first (but, or, and, though)[6] most important teachers. What parents value, (growing, elderly, young, infant)[7] children learn to value – especially in (literacy, education, studies, reading)[8].

Learning to enjoy and value reading (and, or, without, with)[9] writing starts at home. Parents can (think, encourage, make, help)[10] their children see reading and writing (as, very, too, much)[11] important as well as fun by (taking, creating, having, making)[12] these activities part of family life. (The, When, Now, Where)[13] families participate in activities together related (for, with, to, about)[14] reading and writing, it demonstrates the (weightage, importance, impotence, value)[15] placed on those subjects. When you (allot, dedicate, give, permit)[16] your children time and encouragement to (read, study, prepare, develop)[17] and write you help them practice (or, except, but, and)[18] develop these skills.

Summer is the (absolute, perfect, great, true)[19] time for parents to make reading (and, without, or, with)[20] writing a part of regular family, (life, entertainment, problem, trees)[21]. Many studies show that young children (gain, prepare, lose, misuse)[22] some of their reading skills over (a, this, the, one)[23] summer for lack of practice. Activities (in, at, from, from, into)[24] home can help children sharpen their (crafts, skills, intelligence, brain)[25] and be ready for school after (the, a, one, some)[26] break.

This booklet contains over twenty (ideas, items, requests, commands)[27] you can use to help make (those, that, this, the)[28] summer a "family reading" summer. You (can't, won't, shouldn't, don't)[29] need a formal education or a (crore, lot, sum, collection)[30] of money to help your children (hate, love, develop, carry, continue)[31] reading; just a little time, some (ideas, thoughts, theories, philosophy)[32] and desire.

PART – C
GRAMMAR

"The fear of making mistakes is the biggest barrier to making progress".

–Frank Tyger

UNIT – 1

Direct–Indirect

Directions: Change the following passages from Direct to Indirect speech.

The merchant said to the young man: "I beg you to pardon the liberty which I take in asking you how it happens that you always make use of your left hand, and never of the right; some accident surely has happened to it." The young man drew out his right arm from his robe. The merchant saw, to his utter astonishment, that his hand was cut off. He then said to the merchant: " You are no doubt much shocked at seeing me eat with my left hand, but will now see that I cannot do otherwise." The merchant asked him: " May I inquire how you had the misfortune to lose your right hand?"

UNIT – 2

Punctuation

Directions: Punctuate the following passage, to make it a coherent paragraph.

The writers intentions asking what is the writer trying to achieve may not be such an important query where the material is objectively factual but it is essential to ask it of advertising or propagandist in the widest sense writing failure to do this may result in the acceptance of a statement as fact when it is really an inference or a value judgement both of which are open to opinion and discussion.

UNIT – 3

Prepositions

Directions: Fill in the blanks in the following passage with the following words: at, on, from, between, in.

The Home Minister of Nepal reached Delhi _____ the 15th of August _______ 10.00 o'clock. He was received _________ the Indira Gandhi Airport by the Governor of Delhi. _______ the airport he went _______ the Rashtrapati Bhawan. _______ the evening he met the Prime Minister _______ his residence. _______ night he addressed the members of the Parliament _______ the Chelmsford Club. He referred to the old friendship _______ Nepal and India. He also talked about the developments taking place _______ Nepal and India. He said that _______ 1989 also when he came to India he was impressed by the progress made by India _______ different fields.

UNIT – 4

Subject Verb Agreement

Directions: Correct, improve or justify the following sentences.

1. Too great a variety of studies distract the mind.
2. He as well as his sisters were present in the meeting.
3. The whole fleet of their ships were captured.
4. My requirements are as follow.
5. Each of these students have done their work.
6. The horse and carriage are at the door.

7. Many a men have yielded to this temptation.
8. None but fools has ever believed it.
9. He is one of the cleverest boys that has passed through the school.
10. Milk and soda are a refreshing drink.

UNIT – 5

Articles

Directions: Rewrite the following sentences, inserting any article that may be required, or removing any that is not required.

1. The jealousy is an evil passion.
2. He gave very wise judgement.
3. The honey is made by bees, and they extract it from the flowers.
4. The Mount Everest is highest in the world.
5. Dead man tells no tales.

UNIT – 6

Directions: Add transitional words to the following paragraph, and underline them, to show more clearly the relationship between the ideas. You will need to use five conjunctive adverbs.

Economic, social and political circumstances on the Atlantic coast are different from those on the Pacific. The administrative structures on the east coast are often unsuitable for the west coast. Federal public servants must divide their attention among the various regions. This is not to say that the Department of Fisheries and Oceans has been unresponsive to the problems of Pacific fisheries. The last dozen years have seen remarkable changes in their regulation and management. These innovations have taken place in a piecemeal fashion. Regulations have been unpredictable and inconsistent.

UNIT – 7

Nouns

(Multiple Choice)

Directions: Fill in the blanks with appropriate Nouns.

The deceptive lure of money: the influence of money on human behaviour pervades the entire story. Magwitch devotes part of his [1] _______ to making Pip a [2] _______, and Pip himself is at first unable to cope with such unexpected [3] _______, getting into [4] _______ and leading his friend Herbert along the same [5] _______. Miss Havisham's [6] _______ (Matthew Pocket and his family excepted) have greedy [7] _______ of enriching themselves at her [8] _______. Pumblechook and Trabb, as Pip discovers, treat [9] _______ according to their wealth, and Compeyson's whole criminal [10] _______ was bound up with the lure of [11] _______.

1.	(*a*) wealth	(*b*) heritage
	(*c*) amount	(*d*) collection
2.	(*a*) human being	(*b*) man
	(*c*) gentleman	(*d*) snob
3.	(*a*) debt	(*b*) wealth
	(*c*) credit	(*d*) affluence
4.	(*a*) debt	(*b*) charity
	(*c*) credit	(*d*) loan
5.	(*a*) direction	(*b*) path
	(*c*) way	(*d*) manner
6.	(*a*) relatives	(*b*) relations
	(*c*) close-ones	(*d*) families
7.	(*a*) intentions	(*b*) longings
	(*c*) hopes	(*d*) dreams
8.	(*a*) cost	(*b*) place
	(*c*) loss	(*d*) expense
9.	(*a*) persons	(*b*) human beings
	(*c*) people	(*d*) mobs
10.	(*a*) period	(*b*) life
	(*c*) duration	(*d*) career
11.	(*a*) money	(*b*) amount
	(*c*) currency	(*d*) property

UNIT – 8

Error Correction

Directions: In questions 1-10 each sentence has four underlined words or phrases. The four underlined parts of the sentence are marked (A), (B), (C) and (D). Identify the <u>one</u> underlined word or phrase that must be changed in order for the sentence to be correct. Then, on your answer sheet, find the number of the question and fill in the space that corresponds to the letter of the answer you have chosen.

1. He has <u>less</u> (A) friends in <u>his</u> (B) classes now <u>than</u> (C) he had <u>last year</u> (D).

2. The town we visited was a four-days journey
A B
from our hotel, so we took the train instead
C
of the bus.
D

3. The influence of the nation's literature, art, and
A
science have captured widespread attention.
B C D

4. The leader emphasised the need for justice and
A B
equality between his people.
C D

5. Many of the population in the rural areas is
A B
composed of manual labourers.
C D

6. Several people have apparent tried to change
A B
the man's mind, but he refuses to listen.
C D

7. Keith is one of the most intelligent boys of the
A B C
science class.
D

8. The girls were sorry to had missed the singers
A B
when they arrived at the air port.
C D

9. When Keith visited Alaska, he lived in a igloo
A B
in the winter months as well as in spring.
C D

10. The harder he tried, the worst he danced before
A B C
the large audience.
D

PART – D
WRITING ABILITY

"Genius begins great works; Labour alone finishes them."

– Joseph Joubert

UNIT – 1

Précis Writing

Directions: Make a precis of the following passage in about one third of its length.

People tend to amass possessions, sometimes without being aware of doing so. Indeed they can have a delightful surprise when they find something useful which they did not know they owned. Those who never have to change house become indiscriminate collectors of what can only be described as clutter. They leave unwanted objects in drawers, cupboards and attics for years, in the belief that they may one day need just those very things. As they grow old, people also accumulate belongings for two other reasons, lack of physical and mental energy- both of which are essential in turning things out and throwing them away, and sentiment. Things owned for a long time are full of associations with the past, perhaps with the relatives who are dead, and so they gradually acquire a value beyond their true worth.

Some things are collected deliberately in the home in an attempt to avoid waste. Among these I would list string and brown paper, kept by thrifty people when a parcel has been opened, to save buying these two requisites. Collecting small items can easily become a mania. I know someone who always cuts out from newspapers sketches of model clothes that she would like to buy, if she had the money. As she is not rich, the chances that she will ever be able to afford such purchases are remote. But she is never sufficiently strong-minded to be able to stop the practice. It is a harmless habit, but it litters up her desk to such an extent that every time she opens it, loose bits of paper fall out in every direction.

Collecting as a serious hobby is quite different and has many advantages. It provides relaxation for leisure hours, as just looking at one's treasure is always a joy. One does not have to go out for amusement, since the collection is housed at home. Whatever it consists of stamps, records, first editions of books, china-glass, antique furniture, pictures, model cars, stuffed birds, toy animals, there is always something to do in connection with it, from finding the right place for the latest edition to verifying facts in reference books. This hobby educates one not only in the chosen subject, but also in general matters which have some bearing on it. There are also other benefits. One wants to meet like-minded collectors, to get advice, compare notes, to exchange articles, to show off the latest find. So one's circle of friend grows. Soon the hobby leads to travels, perhaps to a meeting in another town, possibly a trip abroad in search of a rare specimen, for collectors are not confined to any one country. Over the years one may well become an authority on one's hobby and will very probably be asked to give informal talks to little gatherings and then, if successful, to larger audiences. In this way self-confidence grows, first from mastering a subject, then from being able to talk about it. Collecting helps to occupy spare time constructively and makes a person contented, leaving no time for boredom.

UNIT – 2

Directions: Rewrite the memo to make it direct, easy to read and concise. When you cut deadwood, be careful not to cut ideas. You will need to use the active voice. Further, find a helpful subject title.

> TO: Ms. Janet Kroger
> FROM: S. R. Longwid
> DATE: May 7, 2001
> SUBJECT:
>
> It is hereby requested that the undersigned be permitted the exclusive use of the seventh floor conference room on the date of May 10th for the purpose of conducting a meeting with the personnel who are to be trained by myself.
>
> Occupancy is desired from 10:00 to 11:00 a.m.
>
> If the subject room has been previously engaged by others, from any other department, notification is desired as promptly as possible in order that other more satisfactory or different arrangements, as the case may be, can be made by me.

UNIT – 3

Composition

Question: Compose or design a poster to show the harmful effects of liquor.

UNIT – 4

Multiple Choice

Coherence Testing

Directions: For the following question, read the sentences and choose the order in which they form a coherent piece of writing.

Sentence 1: His life was not confining and the delight he took in this observation could not be explained by its suggestion of escape.

Sentence 2: The day was beautiful and it seemed to him that a long swim might enlarge and celebrate its beauty.

Sentence 3: He seemed to see, with a cartographer's eye, that string of swimming pools, that quasi-subterranean stream that curved across the country.

Sentence 4: He was not a practical joker nor was he a fool but he was determinedly original and had a vague and modest idea of himself as a legendary figure.

Sentence 5: He had made a discovery, a contribution to modern geography; he would name the stream Lucinda after his wife.

(*a*) 1, 2, 3, 5, 4 (*b*) 3, 5, 1, 2, 4
(*c*) 2, 4, 5, 3, 1 (*d*) 1, 3, 5, 4, 2

UNIT – 5

Testing of Analytical Ability

Directions:

'Corruption starts at the top'

–To what extent do you agree or disagree with the statement? Justify your answer with the help of cogent arguments.

UNIT – 6

Essay Writing

Directions: Write 400-500 words on the following topics.

1. Globalization and its impact on the modern society.
2. If I were the Prime Minister of my country.

So, you are heading towards the end of your journey!

> *"To succeed, you must have tremendous perseverance, tremendous will. 'I will drink the ocean', says the persevering soul, 'at my will, mountains will crumble up'. Have that sort of energy, that sort of will; work hard, and you will reach the goal."*
>
> –Swami Vivekananda

ANSWER KEY–III

Reading Comprehension and Reading Ability

Unit-1

1. b	2. c	3. a	4. c	5. b
6. a	7. b	8. d	9. b	10. c
11. a	12. a	13. a		

Unit-2

1. Those who agree absolutely with him.
2. To keep Bolshevism pure and uncorrupted.
3. In a sealed train.
4. The German General Staff.
5. The Germans hoped they would worsen the confusion in Russia.
6. There had been strikes, demonstrations and Soviets before and nothing had come of them.
7. Bolshevism would not have remained pure and uncorrupted.
8. The Bolsheviks would not accept the Provisional Government and would try to overthrow it.
9. A negotiated withdrawal from the war that would not appear to be a surrender.
10. Probably because they thought the Provisional Government was more firmly established and that it would prevent this.

Unit-3

A. 1. The Bishop gave him shelter, fed him well and put him up at night.
2. The convict stole two silver candlesticks lying on the altar, hid them under his coat and disappeared into the darkness of the night.
3. The police arrested hi, tied his hands and brought him back to the Bishop.
4. The Bishop helped the convict out of pity by deciding to forgive him and free him of the charge.
5. The convict would have got severely punished.
6. Yes. It is because by forgiving the Bishop could teach him to follow a right path.
7. In such a situation some of us like the Bishop would forgive him but others would hand him over to the police for severe punishment.

B. 1. T 2. F 3. T 4. F 5. F

C. 1. Convict 2. Expensive 3. Vanished
4. Forgive 5. Strayed

Unit-4

1. to	2. as	3. were
4. pullers	5. cursed	6. for
7. for	8. of	9. every
10. streets	11. at	12. of

Unit-5

I.

1. 18 years 2. Yes.
3. Middle class pass or equivalent to it from a recognized Board.
4. The applicant should send attested copies of certificates and testimonials and a crossed postal order for Rs. 8/-.
5. It is 28.10.01
6. It should be addressed to
The Administrative officer (PV)
Delhi Electric Supply Undertaking
Shakti Bhawan
Nehru Place - 19
7. (i) If it is not sent through a proper channel.
(ii) If it is incomplete.
(iii) If it reaches after the last date.
8. No.
9. No, because as per the eligibility criterion, he is over-age.
10. Because as per the eligibility criterion, he should have passed class 8th before applying for the post.

II.

1. C 2. D

Unit-6

1. c 2. d 3. d 4. c 5. d

Vocabulary

Unit-1

1. a	2. a	3. c	4. d	5. c
6. b	7. a	8. d	9. c	10. b

Unit-2

1. d 2. a 3. c 4. a 5. c

Unit-3

1. a	2. b	3. a	4. c	5. b

Unit-4

1. a	2. d	3. d	4. b	5. d

Unit-5

1. a	2. b	3. a	4. a	5. b

Unit-6

1. b	2. a	3. a	4. c	5. c

Unit-7

1. d	2. a	3. d	4. b	5. a

Unit-8

1. a	2. c	3. a	4. d	5. b

Unit-9

1. d	2. b	3. d	4. c	5. a

Unit-10

1. B	2. A	3. A	4. A	5. B

Unit-11

1. b	2. c	3. b	4. c	5. c

Unit-12

1. learn	2. the	3. the
4. are	5. real	6. and
7. young	8. education	9. and
10. help	11. as	12. making
13. when	14. to	15. importance
16. give	17. read	18. and
19. perfect	20. and	21. life
22. lose	23. the	24. at
25. skills	26. a	27. ideas
28. this	29. don't	30. lot
31. love	32. ideas	

Grammar

Unit-1

The merchant told the young man that he begged him to pardon the liberty which he took in asking him how it happened that he always made use of his left hand, and never of the right; some accident surely had happened to it. The young man drew out his right arm from his robe. The merchant saw to his utter astonishment that his hand was cut off. He then explained to the merchant that he was no doubt much shocked at seeing him eat with his left hand, but he would see that he could not do otherwise. The merchant asked him whether he might inquire how he had the misfortune to lose his right hand.

Unit-2

The Writer's Intentions

Asking 'What is the writer trying to achieve?' may not be such an important query where the material is objectively factual, but it is essential to ask it of advertising or propagandist (in the widest sense) writing. Failure to do this may result in the acceptance of a statement as fact, when it is really an inference or a value judgement, both of which are open to opinion and discussion.

Unit-3

1. on	2. at	3. at
4. From	5. to	6. In
7. at	8. At	9. at
10. between	11. in	12. in

Unit-4

1. Too great a variety of studies distracts the mind.
2. He, as well as his sisters, was present at the meeting
3. The whole fleet of their ships was captured.
4. My requirements are as follows.
5. Each of these students has done his/her work.
6. The horse and carriage is at the door.
7. Many of man has yielded.
8. None but fools have ever believed it.
9. He is one of the cleverest boys that have passed through the school.
10. Milk and soda is a refreshing drink.

Unit-5

1. Jealousy is an evil passion.
2. He gave a very wise judgement.
3. Honey is made by bees, and they extract it from flowers.
4. Mount Everest is highest in the world.
5. A dead man tells no tales.

Unit-6

Economic, social and political circumstances on the Atlantic coast are different from those on the Pacific. Consequently/Therefore/So the administrative structures on the east coast are often unsuitable for the west coast and Federal public servants must divide their attention among the various regions. Yet/Of course this is not to say that the Department of Fisheries and Oceans has been unresponsive to the problems of Pacific fisheries. In fact the last dozen years have seen remarkable changes in their regulation and management. Since these innovations have taken place in a piecemeal fashion, regulations have been unpredictable and inconsistent.

Unit-7

1. a	**2.** c	**3.** d	**4.** a
5. b	**6.** a	**7.** c	**8.** d
9. c	**10.** d	**11.** a	

Unit-8

1. A	**2.** B	**3.** C	**4.** C	**5.** A
6. B	**7.** C	**8.** B	**9.** B	**10.** B

Writing Ability

Unit-1

Most people are in the habit of amassing possessions without any discrimination. They keep unwanted objects in their drawers etc. This shows their sentimental love and attachment towards the belongings. These represent value-based long associations with the articles. It is in reality a harmless habit that avoids wastage of things. With thrifty people it becomes a mania and they cut out sketches etc. from the newspapers. It is a useful practice to adopt collecting things as a hobby. We can relax and amuse ourselves. It is one of the means of education. It even enhances friendship with others. It encourages self-confidence, contentment and leaves no scope for boredom.

Unit-2

Dated: May 7th **2001**

To
Ms. Janet Kroger

Subject: Request for reserving Conference Room

Madam,

Kindly permit me the use of the seventh floor Conference Room on May 10th from 10:00 a.m. to 11:00 a.m. for conducting a meeting for my trainees. If any other department has already engaged the room, please notify me immediately, so that I can make alternative arrangements.

Thanking you
Yours faithfully
S.R. Longwid

Unit-3

ABSTAIN FROM THE LIQUID FIRE

The slowly demoralising liquor
Kills all your vigour.
It makes you its slave
And the right path, you cannot pave
So, stay away from Rum, Scotch,
Vodka, and Gin
And you will find that there's nothing
you can't win
Instead of being sinful, ginful, rum-soaked men
You'll survive for four score years and ten.

KEEP AWAY FROM ALCOHOL
And heed the Nation's call.

Issued in Public Interest

Unit-4

Answer Key: d

Units 5 and 6

Note: Since these are subjective type of exercises and students can write in their original manner, the author would like the students to write on the given topics and get them corrected by a good teacher of English.

PRACTICE TEST — IV

PART – A
READING COMPREHENSION AND READING ABILITY

"A Heavenly Paradise is that place,
Wherein all pleasant fruits do flow:"

–Thomas Campion

UNIT – 1

Multiple Choice Type

Directions: Read through the passage once only as quickly as you can without suffering loss of comprehension and answer the questions that follow.

Everyone, or nearly everyone, thinks of India as a poor down at heel country with half the population wondering where its next meal is coming from. It comes therefore as news to know that if a world economic Olympics were to be held, India would win at least two gold medals, two silvers and two bronzes. The phrase 'at least' is because all the statistics about all the countries are not available and the medal tally is based on figures listed in the latest edition of the *Statistical Outline of India* which is published by the Tatas once every two years.

India produces more groundnuts (30 percent of the world's total output) and tea (also about 30 percent) than any other country and would win a gold medal in these two items hands down. It is the second largest producer of rice (paddy) and butter, which account for two silvers. As far as the bronzes are concerned, there is tobacco and cotton yarn, of which India produces about 10 percent of the world total.

All these, you will see, are farm-based products, which is not surprising, considering that India is the third largest agricultural country in the world, after the US and the Soviet Union. In industrial items, India is near the top, being No. 11 in cement, No. 7 in iron ore and No. 5 in manganese ore, though we are supposed to be among the top 15 industrial countries of the world.

In per capita terms, the picture is even more depressing. Nearly every country in the world with the exception of Burma, Bangladesh and China, consumes more sugar per head than we do, and also more energy (in terms of coal equivalent). In terms of crude steel, we do a little better, but not much, and even Egypt consumes nearly three times as much steel per head as we do. Whether it is passenger cars, radio sets or telephones, only Burma and Bangladesh seem to be doing worse than us, which is not much of a consolation for a country of our size and potential.

Most of us tend to blame the general sluggishness in development on the abnormal increases in population which devours whatever is produced and leaves next to nothing for development. But this may not be entirely true. Assume for the sake of the argument that there was no increase at all in population since 1950, when it was about half the current population. The living standard indicators and the indices of consumption would automatically double and appear much more respectable than they are today, but even then, they would not bring us any closer to the living standards enjoyed by others.

Sugar consumption per head doubles from 8 kg. per year to about 16 kg., still quite low by international standards. The consumption of energy would go up to 400 kg. of coal equivalent, about one-thirteenth of that of the US and one-twentieth of most other advanced nations. Crude steel consumption would be around 40 kg per year, less than 6 per cent of that in Japan and 8 per cent of that in the USSR. Our consumption of newsprint would go up to just about 1 kg per year, still less than 2 per cent of that in the US, and about 4 per cent of that in Japan. There would be one telephone among 125 persons, as against slightly over one in the US, two in Great Britain and Japan, and 11 in the USSR. And there would be one passenger car among 350 persons against two in the US — a ratio of 175 to 1–5 in Japan and 4 in Great Britain.

A slow-down in population would certainly help but what is holding India back is that the country is just not producing enough in relation to its size. As a people, we seem to be content with marginal rates of growth, 1 per cent here, 2 per cent there, and we crow with delight at the slightest sign of a shift in the decimal point. This attachment to decimals is a peculiar Indian phenomenon. There is something in the Indian soul – and possibly in the Indian soil – which is deeply dedicated to stability, another word for stagnation. Nearly, everything is stable, or stagnant, depending upon how you view it. Our growth rate has been stagnant at 3.5 per cent a year, a rate that is lower than the rate of 90 other countries. All over the world and all over Asia, the percentage of workers in agriculture has been steadily coming down but not in India; it was 72 per cent in the census of 1911, that is 70 years ago, when the British were very much here, and it was 72 per cent in the 1981 census, 35 years after they had left our country.

The number of the poor has remained at a steady level of 50 per cent all these years, though the planners keep on fiddling with the figures. The number of the unemployed has also remained stable at 8 per cent, year in and year out, no matter how you choose to define unemployment. "We are a very stable society," said former Planning Commission member, Prof. Raj Krishna, "anything which is unstable somewhere, bring it here, we will make it stable."

Is it too much to ask that a country of India's size and potential should aim, as a matter of natural right, at 10 gold medals, if not more, twice as many silvers and thrice as many bronzes in the international economic Olympics? India should be exporting at least 20 million tonnes of foodgrains a year after feeding every Indian at a much level of nutrition than at present. And it should be in a position to pepper the whole country with steel plants, for it has iron ore, coal and technical manpower to do so. There is surely something we can excel at, something we can do better than the rest of the world, something that can bring us more than a couple of piffling gold medals in nuts and tea. Nuts, indeed.

Questions:

1. India would win one of the 3 medals in all the following items except in
   (*a*) iron ore (*b*) rice
   (*c*) tobacco (*d*) cotton yarn
2. The underlined phrase 'down at heel' in the first paragraph means:
   (*a*) sickly (*b*) sodding
   (*c*) shabby (*d*) shady
3. India's performance in farm-based products wouldn't strike as something astounding when we consider the fact that
   (*a*) it has manpower in surplus.
   (*b*) it has a developed mechanized system of farming.
   (*c*) 72 per cent of its population is employed in agriculture.
   (*d*) it is the 3rd largest agricultural country in the world
4. Among the following items, India's performance is best in
   (*a*) cement (*b*) sugar
   (*c*) iron ore (*d*) manganese ore
5. The underlined phrase 'hands down' in the second paragraph means
   (*a*) decisively (*b*) probably
   (*c*) practically (*d*) essentially
6. Among the countries the author mentions, the one which has the highest per capita newsprint consumption is
   (*a*) the US (*b*) Japan
   (*c*) the UK (*d*) the USSR
7. The country that has greatest number of passenger cars is
   (*a*) the US (*b*) India
   (*c*) Japan (*d*) none of the above
8. The only reason why India's growth rate has not been increasing rapidly is because we
   (*a*) feel satisfied even at a marginal rate of development.
   (*b*) start celebrating the marginal growth prematurely.
   (*c*) lack capacity to work persistently.
   (*d*) remain preoccupied in farming.
9. The number of countries that have a higher growth rate than ours is
   (*a*) 70 (*b*) 14 (*c*) 90
   (*d*) cannot be determined
10. In his remark Prof. Raj Krishna was perhaps pointing out to
    (*a*) lack of growth prospects for India
    (*b*) the persistently slow growth rate of the economy
    (*c*) our lack of dynamism

(*d*) our inability to remove poverty from our midst.

11. The only way the country can grow is by
    (*a*) checking its population growth.
    (*b*) increasing its agricultural output.
    (*c*) enhancing its industrial output.
    (*d*) both (*b*) and (*c*)
12. The underlined phrase 'crow with delight' in the seventh paragraph means
    (*a*) feel satisfied
    (*b*) make hue and cry
    (*c*) celebrate excessively
    (*d*) clamour excitedly
13. The only major contribution of India has been in the area of
    (*a*) industries (*b*) farming
    (*c*) science and technology
    (*d*) population growth
14. The underlined word 'pepper' in the last paragraph means
    (*a*) heat up rapidly
    (*b*) provide enthusiastically
    (*c*) energize vigorously
    (*d*) enliven fruitfully
15. The author concludes on the note that India's progress so far has been
    (*a*) considerable in some fields
    (*b*) very meagre considering its potential
    (*c*) indicative, in general, of its potential
    (*d*) good in respect of farm-products and some industrial products only

UNIT – 2

There Isn't Time

There isn't time, there isn't time
To do the things I want to do

With all the mountain tops to climb
And all the woods to wander through

And all the seas to sail upon,
And everywhere there is to go,

And all the people, every one,
Who live upon the earth to know,

There's only time, there's only time,
To know a few, and do a few,

And then sit down and make a rhyme
About the rest I want to do.

Eleanor Farjeon

Questions:

I.

A. Tick the right answer:

1. The poet says that there is no time because
   (*a*) She is a very busy woman.
   (*b*) Life is short.
   (*c*) She is very old.
2. In the lines "And all the people, every one who live upon the earth to know" the poet means that
   (*a*) everyone should know everyone on earth.
   (*b*) we should know all living things, people and animals on earth.
   (*c*) we would like to know everyone on earth.
3. In this poem, the poet is
   (*a*) sad. (*b*) dissatisfied.
   (*c*) happy.

B. Answer the following questions:

1. What things does the poet want to know and do?
2. What does the poet wish to do about those things for which he does not have any time?
3. Find out the rhyming words in the poem. Can you see a pattern?
4. Poets often repeat a lot of words, phrases or sounds. Pick out the words, phrases or sounds that are repeated in this poem.

II. Underline the odd word out in each of the following groups of words:

1. sea, lake, desert, ocean
2. mountain, grass, hill, plateau
3. people, pupils, persons, public
4. towns, woods, jungles, deserts

UNIT – 3

Multiple Choice

Communicative Passage

Directions: Questions 1 to 5 are based on the following advertisement.

> **LET THERE BE LIGHT VISION CENTRE**
> 1451 Broadview Rd.
> 661-9281
>
> More Than a Quarter of a Century Serving Holly Heights
> Registered Opticians
>
> One-day Prescription Service
> Custom-Fitted Glasses to Suit Your Individual Needs
>
> Hard and Soft Contact Lenses
>
> HRS. M 10-9
> T-F 8:30-5
> Sat 10-4
>
> *Call for an Immediate Appointment*

Questions:

1. Which phrase indicates that the company is an established firm?
   (*a*) More than a Quarter of a Century Serving Holly Heights.
   (*b*) Registered Opticians
   (*c*) One-Day Prescription Service
   (*d*) Call for an Immediate Appointment
2. The establishment deals only in
   (*a*) spectacles
   (*b*) spectacles and hard lenses
   (*c*) soft and hard lenses
   (*d*) spectacles, hard and soft lenses
3. Which evenings will this establishment be open?
   (*a*) Tuesday through Friday
   (*b*) Monday only
   (*c*) Saturday only
   (*d*) Monday and Saturday
4. Who would most likely go to this establishment?
   (*a*) a person needing surgery for an eye disease
   (*b*) a person who has a prescription for antibiotics to be bought
   (*c*) a person who does not have an appointment
   (*d*) a person who needs a new pair of contact lenses
5. Which of the following is **NOT** true about this business?
   (*a*) It is closed on Sundays.
   (*b*) It is open later in the evening on Monday than on other days.
   (*c*) It has the same hours from Tuesday through Saturday.
   (*d*) It does not open as early in the morning on Monday and Saturday as it does on the other days.

UNIT – 4

Cloze Passage Type

Directions: Fill in the blanks with appropriate words in context. You can read the whole passage before beginning the task.

The Land, the human settlements, the forests, the flora and fauna, the water bodies and the envelope of air all constitute a spatial entity. Some of these components are more ________ [1] and fragile than others and are ________ [2] susceptible to degradation due to pollution. ________ [3] planning is vital to protect these ______ [4] areas. However, this concept or tool ________ [5] seldom been used in India. Proper ________ [6] of newly planned industries and industrial ________ [7] is a strong pollution preventive instrument ________ [8] ensures environmental sustainability of industrial ________ [9]. It is the site that ultimately ________ [10] which water bodies might be affected ________ [11] effluents streaming out of an industry, ________ [12] air shed might be affected by air ________ [13] or which ecosystem might be harmed. ________ [14] above urgency can also be emphasised ________ [15] the Bhopal Gas Tragedy'. Had there ________ [16] a sufficient compatibility between the industry ________ [17] the surrounding land uses, the impact ________ [18] the accident would have been less ________ [19].

UNIT – 5

Cloze Passage Type

Directions: Fill in the blanks with appropriate words in context. You can read the whole passage before beginning the task.

The Land, the human settlements, the forests, the flora and fauna, the water bodies and the envelope of air all constitute a spatial entity. Some of these components are more ________ [1] and fragile than others and are ________ [2] susceptible to degradation due to pollution. ________ [3] planning is vital to protect these ______ [4] areas. However, this concept or tool ________ [5] seldom been used in India. Proper ________ [6] of newly planned industries and industrial ________ [7] is a strong pollution preventive instrument ________ [8] ensures environmental sustainability of the industrial ________ [9]. It is the site that ultimately ________ [10] which water bodies might be affected ________ [11] effluents streaming out of an industry, ________ [12] air shed might be affected by air ________ [13] or which ecosystem might be harmed. ________ [14] above urgency can also be emphasised ________ [15] the Bhopal Gas Tragedy'. Had there ________ [16] a sufficient compatibility between the industry ________ [17] the surrounding land uses, the impact ________ [18] the accident would have been less ________ [19].

UNIT – 6

Miscellaneous Type

Directions: The questions are based on the following news item.

THE TIMES OF INDIA

NO. 245 VOL. CLIV. METRO NEW DELHI: MONDAY OCTOBER 21 1991 Rs. 2.20 16+2 Metro Pages

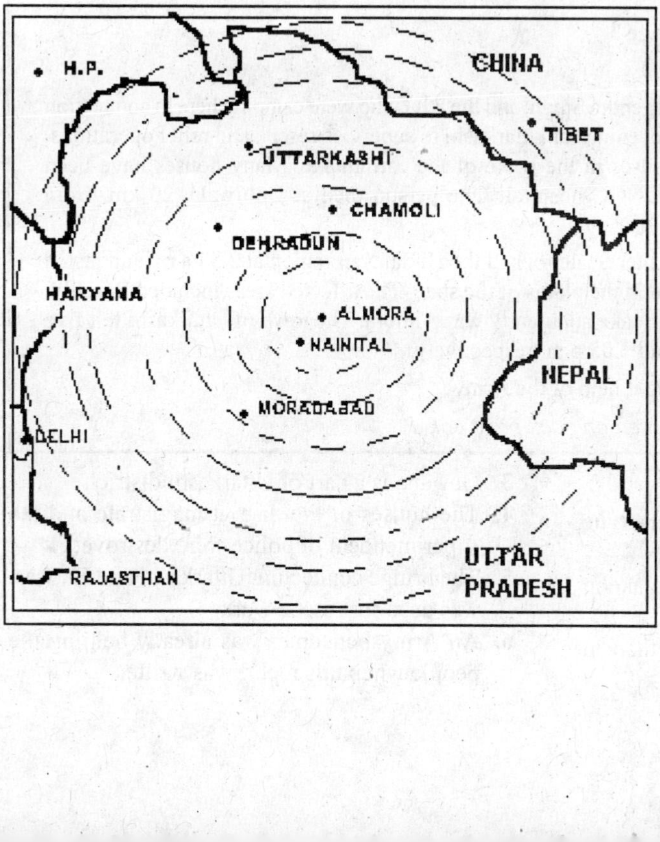

Over 500 killed in UP quake

By R. Nailwal,

SHRINAGAR (Garhwal), October 20 OVER 500 people were feared killed and over 2,000 injured in Uttarkashi district alone in the devastating earthquake which rocked large parts of northern India in the early hours today. Uttarkashi was the worst hit by the quake which caused severe damage in Chamoli, Tehri Garhwal and other adjoining districts.

In Tehri Garhwal 60 people are reported to have lost their lives. In Chamoli the casualty figure was put at 7. In Uttarkashi, according to eyewitnesses, over 200 bodies were seen lying in the hospital mortuary. In Gawana village of the district, nearly 30 people died. It is reported that in the widespread destruction, several houses including that of the district magistrate, the superintendent of police, huge tourist bungalows and the State Bank of India building were totally demolished. Hundreds of other buildings developed huge cracks. Casualty reports about several villages of the district are still awaited.

In Gangwani village in Uttarkashi district several buildings collapsed under the impact of the quake. They included Dandi Ashram, Kali Kamli Dharamshala, and the tourist rest house. Several private and government tourist buses were also damaged by heavy boulders which gave way under the impact of the quake. Meanwhile, rescue teams including doctors and officials from adjoining areas of Pauri, Shrinagar, and Dehra Dun have rushed to Uttarkashi for relief work.

LUCKNOW: The special secretary (home), Mr. Prabhat Kumar, said the collapse of a bridge on the main thoroughfare connecting Uttarkashi to Batwari town has come in the way of rescue operations. He said the help of troops stationed on the Indo-China border had been sought for the rescue operations. An Army helicopter would also be requisitioned. Official sources said a large number of buildings in Uttarkashi town, having a population of about 20,000, had been destroyed. The 14-year-old son of the police superintendent was killed when his house collapsed.

The Vice-President, Mr. Shankar Dayal Sharma, who was staying in a hotel in Dehra Dun was safe, though some rooms in his hotel developed cracks, an official source said. Several other buildings in Dehra Dun, Almora, Ranikhet and Nainital developed cracks. The Tiloh power station and Semri Dam in Uttarkashi were also damaged though the extent was yet to be ascertained, sources said.

At least 34 persons were killed in Pratap Nagar tehsil of Tehri Garhwal district. Fifty persons were killed in Maneri. Villagers have been rendered homeless in the Bhagirathi valley. The number of casualties were not immediately available, said Mr. Sumitra Shankar, DIG Garhwal range. He added that three persons died in Kedar Nath and one in Barkot.

> Two-thirds of India is quake prone - page 3

> Future of Tehri dam threatened - page 3

The commissioner of Garhwal region, Mr. Nagendra Singh, and the DIG who were camping here in connection with the visit of the Vice-President left this evening for Uttarkashi to supervise rescue and relief operations. In Dehra Dun people came out of their houses in the wake of the earthquake. Many houses have been damaged which included the prestigious ONGC hospital. One person died at Dohiwala, 20 km. from Dehra Dun.

The tremors which measured 6.2 on the Richter Scale rocked the Himalayan region at 2.53 a.m. and lasted about 45 seconds. The tremors were also felt in the plains of the state. The affected areas included Bareilly, Kanpur and Lucknow. The epicentre of the quake apparently was Almora. The town of Uttarkashi felt five tremors at 2.53 a.m., 3.10 a.m., 4.15 a.m. and 1.05 p.m. respectively.

ARMY'S HELP: The government has sought help of the Army

Continued on back page col. 1

Questions:

I. **Say whether the following statements are true (T) or false (F):**

1. Five hundred people died in the earthquake in Uttarkashi district.
2. More people died in Tehri Garhwal than in Chamoli.
3. Gawana is a part of Uttarkashi district.
4. The houses of the district magistrate and the superintendent of police were destroyed.
5. The bridge connecting Uttarkashi and Batwari was used for rescue work.
6. An Army helicopter was already helping the people when this report was written.

7. The Vice President was in Dehra Dun when the earthquake hit Uttarkashi.
8. The Tiloh power station and the Semri Dam were completely destroyed.

II. Answer the following questions:

1. On which day did the earthquake hit Northern India?
2. Who is the reporter of this news item?
3. Where was this reporter when he wrote the news?
4. How many pages does this newspaper have?
5. Name two states which are the neighbours of Uttar Pradesh.
6. Name two countries whose borders touch Uttar Pradesh.
7. What efforts were made to help the people affected by the quake?
8. What major difficulty did the rescue team find in reaching Uttarkashi?
9. Can you tell from the map where the centre of the earthquake was?
10. What is the population of Uttarkashi town?

III. Match the words in column A with their meanings in column B. There is an extra word/meaning in Column B.

Column A	Column B
1. widespread	(*a*) many
2. thoroughfare	(*b*) harmed
3. troops	(*c*) found over a large area
4. adjoining	(*d*) save
5. rescue	(*e*) road or street used a great deal for traffic
6. several	(*f*) soldiers
7. severe	(*g*) craftsman
8. damaged	(*h*) nearest or neighbouring
	(*i*) serious

IV. Find words from the passage which are opposite in meaning to the words given below:

1. best
2. late
3. constructed
4. repaired
5. light

V. Fill in the blanks in the following sentences with the verbs given below:

Injured, caused, collapsed, rushed, developed, included, damaged

A burning cigarette ________ the fire and soon the office building started burning. The walls of the building ________ cracks and finally they ________ and fell. More than ten people were ________ in the fire and they were ________ to the hospital. The wounded ________ the chowkidar of the office. Some adjoining buildings were also ________ by the fire(Revised)

UNIT – 7

Single Sentence Readings

Directions: Read each of the following sentences carefully. You are instructed to choose an alternative nearest to the meaning of the underlined part in each one of them.

1. <u>Unintentionally, some cities are squeezing out the middle class by forcing them to support the poor.</u>
   (A) Unintentionally the poor are supporting a movement to squeeze the middle class out of some cities.
   (B) The middle class in some cities is unfortunately squeezing out the support of the poor.
   (C) In some cities, the middle class is forcing the poor to support them.
   (D) By being forced to support the poor, the middle class is unintentionally being squeezed out of the cities.
2. <u>The current was black and mindless, with a beauty that almost masked its danger.</u>
   (A) Although it appeared dangerous, the current had a beauty that was only black and mindless.
   (B) The current was black and mindless but not as dangerous as it seemed.
   (C) Although the current was black and mindless, its beauty nearly disguised the danger.

(D) Despite its danger, the blackness and mindlessness of the current made it more beautiful.

3. Despite the breathtaking natural beauty of the crystalline Great Lakes during the winter, man is reluctant to venture into this snowy wonderland.
   (A) Even though the crystalline Great Lakes are breathtaking in the winter, man is afraid to explore this snowy wonderland.
   (B) Man is reluctant to venture into the snowy wonderland in the winter in spite of the breathtaking natural beauty of the crystalline Great Lakes.
   (C) Man is reluctant to venture into the crystalline Great Lakes during the winter because it makes breathing beautiful.
   (D) Although reluctant to venture into the Crystalline Great Lakes, man does so to appreciate their breathtaking natural beauty.

4. Spain has changed over the years, but the fascination and enchantment still remain for the susceptible romantic to savour and treasure.
   (A) Susceptible romantics are swept up by the fascinating and enchanting changes being made in Spain today.
   (B) Spanish treasures are fascinating and enchanting for the susceptible romantic.
   (C) Despite the changes in Spain, susceptible romantics are still enchanted and fascinated by its culture.
   (D) The changes in Spain are fascinating and enchanting to the savour of susceptible romantics.

5. Tort laws differ from criminal laws — the former offer civil remedies in the form of monetary compensation for the injured individual, while the latter are concerned primarily with punishment for the satisfaction of the State.
   (A) In former times, tort laws and criminal laws were the same, but now they are quite distinct in the methods of compensation.
   (B) A tort law is intended to punish a wrongdoer, while criminal law is intended to offer monetary remedies.
   (C) Tort laws and criminal laws are quite the same because they both are intended to compensate the State with money and to punish the criminal.
   (D) Tort laws are remedial and intended to benefit the individual who as been harmed, but criminal laws are punitive and intended to benefit the State.

PART – B
VOCABULARY

"To the Ocean now I fly,
And those happy climes that lie
Where day never shuts his eye,"

– John Milton

UNIT – 1

C-Type Test

Directions: Fill in the blanks. Each blank begins with one or more than one letter. Taking clue from that, you are directed to fill in the blanks in the following passage:

As Professor Brown got up there was great applause.

He looked about, put his right hand in his trouser po ___ [1], held his temples with his left hand, a ____ [2] began. He looked at Chandran and said t___ [3] he had not bargained for this, a me ___ [4] of this dimension and importance, when he ac ___ [5] to the secretary's request. Chandran tapped the ar ___ [6] of his chair with his fingers, looked d ___ [7] and smiled, almost feeling that he had pl ___ [8] a deep game on the Principal. The lec ___ [9] said that he had consented to deliver a___ [10] address this evening, thinking that he was t __ [11] be at the opening of a very si ___ [12] Association. From what Ragavachar said, he understood i ___ [13] to be something that was of national im _ _. [14] If he had known this, his place n _ __ [15] would be in one of the chairs t___ [16] he saw before him, and he would h___ [17] left the responsible task to better persons. Ho__ [18], it was too late to do anything n___ [19]. He hoped that he would have an oc__ [20] to settle his score with Chandran.

UNIT – 2

Words Often Confused

1. The weather had turned very hot for May, and it seemed only (A. human; B. humane) to clip the dog's hair.
2. Directions for the procession were confused, but all the participants found their (A. respective; B. respectful) places.
3. Although Father rarely scolded us, his high standards were (A. explicit; B. implicit) in everything he did.
4. This final and most crucial debate on television between the two candidates was (A. figuratively; B. literally) a battle to the death.
5. One of the finest sights in Stockholm is an exhibition of her (A. sculptor; B. sculpture) at her home far above the sea.

UNIT – 3

One Word Substitution

Directions: For each sentence given in the exercise, you will find one word in the list of words given below. Choose an appropriate word to fill in the blanks:

List of Words:

(*a*) Omnipresent	(*f*) Philanthropist
(*b*) Misanthrope	(*g*) Atheist
(*c*) Polyandry	(*h*) Celibacy
(*d*) Triennial	(*i*) Polygamy
(*e*) Omnipotent	(*j*) Omniscient

Exercise

1. That which happens once in three years is known as ________.
2. Onc who is present everywhere is called ________.
3. One who is all-powerful is called ________.
4. One who knows everything is called ________.
5. The practice of having more than one wife at a time is known as ________.
6. The practice of having more than one husband at a time is known as ________.
7. The practice of remaining chaste is known as ________.
8. A person who hates mankind is known as a ________.
9. A man who loves mankind and works for human welfare is known as a ________.
10. One who does not believe in the existence of God is known as an ________.

UNIT – 4

Idioms and Phrases

Directions: Each item below consists of an idiom or a phrase, followed by four lettered expressions. Choose the lettered expression that most nearly expresses the meaning of the given idiom or phrase.

1. To crow over
   (*a*) To criticise bitterly
   (*b*) To become unwanted
   (*c*) To exult in triumph
   (*d*) To compromise
2. To be at sea
   (*a*) To wait for an opportunity
   (*b*) To be perplexed and confused
   (*c*) To watch the events
   (*d*) To make futile efforts
3. A bird's eye view
   (*a*) A general view
   (*b*) A narrow view
   (*c*) Honest like a bird
   (*d*) Flying fast like a bird
4. To set one's heart upon
   (*a*) To think of something imaginary
   (*b*) To desire something that cannot be achieved
   (*c*) To become intensely desirous of
   (*d*) To assure help in hour of nccd
5. To bring to light
   (*a*) To shape nicely
   (*b*) To reveal clearly
   (*c*) To revive
   (*d*) To cause

UNIT – 5

Multiple Choice

Vocabulary (In Context)

1. What ________ indeed my husband must have had, to put up with me uncomplainingly during these early days of our married life!
   (*a*) intellect (*b*) patience
   (*c*) nerves (*d*) impatience
2. The ________ of Mr Saxena is the only factor leading to an unreasonable delay in initiating the new project.
   (*a*) co-operation (*b*) impatience
   (*c*) perseverance (*d*) indecision
3. Through the play 'All my sons', Miller points to our ________ social responsibilities, and thus the play becomes relevant and acceptable to modern society.
   (*a*) escapable (*b*) inescapable
   (*c*) detestable (*d*) high-flown
4. It meant that those killed in the war had sacrificed themselves in ________.
   (*a*) vain (*b*) futility
   (*c*) compulsion (*d*) danger
5. The neighbours were inclined to believe that Joe was ________ of his wife's murder.
   (*a*) guilty (*b*) criminal
   (*c*) commited (*d*) abused

UNIT – 6

Multiple Choice

Directions: Choose one word or phrase from the given options closest to the meaning of the word in bold letters.

1. Meritocracy
   (*a*) system based on achievement
   (*b*) nepotism
   (*c*) the democratic process
   (*d*) temporary authority
2. Acumen
   (*a*) exactness (*b*) potentiality
   (*c*) shrewdness (*d*) assurance
3. Premonition
   (*a*) understanding (*b*) forewarning
   (*c*) determination (*d*) mistrust
4. Criterion
   (*a*) explanation (*b*) essence
   (*c*) standard (*d*) turning-point
5. Extricate
   (*a*) frustrate (*b*) isolate
   (*c*) get rid of (*d*) set free
6. Convivial
   (*a*) persuasive
   (*b*) penitent
   (*c*) sociable, friendly
   (*d*) argumentative
7. Wintergreen
   (*a*) wreath of holly (*b*) aromatic plant
   (*c*) vegetable dye (*d*) mild winter
8. Equipoise
   (*a*) pretension (*b*) patience
   (*c*) balance (*d*) modesty
9. A cappella
   (*a*) a temple without any ringing bells
   (*b*) a person without a hat
   (*c*) singing without any accompaniment
   (*d*) a cottage without a roof
10. Apercu
    (*a*) witticism (*b*) insight
    (*c*) dramatisation (*d*) small opening

UNIT – 7

M.C.P.

Like all sports, hunting has its own rules but there is no referee present to make sure that rules are (pursued, followed, accepted, rejected)[1]. The entire responsibility of following the rules depends (in, to, over, on)[2] the sportsman himself. The forest and wild life (people, persons, staff, members)[3] are there to keep a check but it (was, is, may be, isn't)[4] the sportsman who has to keep a control (upon, in, within, on)[5] himself and has to ensure that our wild (forest, nature, greenery, life)[6] is not destroyed completely. The most serious and (great, heavy, dangerous, light)[7] damage to our wild life is caused by (thieves, robbers, poachers, rogues)[8] from villages next to the forest. Damage is (just, only, merely, also)[9] done by gangs from big towns who kill (green, wild, environmental, natural)[10] life so that they can sell skins (but, including, excluding, and)[11] horns. If we are careful and follow the rules (of, about, regarding, for)[12] the game strictly, we can continue to hunt (with, without, for, about)[13] any loss of our fauna at present.

In order to (serve, develop, improve, save)[14] our wild life, a number of national parks (or, and, with, along)[15] game sanctuaries have been established. The difference between (a, the, one, any)[16] national park and a game sanctuary is that (as, though, while, however)[17] a national park is established through an Act (with, of, in, by)[18] parliament or a state legislature, sanctuaries are established (with, from, about, through)[19] an administrative order of the government. National parks (may be, are, were, have been)[20] permanent and their boundaries cannot be changed whereas (parks, zoos, sanctuaries, playgrounds)[21] are established for a fixed period of time (who, whom, what, which)[22] may or may not be increased; and also (the, many, some, all)[23] boundaries can be changed or modified. In India (they, people, we, states)[24] have forty five national parks. The most famous (is, was, were, are)[25] the Kanha National Park in Madhya Pradesh, (a, the, one, some)[26] Corbet National Park and Dudwa National Park (in, at, for, on)[27] Uttar Pradesh.

In these National Parks, the wild (animal, life, forest, plant)[28] gets an opportunity to exist and multiply in (the, a, some, any)[29] natural manner without any interference or danger from (mankind, life, man, humanity)[30]. In the game sanctuaries (210 at present), similar (safety, protection, cover, shelter)[31] is given to all forms of wild life. (A, The, One, Only)[32] most famous game sanctuary in India is (the, a, only, also)[33] Gir Lion Sanctuary in Gujarat. Here lives the Asiatic (lion, animal, giant, bird)[34] which once roamed freely all over Northwest (country, India, Continent, land)[35] Pakistan, Iraq and Arabia. This is the only (part, nation, zoo, land)[36] of the earth where the Asiatic lion still (stays, dwells, puts up, exists)[37] in its natural environment owing to the strict (vigilance, discipline, protection, food)[38] given to it for the last eighty years (and, or, also, nearly)[39] more.

All our national parks and sanctuaries are (a, the, only, also)[40] source of great pleasure and recreation to thousands (of, accountable, countable, countless)[41] visitors each year because they give an opportunity (for, to, through, about)[42] people to see the rich fauna of our (village, forest, city, country)[43] in their natural surroundings.

UNIT – 8

Antonyms

Directions: Give the antonyms of the following words:

1. Alert **2.** Expedient **3.** Equitable
4. Prudent **5.** Ruthless

UNIT – 9

Directions: Given below are the meaning of words all of which begin with 'pro'. Write down the words.

1. testing of a man's ability before he is finally employed
2. to investigate deeply
3. uprightness of character
4. question to be solved
5. order of doing things
6. number of persons moving forward and following each other in an orderly way
7. showing contempt for God or sacred things.

UNIT – 10

Spelling Test

Directions: Six of the following words are spelt correctly and six are spelt incorrectly. Correct those which are spelt incorrectly.

attendent; impertinent; amusment; condence; succession; maintenance; definiton; admittance; repentence; magnificence; compulsury; exclamatory.

UNIT – 11

Multiple-Choice Spelling Test

1. The Sangam of the rivers is [1]**<u>complimented</u>** by a [2]**<u>confluncè</u>** of [3]**<u>spiritual</u>** [4]**<u>sublimity</u>** and professional [5]**<u>governence</u>**. The Kumbh township, spread over 5,000 [6]**<u>hectres</u>**, is divided into 31 administrative and planning sectors for services and security purposes. Each sector is self-

sufficient with regard to civic [7]**aminities**, including drinking water, health, [8]**sanitation**, roads, electricity, housing and [9]**bazaars** along with police and firestations.

The five **incorrectly** spelt words are:

(*a*) 1, 3, 4, 6, and 8
(*b*) 2, 4, 5, 7, and 8
(*c*) 2, 4, 5, 6, and 8
(*d*) 1, 2, 5, 6, and 7

2. Unfolding in the past few months is the largest and most [1]**enigmetic** agriculture crisis faced by [2]**independant** India. Largest, because it [3]**engulfs** every state from Punjab to Kerala and Gujarat to Assam, [4]**afflicting** every crop-foodgrains to oilseeds to fruits. [5]**Enigmatic**, because it is a crisis that has built up [6]**amist** an [7]**unprecedanted** 12 [8]**succesive** normal [9]**monsoons** and is marked by falling (or stagnating) output and falling prices.

The five **incorrectly** spelt words are:

(*a*) 1, 3, 5, 7, and 9
(*b*) 1, 2, 6, 7, and 8
(*c*) 2, 3, 5, 6, and 8
(*d*) 2, 4, 6, 7, and 9

3. A BJP [1]**idoelogue**, an [2]**erudite** [3]**scholar**, a [4]**farmer** teacher, Dr. Murli Manohar Joshi, union [5]**minster** for human [6]**resourse** [7]**development** shares his ideas, [8]**vision**, and future plans for the education [9]**sectar** with us.

The five **incorrectly** spelt words are:

(*a*) 1, 2, 5, 6, and 8
(*b*) 1, 2, 5, 8, and 9
(*c*) 2, 3, 6, 8, and 9
(*d*) 1, 4, 5, 6, and 9

4. In this study, tea consumption was [1]**asociated** with a slightly higher [2]**critical** [3]**fliker** [4]**fushion** [5]**threshold**, which is a measure of a person's ability to [6]**distinguish** [7]**descrete** [8]**sensory** data. Black tea rapidly [9]**revives** by improving and maintaining mental alertness and its regular consumption throughout the day definitely helps to reduce feelings of [10]**fatige**.

The five **incorrectly** spelt words are:

(*a*) 1, 2, 4, 6, and 9
(*b*) 2, 3, 5, 7, and 8
(*c*) 1, 3, 4, 7, and 10
(*d*) 2, 4, 5, 6, and 10

5. After the kidnapping, these urban thugs act as [1]**intermedaries** between the victims' families and their kidnappers, [2]**negotiating** the ransom money and the [3]**modelities** of payment. During the negotiations, the victims are kept at hideouts in small towns and villages in the [4]**revines**. Behind in Madhya Pradesh and the Etawah in Uttar Pradesh have [5]**amerged** as the [6]**favorite** [7]**havens** for hiding victims picked up from as far as Delhi, Kanpur and Gaziabad.

The five **incorrectly** spelt words are:

(*a*) 1, 3, 4, 5, and 6
(*b*) 1, 2, 4, 6, and 7
(*c*) 2, 3, 4, 5, and 6
(*d*) 2, 4, 5, 6, and 7

PART – C
GRAMMAR

"The moving Moon went up the sky
And nowhere did abide;. . ."

– S. T. Coleridge

UNIT – 1

Prepositions

Directions: Fill in the blanks with appropriate Prepositions.

Yet Dickens stresses that it is not money as such but the love [1] _____ money which is [2] _____ the root [3] _____ evil [4] _____ society. And Pip is redeemed [5] _____ his generosity [6] _____ Herbert [7] _____ secretly buying him a partnership. The author raises no moral objection [8] _____ Matthew Pocket' inheriting £ 4,000 [9] _____ Miss Havisham.

UNIT – 2

Verbs

Directions: Choose appropriate Verbs from the alternatives below and fill in the blanks.

Dickens [1] _____ sensitive to every facet of external reality. Very often the effect [2] _____ by the illusion of photography: Miss Havisham's room, which [3]_____ untouched for years as a constant reminder of the betrayal she [4]____ upon her wedding day, [5]_____ most easily as a set in a film studio. The oddity of Wemmick's house — a wooden cottage with a Gothic door and windows, a flagstaff, a drawbridge which [6]____ a moat four feet wide, and a gun, protected by a tarpaulin umbrella, which [7]____ at nine o'clock every night - [8]____ by the straightforward way in which it [9]_____. Jaggers's office [10]______ another instance, with its solid furniture, legal papers, and the two plaster-casts of executed criminals.

1. (*a*) was
   (*b*) has been
   (*c*) had been
   (*d*) will be
2. (*a*) is gathered
   (*b*) is collected
   (*c*) is achieved
   (*d*) is obtained
3. (*a*) has been deserted
   (*b*) has been left
   (*c*) has been dropped
   (*d*) has been kept
4. (*a*) experienced (*b*) brought
   (*c*) suffered (*d*) got
5. (*a*) can be conceived
   (*b*) can be planned
   (*c*) can be thought
   (*d*) can be watched
6. (*a*) measures (*b*) reaches
   (*c*) crosses (*d*) covers
7. (*a*) is fired (*b*) is shot
   (*c*) is activated (*d*) is used
8. (*a*) is similarly aggravated
   (*b*) is similarly increased
   (*c*) is similarly enhanced
   (*d*) is similarly elevated
9. (*a*) is described
   (*b*) is mentioned
   (*c*) is explained
   (*d*) is criticized
10. (*a*) supplies
    (*b*) provides
    (*c*) harbours
    (*d*) gives

UNIT – 3

Directions: Use the following words as the part of speech indicated :

1. 'Long' – as a noun; adjective; verb and adverb.
2. 'Round' – as a noun; adjective; verb; adverb and preposition.

UNIT – 4

Pronouns

Directions: Correct the following sentences for Pronoun errors. (Note: Some sentences may be correct).

1. You are expected to meet Allan and he in the convention centre.
2. Could you try to sit between Mary and her when we go in to dinner?
3. They all work much harder than us.
4. Everybody should bring their own recommendations.
5. Marion and I will make a great team for the next election.

UNIT – 5

Error Correction

Directions: Correct, improve or justify the following sentences.

1. I will be drowned, nobody shall save me.
2. Unless he will be more careful, he will not recover.
3. The end was come as the end of such matters generally comes by gradual decay.
4. The United States easily take the lead in the production of steel.
5. A fair means do not always bring success.

UNIT – 6

Directions: Join the following pairs of simple sentences to form compound sentences. Be careful to punctuate your answers correctly. Don't use the same joining word twice.

1. Mr. Jones spent three days trying to sell the house. The client decided not to buy.

2. I spend too much time walking to work. I bought a bicycle.
3. Glen Frisch draws the pictures. Glenda Rennick writes the captions.
4. You have been carrying the whole department for the last six months. I am giving you a 20% raise.
5. He has all the right qualifications. We can't offer him the job.

UNIT – 7

Adjectives

Directions: Fill in the blanks with the Adjectives opposite in meaning to those written in *italics*.

1. A *brave* man hates a ______ fellow.
2. The land was not *fertile*; it was ______.
3. This cloth is *superior* to that; that cloth is ______ to this.
4. The knife was not *sharp*; it was ______.
5. We all praise an *innocent* person but hate a ______ one.

UNIT – 8

Error Correction

Directions: In questions 1-10 each sentence has four underlined words or phrases. The four underlined parts of the sentence are marked (A), (B), (C) and (D). Identify the one underlined word or phrase that must be changed in order for the sentence to be correct. Then, on your answer sheet, find the number of the question and fill in the space that corresponds to the letter of the answer you have chosen.

1. Had the committee members (A) considered the alternatives more carefully (B), they would have realised that the second was (C) better as the first (D).
2. Malnutrition is a major (A) cause of death in those (B) countries where the cultivation of rice have (C) been impeded by recurrent drought (D).
3. The decision to withdraw (A) all support (B) from the activities of the athletes are causing (C) an uproar among (D) the athletes' fans.
4. Use of underutilised (A) species of fish have been (B) proposed as (C) a solution to the famine (D) in many underdeveloped countries.
5. Because (A) the residents had worked (B) so diligent (C) to renovate (D) the old building, the manager had a party.
6. John's wisdom teeth were troubling (A) him, so he went to a dental surgeon to see about (B) having them (C) pull (D).
7. Hardly he had (A) entered the office (B) when he realised that he had (C) forgotten (D) his wallet.
8. Suzy had (A) better to change (B) her study habits if she hopes to be (C) admitted to a good university (D).
9. The teacher told (A) the students to don't (B) discuss (C) the take-home exam with each other (D).
10. Some bacteria are extremely (A) harmful, but anothers (B) are regularly (C) used in producing cheese, crackers, and many other foods (D).

PART – D
WRITING ABILITY

"Knowledge is an arch wherethro' gleams
That untravelled world"

– Lord Tennyson

UNIT – 1

Precis Writing

Directions: Make a precis of the following passage in about one third of its length.

The other day we heard someone smilingly refer to poets as dreamers. Now it is accurate to refer to poets as dreamers but it is not discerning to infer, as this person did, that the dreams of poets are just as practical as people who build bridges or look into microscopes, and are just as close to reality and truth. There they differ from the logician and the scientist in the temporal sense alone; they are ahead of their time, whereas logicians and scientists are abreast of their time. We must not be so superficial that we fail to discern the practicableness of dreams. Dreams are the sunrise steamers heralding a new day of scientific progress— another forward surge. Every forward step that man takes in any field of life is first taken along the dreamy paths of imagination. Robert Foulton did not discover his steamboat with full steam up. Straining at a hawser at some Hudson River dock, first he dreamed the steamboat and then scientific wisdom converted a picture in the mind into a reality of steel and wood. The automobile was not dug out of the ground like a nugget of gold; first men dreamed the automobile and afterwards the practical minded engineers caught up with what had been created by winging fantasy. He who looks deeply and with a seeing eye into poetry of yesterday finds there all the cold scientific magic of today and much we shall not enjoy until some time tomorrow. If the poet does not dream so clearly that blueprint of this vision can immediately be drawn, and the practical conversations immediately affected, they must not for that reason be smiled upon as merely the mental host for a sort of harmless madness. For the poet, like the engineer, is a specialist. His being turned to the life of tomorrow, cannot be turned simultaneously to the life of today. To the scientist he says, "Here I give you a flash of the future." The wise scientist thanks him and takes that flash of the future and makes it over into a fibre of today.

UNIT – 2

Dialogue Writing

Write an imaginary conversation between two boys, one of whom is habitually despondent and thinks luck is against him, whereas the other is of a more practical bent of mind.

UNIT – 3

Composition

You want to start a Coaching Centre for aspiring Engineers, Doctors, Management and Computer Professionals. Design a circular to that effect.

UNIT – 4

Coherence Testing

Directions: For the following question, read the sentences and choose the order in which they form a coherent piece of writing.

Sentence 1: Updike graduated from high school in 1950; he was the president and the covaledictorian of class.

Sentence 2: He was born in Reading, Pennsylvania on March 18, 1932.

Sentence 3: Updike was an only child; he lived with his father, his mother and his mother's parents.

Sentence 4: John Updike was one of the greatest modern writers of our time.

Sentence 5: At age thirteen his family moved to a farm in Shillington, Pennsylvania.

Sentence 6: He attended Harvard University from 1950 to 1954 and majored in English; he wrote stories and drew cartoons for the *Harvard Lampoon.*

Sentence 7: Then he and his wife moved to England, and Updike attended the Ruskin School of Drawing and Fine Arts at Oxford until 1955.

Sentence 8: In 1953 he married Mary E. Pennington.

(*a*) 1, 2, 3, 7, 8, 6, 4, 5
(*b*) 4, 2, 3, 5, 1, 6, 8, 7
(*c*) 4, 2, 5, 3, 6, 1, 7, 8
(*d*) 2, 1, 3, 8, 7, 6, 4, 5

UNIT – 5

Analytical Ability

'Trust no future, however pleasant
Let the dead past bury it's dead,
Act, act in the living present.....'

– To what extent do you agree or disagree with the above lines written by Mr. H. W. Longfellow? Justify your answer with the help of cogent arguments.

UNIT – 6

Essay Writing

Directions: Write an essay on one of the following subjects. (Word limit 400–500 words).

1. Politics and Religion

Or

2. Sweet are the uses of adversity

And here you finish your exciting journey with the tests

ANSWER KEY - IV

Reading Comprehension and Reading Ability

Unit-1

1. a	**2.** c	**3.** d	**4.** d	**5.** a
6. a	**7.** a	**8.** a	**9.** c	**10.** c
11. d	**12.** c	**13.** b	**14.** b	**15.** b

Unit-2

I.

A. 1. – b **2.** – c **3.** – a

B. 1. The poet wants to know everyone existing on this earth. She wants to climb all the mountains, wander through all the forests and sail upon all the seas.

2. For those things for which the poet does not have any time, she wants to sit down and compose a poem.

3. time, climb
do, through
upon, one (the poet intends to pronounce them alike)
go, know
time, rhyme
few, do (the poet intends to pronounce them alike)
Yes, we can see a regular rhyming pattern:

a	b	a	b
c	d	c	d
a	b	a	b

4. words: time, do, all, know, few, want
sounds: (*a*) isn't
(*b*) time, climb, rhyme (sound: ^I)
do, through (sound: u)
upon, one (here the poet wants us to pronounce the two words alike)
go, know (sound: au)

II.

1. desert	**2.** grass	**3.** pupils
4. towns		

Unit-3

1. a	**2.** d	**3.** b	**4.** d	**5.** c

Unit-4

1. sensitive	**2.** more	**3.** Environmental
4. sensitive	**5.** has	**6.** siting
7. estates	**8.** that	**9.** development
10. determines	**11.** by	**12.** which
13. pollutants	**14.** The	**15.** by
16. been	**17.** and	**18.** of
19. severe		

Unit-5

I.

1. T	**2.** T	**3.** T	**4.** T
5. F	**6.** F	**7.** T	**8.** F

II. 1. Sunday **2.** R. Nailwal
3. Shrinagar (Garhwal) **4.** Eighteen
5. Haryana, H.P. **6.** China, Nepal
7. Rescue teams, including doctors and officials from adjoining areas of Pauri, Shrinagar and Dehra Dun, and troops stationed on the Indo-China border were rushed to help the people affected by the quake. An Army helicopter would also be put into operation for their help.
8. The collapse of a bridge on the main thoroughfare connecting Uttarkashi to Batwari town came in the way of the rescue team in reaching Uttarkashi.
9. Almora **10.** About 20,000.

III.

1–c	2–e	3–f	4–h
5–d	6–a	7–i	8–b

IV.

1. worst	2. early	3. demolished
4. damaged	5. heavy	

V.

1. caused	2. developed	3. collapsed
4. injured	5. rushed	6. included
7. damaged		

Unit-6

1. D 2. C 3. B 4. C 5. D

Vocabulary

Unit-1

1. pocket	2. and	3. that
4. meeting	5. acceded	6. arms
7. down	8. played	9. lecturer
10. an	11. to	12. simple
13. it	14. importance	15. now
16. that	17. have	18. however
19. now	20. occasion	

Unit-2

1. B 2. A 3. B 4. A 5. B

Unit-3

1. d	2. a	3. e	4. j	5. i
6. c	7. h	8. b	9. f	10. g

Unit-4

1. c 2. b 3. a 4. c 5. b

Unit-5

1. b 2. d 3. b 4. a 5. a

Unit-6

1. a	2. c	3. b	4. c	5. d
6. c	7. b	8. c	9. c	10. b

Unit-7

1. followed	2. on	3. staff
4. is	5. on	6. life
7. heavy	8. poachers	9. also
10. wild	11. and	12. of
13. without	14. save	15. and
16. a	17. while	18. of
19. through	20. are	21. sanctuaries
22. which	23. the	24. we
25. are	26. the	27. in
28. life	29. a	30. man
31. protection	32. The	33. the
34. lion	35. India	36. part
37. exists	38. protection	39. or
40. a	41. of	42. to
43. country		

Unit-8

1. Absent-minded		2. Inexpedient
3. Unjust	4. Imprudent	5. Humane

Unit-9

1. probation	2. probe	3. probity
4. problem	5. process	6. procession
7. profanity		

Unit-10

Attendant; amusement; condenses; definition; repentance; compulsory

Unit-11

1. d 2. b 3. d 4. c 5. a

Grammar

Unit-1

1. of	2. at	3. of
4. in	5. by	6. to
7. in	8. to	9. from

Unit-2

1. a	2. c	3. b	4. c	5. a
6. c	7. a	8. c	9. a	10. b

Unit-3

1. Long : This is the long and short of the whole matter. (noun)
   Do not give him a long rope. (adjective)
   I long for a cosy corner. (verb)
   May you live long. (adverb)
2. Round : The principal is on his daily round. (noun)
   The swan has a round head. (adjective)
   The ship rounded the cape in safety. (verb)
   I cannot bring him round to my views. (preposition)

Unit-4

1. You are expected to meet Allan and him in the convention centre.
2. This sentence is correct.
3. They all work much harder than we.
4. Everybody should bring his / her own recommendations.
5. This sentence is correct.

Unit-5

1. If am drowned, nobody will save me.
2. Unless he is more careful, he will not recover.
3. The end has come, as the end of such matters generally comes, by gradual decay.
4. The United States easily takes the lead in the production of steel.
5. Fair means does not always bring success.

Unit-6

1. Mr. Jones spent three days trying to sell the house, but the client decided not to buy.
2. I spent too much time walking to work, so I bought a bicycle.
3. Glen Frisch draws the pictures, and Glenda Rennick writes the captions.
4. You have been carrying the whole department for the last six months; hence/ consequently, I am giving you a 20% raise.
5. He has all the right qualifications; still/yet, we can't offer him the job.

Unit-7

1. timid / cowardly **2.** barren
3. inferior **4.** blunt **5.** guilty

Unit-8

1. D **2.** C **3.** C **4.** B **5.** C
6. D **7.** A **8.** B **9.** B **10.** B

Writing Ability

Unit-1

The common opinion is that the poetic dreams are not as sharp as those of the scientists. The truth however is that their dreams are different only in the sense that they think of tomorrow while the scientist thinks of only today. Yet dreams are necessary for both and what we see today would not have been possible, had some poet not had a vision of it long back. The scientist is therefore always thankful to the poet for his dreams.

Unit-2

Nasarullah Jan. : Come, Hussain, you are taking your failure too much to heart. I know it is a great disappointment, and I sympathise with you; but you must not allow it to make you so unhappy.

Mohd. Hussain : It is all very well for a lucky chap like you, Nasarullah. You have passed the first time, and this is my second failure. You would not feel so cheery if you were in my place.

N.J. : I know; but you must pull yourself together, and make up your mind. You will pass the next time. Remember the old saying, " If at first you don't succeed, try, try, try, again!"

M.H. : I think the other version of the saying has more sense in it- "if at first you don't succeed, quit, quit, quit at once!"

N.J. : Oh nonsense! You'll never do anything if you don't persevere. Now why do you think you failed?

M.H. : This entire year fate has been against me. First, I was ill with enteric, which lost me a whole term. Then just before my examination, my grandfather died, and that so upset me that I could not prepare properly.

N.J. : Well you certainly did have bad luck. I am sorry. But I am sure that you will succeed next time. So you must make up your mind to win through.

M.H. : It's no use. I think I was born unlucky. I seem to fail in everything I touch. I tried several times to get a scholarship, but some other boy always got it instead. I shall give it up.

N.J. : Indeed you must not. Remember that it's the darkest hour before the dawn. Often when things are at it's worst, they begin to improve. I don't believe the talk about bad and good luck. A brave man makes his own luck. You have a whole year before you; you have brains, and if you will only pull yourself together, and put your heart into your work, you will win through.

M.H. : I wish I had your hopeful disposition. Still I will take your advice and have another try.

N.J. : That's the style! And I am sure you will succeed and break your so-called "bad luck" once and for all.

Unit-3

We prepare you for Engineering, Medical, MBA, BBA & BCA Entrance Exams.

Our result is par excellence with 90% of the students getting admission in their desired colleges. We provide extensive study material, question banks, and have periodical tests for the assessment of the progress made by the students.

SCHOLARSHIPS SCHEMES AVAILABLE

Note: Prospectus available for Rs. 50 at the above-mentioned address.

Unit-4

Key Answer: b

Unit-5 and 6

Let these be corrected by a good English Teacher.

PRACTICE TEST — V

PART – A
READING COMPREHENSION AND READING ABILITY

UNIT – 1

Multiple Choice Type

Directions: Read through the passage once only as quickly as you can without suffering loss of comprehension and answer the questions that follow.

'Nothing that exists can be against or outside Nature', wrote Diderot; Montesquieu declared that slavery was against Nature, and Rousseau popularised the idea of the natural noble savage. It was believed that science could teach man to behave naturally and to shape his society intelligently. If society was natural and rational, man's inborn goodness would develop towards happiness and perfection. This was very different from the Christian point of view, that man is born sinful and that our surroundings are of secondary importance.

The most important contribution to progress of this group was the Encyclopedia, published in 21 volumes between 1751 and 1765. Its chief editor was Diderot, and among its contributors were most of the great French writers and thinkers of the time – Voltaire, Rousseau, Montesquieu, d'Alembert, Buffon and Turgot. They did not all hold the same ideas, but most of them were progressive thinkers. Many of the things they wrote were unfriendly to the Christian religion, but they tried to disguise this. Even so, the Encyclopedia was forbidden and publicly burned. Public opinion did not support the action of the police, but the last 14 volumes had to be published secretly.

Many French intellectuals were deists, that is to say that they accepted the existence of a God and held a 'natural religion': others were atheists who did not admit the existence of God. David Hume was dining one night in the house of Baron d'Holbach, a German scientist living in Paris. Hume said that he did not believe there were any atheists and that the had never met one. 'Then you have been unlucky', replied the Baron. 'Here you are at the table with seventeen.'

Voltaire, the great French writer, was a deist. For him God was the First Cause and the architect of Newton's universe. 'Nobody can doubt that a painting is the work of a skilful artist', he wrote: 'Could copies possibly be produced by intelligence and the original note?' Yet he was always attacking established religion. He said that he wanted to prove that it needed only one man to destroy it. He ended most of his letters with the phrase 'Ecrasons l'inflame' – 'We must destroy the vile thing'. The vile thing was superstition, both in religion and in ordinary life, and its destruction was the principal idea of the French philosophers.

Towards the end of the eighteenth century, there grew up in Germany a school of thought very opposed to the philosophy of the Encyclopedists. This was the school of Naturphilosophie (Nature Philosophy), of which the most important figures were the poet Goethe (1749–1832), the philosopher Schelling and the biologist Oken (1779–1851).

Naturphilosophie was part of a wider movement, the Romantic Movement, which began in Germany as a protest against rationalism, giving more importance to feeling than to reason.

–J.G. Bruton

COMPREHENSION TEST

Select the most suitable answer.

1. The idea of the natural noble savage was made famous by
   (*a*) Rousseau (*b*) Diderot
   (*c*) Montesquieu (*d*) Hume
2. Voltaire was
   (*a*) a German scientist
   (*b*) an English philosopher
   (*c*) a great French writer
   (*d*) a great Italian architect
3. The principal aim of the French philosophers was:
   (*a*) the creation of aggressive ideas
   (*b*) the condemnation of science
   (*c*) the creation of new forms of Christianity
   (*d*) the destruction of superstition

4. The Romantic Movement began in
   (*a*) England (*b*) France
   (*c*) Italy (*d*) Germany
5. The Encyclopedists had to disguise their attacks on the Christian religion because:
   (*a*) the politicians did not wish to offend the king
   (*b*) The attacks could be mistaken to appear foolish
   (*c*) the authorities would not allow public criticism of religion
   (*d*) the Christians did not understand science
6. In the eighteenth century, French intellectuals were generally:
   (*a*) not interested in religion
   (*b*) slightly interested in religion
   (*c*) greatly interested in religion
   (*d*) obsessed with religion
7. The French philosophers wanted the destruction of superstition because
   (*a*) it was inimical to the scientific approach
   (*b*) it was same as religion
   (*c*) they were atheists
   (*d*) Voltaire had said they 'must destroy the vile thing'
8. The Romantic Movement was:
   (*a*) a natural development of the progress of science
   (*b*) an answer to the problem of superstition
   (*c*) a movement confined only to Germany
   (*d*) a reaction against the preoccupation with science
9. One of Voltaire's primary aims was
   (*a*) attacking science
   (*b*) Attacking the established religion
   (*c*) attacking anyone who believed in God
   (*d*) attacking German philosophers

UNIT – 2

A Sad Song about Greenwich Village

She lives in a garret
Up a haunted stair,
And even when she's frightened
There's nobody to care.

She cooks so small a dinner
She dines on the smell,
And even if she's hungry
There's nobody to tell.

She sweeps her musty lodging
As the dawn steals near,
And even when she's crying
There's nobody to hear.

I haven't seen my neighbour
Since a long time ago,
And even if she's dead
There's nobody to know.

Questions:

Directions: Tick the right answer:

1. What does the poem convey?
   (*a*) Fright/fear (*b*) Hunger
   (*c*) Poverty (*d*) Loneliness
2. This poem is about
   (*a*) a young woman
   (*b*) an old woman
   (*c*) a mad woman
   (*d*) a dead old woman
3. The 'I' and 'She' in the poem are:
   (*a*) colleagues
   (*b*) friends
   (*c*) strangers
   (*d*) neighbours
4. The last two lines of stanzas 1 to 4 convey:
   (*a*) helplessness of the old woman
   (*b*) courage of the lonely woman
   (*c*) sad plight of a woman in distress
   (*d*) death of the old woman
5. Another title of the poem can be:
   (*a*) Women in Villages
   (*b*) Old woman
   (*c*) Women's plight
   (*d*) Age and Despair

UNIT – 3

Multiple Choice

Communicative Passage

Directions: Questions 1 to 5 are based on the following advertisement.

AIR HOSTESS
FLIGHT STEWARD

The evolving commercial aviation industry in India and abroad are throwing up new career opportunities. This is where **IAAN PATHSHALA** comes up with a 15 day training workshop for people who want to take up ground jobs at the airport and want a career as an Air Hostess/Flight Steward. The workshop will focus on pre-flight duties, customer care, basics of airline, grooming, inflight announcements etc.
Minimum qualification 10 + 2.
For details call:-

Iaan Pathshala

6332137, 6328973

100% Placement Assistance

Questions:

1. The Iaan Pathshala aims at training only:
   (*a*) Air Hostess (*b*) Freshers
   (*c*) Flight Stewards (*d*) both *a* and *c*
2. The Iaan Pathshala assures
   (*a*) a placement
   (*b*) a placement assistance
   (*c*) both *a* and *b*
   (*d*) training only
3. For further details, you can contact Iaan Pathshala:
   (*a*) on the address given
   (*b*) on the telephone numbers given
   (*c*) by visiting them personally
   (*d*) by any means
4. You can attend the training workshop:
   (*a*) if you are a graduate only
   (*b*) if you are studying in B.A. first year
   (*c*) if you are studying in class XII
   (*d*) if you are X pass
5. The commercial aviation industry:
   (*a*) is an established industry
   (*b*) is a developing industry
   (*c*) has just come up
   (*d*) has yet to come up

UNIT – 4

Cloze Passage Type

Directions: Fill in the blanks with appropriate words in context. You can read the whole passage before beginning the task.

Once a day, towards noon, one ________[1] us had to drag the uncle________[2] to Grandma. Then with her withered ________[3] she would feel him all over. ________[4] made her day. If we forgot ________[5] take him to her, her moans ________[6] rise to screeches. Then my mother ________[7] say, go on, someone, bring him ________[8], and the uncle would be dragged ________[9] for the daily inspection. So you ________[10], we could hardly send him to ________[11] madhouse.

PART – B
VOCABULARY

UNIT – 1

Idioms and Phrases

Directions: Each item below consists of an idiom or a phrase, followed by four lettered expressions. Choose the lettered expression that most nearly expresses the meaning of the given idiom or phrase.

1. Your opinion <u>carries no weight</u>.
   (*a*) is not heavy
   (*b*) has no importance
   (*c*) has no force (*d*) is insufficient
2. Do not <u>make light of</u> the advice of your elders.
   (*a*) take advantage of
   (*b*) treat with indifference
   (*c*) abhor (*d*) disclose
3. Do not work so hard, otherwise it will <u>tell upon</u> your health.
   (*a*) destroy (*b*) over-strain
   (*c*) effect (*d*) affect
4. My daughter <u>takes after</u> her mother.
   (*a*) resembles (*b*) waits for
   (*c*) follows (*d*) takes from
5. This rule <u>holds good</u> everywhere.
   (*a*) is respected (*b*) applies
   (*c*) is adopted (*d*) is inspired from

UNIT – 2

Multiple Choice

Vocabulary (In Context)

Dear Hameed,

Do you recall that I was trying to get a commission in the Indian Air Force? ________[1], I did manage to get one after a year's training! I haven't done much flying yet, ________[2] I can already say that it's a wonderful experience. When we meet in the officer's mess ________[3] our seniors are very friendly; and ________[4] there are marvellous facilities for officers. ____[5], we have free rations and very fine accommodation at nominal rent.

1. (*a*) Well (*b*) But (*c*) Nonetheless (*d*) Moreover
2. (*a*) hence (*b*) therefore (*c*) but (*d*) instead
3. (*a*) though (*b*) but (*c*) even though (*d*) even
4. (*a*) what's more (*b*) worse thing (*c*) best part (*d*) sadly
5. (*a*) Besides (*b*) For instance (*c*) In addition (*d*) Too happy

UNIT – 3

Multiple Choice

Directions: Choose one word or phrase from the given options closest to the meaning of the word in bold letters.

1. Congregate
   (*a*) To instruct in a gathering
   (*b*) To gather together
   (*c*) To pray in a holy place
   (*d*) To donate for a purpose
2. Abscond
   (*a*) To confront openly
   (*b*) To run off secretly
   (*c*) To cover from public view
   (*d*) To hide to ensure success
3. Dictatorial
   (*a*) one who plans carefully
   (*b*) one who is evenly-balanced
   (*c*) one who is commanding
   (*d*) one who is questioning
4. Benefactor
   (*a*) One who comforts
   (*b*) One who sponsors
   (*c*) One who gives company
   (*d*) One who supports
5. Imperishable
   (*a*) That which is impartial
   (*b*) That which is inevitable
   (*c*) That which is indestructible
   (*d*) That which has potential

UNIT – 4

Vocabulary In Context

MCP

Narayan's portrayal of life is thus severely restrained by a rigorous discipline of art. It precludes all that falls outside his [1](route, periphery, context, control) of observation and knowledge. The urban middle class [2](setting, family, area, economy) in the south of India — this is [3](her, its, his, their) milieu as a painter of life. The [4](summary, sum-total, substance, plot) of his work — in eleven novels and [5](numerous, few, some, numbered) short stories- has thus an essential homogeneity. [6](His, Its, Her, This) characteristic stand as a delineator of men [7](however, as also, and, also) manners comes out in Dr. Iyengar's oft quoted [8](quotation, word, opinion, comment): "…he is content, like Jane Austen with [9](his, her, its, this) 'little bit if ivory', just so many inches [10](long, high, deep, wide): he would like to be a detached [11](watcher, observer, man, creature), to concentrate on a narrow scene, to [12](measure, sense, gather, estimate) the atmosphere of the place, to snap a small group of characters in their oddities [13](moreover, and, but, as also) angularities; he would, if he could explore [14](such, an, a, the) inner countries of the mind, heart and [15](sentiments, soul, spirit, body), catch the uniqueness in the ordinary, the [16](tragic, tragedy, tragically, tragedies) in the prosaic."

UNIT – 5

Multiple Choice Spelling Test

Directions: Pick out the option which shows the correct spelling out of the choices given below.

1. (*a*) orchesterats (*b*) orchesterates
   (*c*) orchestrats (*d*) orchestrates
2. (*a*) campains (*b*) campaigns
   (*c*) campeins (*d*) campeigns
3. (*a*) vulnerabal (*b*) vulnerble
   (*c*) vulnerable (*d*) vulnerbal
4. (*a*) bihaaf (*b*) behaaf
   (*c*) bihalf (*d*) behalf
5. (*a*) indegenious (*b*) indegenuous
   (*c*) indigenous (*d*) indigenuous

PART – C
GRAMMAR

"As to the Adjective; when in doubt, strike it out."
– Mark Twain

UNIT – 1

Multiple Choice Type

Directions: Choose appropriate Tenses from the alternatives below and fill in the blanks.

The battle of Haldighati [1] ______ in the sixteenth century. Maharana Pratap [2] ______ in the battle. A number of his soldiers [3] ______. Many of them [4] ______ prisoner. He [5] ______ to the jungles of Mewar. He [6] ______ by the Mughal army but [7] ______.

1. (*a*) was fought
   (*b*) were fought
   (*c*) had been fought
   (*d*) has been fought
2. (*a*) was defeated
   (*b*) were defeated
   (*c*) had been defeated
   (*d*) has been defeated
3. (*a*) was killed
   (*b*) were killed
   (*c*) had been killed
   (*d*) have been killed
4. (*a*) was taken
   (*b*) were taken
   (*c*) had been taken
   (*d*) have been taken
5. (*a*) escaped
   (*b*) has escaped
   (*c*) had escaped
   (*d*) shall escape
6. (*a*) was pursued
   (*b*) were pursued
   (*c*) had been pursued
   (*d*) has been pursued
7. (*a*) was not captured
   (*b*) were not captured
   (*c*) had not been captured
   (*d*) has not been captured

PART – D
WRITING ABILITY

UNIT – 1

Coherence Testing

Directions: For the following question, read the sentences and choose the order in which they form a coherent piece of writing.

Sentence 1: When the man passed me at the foot of the gangway I suspected he was suffering from cholera.

Sentence 2: In reply to my question the man said he was travelling alone, and had no friends at Mokameh Ghat.

Sentence 3: It was the mango season, the hottest time of the year, when cholera is always at its worst.

Sentence 4: My suspicions were confirmed when I saw him being violently sick.

Sentence 5: Then I made him comfortable in my punkah coolie's house, which was empty, and detached from the servants' quarters.

Sentence 6: I helped him to his feet and led him the hundred yards that separated my bungalow from the Ganges.

ANSWER KEY - V

Reading Comprehension and Reading Ability

Unit-1

1. a 2. c 3. d 4. d 5. c
6. c 7. a 8. d 9. b

Unit-2

1. d 2. b 3. d 4. a 5. d

Unit-3

1. d 2. b 3. b 4. b 5. b

Unit-4

1. of 2. up 3. hand
4. That 5. to 6. would
7. would 8. up 9. up
10. see 11. the

Vocabulary

Unit-1

1. b 2. b 3. d 4. a 5. b

Unit-2

1. a 2. c 3. d 4. a 5. a

Unit-3

1. b 2. b 3. c 4. d 5. a

Unit-4

1. context 2. setting 3. his
4. sum-total 5. numerous 6. His
7. and 8. comment 9. her
10. long 11. observer 12. sense
13. and 14. the 15. soul
16. trajedies

Unit-5

1. d 2. b 3. c 4. d 5. c

Grammar

Unit-1

1. a 2. a 3. b 4. b
5. a 6. a 7. a

Writing Ability

Unit-1

Ans. b

CHAPTER 7

SOLVED PAPERS

PAPER — I

(Reading Comprehension and Written English)

Q. Read the following passage and answer the questions given below:

It is heartening to note that we in India have educated ladies, who are keen on taking up administrative work. We are amazed to see what wonderful work women are doing in offices as typists, clerks, receptionists and officers. It has been noticed that they are quick to understand and very efficient in work and they have won the applause from the bureaucracy. Moreover, they cheer up others with a sweet smile and they can win over others to their point of view. All important services have been thrown open to them. They are competing for the I.A.S. and Allied services. We have women as magistrates, judges and revenue officers. They are cool-headed, dispassionate, objective and impartial.

There is a special sphere in which women are better suited than men. It is the sphere of social service, canvassing and propaganda. Their services are particularly needed in villages where they can more successfully perform the difficult task of canvassing the canons of family planning and child-welfare. In the urban area, they can efficiently take up the task of visiting and teaching the orphans, helpless widows and fallen women in orphanages and welfare centres. They can train their unfortunate sisters in sewing, knitting, spinning embroidery and other handicrafts in which women excel by nature. They can also render social services whenever there is flood, famine, earthquake or some other natural calamity.

Women surely have a very important role to play in modern India. We are busy with our plans of national reconstruction, rural uplift and all-round development of our country for its progress and prosperity. In the social, economic and political sphere women too have to shoulder the responsibilities along with men. The day is not far when the Indian women would not only catch up with their western counterparts but also regain the honourable status they enjoyed in the distant past (310 words).

(*i*) In what various capacities are women working in offices?

(*ii*) Why are women considered more efficient in work?

(*iii*) What service can women render in villages?

(*iv*) What task can be assigned to women in urban areas?

(*v*) Give one word substitution for the following: (You will find the words in the passage.) Very deep distress, equally fair and just to all.

(*vi*) Make a *précis* of the following in 1/3 of its length, giving it a suitable title.

Ans.

(*i*) Women are working as administrators, typists, clerks, receptionists and officers. They are magistrates, judges and revenue officers.

(*ii*) Women are quick to understand things and work efficiently. They have initiative and drive. They can win others to their point of view.

(*iii*) They can do a wonderful job in villages persuading women for family planning and child welfare.

(*iv*) In cities they can manage orphanages, widow homes and welfare centres. They can teach destitute and fallen women vocational subjects. They can help during emergencies.

(*v*) (*a*) calamity (*b*) impartial

(*vi*) **Women and Society**

Women are discharging very important administrative, judicial and office jobs with success. They are more efficient and intelligent than men. Women are better suited for canvassing family planning ideas in the villages. They can do a better job in cities, manning orphanages, widow homes and welfare centres. They can teach women useful vocational subject. They can offer help during emergencies. Women are taking part in economic political spheres. Very soon they will progress beyond their western counterparts.

PAPER — II

(Reading Comprehension and Written English)

Time allowed: 3 Hours **Maximum Marks : 100**

Note: Attempt **all** the questions.

Q.1 Read the passage given below and answer the questions that follow:

The world today is divided into smokers and non-smokers.

It is true that the smokers cause some nuisance to the non-smokers, but this nuisance is physical while the nuisance that the non-smokers cause the smokers is spiritual. There are, of course, lots of non-smokers who don't try to interfere with the smokers, and wives can be trained even to tolerate their husbands smoking in bed. That is the surest sign of a happy and successful marriage. It is sometimes assumed, however, that non-smokers are morally superior and they have something to be proud of, not realising that they have missed one of the greatest pleasures of mankind. I am willing to allow that smoking is a moral weakness, but on the other hand, we must beware of the man without weaknesses. He is not to be trusted. He is apt to be always sober and he cannot make a single mistake. His habits are likely to be regular, his existence more mechanical and his head always maintains its supremacy over his heart. Much as I like reasonable persons, I hate completely rational persons. For that reason I am always scared and ill at ease when I enter a house in which there are no ash-trays. Things in the room are apt to be in their right places, and people are apt to be correct and unemotional. And immediately I am put on my best behaviour, which means the same thing as the most uncomfortable behaviour.

(*i*) What are the two categories of people in the world today?
(*ii*) What kind of nuisance do smokers cause the non-smokers?
(*iii*) What kind of nuisance do non-smokers cause the smokers?
(*iv*) What do the non-smokers at times not realise?
(*v*) Why must we beware of a non-smoker?
(*vi*) What kind of life does a non-smoker lead?
(*vii*) When is the author scared and ill at ease?
(*viii*) What kind of people does the author hate?
(*ix*) What is the surest sign of a happy and successful marriage?
(*x*) Give the antonyms of (*a*) superior (*b*) moral.
(*xi*) Use in your own sentences the words (*a*) nuisance, (*b*) interfere.
(*xii*) What according to the author is the most uncomfortable behaviour?

Ans.

(*i*) The two categories of people in today's world are (*a*) smokers and (*b*) non-smokers.
(*ii*) The smokers cause physical nuisance to the non-smokers.
(*iii*) The non-smokers interfere with and try to change the habits of smokers.
(*iv*) The non-smokers at times don't realise that the smokers also live a happy life.
(*v*) A non-smoker should never be trusted, according to the author.
(*vi*) The non-smokers lead a mechanical, colourless and dull life.
(*vii*) The author is ill at ease with those who are very formal.
(*viii*) The author hates those people who are totally rational.
(*ix*) The surest sign of happiness in marriage is toleration and understanding of the partner's weaknesses, e.g. letting the smoker smoke in bed.
(*x*) (*a*) inferior (*b*) immoral.
(*xi*) (*a*) Loudspeakers at night have their nuisance value.
(*b*) He always interferes in my work.
(*xii*) The most uncomfortable behaviour is when people are ceremonious and formal.

Q.2 Read the above passage once again and make a précis of it in not more than one third of its length and provide a suitable title.

Ans. Smokers and Non-Smokers:

Both smokers and non-smokers harm each other. The smokers disturb the non-smokers physically but the non-smokers upset the smokers spiritually. Wives of the smokers tolerate their husbands and lead a happy life. It is a truth that smoking is a weakness but a non-smoker is not essentially a better man. A non-smoker should never be trusted. It is very difficult to be with non-smokers who are unemotional and formal.

Q.3 Write a paragraph of about 150 words on "The Habit of Reading Newspapers".

Ans. The Habit of Reading Newspapers:

Newspapers are as important as is our diet. Breakfast is an enjoyable meal. But breakfast without the newspaper is colourless. The press through newspapers gives us news and views about everything around, and reaches everywhere. Newsmen scattered all over the world, send news as quickly as possible. The newspapers keep us alive. Newspapers also give us short and interesting pieces on diverse topics. The magazine section has food for all tastes. It has sports section. It has fashion columns and literary portions as well. There are sections for children. One can improve one's general knowledge and vocabulary through newspapers. It has been said by Gandhiji that a newspaper is stronger than a gun. The press makes and spreads public opinion. No government howsoever powerful can ignore the press. Those who read the newspapers, magazines and journals are alert people and can take part in any discussion.

Q.4 Write a letter to the Editor of a newspaper calling attention to the vulgarity of a serial being shown on the T.V.

Ans. 43 Raghubir Nagar New Delhi
19-4-1997
The Editor
The Hindu
New Delhi-110002

Dear Sir,

I am disturbed at the vulgar television serials telecast by Star Plus. These sexualised and vulgar programmes are telecast at prime time. One can not have lunch with one's children and sisters. Similarly, at night time, it is impossible to have dinner. There are suggestive dialogues. There are semi-nude scenes. There are vulgar remarks. Cinema dances are very obscene. These programmes are harming our children's young minds. I request the government to put a ban on such programmes so that social health is not harmed further.

Yours truly
Radha Krishan Sharma

Q.5 Write a dialogue between Geeta and Rajni discussing the reforms they would like to see introduced in the present system of examinations.

Ans. **Geeta:** My annuals have unnerved me. How about you?

Rajni: I don't care. I'm all on the rock.

Geeta: I have prepared so many topics. But then who knows what the examiner wants?

Rajni: I have mugged only seven topics. I don't want to mug more.

Geeta: I hate the mugging part of our exams. Why don't they ask us to be original and innovative?

Rajni: I understand in America there is no annual exam. The students choose their own subjects and their own teachers.

Geeta: Raju, we are in India. Don't you think things travel too slowly in India. We'll have such a system over here too but after we are dead.

Rajni: I am a brilliant child and can write marvellously if I am given freedom to choose my subjects.

Geeta: Wait for a life time.

Q.6 Complete the following dialogue between.

Ram : You are much absorbed in the novel you are reading. I wonder why you have taken such a fancy to novels.

Mohan: ....

Ram: ....

Mohan: Yes, this is all true but a moderate amount of novel reading is beneficial.

Ram: ....

Mohan: Historical novels give us a brilliant picture of history.

Ram: I agree with you. Are novels of any intellectual utility also?

Mohan: ....

Ram: It is very kind of you to have thrown light on this important subject.

Mohan: ....

Ans. **Ram:** You are much absorbed in the novel you are reading. I wonder why you have taken such a fancy to novels.

Mohan: I love historical novels.

Ram: Don't you agree with me that excess novel reading is bad?

Mohan: Yes, that is true but a moderate amount of novel reading is beneficial.

Ram: But why do you read historical stuff?

Mohan: Historical novels give us a brilliant picture of history.

Ram: I agree with you. Are novels of any intellectual value also?

Mohan: Yeah, they keep us mentally agile and alive.

Ram: It is very kind of you to have thrown light on this important subject.

Mohan: That's my pleasure.

Q.7 There are fourteen blanks in the following passage. Fill in these blanks with words that suit the sense of the passage.

The most important thing is that we should have freedom of thought. This is not as easy ______ it sounds for everyone ______ to have this freedom for ______, but is not ready to ______ it to others when they ______ different opinion. This is particularly ______ case when differences of ______ arise on important matters like ______ or politics. But if we ______ to let other people hold ______ opinion on these matters, and ______ if we try to force ______ to accept our own, progress ______ impossible. If everyone went on thinking the ______ things, progress would come to end. Therefore, we must try to study all sides of the topic that comes before us.

Ans. 1. as 2. likes 3. himself 4. give 5. hold/have 6. the 7. opinion 8. religion 9. refuse 10. their 11. also 12. them 13. is 14. same.

PAPER — III

(Reading Comprehension and Written English)

Time allowed: 3 Hours **Maximum Marks : 100**

Attempt **all** the questions.

Q.1 Read the passage given below and answer the questions that follow:

More damaging than ozone depletion, and far harder to control, is the greenhouse effect caused in large part by carbon dioxide. The effect of carbon dioxide in the atmosphere is comparable to the glass of a greenhouse. It lets in the warming rays of the sun but keeps the excess heat from re-radiating back into space. Man contributes to the greenhouse effect through carbon dioxide generated by the burning of fossil fuels. This is hastening a global warming trend. In the decades ahead, scientists predict drastically altered weather patterns, major shifts of deserts and fertile regions, intensification of tropical storms and rise in sea-level caused mainly by the expansion of sea water as it warms up.

Unlike ozone depletion, the greenhouse effect has some positive consequences. It prevents the earth from being an ice frozen planet. But the massive burning of coal, for instance, which pumps large quantities of carbon dioxide into the atmosphere, might be too much of a good thing. By the year 2050, if the present rate of burning of fossil fuel continues, the earth will be much warmer. The consequences would be disastrous. The plains could become a dust bowl.

Some of the excess heat would be trapped by the oceans which have an enormous heat absorbing capacity, but this heat would have to be released over the year. Nations are already worried over deforestation, especially of the Amazon rain forest in Brazil, which has been slashed for mining and agriculture. When trees are burnt, or when they rot, carbon dioxide and other gases are released. In 1987, some nations signed an accord to limit production and use of chlorofluorocarbons. A more important step is to protect the tropical rain forests and cut back on the use of fossil fuels by using alternative forms of fuel.

(*a*) What are the causes of the Greenhouse effect and how does man contribute to it?

(*b*) Are there any positive consequences of the Greenhouse effect?

(*c*) Why are nations worried about deforestation?

(*d*) Give antonyms of the following words: expansion, accord, depletion.

(*e*) Write a paragraph of about 100 words on 'Problems of Pollution Today'.

Ans.

(*a*) Carbon dioxide causes the greenhouse effect, *i.e.* heat is trapped on earth. Man contributes to the greenhouse effect through carbon dioxide generated by the burning of fossil fuel.

(*b*) The greenhouse effect prevents the earth from being an ice frozen planet.

(*c*) The nations are worried about deforestation because burning of trees releases carbon dioxide and other harmful gases. Trees help by releasing oxygen into the atmosphere.

(*d*) (*i*) curtailment/decrease

(*ii*) discord/disagreement/conflict

(*iii*) repletion, plenty

(*e*) **Problems of Pollution Today**

Pollution rather superpollution is a global problem. The world is caught in a vicious circle. Medicinal advancement has reduced death rate but that has increased population manifold. Each state has cleared forests to set plants, nuclear thermal units to provide mass produced goods for more mouths. If we don't have automatic plants we will starve crores of people. If we have them, then we will die a slow poisonous death. Each megacity is a burning volcano and inferno and people are boiling in it like popcorn. No metropolis can afford pure water, pure air, and pure environment because of industry associated arteries such as transport system, slums etc. Today man has much to eat but less to enjoy. In Japan, Tokyo and Osaka are most polluted cities. London, New York and Delhi are no better. We have to decongest and depopulate cities and rehabilitate people in villages. We have to deurbanise and reruralise people's psyche. People in megacities are prone to many illnesses due to pollution.

Q.2 Read the poem and answer the questions given below

Some of us may die
Remember, statistically
It is not likely to be you
All flags are flying full dressed
On Government buildings—the sun is shining.
Death is the least we have to fear.
We are all in the hands of God.
Whatever happens by His will.
Now go quickly to your shelters.

(*a*) Identify the figure of speech in these lines and discuss its significance.

(*b*) Discuss the poet's attitude to God and religion in this poem.

Ans.

(a) There are three similes suggesting destruction. Bombers are heralders, flags of death, the sun which brings light here brings death and shelter that protects here brings death, and shelter that protects here ruins. In the whole poem Death is the central metaphor which shows no escape from nuclear bombing.

(b) The poet ridicules man's faith in God. It is nuclear bombing by the state that, ruins man. How is God responsible for such horrendous acts? It is not God's will to eliminate mankind through bombing. In fact the author appears to be a leftist atheist.

Q.3 Read the passage and answer the questions given below.

Cataract is the major cause of blindness. Blindness is also caused by damage to the cornea. As one starts growing old, the lens of the eye hardens, loses its transparency and becomes opaque. It obstructs the light rays from entering the eye. This opaque lens is called cataract.

The onset of cataract blurs the vision. Sometimes, the cataract patient sees multiple images instead of a single object image. Some patients complain of watering in the eyes. Because of the gradual development of cataract, the afflicted person loses his/her vision and the world becomes dark to him/her.

The development is a complex, multifactorial process. However, the following factors can be attributed to its formation and development. Cataract generally develops in old age though the process starts when a man is in his forties. Sometimes, children are born with cataract because of hereditary defects. Eye injuries can cause cataract too. Diabetes is one of the common causes of the formation of cataract. Under-nutrition, especially the deficiency of vitamin A, B and C, proteins, etc., in our diet plays a vital role in the formation of cataract.

People exposed to sun rays for longer periods because of the nature of their jobs develop cataract earlier than others. It has been discovered that cataract is formed because of smoking also. Researchers opine the smoke, which is inhaled, carries substances internally damaging to the eyes, and may cause harm to them.

Ultra-violet radiation, invisible to the human eye, is linked to cataract and skin cancer. The patient 'victim' loses vision and the world becomes dark to him. No eye-drops or tablets can cure this cataract. The only cure of cataract is an operation. The eye surgeon removes the opaque lens and transplants an intralocular lens in its place.

(*a*) What are the causes of cataract?

(*b*) Write down *five* main topic sentences from the given passage.

(*c*) Make a précis of the given passage in about 1/3 of the length, giving a suitable title.

Ans.

(*a*) The causes of cataract are: old age, hereditary defect, eye injuries, diabetes, under-nutrition (deficiency of vitamins A, B and C)

(*b*) 1. Cataract is the main cause of blindness.
2. The development is a complex, multifactorial process.
3. People exposed to sun rays for longer periods because of the nature of their jobs develop cataract earlier than others.
4. Ultra-violet radiation invisible to the human eye is linked to cataract.
5. No eye drops or tablets can cure this cataract.

(*c*) Cataract is a major disease which causes blindness. Old age damages the cornea and it becomes opaque. A cataract patient sees blurred or multiple images. Eye injuries, diabetes, undernutrition, deficiency of vitamins A, B, C, proteins continued job based exposure to violet sun rays, smoking are a few main causes that bring cataract. Ultra-violet rays can not be seen by naked eyes. They cause cancer and cataract. Ultra-violet caused cataract can not be cured by eye drops. Operation is the only cure.

PAPER — IV

(Reading Comprehension, Reading Ability and Written English)

Time allowed: 3 Hours **Maximum Marks : 100**

Attempt **all** the questions.

Q.1 Read the following passage and answer the questions that follow:

To be a good teacher, you need some of the gifts of the good actor: you must be able to hold the attention and interest of your audience : you must be a clear speaker, with a good, strong, pleasing voice which is fully under your control; and you must be able to act what you are teaching, in order to make your meaning clear.

Watch a good teacher, and you will see that he does not sit motionless before his class: he stands the whole time he is teaching; he walks about using his arms, hands and fingers to help him in his explanation, and his face to express feeling, listen to him, and you will hear the loudness, the quality and the musical note of his voice always changing according to what he is talking about.

The fact that a good teacher has some of the fits of a good actor does not mean that he will indeed be able to act well on the stage; for there are very important differences between the teacher's work and the actor's. The actor has to speak words which he has learnt by heart, he has to repeat exactly the same words each time he plays a certain part: even his movements and the ways in which he uses his voice are usually fixed before. What he has to do is to make all these carefully learnt words and actions seem natural on the stage. The good teacher works in quite a different way. His audience takes an active part: they ask and answer questions, they obey orders, and if they do not understand something they say so. The teacher, therefore, has to suit his act to the needs of his audience, which is his class. He cannot learn his part by heart, but must invent it as he goes along.

I have known many teachers who were fine actors in class but were unable to take part in a stage-play because their brains would not keep discipline: they could not keep strictly to what another had written.

(*i*) Name one quality of a good teacher.

(*ii*) What is the similarity between a teacher and an actor?

(*iii*) What does a teacher do while teaching?

(*iv*) What does a teacher do with his voice as he is teaching?

(*v*) What is the difference between the teacher's work and the actor's?

(*vi*) How does the teacher's audience take part in his 'play'?

(*vii*) Why must a teacher invent as he goes along?

(*viii*) What has an actor to do when he is on the stage?

(*ix*) Why does a teacher not sit motionless before his class?

(*x*) What does a teacher do in order to make his meaning clear?

(*xi*) Give the opposite of :

(*a*) active

(*b*) discipline.

(xii) Why are some of the finest teachers unable to take part in a stage-play?

Ans.

(*i*) A good teacher is also a gifted actor.

(*ii*) A good teacher and an actor are both clear speakers, have pleasing voices, and fascinate the audience with a clear meaning.

(*iii*) A teacher stands, walks about, expressing his feelings.

(*iv*) His voice is clear, musical and changes with the subject and feel of his teaching.

(*v*) An actor has to speak words which he has learnt by heart, he has to repeat exactly the same words each time he plays a certain role. Even his movements and expressions should not change. He utters learnt words naturally on the stage. But a teacher's audience is actively involved in his teaching. They ask questions, they obey orders, and feel resentment if they do not understand something. A teacher learns and adjusts his role daily.

(*vi*) A teacher's audience asks questions and seeks clarification on doubts.

(*vii*) He must invent as he teaches to engage the interest of his live and active audience.

(*viii*) On the stage an actor must play his part naturally.

(*ix*) He can not do so for fear of the class losing interest in his teaching.

(*x*) He modulates, fluctuates his voice, moves around while teaching.

(*xi*) (*a*) passive/inaetive.

(*b*) indiscipline.

(*xii*) They cannot do so because they can not cram and execute roles mechanically.

Q.2 Read the passage given above once again and make a précis of it. Also give it a suitable title.

Ans. A Good Teacher

A good teacher and good actors are similar. They have clear voices and make their meaning clear. Neither a good teacher nor a good actor sits motionless. A good teacher moves about as he teaches. He modulates his voice. He addresses a live audience. A good actor can perform his role after good learning. He cannot change the script or the tone. He has no freedom. A good teacher has to answer his audience's doubts. He invents new ways of controlling and explaining things to his class. A good teacher is an actor but not a stage actor.

Q.3 Write a letter to the Deputy Commissioner of Police, North Zone, New Delhi, complaining about the theft of your car and the inaction on the part of the local police.

Ans.

Dated: 17th July, 1999

212 Ram Nagar, Delhi

The Deputy Commissioner of Police

North Zone, New Delhi.

Subject: Complaint regarding theft of car & Police Inaction

Dear Sir

My car DLW 7080 Maruti 800 was stolen from my home on the night of 13th July, 1999 between 10 pm and 11:30 pm. I lodged a complaint with the police after their reluctance to take suitable action. The police staff was rude and crude and totally discourteous. One month has passed but nothing has been done.

I shall be obliged if you direct the police to take an active line of investigation.

Thanking you

Yours truly

R.K. Khanna

Q.4 Write a paragraph of about 100 words on 'The Advantages' of a Morning Walk'.

Ans. The Advantages of a Morning Walk

Wee hours are happy hours. The world is asleep. You get up early. You get ready and go for a morning walk. Nature is at its best. All is cool and quiet. The great gigantic monstrous Delhi is still sleeping. There is no voice, no sound. You breathe pleasant breeze, fragrant wind with the chirping birds around. There is no traffic, no crowd, you are your own master. You sing, you dance, you giggle, you are away from all anxieties. Pure air in the morning purifies your lungs. You get oxygen for the whole day. Those who get up early finish their day's work before others leave their beds. They feel active the whole day.

Q.5 Write a dialogue between two friends Geeta and Mohini on whether students should take part in politics or not. Geeta favours it while Mohini is against it.

Ans.

Geeta : Hi ! Mohini. How are you?

Mohini : I've been away to Shimla for ten days. How are you?

Geeta : We're fine. Don't you know I'm contesting college union elections this year?

Mohini : It's news to me. I feel such elections are too political and waste precious time of youth.

Geeta : No, these are prepolitical elections. They prepare leaders for the nation. They teach them how to be responsible.

Mohini : That's true. But in actual practice, each election is a display of muscle power or money power. And what do our students fight for?

Geeta : They fight for the students' rights and against the high handedness of the authorities.

Mohini : Well, that's what you think. I'm dead opposed to all such things.

Q.6 Complete the following dialogue:

Rajesh : Good Morning, Mohan, You are reading 'The Indian Express'. I don't understand what good onc gets from newspapers.

Mohan : (*i*)..........................

Rajesh : (*ii*)..........................

Mohan : Most of the newspapers which people read are either very poor reading or positively harmful.

Rajesh : (*iii*)..........................

Mohan : (*iv*)............................

Rajesh : But there are many newspapers that maintain a very high standard.

Mohan : (*v*)...................................

Rajesh : Yes, to some extent. But the Press is also a power in today's world.

Ans.

(*i*) Well, it makes me aware of the world around me.

(*ii*) Why don't you read vernacular papers ?

(*iii*) But, not all of them.

(*iv*) Of course, you are right. But I have my choice.

(*v*) Some focus on trivial issues.

Q.7 Read the following passage. Every seventh word in the passage is missing. Fill in the blanks with words that suit the sense of the passage. The first and last sentences are given in full.

The English people are not capable of choosing their leaders because they have never given serious thought to education for citizenship. They believe that a good liberal ...1... fits them well for the vocation ...2... citizenship. This is true in the ...3... of a University graduate who, after ....4.... his education, devotes enough time to ...5... public affairs. But a businessman or ....6.... man who is preoccupied with his ...7... trade or profession does not learn ...8... about politics to form independent views. ...9... education in languages or sciences does ...10... make one a competent citizen. A man who is an expert in languages or physical sciences knows little about the political and economic affairs of his country.

Ans.

1. education	**2.** of	**3.** case
4. completing	**5.** learn	**6.** trades
7. individual	**8.** enough	**9.** Liberal
10. not		

PAPER — V

(Reading Comprehension and Written English)

Time allowed: 3 Hours **Maximum Marks : 100**

Attempt **all** the questions.

SECTION A

Q.1 Draft an application in response to the following Advertisement:

"We require the following persons immediately :

(*i*) Accountants

(*ii*) Accounts Assistants.

Suitable candidates with detailed bio-data may apply immediately. Lakshmi Motor Company, S. P. Mukerjee Marg, Delhi 110 006.

OR

Draft a sales letter to be sent to all retailers/ Department stores to promote the sale of new hosiery items, that your company (H.Lon Hosiery Ltd) manufactures with Japanese collaboration.

Ans.

April 23, 1994

M/s. Lakshmi Motor Company

S.P. Mukherjee Marg

Delhi 110006

Sub : Application for the post of Accounts Assistant

Dear Sir,

In response to your advertisement that appeared in 'The Hindustan Times' of April, 12, 1994, I wish to offer my candidature for the post of Accounts Assistant in your firm. Attached herewith is my bio-data and I would be glad if I am considered for the above position with your company.

Name : Mohinder Narain

Father's Name : Late Shri Partap Narain

Date of Birth : May 26, 1967

Educational Qualification:

(*i*) Passed Senior Secondary Examination from C.B.S.E. with Commerce as one of subjects with 58% marks.

(*ii*) Passed B.Com. (Pass) from Delhi University with 55% marks.

(*iii*) Passed Diploma in Financial Accounting from Indira Gandhi National Open University.

Professional Experience : Worked as Accounts Assistant with M/s Bharat Gas for a period of six months.

Salary Expected : Rs 3000/- P.M.

In the event of my selection to the post, I can assure you of my best performance. I am confident that I am the right candidate for the post advertised by you.

Thanking you.

Yours faithfully

Mohinder Narain

OR

H. LON HOSIERY LTD

(A Japanese Collaboration)

Date : 2-4-1994.

Through this circular, the company intends to approach its valued Retailers and Department Stores spread out in the length and breadth of the country to promote the sale of our new hosiery items such as socks, underwear, and vests. You must have seen by now that the new hosiery items manufactured by our company are far superior to any of the similar items produced by other companies in the market. We use the finest thread for the manufacture of these items and these last longer and are very comfortable. These items do not effect the skin in any kind of harmful manner. Considering all these advantages, we expect more and more customers to opt for these items in preference to similar items in the market. We, therefore, call upon our Retailers and Department Stores to bring home these advantages to the notice of their valued customers and even offer replacements in case of any defect within a specified period. Hope these observations would act as good guidelines for the promotion of these new items.

For General Manager

Q.2 As Personnel Manager of B.E.L., write a report for circulation among all department heads of different units for staff punctuality and attendance and also give suggestions for remedial action.

Or

Imagine you are the marketing manager of a company dealing in tyres and tubes. Write a report for your boss explaining why sales have fallen and what steps you are taking to control and improve the situation.

Ans.

BHARAT ELECTRONICS LIMITED
Bhikhaji Cama Place, New Delhi

To
The Heads of the Departments
of the Company

Dear Sirs,

Reports of irregularity of attendance of the employees in all the departments of the company have reached the Head office. The employees are not checked on coming late to the office and they often leave early without seeking permission from the competent authorities. This indifferent attitude regarding the attendance of the employees is not proper because it adversely affects the production of the company. It also sets a bad example for the new employees and interferes with the proper discipline of the company. The company would therefore, call upon all of you to follow the norms of attendance strictly and insist on the punctuality of all the employees without any distinction. Relaxation may be made only in very special cases. Those, who are regular late comers, should be strictly dealt with and follow up action should be taken against them for their irregular attendance immediately. This may kindly be enforced very strictly.

Personnel Manager

OR

MRF Tyres
New Delhi-15

Sir,

The sale accounts of the preceding year show a sharp decline in the sale of all kinds of our tyres. This may be due to the influx of a number of new varieties of tyres in the market. But there should certainly be no reason for the decline in the sales as the tyres and tubes manufactured by our company have stood the test of time and have proved their superiority over almost all the tyres available in the market. The reason for this decline has to be ascertained and efforts made for the situation to be remedied. We will have to call upon our agencies to make proper advertising on mass media and offer certain incentives to our valued customers. We should also make sure that our tyres and tubes are made available easily in accordance with the customer's requirement. If we are able to make our tyres and tubes available at all popular showrooms and also at several service stations and petrol pumps, we are sure to boost the sales.

Sd/- Marketing Manager

Q.3 Read the following paragraph carefully and answer the question that follow:

Two thousand years of incessant thought and analysis have not answered Pontius Pilate's question: "What is Truth?" Many definitions have been attempted and given up as inadequate. Many more will be considered and abandoned. But the quest for a truthful life never ceases. It is more than urgent to-day when values are crumbling and the age-old platitudes fail to act as social or moral analgesics. The disintegration of the social order and the values that sustained it began long ago, even though in a muted form initially. The feudal order had a place for everybody, though not necessarily under the Sun. Social and individual relationships were based on land and tempered by romanticism, religion, and built-in checks and balances. In fact like the 'overmighty Barons' in England during the Hundred Year War and before the Rise of the Tudors, they often held kings virtually captive. Monarchy reasserted itself with the rise of the nation-states. But in some countries it soon had to face fresh challenges. In England, its powers ceased to be absolute after the 1688 revolution. Elsewhere, it frequently reasserted its primacy. This is because no institutional barrier could be set up against absolutism.

(*i*) Are no definitions of Truth attempted now?

(*ii*) Has the quest for Truth stopped now?

(*iii*) What was the purpose of giving lands to the feudal lords?

(*iv*) What were the bases for social and individual relationships during the feudal days?

(*v*) What happened to the system of Monarchy in England and else where after the 1688 revolution?

Ans.

(*i*) Definitions of Truth are attempted even now even though they may be given up as inadequate.

(*ii*) No, it has not ceased as yet.

(*iii*) The feudal lords were given land in order to keep the social order intact. It was a contract between the lords and the king, that the Lords would provide soldiers to the king in times of war.

(*iv*) Social and individual relationships were based on land and tempered by romanticism, religion and built-in checks and balances during the feudal days.

(*v*) In England, the powers of Monarchy ceased to be absolute after the 1688 Revolution. Elsewhere, it frequently re-asserted its primacy.

Q.4 Prepare a précis of the passage in Q.3 in about 90 words and give a suitable title.

Ans.

Title: Eternal Quest for Truth

It is difficult to have a precise definition of Truth though it has been attempted in the past and the answers given up as inadequate.

But the question for a truthful life never ceases and it is more urgent today when values are crumbling. The disintegration of social order and the values that sustained it, began long ago. During the feudal days, social and individual relationships were based on land. Monarchy reasserted with the rise of the nation-states though its powers were lost after the 1688 revolution in England but it reasserted its primacy elsewhere.

Q.5 (*a*) Rewrite the following sentences, making corrections wherever necessary:

(*i*) He entered in the compartment single-handed.

(*ii*) They are confident to win the elections without any alliance.

(*iii*) Shyam is holding the post for the last six months.

(*iv*) The dowry system has been in vogue since time immemorial.

(*v*) At present there is a little hope of survival for those infected with AIDS.

(*vi*) He has returned back the money only a little ago.

(*vii*) He denied to accept my invitation for a friendly match.

(*viii*) Have either of you seen my book?

(*ix*) I feel hesitance in going to meet the Principal.

(*x*) I inquired from him that why he is so negligent in his studies.

(*b*) Write down the odd word in each of the following groups of words:

(*i*) Adversity, Poverty, Severity, Charity

(*ii*) Chairman, President, Citizen, Boss

(*iii*) Appreciation, Incentive, Rebuff, Approval

(*iv*) Corporation, Company, Association, Undertaking.

(*v*) Arthritis, Meningitis, Citrus, Sinusitis.

Ans.

(*a*) (*i*) He entered the compartment single-handed.

(*ii*) They are confident of winning the elections without any alliance.

(*iii*) Shyam has been holding the post for the last six month.

(*iv*) The dowry system has been in vogue from time immemorial.

(*v*) At present there is little hope of survival for those infected with AIDS.

(*vi*) He returned the money only a little while ago.

(*vii*) He refused to accept my invitation for a friendly match.

(*viii*) Has either of you seen my book?

(*ix*) I feel hesitant in going to meet the Principal.

(*x*) I inquired of him why he was so negligent in his studies.

(*b*) (*i*) Charity (*ii*) Citizen (*iii*) Rebuff (*iv*) Association (*v*) Citrus

PAPER — VI

Time allowed: 3 Hours **Maximum Marks : 100**

Attempt **all** the questions.

Directions: **Q. 1–6 :** In the following question, each sentence has four underlined words or phrases. Choose the one word or phrase that must be changed for the sentence to be correct.

1. Species <u>like</u> (I) snakes, lizards, coyotes and squirrels <u>seems</u> (II) to exist <u>quite happily</u> (III) in <u>the</u> (IV) desert.

(*a*) I (*b*) II
(*c*) III (*d*) IV

2. Cholesterol <u>help</u> (I) the body <u>by making</u> (II) hormones and building cell walls but <u>too much</u> (III) cholesterol <u>can cause</u> (IV) heart problems.

(*a*) I (*b*) II
(*c*) III (*d*) IV

3. <u>Many</u> (I) people say that Kerala <u>is a State</u> (II) of remarkable <u>geographic</u> (III) <u>diversity</u> (IV).

(*a*) I (*b*) II
(*c*) III (*d*) IV

4. <u>Certain</u> (I) pollens are more <u>likely</u> (II) to cause <u>an allergic</u> (III) reaction than <u>another.</u> (IV)

(*a*) I (*b*) II
(*c*) III (*d*) IV

5. The child was so <u>spoiled</u> (I) by her <u>parents</u> (II) that she pouted and <u>sullen</u> (III) when she did not receive all of their <u>attention.</u> (IV)

(*a*) I (*b*) II
(*c*) III (*d*) IV

6. Your <u>dilatory</u> (I) tactics may <u>compels</u> (II) me to cancel <u>the contract</u> (III) as the job must be finished <u>on time.</u> (IV)

(*a*) I (*b*) II
(*c*) III (*d*) IV

Directions: **Q. 7–12:** In the following questions, choose the word that is almost similar in meaning to the word in capital letters.

7. QUACK
(*a*) Pyromaniac (*b*) Charlatan
(*c*) Dilemma (*d*) Victim

8. VISAGE
(*a*) Appearance (*b*) Doubt
(*c*) Hermitage (*d*) Armour

9. MASTICATE
(*a*) Swallow (*b*) Organise
(*c*) Meander (*d*) Chew

10. MAWKISH
(*a*) Certain (*b*) Devious
(*c*) Sentimental (*d*) Carefree

11. MILITANT
(*a*) Dramatic (*b*) Religious
(*c*) Combative (*d*) Quaint

12. OSTENSIBLE
(*a*) Apparent (*b*) Elaborate
(*c*) Traditional (*d*) Showy

Directions: **Q. 13–18:** In the following question, a word is given in capital letters, choose the word that is almost opposite in meaning to it.

13. OMNISCIENT
(*a*) Ignorant (*b*) Isolated
(*c*) Trivial (*d*) Weak

14. PARANOIA
(*a*) Fracture (*b*) Sanity
(*c*) Quantity (*d*) Statement

15. PERMEABLE
(*a*) Perishable (*b*) Impenetrable
(*c*) Porous (*d*) Everlasting

16. SQUANDER
(a) Fortify (b) Forfeit
(c) Depart (d) Preserve
17. NOTORIOUS
(a) Invincible (b) Clever
(c) Successful (d) Renowned
18. GIGANTIC
(a) Elegant (b) Lilliputian
(c) Barren (d) Destructive

***Directions:* Q. 19–24:** In the following questions, a related pair of word is followed by four pairs of words. Choose the pair that best expresses a relationship similar to that expressed in the original pair.

19. Musician : Conservatory ::?
(a) Lawyer : Litigation
(b) Carpenter : Saw
(c) Miner : Quarry
(d) King : Coronation
20. Braggart: Boast ::?
(a) Trickster : Risk
(b) Stickler : Insist
(c) Mumbler : Enunciate
(d) Haggler : Concede
21. Reverie : Dreamy ::?
(a) Acquaintanceship: Brief
(b) Tryst : Clandestine
(c) Journey : Leisurely
(d) Expectation : Hopeless
22. Sadist : Pain ::?
(a) Alcohol : Dipsomaniac
(b) Injury : Bandage
(c) Teacher : Pupil
(d) Killer : Death
23. Flow : Ebb :: ?
(a) River : Flow (b) Tide : Sea
(c) Wax : Wane (d) Edge : Cliff
24. Metaphor : Figurative :: ?
(a) Epic : History
(b) Fable : Contemporary
(c) Irony : Dramatic
(d) Precept : Instructive

***Directions:* Q. 25–30 :** In the following questions, select the words that best fill the blanks.

25. Sheila could endure the __________ of society, but her family's aloofness was of greater concern.
(a) solecism (b) ostracism
(c) bonhomie (d) solarism
26. The law imposing penalties for frivolous suits should dampen the __________ instincts of opportunists.
(a) litigious (b) vacuous
(c) puerile (d) ambivalent
27. Many people in a democracy fail to exercise their hard-won __________.
(a) suffrage. (b) subsistence.
(c) anarchy. (d) jurisprudence.
28. Since she believed him to be both candid and trustworthy, she refused to consider the possibility that his statement had been __________.
(a) irrelevant. (b) mistaken.
(c) insincere. (d) critical.
29. This paper intends to __________ fearlessly all forms of corruption and falsehood in public life.
(a) expose (b) present
(c) uncover (d) influence
30. The world is __________ a serious energy problem.
(a) heading (b) braving
(c) facing (d) confronting

***Directions:* Q. 31–35 :** Read the following passage carefully and then answer the question that are based on what is stated or implied in the passage.

When the same parameters and quantitative theory are used to analyse both termite colonies and troops of rhesus macaques, we will have a unified science of socio-biology. Can this ever really happen? As my own studies have advanced, I have been increasingly impressed with the functional similarities between insect and vertebrate societies and less so with the structural differences that seem, at first glance, to constitute such an immense gulf between them. Consider for a moment termites and macaques. Both form cooperative groups that occupy territories. In both kinds of society there is a well-marked division of labour. Members of both groups communicate to each others hunger, alarm, hostility, caste status or rank, and reproductive status. From the specialist's point of view, this comparison may at first seem

facile— or worse. But it is out of such deliberate oversimplification that the beginnings of a general theory are made.

31. Which of the following best summarises the author's main point?
(*a*) Understanding the ways in which animals as different as termites and rhesus macaques resemble each other requires training in both biology and sociology.
(*b*) Animals as different as termites and rhesus macaques follow certain similar and predictable patterns of behaviour.
(*c*) A study of the similarities between insect and vertebrate societies could provide the basis for a unified science of sociobiology.
(*d*) Most animals organise themselves into societies that exhibit patterns of group behaviour similar to those of human societies.

32. What is the central theme of the passage?
(*a*) Biological research
(*b*) Termites and rhesus between insects and vertebrates.
(*c*) Sociobiology.
(*d*) Structural dissimilarities between insects and vertebrates.

33. In discussing insect and vertebrate societies the author suggests which of the following?
(*a*) The caste structure of insect societies is similar to that of vertebrate societies.
(*b*) There are significant structural differences between insect and vertebrate societies.
(*c*) The means of communication among members of insect societies is similar to that among members of vertebrate societies.
(*d*) Most insect and vertebrate societies form co-operative groups in order to occupy territory.

34. Which of the following words could best be substituted for: "facile" (printed in **bold**) without substantially changing the author's meaning?
(*a*) Paltry (*b*) Specific
(*c*) Whimsical (*d*) Remarkable.

35. The author's attitude towards the possibility of a unified theory in sociobiology is best described as of:
(*a*) guarded optimism.
(*b*) objective indifference.
(*c*) dissatisfaction.
(*d*) enthusiasm.

***Directions:* Q. 36–40 :** Read the following passage carefully and then answer the question which are based on what is stated or implied in the passage.

Langston Hughes was one of the greatest American writers of the 20th century. He was born in Joplin, Missouri, and moved to Cleveland at the age of fourteen. Several years later he spent one year in Mexico before attending Columbia University in New York. For a few years after that he roamed the world as a seaman, visiting ports around the world and writing some poetry. He returned to the United States and attended Lincoln University, where he won the Witter Bynner Prize for under-graduate poetry. After graduating in 1928, he travelled to Spain and to Russia with the help of a Guggenheim fellowship. His novels include *Not Without Laughter* (1930) and *The Big Sea* (1940). He wrote an autobiography in 1956 and also published several collections of poetry. *The Dream Keeper* (1932), *Shakespeare in Harlem* (1942), *Fields of Wonder* (1947), *One Way Ticket* (1947), and *Selected Poems* (1959). A man of many talents, Hughes was also a lyricist, librettist, and a journalist. As an older man in the 1960s he spent much of his time collecting poems from Africa and from African-Americans to popularise black writers. Hughes is one of the most accomplished writers in American literary history, and he is seen as one of the artistic leaders of the Harlem Renaissance, the period when a neighbourhood that was predominantly black produced a **flood** of great literature, music, and other art forms depicting daily city life for African-Americans.

36. What is the main topic of this passage?
(*a*) African-American Writers.
(*b*) The Life of Langston Hughes.
(*c*) The Harlem Renaissance.
(*d*) American 20th Century Writer.

37. What provided Hughes with assistance for his travel to Spain and Russia?
    (*a*) A literary fellowship.
    (*b*) His job as a reporter.
    (*c*) His career as a soldier.
    (*d*) A college study programme.
38. According to the author, what did Hughes do during the later years of his life?
    (*a*) Wrote short stories.
    (*b*) Popularise African-American writers.
    (*c*) Advocate racial equality.
    (*d*) Wrote about life.
39. The author uses the word "flood" (printed in **bold**) to refer to
    (*a*) an outpouring. (*b*) a drought.
    (*c*) a cloud burst. (*d*) a streak.
40. According to the passage. Hughes was all of the following except.
    (*a*) a novelist. (*b*) a poet.
    (*c*) a historian. (*d*) a journalist.

ANSWERS

1. **(*b*)**: 'Seems' should be replaced with 'seem'.
2. **(*a*)**: 'help' should be replaced with 'helps'.
3. **(*c*)**: 'geographic' should be replaced with 'geographical.'
4. **(*d*)**: 'another' should be replaced with 'others'.
5. **(*c*)**: 'sullen' should be replaced with 'became sullen'.
6. **(*b*)**: 'compels' should be replaced with 'compel'.
7. **(*b*)**: Quack means a person who pretends to have special knowledge and skill especially in medicine. Its synonym is 'charlatan.'
8. **(*a*)**: Visage means face or expression. Its synonym is 'appearance'.
9. **(*d*)**: Masticate means to reduce. Its synonym is 'chew'.
10. **(*c*)**: Mawkish means tending to indulge in the emotions excessively. Its synonym is 'sentimental'.
11. **(*c*)**: Militant means aggressive or vigorous. Its synonym is 'combative'.
12. **(*a*)**: Ostensible means stated, though perhaps not true. Its synonym is 'apparent'.
13. **(*a*)**: Omniscient means having infinite knowledge or understanding. Its antonym is 'ignorant'.
14. **(*b*)**: Paranoia means abnormal tendency to suspect and mistrust other people. Its antonym is 'sanity'.
15. **(*b*)**: Permeable means that can be permeated by fluids or gas. Its antonym is impenetrable.
16. **(*d*)**: Squander means waste. Its antonym is 'preserve'.
17. **(*d*)**: Notorious means known for some bad quality or deed. Its antonym is 'renowned'.
18. **(*b*)**: Gigantic means very great in size or extent. Its antonym is 'Lilliputian'.
19. **(*c*)**: Conservatory is school where music is taught whereas miner works in a quarry.
20. **(*b*)**: Boast is related to braggart, while stickler is related to insist.
21. **(*c*)**: Reverie is related to dreams, while journey is related to leisure.
22. **(*d*)**: Pain is related to sadist (person who practises sadism), while killer is related to death.
23. **(*c*)**: Ebb and flow are opposite as are wax and wane.
24. **(*c*)**: Metaphor is used to indicate something different from the literal meaning, while irony is an expression of one's meaning by saying the direct opposite of one's thoughts in order to be emphatic.

25. (*b*)	**26.** (*a*)	**27.** (*a*)	**28.** (*c*)	**29.** (*a*)
30. (*c*)	**31.** (*c*)	**32.** (*c*)	**33.** (*d*)	**34.** (*a*)
35. (*a*)	**36.** (*b*)	**37.** (*a*)	**38.** (*b*)	**39.** (*a*)
40. (*c*)				

PAPER — VII

Time allowed: 3 Hours **Maximum Marks : 100**

Attempt **all** the questions.

***Directions:* Q. 1–6:** In the following question, each sentence has four words or phrases underlined and marked I, II, III and IV. Select the one which is not correct in standard written English.

1. Engines used (I) in space shuttles are much larger (II) and more strong (III) than the ones used (IV) in jet planes.
   (*a*) I (*b*) II
   (*c*) III (*d*) IV

2. Bangalore is a beautiful city (I) which in (II) people have successfully blended (III) the modern with (IV) the traditional.
   (*a*) I (*b*) II
   (*c*) III (*d*) IV

3. The bus (I) was hired (II) by (III) the ladies for its picnic. (IV)
   (*a*) I (*b*) II
   (*c*) III (*d*) IV

4. The ways of (I) travelling has changed (II) dramatically since (III) the late nineteenth (IV) century.
   (*a*) I (*b*) II
   (*c*) III (*d*) IV

5. Usually (I) the climate in mountainous areas becomes much (II) windy (III) at higher (IV) altitudes.
   (*a*) I (*b*) II
   (*c*) III (*d*) IV

***Directions:* Q. 6–10:** In the following question, a disarranged sentence is given. Arrange these in proper order.

6. is (P) Hindu Sculpture (Q) movement (R) full of (S)
   (*a*) QSRP (*b*) PSRQ
   (*c*) QPSR (*d*) RSQP

7. to the total cost of the product (P) in reasonable (Q) proportion (R) advertising costs are no longer (Q)
   (A) RSQP (B) RPQS
   (C) RQSP (D) PSRQ

8. unsurpassed power (P) modern society (Q) in (R) women enjoy (S)
   (A) SPQR (B) RPQS
   (C) RQSP (D) PSRQ

9. American (P) as men (Q) earn as much (R) working women (S)
   (A) PSQR (B) PRQS
   (C) SRQP (D) PSRQ

10. adventure programmes (P) adult programmes (Q) more than (R) children watch (S)
    (A) PSRQ (B) SQRP
    (C) PRSQ (D) SPQR

***Directions:* Q. 11–15:** Each of the following questions consists of a word in capital letters, followed by four words. Choose the word that is most nearly similar in meaning to the word in capital letters.

11. MACABRE
    (A) innocent (B) tarried
    (C) gruesome (D) pleasing

12. DENOUEMENT
    (A) outcome (B) eschew
    (C) action (D) character

13. MANACLE
(A) fetter (B) ornament
(C) spectacles (D) order

14. FEIGN
(A) hesitate (B) pretend
(C) spectacles (D) attend

15. ASSAY
(A) attack (B) accept
(C) case (D) evaluate

Directions: **Q. 16–20:** In each of the following questions, a word is given in capital letters followed by four words. Choose the word that is most nearly opposite in meaning to the word in capital letters.

16. SOLICITOUS
(A) concerned (B) indifferent
(C) eager (D) noisy

17. RAMPANT
(A) furious (B) stylish
(C) restrained (D) healthy

18. PROLIFIC
(A) barren (B) backward
(C) reckless (D) profound

19. SEQUESTER
(A) slump (B) isolate
(C) unify (D) simple

20. TRITE
(A) hackneyed (B) correct
(C) original (D) certain

Directions: **Q. 21–25:** In each of the following questions, related pairs of words in capital letters is followed by four pairs of words. Choose the pair that best expresses a relationship similar to that expressed in the original pair.

21. PLANT : PARASITE : : ?
(A) transient : permanent
(B) wild : prey
(C) flora : fauna
(D) sailor : pirate

22. MANAGER : OFFICE : : ?
(A) doctor : patient
(B) curator : museum
(C) bank : account
(D) fruit : seed

23. INSINUATE : CHARGE : : ?
(A) say : deny
(B) refer : reject
(C) hint : affirm
(D) change : pardon

24. BRAVE : VALOUR : : ?
(A) look : see (B) cynic : doubt
(C) scholar : books (D) frame : picture

25. MAN : HUMANITY
(A) Drop : Ocean (B) People : Life
(C) Author : Book (D) River : Stream

***Directions*:** **Q. 26–30:** In each of the following questions, a sentence has a blank, indicating something has been omitted. Beneath the sentence are four words or phrases. Choose the word or phrase that best fits the meaning of the sentence as a whole.

26. A _______________ firms are having trouble with industrial relations.
(A) considerable amount of
(B) great deal of
(C) large part of
(D) great many

27. He was frightened _______________
(A) to be killed. (B) to being killed.
(C) for being killed. (D) of being killed.

28. Capitalist society _______________ profit as a valued goal.
(A) which regards (B) regarding
(C) regards (D) was regard

29. _______________ the rainfall was adequate this year, the mango trees still did not produce a high yield.
(A) Since (B) Although
(C) Due to (D) In spite of

30. The impact of two vehicles can cause a lot of _______________ to both.
(A) damage (B) damages
(C) damaging (D) damagings

Directions: **Q. 31–40:** Read the two passages given below carefully and answer the questions that follow according to the contents of the passage.

PASSAGE I

Patriotism is a very complex feeling, built up of primitive instincts and highly intellectual convictions. There is love of home and family and friends, making us peculiarly anxious to preserve our own country from invasion. There is the mild instinctive liking for compatriots as against foreigners. There is pride, which is bound up with the success of the community to which we feel that we belong. There is a belief, suggested by pride but reinforced by history, that one's own nation represents a great tradition and stands for ideals that are important to the human race. But besides all these, there is another element, at once nobler and more open to attack, an element of worship, of willing sacrifice, of joyful merging of the individual life in the life of the nation. This religious element in patriotism is essential to the strength of the State since it enlists the best that is in most men on the side of national sacrifice.

31. A suitable title for the passage could be
(A) Elements of Patriotism.
(B) Historical Development of a Nation.
(C) The Role of Religion and History in Patriotism.
(D) Religion and Patriotism.

32. Describing the element of worship "open to attack" the author implies that it:
(A) is unnecessary.
(B) leads to national sacrifice.
(C) has no historical basis.
(D) cannot be justified on rational grounds.

33. The tone of the passage can best be described as
(A) critical. (B) descriptive.
(C) persuasive. (D) analytical.

34. Which of the following can early be grouped under "intellectual convictions" the author mentions in the opening sentence?
(A) Love of family.
(B) Love of compatriots.
(C) The element of worship.
(D) None of the above.

35. Which one of the following statements is false?
(A) We tend to like our own countrymen better than we like foreigners.
(B) Nations always stand for ideals that are important to the human race.
(C) It is the religious element in patriotism that motivates us for sacrificing ourselves for our nation.
(D) Our pride of the community is bound with the community's success.

PASSAGE II

Compact Discs (CDs) have revolutionised the music industry with their surprisingly realistic sound. The six-inch discs look like thin plastic sandwiches with aluminium at the centre. They have digitally recorded material that is read by laser beams, so the sound has none of the crackling of vinyl records. CDs are also virtually indestructible, and they are lighter and smaller than conventional records. Since their introduction, CDs have become more affordable and widely available. In fact, they are now sold in electronics and video stores that didn't formerly carry records or cassettes.

There has been a phenomenal growth in the sale of CDs. Sales climbed dramatically during the second half of the 1980s. In the 1990s sales have been greater. CDs have all but replaced records in stores and, in spite of their being less affordable than cassettes, continue to gain in popularity.

36. The main appeal of CDs is their
(A) price. (B) size.
(C) availability (D) sound.

37. The word 'revolutionised', as used in line 1 could best the replaced by
(A) changed (B) taught
(C) surprised. (D) marked.

38. The author refers to CDs as 'sandwiches' because they
(A) are light. (B) are small.
(C) are layered. (D) don't crackle.

39. According to the passage, which one of the following is true ?
(A) CDs have replaced the vinyl records without much success.
(B) CDs are really very expensive.
(C) CDs reproduce human sound in almost realistic way.
(D) CDs may take more time to grow popular among the music lovers.

40. The author's main purpose is to
(A) tell how CDs are made.
(B) discuss the growth of CDs.
(C) compare CDs to sandwiches.
(D) describe the stores that sell CDs.

ANSWERS

1. **(C):** 'more strong' should be replaced with 'stronger'.
2. **(B):** 'Which in' should be replaced with 'in which'.
3. **(D):** 'its' should be replaced with 'their'.
4. **(B):** 'has' should be replaced with 'have'.
5. **(C):** windy' should be replaced with 'windier'.
6. **(C):** The proper order is: "Hindu Sculpture is full of movement."
7. **(A):** The proper order is: "Advertising costs are no longer in reasonable proportion to the total cost of the product."
8. **(C):** The proper order is: "In modern society women enjoy unsurpassed power."
9. **(D):** The proper order is: "American working women earn as much as men."
10. **(B):** The proper order is: "Children watch adult programmes more than adventure programmes."
11. **(C):** Macabre means connected with death. Its synonym is 'gruesome'.
12. **(A):** Denouement means last part. Its synonym is 'outcome'.
13. **(A):** Manacle means a pair of chains. Its synonym is 'fetters'.
14. **(B):** Feign means affect. Its synonym is 'pretend'.
15. **(D):** Assay means attempt. Its synonym is 'evaluate'.
16. **(B):** Solicitous means concerned. Its antonym is 'indifferent'.
17. **(C):** Rampant means widespread. Its antonym is 'restrained'.
18. **(A):** Prolific means abundant. Its antonym is 'barren'.
19. **(C):** Sequester means isolate. Its antonym is 'unify'.
20. **(C):** Trite means hackneyed. Its antonym is 'original'.
21. **(D):** Parasites are inimical to plants, while sailors are attacked by pirate.
22. **(B):** An office has a manager, while a museum has a curator.
23. **(C):** We insinuate a charge, while we affirm a hint.
24. **(B):** Brave and valour (both nouns) are synonyms. So, are cynic and doubt.
25. **(A):** Man is an infinitesimal part of humanity, while a drop is an infinitesimal part of an ocean.

26. (D)	**27.** (D)	**28.** (C)	**29.** (B)	**30.** (A)
31. (A)	**32.** (D)	**33.** (D)	**34.** (C)	**35.** (B)
36. (D)	**37.** (A)	**38.** (C)	**39.** (C)	**40.** (B)

PAPER — VIII

Time allowed: 3 Hours **Maximum Marks : 100**

Attempt **all** the questions.

Directions: **(Qs. 1–15):** Read each paragraph carefully and answer the question(s) given below them. Certain words are given in bold to help you to locate them while answering some questions.

PARA-I

Rationalism has been defined as the mental attitude which **unreservedly** accepts the supremacy of reason and aims at establishing a system of philosophy and ethics verifiable by experience and independent of all arbitrary assumptions or authority. This definition of rationalism was framed at the inauguration of the Rationalist Press Association (RPA) in London in the year 1899.

1. This paragraph best supports the statement that.
   - **A.** Ethics does not constitute a part of philosophy.
   - **B.** One has to accept certain beliefs to find the final truth.
   - **C.** Rationalism is not a set of beliefs which are incapable of verification.
   - **D.** Mental attitude is independent of all assumptions.
   - **E.** Only RPA can establish philosophy of Rationalism.
2. Which of the following words is most nearly the **SAME** in meaning as the word **unreservedly** as used in the paragraph?
   - **A.** conditionally **B.** fully
   - **C.** partially **D.** collectively
   - **E.** unilaterally

PARA-II

In today's world where teachers have a busy schedule, it is noticed that only a few teachers have time for the student's learning experience. One thing which is lacking in almost all classrooms is teachers motivating students to do better. What happens is that teachers would like to give attention to the students who have high intelligence and who are academically good. A larger portion of the student population is neglected. Teachers blame them for not trying to do their best.

3. The author would like the teachers to
   - **A.** motivate bright students to enhance their academic achievements.
   - **B.** improve their own academic standards to motivate students.
   - **C.** keep their schedule busy carrying out various duties.
   - **D.** encourage and give planned learning experiences to all students.
   - **E.** encourage good students to help poor students.
4. According to the author, why are teachers not in a position to perform their expected role?
   - **A.** Majority of the students neglect the classroom teaching.
   - **B.** The students are very busy and have less time to learn.
   - **C.** Intelligent students are after teachers, seeking their help in studies.
   - **D.** They are forced to spend more time in motivating good students.
   - **E.** None of these.

PARA-III

Due to the development of individualism and permissiveness, social norms have become slack and parents and teachers are unable to play their traditional role of shaping the character of their children and pupils. The growing complexity of society due to technological development and the **slackness** of social norms as a result of the growth of individualism and permissiveness are the two causes of the moral crisis of our time.

5. According to the author, which of the following is one of the outcomes of the present crisis of our time?
   - **A.** inability of parents and teachers to develop value base of children.
   - **B.** more than expected growth of science and technology.
   - **C.** increasing social cohesiveness in spite of violence and disturbances.

D. Emergence of new social norms which obstruct growth of individualism.
E. None of these.

6. Which of the following words is most **OPPOSITE** in meaning of the word **slackness** as used in the paragraph?
A. rigidity B. vigorous
C. sluggishness D. business
E. tightness

PARA-IV

Marx, the founder of communism, had predicted the failure and eventual overthrow of capitalism because of what he **regarded** as its inherent contradiction. He visualised that capitalism would maintain the wages of labour at a low Subsistence level, while progressively increasing its productivity by the employment of technologically advanced means of production. During the last many decades the real wages of workers in advanced capitalist countries have gradually and progressively increased. The prediction of Marx has not been borne out by history.

7. Which of the following supports the statement "the prediction ... borne out by history"?
A. Capitalism has just survived but not taken firm roots.
B. The salaries of all the employees have gone up in advanced countries.
C. Technological development has not taken place in capitalist countries.
D. The salaries of all the employees have gone down in all the countries.
E. There is no increase in the productivity of workers.

8. Which of the following words is most nearly the SAME in meaning to the word **regarded** as used in the paragraph ?
A. respected B. valued
C. related D. thought
E. estimated

PARA-V

Literature is a medium through which a person can convey his ideas towards or protest against different norms of society. Those works that deal with a moral issue are of particular importance in literature. They are written with a particular purpose in mind. A literary work with a moral issue will live on to be reinterpreted by different generations. These works involve the reader for he forms his own moral judgement towards the issue.

9. Why does the author consider write-ups 'that deal with a moral issue' more important in literature?
A. They are open for rethinking by coming generations.
B. They are written with a specific approach.
C. They help the reader in forming or consolidating his values and approaches.
A. Only A B. Both A and B
C. Both A and C D. Only C
E. None of these

10. The first sentence of the paragraph implies...
A. literature is not one of the best media of expression for society.
B. society does not observe same standard for all its members.
C. only literature allows individuals to express their different views.
D. society can change its value system after it reinterprets literature.
E. None of these.

PARA-VI

The phenomena of child labour is quite complex. Children work because they belong to poor families who cannot survive without the benefit of the income which accrues to the family on account of child labour. Any attempt to abolish it through legal recourse would, under the circumstances, not be practical. The only alternative is to ban child labour in hazardous areas and to regulate and **ameliorate** the conditions of work in other areas. Many developing countries including India have accepted this approach.

11. According to the paragraph abolishing child labour through legal means is most likely to result into......
A.. dragging/pushing the family of the child in acute economic stress.
B. shortage of labour in other areas of work.

C. regulation of services of adult workers.
D. betterment of working conditions of adult labourers.
E. better understanding of reality.

12. What can be inferred about the policy being followed about child labour in India?
A. Giving economic benefit to the families of child labourers.
B. Reducing/controlling child labour in unhealthy areas of work.
C. Monitoring and improving working conditions for children.
A. Only A and B B. Only B and C
C. Only A and B D. Only B
E. None of these.

13. Which of the following words is most nearly the **SAME** in meaning as the word **ameliorate** as used in the paragraph ?
A. cover B. adjust
C. remove D. mitigate
E. fix

PARA-VII

In recent years our society has shown readiness to **address** the educational and developmental needs of adolescents. Be it the Government or people in the community, there is a realisation that something needs to be done to build on the energy and enthusiasm of this crucial section of the population. Growing social unrest, violence, crime and increasing visibility of the young has contributed to this readiness.

14. Which of the following words is most **OPPOSITE** in meaning of the word **address** as used in the paragraph?
A. discourage B. diffuse
C. locate D. disorganise
E. ignore

15. Which of the following is not a likely cause of readiness to address needs of adolescents, shown by people?
A. Increase in crime.
B. Growing violence.
C. Equality of opportunity.
D. Physical presence of youth.
E. Increased social unrest.

Directions: **(Qs. 16–25):** In the following passage there are blanks, each of which has been numbered. These numbers are printed below the passage and against each, five words are suggested, one of which fits the blanks appropriately. Find out the appropriate word in each case.

The Tea plant, a native of Southern China, was known **16** very early times of Chinese botany and medicine. It is **17** in the classics **18** the various names of Tou, Tseh, Chung kha and Ming and was **19** praised for possessing the virtues of **20** fatigue, delighting the soul, strengthening the will and repairing the eyesight. It was not only administered as an internal dose, but often **21** externally in the form of paste to **22** rheumatic pains. The Taoists claimed it **23** an important **24** of the elixir of immortality. The Buddhists used it extensively to prevent drowsiness during **25** long hours of meditation.

16. A. to B. after
C. from D. beyond
E. behind

17. A. taken B. resorted
C. awarded D. alluded
E. mentioned

18. A. under B. between
C. among D. besides
E. like

19. A. rarely B. loosely
C. under D. severely
E. highly

20. A. absorbing B. relieving
C. avoiding D. resolving
E. recognising

21. A. inserted B. developed
C. conceived D. controlled
E. applied

22. A. recuperate B. alleviate
C. conceal D. indicate
E. slow

23. A. to B. also
C. although D. as
E. hardly

24. A. ingredient B. also
C. offshoot D. outcome
E. discovery

25. **A.** that **B.** these
C. their **D.** our
E. remote

***Directions:* (Qs. 26–30):** In each question below four words numbered (A), (B), (C) and (D) have been printed, one of which may be either inappropriate in the context or wrongly spelt. The number of that word is the answer. If all the four words are correctly spelt and are appropriate in the context, mark (E), i.e. 'All correct', as the answer.

26. Kindly **note** (A) our **address** (B) and use it **in** (C) all **farther** (D) communication. All correct (E)
27. We are **already** (A) to **fight** (B) the **battle,** (C) let the **enemy** (D) come.
All correct (E)
28. Many people in India **cherish** (A) a desire to **immigrate** (B) to **developed** (C) countries to **make** (D) a fortune. All correct. (E)
29. He took great **pains** (A) to **save** (B) many **dyeing** (C) folk arts and helped the artists to live an **honourable** (D) life. All correct (E)
30. Arjun did his MBA from a **prestigious** (A) **institute** (B) by **securing** (C) first class in this **calendar** (D) year. All correct (E)

***Directions:* (Qs. 31–35):** In each of the following questions an idiomatic expression and its four possible meanings are given. Find out the correct meaning of the idiomatic expression and mark the number of that meaning as your answer on the answersheet. If you do not find any correct answer, mark (E), i.e. None of these, as your answer.

31. To strain every nerve
A. To spoil relationship
B. To get a afraid
C. To try one's utmost
D. To take ill
E. None of these
32. To have an axe to grind
A. Pinpoint faults of others
B. To take revenge
C. To make unreasonable demands
D. To have a selfish interest to serve
E. None of these
33. To take heart
A. To become hopeful
B. To love everyone
C. To prepare for a battle
D. To withdraw from activity
E. None of these
34. To draw the line
A. To decide one's occupation
B. To set limits
C. To prepare for a battle
D. To withdraw from activity
E. None of these
35. To beat about the bush
A. To punish an innocent person
B. To hang around
C. To boast about oneself
D. To remain idle
E. None of these

***Directions:* (Qs. 36–40):** Each question below has two blanks. There are five pairs of words below the sentence. Each pair is numbered. Choose the pair of words which can be filled up in the blanks in the sentence in the same order so as to complete the sentence meaningfully.

36. This book is readable, clear and ________ researched with ________ detailed references.
A. fabulously, intricate
B. meticulously, extensive
C. leisurely, complete
D. hardly, notional
E. closely, scattered
37. The interest has ________ innovation related to several sectors of ________ pharmaceutical business and industry.
A. accepted, skeletal
B. insured, fateful
C. affected, plummeting
D. restricted, grown
E. accelerated, burgeoning
38. The Indian hospitality industry which has been ________ a prolonged slump is now entering a new ________ phase ready to enhance profitability.
A. witnessing, ambitious
B. observing, listless

C. demonstrating, efficient
D. recovering, debt
E. succumbing, lean

39. The new policy seeks to ____________ a process of widespread participation of people ____________ the way for more effective implementation.
A. amend, opening
B. halt, propelling
C. generate, paving
D. diagnose, resulting

40. Journalism is a ________ for truth, a crusade to ____________ injustice and wrong-doing.
A. product, limit B. boon, justify
C. travesty, attack D. quest, expose
E. search, optimise

Directions: **(Qs. 41–45):** In each question there are two statements which can be combined into a single statement in a number of different ways without changing their meaning. Below them are given three probable starters of such combined sentence. One, two, three or none of them may be correct. Decide upon which is/are correct, if any, and answer the question.

41. This judgement has been given by the highest court in the land. It therefore assumes finality from legal point of view.
A. Being the judgement of…..
B. In spite of the judgement…..
C. As it is the judgement of …..

A. Only A B. Only B
C. Only C D. Only A and B
E. Only A and C

42. On this special occasion the chief minister of the state would be welcomed first. After that the prime minister would be extended warm welcome.
A. Although the prime minister would…..
B. As per the prevalent practice the prime minister…..
C. In spite of the chief minister…...

A. Only A B. Only B
C. Only C D. Only A and B
E. Only A and C

43. India is rich in bio-resources. It has no clear legislative framework to regulate access to and use of these resources.
A. As India is rich….
B. But India is rich…..
C. Although India is rich…..

A. Only A B. Only B
C. Only C D. Only D
E. Only A and C

44. I did not receive any packet from Dipti. I also not receive any phone call from her.
A. Neither did I receive……
B. Clearly I did not……
C. Because I did not……

A. Only A B. Only B
C. Only C D. Only A and B
E. Only A and C

45. I was to reach home a little early but I got delayed. On reaching home I found that guests had left a little while ago.
A. Hardly had I reached…..
B. As long as I reached…..
C. Besides few minutes…..

A. Only A B. Only B
C. Only C D. Only A and B
E. Only A and C

Directions: **(Qs. 46–50):** Which of the following phrases (A), (B), (C) and (D) given below each sentence should replace the phrase printed in bold to make the sentence grammatically correct? If the sentence is correct as it is, mark (E) as the answer.

46. **When the boy regain** consciousness he wanted to eat something.
A. If the boy regain
B. When the boy regained
C. Despite the boy regain
D. On the boy regaining.
E. No correction required

47. The social worker wanted **to bring about** little changes in the lives of the people of that village.
A. to bring back B. to bring up
C. to bring forth D. bringing about
E. No correction required

48. Raghunath proposes to lay claim for the insurance company as soon as he recovers from the accident.

- **A.** lay claim to lay claim on
- **B.** lay claim on
- **C.** laying claim towards
- **D.** lay claim against
- **E.** No correction required

49. The new concession announced by the Government will have only a **marginalised effect on** the lives of the people.

- **A.** marginal effect off
- **B.** margin of effect on
- **C.** marginal effect on
- **D.** No correction required

50. The Charitable Hospital works **under the auspices from** Welfare Trust of an Industry.

- **A.** under the auspices by
- **B.** by the auspices from
- **C.** through the auspices from
- **D.** under the auspices of
- **E.** No correction required

ANSWERS

1. (C)	**2.** (B)	**3.** (D)	**4.** (E)	**5.** (A)
6. (A)	**7.** (B)	**8.** (D)	**9.** (C)	**10.** (E)
11. (A)	**12.** (B)	**13.** (D)	**14.** (E)	**15.** (C)
16. (C)	**17.** (E)	**18.** (A)	**19.** (E)	**20.** (B)
21. (E)	**22.** (B)	**23.** (D)	**24.** (A)	**25.** (C)
26. (D)	**27.** (A)	**28.** (B)	**29.** (C)	**30.** (E)
31. (C)	**32.** (D)	**33.** (A)	**34.** (B)	**35.** (E)
36. (B)	**37.** (E)	**38.** (A)	**39.** (C)	**40.** (D)
41. (E)	**42.** (B)	**43.** (C)	**44.** (A)	**45.** (A)
46. (B)	**47.** (E)	**48.** (D)	**49.** (C)	**50.** (D)

PAPER — IX

Time allowed: 3 Hours **Maximum Marks : 100**

Attempt **all** the questions.

Directions: **(Qs. 1–11):** In the following passage there are blanks, each of which has been numbered. These numbers are printed below the passage and against each, five words are suggested, one of which fits the blank appropriately. Find out the appropriate word in each case.

Bret Bonson loved animals and was 1 on a family owned zoo. He had grown up caring for antelope, deer and wildcats. He was 2, at times stubbornly, protective. Once, when a tiger cub was born with a deformed leg, the local veterinarian and Bret's parents 3 the animal would never live a full life. Even so, the boy bottle-fed the cub and cared for it. 4 Bret's mothering, the cub died, but Bret's mothering 5 lived on.

He worked at a Safari park where, in 1980, he trained his first African elephant and found his true 6. From the beginning Boson was 7 by elephants. They have the 8 force to uproot trees and can outrun the fastest human sprinter. But they also have 9 fine motor skills. The same trunk that could 10 the front end of an automobile or fracture a predator's skull could gently 11 a peanut from the fingers of a small child.

1. **A.** created **B.** constructed **C.** built **D.** erected **E.** raised
2. **A.** methodically **B.** carefully **C.** fiercely **D.** suitably **E.** actually
3. **A.** believed **B.** valued **C.** expressed **D.** imagined **E.** exhibited
4. **A.** Until **B.** Unless **C.** Instead **D.** Despite **E.** Although
5. **A.** belief **B.** instinct **C.** love **D.** passion **E.** care
6. **A.** companion **B.** attitude **C.** calling **D.** friend **E.** abode
7. **A.** absorbed **B.** alarmed **C.** attacked **D.** attached **E.** awed
8. **A.** empowered **B.** brute **C.** tall **D.** high **E.** exhibited
9. **A.** domestic **B.** durable **C.** devastating **D.** delicate **E.** dubious
10. **A.** hoist **B.** puncture **C.** disturb **D.** attack **E.** deflate
11. **A.** protect **B.** tender **C.** abandon **D.** pluck **E.** touch

Directions: **(Qs. 12–18):** Read each sentence to find out whether there is any error in it. The error, if any, will be in one part of the sentence. The number of that part is the answer. If there is no error, the answer is 'E' (Ignore the error, of punctuation, if any).

12. We are happy that A/ our prime minister B/ with the members C/ of his cabinet are to be present at the function D/. No error. E
13. Neither the size nor the colour A/ of clothes which B/ I purchased for him C/ yesterday were right D/. No error. E
14. I heard to my surprise A/ that the present B/ I send him was not C/ to his taste D/. No error. E
15. Let us refer A/ this matter to the principal. B/ We shall abide C/ with his decision D/. No error. E
16. If I would have come A/ a little earlier, I would have B/ got a glimpse C/ of my beloved leader D/. No error E.
17. When you buy something A/ on the instalment system B/ you are not required to pay C/ the whole price at once D/. No error. E
18. I am waiting for you A/ for the last two hours B/ but you did not bother C/ to turn up in time D/. No error. E

***Directions:* (Qs. 19–28):** In each given sentence, a group of words is given in bold. Below each sentence are four other groups of words of which you have to choose to substitute the words given in bold. If the sentence is correct as it is, mark (E) as the answer.

19. I am glad to hear that you narrowly escaped **being run over by** a speeding car yesterday.
- **A.** by being run over by.
- **B.** to run over by.
- **C.** run over down by.
- **D.** being over run by.
- **E.** No correction required.

20. It is with a heavy heart that I pen these few lines to **condole for you on** the death of your beloved mother.
- **A.** condole with you in .
- **B.** condole upon you on.
- **C.** condole with you on.
- **D.** condole for you with.
- **E.** No correction required.

21. You should visit France when **you had been to England.**
- **A.** had gone to England.
- **B.** go to England.
- **C.** were going to England.
- **D.** should have gone to England.
- **E.** No correction required.

22. He is one of the best players **that has ever lived.**
- **A.** that would have ever lived.
- **B.** that have been ever lived.
- **C.** that would have been ever lived.
- **D.** that would ever live.
- **E.** No correction required.

23. He asked me if he **did shut the window.**
- **A.** will shut the window.
- **B.** can shut the window.
- **C.** may shut the window.
- **D.** should shut the window.
- **E.** No correction required.

24. The teacher told us that prize **would be presented the next day.**
- **A.** will be presented tomorrow.
- **B.** would have been presented the next day.
- **C.** shall be presented tomorrow.
- **D.** should be presented tomorrow.
- **E.** No correction required.

25. His speech was optimistic, but at the end of it he **stroke a note of caution.**
- **A.** strike a note of caution.
- **B.** strut for a note of caution.
- **C.** striked a note of caution.
- **D.** struck a note of caution.
- **E.** No correction required.

26. **Men have been known** how important the sun is to them.
- **A.** Men have long known.
- **B.** Men have to know long.
- **C.** Men had long know.
- **D.** Men have long know.
- **E.** No correction required.

27. I did not like his comments on my paper but I had no alternative as **I have agreed to keep quiet.**
- **A.** I have to agree to keep quiet.
- **B.** I had agreed to keep quiet.
- **C.** I had agreed for keeping quiet.
- **D.** I have to agree for keeping quiet.
- **E.** No correction required.

28. Please do not give him any food **if his temperature will rise.**
- **A.** if his temperature rises.
- **B.** if his temperature would rise.
- **C.** if his temperature shall rise.
- **D.** unless his temperature rises.
- **E.** No correction required.

***Directions:* (Qs. 29–36):** Pick out the most effective pair of words from the given words to fill in the blank to make the sentence meaningfully complete.

29. Man needs food not __________ for the body but for the soul also. The satisfaction of his physical wants does not imply his__________.
- **A.** merely-contentment.
- **B.** properly-superiority.
- **C.** only-spirituality.
- **D.** necessarily-commitment.
- **E.** certainly-entitlement.

30. It is said that knowledge is power. The hunger for power is _______ and therefore most difficult to__________

A. accumulative-subsume.
B. enormous-apply.
C. empowering-delegate.
D. insatiable-contain.
E. evolutionary-rationalize..

31. Nothing undermines the communication of a changed vision more than ________ on the part of key ________ that seems inconsistent with the vision.
A. anything-issues.
B. behaviour-players.
C. advocacy-managers.
D. something-personnel.
E. philosophy-problems.

32. Mountains and hills are a ________ sight. I have always ________ to see them.
A. extraordinary-advocated.
B. stupendous-encouraged.
C. loving-prepared.
D. joyful-imagined.
E. fascinating-longed.

33. Poetry is the language of the imagination and the ________. It relates to whatever gives ________ pleasure or pain to the human mind.
A. thinking-permanent.
B. analysis-temporary.
C. passions-immediate.
D. circumspection-sporadic.
E. visualization-constant.

34. Success in business requires two things: a winning competitive ________ and superb organisational ________
A. advantage-satisfaction.
B. planning-advantage.
C. strategy-execution.
D. philosophy-motivation.
E. marketing-strategy.

35. To ________ in today's rapidly changing environment corporations need to ________ their learning capability.
A. develop-enlarge.
B. surpass-align.
C. project-assimilate.
D. service-mitigate.
E. compete-strengthen.

36. A reader gets much greater pleasure from reading books than a miser gets in ________ money.
A. powerful-accumulating.
B. voracious-hoarding.
C. desirous-stocking.
D. proverbial-spending.
E. profound-lavishing.

Directions: **(Qs. 37–46):** Read the following passage carefully and answer the question given below it.

It is an old saying that knowledge is power. Education is an instrument which imparts knowledge and, therefore, indirectly controls power. Therefore, ever since the dawn of civilization persons in power have always tried to supervise or control education. It has been the hand-maid of the ruling class. During the Christian era, the ecclesiastics controlled the institution of education and diffused among the people the gospel of the Bible and religious teachings. These gospels and teachings were no other than a philosophy for the maintenance of the existing society. It taught the poor man to be meek and to earn his bread with the sweat of his brow, while the priests and the landlords lived in luxury and fought duels for the slightest offence. During the Renaissance, education passed more from the clutches of the priest into the hand of the prince. In other words it became more secular. It was also due to the growth of the nation-state and powerful monarchs, education began to devise and preach the infallibility of its masters, the monarch or king. It also invented and supported fantastic theories like the Divine Right Theory and that the king can do no wrong etc. With the advent of the industrial revolution education took a different turn and had to please the new masters. It now no longer remained the privilege of the baron class but was thrown open to the new rich merchant class of society. Yet education was still confined to the few elite. The philosophy which was in vogue during this period was that of 'Laissez Faire' restricting the function of the State to a mere keeping of law and order while, on the other hand, in practice the law of the jungle prevailed in the form of free competition and the survival of the fittest.

37. Who controlled education during the era after the industrial revolution?
   A. The baron class. B. The priests.
   C. The prince. D. The monarch.
   E. None of these.
38. What does theory of Divine Right of king stipulate?
   A. That kings are gods.
   B. They have the right to be worshipped like gods by their subjects.
   C. That the right of governing is conferred upon kings by god.
   D. That the rights of kings are divine and therefore sacred.
   E. None of these.
39. What does the expression 'handmaid of the ruling class' mean?
   A. Private mistress of the prince.
   B. Something fully under the control of the ruling class.
   C. Private maid-servants of the prince.
   D. The symbol of authority of the prince.
   E. None of these.
40. Who controlled education during the Renaissance?
   A. The common people.
   B. The prince.
   C. The church and the priests.
   D. The secular leaders of the society.
   E. None of these.
41. What does the word "infallibility" mean?
   A. That every man is open to error.
   B. That some divine power is responsible for determining the fate of men.
   C. The virtue of not making my mistake.
   D. Senstivity
   E. None of these
42. What did the ruling class in the Christian era think of the poor man?
   A. That he is the beloved of god
   B. That he deserves all sympathy of the rich.
   C. That he should be strong.
   D. None of these
43. Who controlled the institution of education during the Christian era?
   A. The church and the priests
   B. The monarchs
   C. The secular leaders of society
   D. The common people
   E. None of these.
44. What do you mean by the 'sweat of his brow'?
   A. Very hard work.
   B. The tiny droplets of sweat on the forehead.
   C. The wrinkled visible on the face.
   D. The sign of innocence.
   E. None of these.
45. Why have persons in power always tried to supervise or control education?
   A. Because they wanted to educate the whole public.
   B. Because they wanted to deprive the common man of the benefits of education.
   C. Because it involved a huge expenditure on the state exchequer.
   D. Because it is an instrument of knowledge and therefore power.
   E. None of these
46. What does the philosophy of Laissez-Faire stand for?
   A. Joint control of the means of production by the state and private enterprise.
   B. Individual freedom in the economic field.
   C. State control of the means of production.
   D. Full development of the individual's personality.
   E. None of these.
47. Rearrange the following six sentences (1), (2), (3), (4), (5), and (6) in the proper sequence to form a meaningful paragraph.
   1. But all three have one focus—individual performance improvement.
   2. The importance of each component will vary from organisation to organisation according to the complexity to the operations.
   3. They are individual development, carreer development and organisational development.

4. Since individual performance improvement is the heart of HRD programme, HRD can be described as the area of congruence among the three components.
5. There are three fundamental component areas of human resource development.
6. It will also vary according to the organisation's commitment to improve human resources.

ANSWERS

1. (E)	**2.** (C)	**3.** (A)	**4.** (D)	**5.** (B)
6. (C)	**7.** (E)	**8.** (B)	**9.** (D)	**10.** (A)
11. (D)	**12.** (D)	**13.** (D)	**14.** (C)	**15.** (D)
16. (A)	**17.** (E)	**18.** (A)	**19.** (E)	**20.** (C)
21. (B)	**22.** (E)	**23.** (D)	**24.** (E)	**25.** (D)
26. (A)	**27.** (B)	**28.** (A)	**29.** (A)	**30.** (D)
31. (D)	**32.** (E)	**33.** (C)	**34.** (C)	**35.** (E)
36. (B)	**37.** (E)	**38.** (C)	**39.** (B)	**40.** (B)
41. (C)	**42.** (D)	**43.** (A)	**44.** (A)	**45.** (D)
46. (B)	**47.** 5, 3, 2, 6, 1, 4			

PAPER — X

Time allowed: 3 Hours **Maximum Marks : 100**

Attempt **all** the questions.

ORDERING OF WORDS IN A SENTENCE

***Directions:* (Qs. 1 to 10)**: In these questions, some parts of the sentence have been jumbled up. You are required to rearrange these parts which are labelled P, Q, R and S to produce the correct sentence. Choose the proper sequence from the given alternatives (*a*), (*b*), (*c*) and (*d*).

1. Man cannot create a species (P)/ the one that he has destroyed (Q)/ nor can be recreate (R)/ for all his genius (S)
The proper sequence should be
(*a*) P S Q R (*b*) S P R Q
(*c*) P Q R S (*d*) S P Q R

2. With only five rupees in her pocket, the brave Mother Teresa (P)/ among the poor of India (Q)/ learned a few basic medical skills (R)/ and began to live (S)
The proper sequence should be
(*a*) P R S Q (*b*) Q S R P
(*c*) P R Q S (*d*) Q R S P

3. The great advantage of early rising (P)/ in our day's work (Q)/it gives us (R)/ is the good start (S)
The proper sequence should be
(*a*) S P Q R (*b*) P S R Q
(*c*) S P R Q (*d*) P S Q R

4. Religion can be defined as try to understand life (P)/ by means of which (Q)/ a group of people (R)/ a system of beliefs (S)
The proper sequence should be
(*a*) R Q S P (*b*) P S R Q
(*c*) S P R Q (*d*) S Q R P

5. If you really believe my advice to you is (P)/ that he is a liar (Q)/ from his present job (R) that you must dismiss him (S)
The proper sequence should be
(*a*) R P S Q (*b*) Q P S R
(*c*) Q S P R (*d*) R S P Q

6. The student working on their compositions (P)/ writes well (Q)/ behind the two girls (R) who is sitting on the last row (S)
The proper sequence should be
(*a*) S P R Q (*b*) Q R P S
(*c*) Q S P R (*d*) S R P Q

7. Work is (P) which was ever invented (Q) one of the greatest safety valves (R), and youth especially needs it (S)
(*a*) Q R P S (*b*) S P R Q
(*c*) R P S Q (*d*) P R Q S

8. A hare who crept slowly on the ground (P)/ once laughed at a tortoise (Q)/ who was very proud of his speed (R)/ as a runner (S)
The proper sequence should be
(*a*) R S Q P (*b*) P Q S R
(*c*) P S Q R (*d*) R Q P S

9. Henry; Ford was a complex personality in which the (P)/ visionary and the eccentric fought for mastery. (Q)/ who built the Model T car (R)/ and pioneered the modern assembly line (S)
The proper sequence should be
(*a*) P Q R S (*b*) R P S Q
(*c*) Q P S R (*d*) R S P Q

10. Even when he would one day grow into (P)/ he showed signs that (Q)/ he was a child (R)/ an extraordinary person (S)
The proper sequence should be
(*a*) R Q P S (*b*) S P Q R
(*c*) S Q P R (*d*) R P Q S

ORDERING OF SENTENCES

***Directions:* (Qs. 11 to 15)**: In these questions, each passage consists of six sentences. The first and the sixth sentences are given in the beginning. The middle four sentences in each have been removed and jumbled up. These are labelled P, Q, R and S. You are required to find out the proper sequence of the four sentences from the given alternatives (*a*), (*b*), (*c*) and (*d*).

11. S_1 : In 1945, America faced two powerful enemies in the World War.

S_6 : This was the weapon that ended the Second World War.

P : America found conventional weapons insufficient to crush them.

Q : These were Germany and Japan, who posed strong opposition to America.

R : The result of this was the production of the Atom Bomb.

S : The Government ordered scientists to conduct research and produce a new, deadly weapon.

The proper sequence should be

(*a*) Q P S R (*b*) P Q R S
(*c*) Q P R S (*d*) P Q S R

12. S_1 : Advertising is also advantageous to the consumer in that if it increases the sale of goods, industry prospers and prices may be reduced.

S_6 : Advertising of this particular kind is planned to stimulate new wants or to induce buyers to change their habits.

P : There is no obvious connection, for example, between a picture of a smiling girl and a certain brand of sweets.

Q : The advertiser's assumption is that by looking at such pictures, the consumer would be influenced to buy his products.

R : On the other hand, much of the canvassing of which the consumer is the object does not convey information but endeavours merely to draw the public attention to certain products.

S : But most people like looking at pictures of pretty girls.

The proper sequence should be

(*a*) R Q S P (*b*) S P R Q
(*c*) R P S Q (*d*) S Q R P

13. S_1 : We are living in an age in which technology has suddenly 'annihilated distance'

S_6 : In that event, we should be dooming ourselves to wipe each other out.

P : We have never been so conscious of our variety as we are now that we have come to such close quarters.

Q : Physically we are now all neighbours, but psychologically we are still strangers to each other.

R : Are we going to let this consciousness of our variety make us fear and hate each other ?

S : How are we going to react ?

The proper sequence should be

(*a*) Q P S R (*b*) Q P R S
(*c*) P R Q S (*d*) S R P Q

14. S_1 : Mom was pleased to receive your wishes on her birthday.

S_6 : Your Mom has forgotten all the bitterness and sends her blessings to you.

P : Girl! Wishes are more powerful than any other things in the world.

Q : Both of us had forgotten the day.

R : Your letter holds a proof of it.

S : It was your letter and the card which reminded us of it.

The proper sequence should be

(*a*) P S Q R (*b*) Q R S P
(*c*) R Q S P (*d*) Q S P R

15. S_1 : A century ago, the cinema was just a mechanical toy.

S_6 : Finally it has evolved as the century's most potent and versatile art form.

P : Thus it gained respectability and acceptance.

Q : It gradually came to be considered as an art form of the new era.

R : By the 1920s, even its worst critics had to take it seriously.

S : Later it was viewed as an extension of photography.

The proper sequence should be

(*a*) P Q R S (*b*) S Q R P
(*c*) S P Q R (*d*) Q R S P

SELECTING WORDS/PHRASES

Directions: **(Qs. 16 to 30)** : In the following passage, there are some blanks which are numbered as 16 to 30. Below the passage against these numbers, a choice of three words/phrases (*a*), (*b*), (*c*) is given. Choose the best word/phrase out of these choices.

Catherine Geach was three when she heard the music. Her mother, a sculptor **....(16)....**put a violin concerto on the turntable in her studio outside London**....(17).....** child was transfixed by the rich sounds .....**(18)**....from an instrument whose name she didn't even ....**(19)**.... She wanted to make music like that. Soon she was ....**(20)**.... the Violin. Beyond doubt, her talent ....**(21)**.... exceptional. By the time she was five, she ....**(22)**.... performed solo in public. At seven, she ....**(23)**.... practising two hours a day. Absorbed in music, Catherine ....**(24)**.... forget the hardships of home. Her parents ....**(25)**.... divorced and money was tight. By the time, Catherine ....**(26)**.... her teens, her mother was .....**(27)**.... severe depression. After school, the teenager ....**(28)**... come home to their small ....**(29)**.... and help with chores and cooking. Then alone in her room she ...**(30)**... her violin out of its case, and practice, and practise.

16. (*a*) Has (*b*) Had (*c*) Will have

17. (*a*) A (*b*) The (*c*) One

18. (*a*) Coming (*b*) Emanating (*c*) Emerging

19. (*a*) Recognise (*b*) Know (*c*) Remember

20. (*a*) Learning (*b*) Practising (*c*) Studying

21. (*a*) Was (*b*) Will be (*c*) Had been

22. (*a*) Had (*b*) has (*c*) Must have

23. (*a*) Will be (*b*) Is (*c*) Was

24. (*a*) Could (*b*) Would (*c*) Can

25. (*a*) Were (*b*) Will (*c*) Have been

26. (*a*) Entered (*b*) Had entered (*c*) Was entering

27. (*a*) Undergoing (*b*) Suffering (*c*) Having

28. (*a*) Would (*b*) Should (*c*) Might

29. (*a*) Apartment (*b*) Department (*c*) Compartment

30. (*a*) Would have taken (*b*) Will be taking (*c*) Would take

SPOTTING ERRORS

Directions: **(Qs. 31 to 45):** In this section, a number of sentences are given. The sentences are in three separate parts and each one is labelled (*a*), (*b*) and (*c*). Read each sentences to find out whether there is an error. When you find an error in any one of these parts choose that part as you response. You may feel that there is no error in a sentence, in that case choose (*d*) as your response.

Error may be in grammar, word missing or a word which should be removed.

31. Don't think you can say unpleasant things (*a*)/ about someone behind his back (*b*)/ and not found out. (*c*)/ No error. (*d*)

32. The Americans speak (*a*)/ different from us (*b*)/ though our grammar is the same(*c*)/ no error. (*d*)

33. This is a instance (*a*)/ of the blind (*b*)/ leading the blinds. (*c*)/ No error. (*d*)

34. He took to drink (*a*)/ to lessen (*b*)/ his mental worries. (*c*)/ No error. (*d*)

35. My father could lead (*a*)/ a full and happy life (*b*)/ without spending lot of money. (*c*)/ No error. (*d*)

36. All India Radio broadcasted (*a*)/ a very good programme (*b*)/ this morning. (*c*)/ No error. (*d*)

37. There were so much cattle (*a*)/ on the road that (*b*)/ it was difficult to drive safely. (*c*)/ No error. (*d*)

38. What could have provoked him to behave (*a*)/ in such a rude manner (*b*)/ at dinner last night? (*c*)/ No error. (*d*)

39. They were rich zamindars in the thirties (*a*)./ but now they have become poor (*b*)/ and lost much of their property. (*c*)/ No error. (*d*)

40. The foreign ambassador was (*a*)/ both noted for his charm manners (*b*)/ as well as his wide knowledge of languages. (*c*)/ No error. (*d*)

41. Education helps us understand and tolerate differences (*a*)/ and so holds out the promise (*b*)/ that we can live together harmoniously. (*c*)/ No error. (*d*)

42. He refused to disclose to his friends (*a*)/ whether he will leave for England(*b*)/ immediately after finishing his studies. (*c*)/ No error.

43. Despite for her protests (*a*)/ I decided to buy (*b*)/ the saree which she did not like. (*c*)/ No error (*d*)

44. The government warned the shopkeepers (*a*)/ that if they persist in charging unfair prices (*b*) their licences would be cancelled. (*c*)/ No error. (*d*)

45. The famous poet and the scholar (*a*)/ Dr. Suman has been ailing for (*b*)/ the last one month. (*c*)/ No error. (*d*)

SENTENCE IMPROVEMENT

Directions: **(Qs. 46 to 60):** In these questions, look at the underlined apart of each sentence. Below the sentence are given three possible substitutions for the underlined part. If any one of substitutions (*a*), (*b*) or (*c*) is better than the underlined part, choose that substitution as your response. If none of the substitutions improves the sentence, choose (*d*) as your response. Thus a 'No improvement' response will be signified by the letter (*d*).

46. The sun was shining such brightly that Leela had to put on her sun-glasses.
(*a*) Very (*b*) Too
(*c*) So (*d*) No improvement

47. If I were you, I would report the matter at once.
(*a*) Be (*b*) Am
(*c*) Was (*d*) No improvement

48. The document is concerning your health and that of your family.
(*a*) Concerns with (*b*) Is concerned with
(*c*) Concerns (*d*) No improvement

49. The lady laid out a special dinner for her husband on his birthday.
(*a*) Laid (*b*) Laid up
(*c*) Laid by (*d*) No improvement

50. Epidemics are like to break off in the areas from where flood-water has receded.
(*a*) Break out (*b*) Break up
(*c*) Break in (*d*) No improvement

51. There is no objection to him joining the party.
(*a*) On him (*b*) To his
(*c*) Upon his (*d*) No improvement

52. You are too big to go out alone.
(*a*) Big enough (*b*) So big
(*c*) Very big (*d*) No improvement

53. One of my old friends has invited me for tea in the evening.
(*a*) To take tea (*b*) To tea
(*c*) On tea (*d*) No improvement

54. Hardly had he saddled the horse then the mare broke loose and galloped down the hill.
(*a*) That (*b*) When
(*c*) Than (*d*) No improvement

55. The speaker tried to work up team emotions of his audience.
(*a*) Round (*b*) Off
(*c*) In (*d*) No improvement

56. Until the sky is overcast, I take my raincoat with me.
(*a*) When (*b*) Even if
(*c*) Whenever (*d*) No improvement

57. His discourse about the meteorologist was very stimulating.
(*a*) On (*b*) Of
(*c*) Concerning (*d*) No improvement

58. Mira told her brother that she had made a mistake.
(*a*) Said to (*b*) Pleaded to
(*c*) Admitted to (*d*) No improvement

59. You don't want a beggar to look happy, isn't it?
(*a*) Aren't you (*b*) Do you?
(*c*) Don't you (*d*) No improvement

60. The instructor told the student to hold the club lightly, to keep his eye on the ball, but should not use too much force.
(*a*) And not (*b*) And not to
(*c*) Still not to (*d*) No improvement.

SYNONYMS

Directions: **(Qs. 61 to 70):** In this section, you find a number of sentences, parts of which are underlined. You may also find only a group of words which in underlined. For each underlined part, four words/ phrases are listed below. Choose the word/ phrase nearest in meaning to the underlined part.

61. We were taken aback at the fulsome praise he heaped upon his former enemy.
(*a*) Elaborate (*b*) Extravagant
(*c*) Excessive (*d*) Exorbitant

62. You may think at first that it is <u>queer</u> to talk of having too much paper money and that money is so nice and useful that you cannot have too much of it.
(*a*) Ridiculous (*b*) Absurd
(*c*) Anomalous (*d*) Odd

63. The Government is under no obligation to offer contracts to companies which choose to <u>flout</u> guidelines.
(*a*) Condemn (*b*) Ignore
(*c*) Defy (*d*) Neglect

64. Soon he felt uncomfortable, for the coach was now moving over a <u>rugged</u> road.
(*a*) Rough (*b*) Narrow
(*c*) Dusty (*d*) Sturdy

65. Indians exhibited a remarkable <u>solidarity</u> at the time of war.
(*a*) Coalition (*b*) Cooperation
(*c*) Unification (*d*) Unity

66. A great statesman is <u>actuated</u> by love of his country.
(*a*) Compelled (*b*) Induced
(*c*) Impelled (*d*) Persuaded

67. The cutting curved sharply, and in the darkness the black entrance to the tunnel, loomed up <u>menacingly</u>
(*a*) Harmfully (*b*) Imminently
(*c*) Dangerously (*d*) Threateningly

68. Had he delivered his speech without a long and winding <u>preamble</u>, people would have understood him better.
(*a*) Digression (*b*) Introduction
(*c*) Explanation (*d*) Background

69. His <u>impeccable</u> style caught the attention of all critics.
(*a*) Faultless (*b*) Inoffensive
(*c*) Upright (*d*) Harmless

70. We should not <u>look down on</u> people who are not educated.
(*a*) Dislike (*b*) Despise
(*c*) Disown (*d*) Denounce

ANTONYMS

***Directions:* (Qs. 71 to 80):** In this section, each item consists of a word or a phrase which is underlined in the sentence given. It is followed by four words or phrases as (*a*), (*b*), (*c*) and (*d*). Select the word or phrase which is closest to the opposite in meaning of the underlined words or phrase.

71. My brother is very <u>sensitive</u> about hurting animals.
(*a*) Callous (*b*) Senseless
(*c*) Indifferent (*d*) Unconcerned

72. He did it <u>purposely.</u>
(*a*) Half-heartedly (*b*) Timidly
(*c*) Unintentionally (*d*) Hesitatingly

73. After a week-long strike, the workers took to the path of <u>collision</u> when the chairman intervened.
(*a*) Relation (*b*) Atonement
(*c*) Reconciliation (*d*) Expiation

74. He <u>yielded to</u> temptation.
(*a*) Succumbed (*b*) Rescinded
(*c*) Skirted (*d*) Resisted

75. The <u>dishevelled</u> appearance of the two men on the street made everyone take notice of them.
(*a*) Composed (*b*) Tidy
(*c*) Confident (*d*) Complacent

76. He has a <u>penchant</u> for writing satirical poems.
(*a*) Dislike (*b*) Bias
(*c*) Repulsion (*d*) Hatred

77. The lawyer was convinced that his client had made an <u>authentic</u> statement.
(*a*) Absurd (*b*) False
(*c*) Unreasonable (*d*) Ridiculous

78. He was <u>on pins and needles</u> while his wife was undergoing an operation.
(*a*) Unexcited (*b*) At rest
(*c*) Undisturbed (*d*) Relaxed

79. The coach was too <u>lax</u> about the training of the team.
(*a*) Stern (*b*) Strict
(*c*) Firm (*d*) Steadfast

80. The rebels <u>held out</u> in the face of stiff odds.
(*a*) Gave in (*b*) Deserted
(*c*) Fled away (*d*) Betrayed

SELECTING WORDS (Simple Sentences)

***Directions:* (Qs. 81 to 90):** In each of these questions, the sentence has a blank space and four words (*a*), (*b*), (*c*) and (*d*) are given after the sentence. Select whichever word you consider most appropriate for he blank space as your answer.

81. The train's crossing the bridge just before the bridge collapsed was__________
(*a*) Accidental (*b*) Providential
(*c*) Fatal (*d*) Deplorable

82. The Court has directed the University to__________ the publication of results until further orders.
(*a*) Quicken (*b*) Accelerate
(*c*) Defer (*d*) Cancel

83. The US Ambassador to India submitted his__________ to the President of India.
(*a*) Orders (*b*) Certificates
(*c*) Bio data (*d*) Credentials

84. In the boat disaster that took place near Patna, more than thirty passengers were__________ to be drowned.
(*a*) Thought (*b*) Feared
(*c*) Believed (*d*) Presumed

85. Many young people grow excited, even_____, when they see before them a popular film star.
(*a*) Overjoyed (*b*) Enthusiastic
(*c*) Rapturous (*d*) Hysterical

86. Bandits quarrelled__________ the division of the booty.
(*a*) On (*b*) Upon
(*c*) For (*d*) Over

87. Rajat was unreasonably incensed__________ me.
(*a*) With (*b*) At
(*c*) On (*d*) Against

88. I shall avail__________ of your advice.
(*a*) Him (*b*) Me
(*c*) Yourself (*d*) Myself

89. No one really likes her__________ jokes which come so abundantly and unexpectedly.
(*a*) Hilarious (*b*) Outrageous
(*c*) Mirthful (*d*) Mighty

90. As the crowd didn't heed the warning, the police__________ to lathi charge.
(*a*) Resorted (*b*) Retaliated
(*c*) Moved (*d*) Marched

COMPREHENSION

Directions: **(Qs. 91 to 120):** In this section, you have six short passages. After each passage you will find several questions based on the passage. First, read Passage I and answer the questions based on it. Then go on to the other passages.

PASSAGE I

At low tide he walked over the sands to the headland and round the corner to the little bay facing the open sea. It was inaccessible by boat, because seams of rock jutted out and currents swirled round them treacherously. But you could walk there if you chose one of the lowest ebb tides that receded a very long way. You could not linger on the expedition, for once the tide was on the turn, it came in rapidly. For this reason very few people cared to explore the little bay and the cave at the back of it. But the unknown always drew this man like a magnet. He found the bay fresh and unlittered, as it was completely covered by the sea at high tide. The cave looked mysteriously dark, cool and inviting, and he penetrated to the farthest corner where he discovered a wide crack, rather like a chimney. He peered up and thought he could see a patch of daylight.

91. According to the writer, the bay could not be reached by boat, because
(*a*) It had numerous layers of rock
(*b*) There were too many eddies
(*c*) It was facing the open sea
(*d*) There were seams of rock and treacherously swirling currents

92. One could visit the bay
(*a*) At any time one chose
(*b*) On certain specified occasions
(*c*) When there was a low tide
(*d*) During the evening walk

93. It was not possible to "linger on the expedition" because
(*a*) The water rose rapidly
(*b*) The tide turned quickly
(*c*) The tide turned sprightly
(*d*) The water rushed in with a great force

94. He found the bay "fresh and unlittered" because
(*a*) The sea water had receded
(*b*) He was the first visitor there
(*c*) The high tide had just washed the litter away
(*d*) It was not frequented by people who would pollute it

95. While passing through the cave, the writer discovered a
(*a*) Cool and secluded corner
(*b*) Large opening
(*c*) Chimney-shaped rock
(*d*) Big crack through which light came in

PASSAGE II

Regular physical activity provided numerous health benefits—from leaner bodies and lower blood pressure to improved mental health and cognitive functioning. As the school physical education programme promotes physical activity and can teach skills as well as form or change behaviour, it holds an important key to influencing health and well-being across the life span. To improve the fitness of students, we need to rethink the design and delivery of school-based physical education programme. Adults in the United States think that information about health was more important for students to learn than content in language arts, mathematics, science, history or any other subject. Despite this high ranking, most schools devote minimal curriculum time to teaching students how to lead healthy lives. Our first step might be to consider ways to increase curriculum time devoted to physical education. In addition, schools need to thoughtfully analyse the design and delivery of school physical education programme to ensure that they are engaging, developmentally appropriate, inclusive and instructionally powerful.

96. According to this passage, regular physical activity is needed to
(*a*) Control one's blood pressure
(*b*) Lose one's weight
(*c*) Improve one's cognitive skills
(*d*) Improve one's physical as well as mental health

97. In order to tone up the physical education programme
(*a*) It should be made compulsory at school
(*b*) An assessment of the existing programme should be made
(*c*) A committee should be set up in every school
(*d*) The programme should be reoriented and implemented

98. According to Americans, health education is more important than teaching
(*a*) Social sciences
(*b*) Liberal arts
(*c*) Any subject
(*d*) Natural science

99. The author wants the reoriented physical education programme to be
(*a*) Given minimal curriculum time
(*b*) Very comprehensive
(*c*) Relevant to the modern society
(*d*) Thoughtful

100. In order to improve the physical education programme, we should first of all
(*a*) Allot more time to the teaching and learning of physical activity
(*b*) Decide on the number of activities to be taught
(*c*) Employ qualified instructors
(*d*) Increase the teaching load of instructors

PASSAGE III

The highbrows reverse the numerical argument and imply that, because they are so few, they must therefore be right. But where they chiefly offend is in their excessive self-congratulation and contempt for others. In the past, the highbrows were alone in expressing a feeling of superiority; the lowbrows humbly accepted the position assigned to them. Recently, however, there has been a change, and the lowbrows now adopt towards the highbrows exactly the same attitude as the highbrows adopted towards them.

101. The reversal of the numerical argument in the context of the passage means that the highbrows
(*a*) Have no regard for the majority
(*b*) Respect the majority
(*c*) Are indifferent to numbers
(*d*) Have regard for the minority

102. A highbrow is
(*a*) A liberal-minded person
(*b*) A believer in conservative values
(*c*) A self-opinionated intellectual
(*d*) A democrat

103. The phrase 'self-congratulation' can best be replaced by
(*a*) Self-effacement (*b*) Self-admiration
(*c*) Self-negation (*d*) Self-criticism

104. The attitude of the lowbrows towards the highbrows in the past was one of
(*a*) Violent rejection
(*b*) Resentful acceptance
(*c*) Open rebelliousness
(*d*) Unprotesting submission

105. The recent change in the attitude of the lowbrows towards the highbrows suggests that
(*a*) The lowbrows reject the superiority of the highbrows
(*b*) The lowbrows have become highbrows
(*c*) The lowbrows have become indifferent to the highbrows
(*d*) The highbrows have become meek and humble

PASSAGE IV

Crude mineral oil comes out of the earth as a thick brown or black liquid with a strong smell. It is a complex mixture of many different substances, each with its own individual qualities. Most of them are combinations of hydrogen and carbon in varying proportions. Such hydrocarbons are also found in other forms such as bitumen, asphalt and natural gas. Mineral oil originates from the carcasses of tiny animals and from plants that live in the sea. Over millions of years, these dead creatures form large deposits under the sea-bed, and ocean currents cover them with a blanket of sand and silt. As this material hardens, it becomes sedimentary rock and effectively shuts out the oxygen, so preventing the complete decomposition of the marine deposits underneath. The layers of sedimentary rock become thicker and heavier. Their pressure produces heat, which transforms the tiny carcasses into crude oil in a process that is still going on today.

106. Marine deposits under the sea do not get decomposed because they
(*a*) Become rock and prevent oxygen from entering them
(*b*) Are covered by the sand and silt brought by the current
(*c*) Contain a mixture of hydrogen and carbon
(*d*) Are constantly washed by the ocean current

107. Sedimentary rock leads to the formation of oil deposits because
(*a*) It becomes hard and forms into rocks which produce oil
(*b*) Its pressure produces heat and turns the deposits of animal carcasses and plants into oil
(*c*) It turns heavy and shuts out the oxygen
(*d*) It becomes heavy and hard, and applies pressure to squeeze oil

108. In order to have mineral oil, hydrogen and carbon are combined in
(*a*) Equal proportions
(*b*) Fixed proportions
(*c*) Varying proportions
(*d*) The proportion of two and one

109. The time it takes for the marine deposits to harden into rocks is
(*a*) A few years
(*b*) Thousands of years
(*c*) Hundreds of years
(*d*) Millions of years

110. The most apt title for the passage is
(*a*) Crude Mineral Oil
(*b*) How Sedimentary Rock Is Formed ?
(*c*) How Mineral Oil Is Formed ?
(*d*) Marine Deposits Under The Sea

PASSAGE V

To avoid the various foolish opinions to which mankind is prone, no superhuman brain is required. A few simple rules will keep you free, not from all errors, but from silly errors. If the matter is one that can be settled by observation, make the observation yourself. Aristotle could have avoided the mistake of thinking that women have fewer teeth than men, by the simple device of asking Mrs. Aristotle to keep her mouth open while he counted. Thinking that you know when in fact you do not is a bad mistake, to which we are all prone. I believe myself that hedgehogs eat black beetles, because I have been told that they do; but if I was writing a book on the habits of hedgehogs, I should not commit myself until I had seen one enjoying this diet. Aristotle, however, was less cautious. Ancient and medieval writers knew all about unicorns and salamanders; not one of them thought it necessary to avoid dogmatic statements about them because he had never seen one of them.

111. The author portrays mankind as
(*a*) Very intelligent
(*b*) Having superhuman qualities
(*c*) Nervous and weak
(*d*) By and large, lazy and ignorant

112. The author is in favour of drawing conclusions on the basis of
(*a*) Reasoning
(*b*) Study of eminent thinkers
(*c*) Empirical evidence
(*d*) Discussion and consultation

113. According to the author, unicorns and salamanders
(*a*) Existed in the past but now have become extinct
(*b*) Are invisible
(*c*) Never really existed
(*d*) Have caused strange stories to be written about them

114. The author implies that
(*a*) Hedgehogs eat black beetles
(*b*) Hedgehogs do not really eat black beetles
(*c*) He is writing a book about hedge hogs
(*d*) He has never seen a hedgehog eating beetles

115. The attitude of the author is
(*a*) Philosophical (*b*) Scientific
(*c*) Cultural (*d*) Commonsensical

PASSAGE VI

Long ago Emerson wrote : "A man's task is his life-preserver." This seems to be remarkably correct in our modern life. The man without task is like a ship without a ballast and anchor; he is all too often merely a drifter. Few men seem to have initiative enough to choose a task for themselves if they do not need to work. When the inevitable disappointments come, as they assuredly will they are completely overwhelmed. But the man who has his task has no time for vain regrets; he escapes the disastrous fate which overtakes his less fortunate brother. Work is one of the greatest safety-valves which was ever invented, and youth especially needs it.

116. It seems to be remarkably correct in modern life that
(*a*) A man has enough leisure
(*b*) Youth needs less work and more rest
(*c*) The correct choice of the task preserves one's life
(*d*) Men fail to choose a task for themselves

117. The expression 'safety-valve' means
(*a*) Something which blows up safety
(*b*) An outlet for pent-up energy
(*c*) Something which guarantees safety
(*d*) A leaf of a folding door

118. A ship without ballast and anchor
(*a*) Is in great danger
(*b*) Merely drifts
(*c*) Is very safe
(*d*) May not go in the right direction.

119. A man who suffers from vain regrets must have
(*a*) Chosen his life's work rather carelessly
(*b*) Met with disastrous fate
(*c*) Been a victim of adverse circumstances
(*d*) Accepted whatever work he got to do

120. A person who has chosen the right task has no time to regret because he
(*a*) Is engrossed in his work
(*b*) Has too much to do
(*c*) Has succeeded in life
(*d*) Has a safe and secured life

ANSWERS

1. (*b*)	**2.** (*a*)	**3.** (*b*)	**4.** (*d*)	**5.** (*b*)
6. (*d*)	**7.** (*d*)	**8.** (*a*)	**9.** (*d*)	**10.** (*a*)
11. (*a*)	**12.** (*c*)	**13.** (*a*)	**14.** (*d*)	**15.** (*d*)
16. (*b*)	**17.** (*b*)	**18.** (*b*)	**19.** (*b*)	**20.** (*a*)
21. (*a*)	**22.** (*a*)	**23.** (*c*)	**24.** (*b*)	**25.** (*a*)
26. (*a*)	**27.** (*a*)	**28.** (*a*)	**29.** (*a*)	**30.** (*c*)

31. (*c*) : Part 'c' should be 'and and not be found out'
32. (*b*) : Part 'b' should be 'differently'.
33. (*c*) : Part 'c' should be 'leading the blind'.

34. (*a*) : Part 'a' should be 'He took to drinking'.
35. (*c*) : Part 'c' should be 'without spending a lot of money'.
36. (*a*) : Part 'a' should be 'All India Radio broadcast'.
37. (*a*) : Part 'a' should be 'There were so many cattle'.
38. (*d*)
39. (*a*) : Part 'a' should be 'They had been rich Zamindars in the thirties'.
40. (*b*) : Part 'b' should be 'noted both for his charming manners.'.
41. (*b*) : Part 'b' should be 'and thus hold out the promise'.
42. (*b*) : Part 'b' should be 'whether he would leave for England'.
43. (*a*) : Part 'a' should be 'Despite her protests'.
44. (*b*) : Part 'b' should be 'that if they persisted in charging unfair prices'.
45. (*a*) : Part 'a' should be 'The famous poet and scholar'.

46. (*c*)	**47.** (*d*)	**48.** (*c*)	**49.** (*d*)	**50.** (*a*)
51. (*b*)	**52.** (*d*)	**53.** (*b*)	**54.** (*c*)	**55.** (*d*)
56. (*c*)	**57.** (*c*)	**58.** (*c*)	**59.** (*b*)	**60.** (*b*)
61. (*c*)	**62.** (*d*)	**63.** (*c*)	**64.** (*a*)	**65.** (*d*)
66. (*c*)	**67.** (*d*)	**68.** (*b*)	**69.** (*a*)	**70.** (*b*)
71. (*a*)	**72.** (*c*)	**73.** (*c*)	**74.** (*d*)	**75.** (*b*)
76. (*c*)	**77.** (*b*)	**78.** (*d*)	**79.** (*b*)	**80.** (*a*)
81. (*b*)	**82.** (*c*)	**83.** (*d*)	**84.** (*b*)	**85.** (*d*)
86. (*d*)	**87.** (*a*)	**88.** (*d*)	**89.** (*b*)	**90.** (*a*)
91. (*d*)	**92.** (*c*)	**93.** (*b*)	**94.** (*c*)	**95.** (*d*)
96. (*d*)	**97.** (*d*)	**98.** (*c*)	**99.** (*d*)	**100.** (*a*)
101. (*a*)	**102.** (*c*)	**103.** (*b*)	**104.** (*d*)	**105.** (*a*)
106. (*b*)	**107.** (*b*)	**108.** (*c*)	**109.** (*d*)	**110.** (*c*)
111. (*d*)	**112.** (*c*)	**113.** (*c*)	**114.** (*d*)	**115.** (*b*)
116. (*c*)	**117.** (*b*)	**118.** (*d*)	**119.** (*a*)	**120.** (*a*)

"O Captain! O Captain! Our fearful trip is done, The ship has weather'd every rock, the prize we sought is won, ..."

– Walt Whitman